Greater Puget Sound Edition

Event RESOURCE Guide

The Area's Most Comprehensive Guide to Services for Meeting & Event Planning

2002

Bravo! Publications
3435 California Avenue S.W., Suite 100A
Seattle, Washington 98116
(206) 937-3264 or (888) 832-7286
Fax (206) 937-1229

Visit our Web site:
www.bravoseattle.com

E-Mail:
info@bravoseattle.com

Printed in the United States of America

ISBN: 1-891492-09-8

TABLE OF CONTENTS

Ad Specialties, Awards & Corporate Gifts continued...

BANQUET, GETAWAY & RETREAT SITES 99–126

BANQUET, MEETING & EVENT SITES/BOATS 127–134

BANQUET, MEETING & EVENT SITES 135–320

Banquet, Meeting & Event Sites continued...

Banquet, Meeting & Event Sites continued...

Catering/Food & Beverage Services continued...

CONVENTION & EXHIBITION FACILITIES 377–388

CONVENTION & EXHIBITION SERVICES 389–392

DECORATIONS, THEMES & PROPS 393–402

ENTERTAINERS & PERFORMERS 403–426

Entertainers & Performers continued...

GAMES & TEAM BUILDING ACTIVITIES 459–480

GOLF COURSES 481–492

ICE CARVINGS 493–496

MEETING & EVENT PLANNERS 497–516

TABLE OF CONTENTS

SPEAKERS .575–580

TRANSPORTATION & VALET SERVICES .581–590

TUXEDOS & FORMAL WEAR .591–594

VIDEO SERVICES .595–598

LISTINGS .599–664

INDEX .665–680

ACKNOWLEDGEMENTS

This Guide would not have been possible without the hard work, dedication, and endless hours from the following individuals and companies:

Publisher:
Marion Clifton

Bravo! Seattle Sales Consultants:
Jane Egger
Mindy Milton
Penny Picket Simmons

Web Site Design:
Danger Island:
Matt Morgan
Joe LeBlanc

Web Page Maintenance:
Greendale Associates:
Lillian Sugahara

Copywriters:
Andrew Willems
Kim Shinsato

Cover Design:
Roz & Co.
Roz Duavit-Pasion

Production:
Bravo! Staff:
Kim Shinsato
Alanna Barsamian-Moncrief
Greendale Associates:
Lillian Sugahara

Printer:
GAC Allied:
Lynda Ross

HELPFUL HINTS UPDATES & ARTICLES

Etiquette & Gift Giving and **Tipping Etiquette** Helpful Hints
©Pacific Rim Protocol—Stephanie Horton, CMP
See page 580 under Speakers & Presentations
How To Write A Press Release—Steve Brown, *The Tacoma Daily News*
Rental Services & Equipment—Lynn Carpenter, CMP and Andrew Willems

PHOTOGRAPHIC ACKNOWLEDGEMENTS

BACK COVER PHOTOGRAPHS:
2001 Bravo! LIVE Meeting & Event Planners Trade Show
at the Washington State Stadium Exhibition Center

TITLE PAGE PHOTOGRAPHS:
Upper left: "Clown"—©**Action Events**
see page 463 under Games & Team Building Activities
Middle: "Dining"—©**Spirit of Washington Dinner Train**
see pages 64 & 367 under Attractions & Activities and *Catering/Food & Beverage*
Lower right: "Table"—©**Event Success**
see page 507 under Meeting & Event Planners

ABOUT THE BRAVO! TEAM

Bravo! Publications was started in 1989 by Marion Clifton and Mary Lou Burton in Portland, Oregon, shortly after Mary Lou's own wedding. During these past twelve years, a lot has happened! We've reorganized the company so that each market runs independently from each other, added trade shows to our list of "products," and expanded our services to include the web. More importantly, we've welcomed eleven children into the world, and said goodbye to treasured loved ones.

As we reflect back on the past decade, it becomes very clear that what we have built is something rather incredible. No one individual on the Bravo! team does just one thing—they do it all. Everyone involved has become more than a friend, they are "family" members who are there to support each other through the good and bad, as well as the ups and downs on life's highway. I would like to personally thank each member of the Bravo! team, both past and present, for all of their contributions and for being such valued friends.

Sincerely,
Marion Clifton
Publisher

BRAVO!® RESOURCE GUIDES

When you want information, not glossy ads—you want Bravo!
Bravo! Publications is proud to offer four regional *Resource Guides* for planning meetings, events and weddings. Each of the Guides featured on this and the following page is filled with important information and details about the area's finest businesses and services providers, and is presented in easy-to-read, resumé style formats, alphabetically, by category. Designed to be user-friendly, each of these Guides truly are your planning *Resource*!

Greater Puget Sound *Bravo!® Event Resource Guide*

Venues, Attractions & Activities, Audience Participation, Ad Specialties, Corporate Gifts & Awards, Food & Beverage Services, Accommodations, and more...

The 2002 Edition features 704 pages of easy-to-read, resumé-style write-ups on area businesses and service providers, listings of area Banquet and Event Sites, how-to's, check lists, and all the helpful hints you've come to expect from Bravo!

Suggested Retail: $9.95
(Complimentary to pre-qualified Meeting and Event Planners...*see page XXI for details*)

Greater Puget Sound *Bravo!® Bridal Resource Guide*

Churches, Chapels, Banquet & Reception Sites, Caterers, Florists, Photographers, Videographers, Invitations, Bridal Attire, Tuxedo Rentals, Bridal Registry, Favors, Accessories, Consultants and more...

The 2002 Edition features 672 pages of easy-to-read, resumé-style write-ups on area businesses and service providers, listings of area Banquet and Reception Sites, how-to's, check lists, and all the helpful hints you've come to expect from Bravo!

Suggested Retail: $9.95

SAY YOU SAW IT IN BRAVO!

Every business or service needs to track where their business is coming from. By letting them know you are using one of the Bravo! Resource Guides, you not only ensure that Bravo! will be available for meeting and event planners or brides in the future, but you also let the businesses or services know where their business is coming from.

Portland • Vancouver • Salem
and outlying areas
Bravo!® Event Resource Guide

Venues, Attractions & Activities, Audience Participation, Gifts & Awards, Food & Beverage, Accommodations, and more...

The 2002 Edition features 640 pages of easy-to-read, resumé-style write-ups on area businesses and service providers, listings of Banquet and Event Sites, how-to's, check lists, and all the helpful hints.

Suggested Retail: $8.95
(Complimentary to pre-qualified Meeting and Event Planners...*see page XIX for details*)

Portland • Vancouver • Salem
and outlying areas
Bravo!® Bridal Resource Guide

Churches, Chapels, Banquet & Reception Sites, Caterers, Florists, Photographers, Videographers, Invitations, Bridal Attire, Tuxedo Rentals, Bridal Registry, and more...

The 2002 Edition features 640 pages of easy-to-read, resumé-style write-ups on area businesses and service providers, listings of Banquet and Reception Sites, how-to's, check lists, and all the helpful hints!

Suggested Retail: $9.95

Bravo!® Wedding Organizer

The step-by-step system to track every detail of your event.

Bravo!™ Wedding Organizer
Suggested Retail: $24.95

The *Organizer* features:

- Detailed worksheets designed to double as contracts
- Time schedules, checklists and calendars
- Detailed budget worksheets and "who pays for what forms
- "To Do" forms and "Delegat-ing Duties" lists

BRAVO! RESOURCE GUIDES AND WEDDING ORGANIZER

❒ I am a meeting or event planner, and would like to receive a complimentary copy of the *Bravo!® Event Resource Guide.* — No Charge

❒ *Greater Puget Sound Edition*

❒ *Portland • Vancouver • Salem and outlying areas Edition*

❒ I am planning a wedding, and would like to receive a copy of the *Bravo!® Bridal Resource Guide.* — $9.95

❒ *Puget Sound Edition* ❒ *Portland • Vancouver • Salem Edition*

❒ Bravo! Wedding Organizer in binder — $24.95

Shipping and handling—$3 per product +__________

SUB-TOTAL: $__________

Add 8.8% Sales Tax: +__________

TOTAL ENCLOSED: $__________

Please take the time to fill out the survey on the back of this card. Your input is very important to the success of this publication.

CONTACT: ____________________

TITLE: ____________________

COMPANY NAME: ____________________

ADDRESS: ____________________ **M/S** __________

CITY, STATE, ZIP: ____________________

PHONE: ____________________ **FAX:** ____________________

TYPE OF COMPANY: ____________________ **# EMPLOYEES:** __________

What type of events do you plan? ❒ Meetings ❒ Seminars ❒ Conferences ❒ Conventions ❒ Trade Shows ❒ Parties ❒ Holiday Parties ❒ Golf Tournaments ❒ Picnics ❒ Fund Raisers ❒ Retreats ❒ Other: ____________________

Number of people you plan events for?
❒ 1–50 ❒ 51–100 ❒ 101–200 ❒ 201–500 ❒ 501–1000 ❒ 1001+ ❒ Range: ________

METHOD OF PAYMENT:

❒ Check or money order enclosed ❒ Charge to: Visa or Mastercard

Name of card holder: ____________________

Account No: ____________________

Exp. Date: __________ Signature: ____________________

Please allow 7 to 10 days for delivery

Send order to: **BRAVO! PUBLICATIONS, INC.**
3435 CALIFORNIA AVENUE S.W., SUITE 100A • SEATTLE, WA 98116
(206) 937-3264 or (888) 832-7286; Fax (206) 937-1229
E-mail: info@bravoseattle.com

BRAVO! EVENT RESOURCE GUIDE SURVEY

Please fill in this survey and send back.

Your input is very important for the continued success of this publication. Please take the time to fill out this survey and send it back to us. If you would like to send a complimentary Event Guide to another meeting or event planner, just fill out the order form on the back side of this page and send or fax it to Bravo! Publications, Inc.

Please fill in the following on the back of this survey: Name, Title, Company Name, Address, Phone, Fax, and type of events you plan.

1. How has the *Bravo!® Event Resource Guide* been helpful to you? (Examples)

____

____

____

2. Please list the businesses and services (by name) that you are working with out of the *Bravo!® Event Resource Guide* (caterer, facility, musician, etc.).

____

____

____

____

____

____

3. Your experiences can help others. To ensure the quality of this publication for future users, we'd like to know if you had good or bad experiences with the businesses listed in the Guide.

____

____

____

4. Please add any additional ideas, thoughts or recommendations for how *Bravo!®* can improve this Guide for you.

____

____

____

If You Love The Bravo! Event Resource Guide, Wait Until You Browse Our Bravo! Event Web Site!

Check out the Bravo! Publications Web site at:
www.bravoseattle.com

The Bravo! Web site is:

- **Easy to use!**
- Features all the **detailed information** you're used to seeing in your *Bravo! Event Resource Guide!*
- Features **color photographs**!
- Has a comprehensive **Calendar of Events** that will let you know when and where the next Meeting Planning Trade Shows, Seminars or Events will be taking place.

The Bravo! Event and Wedding Web sites will be...
growing and changing weekly, so be sure to browse them often so you can see what's new!

ADD BRAVO! TO YOUR ROLODEX!
(Just cut out the card below and staple or slip it into your Rolodex.)

Bravo! Publications, Inc.
3435 California Ave. S.W., Suite 100A
Seattle, WA 98116
Phone: (206) 937-3264; **Fax:** (206) 937-1229
E-mail: info@bravoseattle.com
Web site: www.bravoseattle.com

Bravo!®

NOTES

Introduction and How to Use This Book

INTRODUCTION & HOW TO USE THIS BOOK

The objective of the *Bravo!® Event Resource Guide* is to help planners of any experience level reference information from facilities, caterers, florists, speakers, etc. Before businesses or services are listed in the Guide, they are screened to make sure they meet specific criteria for their category. Businesses and services are listed in the book based on merit and not just the amount of money they have paid for an advertisement. Small businesses are portrayed in the same light as their counterparts. Information has to be complete, reliable, and factual, including important details like deposits, cancellation terms, and cost.

The *Bravo!® Event Resource Guide* was created by popular demand! Many meeting and event planners were already using the *Bravo!® Bridal Guide* as a resource for its many facilities and services. Bravo! Publications published the first Bridal Guide in 1990, and its popularity among brides has made it a number-one seller. Meeting and event planners found the information listed in the Guide invaluable to finding a specific location that met their needs, including information like capacity, price, sleeping rooms, etc.

In creating the *Bravo!® Event Resource Guide,* we worked with professional meeting and event planners and vendors in the industry to offer information and helpful hints based on years of knowledge and experience in the industry. We provide a survey in the front of this Guide and appreciate input from readers like you about what they found useful in the Guide. Please take the time to fill out the survey; your input ensures the success of this publication for future users. Every year the Guide is updated, and we want to know businesses with which you had good or bad experiences.

In addition to the Bravo! *Resource Guides* and *Organizers,* we also produce events throughout the year for meeting and event planners to attend, where planners receive information and ideas directly from the businesses and services in the Guides. Your attendance in supporting these events will help us to continue to provide quality products and services! For dates of upcoming Bravo! trade shows and events, check out our web site at: *www.bravoseattle.com.*

IMPORTANT NOTE!

It's important to make sure you mention to the businesses or services, that you selected them from the *Bravo!® Event Resource Guide.* This will help us continue to provide this Guide complimentary.

Keeping Up With Technology

More and more meeting planners are accessing information on the worldwide web. Keeping up on technology, Bravo! has created one of the most advanced web sites for meeting and event planners. Now you can access the entire 2002 *Bravo!® Event Resource Guide* on-line. With our own internal search engine, you can find information on businesses and services featured in the following pages by pull-down category lists, key word, capacity, or area! Just go to *www.bravoseattle.com* for everything you need to plan your next meeting or event!

Planning A Meeting Or Event

❖❖❖

TYPES OF EVENTS & WHERE TO START

MANY TYPES OF EVENTS

- Conventions
- Holiday Parties
- Seminars
- Tours
- Groundbreakings
- Grand Openings
- Festivals
- Concerts
- Trade Shows
- Sporting Events
- Fund Raisers
- Product Announcements
- Anniversaries
- Picnics
- Sales Meetings
- Carnivals/Fairs

PURPOSE OF EVENTS AND MEETINGS

Corporations are planning more meetings and special events than ever before. In fact, these events have become a big part of companies' overall marketing budgets. They have found it is becoming more and more difficult to motivate and attract attention with just a regular in-house memo or announcement.

BENEFITS OF A WELL-PLANNED EVENT

- More sales, higher profits and employees take ownership of ideas
- Media attention and free publicity
- Target marketing
- Education
- Name recognition
- Good will in the community
- Product loyalty
- Problem-solving
- Networking

PLAN...PLAN...PLAN

Ask professional meeting planners how to ensure a successful event or meeting and they will say, "pay close attention to the logistics and details and plan...plan... plan...ahead so that when the day of the event comes, all the good planning will kick into gear, and you can take care of the 'surprises' that Murphy brings to the event!"

DETAILS

When meeting and event arrangements work well, the attendees have no idea of the details that went into the planning. But, when arrangements aren't right, everyone is aware of the details that needed to be handled and weren't! Whether it's too few chairs or faulty audio visual equipment, everyone's attention will be focused on the one who planned the event and how things could have been organized and handled better!

ASKING QUESTIONS

Whether it's for yourself, a corporation, a non-profit convention, or other clients, when planning a meeting or an event, you need to start with the basic questions; and from there you will get your event off to a good start. Without the solid foundation of knowing your meeting goals and attendees' expectations, you have no way of determining if your event was successful.

So, before you can get into the nuts and bolts of planning a great meeting or event, you need to ask lots of questions!

On the following pages we offer you the basic questions to ask to start your planning.

DO YOUR HOMEWORK!!!

WHY? THE PURPOSE...

Why are you, your client, or your boss wanting to have a meeting or event? Whatever the occasion, you, as the planner, need to know WHY! Ask questions!

- Is it for a celebration?
- An annual convention?
- New product introduction?
- A sales meeting?
- Retirement or anniversary party?
- Employee motivation?
- To educate?
- Allow for networking?

WHAT? THE OBJECTIVE...

Along with the WHY is WHAT are the objectives of the event? Is the objective to thank employees for a year of hard work or to provide recognition for some special people or individuals? Is your objective to promote good feelings within the company or with the general public? Is this an event that has many audiences or just one? How do you want your audience to feel when this event is over? Do you want them to buy your products, feel pride in working for an outstanding company, or learn new techniques to make their jobs more productive?

DETERMINE YOUR OBJECTIVES

The meeting may have multiple objectives...keeping within a budget is one of them, along with keeping the planning time to a minimum. What kind of a retirement party can I realistically plan with $1000 and two weeks' notice?

WHO? PROFILE THE AUDIENCE...

Determining objectives of your meeting is an important first step because meeting programs are designed from these objectives to bring about the desired results. In order to measure your success, you need to determine goals and objectives and then create a meeting that accomplishes the results you want.

Who will be your attendees, speakers, sponsors, etc? These are all the different audiences with whom you will be working. You need to have a profile of who they are, where they are coming from, and how old they are. Are they couples? Do any have disabilities? Will any attendees be international? Do they speak English? The more you know about your participants, the more success you will have meeting their expectations!

AMERICANS WITH DISABILITIES ACT (ADA)

The Americans with Disabilities Act (ADA), passed into law in 1991, guarantees protection for disabled persons in the area of public accommodations. The meeting planner is legally responsible to make certain all efforts have been made to comply with the ADA. Know the individual needs of attendees. To be in compliance with the ADA, it is very important to ask you attendees if anyone has disability-related needs. Then follow-up with a call to determine what their specific needs are. Be sure to clearly communicate these needs to the facility. By doing this, you have established the intent to comply with ADA. Contact the ADA Northwest regional office at (800) HELP-ADA to get detailed regulations, or ask your facility.

CHECKLIST, PROFILE & SCHEDULING

PLANNING CHECKLIST

It is helpful to develop a Planning Checklist for your event or meeting; this allows you to jump into planning and delegating without trying to "re-invent" the wheel with a plain notepad. You can even assign each category to qualified attendees.

- Profile the audience
- Determine the needs
- Site selection
- Budget
- Publicity plan
- Work plan or work flow
- Registration, invitations, programs
- Staffing
- On-site coordination
- Evaluation and accounting

WHAT ARE YOUR NEEDS FOR THIS EVENT?

Make a list of what you think will be your immediate needs. Will you need a facility, or can you do it at your own location, home, or business? Will you need to arrange transportation? Air or ground? Will you include food and hotel lodging for your event guests? Will you need meeting rooms and function space? Will you need audio visual equipment? Will you need printed materials, signage, extra staff?

SUB-CATEGORY QUESTIONS

These are general questions, but this is the beginning of a needs list. From this general list you will naturally develop your sub-category of questions including: site selection criteria, room rates, bus or shuttle, etc. And then the fun begins....negotiating what you want!!

SCHEDULING

DETERMINING YOUR SCHEDULE OF EVENTS

Determining the "schedule" of an event needs to start in the initial planning stages! Changes and more changes will occur, but having a sense of timing for the various aspects of a two-hour meeting, a one-day seminar, or a five-day conference will help set the groundwork for selecting the site and vendors. Decide what "TYPES" of activities your group will be involved in during your meeting or event. For example: business portions, social portions, recreation free time, exhibits, etc. Begin to map out a schedule of events.

SCHEDULE OF EVENTS (SAMPLE)

DATE: ____________________

TIME	EVENT	LOCATION	NUMBERS	SETUP
8–9 a.m.	Registration	TBD	300	Flow See Diagram
9–10 a.m.	Breakfast	TBD	300	Rounds
10 a.m.–Noon	General Session	TBD	300	Theatre Style
Noon–1 p.m.	Lunch	Off Property	N/A	N/A
1–3 p.m.	Workshops A B C	TBD TBD TBD TBD	300 100 100 100	Classroom Classroom Classroom Classroom

PREPARING A BUDGET

Preparing a budget is critical to effective meeting or event management. The budget provides you with the control and accountability for all meeting revenues and expenses. Your meeting objectives will influence both the revenues and the expenses of the program. Whatever the goal, it is important to document everything you commit to spending so you know at any time where you stand financially. A well-developed financial plan is a tool to guide the planner in making decisions and identifying priorities throughout the event.

REVENUE

There are two concerns in creating a budget: revenue and expenses. Revenue is determined if you are going to expect income. How will it be generated? Registration fees, exhibitor fees, sponsorships, individual event fees, concession fees, are all ways money is brought in. How much income will you expect to receive in each category?

EXPENSES

After determining your NEEDS PROFILE and your SCHEDULE OF EVENTS, you can develop a list of expenses involved or anticipated with each item. Don't forget the costs of administration, phone, mailings, faxes, staff, and supplies—in other words, your overhead. Experience helps in this process, but if you are a novice, you can do some research with vendors to determine reasonable estimates at this stage.

GOOD PLANNING AND BUDGETING

Good planning results in meeting your objectives. During the budget portion of planning, you need to determine what your financial goals are as well. Determine what the group expects to gain. Should the meeting make money, lose money, or break even? If the group wants to make a profit, the amount or percentage should be determined in this initial stage.

BUDGET WORKSHEET (SAMPLE)

BUDGET WORKSHEET

Meeting Name ______________________________

Meeting Date ____________________ Division/Cost Center ____________

Name of Person Responsible for Meeting______________________________

HOTEL		**MEALS/FUNCTIONS**	
Sleeping rooms	$ ____________	Breakfast	$ __________
($___/night + ___% tax= $___x___ room nights)		Breaks	$__________
Meeting room rental	$ ____________	Lunch	$__________
Audio visual charges	$ ____________	Receptions	$__________
TOTAL:	$ ____________	Entertainment	$__________
		Recreation	$__________
		TOTAL:	$__________

THE PLANNING & TIMELINE PROCESS

MANAGING THE DETAILS

This is what meeting and event planners are famous for and everyone has tools to help them be successful. Everyone develops his or her own style and methods, but generally detail management includes these elements:

- TASKS...determine the tasks needed to be completed to ensure a successful event
- ORDER....determine the order in which these tasks need to be completed
- DEADLINE...determine the time by which they need to be completed
- DELEGATE... determine if, and to whom, they can be delegated

  This is where you'll hear those magic words:

  TIMETABLES, WORKPLANS AND CHECKLISTS

THREE-PART TIMELINE

One simple way to begin managing your information is to break your timeline into three parts:

1. PRE-EVENT or MEETING
2. ON-SITE
3. POST-EVENT or MEETING

You can then add the functional sub-categories under each part, like event design, speaker recruitment, marketing and promotion, registration, site selection, etc. Determine what needs to be accomplished during each phase.

MANAGEMENT TIMELINE

(SAMPLE TIMELINE)

12–18 MONTHS BEFORE THE EVENT

❒ Suggest program and "needs" list subjects

❒ Define audiences

❒ Determine needs

❒ Draft theme/title

❒ Determine pricing

❒ Establish program budget

❒ Select dates

❒ Conduct site inspections

❒ Book meeting, banquet, and sleeping room space

9–12 MONTHS BEFORE THE EVENT

❒ Determine speakers

❒ Determine agenda: business and social

❒ Contact speakers

❒ Contract transportation: ground and air

❒ Coordinate facility needs

❒ Send "save the date" mailings to audiences

❒ Solicit exhibits and sponsors

6–9 MONTHS BEFORE THE EVENT

- ❐ Review program needs
- ❐ Review audio visual needs
- ❐ Review and refine budget
- ❐ Select catering and event menus and themes
- ❐ Communicate with vendors
- ❐ Establish registration procedure
- ❐ Design registration materials

and so on...

USING A WORKPLAN

Once you have determined the tasks, give them a deadline and delegate. Responsibilities may be assigned to individuals, groups, committees, or suppliers, such as hotels, caterers, etc. Even if you are the ONLY person working on your event, suppliers or vendors do have a place in your delegation timeline. They need to get back to you in a timely way that works for you; you need to get signed contracts and guarantees back to them. Through the WORKPLAN you can manage the details.

WORKPLAN (SAMPLE)

WORK ELEMENT	DEADLINE	ASSIGNED TO
PROGRAM:		
Theme design	Oct. 1	Smith/Jones
Draft agenda	Nov. 5	Staff
Determine speakers	Nov. 15	Smith/Staff
BUDGET:		
Draft budget	Oct. 1	Meyer/Staff
Setup ledgers	Dec. 1	Smith/Accounting

SITE SELECTION

SELECTING THE SITE

Decision time...if you have done your homework, you will be armed with information that will help you make good decisions about your site selection. Once your needs are identified, you must match them with the sites that can handle them. Determine the geographic location that best suits your event...the United States, the West Coast, the Northwest, Washington, Puget Sound, Downtown Seattle, Tacoma... These are all decisions that determine from whom to request proposals.

RESOURCES TO SELECT THE SITE

You can call upon many resources to help you determine the best location for your event. Once you have narrowed the possibilities, you will be ready to make some comparisons and decide. Use the expertise of travel agents, Convention and Visitors Bureaus, Chambers of Commerce, professional planners—anyone that you feel understands your needs. ***This publication gives you a good comparison of over 400 local meeting and event facilities in the Greater Puget Sound area.***

MEETING PROFILE

Develop specifications and requirements for your meeting. This is sometimes referred to as a "Meeting Profile." This will be the natural outcome of your Needs List. It may be as simple as, "I need a room and meals for 30 people on this date, at this time." It might include preferred dates, number of sleeping rooms, meeting rooms, types of food functions, range of acceptable rates, exhibit requirements, and special needs of your group. The more information you can provide, the better chance you have of getting what you want. Many groups provide a detailed history of their event or meeting and the monetary value it has to a property. The profile becomes a request to all sites you choose to bid on your business. Once bids begin to come in, the planner can begin the evaluation and elimination process. After selecting an appropriate number to consider—and that number is up to you—it is recommended that you conduct site inspections.

SITE INSPECTION

A site inspection is the best time to ask questions and get a good look at what each facility has to offer. It will be important for you to identify the property that can best meet your space requirements and the level of service you will need. Request references from groups with similar attendance and requirements, then contact them.

NEGOTIATION

NEGOTIATION AND CONTRACTS

Facility negotiations sound serious, but they don't have to be intimidating. These are important conversations because negotiations build relationships, which will lead to contracts. Contracts are serious business and when you, as a planner, enter into a contract, you want to be sure you have all the knowledge and information you need. Keep in mind that negotiable items and practices vary between areas of the country, so what may be standard procedure on the East Coast is not necessarily the same on the West Coast.

HOMEWORK PAYS OFF!

Before you begin negotiating, you need some tools! If you have done your homework (refer to the first section), you'll be set! You need your meeting profile or prospectus, a history of your meeting or event, the value of your meeting to the facility (your budget), and a profile of your group. If you know your requirements, they will dictate the specific items you can negotiate.

NEGOTIATIONS SHOULD BE WIN-WIN

Don't get bogged down in sleeping room rates! Rates are only one item that can be negotiated. The list of negotiable items may be as long as you want ...it never hurts to ask! But, in order to have a successful meeting, negotiations should be a win-win process. For example, if you get the hotel to provide complimentary meeting room space, but in order to afford this, the hotel cuts back on service staff for your meeting...who wins?

CONTRACTS

The most important things to remember are that contracts should be written with an equal amount of risk for both parties, and that all your discussions are put into writing so there will be no confusion when it's time for your event.

VENDOR SELECTION

WORKING WITH VENDORS

Facilities are not the only vendors you will be working with to put on meetings and events. You will communicate with many different suppliers of services. Good planners realize that vendors have their own needs as they relate to your event. You need to select vendors on the basis of criteria that you develop for your event. XYZ bus company may have the most modern and comfortable equipment available, but if they are late, or their drivers are rude, they might cause more problems than the shiny buses are worth!

BE SURE TO CHECK REFERENCES

Take every bit as much care in selecting a caterer, transportation company, or a dance band as you do in selecting a site for your event. Unless you have worked with the same vendors over and over again (personnel does change), make sure you check references and ask for bids for their service. Good vendors know how to make planners look good...and good vendors want and deserve repeat business!

USING THE *BRAVO! EVENT RESOURCE GUIDE*

This Resource Guide is an invaluable resource of goods and services. Everything from caterers to musicians is listed in an easy-to-read format that allows you to make informed "apples to apples" comparisons of hundreds of products and services. You can count on reliable information and reliable references, as each business is screened before being listed in the Guide. Also included are helpful hints on checking references, protecting your deposits, securing dates, and more.

ADMINISTRATIVE NEEDS

DAILY TASKS

In conjunction with site and vendor selection, you, as the planner, will also attend to the daily administration tasks necessary to put on an event or meeting. Administration is where communication with your audiences will take place.

COMMUNICATING WITH YOUR AUDIENCE

This is where you will determine appropriate mailing lists and how to handle RSVP's or registrations. How will the mailing happen? Volunteers or mailing houses? Create the graphics and coordinate the printing of all your written materials as early as possible. This is your promotion and publicity for your event. If staff or volunteers are needed, start recruiting them early.

DEVELOPING A SMOOTH SYSTEM

The administration portions of the task list and budget usually include registration, name badges, financial record keeping, database, and computer work. Developing a smooth system that allows checks and balances along the way will help you feel confident that the paperwork is getting handled. A lot of meeting planning is telephone and paper work! The development of clear instructions to the registrants in all your materials will save time and money throughout the meeting process!

GOOD COMMUNICATION

Good communication with your attendees is only half of the successful meeting equation, the other half is good communication with your selected vendors. This means ordering the food and beverages, the room blocks, the room setup, the flowers and the awards! Hopefully, you have selected a great team, and they are supporting you all the way! But they are not mind readers...let them know in writing, in diagrams, charts, and phone calls what you expect—what you are planning, what you need, and when you need it. Lack of information and lack of feeling for the big picture are two of the biggest problems in planning an event. You, as the planner, want to get a timely response from your vendors, and they want to get direction from you.

STAFFING ASSISTANCE

For a large event or trade show, extra staffing and assistance is going to be necessary. There are companies and coordinators that can even deal with the entire registration for your event—handling reservations, organization, name badges, and staffing. Also, there are staffing companies that can offer assistance on a temporary, as needed basis—data entry of names, greeters, setup help, etc. The benefit of these companies is that they assume all the liability for the employee, you just pay an hourly wage.

THE BIG DAY...BIG AFTERNOON...BIG WEEK...

Whether your event is a lunch or a major exposition, the Big Day always arrives! Your good planning will determine just how BIG that day will be. If you have met your deadlines, used your timelines, checked off your checklists, verified menus, orders, schedules, and agendas, you will be ready for any last-minute disasters!!

PRE-CONFERENCE MEETINGS

It is a good idea to plan rehearsals, run-throughs, and team meetings. Conference planners often have pre-conference meetings where all the players are in attendance: the food and beverage managers, the audio visual people, the registration supervisors, the transportation providers, the off-site providers. This is when the last-minute changes are noted, the lines of communication are finalized, and the team is energized for a successful meeting or event!

THE PLANNER IS THE RINGMASTER

On-site is not the place to be determining agenda, policy, or making arrangements. On-site is reacting to the unexpected situations that arise, no matter how good your planning. On-site is maintaining balance as the months, weeks, and days of preparation kick into gear and the event unfolds. The planner is the ringmaster as the acts perform. What happens backstage will most often go unnoticed if good planning has taken place!

TRUST THE TEAM

Delegate as many tasks as possible so you, as the organizer, can attend to the event and troubleshoot. If you are stuck at a registration desk when the lights go out on the main speaker, who's going to get the wheels moving to fix the problems? When the buffet lines are out in the street, who's going to get another serving station set up? Circulate and be everywhere, but don't be in anyone's way. The team has a job to do. They're there to support you and work together to make the event a success. TRUST THE TEAM you have assembled. They are the cast and crew of your production!

MEETING SURVIVAL SUPPLIES

- ❒ File boxes
- ❒ Date and number stamps
- ❒ Stationery and envelopes
- ❒ Computer and computer supplies (disks, etc.)
- ❒ Pens, pencils, markers (multicolor)
- ❒ Staplers and staples
- ❒ Tape (single and double-faced), duct tape
- ❒ Clips, rubber bands, scissors, rulers
- ❒ Toolbox (hammer, screwdriver, assortment of nails)
- ❒ First aid kit
- ❒ Extension cords
- ❒ Colored dots, file folders, labels
- ❒ Flashlight
- ❒ Emergency numbers (messenger services, all-night copy center, etc.)
- ❒ Local telephone book
- ❒ Cash boxes
- ❒ Message pads
- ❒ Extra name badges, place cards, card stock, ribbons
- ❒ Local tourist information, maps, restaurant guides
- ❒ Three-hole and single punches
- ❒ Hand calculator
- ❒ Chalk and eraser, pointer
- ❒ Projector bulb, batteries, carousel tray
- ❒ Cellular phone
- ❒ Walkie talkies
- ❒ Packing knife
- ❒ Measuring tape
- ❒ Spot remover
- ❒ Cassette tape and recorder
- ❒ Camera, film
- ❒ Typing whiteout
- ❒ Sewing kit
- ❒ Throat lozenges
- ❒ Stopwatch
- ❒ Flashlight
- ❒ Other: ____________________
- ❒ Other: ____________________
- ❒ Other: ____________________

SELL THE AUDIENCE ON ATTENDING THE EVENT

Will they come? Even if this is the 100th annual conference, your attendees have to be sold on attending. Even if this is the biggest awards banquet in the history of your company, the employees have to be motivated to come. As the planner, you are in charge of making sure your event is marketed to the right audience. They need to know where, what, when, and how to sign up!

MARKETING TOOLS

You have many tools available to you, and if your kit has a variety of options, you'll have the most success. Some obvious options include: direct mail, in-house newsletters, press releases, paid advertising, billboards, bus sides, and word of mouth. Don't rely on what has worked before—things change, people change. Good programs and reasons to attend will always be your best tools.

PUBLIC RELATIONS/PRESS RELEASE

Refer to the Advertising and Public Relations section of this Guide for local media (newspapers, radio, and television) addresses and phone numbers. Listed below is information about writing the different types of releases:

MEDIA ALERT (SAMPLE)

WHAT: Press Conference

WHEN: Wednesday, December 17, 2002–10:00 a.m.

WHERE: Convention Center, 455 Grand Ave.

WHO: Mike Jones, President, Meeting Planners

TOPIC: Washington's largest convention coming to town

ADDITIONAL INFORMATION: Press pass available. Photo opportunity. Meeting Planners is the largest meeting planner association in the country.

PRESS RELEASE (SAMPLE)

The press release starts the same as the "media alert," then expands upon the what, when, where, who, and topic. Bold the key information throughout the copy.

CALENDAR ITEM (SAMPLE)

WHAT: Cajun Cooking Seminar

WHEN: Wednesday, December 18, 2002–10:00 a.m.

WHERE: Cajun Restaurant, 252 Pacific Road

WHO: Donald Smith, Chef, Cajun Restaurant

COST: $16 per person, senior citizens $8

REGISTRATION: Space limited to 25 people. Pre-registration is required. Registration deadline is December 10, 2002.

ADDITIONAL INFORMATION: Don Smith is a world renowned Cajun Chef who is sharing his secrets to preparing the hottest food in town.

The calendar continues expanding upon the what, when, where, who and cost. Bold the key information throughout the copy.

HOW TO WRITE A PRESS RELEASE

A Press Release is one of the more effective advertising mediums. Press stories are usually presented in the paper, on television or radio, and in trade publications because what you are offering is of special interest to the audience or readership. A press release should be sent out for a variety of reasons, including: a grand opening, a new office site, a special event, a new product, or other exciting news.

Public relations can be like Russian roulette; sometimes you get the coverage and other times you don't. But always send a press release, whether or not you think your event is newsworthy. At current costs, a year's worth of releases can be sent out for the price of a week's worth of advertising. If the newspaper or television station needs a last-minute story, it may publish your release verbatim—or ask to do a story the day of the event.

Timing

- You have to be creative in order to get attention. Larger, more public events and happenings will always take priority over a smaller event. When possible, try not to let your event conflict with other significant occasions.
- You cannot predict disaster or national news stories, but these can happen. Even stories that are already planned and written may be bumped.
- When you send your press releases may determine whether you will receive exposure before or after the event. You may simply send information about the event, or you can invite the press to a press party or to the actual event for coverage. If you want press after the event, as well as before, send out a follow-up release with photos.
- Press Releases should be sent well in advance of the event, anywhere from two weeks to a month. Call the media ahead of time for information about their deadlines and contact people. Larger newspapers may have more than one contact person, perhaps both a "features" editor and a calendar editor. Be sure to send your release to both. Call to confirm that the release was received and then follow-up with enthusiasm about the event, to see if you can answer any questions or provide any additional information.

Planning and Preparation

- The more information you collect (facts, figures, interesting points, etc.) the easier it will be to write an effective press release.
- Media list: There are hundreds of newspapers, radio and television stations, and trade publications (a listing of all local media is located in the following pages). You can send press information to all of them, or just a selected list. Make sure to keep this list for future use. (Note: always update and call-down the media list prior to using—updates are recommended every six months.)
- During this call-down, confirm which department or editor your information should be sent to. You can develop an ongoing relationship with these people for future events and happenings.
- When the press arrives at an event, provide a fact sheet for reporters to take back to their offices. The best fact sheets include details surrounding the event, information about the organization and any keynote speakers or celebrities, as well as the event's goals.
- Don't overlook smaller newspapers. Send press releases to weekly and specialty newspapers as well as the prominent daily papers. You're much more likely to get press there.
- Invite editors or reporters to events in writing, and call to ask if they will be able to attend.

Features of a Superior Press Release:

- **Provides all basic information:** Press releases often lack contact names, telephone numbers, or other essentials. Reporters are busy people who cannot take the trouble to do your work for you. Unclear or incomplete releases will probably be ignored.
- **Includes photos:** A creative photo will give your release an edge over competing releases. Consider suggesting captions for photos. Always send the information necessary for photo credits.
- **Indicates a willingness to assist** with interviews and photo opportunities at your event.
- **Offers admission passes for reporters;** media seldom pay to cover any but the most significant events.
- **Includes some brief background information about your company or organization.** Reporters may not be familiar with your history and will appreciate knowing where the action is.

Writing and Developing

- Creative writing is a must.
- Try to write the press release in a journalistic manner (no first person). Utilize quotes, but avoid any unnecessary hype. Remember to send photos with the story. If written well, the press release will sometimes be published word-for-word.
- While you need to make it interesting, remember to also keep it brief and to the facts; make sure facts are accurate and specific.
- Creative angle to a press release: insert a sample of the product or a photo. Consider a fun and creative format with special paper or ink, mounting on foam core, etc.
- Format for the press release is listed on the previous page.

SPONSORSHIP

HISTORY OF SPONSORSHIP

Sponsorships came about as a good way to finance community events. Large companies were able to generate product awareness, do direct target marketing, establish their name in the community and receive a tax break for sponsoring such events. This tradition of philanthropy is one of the oldest forms of corporate social responsibility where companies build stronger ties with the communities in which they do business.

CREATING FINANCE

Almost every event begins with a budget. The shorter you are on budget, the more you must creatively finance. One excellent way to stretch your dollars is to obtain a co-sponsor. When planning your event, seek out another organization or company which is not a competitor, but would likely benefit from exposure to your audience.

SPONSORSHIP PARTICIPATION MAY INCLUDE:

- Sharing in the cost of the event
- Donating their service
- Advertising the event to their employees or customers
- Including your business at their next event

Terms of co-sponsorship may vary greatly.

YOUR PARTICIPATION MAY INCLUDE:

- Including their name and logo in all event advertising
- Promoting them at the event by publically acknowledging their participation
- Including some of their literature in the next mailing to your customers
- Giving them the mailing list from your event

To follow through on what was promised, keep samples and photos of sponsor acknowledgements and send them in a thank-you letter following the event.

PROMOTIONAL ADVERTISING:

Always ask if there is extra promotional support that can go along with any dollars spent; it can help stretch your budget. For example, if a radio schedule is purchased, ask if you can be the sponsor of the morning news broadcast "This message brought to you by...," then have your commercial run in conjunction with that announcement.

REMEMBER:

- Select your co-sponsors wisely. Affiliation with a sponsor will impact the image of the event.
- Always put your arrangements in writing.
- Provide promotional coupons for their stores promoting the event.
- Confirm, confirm, confirm. This is the event planners mantra.

This type of teamwork often leads to a very positive, ongoing alliance, which makes it one of the most exciting aspects of event planning. If the event is a win-win for both and the event is recurring, you may have an annual sponsor and funding or promotion for your event.

ADVERTISING YOUR EVENT

The many choices of advertising vehicles: There are hundreds of choices of where to spend your advertising dollars: radio, direct mail, newsprint, magazines, television, billboards, the web, etc. There may be a proven medium that has always been used by your company, or you may be faced with making the confusing decision yourself. Advertising agencies and consultants can be helpful in exploring the many options available to achieve the desired results.

Create the marketing plan and set the goals:

- Critique last year's promotion by reviewing the invitations, brochures, press releases, etc.
- Determine your target market in a brainstorming session.
- Gather examples of outstanding ideas and printed pieces you have seen that grab the reader's attention. Always keep an ongoing library of ideas.

Pick a theme and create a campaign:

- Search for a relevant theme.
- Decide the key components to your campaign: posters, mailers, teasers, promotional gifts, giveaways, invitations, paid advertising, media contacts or press releases, etc.

Plan your activity schedule over a six-month period of time:

- Order ad specialties/giveaways, invitations and teasers no later than six weeks before the event.
- Mail teasers four to six weeks prior to event (some meeting planners mail immediately following an annual event, so attendees will save the date for next year).
- Mail invitations three to four weeks prior to event.
- Write a press release at least two weeks prior to the event, and target media alerts for two days prior (after sending a press release, a follow-up phone call to answer any questions can be effective).

Check the design of any mail pieces at the post office before printing: Make sure your design is within postal requirements before completing the project. Rules are always changing, and it is important to keep up to date.

Bulk Mail: Bulk mail can save dollars when mailing high volume campaigns or invitations. You will need a bulk mail permit, or you can buy bulk mail stamps, or the mail house can inkjet the information on your piece. Remember, with bulk mail you are not guaranteed a quick delivery. Mail that is addressed incorrectly will not be returned to you, unless you type "address correction requested" on the piece. If you plan on sorting your own bulk mail it can be a long process. The post office offers seminars on bulk mail. A mail house may be the best investment in this case; mailing can cost you more in your own time, than if you hired a professional.
Postcards can save you dollars: If printing a post card to save postage dollars, make sure it does not exceed 6"x4" or it will not qualify for the post card rate. Check the post card rates at the post office.

The web: Check into banner ads or a listing for your event on web sites that are used by your attendees.

Tracking your results: The best way to know if advertising is working or not for your company is to track results. It can be as simple as asking "how did you hear about this event?" Keep a list at the phone specifying all the ways you received your RSVPs or sales. This list should include all forms of advertising: yellow pages, newspaper, direct mail, publications, word-of-mouth, etc.

Newspapers/Periodicals

Beacon Hill News — 2314 Third Avenue, Seattle WA 98121
(206) 461-1300

Bellingham Herald — PO Box 1277, Bellingham WA 98227
(360) 676-2600, Fax (360) 647-9260

Business Examiner — 1517 S. Fawcett, Suite 350, Tacoma WA 98402
(253) 404-0891 or (800) 540-8322, Fax (253) 404-0892

Capitol Hill Times — 2314 Third Avenue, Seattle WA 98121
(206) 461-1300 or (206) 461-3333

Eastside Business Journal — 12011 NE First Street, Suite 300, Bellevue WA 98005
(425) 455-9734, Fax (425) 453-4171

Eastside Journal — PO Box 90130, Bellevue WA 98009-9230
(425) 455-2222, Fax (425) 635-0603

The Edmonds Enterprise — 4303-198th Street SW, Lynnwood WA 98036
(425) 673-6500, Fax (425) 774-8622

The Enterprise Newspapers — 4303-198th Street SW, Lynnwood WA 98036
(425) 673-6500, Fax (425) 774-8622

Federal Way Mirror — 1414 S. 324th Street, Suite B-210, Federal Way WA 98003
(253) 925-5565, Fax (253) 925-5750

The Herald — PO Box 930, Everett WA 98206
(425) 339-3000, Fax (425) 339-3435

Issaquah Press — PO Box 1328, Issaquah WA 98027
(425) 392-6434

Kirkland Courier — 733 Seventh Avenue, Suite 204, Kirkland WA 98033
(425) 822-9166, Fax (425) 827-7716

The Lake Forest Enterprise — 4303-198th Street SW, Lynnwood WA 98036
(425) 673-6500, Fax (425) 774-8622

Lynden Tribune — PO Box 153, Lynden WA 98264
(360) 354-4444, Fax (360) 354-4445

The Lynnwood Enterprise — 4303-198th Street SW, Lynnwood WA 98036
(425) 673-6500, Fax (425) 774-8622

Madison Park Times — 2314 Third Avenue, Seattle WA 98121
(206) 461-1300

Magnolia News — 2314 Third Avenue, Seattle WA 98121
(206) 461-1300 or (206) 461-1325

Marysville Globe — PO Box 145, Marysville WA 98270
(360) 659-1300, Fax (360) 658-0350

Mercer Island Reporter — PO Box 38, Mercer Island WA 98040
(206) 232-1215, Fax (206) 232-1284

Military News Publishers — Swarner Communications,
PO Box 98801, Tacoma WA 98498
(253) 584-1212, Fax (253) 581-5962

The Mill Creek Enterprise — 4303-198th Street SW, Lynnwood WA 98036
(425) 673-6500, Fax (425) 774-8622

The Mountlake Terrace Enterprise — 4303-198th Street SW, Lynnwood WA 98036
(425) 673-6500, Fax (425) 774-8622

The News Tribune — PO Box 11000, Tacoma WA 98411
(253) 597-8686, Fax (253) 597-8274

North Central Outlook — 2314 Third Avenue , Seattle WA 98121
(206) 461-1300

North Kitsap Herald — PO Box 278, Poulsbo WA 98370
(360) 779-4464, Fax (360) 779-8276

The Northlake News — PO Box 587, Woodinville WA 98072
425) 483-0606, Fax (425) 486-7593
Northshore Citizen — PO Box 647, Bothell WA 98041
(425) 486-1231, Fax (425) 483-3286
The Olympian — PO Box 407, Olympia WA 98507
(360) 754-5420, Fax (360) 357-0202
Penninsula Daily News — 305 W First Street, Port Angeles WA 98362
(360) 452-2345, Fax (360) 417-3521
Puget Sound Business Journal — 720 Third Avenue,
Suite 800, Seattle WA 98104-1811
(206) 583-0701, Fax (206) 447-8510
Queen Anne News — 2314 Third Avenue, Seattle WA 98121
(206) 461-1300
The Rocket — 2028 Fifth Avenue, Seattle WA 98121
(206) 728-7625, Fax (206) 728-8827
Seattle Post Intelligencer — 101 Elliott Avenue W, Seattle WA 98119
(206) 448-8323, Fax (206) 448-8174
Seattle Weekly — 1008 Western Avenue, Suite 300, Seattle WA 98104
(206) 623-0500, Fax (206) 467-4377
Seattle Times — 1120 John Street/Seattle WA 98111, PO Box 70/Seattle WA 98109
(206) 464-2200, Fax (206) 464-2261
The Shoreline Enterprise — 4303-198th Street SW, Lynnwood WA 98036
(425) 673-6500, Fax (425) 774-8622
Skagit Valley Herald — PO Box 578, Mount Vernon WA 98273
(360) 424-3251, Fax (360) 428-0400
South County Journals — PO Box 130, Kent WA 98035-0130
(253) 872-6600, Fax (253) 854-1006
South District Journal — 2314 Third Avenue, Seattle WA 98121
(206) 461-1300
The Stranger — 1535-11th Avenue, 3rd Floor, Seattle WA 98122
(206) 461-1300, Fax (206) 323-7203
The Sun — PO Box 259, Bremerton WA 98337
(360) 377-3711, Fax (360) 479-7681
Tacoma City Paper — PO Box 98801, Tacoma WA 98498
(253) 584-1212, Fax (253) 581-5962
Tacoma Reporter — 917 Pacific Avenue, Suite 100, Tacoma WA 98402
(253) 593-3931, Fax (253) 272-8824
Tacoma Weekly — PO Box 7185, Tacoma WA 98407
(253) 759-5773, Fax (253) 759-5780
University Herald — 2314 Third Avenue, Seattle WA 98121
(206) 461-1300
University Place Journal — 9105 Bridgeport Way SW, Lakewood WA 98499
(253) 565-8756, Fax (253) 584-6098
The Valley View — 13342 NE 175th, Woodinville WA 98072
(425) 483-0606, Fax (425) 486-7593
Vashon-Maury Island Beachcomber — PO Box 447, Vashon WA 98070
(206) 463-9195, Fax (206) 463-6122
WA CEO — 2505 Second Avenue, Suite 602, Seattle WA 98121-1458
(206) 441-8415, Fax (206) 441-8325
West Seattle Herald — 3500 SW Alaska Street, Seattle WA 98126
(206) 932-0300, Fax (206) 937-1223
WHERE Seattle Magazine — 2505-3rd Avenue, Suite 305, Seattle WA 98121
(206) 728-2624, Fax (206) 728-1423

The Woodinville Weekly — 13342 NE 175th, Woodinville WA 98072
(425) 483-0606, Fax (425) 486-7593

Radio Stations

KARR 1460 AM — 7708-128th Place NE, Kirkland WA 98083
(425) 828-6738

KASE 104.3 FM — PO Box 28160, Bellingham WA 98228
(360) 734-1170, Fax (360) 734-5697

KBCS FM — 3000 Landerholm Circle SE, Bellevue WA 98007-6484
(425) 564-2424

KBFW 930 AM — PO Box D, Bellingham WA 98227
(360) 384-1085

KBKS 106.1 FM — 1000 Dexter Avenue N, Suite 100, Seattle WA 98109
(206) 805-1061, Fax (206) 805-0922

KBLE 1050 AM — 114 Lakeside Avenue, Seattle WA 98122
(206) 324-2000, Fax (206) 322-4670

KBRC 1430 AM — PO Box 250, Mount Vernon WA 98273
(360) 424-4278 or (360) 734-8555, Fax (360) 424-1616 or Fax (360) 734-8557

KBSG 97.3 FM & 1210 AM — 1730 Minor Avenue, Suite 2000, Seattle WA 98101
(206) 343-9700, Fax (206) 343-0481

KCIS 630 AM — 19303 Fremont Avenue N, Seattle WA 98133
(206) 546-7350, Fax (206) 546-7372

KCMS 105.3 FM — 19303 Fremont Avenue N, Seattle WA 98133
(206) 546-7350, Fax (206) 546-7372

KCMU 90.3 FM — University of WA, Box 353755, Seattle WA 98195
(206) 543-5541, Fax (206) 543-2720

KENU 1330 AM — 12401 SE 320th Street, Auburn WA
(253) 288-3388

KGMI 790 AM — 2219 Yew Street Road, Bellingham WA 98226
(360) 734-9790, Fax (360) 733-4551

KGNW 820 AM — 2815 Second Avenue, Suite 550, Seattle WA 98121
(206) 443-8200, Fax (206) 777-1133

KGRG 89.9 FM — 12401 SE 320th, Auburn WA 98092-3699
(253) 833-5004, Fax (253) 288-3439

KGY 1240 AM & 96.9 FM — PO Box 1249, Olympia WA 98507
(360) 943-1240, Fax (360) 352-1222

KING 98.1 FM — 333 Dexter Avenue N, Suite 400, Seattle WA, 98109
(206) 448-3981, Fax (206) 448-0928

KIRO 710 AM & 100.7 FM — 1820 Eastlake Avenue E, Seattle WA 98102
(206) 726-7000, Fax (206) 726-5446

KISW FM 99.9 — 712 Aurora Avenue N, Seattle WA 98109,
Business Office 1100 Olive Way, Suite 550, Seattle WA 98101
(206) 285-7625, Fax (206) 282-7018

KIXI 880 AM — 3650-131st SE; Suite 550, Bellevue WA 98006
(425) 653-9462, Fax (425) 455-8849

KJR 950 AM & KJR 95.7 FM — 190 Queen Anne Avenue N,
Suite 100, Seattle WA 98109
(206) 285-2295, Fax (206) 286-2377

KKBY 104.9 FM — 5303 Pacific Hwy E, Suite 106, Tacoma WA 98424
(253) 926-1450, Fax (253) 922-2495

KKDZ 1250 AM — 200-1st Avenue W, Suite 104, Seattle WA
(206) 281-5300
KKOL 1300 AM — 2815-2nd Avenue, Suite 550, Seattle WA 98121
(206) 777-5469, Fax (206) 777-1133
KLFE 1590 AM — 2815 Second Avenue, Suite 550, Seattle WA 98121
(206) 443-8200, Fax (206) 443-1561
KLKI 1340 AM — PO Box 96, Anacortes WA 98221-0096
(360) 293-3141, Fax (360) 293-9463
KLSY 92.5 FM — 3650-131st SE; Suite 550, Bellevue WA 98006
(425) 454-1540, Fax (425) 455-8849
KLYN 106.5 FM — PO Box 30, Lynden WA 98264
(360) 354-5596; (360) 354-7517
KMPS 1300 AM & KMPS 94.1 FM — 1000 Dexter Avenue N,
Suite 100, Seattle WA 98109
(206) 805-0941, Fax (206) 805-0911
KMTT 850 AM & 103.7 FM — 1100 Olive Way, Suite 1650, Seattle WA 98101
(206) 233-8984, Fax (206) 233-8979
KNDD 107.7 FM — 1100 Olive Way, Suite 1650, Seattle WA 98101
(206) 622-3251, Fax (206) 682-8349
KNHC 89.5 FM — 10750-30th NE, Seattle WA 98125
(206) 366-7815, Fax (206) 421-5018
KNWX 770 AM — 1820 Eastlake Avenue E, Seattle WA 98102
(206) 726-7000, Fax (206) 726-5446
KOMO 1000 AM — 1809 Seventh Avenue, Suite 200, Seattle WA 98101
(206) 223-5700, Fax (206) 516-3110
KPLU 88 FM — Pacific Lutheran University,
121st Street & Park Avenue, Tacoma WA 98447
(253) 535-7758, Fax (253) 535-8332
KPLZ 101.5 FM — 1809 Seventh Avenue, Suite 200, Seattle WA 98101
(206) 421-1015, Fax (206) 292-1015
KQBZ 100.7 FM — 1820 Eastlake Avenue E, Seattle WA 98102
(206) 726-7000, Fax (206) 726-7701
KRPM 1090 AM — 3131 Elliott Avenue, Suite 750, Seattle WA 98121
(206) 282-5477, Fax (206) 282-3531
KRWM 106.9 FM — 3650-131st Avenue SE, Bellevue WA 98006
(206) 292-8600, Fax (206) 292-6964
KSER 90.7 FM — 14920 Hwy 99, Suite 150, Lynnwood WA 98037
(425) 742-4541, Fax (425) 742-4191
KSRB 1150 AM — 3650-131st Avenue SE, Suite 550, Bellevue WA 98006
(425) 373-5536, Fax (206) 441-6322
KUBE 93 FM — 190 Queen Anne Avenue N, Suite 100, Seattle WA 98109
(206) 285-2295, Fax (206) 286-2376
KUOW 94.9 FM — University of WA, Box 353750, Seattle WA 98195
(206) 543-2710, Fax (206) 543-2720
KUPS 90.1 FM — 1500 N Warner, Tacoma WA 98416
(253) 756-3288, Fax (253) 879-3947
KVI 570 AM — 1809-7th Avenue, Suite 200, Seattle WA 98101
(206) 223-5700, Fax (206) 292-1015
KVTI 90.9 FM — 4500 Steilacoom Boulevard SW, Lakewood WA 98499
(253) 589-5884
KXPA 1540 AM — 1100 Olive Way, Suite 950, Seattle WA 98101
(206) 292-7800

MIXX 961 AM KXXO — PO Box 7937, Olympia WA 98507
(360) 943-9937, Fax (360) 352-3643
KYCW 96.5 FM — 1000 Dexter Avenue N, Suite 100, Seattle WA 98109
(206) 805-0965, Fax (206) 805-0932
KZOK 102.5 FM — 1000 Dexter Avenue N, Suite 100, Seattle WA 98109
(206) 805-0941, Fax (206) 805-0909

Television Stations

KBTC-TV Channel 28 — 1101 S Yakima Avenue, Tacoma WA 98405
(253) 596-1528, Fax (253) 596-1623
KCPQ-TV Channel 13 — 1813 Westlake Avenue N, Seattle WA 98109
(206) 674-1313, Fax (206) 674-1713
KCTS-TV Channel 9 — 401 Mercer, Seattle WA 98109
(206) 728-6463, Fax (206) 443-6691
KING-TV Channel 5 — 333 Dexter Avenue N, Seattle WA 98109
(206) 448-5555, Fax (206) 448-4525
KIRO-TV Channel 7 — 2807 Third Avenue, Seattle WA 98121
(206) 728-7777, Fax (206) 441-4840
KOMO-TV Channel 4 — 140 Fourth Avenue N, Seattle WA 98109
(206) 443-4000, Fax (206) 443-3422
KSTW-TV Channel 11 — 2320 S 19th, Tacoma WA 98405\
(253) 572-5789, Fax (253) 272-7581
KTBW-TV Channel 20 — 1909 S 341st Place, Federal Way WA 98003
(253) 927-7720, Fax (253) 874-7432
KTZZ-TV Channel 22 — 1813 Westlake Avenue N, Seattle WA 98109
(206) 282-2202, Fax (206) 281-0207
KVOS-TV Channel 12 — 1151 Ellis Street, Bellingham WA 98225-5203
(360) 671-1212, Fax (360) 647-0824

FINAL WRAP-UP

The event is over, but the work is not. For many meeting and event planners the final wrap-up is the biggest struggle. Not only have you ended months of preparation, now you have to finalize the billings, check the invoices, distribute the monies, etc. The wrap-up may not be fun, but it is crucial.

START THE PROCESS IN THE BEGINNING

Good planners start this final process long before they get on-site. They plan with their vendors how they will verify services during the event, when payments will be due, and what kind of documentation will need to be completed in order to take care of matters in a timely way.

THINGS TO MAKE THIS STEP EASIER

Ask to get all function bills the day of the event so you can verify their accuracy while things are still fresh in your mind. When verifying charges, ask yourself:

- Were you charged for the correct number of people?
- Are there any charges you cannot identify?
- Are there charges you did not anticipate?

DAILY DIARY

Make a daily diary notation of things that worked and didn't work, notes for next year, and things to remember. Write it down or it won't be remembered. Follow-up should include making arrangements in advance to have materials returned or disposed of.

THANK-YOU NOTES

Determine who will receive thank-you notes. Verify addresses, spelling of names, facility, and vendor contacts. Make a note of those people who were especially helpful to you or your attendees!

MEETING WRAP-UP

Schedule a wrap-up meeting in advance with the facility's major department heads, or for small events, your contact. The purpose of this meeting is to find out how well EVERYONE performed, and what could be done differently in the future. This is also a time to ascertain whether you provided the facility and other vendors with appropriate information and instructions. Did you schedule enough time for activities on the agenda? Did you guarantee enough meals within the deadline? Should you have ordered another bar, larger room, or extra servers?

FEEDBACK

While you are evaluating, make sure you ask the attendees what they thought of the event, the facility, and the program? Do they have ideas or suggestions for next year? Their feedback can be one of the most important tools to help you plan the next event. Take time before the event to design questions that will solicit answers which will help you plan future events.

REWARD YOURSELF!

Last, but not least...reward yourself! Many planners make this their first task of the meeting or event. They plan what they will do after the BIG DAY. Whether it is a bubble bath or an island cruise, plan something for yourself—you've done a great job and you deserve it!

ETIQUETTE—CULTURAL AWARENESS MEANS GOOD BUSINESS

In today's global marketplace, it is no longer enough to know the products you are marketing. The way you first connect with someone from a different culture is critical to establishing a mutually beneficial relationship, and understanding cultural differences, styles and expressions is the first step toward success. Every culture has its own time-honored protocols, and savvy Americans learn them while they are still on familiar soil.

Do Your Homework

The first step is to learn as much as possible about your target country—before leaving your office. Research materials are readily available. Do not underestimate the importance of this commitment. People from other countries spend years studying the "American way" of doing business.

Make Detailed Business Plans

Plan all aspects of your trip in advance. Outside of the U.S., you cannot just pick up the hotel room phone and set up appointments. In fact, the objective of your first trip may be to introduce yourself and build all-important credibility and trust, not talk business. If you are committed to a long-term relationship, be prepared to make another trip.

Status is Important

Status is very important to persons in countries outside the U.S. Here, it may happen that, in some companies, the CEO is on a mutual first-name basis with the mail room attendant. You should be prepared for a very formal atmosphere in your dealings abroad. Your position here in the U.S. will dictate whom you meet in your target country. In Japan, for example, a manager from the U.S. will meet a manager from the Japanese firm...a director will meet a director. The same is true throughout Eastern Asia, as well as in Western and Eastern Europe, the Arab World, and Latin America. Sending a mid-level executive to deal with a high-ranking executive is interpreted as an insult. Instant familiarity is not appreciated. You will cause discomfort if you call your new acquaintances by their first names, or if you invite them to call you by your first name.

Introductions

Outside of the U.S., a great deal of emphasis is placed on style and form. Introductions and greetings are critically important, unlike the U.S. where we frequently laugh at wrong introductions and move on to other matters. Do not expect your international counterparts to take a wrong so lightly. Simply, in business introductions, who gets introduced to whom is determined by precedence. The person who holds the highest position takes precedence over other who work there. The most important person's name is always spoken first. For example, "Ms. Senior Executive, may I present Ms. Junior Executive," or, "Mr. Senior Executive, may I present Ms. Junior Executive," or, "Mr. Senior Executive, I would like to introduce Mr. Junior Executive." Always provide additional information..."Mr. Junior Executive is from the accounting department; Mr. Senior Executive is our Director of Public Affairs."

Gift Giving

Gift giving is an important aspect of conducting business abroad, and, while pleasurable, it is also a subject of concern. Choosing the appropriate gift requires careful study of your target country's gift culture, for a blunder in this area can be the cause of a tarnished relationship or media embarrassment. In the business arena, Japan is considered the most gift-giving culture in the world.

Here are a few protocols on gifting in Japan:

- When visiting Japan, always let your Japanese colleague give you a gift before you give him one. You would make him lose face otherwise.
- You should give your Japanese host a reciprocal gift after you have received yours, but always a more modest one than the one he gave you.
- Never give a gift in front of others unless you have something to give everyone in the room. Gift giving is a private, intimate ritual.
- Be aware that your gift may not be opened in front of you. Do not be insulted by this.
- Present and receive a gift with both hands and a slight bow.
- Take a gift with you if you are invited to a private home. A book, candy, or flowers are appropriate.
- The Japanese take great pains in their wrapping of gifts. There should be color in the wrapping, instead of a funeral all-white scheme. Avoid ribbons and bows when gift wrapping.

Favorite Gifts for the Japanese:

- The Japanese enjoy brand name gifts "Made in the USA" such as Tiffany's, Saks Fifth Avenue, Neiman Marcus, or Nordstrom.
- The gift does not have to be elaborate or costly, but the store you shopped in gives it a special value. In fact, printed wrapping paper from the store is much appreciated.
- Special products of your company are excellent choices; however, avoid humorous logo gifts.
- A book is an excellent choice—a beautiful coffee table book with photographs of your geographical area is appropriate.
- CDs or tapes of American symphonic, rock or folk music are appropriate (if you know the personal preference)
- Good quality, somber-colored neckties for men
- Silk scarves and good handbags for women
- Obviously, do not present a gift that was "Made in Japan" or any other Asian country.
- Avoid the numbers "4 and 9"—they mean death and suffering

As you can see, doing your "etiquette homework" is the first step toward successful dealings in the United States and abroad, whether you are a high ranking executive, manager, or important "behind-the-scenes" player in today's competitive marketplace.

For additional information on
Gift Giving Etiquette for China and European Countries,
see pages 38–39.

NOTES

Accommodations

❖❖❖

HELPFUL HINTS

Americans With Disabilities Act (ADA): This law passed in 1991 requires public buildings (convention centers, hotels, restaurants, etc.) to meet minimum standards making their facilities accessible to individuals with disabilities. Expect facilities to comply. It is the planner's responsibility to find out what auxiliary aids are available in the facilities they use. Although it may not be readily apparent, nearly every group has at least one person with a disability. Ensuring barrier-free accommodations for disabled people goes beyond inspecting for wheelchair ramps. Keep other attendees with needs in mind, such as hearing and visually impaired guests and people with special dietary needs (insulin dependent diabetics may need refrigerators in their rooms).

Room Rates: Rates are available in several categories. Be sure to know which ones you qualify for: commercial rates, corporate rates, government rates. Rack rates are common rates that hotels provide. Rack rate is the facility's standard, pre-established guest room rate and is never considered or accepted by groups.

What determines group rates? Group rates are determined by group size. Definition of the group size might vary, or other factors may affect the rate you receive. Rates for sleeping rooms are determined in several ways:

- **Time of year:** "Peak" season, hotels can demand higher rates. Shoulder seasons and off-season rates are usually your best buy.
- **Number of rooms required:** Groups with large numbers are in a better position to negotiate lower room rates.
- **Arrival and departure patterns:** Business hotels tend to have high occupancy mid-week and lower occupancy over the weekend. The opposite is true at resorts.
- **Future business:** If you are, or may be, a repeat customer, you may get more favorable rates.

Be prepared with past history: If the meeting was held at the same place in years past, be sure to know the history and past negotiations. You will be able to negotiate better knowing your previous room block, pickup rate of rooms, and dollars generated by the hotel.

Last minute bookings: Be flexible with the details of the meeting or event to negotiate the best rates. You may not be able to get everything you need, but by changing the starting or ending time of your meeting to accommodate another meeting, you may receive a greater concession on rental fees. Also, the hotels are anxious to fill up any last-minute open space.

Off-season can offer great benefits: Most properties offer a 25-50% discount in what they call off-season and shoulder season.

Amenities provided by hotels: Complimentary items provided by a facility for guests may include toilet articles, writing supplies, bathrobes, or fruit baskets. Some planners say that in-room coffee is one of the best amenities. It is reasonable to ask for extra towels for health club use, or for quick delivery of forgotten items, such as razors, toothbrushes, or hair dryers. Find out before if these supplies are available. Concierge services and business centers are valuable to your guests. Don't be afraid to ask for the extras: an additional room for every block of 50 rooms, complimentary use of hotel limousine for VIP pickups, a few rooms at 50% off the group rate for staff.

Tipping: A tip or gratuity is given to an individual at the time the service is provided. Personnel that most frequently receive this type of gratuity are doormen, bell staff, waitstaff, and housemaids or room attendants. If these tips are meeting or event related, keep a detailed record because they need to be accounted for in the budget.

HELPFUL HINTS

Tipping can be confusing: "Let me see, the garage attendant is bringing my car around." "It is a first-class restaurant. How much should I tip?" "What do I tip if I have less than perfect service in a restaurant?" "What if we have bad service?"

In most cases, servers and attendants rely heavily upon their tipping income. Most try their best to provide good service, and when service blunders do happen, you should try to give them the "benefit of the doubt." If the service is fantastic, leave a generous tip. If not, leave a modest tip and explain to the server/attendant in private your reasoning for doing so. Hopefully, they will benefit from your feedback. The only time you shouldn't leave a tip is when a server/attendant is blatantly rude.

Suggested Tipping Guidelines

- **In a modest restaurant:** Give the waitperson 15% of the bill minus tax; give $1 to the waiter if he goes outside to call you a cab; tip $1 to the garage attendant who brings your car around.
- **In an expensive restaurant:** Give the waitperson 20% of the total bill minus tax, split 12% to the waiter and 8% to the captain. (You may ask the captain to split the bill between him and the waiter, with the waiter receiving 75% of it.) Give $10 to the maitre d'hôtel if he gave you a good table and provided good service on a busy day. Tip $3 to $5 for the wine steward (or 8% of the total cost of the wines). Tip $1 for each coat checked, $2 if there are shopping bags or umbrellas with your coat. Tip $1 to the restroom attendant, $5 for services, like sewing a button or removing a spot on a tie or gown. Tip $3 to the garage attendant who brings your car around.
- **In a limousine:** 20% of the bill in a large city; 15% in a small city
- **In a taxi:** For a $5 ride, give a $1 tip. For a $10 ride, give a $1.50 to $2 tip. For a ride to the airport, pay 15–20%. If you are caught in a traffic jam with a zone taxi driver (not paid by time), tip up to $5 more for his time. It is up to you—if he complains through the whole incident, give him less.
- **In a first-class hotel:** In a nice hotel, you should not carry even one small bag around, unless you are very late for a flight. Bags should be carried by the bellman. Tip $2 to the doorman when you arrive or leave; $3 to the bellman; room service—20% of bill, with a $2 minimum; maid service—$2 per night (left on your pillow, so they know it is for them); $1 to $5 for the bellman who runs an errand for you, depending upon the time commitment; $1 to the doorman for getting you a cab; $2 to $5 for a doorman who goes out in the rain to get you a cab; $5 to a concierge who has provided extra-special service.
- **In a modest hotel:** $1 to the doorman when you arrive or leave; $2 to the bellman—or $3 if there is a lot of luggage; 10–15% of the room service bill (minimum of $1); $1 per night to the maid; 50¢ to $1 for bellman delivery to your room; $3 to the bellman who provides a special service; $1 for the doorman who brings your car around.
- **In a fast-food or take-out restaurant:** Of course, you are not required to tip in a pizza parlor or deli, but if someone has provided extra service in a cheerful manner, a $1–$2 tip is appreciated, especially if you are picking up multiple orders to take back to your office.

A Thank You Is Free

Remember an appreciative "thank you for the excellent service" goes a long way toward making someone's day. In addition, fill out a customer service response card or send a letter to the manager congratulating them on their fine waitperson. It feels great to compliment others! And it's free! If it is a restaurant your business frequents regularly, letters such as those written on company letterhead help build long lasting customer relationships, and good service as well.

THE CLAREMONT HOTEL

2000 Fourth Avenue at Virginia • Seattle, Washington 98121
Contact: Sales Department
(206) 694-7255, (800) 448-8601; Fax (206) 443-1420
E-mail: sales@claremonthotel.com
Web site: www.claremonthotel.com

Seattle's Favorite Classic Hotel

Description of hotel

The Claremont Hotel is a charming, intimate, upscale European-style boutique hotel. Located in the absolute heart of downtown Seattle, within three blocks of the world famous Pike Place Market, all major department stores and the monorail terminal to the Seattle Center. The hotel is delightfully restored with high ceilings and classic architectural detail featuring marble and brass accents.

Accommodations

120 gracious guest rooms and suites, including Junior Suites with wet bars and Executive Suites with a spacious parlor and separate king bedroom. All guest rooms have plush robes, hair dryers, irons and ironing boards and complete Aveda amenities. Enjoy a complimentary *USA Today* delivered to your guest room. For the frequent traveler, each room has a desk, dual line telephone with DID (direct inward dial) line, modem hookup and voice mail. Copy services and in-room fax machines upon request. Ask about our rooms equipped with data linking technology. Corporate and group rates are available. Valet parking available.

Meeting facilities

The centerpiece of the hotel is an intimate and elegant two-story ballroom with wrap-around gallery and sky light. Next to the ballroom is the Virginia Room, with high ceilings, abundant light and a long cherry wood bar. Used separately or together, these two fully restored rooms are extraordinary facilities for meetings of up to 175 or a social event up to 250. Additional breakout rooms and complete meeting banquet and catering services are available.

Assaggio Ristorante

The perfect place to entertain clients is Assaggio Ristorante. Featuring award winning Northern Italian cuisine and voted the Best Italian Restaurant in Seattle by the readers of the *Seattle Weekly*. Open for lunch Monday through Friday and dinner six days a week.

See page 161 under Banquet, Meeting & Event Sites.

THE EDGEWATER

A NOBLE HOUSE HOTEL

2411 Alaskan Way • Pier 67
Seattle, Washington 98121
Dir. of Sales & Marketing: Jodi Forslund
(206) 728-7000 or 1-888-316-4449
Fax (206) 448-0255
E-mail: jforslund@edgewaterhotel.com
Web site: www.noblehousehotels.com

Guest rooms and amenities

- 236 guest rooms with fireplaces, including 3 waterfront suites; 1 penthouse suite
- Waterview Rooms available from $229 to $299
- Cityview Rooms available from $189 to $239
- Suites: $325 to $1,500
- In-room refreshment Center
- Hair dryers, coffee service, umbrellas, irons with ironing boards, and luxurious robes in all rooms
- Gift Shop with Northwest products
- Complimentary use of mountain bikes, April–October
- In-room movies available

Meeting space and services

- Nine different meeting rooms with capacities from 10 people up to 200
- Professional audio/visual equipment available
- Full-service bar available in either host or no-host arrangement
- All catering costs include a professionally trained and quietly efficient staff

Special package

Romance package includes one night's accommodations, bottle of champagne, breakfast from *Six Seven* restaurant, and free parking.

AN AWARD-WINNING HOTEL

The Edgewater has been featured in numerous local, regional and national publications, including *The Wine Press,* the Pacific Northwest edition of *Special Places,* and *The Best Places to Kiss in the Northwest: A Romantic Travel Guide.* The Edgewater is owned and operated by Noble House Hotels and Resorts.

See page 177 under Banquet, Meeting & Event Sites.

1101-4th Avenue
Seattle, Washington 98101
(206) 621-7779
or (800) 715-6513

The 189 guestrooms at the boutique Hotel Monaco balance the business needs away from the office with the pampering comfort of a small luxury hotel. Fully configured for business use, each room surrounds guests in exceptional comfort. Rich color schemes in crimson, ochre and charcoal or vibrant yellow with raspberry and cream are layered upon bold patterns and luxurious textures and furnishings.

In addition to the attention to details for which the downtown Hotel Monaco Seattle is known, guestroom amenities include:

- Two-line phones with 15-foot cords
- Private voicemail
- Private bar
- Gourmet treats in the fully-stocked honor bars
- Amenities of home such as terrycloth bathrobes, in-room coffee makers (with Starbucks coffee), hairdryers, iron and ironing boards
- Double-glazed sound-proof windows
- Suites have a VCR and CD stereos
- Monte Carlo Suites have sofabeds
- Mediterranean suites feature deluxe bathrooms with two-person Fuji jet tubs

The hotel also provides the following services for those business guests that you would like to impress.

- Complimentary in-room coffee serving Starbucks coffee
- Complimentary evening wine service by the lobby fireplace, a chance to relax and unwind after a busy day
- Round-the-clock room service
- Round-the-clock fully equipped fitness facility
- Complimentary USA Today delivered daily to hotel guestroom
- Same-day laundry, dry-cleaning service and complimentary shoeshine
- Secretarial and business services available
- Full concierge staff on site to assist you during your stay
- Safety deposit boxes are available at the front desk
- Bring your pet with you—we are a pet-friendly hotel; upon request, you may have a complimentary goldfish companion delivered to your guestroom
- Valet parking

Located near historic Pioneer Square, the Washington State Convention and Trade Center, and Pike Place Market, the small luxury Hotel Monaco Seattle is also convenient to the waterfront and downtown financial district.

THE INN - APARTMENTS℠

THE MEDITERRANEAN INN

425 Queen Anne Avenue North • Seattle, Washington 98109
(206) 428-4700 or Toll-free (866) 425-4700
Fax (206) 428-4699
E-mail: innaptsglenn@hotmail.com

Discover Seattle's newest hotel located in the vibrant Queen Anne neighborhood adjacent to the Key Arena and Space Needle. Our accommodations include 180 guest rooms beautifully decorated to reflect the Mediterranean style, and the option to stay nightly, weekly or month-to-month.

Guestrooms and amenities

- Waterview and Cityview rooms
- High speed Internet connection, Data ports, Voice Mail
- Kitchenettes with refrigerator, coffee maker, microwave, granite countertops
- Exercise Facility
- Guest Laundry
- Parking on site
- Business Center
- Rooftop deck with Seattle and Elliott Bay views

Meeting facilities

We provide an ideal location for small meetings and events. The Boardroom accommodates 12 people boardroom style seating and The Meeting Room accommodates 20 reception style and 16 classroom.

Our ideal location in the Queen Anne neighborhood provides our guests with the convenience of nearby shopping, theatres, restaurants and the Seattle Center.

See page 235 under Banquet, Meeting & Event Sites.

Notes

Ad Specialties, Awards & Corporate Gifts

❖❖❖

HELPFUL HINTS

Gift giving in the business arena is a task to be taken seriously, as the opportunity to cement a relationship can be lost if the situation is not handled properly. The challenge is to make your gift both appropriate and appreciated:

Choosing the appropriate gift requires a careful study of your target country's gift culture, for a blunder in this arena can be the cause of a tarnished relationship or media embarrassment. No matter what country, always keep in mind:

- A perfect gift shows great research and thought (example: someone who collects something special would appreciate an addition to his/her collection).
- A perfect gift is chosen specifically with the recipient in mind (your customer may have mentioned a passion for poetry, thus a book of poetry would be appreciated).
- If you are not familiar with the gift giving customs of a particular country, ask the advice of a business colleague, an official in the local consulate of that country, or a business person from that country who is now living in the U.S.
- Your gift should not be too costly, or the recipient could consider it a bribe.
- A gift relating to the person's profession is always meaningful (an antique dictionary might be appropriate for an attorney who displays antique furniture in the office).
- Steer clear of corporate logo gifts, they can seem like an advertisement, not a present. As a general rule, any gift displaying a corporate logo should do so discreetly, not so the logo overshadows the gift item.

In Japan:

Japan is considered the most gift-giving culture in the world. Here are a few tips:

- When visiting Japan, always let your Japanese colleague give you a gift before you give him one. You would make him lose face otherwise.
- You should give your Japanese host a reciprocal gift after you have received yours, but always a more modest one than the one he gave you.
- Never give a gift in front of others unless you have something to give everyone in the room. Gift giving is a private, intimate ritual.
- Be aware that your gift may not be opened in front of you. Do not be insulted by this.
- Present and receive a gift with both hands and a slight bow.
- Take a gift with you if you are invited to a private home. A book, candy, or flowers are appropriate.
- The Japanese take great pains in their wrapping of gifts. There should be color in the wrapping, instead of a funeral all-white scheme. Avoid ribbons and bows when gift wrapping.

Favorite Gifts for the Japanese:

- The Japanese enjoy brand name gifts "Made in the USA" such as Tiffany's, Saks Fifth Avenue, Neiman Marcus, or Nordstrom.
- The gift does not have to be elaborate or costly, but the store you shopped in gives it a special value. In fact, printed wrapping paper from the store is much appreciated.
- Special products of your company are excellent choices; however, avoid humorous logo gifts.
- A book is an excellent choice—a beautiful coffee table book with photographs of your geographical area is appropriate.
- CDs or tapes of American symphonic, rock or folk music are appropriate (if you know the personal preference).
- Good quality, somber-colored neckties for men.
- Silk scarves and good handbags for women.
- Obviously, do not present a gift that was "Made in Japan" or any other Asian country.
- Avoid the numbers "4" and "9"—they mean death and suffering.

In China:

Technically speaking, gift giving is against their law. However, two perfectly legal and honorable gifts are the banquet (which matches the lavishness of the one they held for you) and a collective, symbolic gift "from your side to their side"—this is publicly given for the entire Chinese delegation, and is given to the leader of that delegation.

- High quality pens are a luxury in China.
- Gifts are given after all business negotiations are finished.
- Don't give commemorative medals or tokens, since they may be mistaken for foreign currency, which the Chinese are not allowed to accept as gifts.
- Avoid giving clocks. The English word for "clock" is a homonym for the Chinese word "funeral."
- Avoid writing in red ink, it means you're cutting off a friendship.

In Europe:

- In Italy, don't give chrysanthemums, as they are symbols of mourning. Also, the number 17 is considered unlucky (13 is the luckiest) for flowers as well as overall good fortune. And avoid purple, the color of death in Italy.
- In Germany, flower bouquets should always consist of an uneven number, and never give 13 flowers. Red roses are reserved for lovers only. Excellent gifts are those which give a taste of America and its culture.
- In Great Britain, gifts that demonstrate thoughtfulness and consideration give the most pleasure. Entertainment in the form of meals, drinks or a night at the theater or ballet generally take the place of gift giving.

Female Executives Giving Gifts

- The position of women in other countries may be far less advanced than in the United States, so an American woman executive should refrain from giving gifts to her foreign colleagues until she knows them fairly well. She should wait until a foreign colleague gives her a gift (unless she is the honoree of a party he is giving).
- If she has met the wife of a foreign colleague, she may bring a small gift for the wife when she goes to that country on business, for that is something easy for a male executive to accept. Cosmetics, designer perfume, or costume jewelry are appropriate.
- From one woman executive to another, a travel case, nice tote bag, or an umbrella make suitable gifts, even if they have NOT previously met.
- If a woman does know her foreign colleague well, she must refrain from giving a personal gift (such as a bathrobe). A desk accessory would be appropriate, or perhaps a leather picture frame, with the suggestion he use it to display a family photo. A gift of food is also appropriate.

General International Gift Ideas

- The latest American gadget is usually appreciated by a foreigner, but make sure to include a battery adapter.
- A best-selling American book on foreign policy or on American business practices would be of interest to English-speaking associates.
- A box of fine stationery with a conservative color is always welcome.
- Music tapes or compact discs of classical music, American jazz, folk, country, or rock are also a good idea.
- Clothing is welcome, if you know the size. Consider blue jeans and all Western wear, American-made sweaters and sweatshirts, running shoes, ski caps with American ski organizations and team names, or sports team t-shirts.
- Designer-name accessories (ties, scarves, belts) are always appropriate.

HELPFUL HINTS

Advertising specialties are the items that make an impression and keep your name in the minds of the attendees long after the event is over. These gifts, giveaways, awards, or promotional items feature your meeting name, business logo, or your slogan imprinted on them. Traditional types of imprinted giveaways include pens, coffee mugs, hats, t-shirts, etc. The goal today is that these ad specialties be gifts that will have real meaning and function for the people who receive them.

Get the most from your gift or promotional dollars! Make sure you investigate all the options and come up with the gift or giveaway that has the most importance and value to your audience. Working with a professional company that offers experience and service is important. The experienced company will have a large enough selection available so you won't have to go all over town looking for the perfect gift.

When looking for your gift, promotional item, or giveaway, ask yourself the following questions: How much is the budget? How many pieces will I need? Do I give them to everyone? Do I want a functional or fun item? Is this something I would like to receive? Are the gifts of a quality that reflects my company/meeting standards? What type of imprint is needed on the gifts? What do I want it to say? How much time do I have before I need them?

There is a fine line between a gimmick and a giveaway. A gimmick means you have to do something before you receive the "special gift." Everyone is fed up with scams and phony prizes. A gift or promotional item is given without any strings attached.

Theme and recreational events. There is an idea for every theme or recreational event: golf balls with the company logo imprinted for a golf tournament, imprinted bandanas for a western party, water bottles for a run, travel clocks given to meeting planners reminding them it's time to book a meeting, etc.

Giveaways can be sophisticated. Imprinted calculators, watches, duffel bags, golf bags, towels, beach chairs—just about anything is possible. Refer to this section for lots of wonderful ideas.

Favors: Meal time is the perfect time to give a souvenir. Something portable, like a lapel pin, an imprinted pen, or small box of chocolates or mints. Favors are often a part of the theme of a gala evening. Make it something convenient to carry, not cumbersome.

HELPFUL HINTS

Gift and fruit baskets: The famous welcome basket of fruit has come a long way! Today meeting planners are pressured to provide "VIP" gifts that are creative, easy to travel with, functional, and even recyclable! The fruit basket has evolved into a theme basket for whatever occasion is at hand. Pick the items and the theme, and the basket can be created. Baskets can be personalized, according to hobbies and season, with food additions (coffee, chocolate, etc.). Refer to this section for professionals who custom-design and deliver to your door.

Thank you gifts: These are most often given to vendors, speakers, and volunteers for doing a good job. After a speaker has presented, many planners send a gift to the speaker's office or hand it to him or her personally. Thanking a vendor or the volunteers who helped create a successful meeting or event is very common. Jewelers and gift stores specialize in gifts like designer pen and pencil sets, crystal or silver pieces, lapel pins, etc.

Room gifts: These are usually light snacks, cheese, wine, crackers, and fruit. Logo chocolates are fun to have for a late-night treat. Other items might be mementos of the city, state, or company. Coffee-table books can be easily packed for the return trip home.

Retirement or acknowledgment gifts: These gifts or awards are usually very nice and more personal—watches, jewelry, crystal or silver pieces. Many of these gifts have a personal message engraved on them or can be an item that fits the person's style and personality.

Annual gifts: The holidays are always busy times for the gift-giving businesses. Thanking clients for their business and thanking vendors for a job well done are reasons to give holiday gifts. Keep in minds these gifts need to be tasteful. A gift given during the year for no particular reason is a nice surprise. Also, a thank-you to a client for a large order or big account is a nice gesture.

Awards: Traditional plaques have little purpose aside from placing them on a wall or desk. Today, many awards have a purpose—an engraved clock or a piece of engraved jewelry. It's nice to receive an award you can proudly use and display throughout the year that reminds you of that special acknowledgment you have earned.

Unique gifts: Corporate awards are lasting visual symbols that show how much the award-winner's contributions are valued. Unique, unusual, or uncommonly beautiful awards elicit the most comments from the employees and customers who see them. Every time someone asks about a particularly striking award, the performance which earned it is remembered and reinforced. The best awards are ones which are selected with the people who receive them in mind.

bluedip marketing

4122 Factoria Boulevard S.E., Suite 102 • Bellevue, Washington 98006
(425) 373-3574
Fax (425) 373-3575
E-mail: darron@bluedip.com
Web site: www.bluedip.com

Promotional Products and Marketing Collateral

Bluedip Marketing is a full service promotional marketing firm that specializes in creative solutions and innovative ideas to meet all of your marketing needs.

With over 13 years of experience in the promotional marketing industry, we pride ourselves in offering competitive pricing and unsurpassed customer service.

Bluedip Marketing can extend your company brand in various ways. We source everything from apparel to high-tech toys to executive gifts. We are committed to working with you to find the ideal product that will get your company recognized and remembered.

We do it all!

- Lava Lamps
- Mugs
- Key Chains
- Mousepads
- Fleece Clothing
- Post-Its
- Chocolates
- Shirts/Hats
- Portfolios
- Awards
- Toys
- Picture Frames
- Lanyards
- Cigars/Accessories
- Corporate Gifts
- Pens
- Candles
- Sports Items
- PDA Holders
- Duffel/Laptop Bags
- Watches

Bluedip Marketing. All you need.

Do Me a Favor!®

900-108th Avenue N.E., Suite 104 • Bellevue, Washington 98004
(425) 456-0050 or Toll-free (800) 686-7103; Fax (425) 456-0070
E-mail: domeafavor1@aol.com • ***Web site: www.domeafavor.com***

Business Hours: Tue–Sat 10am–6pm; Other hours by appointment

Free parking, always! Conveniently located in downtown Bellevue.

Business Conferences, Fundraisers, Retirements, Grand Openings, Anniversaries, Sales Meetings, Corporate Functions, Holiday Celebrations, Bar/Bat Mitzvahs, Milestone Accomplishments, Family Reunions, New Babies, Weddings...

We all love a gathering. The people, the conversations, the smiles, sometimes the tears, the celebration, the good times. But the stressful part can be coming up with those details that make your function "special." Walk through the door at 'Do Me A Favor!' and you'll think "Wow!" From the delightful smells, to our comfortable guest chairs, and our wide selection of products and services, you'll feel a great sense of relief. Most importantly, we'll save you time and reduce your stress. Need instant help, or to visit after work hours? Give us a call!

Gifts and Gift Baskets

We offer an impressive selection of specialty gift items for any occasion. Selected for their beauty and special appeal. On display in our showroom you'll find the best of the marketplace, including seasonal gifts. Our custom-made gift baskets, with a range of prices, are a great surprise for out-of-town guests, or a "thank you" for that terrific client. Delivery is available. Special orders and requests, always. Just ask.

Invitations, Announcements, and Holiday Cards

Our stationery department offers you a vast array of choices, with styles and prices to meet your needs. Yours will be printed by outstanding companies including Anna Griffin, Carlson Craft, Checkerboard, Crane, Dempsey & Carroll, Elite, Encore Studios, Family Cards, Oblation, Regency, and others. Personalized holiday cards are a specialty for us. You'll come back year after year like others who have discovered our resources and friendly service.

Imprintable Cards

When you prefer your own printing touches. Our lines include: Anna Griffin, Big Silver Mailbox, Envelopments, George Stanley, Mara Mi, Meri Meri, MM's Designs, Paper Prince, Oddballs, and more, available by the box or in bulk.

In-house Custom Design and Printing

We do all the work so you can relax. Place cards, programs, menu cards, nametags, out-of-town travel packets, t-shirts, computer calligraphy for special addressing, and much more. Let us work our magic!

Party or Special Event Favors

Your event favors should leave a lasting impression. A finishing touch for guests to take with them, and recall memories of a great time. 'Do Me A Favor!' offers unique selections found no where else. Let us "do" a special favor for you!

DON'S GROUP ATTIRE

Bring Your Logo Apparel to Life!

5216-1st Avenue South • Seattle, Washington 98108
Contact: Jan Glithero
(425) 486-7268; Fax (425) 806-5609
E-mail: jan@donsgroupattire.com
Web site: www.donsgroupattire.com

WE USE THE LATEST TECHNOLOGY IN EMBROIDERY AND SCREEN-PRINTING TO BRING YOUR MESSAGE TO THE OUTSIDE WORLD IN STYLE

High quality logo apparel for companies of all sizes:

- Event Merchandise
- Employee Incentives
- Executive Gifts
- Fashion Apparel
- Staff Uniforms
- Sportswear
- T-shirts
- Formal Wear

Ad specialty and promotional products:

- Awards
- Food Gifts
- Glassware
- Sport Items
- Leather Goods
- Mugs
- Pens
- Umbrellas
- Watches
- Key chains
- And Much More...

Pricing and service

You will find our pricing to be extremely competitive with quick turnaround and personalized friendly service. With Don's Group Attire there are no minimum order requirements on apparel items.

WE ARE A LOCALLY-OWNED, FAMILY-OPERATED COMPANY THAT HAS BEEN IN BUSINESS IN SEATTLE SINCE 1946.

LET OUR CREATIVE STAFF HELP YOU ENHANCE YOUR IMAGE.

Please let this business know that you heard about them from the Bravo! Event Resource Guide.

Contact: Stacy Fortier
(206) 632-9867 Seattle or (425) 453-8858 Bellevue
E-mail: info@fremontgiftbaskets.com
Web site: www.fremontgiftbaskets.com

Luxury Gift Baskets

When the ordinary will simply not do…Fremont Gift Baskets can create the perfect "gift solution" for any occasion or special event. Allow us to help you celebrate special occasions or say thank you with a treasured gift for clients, co-workers, friends, and family. Choose from our wide variety of signature gift baskets from the following categories:

Bath · ***Gourmet*** · ***Seasonal***
Outdoor · ***Baby*** · ***Holidays***
Life's Little Luxuries

High Impact Custom Gifts

Any of our signature baskets can be tailored to meet your specific needs, or we can create a custom basket around a theme or central gift. Whether it's special events, employee recognition, corporate recruiting, or just to say "thank you," ***we offer spectacular gift solutions!***

Let us deliver the perfect gift for you!

Call us at (206) 632-9867 in Seattle

or (425) 453-8858 in Bellevue.

Visit our web site at
www.fremontgiftbaskets.com

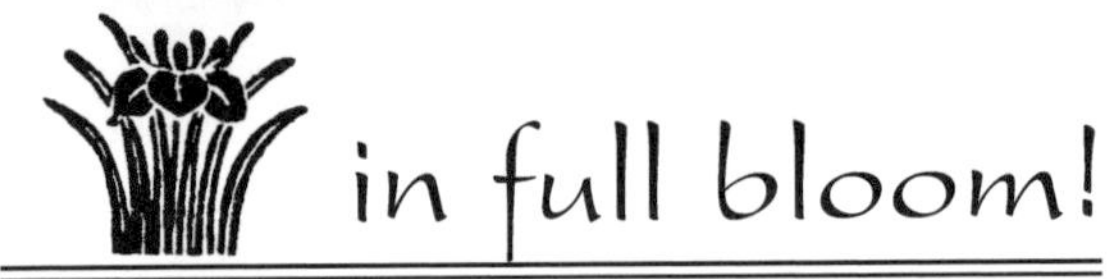

P.O. Box 52743 • Bellevue, Washington 98015
(425) 453-1171; Fax (425) 453-4420
E-mail: infullbloom@msn.com

• Meetings and Conventions • Corporate • Personal

Whether you are looking for a gift basket for a special client, or a range of gifts for your entire convention, our goal is to make gift giving easy for you! Today's busy lifestyles demand convenience, yet there is no substitute for good old-fashioned personalized service. With seven years of experience you can rely on us to assist you in selecting the perfect gift for any occasion.

We package our gourmet foods and gifts in a variety of decorative boxes, bags and baskets. Our floral services include blooming plant baskets and providing permanent arrangements for offices, restaurants and hotels. More than half of our business is from custom orders; we can personalize your gift with your logo and design gift baskets for the theme of your event or meeting.

Gift basket choices include:

- **Mini boxes and totes**—Perfect for small groups and hotel amenities
- **Taste of the Northwest**—*Our most popular*—The Northwest's finest gourmet foods
- **Sip of Seattle or Seattle Coffee Snack**—just hafta have that java!
- **Blooming baskets**—Beautiful blooming plants and tasty snacks

Delivery

We deliver locally and ship domestically

For the very best in creative solutions and customer service call on us today. We look forward to the opportunity to earn your business!

Hi-Performance Marketing Gear

11206 Des Moines Memorial Drive, Suite 100
Seattle, Washington 98168
(206) 378-1900; Fax (206) 378-1919
E-mail: info@progear.com
On-Line Store: www.progear.com

Promotional Products and Printing Services

Promarketing Gear Inc. is a national brand promotion and print management agency providing companies with innovative promotional products and marketing materials.

With access to over 350,000 promotional items, Promarketing Gear helps your company get noticed by strategically recommending the most appropriate item to meet your objectives. We offer the latest methods and ideas in establishing and maintaining a solid and dependable public image.

Promarketing Gear also provides over a decade of experience in supplying cost-effective print management services for one to six color jobs, small and large runs, Mac or Windows files. We will even create original artwork for your product.

Our specialty...finding you the right solution—the best price—and providing you with the best service!

- **Promotional Products**
  - Awards
  - Banners
  - Bags
  - Company stores
  - Calendars
  - Clocks
  - Holiday gifts
  - Employee incentives
  - Sportswear
  - Safety items
  - Mouse pads
  - Mugs
  - Games and puzzles
  - Golf accessories
  - Hats
  - Magnets
  - Executive gifts

  And much more!
- **Print Management Services**
  - Printed forms (letterhead, envelopes, brochures and more)
  - Presentation materials
  - Labels and tags
- **Other Services**
  - Full in-house graphic design
  - Direct mail
  - Packaging and fulfillment

CALL US TODAY FOR A FREE ESTIMATE!

SEATTLE GIFT BASKET CO.

◆ Corporate Gifts

◆ Personal Gifts ◆ All Occasion

Contact: Rachel Merlino
(425) 827-8490 or (800) 334-0113
Fax orders to (425) 827-7459
E-mail: seattlegift@msn.com
Web site: www.seattlegiftbasket.com

A gift basket is always appropriate and appreciated.

Let us help you with special gifts for clients, coworkers, family and friends. We specialize in pairing regional foods and gifts with beautiful presentation, and can help you select the perfect gift for any occasion.

Meetings and special events

Add a little local flavor to any occasion with amenity baskets, speaker gifts, party favors, or centerpieces from Seattle Gift Basket Co. We're experts at working with meeting planners to arrange welcome gifts for arriving guests, and thank you gifts to those who helped make your event a success. We're ready to help you with gift ideas for one or one thousand.

Gift basket ideas

At Seattle Gift Basket Co., we specialize in putting together spectacular gifts that fit with your needs and your budget. Choose from a variety of basket ideas.

The Northwest Gourmet—*a perfect gift for showing off our region's wonderful delights*
The Snack Basket—*great for an office or anyone who might be inclined to share*
The Hats Off Basket—*to celebrate a promotion, anniversary, or any other special occasion*
The Latté Lane Basket—*for the coffee lover*
The Pamper Basket—*a perfect gift for anyone needing a relaxing break*
and much, much more . . .

Delivery

We can deliver your basket locally, or ship it to any location.

VISIT OUR WEB SITE AT
www.seattlegiftbasket.com

Attractions & Activities

❖❖❖

HELPFUL HINTS

The Pacific Northwest features many attractions: From Elliott Bay to the San Juan Islands, there are endless attractions and activities. The majestic mountains are only an hour away. Award-winning wines at local wineries and brew pubs are cropping up all over town. The performing arts, museums, scenic and historical sites will keep you busy. Throw in the recreation, sporting events and tours and there is something for everyone. These unique venues can also make great locations for your next event or meeting.

Tours are perfect for your meeting or event. They provide a quick introduction to the city which enables your attendees and their guests to feel comfortable with downtown, discover opportunities unknown to most visitors, and maximize the Puget Sound area experience. Whether on foot, bus, trolley, or other forms of transportation, these are fun activities to include spouses on. Light adventure and exercise are increasingly desired by Puget Sound area visitors.

Destination Management Companies (DMC): These companies are hired by conventions and out-of-state planners. They specialize in packaging group and VIP events. They can customize local activities to fit the planner's needs.

Local celebrations and sporting events: Take advantage of local celebrations, sporting events, and theatre schedules to provide "group" activities for free time or for individuals to attend. Sporting activities can be attended as a spectator, or local companies can assist in your programming, offering harbor cruises, sport fishing, rafting trips, or ski excursions for your guests' free time.

Utilize historical sites and attractions as venues for your special events: Have a cocktail reception at an aquarium, or a dinner in a museum. Often the exhibits are interesting "decor" at no additional costs. Docents can serve as greeters, and guests can learn something new.

Audience participation activities: Recreational activities for company events are becoming more and more popular. The company picnic is becoming more interesting. There are corporate outing events like ski days, paintball tournaments, laser tag for team-building, and mini "Indy car race tracks." The more interesting an event is, the better the attendance. ***(See pages 459–482 for more game and team building activity ideas.)***

Spirit of Seattle

M.V. Kirkland

Pier 55, Suite 201 • Seattle, Washington 98101
(206) 623-1445; Fax (206) 623-5474
Office Hours: Mon–Fri 8am–5pm, Sat–Sun 8:30am–5pm
E-mail: sales@argosycruises.com • ***Web site: argosycruises.com***

PUBLIC CRUISES

Argosy Cruises offers an experience that is truly unique. For over 50 years, we have provided quality, value and one of the most spectacular panoramas imaginable—views from the water. Let our professional and courteous crew make your cruise a special one.

- **Lake Cruise–Seattle:** this 2-hour cruise departs from AGC Marina–Dock E on Lake Union and takes you by the floating home community, Husky Stadium and luxurious waterfront homes on Lake Washington. Departs daily year-round.
- **Lake Cruise–Kirkland:** this 1½-hour cruise departs from Kirkland City Dock and cruises Lake Washington past beautiful waterfront homes and Husky Stadium. This cruise is often aboard the historic vessel, the *M.V. Kirkland*. Cruises daily May through September and weekends year-round.
- **Locks Cruise:** this 2½-hour cruise takes you on both salt and fresh waters via the famous Hiram Chittenden Locks. See the "Sleepless in Seattle" houseboat while cruising through Lake Union. Departs daily year-round from Pier 56.
- **Harbor Cruise:** this 1-hour cruise is a "must do" for visitors and locals alike. Learn about Seattle's historic waterfront on this cruise of Elliott Bay and the Seattle Harbor. Departs daily year-round from Pier 55.
- **Royal Argosy:** lunch and dinner ship. Departs from Pier 56. This vessel can accommodate up to 800 guests for group events or individual dining. **See page 133 for more information.**

Reservations

Reservations are recommended to ensure space availability. Please call (206) 623-4252 or visit ***www.argosycruises.com*** for cruise information and departure times.

Captain's Club

For people that plan to cruise with Argosy more than once, consider a Captain's Club membership. This membership offers you unlimited trips on board our public cruises, in addition to a variety of other benefits. Once you have cruised 3 times, the membership has paid for itself. The membership is available in 2 person or 4 person options.

Private Charters

Argosy has 12 vessels available for private cruises. We can accommodate groups from 10 to 800. Call (206) 623-1445 for more details on specializing a cruise for you and your guests.

Call (206) 623-1445 or (800) 642-7816 for reservations.

2300 Emerald Downs Drive
Auburn, Washington 98001
(253) 288-7700
Fax (253) 288-7710
Web site: www.emeralddowns.com

WORLD CLASS THOROUGHBRED RACING

Experience the Sport of Kings at America's newest racing showplace. Emerald Downs, a magnificent facility, offers the finest in racing excitement for fans of all ages. The Northwest's best Thoroughbreds can be found racing on the Emerald oval while Mount Rainier provides a stunning backdrop.

Emerald Downs' six-level grandstand is focused on the finish line. Whether you choose a spot trackside, in Champions Sports Bar; or high atop the grandstand in one of our luxurious Triple Crown Suites, you won't miss a bit of the action. Our state-of-the-art video coverage brings the action up close with over 550 monitors located throughout the facility.

Those new to racing and long-time fans alike will appreciate our commitment to customer service. Our friendly staff is available to offer racing information at a variety of locations and various levels of knowledge.

EVERYONE'S A WINNER AT EMERALD DOWNS!

Fans of all ages will enjoy a variety of special events throughout our racing season. Families can gather in the Paddock Park on summer Sundays to enjoy racing and special Family Day activities that include pony rides, face painting, clowns, magicians and much more! Call for other promotional events happening throughout the year.

EMERALD DOWNS IS GREAT FOR GROUPS!

You won't find a better place for your next office party, corporate picnic or birthday party. Emerald Downs makes your event easy to plan with various great Day-at-the-Races packages for groups of 15 or more. Call our Group Sales Department at (253) 288-7700 to get your party started.

GET IN THE WINNER'S CIRCLE!

See page 185 under Banquet, Meeting & Event Sites.

2102 Alexander Avenue
Tacoma, Washington 98421
(888) 831-7655
E-mail: Robbynn_hoff@emeraldqueen.com
Web site: www.emeraldqueen.com

GET A PIECE OF THE ACTION!

The Emerald Queen Casino and Night Club is the Northwest's only true riverboat casino, featuring top name national entertainment, professional boxing and Las Vegas style gaming. The Emerald Queen offers over 850 slot machines, your favorite table games, Black Jack, comedy, lounge acts and a beautiful shore-side casino with multiple bars and exciting dining facilities.

Join the winners at Puget Sound's only true Riverboat Casino for gambling, dancing, entertainment, fine dining and a great time!

Transportation Options

We have several transportation options from our custom van to a 50-seat bus that are FREE for your group of 15 or more! Just tell us where to pick you up (within a 30-mile radius of the casino, please).

"THE QUEEN" IS THE PERFECT DESTINATION FOR YOUR GROUPS, BOTH BIG AND SMALL

With the central location between Olympia and Seattle, easy freeway access, open 7 days a week and boatloads of parking (sorry, we couldn't help it), your group will have a great time, guaranteed! We also have discount packages available, just contact our Group Sales Coordinator, Robbynn Hoff, by e-mail. You can also request a Group Tour Package and we'll get one in the mail for you today.

See page 186 under Banquet, Meeting & Event Sites.

7300 Fun Center Way • Tukwila, Washington 98188
(425) 228-7300; Fax (425) 228-7400
Open 365 days a year; Business Hours: 11am–10pm winter; 9am–12am summer
E-mail: tamarrah@fun-center.com
Web site: www.fun-center.com

Capacity: amusement park, 2,500 people; Bullwinkle's dining room, 300 people
Price range: $9–$28 per person
Catering: in-house
Types of events: corporate picnics, holiday parties, graduation parties, employee incentives, birthday parties, family reunions

Great food and entertainment for all ages

This amazing 8-acre amusement park is located in the city of Tukwila (I-405, Exit 1). The Family Fun Center and Bullwinkle's Restaurant provide a fun and clean atmosphere, safe attractions, great food and entertainment for all ages.

Indoor attractions

- **Laser X-treme:** laser tag arena; 1,500 sq. ft.
- **Kidopolis:** four-level soft play area for children 5 feet and under
- **Arcade:** large arcade room; over 150 video and interactive games
- **Rock Wall:** 30-ft. high with four levels of difficulty

Outdoor attractions

- **Miniature golf:** two 18-hole courses
- **Go karts:** single and double-seater cars available; 1/4-mile track
- **Bumper boats:** enjoy a wild ride on motorized boats with squirt guns
- **Batting cages:** eight batting cages ranging from 40 mph to 70 mph
- **Golf driving range**

Availability and terms

First come, first served. Reservations are required. After-hour packages also are available. Deposits are required.

Special services

Ask about our birthday packages, corporate packages and group discount packages. The Family Fun Center is open 365 days a year, rain or shine. No admission fee. Price per attraction.

See page 191 in Banquet, Meeting & Event Sites.

1025 N.W. Gilman Boulevard • Issaquah, WA 98027
(425) 427-2444
E-mail: info@illusionz.com
Web site: www.illusionz.com

EXPERIENCE THE MAGIC! EXPERIENCE THE FUN!

Voted Best New Family Entertainment Center in the U.S.A. by the International Association for the Leisure and Entertainment Industry!

You've never experienced anything like this before! Take fun to the limit and challenge your imagination with our state-of-the-art games and illusions.

Enjoy world-class magic performances...

in either of the two specially designed theaters. The main 200+ seat theatre is currently running an exclusive engagement of "Mysterian," starring Steffan Soule, the largest, most spectacular magic show from here to Las Vegas! Or see "Experience Magic," our intimate sleight of hand magic shows held in the specially designed, 30-person "close-up" magic theatre.

Additional highlights of the 45,000 sq. ft. space include:

- Challenge yourself and your friends in the world's most amazing laser tag game! Ramps, towers, dragons and interactive targets will have your pulse pounding!
- Play Wackyputt, an incredible 18-hole miniature golf course full of surprises and illusions, where half the challenge is getting the ball in the hole and the other half is getting it out!
- Experience the ride of a lifetime in the roller coaster simulator ride. It allows passengers to design their own unique coaster, and then ride it—loops, corkscrews, even "mystery moves"
- Climb the computerized, interactive climbing wall—"The Rock"
- Play over 100 of the latest games in the state-of-the-art high-tech arcade
- Watch your children play in the three-story, 4,000 sq. ft. "Magicastle" children's play complex. The oversized tubes allow you to play with your kids!
- Test yourself in the specially designed batting cages which use the same system used by major league baseball teams
- Enjoy a great meal in the Magicafe
- See water fall up and fish swim in midair! Talk to a magic parrot!
- Five private meeting/party rooms

Corporate and group events

Illusionz provides complete corporate event and party planning services in addition to its numerous entertainment offerings. Group reservations should be made as early as possible to ensure availability.

Costs and terms

Admission to the center is free. Fees are based on games played. Packages available.

Hours of Operation

Illusionz is open from 10am to 10pm Tuesday through Thursday, from 10am to midnight on Friday and Saturday and noon to 8pm on Sunday. Illusionz can accommodate private functions based on availability. Center rentals are available.

See page 413 under Entertainers & Performers

SEATTLE
731 Westlake Avenue North
Seattle, Washington 98109
Contact: Chris Weaver (206) 223-0300

TACOMA
1114 Broadway Plaza
Tacoma, Washington 98402
Contact: Jeff Weinkauf (253) 572-0300

Are you ready to have a great time?

Jillian's puts it all together with great games, fun atmosphere and classic American cuisine. Come and enjoy our 24,000 sq. ft. of the latest technology in games and sports viewing all under one roof. Your only limitation is your imagination!

- Video Café with Giant Screen TV's
- Two bars
- 28 Billiard Tables
- Ping Pong
- Darts
- A Game Room with the latest electronic simulation games as well as classic favorites

We've got something for every skill level

From traditional to the most technologically advanced, Jillian's offers a full menu of games that will challenge every skill level. It's a great environment for company parties, social events, or just an evening out on the town. A "House Pro" is available to run tournaments, give informal group lessons, and help the fun along!

Jillian's is your Food & Entertainment Universe!

Jillian's creates the perfect setting for parties and get-togethers by providing an active, upscale event atmosphere that encourages interaction and camaraderie. Guests experience total entertainment and enjoyment playing pool, the latest in electronic simulation games, ping pong and darts. Relax in our exclusive private party room or converse in our bar and Sports Café while enjoying our panoramic views of Lake Union.

See page 218 under Banquet, Meeting & Event Sites.

 Please let this business know that you heard about them from the Bravo! Event Resource Guide.

KENMORE AIR

Get Your Event Off to a Flying Start

Two Seattle Terminals: Lake Union & North Lake Washington
(425) 486-1257 or (800) 543-9595
E-mail: reservations@kenmoreair.com • ***Web site: www.kenmoreair.com***

SEAPLANES. WHEN *ORDINARY* WON'T DO.

Flying off the water will spoil you. Travel has never been this fun or easy. City distractions are quickly and easily forgotten as your group soars over stunning landscapes enroute to any of this region's favored waterside destinations within an hour of Seattle. They'll arrive energized, ready to participate in your extraordinary event.

For Work or Play

Whether it's planning corporate strategy, impressing a client at lunch, cruising amidst Orca whales or battling tackle-busting salmon, seaplane travelers will appreciate having more time at their destination, perhaps to golf, fish, indulge at a spa, kayak, beachcomb...

Popular Destinations

The choices are endless:

- Victoria
- Hood Canal
- Semi-ah-moo
- San Juan Islands
- Port Ludlow
- British Columbia Wilderness lodges
- Canadian Gulf Islands
- Whidbey Island

Scheduled Flights from Seattle

In less than 45 minutes, you can land on Victoria's Inner Harbour or in the San Juan Islands on daily, economical flights.

Custom Groups

Our charter fleet is best suited for groups up to 50, although larger is possible. Individual plane capacities range from 3 to 10 passengers.

The Seaplane Leader

Founded in 1946, our seaplane fleet, professional pilot corps and safety record are the envy of the industry.

TAKING PEOPLE TO WHERE THEY'D RATHER BE
(425) 486-1257
E-mail: reservations@kenmoreair.com

NORTHWEST TREK WILDLIFE PARK

11610 Trek Drive East
Eatonville, Washington 98328
For information call:
(360) 832-6117
Web site: www.nwtrek.org

Trek hours

- **April–October:** open daily at 9:30am
- **November–March:** open Friday, Saturday & Sunday and selected holidays at 9:30am

NORTHWEST TREK—It's wild!

Visiting Northwest Trek is a journey into the wild! Home to over 600 acres of native plants and animals, you'll find excitement, adventure and education on every visit. People of all ages thrill to this "wild" journey. Come see our grizzlies, cougar, bison, caribou and more in natural settings with plenty of room to roam.

Admission

Call (360) 832-6117 or visit our web site for current admission prices and hours.

Admission includes

- A 50-minute naturalist guided tram tour through 435 acres.
- Core area animal exhibits: cats, bears, wolves, owls, eagles and wetlands.
- Cheney Discovery Center: hands-on activities for children of all ages.
- Forest Theater: 14-minute presentation on the history of Northwest Trek.
- Five miles of nature trails.
- Northwest Trek offers special events throughout the year. Unique viewing opportunities such as private free roaming area photo tours, elk bugling tours, evening tram rides, salmon bakes, animal care camps for children and much more! Northwest Trek's friendly and professional staff will customize events to meet your needs.

Gifts and souvenirs

Trek's gift shop, featured in "Best of the Northwest," is open during park hours. You'll find a unique array of Northwest gift items including art, jewelry, home decor, children's items and more.

Reservations

Trek offers a discount for groups of 15 or more. To make your reservation, call (360) 832-7182 fifteen days in advance or fill out the request form at our web site ***www.nwtrek.org***.

Group sales

If you are interested in having a company picnic, meeting, reception or retreat, call (360) 832-7182. **See page 244 for more information.**

Location

Located on State Route 161 on the way to Mount Rainier. Only 17 miles south of Puyallup, 35 miles from Tacoma and 55 miles from Seattle. Call (360) 832-6117 for directions.

JOURNEY INTO THE WILD!

PACIFIC SCIENCE CENTER

200 Second Avenue North • Seattle, Washington 98109-4895
General Information (206) 443-2001; Group Sales (206) 443-3625; Fax (206) 443-3631
Web site: www.pacsci.org

Science Fun for Everyone

Robots, dinosaurs and insects! Oh, my! Located under the arches near the Space Needle, Pacific Science Center features five buildings of hands-on exhibits that provide educational entertainment for all ages.

On-going Exhibits Include:

- Willard Smith Planetarium
- Tropical Butterfly House & Insect Village
- Dinosaurs
- Tech Zone
- Water Works
- K5 First Alert Weather Center
- Salt Water Tide Pool
- Naked Mole Rats
- Kids Works
- Science Playground
- Body Works
- Animal Attractions

The Boeing IMAX® Theater. See Where It Takes You.

Experience IMAX® like never before in this state-of-the-art theater. Equipped with 3D technology, the Boeing IMAX® Theater is the only theater of its kind in the Northwest. Breathtaking images projected onto a six-story tall screen. 12,000 watts of digital sound transport you to worlds you've only dreamed of visiting. Come as a group during the day or host a private screening in the evening.

Tropical Butterfly House

Exotic flora and a tropical climate set the stage for the fluttering and soaring of 1,200 free-flying butterflies in the Tropical Butterfly House. Don't be surprised if a butterfly lands on your shoulder as you walk along paths in this colorful environment. A warm and tranquil oasis on even the darkest Seattle day.

Admission

Adults $12.00; Junior and Seniors $10.00; Under age 3 Free. These rates include admission to exhibits and one regular feature IMAX® film. Rates also available for IMAX® 3D, regular IMAX® and exhibits individually. Group discounts available for groups of 15 or more.

IMAX is a registered trademark of Imax Corporation.

See page 247 under Banquet, Meeting & Event Sites.

Point Defiance Park

5400 North Pearl Street
Tacoma, Washington 98407
(253) 305-1000
Web site: www.tacomaparks.com

History, Fun and Entertainment All Rolled Into One Location

Point Defiance Park offers entertainment for everyone. From the world class Point Defiance Zoo & Aquarium, to historic recreations or fishing fun, Point Defiance Park has it all.

- **Boathouse Marina**
  Outdoor enthusiasts may fish free from the pier, rent a small boat and tackle, or walk the half-mile promenade from the marina to Owen Beach and read the poetry carved into the sidewalk. *Direct line (253) 591-5325*
- **Camp 6 Logging Museum**
  This reconstructed logging camp features logging memorabilia, logging films, and a logging train that runs weekends and holidays in the spring and summer. The Santa Train runs the first three weekends of December. *Direct line (253) 752-0047*
- **Fort Nisqually Living History Museum**
  The fort, a restoration of the original Hudson's Bay Company trading post used from 1833 to 1869, depicts the state's fur-trade and exploration eras. The fort offers a variety of special events and programs during the year including living-history demonstrations and exhibits during the summer months. *Direct line (253) 591-5339*
- **Point Defiance Zoo & Aquarium**
  The zoo houses Pacific Rim wildlife in its Arctic tundra, two aquariums, Southeast Asia, and Rocky Shores of Puget Sound exhibits. Visitors can view white beluga whales, sharks, elephants, polar bears, and more. Zoolights is a popular Yuletide attraction, with more than 500,000 dazzling lights depicting zoo animals. Call for hours. *Direct line (253) 591-5337*

A facility of Metro Parks Tacoma.

Point Defiance Zoo & Aquarium

• Located in beautiful
700-acre Point Defiance Park •

5400 N. Pearl Street • Tacoma, Washington 98407
(253) 591-5337; Fax (253) 591-5448
Web site: www.pdza.org

***Winter Hours:** 10am–4pm,*
Labor Day through Memorial Day
(Closed Thanksgiving and Christmas)
***Summer Hours:** 10am–7pm daily,*
Memorial Day through Labor Day
(Closed for Zoobilee, third Friday of July)

DISCOVER THE WONDER

When you're eye-to-eye with icy white beluga whales, giant Pacific octopus, frolicking polar bears and mysterious sharks, the wonder of wildlife unfolds before you. Whether you're six or sixty, you'll find the Pacific Northwest's premiere zoo and aquarium a magical world of discovery—all overlooking beautiful Puget Sound.

But wait, there's more...

The combination of a zoo and two aquariums—a North Pacific cold water aquarium with marine life from Puget Sound and a South Pacific aquarium with tropical fish and sharks—makes a visit to Point Defiance a real value. And, you don't have to drive anywhere to get from the Aquarium to the Zoo!

Admission

Adults: $7.75; Children: $6.00; Seniors: $6.75. Group discounts and behind-the-scenes tours available. Zoo Society members enjoy unlimited admission for a year. For information on affordable membership programs, call (253) 591-5368.

Banquet, picnic and event information

Point Defiance Zoo & Aquarium offers a variety of sites for group picnics of 25 to 1,000 as well as banquet space for receptions, breakfast, lunch or dinner for groups of 25 to 250.

See page 256 under Banquet, Meeting & Event Sites,
and page 547 under Picnic Sites.

11819 Renton Avenue South
Seattle, Washington 98178
(206) 772-1220; Fax (206) 772-9860
E-mail: skywayparkbowl@aol.com
Web site: www.skywayparkbowl.com

Company Parties Our Specialty

Planning a successful company party? Want a place everyone can enjoy and have fun? Interested in team building, increasing company morale and a good time?

Skyway Park Bowl & Casino and Miniature Golf offer the facility and staff to make that next corporate outing spectacular! All under one roof! Regardless of the weather your event will proceed as planned. The most modern bowling center in the northwest plus an 18-hole miniature golf course combine to entertain everyone in your party. The fourteen table Las Vegas-style casino features a variety of games any group can enjoy.

A full service restaurant, snack bar, and lounge can provide all the food and beverages your party will need. There is even Karaoke four nights a week! Regardless of size, a party that has group participation and interaction in a fun atmosphere leaves a lasting memory of the good time shared.

We have a variety of reasonably priced bowling and golf packages. Give us a call and discover what other companies (Microsoft, FX McRory's, WalMart, AT&T, Nordstroms, Onyx Software, Rainforest Café) already know, the fun of a corporate party at Skyway Park Bowl & Casino!

Located at Seattle Center

Entrance at Broad and John Streets

219 Fourth Avenue North • Seattle, Washington 98109

Reservations and General Information: (800) 937-9582 or (206) 905-2111

Business Hours: Open Daily

E-mail: groups@spaceneedle.com

Web site: www.spaceneedle.com

The Space Needle—"Live the View"

We are revitalized and energized at the Space Needle. From our brand new, nautilus-shaped Pavilion, we'll send you skyward on a breathtaking 43-second journey to the 520-foot O Deck or SkyCity, our new world-famous revolving restaurant. During your adventure at the top, you'll discover the most incredible indoor and outdoor viewing Seattle has to offer, the finest Pacific Northwest cuisine and lots of other new and dynamic ways to "Live the View!"

SkyCity Restaurant

Take in the splendor of Puget Sound from SkyCity, the Space Needle's all-new revolving restaurant. Located 500 feet above Seattle, SkyCity features many exclusive and signature menu items and celebrates Pacific Northwest cuisine with freshness and dazzling flavor. The decor is 1960's retro inspired. However, the mood is distinctively modern. Breathtaking views are guaranteed from all tables. Your elevator ride and O Deck visit are complimentary when dining at SkyCity. Join us for lunch, dinner, or brunch on Saturday and Sunday.

SkyLine Level Events

You can give your celebration a real lift by hosting it at Seattle's premier banquet facility, the SkyLine Level at the Space Needle. Located 10 stories above the Seattle Center campus, the Space Needle's SkyLine Level features elegant rooms that can accommodate 20 to 350 guests and is the perfect spot for holiday parties, corporate functions, weddings and receptions, banquets and more.

O Deck

Every adventure at the Space Needle begins with a breathtaking 43-second journey skyward to the O Deck. Perched 520 feet above ground, the newly remodeled O Deck is dedicated to 360 degrees of the most incredible indoor and outdoor viewing Seattle has to offer. Day or night, you will find unparalleled vistas of Puget Sound, Downtown Seattle, Lake Union, Mt. Rainier and beyond. Something exciting is always on the horizon at the Space Needle. Make plans to visit soon.

SpaceBase

Before you take in the view from the O Deck, enjoy the view from ground level in the gleaming new glass-enclosed Pavilion at the base of the Space Needle. From bright blue to blustery, Seattle skies are something to behold—and the gleaming Pavilion is designed to take full advantage of them. The Pavilion is also where you'll find SpaceBase, the Space Needle gift shop with an array of quality gifts made exclusively for the Space Needle.

See page 285 under Banquet, Meeting & Event Sites.

SPIRIT OF WASHINGTON DINNER TRAIN

625 South 4th Street • Renton, Washington 98055
Contact: Marni Ness (425) 277-8408 or (800) 876-7245; Fax (425) 277-8839
Web site: www.spiritofwashingtondinnertrain.com

Dine on the Rails: Experience the nostalgia of passenger rail as you dine in our luxurious, vintage rail cars. The Spirit of Washington Dinner Train takes you on a 3½-hour 45-mile round trip excursion enhanced by scenery of Lake Washington, the Olympic Mountains, the Seattle skyline and Mount Rainier. You'll dine in comfort and elegance as your journey takes you to Woodinville's beautiful Columbia Winery. There, you'll sample fine Northwest wines and visit the cellar before returning to the depot.

Since we began operation in May 1992, we have successfully entertained over 3,000 group events. Client and office parties, weddings, conventions, sales meetings and tour groups have all enjoyed the service and gourmet cuisine aboard the Spirit of Washington. We have seven restored vintage rail cars from the 1930's. 40's and 50's that accommodate between 24 to 72 guests per car. Rent one car or the entire train for your next event no matter what season of the year.

What's New

To mark our seventh anniversary, we are undergoing a $2 million renovation. The depot has been expanded and remodeled including upgrades to our waiting areas. We've refurbished the interiors of the dining cars, enhanced the landscaping of the depot, and upgraded the railway track.

Departure Times

Monday (June to September)	6:30 pm	Saturday	12:00 pm and 6:30 pm
Tuesday thru Friday	6:30 pm	Sunday	11:00 am and 5:30 pm

Group Rates (25 or More Guests), Food Service Gratuity Included

Dinner:	$58.34 per person Parlor Seating	Lunch/Brunch:	$48.59 per person Parlor Seating
	$74.34 per person Dome Seating		$63.59 per person Dome Seating
	$79.34 per person Mystery Events		

Group Policies

- **Payment:** 25% deposit within 14 days of reservation. Balance due 30 days in advance.
- **Cancellation:** 100% refund 30 days or more, 50% refund 14 days or more, no refund if less than 14 days prior to departure date.
- **Entree Selection List:** Name list with entree selections is due 7 days prior to departure.

Special Events

- **Gift Certificates:** A great idea for everyone. Volume discounts available.
- **Fourth of July:** An evening of spectacular fireworks hosted by the city of Woodinville. Dinner and wine tasting included, you provide the oohs and ahhs.
- Come celebrate **New Year's Eve** aboard the Spirit of Washington Dinner Train. Bring in the New Year at Columbia winery with music and complimentary champagne.
- There's mayhem, intrigue and a whodunit good time! Our **Mystery Dinners** are offered year round. Events are available for parties of 40 or more. Seating is in our parlor level.

Tillicum Village

On Blake Island

In the Northwest...

"If you've but one experience, make it Tillicum Village!"

2992 S.W. Avalon Way
Seattle, Washington 98126
(206) 933-8600
or (800) 426-1205
E-mail: mail@tillicumvillage.com
Web site: www.tillicumvillage.com

Under lease operated in conjunction with Washington State Parks and Recreation Commission.

A Four Hour Adventure Awaits You!

Located on Blake Island, Tillicum Village is unlike any other attraction you have ever visited. Your adventure begins at Pier 55/56 aboard an Argosy charter vessel and includes a narrated harbor tour, magnificent scenery and a possible encounter with a sea lion, dolphin or soaring eagle. Your journey will take you back in time to a gathering place once used by Northwest Coast First People as a fishing camp.

Upon entering Tillicum Village, visitors see Pacific salmon being prepared the traditional way. After guests finish their buffet style lunch or dinner, the lights dim, and myth and magic come to life in the Native American Dance performance featuring the Tillicum Village dancers. After the show, visitors witness the intricate craft of carving, view cultural displays, browse through the gift gallery and enjoy other amenities that Tillicum Village has to offer.

Your Adventure Includes:

- **Tour:** Enjoy the warmth of Tillicum Village's "longhouse," styled in the fashion of the ancient dwellings of the Northwest Coast Native Americans.
- **Buffet:** Savor the delicious buffet featuring fresh, Pacific salmon prepared on cedar stakes over alder fires...the traditional method of the Northwest Coastal Tribes.
- **Dance:** Myth and magic come to life in the spectacular stage show, "Dance On The Wind," produced by world famous Greg Thompson Productions.
- **Explore:** Take time to explore the forested trails and picturesque beach walks. Blake Island State Park has a unique beauty all its own.
- **Gift Gallery:** Uniquely Northwest, the gift gallery is filled with one-of-a-kind treasures representing many Native American tribes and features items handcrafted by Tillicum staff.

Additional Services

- **Educational Programs** designed for school age children
- **Senior Programs** with special needs in mind
- **Corporate Retreats** for groups of any size
- **Company Picnics**—Park grounds and Tillicum Village can be reserved for private events

SHARING NORTHWEST TRADITIONS SINCE 1962

Our site and service will add a uniqueness to your event that your guests won't forget. (The facility is under lease and operated in conjunction with Washington State Parks and Recreation Commission.)

Call (206) 933-8600 for a brochure or tour schedule.

See page 295 under Banquet, Meeting & Event Sites.

5500 Phinney Avenue North • Seattle, Washington 98103-5897
Zoo Information (206) 684-4800, TDD (206) 684-4026
Event Planning/Group Sales (206) 233-7272
Zoo Hours: Mar 15–Oct 14 9:30am–6pm, Oct 15–Mar 14 9:30am–4pm
After Hours: Facilities are available on Zoo grounds for evening rental
Web site: www.zoo.org

Where can you explore arthropods in *Bug World*,
trek through the *Trail of Vines*,
stroll through the *Northern Trail*,
and journey to the *Tropical Rain Forest*...all in one day?

Woodland Park Zoo!

Don't expect to see a lot of bars and cramped, dark cages at Woodland Park Zoo! This 92-acre botanical garden has reinvented the word "zoo," with nearly 300 species of wildlife and more than 1,000 species of plants. Standouts among the Zoo's award-winning naturalistic habitats include orangutans and Indian Pythons in the Trail of Vines; grizzlies, bald eagles, and wolves alongside the Northern Trail; gorillas, poison dart frogs, and free-flying birds in the Tropical Rain Forest; elephants in the Elephant Forest and lions, giraffes, and hippos in the African Savanna.

There's always something exciting going on at the Zoo!

- Keeper Talks & Docent Tours
- Pony Rides (seasonal)
- Classes for Children, Adults, & Families
- Elephant & Raptor Programs
- Company Picnics
- Holiday Parties
- Weddings & Receptions
- Summer Concerts

Admission and accessibility: ranges from $9.50 for adults to free for toddlers (subject to change). All King County residents receive an admission discount. Accommodations will be made for people with disabilities

Gifts and souvenirs: The ZooStore, located near the South Gate, is open every day during Zoo hours, except Thanksgiving and Christmas. It offers an abundant supply of animal related books, T-Shirts, cards, and gifts.

Events and catering: From barbecues for 5,000 in the North Meadow, to formal banquets in the Rain Forest Pavilion, to a ceremony in the Rose Garden, Woodland Park Zoo will arrange for all your event needs. **(206) 233-7272**

Have an Adventure at
Woodland Park Zoo!

 Please let this business know that you heard about them from the Bravo! Event Resource Guide.

AUBURN

Emerald Downs — 2300 Emerald Downs Dr., Auburn WA 98071 *See pages 52 & 184*
(253) 288-7700 or Gen. Info. (253) 288-7000, Fax (253) 288-7710

BELLEVUE

Seattle Walking Tours — PO Box 732, Bellevue WA 98005
(425) 885-3173

BREMERTON

Elandan Gardens — 3050 W. State Highway 16, Bremerton WA 98312
(360) 373-8260

U.S.S. Turner Joy Bremerton Historical Ships — 300 Washington Beach Avenue, Bremerton WA 98337
(360) 792-2457

CARNATION

Camlann Medieval Village — 10320 Kelly Road N.E., Carnation WA 98014
(425) 788-8624

EATONVILLE

Northwest Trek Wildlife Park — 11610 Trek Dr. E., Eatonville WA 98328 *See pages 58 & 244*
(360) 832-7181

ELBE

EZ Times Outfitters Horse Rentals — 18703 SR 706, Elbe WA 98330
(360) 569-2449

EVERETT

The Boeing Tour Center — PO Box 3701 - M/S OE-44, Everett WA 98124
(800) 464-1476

Everett Naval Station — West Marine View Drive, Everett WA 98206
(425) 304-5665

FEDERAL WAY

Pacific Rim Bonsai Collection — 33663 Weyerhauser Way S, Federal Way WA 98003
(253) 924-3153

Rhododendron Species Botanical Garden — 33663 Weyerhauser Way S, Federal Way WA 98003
(253) 661-9377

Wild Waves & Enchanted Village — 36201 Enchanted Pkwy., Federal Way WA 98003 *See page 549*
(253) 661-8001 or (253) 925-8001, Fax (253) 925-1332

FIFE

Grand Prix Raceway — 2105 Frank Albert Road, Fife WA 98424 *See page 471*
(253) 922-7722

ISSAQUAH

Boehm's Candies, Inc. — 255 N.E. Gilman Blvd., Issaquah WA 98027
(425) 392-6652, Fax (425) 557-0560

Illusionz Magical Entertainment Center — 1025 N.W. Gilman Blvd., Issaquah WA 98027 *See pages 55 & 413*
(425) 427-2444

KENT

Seattle International Raceway — 31001-144th Avenue S.E., Kent WA 98042
(253) 631-1550

LAKEWOOD

Lakewold Gardens — 12317 Gravelly Lake Dr. S.W., Lakewood WA 98499 *See page 228*
(253) 584-4106, Fax (253) 584-3021

LEWISTON

American Freedom Dinner Train — 610 1/2 Main St., Lewiston ID 83501
(888) RR-Diner

OCEAN SHORES

Quinault Beach Resort & Casino — 78 State Route 115, P.O. Box 2107, Ocean Shores WA 98569 *See page 114*
(360) 289-9466 or (888) 461-2214, Fax (360) 289-5833

PORT GAMBLE

Kitsap Maritime Attractions — PO Box 270, Port Gamble WA 98364
(800) 416-5615

PORT ORCHARD

Janssen's City Tours — 1623 Woods Road E., Port Orchard WA 98366
(800) 922-5044 or (360) 871-2446, Fax (360) 871-0245

Kitsap Harbor Tours — 110 Harrison Ave., Port Orchard WA 98366
(360) 876-1056

PORT TOWNSEND

Kayak Port Townsend Sea Kayaking — 435 Water Street, Port Townsend WA 98368
(360) 385-6240 or (877) 578-2252

REDMOND

Champs Karting — 2207 N.E. Bel-Red Rd., Redmond WA 98052 *See page 160*
(425) 455-9999, Fax (425) 646-2722

Ling Shen Ching Tze Temple
(Magnificent Buddhist Temple) — 17012 N.E. 40th Court, Redmond WA 98052
(425) 882-0916

RENTON

Spirit of Washington Dinner Train — 625 S. 4th St., Renton WA 98055 *See page 64*
(425) 227-8408, Fax (425) 277-8839

SEATTLE

Alpine Adventures Wild & Scenic River Tours — PO Box 22606, Seattle WA 98122
(206) 323-1220

Argosy
Cruises — 1101 Alaskan Wy., Pier 55, #201, Seattle WA 98101 *See pages 51, 130 & 131*
(206) 623-1445, Fax (206) 623-5474

Bill Speidel's Underground Tours — 608 First Avenue, Seattle WA 98104
(206) 682-4646

Biplane Tours C/O Galvin Flying Service — 7001 Perimeter Road, Seattle WA 98108
(206) 763-9706, Fax (206) 767-7662

Cafe Appassionato Coffee Roasting Co. — 4001 21st Avenue W., Seattle WA 98199
(206) 281-8040

Chinatown Discovery, Inc. — P.O. Box 3406, Seattle WA 98114
(425) 885-3085, Fax (425) 869-9170

City Pass, Inc. — Seattle WA
(888) 330-5008, Fax (307) 733-7150

Experience Music Project
(at the Seattle Center) — 325-5th Ave. N., Seattle WA 98109 *See page 187*
(206) 770-2700, Fax (206) 770-2727

GameWorks — 1511-7th Ave., Seattle WA 98101
(206) 521-0952, Fax (206) 521-9293

Grayline of Seattle — 4500 W. Marginal Way SW, Seattle WA 98106 *See page 584*
(206) 624-5077 or (800) 426-7532

Hale's Brewery & Pub — 4301 Leary Way N.W, Seattle WA 98107
(206) 706-1544

IMAX Dome Theater — Pier 59, Waterfront Park, Seattle WA 98101
(206) 622-1868

Jillian's – Seattle — 731 Westlake Avenue N., Seattle WA 98109 *See pages 56 & 217*
(206) 223-0300

Kenmore Air — 6321 N.E. 175th (Lk. Union & Lk. Wash. Terminals), Seattle *See page 57*
(800) 543-9595

Maritime Pacific Brewery — 1514 N.W. Leary Way , Seattle WA 98107
(206) 782-6181

Odyssey - The Maritime Discovery
Center — Bell Street Pier, Pier 66, 2205 Alaskan Wy., Seattle WA 98121 *See page 245*
(206) 374-4000

Pacific Science Center — 200-2nd Ave. N., Seattle WA 98109 *See pages 59 & 247*
Events (206) 443-2899 or General (206) 443-2001, Fax (206) 443-3631

Pier 54 Adventures
(Argosy Cruises) — Pier 55, Suite 201, Seattle WA 98101 *See page 51*
(206) 623-1445

Pier 55 & 56 — Seattle's Central Waterfront, 1109 1st Avenue, Suite 500, Seattle WA 98101
(206) 903-3102

The Pike Pub & Brewery — 1415-1st Ave., Seattle WA 98101
(206) 622-6044, Fax (206) 622-8730

Pike Street Market Merchants' Association — 93 Pike Street, Suite 312, Seattle WA 98101
(206) 587-0351

Pioneer Square Community Council — 223 Yesler Way, Seattle WA 98104
(206) 667-0687

Pyramid Alehouse — 1201 First Ave. S., Seattle WA 98134 *See page 257*
(206) 682-8322 x323, Fax (206) 682-8420

Rainforest Cafe — 290 Southcenter Mall Blvd., Seattle WA 98188 *See page 258*
(206) 248-8882, Fax (206) 248-2026

Redhook Ale Brewery – Seattle — 3400 Phinney Avenue N., Seattle WA 98102
(206) 548-8000

REI — 222 Yale Ave. N., Seattle WA 98109 *See pages 261 & 475*
(206) 223-1944 or (888) 873-1938, Fax (206) 223-1407

Ride the Ducks of Seattle — 516 Broad #201, Seattle WA 98109
(206) 441-DUCK or (800) 817-1116

Royal Argosy Fine Dining
Cruises — 1101 Alaskan Wy., Pier 55, #201, Seattle WA 98101 *See pages 51 & 133*
(206) 623-1445, Fax (206) 623-5474

SAFECO Field -
Home of Winning Events — 1250-1st Ave. S., Seattle WA 98134 *See page 265*
(206) 346-4228, Fax (206) 346-4250

Seattle Aquarium — 1483 Alaskan Wy., Pier 59, Seattle WA 98101 *See page 270*
Events (206) 386-4314 or General (206) 386-4320

Seattle Architectural Foundation/Gallery — 1333 5th Avenue, Level 3, Seattle WA 98101
(206) 667-9184, Fax (206) 667-9183

Seattle Center — 305 Harrison St., Seattle WA 98109
Events (206) 684-7202 or General (206) 684-7200

Seattle Seaplanes — 1325 Fairview Ave. E., Seattle WA 98102
(206) 329-9638, Fax (206) 329-9617

Seattle Tours — 5609 Second Avenue S, Seattle WA 98108
(206) 768-1234

Skagit Tours / Seattle City Light — 700 - 5th Ave., Suite 3300, Seattle WA 98104
(206) 684-3000

Skyway Park & Bowl — 11819 Renton Ave. S., Seattle WA 98178 *See page 62*
(206) 772-1220, Fax (206) 772-9860

The Smith Tower — 506-2nd Ave., Seattle WA 98104 *See page 280*
(206) 682-4004

Space Needle — Broad & John St., Seattle WA *See pages 63 & 574*
(206) 905-2100 or (800) 937-9582

Stone Gardens, Inc. — 2839 N.W. Market St., Seattle WA 98107
(206) 781-9828, Fax (206) 781-9837

Tillicum Village — 2200-6th Ave., #804, Seattle WA 98121 *See pages 65 & 295*
(206) 933-8600 or (800) 426-1205

Victoria Clipper — 2701 Alaskan Wy., Pier 69, Seattle WA 98121
Resv. (206) 448-5000 or General (206) 443-2560, Fax (206) 443-2583

Woodland Park Zoo — 5500 Phinney Ave. N., Seattle WA 98103 *See page 66*
Events (206) 233-7272 or General (206) 684-4800

SEQUIM

Olympic Game Farm — 1423 Ward Road, Sequim WA 98382
(360) 683-4295 or (800) 778-4295

SNOQUALMIE

Puget Sound Railway Historical Association — 109 King Street, Snoqualmie WA 98065
(425) 888-3030

SUMNER

Sunshine Venture Tours — 909 Alder Avenue, Sumner WA 98390
(253) 627-1370

TACOMA

Harmon Pub & Brewing — 1938 Pacific Ave., Tacoma WA 98402
(253) 383-2739

Jillian's – Tacoma — 1114 Broadway Plaza, Tacoma WA 98402 *See pages 56 & 217*
(253) 572-0300, Fax (253) 572-2103

Point Defiance Lodge — 5400 N. Pearl St., Tacoma WA 98407 *See page 253*
(253) 305-1010

Point Defiance Park Pagoda — 5400 N. Pearl St., Tacoma WA 98407 *See page 254*
(253) 305-1010

Point Defiance Zoo & Aquarium — 5400 N. Pearl St., Tacoma WA 98407 *See pages 61, 255 & 547*
(253) 404-3643 or Gen. Info.: (253) 591-5337, Fax (253) 591-5448

Spanaway Speedway — 16413 22nd Avenue E, Tacoma WA 98445
(253) 531-4249 or (253) 537-7551

Tacoma Inns.com — PO Box 7957, Tacoma WA 98407
(253) 593-6098

The Villa B&B (A 1925 Historic Mansion) — 705 N. 5th St., Tacoma WA 98403
(253) 572-1157 or (888) 572-1157, Fax (253) 572-1805

TENINO

Wolf Haven International — 3111 Offut Lake Road, Tenino WA 98589
(360) 264-4695

TUKWILA

Family Fun Center – Bullwinkle's Restaurant — 7300 Fun Center Wy., Tukwila WA 98188 *See pages 54 & 190*
(425) 228-7300, Fax (425) 228-7400

WESTPORT

Ocean Charter, Inc./ Westport Whale Watch — PO Box 548, 2315 Westhaven Drive, Westport WA 98595
(360) 268-9144 or (800) 562-0105

WOODINVILLE

Chateau Ste. Michelle — P.O. Box 1976, Woodinville WA 98072
(425) 488-1133, Fax (425) 415-3657

Columbia Winery — 14030 - 145th Street, Woodinville WA 98072 *See page 163*
(425) 488-2776 or (800) 488-2347, Fax (425) 488-3460

The Herbfarm — 14590 N.E. 145th St., Woodinville WA 98072
(206) 789-2279

Molbak's — 13625 N.E. 175th Street, Woodinville WA 98072
(425) 483-5000

Redhook Ale Brewery – Woodinville — 14300 N.E. 145th, Woodinville WA 98072 *See page 260*
(425) 483-3232 x222, Fax (425) 481-4010

Silver Lake / Spire Mountain Ciders — 15029-A Woodinville-Redmond Rd., Woodinville WA 98072
(425) 486-1900, Fax (425) 481-3308

ANACORTES

Swinomish Casino — 12885 Casino Drive, Anacortes WA 98221
(360) 293-2691

AUBURN

Muckeshoot Indian Casino — 2402 Auburn Way S, Auburn WA 98002
(253) 804-4444 or (800) 804-4944

BOW

Skagit Valley Casino Resort — 5984 N. Darrk Lane, Bow WA 98232 *See pages 119 & 277*
(877) 275-2448, Fax (360) 724-0222

DEMING

Nooksack River Casino — 5048 Mt. Baker Hwy., Deming WA 98244
(360) 592-5472

GRAND RONDE

Spirit Mountain Casino — PO Box 39, Grand Ronde OR 97347 *See pages 121 & 285*
(800) 760-7977

LAKEWOOD

Jimmy G's Casino Lakeview Room — 8200 Tacoma Mall Blvd., Lakewood WA 98499
(253) 581-4353, Fax (253) 581-4375

MARYSVILLE

Tulalip Casino — 6410 33rd Avenue N.E., Marysville WA 98271
(360) 651-1111

ROCHESTER

Lucky Eagle Casino — 12888 188th Sw, Rochester WA 98579
(360) 273-2000 or (800) 720-1788

SEATAC

Funsters Grand Casinos — 15221 International Blvd., SeaTac WA 98188 *See page 193*
(206) 988-4888, Fax (206) 988-6166

SEATTLE

Skyway Park & Bowl — 11819 Renton Ave. S., Seattle WA 98178 *See page 62*
(206) 772-1220, Fax (206) 772-9860

SEQUIM

Seven Cedars Casino — 270756 Hwy. 101, Sequim WA 98382
(360) 683-7777 or (800) 458-2597

SHELTON

Little Creek Casino — West 91 Hwy. 108, Shelton WA 98584
(360) 427-7711

SUQUAMISH

Clearwater Casino — 15347 Suquamish Way NE, Suquamish WA 98392
(360) 598-1835

TACOMA

Emerald Queen Casino &
Night Club — 2102 Alexander Ave., Tacoma WA 98421 *See pages 53 & 185*
(888) 831-7655, Fax (253 272-6725)

TUKWILA

Grand Central Casino — 14040 Interurban Ave. S., Tukwila WA 98168 *See page 195*
(206) 244-5400, Fax (206) 244-4542

BALLARD

Nordic Heritage Museum — 3014 N.W. 67th Street, Ballard WA 98117
(206) 789-5707

BELLEVUE

Bellevue Art Museum — 510 Bellevue Way NE, Bellevue WA 98004
(425) 519-0770, Fax (425) 637-1799

Rosalie Whyel Museum of Doll Art — 1116-108th Ave. N.E., Bellevue WA 98004
(425) 455-1116, Fax (425) 455-4793

BOTHELL

Bothell Historical Museum — 9919 N.E. 180th Street, Bothell WA 98001
(425) 486-1889

EATONVILLE

Rainier Legacy–Pioneer Farm–Ohop Indian Village — 7716 Ohop Valley Road E., Eatonville WA 98328
(360) 832-6300

EVERETT

Children's Museum of Snohomish County — 3013 Colby Avenue, Everett WA 98201
(425) 258-1006

FORT LEWIS

Fort Lewis Military Museum — Building 4320, Fort Lewis WA 98433
(253) 967-7206

FRIDAY HARBOR

The Whale Museum — 62 First Street N., Friday Harbor WA 98250
(360) 378-4710

GIG HARBOR

Gig Harbor Peninsula Historical Museum — 4218 Harborview Drive, Gig Harbor WA 98335
(253) 858-6722

ISSAQUAH

Gilman Town Hall Museum — 165 S.E. Andrews Street, Issaquah WA 98027
(425) 392-3500

KEYPORT

Naval Undersea Museum — PO Box 408, Keyport WA 98345-0408
(360) 396-4148

MCCHORD AIR FORCE BASE

McChord Air
Museum — Box 4205, Building 517, McChord Air Force Base WA 98438-0205
(253) 982-2485

NORTH BEND

Snoqualmie Valley
Historical Museum — 320 North Bend Blvd. S. / PO Box 179, North Bend WA 98045
(425) 888-3200

OLYMPIA

Hands on Children's Museum — 106 11th Avenue S.W., Olympia WA 98501
(360) 956-0818, Fax (360) 754-8626
Olympic Flight Museum — 7637A-Old Hwy. 99 S.E., Olympia WA 98501
(360) 705-3925, Fax (360) 236-9839
State Capitol Museum — 211 W. 21st Avenue , Olympia WA 98501
(360) 753-2580

REDMOND

Marymoor Museum — 6046 W. Lake Sammamish Pkwy. N.E., Redmond WA 98052
(425) 885-3684

RENTON

Renton Historical Museum — 235 Mill Avenue S., Renton WA 98055
(425) 255-2330

SEATTLE

The Burke Museum of Natural History &
Culture — (UofW Campus) N.E. 45th St. & 17th Ave. N.E., Seattle WA 98195 *See page 155*
(206) 221-2853 Banquets or (206) 543-5590 Museum
The Children's Museum — 305 Harrison St., Seattle WA 98109
(206) 441-1768, Fax (206) 448-0910

Frye Art Museum — 704 Terry Avenue, Seattle WA 98104
(206) 622-9250, Fax (206) 223-1707

General Petroleum Museum — 1526 Bellevue Avenue, Seattle WA 98122
(206) 323-4789

Henry Art Gallery — University Of Washington, 15th Ave. N.E. & N.E. 41st St., Seattle WA 98195
(206) 543-2280 or (206) 616-8627, Fax (206) 685-3123

Klondlike Gold Rush Museum — 117 S. Main, Seattle WA 98104
(206) 553-7220

Museum of Flight — 9404 East Marginal Wy. S., Seattle WA 98108 *See page 238*
Events (206) 764-5706 or Museum (206) 764-5720 , Fax (206) 764-5707

Museum of History & Industry (MOHAI) — 2700-24th Ave. E., Seattle WA 98112 *See pages 95 & 240*
(206) 324-1126, Fax (206) 324-1346

Northwest Puppet Center — 9123-15th Avenue N.E., Seattle WA 98115
(206) 523-2579

Odyssey - The Maritime Discovery Center — Bell Street Pier, Pier 66, 2205 Alaskan Wy., Seattle WA 98121 *See page 245*
(206) 374-4000

Seattle Art Museum — 100 University St., Seattle WA 98101 *See page 271*
Events (206) 654-3140 or General (206) 625-8900

Seattle Asian Art Museum — 1400 E. Prospect, Seattle WA 98112 *See page 272*
Events (206) 654-3140 or General (206) 654-3206

Wing Luke Asian Museum — 407 7th Avenue S, Seattle WA 98104
(206) 623-5124

SHORELINE

Shoreline Historical Museum — 749 N. 175th, Shoreline WA 98133
(206) 542-7111

SNOQUALMIE

Northwest Railway Museum / Snoqualmie Valley Railroad — 38625 S.E. King Street, Snoqualmie WA 98065
(425) 888-3030

STEILACOOM

Steilacoom Historical Museum Association — 112 Main St., Steilacoom WA 98388
(253) 584-4133

Steilacoom Tribal Cultural Center & Museum — 1515 Lafayette Street, Steilacoom WA 98388
(253) 584-6308

TACOMA

Camp 6 Logging Museum — 5400 North Pearl Street, Tacoma WA 98407
(253) 752-0047

Children's Museum of Tacoma — 936 Broadway, Tacoma WA 98402
(253) 627-6031

Karples Manuscript Library Museum — 407 South G Street, Tacoma WA 98405
(253) 383-2575

Museum of Glass — 934 Broadway, Tacoma WA 98402 *See page 239*
(253) 396-1768 x.2148, Fax (253) 396-1769

Tacoma Art Museum — 1123 Pacific Avenue, Tacoma WA 98402
(253) 272-4258

Tacoma Dome Sports Museum — 2727 E. D St., Tacoma WA 98421
(253) 627-5857

Washington State
History Museum — 1911 Pacific Ave., Tacoma WA 98402 *See pages 98 & 309*
(253) 798-5895 or (253) 798-5893 or Gen. Info. (888) 238-4373,
Fax (253) 272-9518

The Working Waterfront Museum — 705 Dock Street, Tacoma WA 98402
(253) 272-2750

Performing Arts

LAKEWOOD

Lakewood Community Players — 10101 Plaza Drive, Lakewood WA 98499
(253) 588-0042

PUYALLUP

Jesus Of Nazareth
Drama — The Amphi Theatre, 14422 Meridian Avenue E., Puyallup WA 98373
(253) 848-3411

SEATTLE

5th Avenue Theatre — 1308 Fifth Avenue, Seattle WA 98101
(206) 625-1418, Fax (206) 292-9610

A Contemporary Theatre — 700 Union Street, Seattle WA 98101
(206) 292-7676

Arts West — 4711 California Ave. S.W., Seattle WA 98116
(206) 938-0339

Broadway Performance Hall — 1625 Broadway, Seattle WA 98122 *See page 92*
(206) 325-3113, Fax (206) 325-3420

Empty Space Theatre — 3509 Fremont Avenue N., Seattle WA 98103
(206) 547-7500, Fax (206) 547-7635

Intiman
Theatre — (In The Seattle Center), 3rd & Mercer Street, Seattle WA 98109
(206) 269-1900

Northwest Actor's Studio — 1100 E. Pike Street, Seattle WA 98122
(206) 324-6328

Pacific Northwest Ballet — 301 Mercer Street, Seattle WA 98109
(206) 441-2424

The Paramount Theatre
& Ballroom — 911 Pine St., Seattle WA 98101 *See pages 96 & 249*
(206) 467-5510, ext. 150 or Gen. Info. (206) 682-1414,
Fax (206) 682-4837

Seattle Children's Theatre — 201 Thomas St., Seattle WA 98109
(206) 441-3322

Seattle Repertory Theatre — 155 Mercer St., Seattle WA 98109 *See page 274*
(206) 443-2210, Fax (206) 443-2379

Seattle Symphony
Orchestra — At Benaroya Hall, 200 University Street,
PO Box 21906, Seattle WA 98109-4645
(206) 215-4747

TACOMA

Broadway Center for the Performing Arts – Rialto, Pantages, Theatre in the Square — 901 Broadway, Tacoma WA 98402
(253) 591-5890

Tacoma Actors Guild — 915 Broadway, 6th Floor, Tacoma WA 98402
(253) 272-2145

Tacoma Little Theatre — 210 North I Street, Tacoma WA 98403
(253) 272-2281

Tacoma Master Chorale — 7116 6th Ave., Tacoma WA 98407
(253) 565-6867

Tacoma Musical Playhouse — 7116 6th Avenue, Tacoma WA 98406
(253) 565-6867

Festivals

BELLEVUE

Bellevue Art Museum Fair — 510 Bellevue Way, Bellevue WA 98004
(425) 519-0742, Fax (425) 637-1799

PUYALLUP

Western Washington Fair Association — 9th & Meridian, Puyallup WA 98371
(253) 841-5045

SEATTLE

Northwest Folklife — 158 Thomas Street, 3rd Floor, Seattle WA 98109
(206) 684-7300

Olympic Music Festival –
Friends of the Philadelphia String Quartet — 4730-1/2 University Way N.E.,
PO Box 45776, Seattle WA 98105
(206) 527-8839, ext. 110

One Reel/Bumbershoot — PO Box 9750,
1725 Westlake Avenue N., 2nd Floor, Seattle WA 98109
(206) 281-7788

Seafair — 2200 6th Avenue, Suite 400, Seattle WA 98121
(206) 728-0123

TACOMA

Victory Music — PO Box 2254, Tacoma WA 98401
(253) 428-0832

Professional Sports

BELLEVUE

Seattle Sounders — 14120 N.E. 21st Street, Bellevue WA 98007
(206) 622-3415

Seattle Thunderbirds Hockey Club, Inc. — 1813 130th Avenue N.E., Suite 210, Bellevue WA 98005
(425) 869-7825

EVERETT

Everett AquaSox Baseball — 3802 Broadway, Everett WA 98201
(425) 258-3673 or (800) GO-FROGS

KIRKLAND

Seattle Seahawks — 11220 N.E. 53rd Street, Kirkland WA 98033
(425) 827-9777

SEATTLE

Seattle Mariners Baseball Club — 1250-1st Ave. S., Seattle WA 98134
(206) 346-4000

Seattle Super Sonics — 351 Elliott Ave. W., Seattle WA 98119
(206) 281-5800

TACOMA

Tacoma Rainiers Baseball Club — 2502 S. Tyler Street, Tacoma WA 98405
(253) 752-7700 or (800) 281-3834

Tacoma Sabercats Hockey Club — 521 E. 27th, Tacoma WA 98402
(253) 627-2673

Recreational Activities

HOOD RIVER

River Riders — 2149 W. Cooascade #106A-178, Hood River OR 97031
(206) 448-RAFT or (800) 448-RAFT

KIRKLAND

Rivers, Inc. — PO Box 2092, Kirkland WA 98083
(425) 822-5296

MONROE

Downstream River Runners, Inc. — 13414 Chain Lake Road, Monroe WA 98272
(800) 234-4644 or (360) 805-9899

PORT TOWNSEND

Kayak Port Townsend Sea Kayaking — 435 Water Street, Port Townsend WA 98368
(360) 385-6240 or (877) 578-2252

SEATTLE

Alpine Adventures Wild & Scenic River Tours — PO Box 22606, Seattle WA 98122
(206) 323-1220

Northwest Outdoor Center, Inc. — 2100 Westlake Avenue N., Seattle WA 98109
(206) 281-9694

Pier 57 Parasail — Pier 57, 1301 Alaskan Way, Seattle WA 98101
(206) 622-5757

REI — 222 Yale Ave. N., Seattle WA 98109 *See pages 261 & 475*
(206) 223-1944 or (888) 873-1938, Fax (206) 223-1407

Stone Gardens, Inc. — 2839 N.W. Market St., Seattle WA 98107
(206) 781-9828, Fax (206) 781-9837

Terrene Tours Sports & Recreation — 3810 E. Galer Street, Seattle WA 98112
(206) 325-5569

WOODINVILLE

Over the Rainbow Balloon Flights — PO Box 2772, Woodinville WA 98072
(206) 364-0995

Ski Resorts

ASHFORD

Mt. Rainier National Park Guest Services — PO Box 108, Ashford WA 98304
(360) 569-2275 or (360) 569-2411

BELLINGHAM

Mt. Baker Ski Area — Office: 1019 Iowa Street, Bellingham WA 98226
(360) 734-6771 or (360) 671-0211

CRYSTAL MOUNTAIN

Crystal Mountain Resort — Crystal Mountain Blvd., Crystal Mountain WA 98022
(360) 663-2265, Fax (360) 663-3001

GREENWATER

Alta Crystal Resort — 68317 SR 410 E., Greenwater WA 98022
(360) 663-2500 or (800) 277-6475

LEAVENWORTH

Stevens Pass Ski Area — Office:, PO Box 98, Leavenworth WA 98288
(360) 973-2441 or (206) 812-4510

MERCER ISLAND

The Summit:
Alpental*Hyak*Ski Acres — Office: 7900 S.E. 28th St., #200, Mercer Island WA 98040
(425) 434-7669

WENATCHEE

Mission Ridge — PO Box 1668, Wenatchee WA 98807
(509) 663-6543

AUBURN

Super Mall of the Great Northwest — 1101 Super Mall Way, Suite 1268, Auburn WA 98001
(253) 833-9500

BELLEVUE

Bellevue Place — 575 Bellevue Place, Bellevue WA 98004
(425) 453-5634, Fax (425) 646-3661

Bellevue Square — 302 Bellevue Way & NE 8th, Bellevue WA 98004
(425) 454-8096

Crossroads Shopping Center & Public Market — 15600 N.E. 8th Street, Bellevue WA 98008
(425) 644-1111, Fax (425) 644-1156

Factoria Square Mall — PO Box 5787, Factoria Mall Blvd. S.E., Bellevue WA 98006
(425) 747-7344

Country Village — 23730 Bothell-Everett Hwy., Suite K, Bothell WA 98021
(425) 483-2250

BURLINGTON

Prime Outlets at Burlington — 234 Fashion Way, Burlington WA 98233
(360) 757-3549

CENTRALIA

Centralia Factory Outlet Stores — 1342 Lum Road (exit 82 Off I-5), Centralia WA 98531
(360) 736-3327, Fax (360) 736-3328

EVERETT

Everett Mall — 1402 S.E. Everett Mall Way, Everett WA 98208
(425) 355-1771

FEDERAL WAY

SeaTac Mall — 1928 SeaTac Mall, Federal Way WA 98003
(253) 839-6150

ISSAQUAH

Gilman Village — 317 N.W. Gilman Blvd., Suite 32, Issaquah WA 98027
(425) 392-6802

LAKEWOOD

Lakewood Mall — 10509 Gravelly Lake Drive S.W., Lakewood WA 98499
(253) 984-6100

LYNNWOOD

Alderwood Mall — 3000 184th Street S.W., Lynnwood WA 98037
(425) 771-1211

NORTH BEND

Factory Stores at North Bend — 461 S. Fork Avenue S.W., Suite E1, North Bend WA 98045
(425) 888-4505

PUYALLUP

South Hill Mall — 3500 South Meridian, #494, Puyallup WA 98373
(253) 840-2828

SEATTLE

Northgate Mall — 401 N.E. Northgate Way, Suite 210, Seattle WA 98125
(206) 362-4777

Pacific Place — Sixth & Pine, 600 Pine Street, Seattle WA 98101
(206) 405-2655

Pier 55 & 56 — Seattle's Central Waterfront, 1109 1st Avenue, Suite 500, Seattle WA 98101
(206) 903-3102

Pike Place Market — 85 Pike Street, Room 500, Seattle WA 98101
(206) 682-7453

Pioneer Square — 1st & Main Pioneer Square, Seattle WA 98104
(206) 622-6235

Southcenter Mall — 633 Southcenter Mall, Seattle WA 98188
(206) 246-7400

University Village — 2673 N.E. University Village, Suite 7, Seattle WA 98105
(206) 523-0622

Westlake Center — 1601 Fifth Avenue, Suite 2210, Seattle WA 98101
(206) 467-1600

TACOMA

Tacoma Mall — 5225 Tacoma Mall Blvd., Tacoma WA 98409
(253) 475-4570

Audio Visual Services

HELPFUL HINTS

Planning for audio visual equipment, lighting, and staging for your meeting or event is very important. Exciting new technologies like interactive computer use, live video enhancement of speakers, and teleconferencing have arrived, but the budgets that have arrived with them are steep. The type of AV support you will need for your meeting or event may be simple or more complex. Be sure to review all your options.

Think ahead to what your audio visual needs will be:

- Get a list of the speakers' needs well in advance of your event and schedule a rehearsal. You will avoid last-minute and rush labor charges this way.
- Book rehearsal and set-up time in your meeting rooms.
- Give speakers a chance to rehearse with equipment.
- Test equipment immediately prior to the beginning of the event.
- Have spare bulbs and extra extension cords on hand.
- Having a technician available to attend to your needs throughout the meeting may be your best insurance policy.
- Many facilities have in-house equipment (check availability and working condition).
- Remember that poor-quality AV equipment can ruin a meeting.

To maximize your audio visual budget, try the following:

- **Reserve equipment early** so you have what you need from a reputable company. If you have never worked with the company, ask for references and check them. This is an important part of the meeting.
- **Negotiate all costs.** Package deals are good for you and the rental companies. If they know your needs and have your timelines, it will be more cost effective.
- **Put your agreements in writing.** If one company is not able to meet your needs, look at other companies until your needs are met.
- **Write all instructions.** Include agendas and room layouts so your vendors know exactly what you expect. This will eliminate surprises or the need for mind reading.
- **Save yourself headaches.** If you are too busy doing the many other jobs needed for a meeting, seek out and use experienced production managers and technicians to oversee the AV portions of your event. Introduce yourself to the technicians who will be working your event, and find out how to contact them should the need arise.
- **Barter goods and services with your rental companies.** They may want to advertise in your publications, exhibit at your trade show, or acquire leads from your attendees.
- **Guaranteed performance is often a policy of AV companies.** They will compensate clients for rental costs in the event of equipment failure. Even better, many will provide on-site back-up.

Check the audio visual equipment: Many facilities have their own in-house audio department. Ask if any audio visual equipment is included in your room charge, then be sure to check out the quality and age of the equipment.

Most facilities only provide a podium and microphone, so you will need to rent additional equipment from a qualified audio visual rental company.

Audio-Visual Products, Inc.
825 South Dakota Street Seattle, WA 98108-5227

(206) 343-3123; Fax (206) 343-3063
Office Hours: Mon–Fri 8am–5pm, Sat by appointment
E-mail: info@av-pro.net
Web site: www.av-pro.net

AUDIO-VISUAL SERVICES FOR YOUR SPECIAL EVENT NEEDS

Exceptional Production Services
- Corporate Meetings
- Fund Raiser Auctions
- Trade Shows
- Special Events
- Festivals

Presentation Equipment
- Data/Video Projectors
- Screens with Drapery Kits
- Slide, Overhead & Opaque Projectors
- Easels & Laser Pointers
- Podiums

Light Systems
- Presentation Lighting
- Stage Lighting
- Special Effects
- Intelligent Lighting

Sound Reinforcement Systems
- Sizes to fit any audience
- Wireless Microphone Systems

Special Event Equipment
- Pipe & Drape
- Portable Staging
- Stage Roofs
- Wireless Intercom Systems

We have qualified systems, operators and experienced event consultants ready to work with you to make your event a complete success.

AUDIO VISUAL MANAGEMENT & SOLUTIONS

617-8th Avenue South
Seattle, Washington 98104
(206) 694-4444; Fax (206) 694-4445
E-mail: scott@mrprojector.com

SOLUTIONS

AUDIO VISUAL CONVENTION SERVICES AND MANAGEMENT

Offering premium audio visual services and solutions to quality companies and organizations

HOSPITALITY AUDIO VISUAL SOLUTIONS

AVMS is the preferred provider of audiovisual services to some of the finest hotels and resorts in the Pacific Northwest

SOUND SYSTEMS AND LIGHTING SYSTEMS

Whether you need a full-blown concert sound system or a complete lighting design, our rental office is up to the challenge. We offer the latest in sound and lighting systems to make you look and sound your best!

CUSTOMERS

- **Corporate:** Windermere Services – AT&T Wireless – The Computer Store – Wells Fargo Bank – Merrill Lynch – Pharmacia – NIKE – BD&A
- **Association:** Fuel Cell – Women's Funding Alliance – Families Northwest Development – Ski Alliance – Education Audiology Association
- **Non-Profit:** Boys & Girls Clubs – Cystic Fibrosis Foundation – Poncho Wine Auction – Woodland Park Zoo – Kent Chamber of Commerce – Children's Hospital – UW

VISION

We believe in the idea that audiovisual service should be seamless to our customers...

1-800-503-3433

www.daywireless.com

Rental Services

Day Wireless Systems specializes in the rental of wireless equipment. Whether your needs are short term or long term, whether you're equipping a legion of employees or just a few, we can design a Rental Program that's just right for you.

Renting provides numerous advantages for today's business:

- Improve your productivity and profitability
- Increase your efficiency
- Keep in touch with key personnel
- Provide greater safety on the job site

We offer Daily, Weekly or Monthly Rental of Portable Two-Way Radios, Cellular Phones, Nextel Phones, Satellite Phones and more. All available for shipment within 24-hours, and at terms to meet your budget. You can also look to Day for a complete range of accessories to make your rental products even more effective.

Rental products are ideal for:

- Construction
- Fairs
- Corporate moves
- Conventions
- Festivals
- Facility management

Please contact us at 1-800-503-3433
or visit our website at *www.daywireless.com*
for more information.

300 Fairview Avenue North
Seattle, Washington 98109
Production Lighting Contact: Jay Markham
Electrical Services Contact: Star Moser
Rentals/Sales Contact: Brian Kameoka
(206) 292-2353 or (800) 547-2353
Fax (206) 215-9370
Showroom Hours: Mon–Fri 8am–6pm
E-mail: info@hollywoodlights.com
Web site: www.hollywoodlights.com

Hollywood LIGHTS INC.

Services Available

- **Production Lighting:** From corporate meetings and industry trade shows to special events and rock concerts—the creative team at Hollywood Lights will design and implement a show that will exceed your expectations. The expert Hollywood Lights production team will set up, focus, operate and tear down your show quickly, safely, and efficiently, keeping your event on time and on budget. Hollywood Lights' complete inventory of state-of-the-art automated lighting equipment will set your event apart. Clients include: Nike, Adidas, Intel, In Focus, Columbia Sportswear, Microsoft XP rollout, Nordstrom, Portland Trail Blazers, Mentor Graphics, and more.

- **Temporary Electrical Services:** When your event requires power throughout the Northwest, call Hollywood Lights. Whether you are planning a corporate meeting, trade show, outdoor festival, political event, private party, concert, grand opening, wedding/memorial, sporting event, RV rally, or you need an emergency back up system—our professional team of electrical technicians make it happen. Hollywood Lights provides every detail of temporary electrical services from the permit process through all distribution, no matter how remote your location. Additional services include tent lighting, corporate Christmas lighting, and supplemental lighting for warehouse sales.

- **Rentals:** Hollywood Lights offers a complete inventory of equipment you can rent—from mirror balls to fog machines and Christmas lights to deejay-style, dance club effects—all for the creatively inspired do-it-yourselfer. A dazzling addition to your party or event is one call away with Hollywood Lights.

- **Sales:** Where do you go for ideas? Hollywood Lights has a 2,000 square foot showroom featuring creative applications of lighting and effects for holidays decorations, parade floats, weddings, and unique special events. Please visit or call for additional information—our team is full of innovative suggestions.

Why Hollywood Lights?

- Founded in Portland in 1948, Hollywood Lights has a history of servicing special events in the Northwest. Whatever your vision, Hollywood Lights will make it happen.

- Hollywood Lights offers 24-hour emergency pager service, insuring your event runs as planned. Or arrange a standby technician on site at your event.

- With a growing office in Seattle, Hollywood Lights covers the Northwest.

- At Hollywood Lights, we believe our people are simply the best. The Hollywood Lights team comprises lighting and electrical professionals who offer technical expertise, creative solutions, and exceptional customer service.

- The lighting and electrical equipment in Hollywood Lights' inventory is extensive. From automated, moving light fixtures to special effect equipment, Hollywood Lights has it.

Auditoriums, Theatres & Classrooms

❖❖❖

Auditoriums, Theatres and Classrooms

Broadway Performance Hall

1625 Broadway
Seattle, Washington 98122
Contact: Meg Stevenson
or Darrell Jamieson
at The Broadway Management Group
(206) 325-3113
Fax (206) 325-3420
E-mail: meg@broadwayperfhall.com
Web site: www.broadwayperfhall.com

Capacity: accommodates up to 295

Event/Performance price range: up to 5 hours of event/performance time: $495; up to 10 hours with 2 performances per day: $900; weekly and monthly rates also available; rehearsal rates: $23 per hour for an 8 hour day; labor and equipment charges additional—please inquire

Conference and meeting price range: $450 for half day (4 hours); $700 for full day (up to 8 hours); Lobby available for receptions for $100 per hour

Types of events: corporate, social and cultural; music, concerts, theatre, dance, film, video presentations, lectures, meetings, seminars, and more

Availability and terms

The Broadway Performance Hall is Seattle's most popular medium-size theatre. Renovated as a performing arts center, this 295-seat venue offers an intimate, professional setting for all kinds of events. A deposit is required with the balance due upon signing of rental agreement.

Description of services and facility

ADA: fully accessible

Parking: secured covered parking across street for $3 per car, up to 8 hours

Auditorium

- **Seating:** fixed seating, raked and numbered for your convenience; all chairs padded
- **Stage:** wood flooring; dimensions approximately 36' wide x 40' deep x 26' high
- **Sound:** Mackie sound board with a large inventory of sound equipment
- **Lighting:** computerized light board; full complement of stage lighting equipment plus stage masking, scrim, cyclorama

Meeting and event services

- **Audio visual:** slide, overhead, and 35mm or 16mm projectors; video projector; 2 projection screens; please inquire for a complete list of our extensive inventory of A/V equipment
- **Equipment:** podium, risers, easels and more
- **Lobby:** ideal for receptions up to 150; tables and chairs provided
- **Breakout rooms:** additional rooms available
- **Catering:** provide your own caterer or we'll be happy to refer you to one

MAKE A STATEMENT AND AN IMPRESSION
• Affordable Elegance at The Broadway Performance Hall •

Surround your staff and business guests with the beauty and history of turn-of-the century Seattle, by holding your next meeting, conference or product rollout at The Broadway Performance Hall—minutes from downtown Seattle, yet affordably priced.

Built in 1911, The Broadway Performance Hall was an addition to Seattle's first high school. The renovated brick building maintains most of its original architectural detail and houses an impressive Northwest art collection that is closely linked to the school's past.

City of Renton's

CARCO THEATRE

1717 Maple Valley Highway • Renton, Washington 98055
(425) 430-6706; Fax (425) 430-6701
Office Hours: Mon–Fri 8am–5pm

Capacity: accommodates up to 310
Price range: $20 to $75 per hour according to type of event; non-profit and government rates available; please inquire about our all-day or half-day rates
Types of events: business meetings, seminars, conferences, training, performing arts or theatrical performances

Availability and terms

Reservations can be made up to one year in advance. Availability possible on shorter notice when space allows. A deposit is required at the time of reservation.

Description of services and facility

ADA: facility complies with all ADA requirements; handicap accessible; assisted listening
Parking: on-site complimentary parking for up to 300 vehicles

Auditorium

- **Ticket booth:** available for ticket sales or for group registration
- **Seating:** fixed seating, raked and numbered for your convenience; all seats are padded for your attendees comfort; two aisles for easy access
- **Stage:** 40' wide x 40' deep x 40' high; 18' high to lighting grid
- **Sound:** full sound capabilities for any event
- **Lighting:** fully updated and complete lighting system

Meeting and event services

- **Audio visual:** video projector, 20'x20' motorized projection screen, podium, overheads, slide projectors, microphones
- **Equipment:** most incidental equipment is available

Banquet and meeting rooms

- **Lobby:** accommodates up to 40
- **Banquet and meeting facility:** Carco Theatre is adjacent to the Renton Community Center which can accommodate groups of 30 to 800
- **Catering:** provide your own caterer or we'll by happy to refer you to one
- **Cleanup:** please remove anything you bring in; we'll handle the rest

Special services

One of our in-house audio visual technicians is included in every rental fee to assist you with sound and lighting, technical expertise, and to ensure your event runs smoothly.

A PROFESSIONAL MEETING LOCATION IN A RELAXED ATMOSPHERE

Finally, a meeting location that offers professionalism in a relaxed atmosphere. Conveniently located just off I-405 on the Maple Valley Highway, the Carco Theatre sits on the banks of the Cedar River in the heart of the 20-acre Cedar River Park. An adjacent 35,000-square-foot recreational and banquet facility and over four miles of walking and biking trails create the perfect environment for between-session gatherings and recreation. Hold your next event in the pleasant surroundings of Carco Theatre.

See page 263 under Banquet, Meeting & Event Sites.

3200 S.W. Dash Point Road • Federal Way, Washington 98023
Contact: Knutzen Family Theatre Coordinator
(253) 835-2025; Fax (253) 835-2010
Business Hours: Mon–Fri 8am–5pm
E-mail: webmaster@ci.federal-way.wa.us • ***Web site: www.ci.federal-way.wa.us***

Capacity: accommodates up to 250
Price range: varies according to space required and type of event
Types of events: performing arts or theatrical performances, meetings, seminars, video presentations

Availability and terms

Reservations may be made up to one year in advance. Deposit required at time of reservation.

Description of services and facility

ADA: fully accessible; assistive listening system available
Parking: on-site complimentary parking for up to 200 vehicles

Auditorium

- **Seating:** fixed seating, raked and numbered for your convenience; all seats are padded; two aisles
- **Stage:** 36' wide x 28' deep x 19' high
- **Sound:** brand new system can handle any event; 24-channel Mackie board, effects, ClearCom, and more
- **Lighting:** brand new, state-of-the-art lighting system

Meeting and event services

- **Audio visual:** video/data projector, 20'x15' motorized projection screen, TV, VCR, DVD, MiniDisc, overheads, slide projectors, wireless microphones
- **Equipment:** lectern, flip charts, easels

Banquet and meeting rooms

- **Rehearsal hall:** accommodates up to 72 people
- **Lobby:** accommodates up to 42 people
- **Banquet and meeting facility:** Knutzen Family Theatre is located at Dumas Bay Centre, a full-service business conference and retreat facility
- **Cleanup:** please remove anything you bring in, we'll do the rest

THE BENEFITS ARE ENDLESS

When you combine a state-of-the-art performance and meeting space with a full-service conference and retreat center and an award-winning caterer, you open up a world of possibilities. Add in a friendly, professional staff, a relaxing atmosphere and stunning views of Puget Sound and the Olympic Mountains and it's easy to see why people love doing business here, time and time again.

For more information about Dumas Bay Centre,
see page 174 under Banquet, Meeting & Event Sites.

2700-24th Avenue East
Seattle, Washington 98112
(206) 324-1126
Fax (206) 324-1346
Special Event Facilities
Available: 7am–Midnight
E-mail:
specialevents@seattlehistory.org

Capacity: McEachern Auditorium/Theatre accommodates up to 373
Price range: price varies depending on specific event requirements
Types of events: corporate, social/cultural; video presentations, film festivals/screenings, auctions, lectures, meetings, seminars, workshops, concerts, performances, shareholders meetings

Availability and terms

We schedule events from three weeks to three years out. Available for convention overflow. Security damage deposit is required to reserve date; full event fees due three weeks prior to event.

Description of services and facility

ADA: fully accessible
Parking: ample free parking on site
Auditorium

- **Seating:** fixed seating, raked and numbered for your convenience; all chairs padded
- **Stage:** oak parquet flooring; dimensions approximately 38' wide x 22' deep x 32" high
- **Sound:** complete sound system with stereo front speakers and mono back fill (sub woofers available); a 16-channel mixing board and snake, effects processor with two stage monitors, various microphones including wireless or lapel, breakout panel, booth monitors and intercom system
- **Lighting:** versatile repertory plot; 48 instruments; 24 dimmers
- **Lobby:** adjacent space for registration, displays or receptions
- **Dressing rooms:** easy access to backstage

Meeting and event services

- **Audio visual:** slide, overhead, 16mm projectors, 35mm film projectors; screens: standard, portable, 13'x20' screen fixed in auditorium; perforated screen for films (fixed); CD player, cassette player, VCR/TV; please inquire for current list
- **Equipment:** podium, risers, easels, flipcharts

Event and meeting rooms

- **McCurdy Gallery:** up to 300 for receptions, 200 for sit-down functions
- **Founders Room:** up to 25
- **Clise Gallery:** up to 50 for sit-down, up to 150 for reception
- **1880s Room:** up to 40 for sit-down, up to 75 for reception
- **Seating:** 20 - 60" rounds, 20 - 6' buffets, and 200 folding chairs provided
- **Catering:** provided by Museum-approved caterers; please call for concession policy
- **Cleanup:** restore facility to original condition; all event materials and garbage removed

Special services

Additional tech and security staff as required for additional charge. Access to other galleries for nominal fee. Special rates for Benefactor-level MOHAI members.

BRING US YOUR SPECIAL EVENT AND WE'LL HELP YOU MAKE HISTORY

Located less than ten minutes from both downtown and the eastside, plus attractive pricing and ample free parking make this the perfect venue for your business, social or cultural gatherings. Please call (206) 324-1126 to reserve this unique setting for your upcoming event!

911 Pine Street
Seattle, Washington 98101
Contact: Jason Ferguson
(206) 467-5510, ext. 150
Fax (206) 682-4837
E-mail: jasonf@theparamount.com • ***Web site: www.theparamount.com***

Capacity: Total seating: 2,946; Main Level: 1,523 seats; Balcony: 1,423 seats
Price range: rates vary according to time of day and day of the week; please inquire
Types of events: private performances, large meetings, seminars, films, lectures, product rollouts, and more

Availability and terms

A deposit of 50% of the rental fee reserves your date, with the balance due 30 days prior to your event.

Description of services and facility

ADA: The Paramount is in full compliance with the ADA theatre standards
Parking: convenient pay lots and parking garages nearby, plus street parking
Auditorium

- **Box office:** original built-in ticket booth available for registration or admission
- **Seating:** fixed, traditional raked theatre seating; all chairs padded
- **Stage:** proscenium: 31' 6" high x 51' 10" wide; stage: 85' wide x 47' deep x 68'10" high
- **Sound:** Claire Brothers professional touring system with Yamaha PM 400 counsel
- **Lighting:** full theatre lighting available
- **Video:** theatre video system projects events on monitors throughout the venue

Meeting and event services

- **Audio visual and equipment:** we are happy to coordinate any A/V or equipment needs

Banquet and meeting rooms

- **Rooms available:** "star" dressing room or private backstage lounge are ideal for intimate gatherings of 15 to 20; the lobby area, converted stage and ballroom elegantly hosts 100 to 2,500
- **Seating:** tables, chairs and linens arranged according to your event needs
- **Catering:** select the caterer of your choice from our preferred list

Special services

Your keynote speaker or VIP's will be sure to enjoy the comforts of our state-of-the-art "star" dressing room with fireplace and jacuzzi.

WHERE DID ALL THE SEATS GO?

They're still here...we've just tucked them under the floor.

The convertible floor technology we installed transforms The Paramount's auditorium into a stunning ballroom. The historic landmark's inspiring architecture and elegant surroundings create a one-of-a-kind environment, perfect for groups of 100 to 2,500. Call us about staging your next event at The Paramount, a refreshingly different event atmosphere.

See page 249 under Banquet, Meeting & Event Sites.

EDUCATION CONFERENCE CENTER

400 South 43rd Street • Renton, Washington 98055
Contact: Kathy Christensen (425) 656-5375; Fax (425) 656-5095
Office Hours: Mon–Fri 8am–5pm
E-mail: Kathleen_Christensen@Valleymed.org
Web site: www.Valleymed.org

Capacity: accommodates up to 200 with flexible setup options
Price range: $25 to $117 per hour depending on meeting room; half-day or all-day rates available; non-profit rates available
Types of events: conferences, trainings, seminars, business meetings, and more

Availability and terms

Reservations can be made up to one year in advance. Availability possible on short notice when space allows. Deposit required upon signing of rental agreement.

Description of services and facility

ADA: fully accessible
Parking: complimentary on-site covered parking
Auditorium

- **Seating:** fixed seating; 200 padded seats with fold-down writing desks; 2 entrances and 2 aisles for easy access
- **Stage:** carpeted stage; fixed podium with touchscreen control panel
- **Sound:** THX surround sound system, soundboard and a large inventory of sound equipment
- **Lighting:** system offers variety of light levels for AV presentations, note-taking and lectures

Meeting and event services

- **Audio visual:** full array of audio visual equipment available for rent
- **Equipment:** podiums and other equipment available; each room is equipped with a conference cabinet containing a projection screen, whiteboard and paper pads

Banquet and meeting rooms

- **Rooms available:** 7 rooms including auditorium; rooms can accommodate between 20 and 200 people depending on type of setup
- **Seating:** flexible set-up options, including movable walls; round and rectangular tables
- **Catering:** provided by Rainbows Catering, who offers a full range of catering services
- **Cleanup:** provided by Valley Medical Center; please remove anything you bring in

CENTRALLY LOCATED

Valley Medical Center's Education Conference Center is centrally located in the Puget Sound area. It is conveniently located just off Highway 167, near I-405 and close to Sea-Tac Airport and an array of hotel accommodations. The 21,000 square foot facility includes 6 meeting rooms, and a 200-seat, state-of-the-art auditorium. We offer a full complement of audiovisual equipment. Full catering for any type of function is available.

WASHINGTON STATE HISTORY MUSEUM

1911 Pacific Avenue • Tacoma, Washington 98402
Contact: Amice Barreras or JoAnn Puccia (253) 798-5895,
or Gary Larson (253) 798-5893; Fax (253) 272-9518
Office Hours: Mon–Fri 10am–5pm
Web site: www.wshs.org

Capacity: accommodates up to 215 in the auditorium
Price range: varies depending on type of event and space required; catering and rental packages available
Types of events: corporate, social and cultural; concerts, theatre, film, video presentations, lectures, meetings, seminars, and more

Availability and terms

Many dates are presently available on short notice. A 25% non-refundable deposit is required at booking with balance due two weeks prior to the event. A $300 refundable damage deposit is required.

Description of services and facility

ADA: fully accessible; wheelchair ramp leading into the auditorium and spaces for 4 wheelchairs; front row of seats can be removed to accommodate additional wheelchair seating; projection booth also is wheelchair accessible
Parking: nominal fee in adjacent lots
Auditorium
- **Ticket booth:** built in ticket counter available for registration
- **Seating:** fixed, racked seating; all chairs padded
- **Stage:** dimensions: 32' long x 7'6" wide at center, 4'6" wide on each end; stairs on each end of stage, and one stage door entrance
- **Sound:** built-in sound system

Meeting and event services
- **Audio visual:** projection booth has audio-visual equipment available such as slide projector, video/laser disk projector, and 16mm projector; microphones, overhead projectors, LCD projection panel, and hearing-assisted devices are also available at no charge to renters
- **Equipment:** podium, easels

Banquet and meeting rooms
- **Rooms available:** a variety of banquet, meeting or reception rooms that are ideal for groups of 10 to 350 in addition to our outdoor Plaza and Amphitheater
- **Seating:** 20 round tables, 18 rectangular tables and 215 chairs provided
- **Catering:** full-service in-house catering provided by The Vault Catering Company
- **Cleanup:** restore facility to original condition; all event-related materials removed

ELEGANCE AND CONVENIENCE

The Washington State History Museum opened in 1996 and is the most elegant and unique venue in Tacoma for performances, presentations, meetings, seminars, receptions, banquets, and any other type of private or business functions.

BANQUET, GETAWAY & RETREAT SITES

❖❖❖

AMERICAN KITCHEN

Peace Arch State Park

Washington State Parks
Unique Heritage Facilities

(360) 332-8221

Web site: www.parks.wa.gov *[Click on Rental Places, then on Heritage Places]*

Capacity: 100 inside, 400 inside and outside combined
Price range: $2.52 per person per day; $50 damage deposit; please inquire about rates
Catering: client arranges own catering
Types of events: reunions, ethnic celebrations, company picnics, weddings, and receptions

Availability and terms

Reservations may be made beginning the second Monday in January for dates in that calendar year. The full fee plus a $50 damage deposit is required two weeks prior to the event. Cancellations made within two weeks of the event result in forfeiture of the damage deposit.

Description of services and facility

ADA: accessible to people in wheelchairs
Parking: ample parking nearby
Banquet services

- **Seating:** chairs for 100 indoors, with eight rectangular and eight round tables. Outdoor seating is 20 picnic tables
- **Servers and bar facilities:** caterer or client provides
- **Linens, china and serviceware:** caterer or client provides
- **Decorations:** please call to learn about possibilities and restrictions
- **Cleanup:** client is responsible for cleanup

Special services

The American Kitchen is heated and has a kitchen with a triple sink, a refrigerator, and a stove. The carpeted dining or meeting area has a fireplace (guests should take along their own firewood). A large picnic area just outside the building has 20 picnic tables and a stage with electricity.

WITH A VIEW OF THE PEACE ARCH

Vast lawns, gardens, and the magnificent Peace Arch on the Canada-United States border set the tone for any event planned at the American Kitchen. The building has all the practical amenities, and the graceful grounds that surround the facility have a grove of giant oak trees and 20,000 flowers, including hundreds of rhododendrons and azaleas throughout the park. Views include Point Roberts, Vancouver Island, and the San Juans, and there are spectacular sunsets over Semiahmoo Bay.

Leavenworth's Only Full Service Hotel

505 Highway 2
Leavenworth, WA 98826
Reservations (800) 558-2438
Seattle (888) 353-0595
On-site (509) 548-7000
E-mail: info@icicleinn.com
Web site: www.icicleinn.com

Capacity: over 4,500 square feet of conference space in six rooms, three with mountain and pool views seating up to 250 guests, an executive boardroom, a sloped projection theater, and an outdoor barbeque lawn with mountain views

Price range: group rates depend on season and begin at $79 during the winter and include a complimentary European breakfast buffet

Catering: full catering service offered in-house

Types of events: conferences, meetings, retreats, board meetings, team building, reunions, incentive trips, adventure and activity retreats, and spousal programs

Availability and terms

Leavenworth is approximately 2.5 hours from Seattle along scenic mountain drives. We encourage early reservations; last-minute planning is based on availability.

Description of services and facility

ADA: fully accessible

Parking: ample and complimentary at the Inn; free scheduled shuttle service to downtown

Banquet services

- **Seating:** tables and chairs provided and set up to your specifications
- **Servers:** courteous and professional catering staff
- **Bar facilities:** full service bar located in restaurant, host/no-host bars for events
- **Dance floor:** available
- **Linens, napkins, china and glassware:** included in menu and conference fees
- **Decorations and cleanup:** included in menu and conference fees; special needs (rentals, extra labor) accommodated in advance for a small handling fee

Meeting and event services

- **Audio visual and equipment:** upon availability complimentary overhead and screen, TV and VCR, slide projector, flip chart easel, podum and mike

Special services

Five-acre Entertainment Park with bumper boats, miniature golf, historical train tour, remote control boats, video arcade, movie theatre, and more! Golf packaging with Kahler Glen and Desert Canyon, the #1 rated public course in Washington and special rates with Stevens and Mission Ridge ski areas. A complimentary European breakfast is served daily with view of the Cascade Mountains.

WE HAVE MORE SUNSHINE!

Sparkling clear rivers, towering pines, and lush orchards surround the Icicle Inn, providing an exciting adventure for every group. Experience interpretive hiking trails, river floats, rafting, breathtaking golf courses, two mountain Alpine and Nordic sports, miniature golf, bumper boats, replica historical train tour, sleigh rides, snowmobile tours, hayrides, barn dances, and mouth-watering barbecues... an ideal destination in Central Washington.

"Northwest Country" INNS MEMBER

104 W. Woodin Avenue, Chelan, WA 98816 • 509 682-2561 • email: groups@campbellsresort.com

---

Capacity: 14,000 sq. ft.; accommodates up to 300 in various configurations
Price range: varies with menu selection; please inquire
Catering: full service, in-house catering
Types of events: ideal for banquets, meetings, conferences, seminars, retreats

Availability and terms

Call or check our web site for seasonal packages.

Description of services and facility

ADA: fully accessible
Parking: complimentary parking on-site
Banquet services

- **Seating:** tables and chairs provided and arranged to your specifications
- **Servers:** fully trained banquet servers and set crew included
- **Bar facilities:** full-service and satellite bars; certified servers available
- **Dance floor:** available at an extra charge; up to 450 sq. ft.
- **Linens, china and glassware:** white china, silverware, glassware and stemware provided
- **Decorations:** centerpieces and some themes available; please inquire

Meeting and event services

- **Audio visual and equipment:** state-of-the-art equipment available on site, including wireless technology; ethernet access to the internet also available

Special services

Business Center, guest room voice mail, fitness center and spa services on property.

SUPERIOR FACILITIES IN A SPECTACULAR SETTING

Campbell's Resort is located on the shores of one of the most pristine natural fresh water lakes in the nation—Lake Chelan. 14,000 sq. ft. of state-of-the-art meeting space, accommodating groups up to 300 makes Campbell's the finest midsize meeting center in Washington.

Mention that you saw Campbell's Resort in the Bravo! Event Resource Guide and receive dinner for two at the Campbell House Café and Second Floor Pub.

THE COEUR D'ALENE RESORT

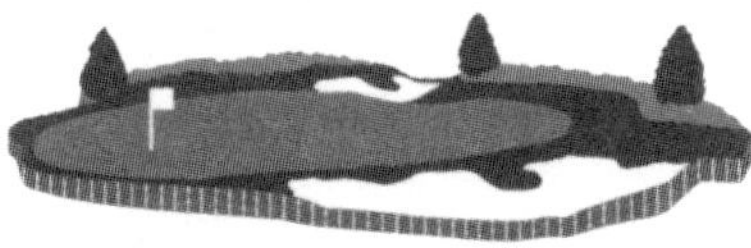

115 South 2nd Street • Coeur d'Alene, Idaho 83814
(208) 765-4000 or Toll free (800) 365-8338
Fax (208) 664-7278
Web site: www.cdaresort.com

Capacity: over 24,000 square feet of flexible meeting space in over 29 different meeting locations; up to 2,000 theatre style in conference center

Price range: varies according to group size and needs; please inquire

Catering: in addition to three on-site restaurants and three lounges, the Coeur d'Alene Resort features world class in-house catering

Types of events: conferences, conventions, banquets, receptions, retreats, reunions, meetings, seminars, business and social events

Availability and terms

Reserve early for best availability. A deposit is required to confirm your reservations.

Description of services and facility

ADA: complies with all ADA requirements

Parking: self parking in the Resort's secured, covered parking garage; valet parking available

Banquet services

- **Seating:** tables and chairs provided to meet your event specifications
- **Servers:** included in catering costs; 19% gratuity and 5% tax applied to all F&B sales
- **Bar facilities:** full service hosted or cash bar available
- **Linens, china and serviceware:** included in catering cost
- **Decorations:** please inquire; nothing that will damage the facility
- **Cleanup:** please remove anything you bring in, we'll handle the rest

Meeting and event services

- **Audio visual and equipment:** complete in-house A/V and equipment service
- **Guest accommodations:** 337 lakeside guestrooms and suites

Special services

The Coeur d'Alene Resort features an 18-hole golf course as well as a European Spa and Fitness Center. Other activities include lake and fly fishing, mountain biking, hiking, sailing, canoeing, sea plane rides, kayaking, jet skiing, cross country and nordic skiing, and shopping.

OFFERING THE FINEST YEAR-ROUND WATERFRONT RESORT ACCOMMODATIONS IN THE NORTHWEST

The Coeur d'Alene Resort is a world-class resort located on the shores of beautiful Lake Coeur d'Alene in Idaho, and features 337 lakeside guestrooms and suites, over 24,000 sq. ft. of flexible meeting space, three restaurants and three lounges, a fleet of lake cruise boats and a world-class golf course with the world's only floating, moveable golf green. **Awards:** America's Best Mainland Resort—*Conde Naste Traveler* magazine*;* America's Most Beautiful Resort Golf Course—*Golf Digest;* Five Star Award—*Golf Digest;* Gold Medal Award—*Golf* magazine.

1131 Skamania Lodge Way • Stevenson, WA 98648
Sales Office (509) 427-2503 or (800) 376-9116
Reservations (800) 221-7117
Office Hours: Mon–Fri 8am–5pm
E-mail: lodge@Gorge.net
Web site: www.skamania.com

Capacity: 450 to 500 people
Price range: $25 to $50
Catering: our Catering Coordinator will take care of all your catering needs
Types of events: retreats, meetings, seminars, conventions, banquets, parties and more

Availability and terms

Our Conference Center consists of two large ballrooms, each divisible into four smaller spaces by state-of-the-art acoustic walls. The ballrooms are accessible to vehicles through large outside doors. Each ballroom is attractively decorated with wainscoting, handsome acoustic panels, and open wood-beamed ceiling. The large ballroom features a fireplace for a special dinner or cozy event. Two comfortable open areas provide flexible reception or breakout options. A moderately-sized board room is located off the main lobby for executive sessions.

Description of services and facility

ADA: meets ADA requirements
Parking: 500 parking spaces
Banquet services

- **Seating:** tables and chairs for up to 500 provided
- **Servers:** appropriate service staff provided
- **Bar facilities:** full-service bar, portable bars, and bartender; all beverages and liquor liability provided by Dolce Skamania Lodge
- **Dance floor:** 21'x30' dance floor; electrical outlets available
- **Linens and napkins:** available in all colors at an additional charge
- **China and glassware:** house china and a variety of glassware included in catering costs
- **Cleanup:** please remove anything you bring in, Dolce Skamania Lodge staff will handle the rest

Meeting and event services

- **Audio visual and equipment:** on-site A/V and equipment to accommodate any of your needs

Overnight accommodations

Dolce Skamania Lodge features 195 elegantly appointed guest rooms. Dolce Skamania Lodge is expanding to 254 guest rooms and 24,000 sq. ft. of conference space, to be completed summer 2002.

IDEAL EVENT FACILITY FOR GROUPS OF ALL SIZES

In the Columbia River Gorge National Scenic Area lies a rustic mountain resort and conference center. Just 45 minutes from Portland International Airport, Dolce Skamania Lodge offers 195 cozy guest rooms, and 12,000 sq. ft. of dedicated conference space. The warmth of the Lodge is characterized by the Native American-inspired rugs, original stone rubbings, warm Pendleton fabrics and mission-style wood furnishings and some of the most spectacular scenic views in the world.

 Please let this business know that you heard about them from the Bravo! Event Resource Guide.

Dumas Bay Centre

3200 S.W. Dash Point Road
Federal Way, Washington 98023
Contact: Dumas Bay Centre (253) 835-2000
Fax (253) 835-2010
Office Hours: Mon–Fri 8am–5pm • ***Web site: www.ci.fed-way.wa.us***

Capacity: banquet room up to 98; meeting rooms for conferences to break into smaller groups; theatre available for larger groups up to 250
Price range: prices vary according to event size and hours; please call
Catering: in-house caterer available
Types of events: overnight and weekend retreats, banquets, meetings, seminars, reunions, conferences, holiday parties, social or business gatherings, weddings and receptions, performing arts or theatrical performances, video presentations

Availability and terms

In addition to overnight accommodations for up to 80, the Dumas Bay Centre has four banquet rooms and meeting rooms. Minimum rental period is three hours. A 50% deposit and 100% damage deposit are due at the time of application with the balance due at least 45 working days prior to your event. Call for prices on overnight packages.

Description of services and facility

ADA: fully complies with ADA requirements

Banquet services
- **Seating:** tables and chairs provided for indoor use
- **Servers:** caterer provides
- **Bar facilities:** bar service set-up by in-house caterer only
- **Linens, china and glassware:** available through caterer
- **Cleanup:** renter is responsible for cleanup
- **Decorations:** nothing that will damage the facility, equipment or furniture; decorating time is included in the rental time; renter is responsible for set-up

Meeting and event services
- **Audio visual and equipment:** TV, VCR; other A/V or equipment needs

Retreat services

- **Overnight accommodations** are available to groups of 12 people or more (up to 80); dormitory-style rooms
- **Extensive grounds and gardens** overlooking bay create a tranquil setting for retreat attendees

ENJOY OUR LUSH, SECLUDED GROUNDS AND VIEW OF PUGET SOUND AND THE OLYMPICS

Located on the water's edge on over 12 acres of manicured lawns and gardens, the Dumas Bay Centre is ideal for social or work gatherings. This former monastery features well-kept banquet and guest rooms with expansive views and is centrally located between Seattle and Tacoma, close to the SeaTac Airport.

See page 174 under Banquet, Meeting & Event Sites.

Enzian Inn

590 Highway 2
Leavenworth, Washington 98826
Group Sales (509) 548-5269
Toll free (800) 223-8511
Fax (509) 548-9319
E-mail: enzgrps@rah.net
Web site: www.enzianinn.com

Capacity: 5,706 sq. ft. meeting space to 225; additional 3,334 sq. ft. for banquets up to 250
Price range: prices vary; please call for current pricing information
Catering: in-house catering provided
Types of events: corporate retreats, conferences, conventions, banquets, board meetings, seminars, receptions, team-building

Availability and terms

We suggest that you make reservations as early as possible, to ensure the best availability. A deposit and signed contract are required.

Description of services and facility

ADA: fully accessible
Parking: ample complimentary parking provided
Banquet services
- **Seating:** all tables and chairs provided at no additional cost
- **Servers:** all service staff provided by Enzian Inn
- **Bar facilities:** client with license or licensed bartender provides permit and all alcoholic beverages
- **Dance floor:** available for a nominal set-up fee
- **Linens, napkins, china and glassware:** provided at no additional charge
- **Decorations:** must be pre-approved; decorating must be done during rental hours
- **Cleanup:** client responsible for removing decorations; Enzian staff handles the rest

Meeting and event services
- **Audio visual and equipment:** full range of equipment available, if reserved

Accommodations and special services

104 guest rooms, including VIP fireplace and spa suites; please call for prices. Indoor/outdoor pool/spa, exercise room. Enzian Falls, our 18-hole championship putting course is located directly across the street from Enzian Inn. Let us help you plan a team-building event or lighthearted group tournament. Featuring natural bent grass greens and a walk-under waterfall, the course offers views of the river, mountains, and grazing goats.

OLD-WORLD CHARM & GRACIOUS HOSPITALITY

Located in beautiful Leavenworth, Enzian Inn brings gracious hospitality and old-world charm to the Cascade foothills. We invite you to enjoy the elegance of authentic Austrian furnishings and relax under our cozy down comforters. Guests awaken to our famous complimentary breakfast buffet served in our fourth-floor solarium and accompanied by an Alpenhorn serenade. Views of surrounding mountains and the Bavarian Village complete the charming ambiance. Our fitness room and racquetball court provide an ideal way to begin your day's activities. Indoor and outdoor pools and hot tubs offer a refreshing way to complete the day's business or pleasure. We look forward to hosting your next special event or retreat.

See page 186 under Banquet, Meeting & Event Sites.

 Please let this business know that you heard about them from the Bravo! Event Resource Guide.

FORT WORDEN STATE PARK CONFERENCE CENTER

Fort Worden State Park

Washington State Parks
Unique Heritage Facilities

200 Battery Way
Port Townsend, Washington 98368
(360) 344-4400; Fax (360) 385-7248
Web site: www.olympus.net/ftworden/confer.html

Capacity: nearly two dozen meeting rooms to accommodate groups of 12–280; conference lecture space for up to 325; theater for 275; chapel for 160; performance pavilion for 1,200; overnight space for 32–365; and 33 Victorian houses for 2–23 are part of a total 39 units with a total capacity of 620

Price range: meeting room prices range from $30–$180; Victorian house rates range from $107 a night to $375 a night for the 11-bedroom house; the chapel is available for $110; a pavillion for 1,200 is as low as $300; please inquire

Catering: all catering is through Fort Worden's in-house caterer, Community Enterprises of Port Townsend, which also runs The Cable House on campus; some catered meals are mandatory with overnight conference group accommodations; to reach the caterer, call (360) 344-4441 or (800) 890-9952, TDD (360) 379-9385

Types of events: business retreats, youth camps, conferences, workshops, meetings, weddings, family reunions, and vacation groups

Availability and terms

For overnight stays for groups of 32 or more, reservations may be made up to two years in advance. For day uses such as meetings or day-long retreats, you can make reservations 90 days in advance. Reservations for 2002 are now being taken. Deposits are charged to secure dates, and refunds vary; fees are charged for cancellations.

Special services

Choose a combination of meeting spaces, banquet rooms, and overnight accommodations that suits your group's needs. Make your stay special; rent a Victorian house with linen service and modern conveniences. Fort Worden also offers more than a dozen attractions, including the 1902 gun batteries, the Coast Artillery Museum, the Marine Science Center, the Centennial Rhododendron Garden, and the galleries, restaurants, historic waterfront and residential areas of Port Townsend.

RETREAT TO A PLACE WITH HISTORY

History is the main attraction at Fort Worden State Park Conference Center, set high on a wooded bluff overlooking the entrance to Puget Sound. The 1902-vintage Fort offers a beautiful setting, with the old-fashioned ambiance of Officers' Row Victorian houses, gun batteries, museums and gardens, as well as the galleries, restaurants and historic waterfront of nearby Port Townsend. Mix and match lodgings and services to suit your group's needs.

31 Early Winters Drive
Mazama, Washington 98833
The Freestone Inn is located in the Methow Valley, 1.5 miles west of Mazama. It is accessible via Highway 20, Highway 2, or Interstate 90.

For reservations, more information, and a free brochure, call 1-800-639-3809
Fax (509) 996-3907 • ***Web site: www.freestoneinn.com***

Named one of the 25 Great American Lodges by *Travel & Leisure* magazine, July 1998.

A Scenic Retreat in a Recreational Paradise

Experience the first-class comfort and luxury of the Methow Valley's newest and finest resort getaway. This renowned Inn, located in a setting of extraordinary natural beauty on the shores of a secluded lake, features a superb restaurant, two outdoor hot tubs, and access to year-round recreation on the many hiking, biking, cross-country skiing, and horseback trails. Special seasonal activities are available, from heli-skiing in winter to white-water rafting and adventure treks in spring and summer. Additional resort accommodations include spacious and luxurious lakeside lodges and cozy creek-side cabins.

Accommodations

The Freestone Inn has 21 rooms, with a fireplace and lake view in every room. The first-class restaurant and a lobby/reception area feature opposite sides of a spectacular, soaring stone fireplace. The Steelhead Lodge offers three bedrooms and a full kitchen; the Rainbow Lodge has two bedrooms and a full kitchen. Fifteen comfortable, creek-side cabins offer scenic seclusion and are available in studio, one or two bedrooms.

Wedding and Meeting Facilities

The Freestone Inn, lakeside lodges, and cabins offer the perfect setting for small corporate retreats, board meetings, planning sessions, or any group of 5 to 100 people. Breakfast, lunch, and dinner can be served in our three meeting rooms, or in the beautiful lakeside restaurant equipped with a full-service bar and class H license. The comfortable meeting rooms offer stunning views of the Methow Valley and surrounding mountain peaks, and are equipped with the finest amenities, including: podiums, microphones, easels, flip-charts, overhead and slide projectors, VCR's, and monitors. Freestone Inn is also the perfect place for weddings, anniversaries, reunions, and other family celebrations.

Your meeting or special event will be a great success in this setting of extraordinary natural beauty and seclusion, tinged with the bracing fragrance of pine trees.

Capacity

Wilson Mews: 1,081 sq. ft., 100 reception, 60 seated; **Merrill AB:** 920 sq. ft., 100 reception, 60 seated; **Merrill A:** 460 sq. ft., 50 reception, 30 seated; **Merrill B:** 460 sq. ft., 50 reception, 30 seated; **Merrill Veranda:** 520 sq. ft., 50 reception, 40 seated; **Lakeside Patio:** 1,536 sq. ft., 100 reception; **Valley View Lawn:** 5,000 sq. ft., 100 reception; **Lake View Dining Room:** 775 sq ft., 75 reception, 50 seated; **8 Fireside Breakout Areas:** 6–10 people each.

We are happy to negotiate exclusive use of the entire facility for your group.
The Freestone Inn is fully ADA accessible and offers plenty of complimentary parking.
Be sure to visit our web site at ***www.freestoneinn.com***

One Bellwether Way • Bellingham, WA 98225
(360) 392-3100 or (877) 411-1200
Fax (360) 392-3101
Web site: www.hotelbellwether.com

HOTEL BELLWETHER
ON BELLINGHAM BAY

Capacity: up to 350 seated, up to 700 reception; includes our Bayview Terrace on the waterfront and our Bellwether Ballroom with spectacular views of Bellingham Bay
Price range: varies according to group size and menu selection
Catering: full-service in-house catering by Harborside Bistro
Types of events: meetings, retreats, seminars, conferences, receptions, banquets, reunions, ballroom and terrace weddings, holiday parties and more

Availability and terms

We recommend reserving your date as soon as possible. Reservations confirmed one year in advance with deposit.

Description of services and facility

ADA: fully accessible as well as guest rooms
Parking: secured underground parking and public parking
Banquet services
- **Seating:** tables and chairs provided
- **Servers:** professional service staff provided
- **Bar facilities:** full service; host or no host; bartenders
- **Dance floor:** permanent dance floor in ballroom
- **Linens and napkins:** white linens and napkins are provided
- **China and glassware:** all provided
- **Decorations:** please inquire for guidelines
- **Cleanup:** handled by our staff

Meeting and event services
- **Audio visual and equipment:** in-house screen; microphone; rental service is available

Special services

Fleet of two yachts for guest charters. 100% Smoke Free Hotel. Terrace canopy available.

SUBTLE CHARM, CONTEMPORARY COMFORTS

Nestled in a quaint cove on Bellingham Bay, Hotel Bellwether offers the subtle charms of a European Inn along with the contemporary comforts today's guests require. Whether you are planning a corporate brainstorming retreat or a magical waterside wedding, Hotel Bellwether offers unique meeting and event space along with assistance from a talented staff to help you attain your vision of perfection. The unrivaled atmosphere and decadent catering options are sure to please you and your guests.

LA CONNER COUNTRY INN & CHANNEL LODGE

P.O. Box 573 • LaConner, Washington 98257 • Contact: Melinda Burghduff (360) 466-3101
Business Hours: Hotel 24 hours, Sales Office 8am–5pm; Mon–Fri
Reservations 1-888-466-4113
Web site: www.laconnerlodging.com

Capacity: Maple Hall: 2,271 sq. ft., 200 guests; **Maple Center:** 815 sq. ft., 35 guests; **Two Forks:** 1,035 sq. ft., 70 guests; **North Fork:** 570 sq. ft., 20 to 30 guests; **South Fork:** 470 sq. ft., 15 to 20 guests; **Dunlap:** 438 sq. ft., 18 guests; **Vantage:** 1,200 sq. ft., 100 guests; **Bird's Nest:** 200 sq. ft., 7 guests
Price range: please inquire; prices may vary
Catering: full-service, in-house catering available
Types of events: meetings, seminars, retreats, conferences, reunions and more

Availability and terms

Room reservation, cancellations and deposits due 45 days prior to arrival.

Description of services and facility

ADA: Lodge and Inn are accessible
Parking: ample complimentary parking provided
Banquet services
- **Seating:** up to 150 people; arrangements vary according to room
- **Servers:** provided by caterer
- **Bar facilities:** provided by caterer or client
- **Dance floor:** available upon request
- **Linens and napkins:** provided by caterer
- **China and glassware:** silver, china and glassware provided by caterer
- **Decorations:** please inquire
- **Cleanup:** handled by staff and caterer

Meeting and event services
- **Audio visual equipment:** please inquire

Overnight accommodations

Channel Lodge: 40 rooms on the Swinomish Channel; 11 suites with Jacuzzis; all rooms have refrigerators, gas fireplaces, coffee pots, irons and ironing boards and hair dryers. **Country Inn:** Features 28 spacious rooms with highbeam ceilings, coffee pots and gas fireplaces. Room service and Homemade Continental Breakfast at both hotels.

"THE TOWN THAT CAPTURES THE NORTHWEST SPIRIT"

Evening Magazine survey 1997

Halfway between Seattle and Vancouver, B.C., located in the charming historical Town of LaConner are our two Hotels. We offer unique accommodations and services not found in your typical destination resort. The Country Inn has cathedral ceiling and quaint finishings that add to the country atmosphere. The Channel Lodge is LaConner's only waterfront hotel that offers private balconies which overlook the Swinomish Channel, the gateway to the San Juan Islands. The two Hotels and the Town of LaConner provide the area's finest facilities for conferences.

 Please let this business know that you heard about them from the Bravo! Event Resource Guide.

MOUNTAIN SPRINGS LODGE & CONFERENCE CENTER

19115 Chiwawa Loop Road
Leavenworth, Washington 98826
Contact: Lyn Kay
(509) 763-2713 or (800) 858-2276
Web site: www.mtsprings.com

Capacity: indoor meeting and banquet facilities consist of several elegantly rustic areas with river rock fireplaces and mountain views, accommodating up to 100; outdoor facilities consist of our corral and barn area, complete with covered wagons, garden ponds, and surrounding lawn areas, accommodating up to 400

Price range: prices vary depending on facilities used, service and menu selections

Catering: full-service catering provided for all events, from formal gatherings to Western barbecues

Types of events: Mountain Springs Lodge and its sister property, Kahler Glen Golf & Ski Resort, offer facilities for a complete range of activities: conferences, corporate retreats, team building programs, reunions, weddings, and outdoor events

Availability and terms

A reservation and deposit are required in advance of your event. We recommend that you make your reservations as soon as possible, especially for summer and winter months.

Description of services and facility

ADA: fully accessible

Parking: complimentary parking is available

Banquet services

- **Seating:** indoor facilities include table and chairs for the seating capacity of each facility; additional furniture is available for outdoor functions
- **Servers:** professional and courteous staff is included in your catering costs
- **Bar facilities:** you are welcome to arrange for service through our licensed suppliers
- **Linens and china:** provided; please inquire about special color requests
- **Decorations:** centerpieces, floral arrangements, and special theme décor available
- **Cleanup:** full cleanup is provided

Meeting and event services

- **Audio visual and equipment:** available at no charge—VCR and TV, overhead and slide projectors, screen, flip charts, easels, whiteboard; we can arrange for the rental of additional equipment as needed

"ON THE SUNNY SIDE OF THE CASCADES"

Enjoy the beauty and serenity of a truly unique mountain resort just two hours from Seattle, between Lake Wenatchee and Leavenworth. Our lodge offers a perfect location for your group to recreate, network, relax, and rejuvenate from the rigors of today's all-too-busy lifestyles. Recreational opportunities include snowmobile tours, sleigh rides, cross-country skiing, downhill skiing at nearby Stevens Pass, horseback and wagon rides, hiking, and golf. The owners and staff look forward to discussing your special needs and matching those to our special facilities.

Be sure to visit our web site at *www.mtsprings.com*

Friday Harbor House

The Inn at Langley

The Resort at Deer Harbor

NORTHWEST WATERFRONT INNS & RESORTS

Seattle Office: 2205 Alaskan Way • Seattle, Washington 98121
(206) 239-1806; Fax (206) 239-1801

Three Unique Inns. At one with their surroundings.

Each of the three Northwest Waterfront Inns & Resorts has unique personal charm and unmistakable character. Nestled along some of the Pacific Northwest's most scenic shorelines, Friday Harbor House, The Inn at Langley, and The Resort at Deer Harbor, offer guests a private sanctuary, gourmet food, and personal service.

• Friday Harbor House

Located on San Juan Island, just three hours from Seattle by car/ferry, or 45 minutes by float plane.

Located in the Pacific Northwest's "Banana Belt," the 20-room Friday Harbor House sits high on a bluff over San Juan Island and receives an average of 257 days of sunshine each year. Guest rooms feature magnificent floor-to-ceiling views, fireplaces, and oversized whirl bathtubs.

The intimate dining room and its ever-changing seasonal menu are favorites with both longtime local residents and guests of the Inn. The culinary team takes special care to use only the finest local products. Guests are invited to enjoy a signature complimentary continental breakfast of homemade scones, breads and granola, assorted cereals, orange juice, and gourmet local coffee.

Ideal for exploring on foot, the town of Friday Harbor offers a wide variety of unique shops, cafes, art galleries and museums highlighting local history, artifacts and island lore.

20 guest rooms • Nationally acclaimed dining • 130 West Street • P.O. Box 1385 • Friday Harbor, WA 98250
(360) 378-8455 • Web site: *www.fridayharborhouse.com*

• The Inn at Langley

Located on Whidbey Island, just 90 minutes from Seattle by car/ferry.

Providing a peaceful Zen-like environment, the 26-room Inn at Langley creates a personal refuge with its use of space, natural fabrics and rich furnishings. Built into a bluff overlooking Saratoga Passage, guest rooms feature an oversized whirl bath jetted tub, fireplace, and private deck with 180º water view.

Overlooking a formal herb garden, the heart of the Inn is The Country Kitchen, complete with a double-sided river rock fireplace and an open display kitchen. The innkeeper/chef prepares elaborate five-course dinners every Friday and Saturday night, and Sunday Suppers seasonally. Guests are also treated to a complimentary continental breakfast featuring fresh fruit, homemade muffins, and the chef's own muesli. You will enjoy inventive, personalized menus that use the season's best bounty and can be accompanied by wines from the Inn's extensive cellar, which features the best available wines from premium Northwest wineries. Just outside the Inn, the charming village of Langley awaits you, famous for its art galleries, antique stores and quaint boutiques.

26 guest rooms • On-site day spa • 400 First Street • P.O. Box 835 • Langley, WA 98260
(360) 221-3033 • Web site: *www.innatlangley.com*

• The Resort at Deer Harbor

Located on Orcas Island, just three hours from Seattle by car/ferry, or 45 minutes by float plane.

Perched on a peaceful beachfront, The Resort at Deer Harbor offers the ultimate in privacy and natural beauty. Each freestanding cottage offers beautiful views of famous Pacific Northwest sunsets from private outdoor hot tubs, or from spacious suites warmed by a cozy fireplace. And guests always enjoy our harbor view outdoor swimming pool during hot island summers.

The Starfish Grill, recently opened by renowned island restaurateur Christina Orchid, overlooks the Deer Harbor Marina and offers the finest in island cuisine. Guests also enjoy the resort's complimentary continental breakfast each morning in the casual fireside lobby.

Many enjoyable leisure activities await you on Orcas Island. The Deer Harbor Marina, just steps away from the resort, offers boat and bike rentals, whale-watching excursions, and kayak wildlife tours.

26 cottages • Private decks with hot tubs • P.O. Box 200 • Deer Harbor, Washington 98243
(360) 376-4420 • Web site: *www.deerharbor.com*

18660 Highway 305
Poulsbo, Washington 98370
Contact: Terri Douglas
(360) 779-3921
Fax (360) 779-9737
E-mail: salesmgr@poulsboinn.com

A HOME AWAY FROM HOME, FOR BUSINESS OR PLEASURE

Just a few blocks from the marina and picturesque waterfront, The Poulsbo Inn offers breathtaking views of the Olympic Mountains and Puget Sound. Spacious and comfortable rooms allow you to relax after a day of work or just to enjoy the beautiful sunsets.

Guest rooms

The Poulsbo Inn offers 72 rooms, including extended stay suites. All rooms feature king or queen size beds and cable TV; some units have kitchens available. Our facility is fully ADA accessible.

Prices, discounts, and terms

Our standard room rates range from $80 to $95. Executive suites are available from $98 to $113. We offer AAA, AARP, corporate, and government rates. Consider making reservations well in advance during peak seasons. Reservations are held until 6pm, unless guaranteed with a credit card. Reservations must be canceled 24 hours prior to arrival date to avoid charges.

Amenities

The Poulsbo Inn provides guests with a complimentary continental breakfast; coffee and coffeemakers are also available in every guestroom. Meeting space will accommodate groups of up to 25 people. Conference facilities for larger groups are available at nearby off-site locations. Guests can enjoy an outdoor seasonal swimming pool, Jacuzzi, and Exercise Room. A play area for children makes The Poulsbo Inn an ideal location for a family getaway. Business travelers enjoy the convenience of free local calls and phones with data ports. Each guestroom features hair dryers, ironing boards, and irons. Coin-operated guest laundry facilities are available for your convenience. Parking at The Poulsbo Inn is complimentary.

78 State Route 115, P.O. Box 2107
Ocean Shores, Washington 98569
(360) 289-9466
or Toll-free (888) 461-2214
Fax (360) 289-5833

E-mail: nhoggan@qbr1.com • ***Web site: www.thequinaultbeachresort.com***

Capacity: beautifully appointed, rich lodge-style facilities; 16,000 square feet; seating for 400 banquet, 1,100 theater/concert; divisible into six breakout rooms; large adjacent lobby/display area

Catering: full-service, in-house food and beverage services; customized menus

Price range: varies depending on type of event, menu selection, other needs

Types of events: meetings, retreats, conventions, trade shows, weddings, reunions, special events of all types

Description of services and facility

ADA: accessible, ADA guest rooms

Parking: free on-site; valet parking available; bus parking also available

Banquet services

- **Seating:** banquet seating up to 400
- **Servers:** provided by resort
- **Bar facilities:** Ocean Lounge, Lobby Fireplace Bar, portable bars available, complete wine list
- **Dance floor:** risers available, dance floor, other special needs can be accommodated by the resort or by area vendors
- **Linens and napkins:** provided by resort; inquire about special color requests
- **China and glassware:** silver, china, and classic stemware provided
- **Decorations:** personalized, special decorations, or themes available by special request

Meeting and event services

- **Audio visual and equipment:** basic inventory in-house, rentals also available; broadband internet access also available

Accommodations

150 guest rooms (117 oceanfront rooms with spectacular views), plus nine oceanfront suites. Each room features a coffee maker, terry robes, luxurious furnishings, fireplace, and other world-class in-room amenities.

THE NORTHWEST'S ULTIMATE BEACH ESCAPE—AFFORDABLY PRICED!

A travel writer recently stated, "The new $60 million Quinault Beach Resort is one of the top three destination resorts on the Pacific Coast." Located approximately 125 miles from SeaTac Airport, the resort is situated on the beach just north of Washington's most popular seaside destination, Ocean Shores. The resort is home to Emily's—a fine dining oceanfront restaurant, the popular Sidewalk Bistro (a café), Ocean Lounge, international-style casino, a variety of nightly entertainment options, gift shop, full-service spa, oceanfront pool and spa, sauna, steam room, state-of-the-art fitness center, and children's activity center.

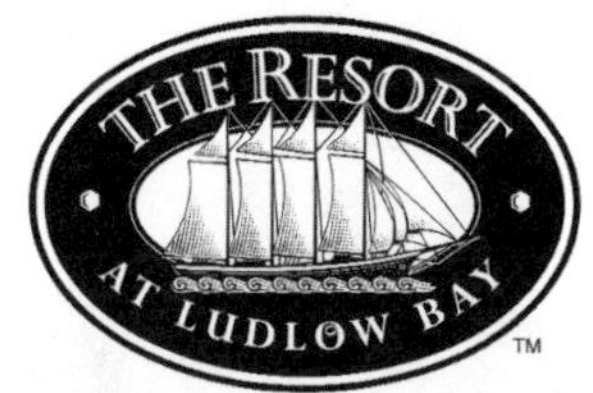

200 Olympic Pl. • Port Ludlow, WA 98365
Contact: Debi Bainbridge, Sr. Sales Manager
(360) 437-2222; Fax (360) 437-2482
Web Site: www.ludlowbayresort.com

Poised on the eastern shores of the Olympic Peninsula, the natural setting of The Resort at Ludlow Bay celebrates the native drama of the Northwest. With over a half mile of shoreline and beach surrounding The Resort, rooms have spectacular views of the Olympic and Cascade mountain ranges, Mt. Baker and our 300-slip marina.

Inn guest rooms feature fireplaces, oversized whirl bath jetted tubs with luxurious bathrobes, European mattresses and down-filled duvets. Villas feature condominium living with full size kitchens and living areas with fireplaces and balconies.

Enjoy the wealth of activities in Port Ludlow. Take a hike to the stunning Ludlow Falls, get a massage, charter a boat from the marina, play a round of golf on our award-winning golf course—the list is endless. And if we don't tire you out, explore the area in depth and navigate the Olympic National Park on foot, horseback, or by car or take a trip to Port Townsend, one of the quirkiest and most beloved spots in Western Washington.

Capacities

Inn: Olympic Room: 656 sq. ft. accommodates up to 48 guests; **Heron Room:** 420 sq. ft. accommodates up to 28 guests; **Andrews Suite:** 562 sq. ft. accommodates up to 12 guests; **Main Dining Room:** 1,155 sq. ft. accommodates up to 75 guests; **Sun Room:** 763 sq. ft. accommodates up to 48 guests

Conference Center Space: Olympic Conference Room: 2,166 sq. ft. accommodates up to 200 guests; **Quinault (can be combined with Olympus):** 722 sq. ft. accommodates up to 60 guests; **Olympus:** 722 sq. ft. accommodates up to 60 guests; **Elwha (can be combined with Kalaloch):** 361 sq. ft. accommodates up to 18 guests; **Kalaloch:** 361 sq. ft. accommodates up to 18 guests

Bay Club: Auditorium: 2,400 sq. ft. accommodates up to 240 guests

Harbormaster Building: Chart Room: 784 sq. ft. accommodates up to 45 guests; **Anchor Room:** 319 sq. ft. accommodates up to 12 guests; **Compass Room:** 405 sq. ft. accommodates up to 24 guests

Beach Club: Bayview Room: 1,672 sq. ft. accommodates up to 130 guests

Outdoor facilities: Patio Tent accommodates up to 60 guests; **Cascade/Lookout Tent** accommodates up to 140 guests

Price range: varies according to group size and menu selections

Catering: full service in-house catering provided by The Resort at Ludlow Bay

Types of events: business meetings, retreats, weddings and social gatherings

Availability

As much advance notice as possible. Event space can be reserved on short notice, based on availability.

68010 East Fairway Avenue
Welches, Oregon 97067
(at the western base of Mount Hood)
(800) 733-0800
Web site: www.theresort.com

Capacity: 18,000 square feet; groups of up to 700; 14 meeting rooms available
Price range: moderate to customized events; please inquire
Catering: in-house catering only
Types of events: business meetings, themed galas, banquets, retreats and golf outings

Availability and terms

Advance bookings are encouraged. Deposits required with payment due in full upon arrival.

Description of services and facility

ADA: fully complies
Parking: ample complimentary parking
Banquet services

- **Seating and servers:** provided to accommodate group size
- **Bar facilities:** liquor and liability provided by The Resort
- **Dance floor:** provided; accommodates up to 200; electrical hookups provided
- **Linens, china and glassware:** provided at no charge
- **Decorations:** prior approval must be obtained by Convention Services
- **Cleanup:** provided by The Resort

Meeting and event services

- **Audio visual:** well-equipped with in-house audio visual; equipment and technicians
- **Equipment:** all necessary meeting/convention equipment provided

Special services

The Resort at The Mountain offers 160 luxury guest rooms and a variety of activities for groups.

GET AWAY FROM IT ALL AT THE RESORT

The Resort at The Mountain offers the Spirit of Scotland in the Highlands of Mount Hood, just an hour from Portland, Oregon. It is the perfect location for events, meetings or conferences. In addition to one of the most beautiful 27-hole golf courses in the Northwest, The Resort at The Mountain offers restaurants, lounges, shops, Scottish artifacts and decor, croquet and lawn bowling, a fitness center, Jacuzzi, pool (seasonal), tennis courts, and a mountain of other activities such as fly fishing on the Salmon River, miles of nearby hiking trails and skiing on Mt. Hood just 20 minutes away.

For more information on events or meetings at
The Resort at The Mountain, please call our sales department.

RESORT

Inn Spa Golf Marina Real Estate

SEMIAHMOO

9565 Semiahmoo Parkway
Blaine, Washington 98230
(360) 318-2000 or (800) 770-7992
Fax (360) 318-5490
Web site: www.semiahmoo.com

Capacity: over 20,000 sq. ft. of newly renovated banquet facilities offer a variety of options that include: exterior view of surrounding bay and Puget Sound, two flexible ballrooms, a tiered theatre, a 7,200 sq. ft. exhibit hall, executive boardroom, two meeting parlors, outdoor tented pavilion along the water, outdoor terrace and function area, two golf clubhouses; 186 guestrooms and 12 suites, many with a waterview and fireplaces
Price range: prices vary depending on menu selection and service needs
Catering: in-house, full service catering provided
Types of events: sit-down or buffet, brunch, lunch, or dinner; ceremonies, receptions, rehearsal dinners, reunions, retreats, parties, or any other types of social event

Availability and terms

We suggest you make your reservations as soon as possible, especially for summer and holiday events; however, we will attempt to accommodate your needs on short notice if possible.

Description of services and facility

ADA: fully accessible and meets current codes
Parking: ample complimentary parking on-site
Banquet services

- **Seating:** table, chairs and patio furniture provided
- **Servers:** courteous, professional staff to meet your needs
- **Bar facilities:** full-service bar and complete wine list
- **Linens and napkins:** provided; please inquire about special color requests
- **China and glassware:** silver, china and classic stemware included in menu prices
- **Cleanup:** please remove anything you bring in; we'll handle the rest
- **Decorations:** we will be happy to discuss personalized decorations to augment our special setting

Special services

Consider one of our two championship golf courses, miles of hiking and biking trails or our spa and fitness center for additional activities for your guests. Our professional event staff is available to assist you in coordinating a truly memorable and first-class event that you and your guests will remember for years to come.

SPECTACULAR WATERFRONT RESORT WITH FIRST-CLASS SERVICE

Nestled on a 1,100-acre natural wildlife preserve just two hours north of Seattle and 45 minutes south of Vancouver, B.C., our AAA Four-Diamond resort is a member of Preferred Hotels and Resorts Worldwide. The waterfront location and expansive meeting and banquet space is ideal for intimate gatherings, larger guest receptions, corporate meetings and events.

The beautiful setting, luxurious guest accommodations, first-class banquet and dining facilities and gracious staff are all reasons that Resort Semiahmoo is Washington's premier waterfront destination and is ranked as "One of the Best Places to Stay in the Whole World" by *Condé Nast Traveler* Gold List.

Shilo INNS
Suites Hotel

SHILO INN–OCEAN SHORES

707 Ocean Shores Boulevard N.W.
Ocean Shores, Washington 98569-9593
Reservations (800) 222-2244;
Group Sales (360) 289-0783
Web site: www.shiloinns.com

OCEANFRONT HAVEN FOR BUSINESS OR PLEASURE

Shilo Oceanfront Resort—Ocean Shores overlooks the gorgeous Pacific Ocean. It features over 12,000 square feet of flexible meeting space. Each of the 113 oceanfront deluxe suites features a sunset-viewing balcony, a microwave, refrigerator, wet bar, three televisions, four telephones, data ports and fax capabilities. In-room movies, games and entertainment, coffee service and iron and ironing board are thoughtfully provided. Guests can relax in the indoor swimming pool, spa, steam room or sauna. Take a moment to unwind and watch our exotic sea life in the 3,000-gallon aquarium in the lobby.

After indulging in a scrumptious meal in Shilo's oceanfront restaurant, work out in the fully-equipped fitness center. Shop, take a ferry boat ride across the bay or enjoy a game of golf at the 18-hole PGA-rated golf course. Walk on the beach, ride horses or rent a moped to visit the 6,000-acre peninsula of Ocean Shores.

Special services

Shilo Inn's catering and event-planning staff will assist you with your menu selection and theme planning for your business or social event. A Shilo Inn representative will be on hand at your event to answer questions and to make sure things run smoothly.

Capacity: 12,200 sq. ft. of flexible meeting space which can accommodate up to 750 people; we are also adjacent to the city convention center
Price range: varies
Catering: full-service catering to meet your needs
Types of events: intimate business meetings to formal affairs

Availability and terms

Call for available dates, and terms will be discussed.

Description of services and facility

ADA: complies
Banquet services

- **Seating:** up to 350
- **Bar facilities:** hosted or no-host bar; liquor and bartenders provided
- **Dance floor:** available upon request
- **Linens:** we have an array of colors available
- **China and glassware:** elegant coordinating china; a variety of glassware

Meeting and event services

- **Audio visual:** state-of-the-art equipment available on rental basis

Reservations

For toll-free reservations to any of 46 Shilo Inns, phone 1-800-222-2244.

Remember, we're just over two hours from Seattle and boast one of the most pristine coasts in the Northwest!

 Please let this business know that you heard about them from the Bravo! Event Resource Guide.

5984 North Darrk Lane • Bow, Washington 98232
(877) 2-SKAGIT or (877) 275-2448 • ***Web site: www.theskagit.com***

Capacity: 460-seat Pacific Showroom, 460-seat Northwest Ballroom, 6 meeting rooms
Price range: varies according to room and menu selections
Catering: full-service in-house catering
Types of events: corporate meetings, retreats, conventions, trade shows, private gatherings, specialty theme parties, weddings

Availability and terms

The Skagit consists of 26,075 square feet of gaming, 103 deluxe rooms including 29 luxurious suites as well as 14,000 square feet of meeting/conference space for groups of various size. Reservations may be confirmed three months in advance. A 50% deposit with signed contract confirms your date.

Description of services and facility

ADA: fully accessible
Parking: ample free parking available
Amenities: luxury hotel, Las Vegas-style Casino, indoor heated pool and spa, fitness center, newly expanded convention center

Banquet services

- **Seating:** all seating layouts available
- **Servers:** provided by The Skagit
- **Bar facilities:** full service bar
- **Dance floor:** available upon request
- **Linens, napkins, china, and glassware:** provided by The Skagit
- **Decorations:** client may provide, or The Skagit can provide all decorations as well as assistance with theme parties
- **Cleanup:** provided by The Skagit

Meeting and event services

- **Audio visual and equipment:** all in-house please inquire

RETREAT, MEET, STAY AND PLAY... THE SKAGIT HAS IT.

At The Skagit work and play are interchangeable. Set in the glorious atmosphere of the Pacific Northwest's Skagit Valley, The Skagit combines the grace and elegance of a four star resort with the energy and excitement of a real Las Vegas style casino. Offering 103 deluxe guest rooms, 29 luxurious suites, a Casino with more than 600 slot machines, table games, three restaurants, live entertainment, and fully appointed conference rooms. Not to mention our new indoor pool with retractable roof, hot tub, sauna, fitness center, sundeck and a spacious 450-seat showroom/ballroom. Coming soon, a spectacular par 72, 18-hole golf course. The Skagit offers all the amenities to make any event perfect.

SLEEPING LADY

7375 Icicle Road • Leavenworth, WA 98826
Contact: Michael Molohon
(800) 574-2123; Fax (509) 548-6312
E-mail: info@sleepinglady.com
Web site: www.sleepinglady.com

Sleeping Lady is a mountain conference retreat located on 67 woodland acres beside Icicle Creek

---

Capacity: 10 meeting spaces, from 352 to 2,020 square feet, accommodate up to 200
Price range: $91 to $202 per person per night, includes lodging, three gourmet buffet meals, meeting space, beverage breaks, A/V equipment and general meeting supplies; day conference rates available
Catering: full service, in-house catering provided
Types of events: conferences, meetings, corporate retreats, board meetings, team building programs, reunions, receptions, holiday dinners, and parties

Availability and terms

Year-round conference center and mountain retreat; deposit required.

Description of services and facility

ADA: fully accessible
Parking: complimentary parking
Banquet services
- **Seating:** all tables and comfortable chairs provided and set up to meet your needs
- **Servers:** courteous, well-trained and experienced professional staff
- **Bar facilities:** beer, wine and spirits; host or no-host events; Grotto bar
- **Dance floor:** space available for dancing
- **Linens and china:** tablecloths and china included in costs

Meeting and event services
- **Audio visual and equipment:** state-of-the-art equipment included in room rate

Special services

Our experienced event planners will assist you throughout the conference planning process. Sleeping Lady's exceptional customer service inspires most groups to book their next event with us before they check out! Ask about our complimentary winter charter transportation for groups.

A CONFERENCE EXPERIENCE THAT ENHANCES COMMUNICATION AND ENCOURAGES CREATIVE THINKING

Sleeping Lady, a mountain conference retreat, is designed for professional and personal renewal. We offer advanced electronic conference support in a casual meeting environment. Feast on the freshest of good foods, sleep in down-fluffed comfort, stroll our woodland trails, work out in the fitness room, arrange for a massage. Outdoor recreation at Sleeping Lady includes hiking, cycling, cross-country skiing, and snowshoeing. Enjoy nature walks, birdwatching, and stargazing led by our staff naturalist. Golf, whitewater rafting, horseback riding, and downhill skiing are available nearby.

P.O. Box 39 • Grand Ronde, OR 97347
Contact: Group Sales (800) 760-7977
Business Hours: Mon–Fri 8am–5pm
Casino Hours: 24 hours
E-mail: groupsales@spiritmtn.com
Web site: www.spiritmountain.com

Capacity: Rogue River Room: 2,500 square-foot room that divides into two equal sections, up to 200 banquet-style or 250 theater-style; **Kalapuya Room:** 2,200 square-foot room that divides into two sections, up to 160 banquet-style or 225 theater-style

Price range: room is complimentary with a $150 minimum food and beverage purchase

Catering: full-service, in-house

Types of events: meetings, seminars, conventions, luncheons, dinners, receptions, parties, weddings, corporate functions

Availability and terms

Contact Group Sales at (800) 760-7977. Online RFP available at ***www.spiritmountain.com***.

Description of services and facility

ADA: fully complies

Parking: ample free parking, including complimentary valet service

Banquet services

- **Seating:** maximum seating capacity is 250 theater-style in the Rogue River Room; other seating styles available for both rooms
- **Servers:** provided
- **Stage/dance floor:** complimentary with advance notice
- **Linens, napkins, china and glassware:** provided
- **Decorations:** allowed with prior approval
- **Cleanup:** provided

Meeting services

- **Audio visual and equipment:** overhead, slide projector, LCD projector, TV, VCR, flip charts, podium, cordless hand-held and lavaliere microphones

Entertainment: At Oregon's most popular attraction, you'll find 1,500 slots machines, blackjack, poker, roulette, craps, Pai Gow and Let It Ride poker, Keno, a Big 6 Wheel, off-track betting, and an 850-seat bingo hall which also hosts live headline entertainment. Live weekend entertainment is featured in the Summit View Lounge. The 5,200 sq. ft. non-smoking casino features all the games and slots found in the regular casino in a non-smoking environment.

Dining: Legends restaurant features Northwest cuisine. Coyote's Buffet presents a rotating menu with over 300 dishes. Other options include the Summit View, a casual dining experience; Rock Creek Court featuring an American Grill, a New York-style deli and traditional Asian Cuisine; and Spirit Mountain Café, proudly brewing Starbucks® Coffee.

Lodging: Spirit Mountain Lodge has 100 guest rooms and suites featuring Northwest-style furnishings and original cultural art. A hospitality suite to accommodate up to 15 people is also available. Group rates available.

We're located about an hour from Portland and a half hour from Salem.
Groups may be eligible for free luxury motorcoach transportation.

Sun Mountain Lodge

P.O. Box 1000
Winthrop, Washington 98862
(800) 572-0493
Seattle Office: Lisa Adair
(425) 487-6638; Fax (425) 487-1278
E-mail: smtnsale@methow.com
Web site: www.sunmountainlodge.com

Capacity: 384 to 2,112 square feet of event space accommodating groups up to 200
Price range: prices vary depending on food and beverage selections
Catering: provided by Sun Mountain Lodge's award winning restaurant
Types of events: corporate retreats, conferences, meetings, team building, outdoor events; banquets, receptions, weddings, rehearsal dinners, and more

Availability and terms

This popular Northwest resort accepts reservations up to five to ten years in advance (shorter notice available depending on space availability; room rates not confirmed until one year out). A $500–$1,000 deposit is required on booking with the balance due 90 days prior to arrival.

Description of services and facility

ADA: fully accessible
Parking: ample complimentary parking adjacent to Lodge
Banquet services

- **Seating:** all tables, chairs and/or patio furniture provided and set up to meet your needs
- **Servers:** professional service staff included in catering costs
- **Bar facilities:** full service bar; host or no-host; cocktail stroller also available
- **Dance floor:** available at additional charge
- **Linens, china and glassware:** included in catering costs
- **Decorations:** please inquire; nothing that will damage the facility
- **Cleanup:** handled by Sun Mountain Lodge

Meeting and event services

- **Audio visual and equipment:** podium, microphones, easels, flipcharts, overhead and slide projectors provided; we'll be happy to coordinate any additional A/V needs

Special services

Let our experienced event staff design non-traditional group or team building activities for your retreat, conference, or event.

DELUXE RESORT SET ON 3,000 PRIVATE ACRES OF MAGNIFICENT WILDERNESS

Sun Mountain Lodge has won distinguished interior design awards for creating space that meets your highest expectations. 115 guestrooms featuring beautiful rustic furniture with bedspreads and decor handcrafted by local artisans. Many rooms feature fireplaces and jetted tubs. Several of our meeting rooms offer the spectacular backdrop of the entire Methow Valley and during breaks, your group can wander out to a courtyard and recharge on fresh mountain air. Sunny 300 days a year, Sun Mountain offers a year-around playground with mountain biking, horseback riding, cross-country skiing, heli-skiing, ice skating, fly fishing and miles of hiking trails. Complete spa services available. Team building has never been so fun! Ask about our non-traditional group activities designed to celebrate the uniqueness of our surroundings. Scheduled air service is just 90 minutes away in Wenatchee or take the 170 mile scenic route by car from Seattle.

CITY OF TUKWILA

16400 Southcenter Parkway, Suite 210
Tukwila, Washington 98188
Contact: Katherine Kertzman
(206) 575-2489 or Toll-free (877)-TUK-WILA
Fax (206) 575-2529
E-mail: tukwila@SWKCC.org
Web site: www.thinktukwila.com

Just 15 minutes away from Seattle, but a world away from downtown prices

Tukwila continues to attract visitors who appreciate its convenient access to Seattle and exceptional values in lodging and other services. Within easy reach of Seattle-Tacoma International Airport, Tukwila offers an ideal location to host out-of-town guests. Convenient access to Interstates 5 and 405 allows for easy transportation around the Puget Sound area. Many Tukwila hotels offer scheduled express van service to downtown Seattle for as little as $10 roundtrip. These hotels are typically priced 20-30% less than lodging in downtown Seattle.

Tukwila offers recreation for everyone

Choose from over 60 high quality restaurants featuring fine Northwest specialties, pizza, and everything in between. An assortment of local casinos and bars also offer live music, dancing, and billiards. Shop **Southcenter Mall**, one of Washington State's largest indoor shopping malls. It offers a selection of over 150 fine stores where you're certain to find the perfect gift or the perfect fit. Indulge yourself with complete beauty and wellness services at the new **Gene Juarez Salon & Spa**. Or surround yourself with exotic sights and sounds while enjoying delicious food and beverages at the **Rain Forest Café**. Visit the world-famous **Museum of Flight**, which features 54 of the most awe-inspiring aircraft; sit in the cockpit of a real SR-71 Blackbird or F/A-a8 Hornet. Whether you're a kid or just a kid at heart, you won't want to miss Tukwila's eight-acre **Family Fun Center**; enjoy go-karts, bumper boats, miniature golf, laser tag, and batting cages. More than 30 miles of **paved trails** follow the peaceful Green and Duwamish Rivers north from Algona to Seattle. Once used by trolley cars, this route offers scenic bicycling, jogging, walking, and skating. Parking and picnic sites are available at many points along the trail. Looking for a golfing getaway? Visit Foster Golf Links, an 18-hole public course, just under 5,000 yards and a par 69.

Tukwila features a full range of accommodations, and meeting space suitable for small gatherings or receptions hosting several thousand guests. Free parking abounds in Tukwila, and most hotels offer complimentary airport shuttle services. A directory with complete listings of available space and services can be viewed on the Tukwila tourism web site at ***www.thinktukwila.com***.

For more information about Tukwila,
please call toll-free 1.877.885.9452

WALLACE FALLS LOG LODGE

(360) 793-8784
or (888) 337-7492
E-mail: lodging@wallacefallslodge.com
www.wallacefallslodge.com

A place of quiet seclusion with fabulous Cascade views, Wallace Falls provides a fantastic setting for off-site informal meetings, company retreats, teambuilding activities, and other special events. We offer a recreational and retreat facility ideal for hosting family or employees. A stress-releasing retreat can be arranged, complete with yoga, meditation, and massage.

Description of the Lodge

A 10-bedroom, 6000 sq. ft. lodge of log and stone, with ceilings soaring three stories high, Wallace Falls displays a remarkable old-world ambiance. A sizeable collection of antique clocks and a large elk-head over a stone fireplace contribute to its rustic charm. All rooms have private baths, handcrafted pine doors, and queen-size beds built from knotty pine

Our amenities include a therapy spa and hot tub, a volleyball court and horseshoe pit, campfire facilities, a game room, and a TV room. A licensed massage therapist is also available. With so much to do, your guests will sleep well between our soft flannel sheets.

Stay with us in winter, and enjoy generous discounts at Stevens Pass Ski Resort. Other nearby recreational activities include whitewater rafting, kayaking, and fishing in the Skykomish River, all available seasonally. Trails are open for hiking year-round, allowing you easy and scenic access to the waterfalls, Wallace Lake, and Wallace Falls State Park.

Reserve the entire Lodge for your special event—your organization can enjoy exclusive use of the lodge for an entire week, just the weekend, or a few weekdays. The price includes banquet tables, and chairs for 60 people. Kitchen facilities are available for your use, but we also welcome caterers or the opportunity to provide meals. A permit is required for alcohol.

Capacity: Wallace Falls can accommodate up to 100 guests for daytime outdoor events, and can provide overnight accommodations for up to 25.

Price range: for an exclusive-use booking, Monday–Thursday $500–$700; Friday–Sunday $675–$1,000

Visit our web site for a virtual tour: *www.wallacefallslodge.com*

Located just off of scenic Highway 2 in Gold Bar, we offer the beauty of the Cascade Mountains only 70 minutes from SeaTac Airport. We look forward to hosting your next corporate retreat. Please e-mail us or call for more information.

116 North Wenatchee Avenue • Wenatchee, Washington 98801
(800) 572-7753; Fax (509) 663-3983
E-mail: jillwood@wenatcheevalley.org
Web site: www.wenatcheevalley.org

Capacity: in the Wenatchee Valley we have 16 unique and affordable accommodations with convention capabilities that are located within 5 miles of each other; the **Wenatchee Center** has 20 individual meeting rooms in 50,000 sq. ft. of meeting space and can accommodate up to 1,500 people; the **Red Lion Hotel** has 7 meeting rooms in 7,500 square feet of meeting space and can accommodate up to 600 people
Price range: varies depending on event and menu selections; please call for a proposal
Catering: full service in-house catering at banquet facilities as well as catering referrals for off-site events
Types of events: conventions, meetings, gatherings, reunions, corporate retreats, seminars and trade shows

Availability and terms
Please inquire about available dates and facilities. You will want to reserve space well in advance, though short-term bookings are possible depending on availability.

Description of services and facility
ADA: fully accessible
Parking: plenty of FREE parking
Banquet services
- **Seating:** tables and chairs are provided to fit your needs
- **Servers:** experience small town hospitality in a world class setting
- **Bar facilities:** full service bars available that include all beverages, bartenders, and servers
- **Dance floor:** available upon request
- **Linens, napkins, china and glassware:** included in meeting room rental
- **Decorations:** available upon request or client may bring own
- **Cleanup:** provided by facility

Special services
We help you with all the details for holding a successful and hassle-free convention, event or meeting. Best of all, we do it for free. Simply call us and let us know your basic needs and we will work with you from start to finish.

THERE'S MORE TO WENATCHEE THAN APPLES
If you've ever heard about Wenatchee, more that likely it had something to do with apples. After all, we're world famous for our apples. But you might not have heard that we receive over 300 days of sunshine a year! Located smack dab in the middle of Washington State on the eastern slopes of the Cascade mountains, Wenatchee is a short drive form Seattle and Spokane.

THE WESTIN SALISHAN

LODGE & GOLF RESORT

Gleneden Beach, Oregon

7760 Highway 101 North • Gleneden Beach, Oregon 97388
Contact: Group Sales
(800) 890-9316; Fax (503) 764-3510
Web site: www.salishan.com

Capacity: 14,000 square feet of flexible meeting space for groups of 5 to 500
Price range: price varies depending on event
Catering: full-service in-house catering
Types of events: conferences, receptions, banquets, catered functions

Availability and terms

Reservations are recommended six months to one year in advance.

Description of services and facility

ADA: yes
Parking: plenty of parking available
Banquet services

- **Seating:** tables and chairs provided for up to 600
- **Servers:** one server per 25 guests
- **Bar facilities:** full-service in-house bar
- **Dance floor:** 400-square-foot dance floor available
- **Linens and napkins:** a variety of colors are available at no charge
- **China and glassware:** china and crystal available
- **Cleanup:** provided at no charge

Meeting and event services

- **Audio visual and equipment:** full service available; podiums, easels and risers available at no charge

Special services

The Westin Salishan Lodge features 205 oversized guest rooms with fireplaces, private balconies, forest or bay views; golf course, golf links, tennis courts, Westin Kids Club, and putting course.

EXPERIENCE YEAR-ROUND ATTRACTIONS OF THE OREGON COAST

The Westin Salishan Lodge and Golf Resort offers conference groups, individuals, couples and families a unique opportunity to experience the year round attractions and activities of the Oregon coast. Recreational activities include Oregon coast eco tours, hiking, beach combing, shopping at the local factory stores and marketplace, classic tours of the nationally renown wine cellar, wine tasting, horseback riding, tennis, golf, massages and storm watching. In addition to two unique on-site restaurants, Salishan is located within a seven mile radius of over 60 restaurants.

Banquet, Meeting & Event Sites/ Boats

❖❖❖

HELPFUL HINTS

- **You can hold a variety of events on a boat.** From a simple cruise to a very formal sit-down dinner, a boat offers a wonderful way to see Puget Sound and Lake Washington at their finest.
- **Certification:** If you decide to hold your function on a boat, make sure it is Coast Guard certified. This not only ensures you and your guests' safety, but also makes sure you avoid all kinds of legal, tax and liability problems.
- **Capacity:** Never plan a function on a boat where more people 'might' attend than the boat can legally accommodate. Coast Guard certified boats have a maximum capacity of passengers allowed on board. Make sure you have an accurate estimate of how many people will be attending —it would be very embarrassing to have to leave someone behind.
- **Catered events:** Many of the boats in the Greater Puget Sound area are known for their fine dining. You'll be surprised by the variety of choices available to you—from formal to informal, even theme parties.
- **Budget:** When reserving a boat, make sure you have a detailed estimate of the time you will be out, and the charges for any additional hours. Remember, if you are holding the boat because someone is late, the clock is ticking, and your budget can be blown.
- **Boarding and sailing times:** Be very clear with your guests about the exact boarding time. It's best to allow at least one-half hour between the boarding and sailing times.

218 Main Street, #143 • Kirkland, Washington 98033
(425) 481-1077; Fax (425) 481-0832 • E-mail: fun@amzcruises.com

Capacity: 30 to 200 guests

Price range: we have all inclusive discount packages that start at $1499 which includes our catered hors d'oeuvres buffet, two beverages per guest; Fantasy Casino, prizes from our corporate sponsors, and a musical theme of your choice; rates vary according to season, day, menu selection and group size

Catering: we have professional caterers dedicated to creating a delectable dining experience for your event; anything from buffet hors d'oeuvres to a seated dinner extravaganza

Types of events: corporate and individual events, holiday parties, club and group functions with many theme choices, like our Reggae Sun Splash, Down Home Blues, Smooth Jazz, and Classic Rock Cruises

Availability and terms

We're available for you year round. Reservations require a 50% deposit with the balance due 30 days prior to cruise.

Description of services and vessel

Parking: ample free parking near each yacht

Banquet services

- **Seating:** once you've exhausted yourself from playing blackjack, partying, and libations, we'll have chairs and tables for your relaxation
- **Bar facilities:** staffed full-service bar and script bars available
- **Cleanup:** provided by Absolutely Amazing Cruises

Meeting and event services

- **Audio visual and equipment:** you want to see or hear it...we can arrange it

RECOMMENDATIONS FROM OUR GUESTS!

"The cruise received rave reviews from all who attended...We were thoroughly impressed!"
—Frank Leach, John L. Scott

"Our wedding rehearsal dinner was a lot of fun for us and our guests."
—Valerie Bryson, Happy Customer

"You and your staff have always provided professional, courteous service that has exceeded expectations."
—Bradford Maynard, Allstate Insurance

Spirit of Seattle

M.V. Kirkland

Lady Mary

Pier 55, Suite 201
Seattle, Washington 98101
(206) 623-1445; Fax (206) 623-5474
Office Hours: Mon–Fri 8am–5pm, Sat–Sun 8:30am–5pm
E-mail: sales@argosycruises.com
Web site: argosycruises.com

Capacity: up to 800 people for private cruises
Price range: varies according to vessel, day, and menu; packages to fit every budget
Catering: full-service catering available, or you choose your own caterer
Types of events: corporate meetings and events, club and group functions, sit-down dinners, buffets, brunches, casual or formal functions, weddings, receptions, reunions, birthdays, school events, client entertaining, bar mitzvahs, bat mitzvahs, and holiday parties

Availability and terms

All 12 vessels in the Argosy fleet are available to privately charter. A 50% deposit is required to reserve a vessel, with the balance due one month prior to cruise.

Description of services and vessels

ADA: vessel layouts differ; please inquire
Parking: parking is available in lots nearby our departure locations on the Seattle, Lake Union and Lake Washington waterfronts

Banquet services

- **Seating:** tables and chairs to meet your needs
- **Bar facilities:** staffed, full-service bars; host/no-host and bar packages available
- **Dance floor:** available on selected vessels
- **Linens and napkins:** provided by our caterers
- **China and glassware:** china and glassware vary according to menu
- **Cleanup:** cleanup, plus table setup and take-down is provided by Argosy staff
- **Decorations:** please inquire; special occasion packages available

Meeting and event services

- **Audio visual and equipment:** can be arranged; please inquire

Special services

Photography, music/DJs, entertainment, espresso, theme cruises, additional cruising time and departures from locations of your choice. Let our professional sales managers assist you in planning all aspects of your event.

SEATTLE'S BEST VENUES

Argosy Cruises offers an experience that is truly unique. For over 50 years we have provided quality, value and one of the most spectacular panoramas imaginable—views of Seattle from the water. Our professional and courteous crew will make your cruise special.

continues on next page

ARGOSY CRUISES

continued from page 130

Regularly scheduled cruises

In addition to private charters for all occasions, Argosy also offers exciting regularly-scheduled public cruises.

- **Lake Cruise–Seattle:** this 2-hour cruise departs from AGC Marina–Dock E on Lake Union and takes you by the floating home community, Husky Stadium and luxurious waterfront homes on Lake Washington. Departs daily year-round.
- **Lake Cruise–Kirkland:** this 1½-hour cruise departs from Kirkland City Dock and cruises Lake Washington past beautiful waterfront homes and Husky Stadium. This cruise is often aboard the historic vessel, the *M.V. Kirkland.* Cruises daily May through September and weekends year-round.
- **Locks Cruise:** this 2½-hour cruise takes you on both salt and fresh waters via famous Hiram Chittenden Locks. See the "Sleepless in Seattle" houseboat while cruising through Lake Union. Departs daily year-round from Pier 56.
- **Harbor Cruise:** this 1-hour cruise is a "must do" for visitors and locals alike. Learn about Seattle's historic waterfront on this cruise of Elliott Bay and the Seattle harbor. Departs daily year-round from Pier 55.

Reservations are recommended to ensure space availability. Please call (206) 623-4252 or visit ***www.argosycruises.com*** for cruise information and departure times.

***For groups/individuals that cruise frequently,
ask about Argosy's Captain's Club membership.***

Boats available

Our fleet of climate-controlled boats can accommodate your next special event.

- ***Spirit of Seattle:*** this 115' vessel has a maximum capacity of 400 guests; features two large fully enclosed decks with double bars and a third open-air deck
- ***M.V. Kirkland:*** 110' original 1924 wooden hull ferry, completely restored; features both interior and extensive exterior decks, 14' ceiling surrounded by 12' windows, dance area and two full-service bars
- ***Lady Mary:*** this 98' vessel offers spacious interior decks and a second deck with plenty of open air space and the option to enclose it during the winter months; newly renovated interior and a new baby grand piano; maximum capacity is 200 guests
- ***Goodtime:*** maximum capacity of 300 guests; features two enclosed decks, a large open-air area on the upper deck and one bar
- ***Goodtime II:*** the sister ship to the *Goodtime;* features two enclosed decks, a large open-air area and two bars with a maximum capacity of 300 guests
- ***Goodtime III:*** maximum capacity of 175 guests; features one-and-a-half climate-controlled decks, a large open-air deck area and a double bar on the lower deck
- ***Celebrations:*** 73' of dynamic beauty; maximum capacity of 90 guests, features both interior and exterior decks, dance area, baby grand piano and full-service bar
- ***Champagne Lady:*** the sister ship to the *Celebrations*; features an additional exterior bar with maximum of 80 guests
- ***Sightseer:*** maximum capacity of 150 guests; features two enclosed decks and one bar
- ***Queen's Launch:*** small and fun; maximum capacity of 40 guests; features one enclosed deck and one open deck along with a beer and wine bar

See page 133 for information on Argosy's new fine dining lunch and dinner ship, the Royal Argosy. This vessel can accommodate up to 800 guests for group events or individual dining.

Cristal Charters, LLC

6037-35th Place N.W.
Seattle, Washington 98107
Contact: Ralph
(206) 286-9711; Fax (801) 881-8372
Web site: www.cristalcharters.com

Capacity: Day Charters: up to 49 guests; **Overnight:** sleeping accommodations for 8+
Price range: our most popular yacht cruise is $1,495
Catering: we are happy to work with the caterer of your choice; for your convenience, we offer a full-service galley located on main deck
Types of events: private parties, meetings, celebrations, client appreciations, product presentations, and more...

Availability and terms

We suggest making reservations as early as possible to reserve Cristal Charter's Match Maker. A 50% deposit will reserve your date with the balance due prior to departure. A refundable damage deposit is required. Ask about other vessels available.

Description of services and vessel

ADA: the Match Maker's main deck is fully accessible
Parking: ample parking adjacent to dock
Banquet services

- **Seating:** all tables and chairs included at no additional charge; the comfortable furnishings in the salon can be rearranged to fit the needs of your group
- **Servers:** our three-man crew will look after all your needs; caterer provides any necessary food service personnel
- **Bar facilities:** client or caterer provides all beverages
- **Dance floor:** the main deck and sun deck are ideal for dancing; standard 110 volt outlets conveniently located on-board; great on-board sound system
- **Linens, china and glassware:** provided by caterer
- **Cleanup:** provided by the Match Maker crew
- **Decorations:** please inquire; nothing that will damage the vessel

Meeting and event services

- **Audio visual and equipment:** we'll be happy to help arrange for any of your needs
- **Guest rooms:** master stateroom located below deck with private bath; four additional staterooms, each with private head and shower

WELCOME ABOARD THE YACHT "MATCH MAKER"— 67 FEET OF LUXURY AND ELEGANCE

Treat family, friends or business associates to a uniquely Northwest experience aboard the Match Maker, Cristal Charters' 67-foot luxury yacht. Yours for an afternoon, evening or longer cruise, it is the perfect place to host an unforgettable event. Entertain business associates in a relaxed atmosphere of beauty, comfort and style. Celebrate with an unforgettable wedding, birthday, anniversary or graduation party.

Royal Argosy Fine Dining Cruises

Pier 56
Seattle, Washington 98101
(206) 623-1445; Fax (206) 623-5474
Office Hours: Mon–Fri 8am–5pm, Sat–Sun 8:30am–5pm
E-mail: sales@argosycruises.com
Web site: royalargosy.com

Capacity: up to 600 guests for seated meals, reception facility for up to 800 guests

Price range: varies according to day, cruise type, menu selection and group size, packages available to fit every budget

Catering: guests will be able to select from a rotating seasonal menu of favorites showcasing the Pacific Northwest, all freshly prepared aboard the ship; table-side service will be offered in four dining areas by an experienced wait staff employed by Consolidated Restaurants who own Elliott's Oyster House, The Metropolitan Grill and Union Square Grill

Types of events: corporate events, club and group functions, sit-down dinners, brunches, informal or formal functions, weddings and receptions, client entertaining, birthdays, anniversaries, holiday parties, bar mitzvahs and bat mitzvahs

Availability and terms

The Royal Argosy takes individual reservations. Groups can charter the entire ship or private rooms for functions. A 50% deposit is required to reserve a private room for groups. The balance is due one month prior to your cruise.

Description of services and vessel

ADA: fully accessible on main and 2nd deck, please inquire

Parking: parking is available in nearby lots; please inquire

Banquet services

- **Seating:** tables and chairs for sit-down service up to 600 guests
- **Bar facilities:** full service bar on each deck, host/no-host and bar packages available
- **Dance floor:** two decks have dance floors; electrical outlets available
- **Linens and napkins:** linen tablecloths and napkins
- **China and glassware:** fine white china and classic stemware provided
- **Cleanup:** clean up plus table setup and take-down is provided by Royal Argosy staff
- **Decorations:** please inquire; special occasion packages available

Meeting and event services

- **Audio visual and equipment:** state-of-the-art video and audio capability throughout; podium, microphone, TV/VCR, Powerpoint

Special services

Photography, baby grand piano, music/DJs, entertainment, theme cruises, additional cruising time; let our professional sales managers assist you in planning all aspects of your event.

SEATTLE'S BEST VENUE

The Royal Argosy is the newest addition to Argosy's fleet. Fine dining lunch and dinner cruises offering breathtaking views and a sensational menu, freshly prepared onboard. Departs from Pier 56.

809 Fairview Place North, Suite 110 • Seattle Washington 98109
(206) 223-2060; Fax (206) 223-2066
Office Hours: Mon–Fri 8:30am–5:30pm; or by appointment
Web site: www.waterwayscruises.com

Capacity: our fleet accommodates individuals and groups of every size; our luxury yachts include the Emerald Star, Olympic Star, Weststar, Entertainer, and High Spirits

Price range: will vary depending on vessel, length of cruise, season, or time of day

Catering: our exclusive caterer offers a full range of options; we'll work with you to create a menu that complements your specific needs and budgets; whether you want a formal sit-down dinner, an exquisite buffet or an elegant hors d'oeuvres reception, you will enjoy superior cuisine carefully prepared and presented with style

Types of events: corporate events, client entertaining, holiday festivities, theme parties, new product kick-offs, summer picnics, social events and special celebrations; we also offer overnight or extended cruises for up to 8 people to many different destinations in the Pacific Northwest

Availability and terms

Our vessels are available for private charter throughout the year. Reservations should be made as early as possible to ensure availability.

Description of services and vessels

ADA: fully complies with ADA requirements

Banquet services

- **Seating:** tables and chairs provided
- **Servers:** friendly, professional service staff included in catering costs
- **Bar facilities:** full-service bar on each yacht
- **Linens, china and glassware:** included in catering costs
- **Decorations:** discuss your thoughts with our event coordinator, or we'd be happy to share our ideas
- **Cleanup:** provided by Waterways

Meeting and event services

- **Audio visual and equipment:** each vessel equipped with an audio system; additional equipment available for rental

Special features

Our fleet includes Seattle's newest and most luxurious yachts. Come aboard and enjoy impeccable surroundings, inviting ambiance and inspired cuisine. At Waterways, our standards for exceptional quality match yours. Our expert staff caters to all your needs, so you can sit back and enjoy the true camaraderie among your group.

 Please let this business know that you heard about them from the Bravo! Event Resource Guide.

Banquet, Meeting & Event Sites

❖❖❖

BANQUET, MEETING & EVENT SITES AREA MAP

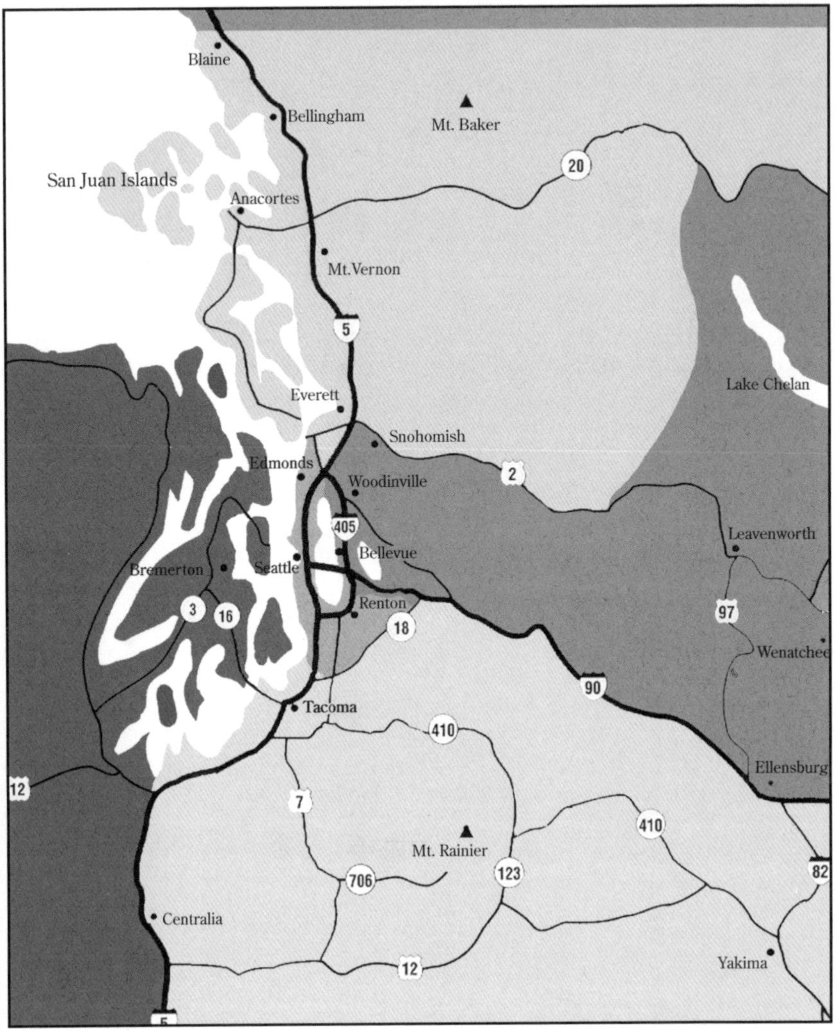

Blaine
Bellingham
Mt. Baker
San Juan Islands
Anacortes
20
Mt.Vernon
5
Lake Chelan
Everett
Snohomish
Edmonds
2
Woodinville
405
Leavenworth
Bellevue
Bremerton
Seattle
Renton
3
16
97
18
Wenatchee
90
Tacoma
410
Ellensburg
12
7
410
Mt. Rainier
123
82
706
Centralia
Yakima
12
5

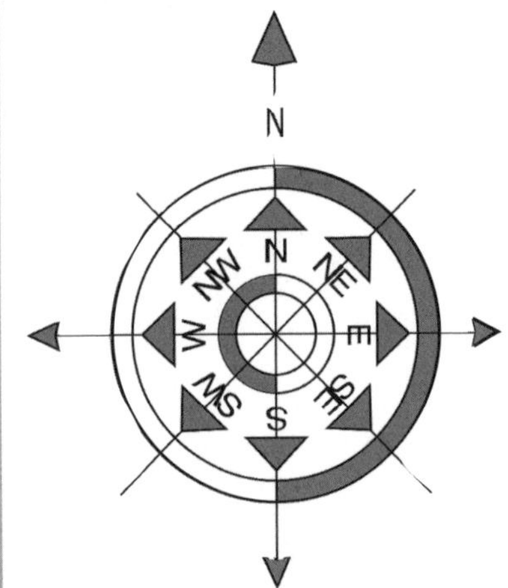

Banquet, Meeting & Event Sites listed alphabetically according to following areas:

- ***Greater Seattle***
- ***Eastside***
- ***Northend***
- ***South Sound***
- ***Destination Sites–Washington***
- ***Destination Sites–Idaho***
- ***Destination Sites–Oregon***

GREATER SEATTLE

Absolutely Amazing Cruises***
Argosy Cruises***
Alexis Hotel - The Painted Table
Aljoya Conference Center of Seattle
The Bay Pavilion
Bell Harbor International Conference Center
Benaroya Hall
Big Picture
Blue Ribbon Cooking
BluWater Bistro
Broadway Performance Hall*
The Burke Museum
Canlis Restaurant
CaterArts at The Lakeside
Century Ballroom
The Claremont Hotel
Columbia Tower Club
Court In The Square
Cristal Charters, LLC***
Crowne Plaza
Cutter's Bayhouse
Dahlia Lounge Seattle
Daniel's Broiler - Leschi Marina
Daniel's Broiler- South Lake Union
The Dome Room
Doubletree Guest Suites - Seattle
Doubletree Hotel - Seattle Airport
The Drachen Foundation
Dragonfish
Eagles Aerie #1, Fraternal Order of
The Edgewater
Edmonds Floral Conference Centre
El Gaucho
Elliott Grand Hyatt
Embassy Suites Hotel - Seattle North/ Lynnwood
Emerald Center
Experience Music Project
F.X. McRory's
The Fairview Club
Family Fun Center - Bullwinkle's Restaurant
Fauntleroy, The Hall at
Flying Fish
Funsters Grand Casinos
Greenwood Square
Grand Central Casino
The Harbor Club - Seattle
Harborside, McCormick & Schmick's
Hilton Seattle
Hilton Seattle Airport & Conference Center
Hotel Monaco*****
Holiday Inn Express - SeaTac
Hunt Club
Icon Grill
Ivar's Acres of Clams
Ivar's Salmon House
The Jerry M. Brockey Center at South Seattle Community College
Jillian's - Seattle
Kaspar's
Kingstad Meeting Center
Knights of Columbus
Lake Union Cafe
Lake Union Crew
Lake Washington Rowing Club
Lowell-Hunt
Marina Club at Shilshole Bay
Mayflower Park Hotel
Mediterranean Inn
Museum of Flight
Museum of History & Industry
New Holly Neighborhood Campus
Nile Golf & Country Club
Odyssey, The Maritime Discovery Center
Pacific Science Center
Palisade
The Paramount
Ponti Seafood Grill
Pyramid Brewery
Rainforest Cafe
Ray's Boathouse
REI
The Renaissance Madison Hotel
Royal Argosy Fine Dining Cruises***
SAFECO Field - The Seattle Mariners
Saint Edward Grand Dining Hall
Salty's on Alki
Scottish Rite Masonic Center
The Seattle Aquarium
Seattle Art Museum
Seattle Asian Art Museum
The Seattle Design Center
Seattle Repertory Theatre
Sheraton Seattle Hotel & Towers
Shilshole Bay Beach Club
Skansonia Ferryboat
Skyway Park Bowl & Casino****
The Smith Tower - Chinese Room
Sorrento Hotel
The Space Needle
The Stimson-Green Mansion

continues on page 138

GREATER SEATTLE,
continued from page 137
Studio 7000
Studio One-Sixteen
Tillicum Village
Top of the Market
Town Hall Seattle
Tukwila Community Center
Tulio Ristorante
Tyee Yacht Club
Union Station - Seattle
Valley Medical Center Education Conference Center*
W Seattle
Washington Athletic Club
Waterways Cruises***
WestCoast Grand Hotel on Fifth Avenue
The Westin - Seattle
Wilsonian Grand Ballroom
Woodland Park Zoo****
World Trade Center - Seattle
Yale Street Landing

EASTSIDE

Bear Creek Country Club
Bellevue Club Hotel
Best Western Bellevue Inn
Carco Theatre, City of Renton*
Champs Karting
Columbia Winery
Daniel's Broiler - Bellevue Place
Doubletree Hotel - Bellevue
Echo Falls Country Club
Embassy Suites - Bellevue
The Harbor Club - Bellevue
Hedges Cellars
The Hollywood Schoolhouse
Hyak Lodge
Hyatt Regency - Bellevue
Illusionz Magical Entertainment Center
Issaquah Community Center
Kingstad Meeting Centers
Lake Wilderness Center
Lake Wilderness Golf Course
Maplewood Greens
The Monte Villa Farmhouse
The Golf Club at Newcastle
Overlake Square Conference Center
Pickering Barn
The Plateau Club
Pleasant Hill Estate
Redhook Brewery-Woodinville
Remlinger Farms
Renton Community Center, City of
Salish Lodge & Spa
Snoqualmie Ridge Golf Club
Spirit of Washington Dinner Train****
Tibbetts Creek Manor
Valley Medical Center - Education Conference Center*
WestCoast Bellevue Hotel
Willows Lodge
The Woodmark Hotel
Yarrow Bay Grill

NORTHEND

Best Western Cotton Tree Inn & Conference Center
Craven Farm
Edmonds Floral Conference Centre
The Farm
Hotel Bellwether on Bellingham Bay
Gleneagle
Lord Hill Farms
Marine View Banquet Center
Nile Golf & Country Club
Remlinger Farms
Resort Semiahmoo
Skagit Valley Casino Resort

SOUTH SOUND

Centre at Norpoint
Dumas Bay Centre
Emerald Downs
Emerald Queen
Harbor Creek Lodge
Indian Summer Golf & Country Club
Inn at Gig Harbor
Jillian's- Tacoma
King County Aquatic Center
King Oscar Motel & Convention Center
Knutzen Family Theatre*
Lakewold Gardens
Mulligans at Meadow Park Golf Course
Museum of Glass
Nature Center, The Tacoma
Norpoint, Centre at
Northwest Trek Wildlife Park
Point Defiance Lodge
Point Defiance Pagoda
continues on page 139

SOUTH SOUND
continued from page 138
Point Defiance Zoo & Aquarium
Salty's at Redondo
South Park Community Center
Tacoma Rhodes Center
Tacoma's Landmark Convention Center
Titlow Lodge Community Center
The Top Floor at The Vault
Trattoria Grazie Ristorante
Union Station-Tacoma
Valley Medical Center Education Conference Center*
The Vault
The Top Floor at the Vault
Verrazano's
Washington State History Museum
Wild Waves Enchanted Village

DESTINATION SITES–WASHINGTON

American Kitchen
Best Western Icicle Inn
Campbell's Resort on Lake Chelan
Deer Harbor Resort**
Dolce Skamania Lodge**
Enzian Inn
Fort Worden State Park Conference Center
Freestone Inn**
Friday Harbor House**
Hotel Bellwether on Bellingham Bay
The Inn at Langley**
La Conner Country Inn**
La Conner Channel Lodge**
Mountain Spring Lodge**
Poulsbo Inn*****
Quinault Beach Resort & Casino**
Red Lion Hotel - Wenatchee
Resort at Ludlow Bay
Resort Semi-ah-moo
Shilo Inns - Ocean Shores**
Skagit Valley Casino
Sleeping Lady Conference Center
Sun Mountain Lodge
Tillicum Village
Wallace Falls Lodge**
Wenatchee Center**

DESTINATION SITES–IDAHO

Coeur d'Alene Resort**

DESTINATION SITES–OREGON

The Resort at the Mountain**
Spirit Mountain Casino
Westin Salishan**

* *See Auditorium, Theatres & Classrooms section (Pages 91–98)*

** *See Banquet, Getaway & Retreat Sites section (Pages 99–126)*

*** *See Banquet, Meeting & Event Sites/Boats section (Pages 127–134)*

**** *See Attractions & Activities section (Pages 49–84)*

***** *See Accommodations section (Pages 29–36)*

HELPFUL HINTS

- **Begin looking for your banquet or meeting site immediately:** As soon as the event date is decided upon, the first decision that needs to be made is where the event or meeting will be held. Some hotels and facilities will book one to three years in advance, depending on the time of year and size of the event. It is not uncommon for a large convention to be booked five years in advance.
- **Visit the location:** When you narrow down the options of sites available, it is always a good idea to look at the room in person before you reserve it or send the deposit. The look and setup of the room or location will make a difference for the type of event. Also, the room setup will determine the room layout, which is essential to the rest of the planning.
- **Visit your site with vendors:** A site inspection of the facility is important. You might also consider bringing your vendors. These visits can answer questions for caterers, decorators and musicians about parking and unloading, lighting, electrical requirements and permitted work areas.
- **Most common room layouts:**
  - Banquet Seating
  - Classroom Style
  - Conference Style
  - Hollow Square
  - Theatre Style
  - U-Shape
- **Be honest about your budget:** Do not be afraid to tell the facility coordinator or event planner what your budget is. This important information can be used as a guideline that can save time and effort on everyone's part. Make sure to work as a team with your facility staff because they will be the ones that will help create a successful event for you. They can also offer time and budget-saving ideas based on their experience.
- **Deposits are important:** Remember that when you reserve a facility, a deposit is usually required to confirm the date. Do not count on a verbal commitment, everything needs to be confirmed in writing. Facility staff can frequently change, so verbal commitments may be forgotten.
- **Find out what equipment is available at the facility:** (AV, staging, tables and chairs). Find out what you can get at no charge, as well as the quality and quantity of the various equipment. If you are planning to use the equipment, make sure it is reserved in writing. The day of the event, thoroughly check the equipment to make sure it is in working order.
- **In-house audio visual departments:** Many hotels have their own in-house audio visual department. Ask if AV equipment is included in your room charge, then be sure to check out the quality and age of the equipment. If the facility has in-house specialists, they usually know the rooms well enough to help determine the most effective room set-up and equipment requirements.

In most cases, facilities only provide a podium and microphone, so you will need to rent additional equipment from a qualified audio visual rental company. Remember: poor quality audio visual equipment can ruin a meeting.

1007 First Avenue at Madison
Seattle, Washington 98104
Main phone (206) 624-4844

Contact: Elizabeth Bernstein (206) 340-6710
Please call for an appointment
E-mail: private.dining@alexishotel.com
Web site: www.alexishotel.com

Capacity: 10–120 guests
Price range: $30–$60 per person
Catering: innovative cuisine provided by the Painted Table Restaurant, featuring award winning catering menus
Types of events: corporate dinners and lunches, conferences, and special events

Availability and terms

Our private dining facilities are available for any of your special event needs.

Description of services and facility

ADA: yes, enter through First Avenue entrance
Parking: limited valet parking available
Banquet services

- **Seating:** tables and padded chairs provided
- **Servers:** high ratio of server/guest included with the catering
- **Bar facilities:** full service bar available for a $50 fee; we provide the bartender; a labor charge will be applied for a no-host bar
- **Linens and napkins:** cloth tablecloths and napkins are provided
- **China and glassware:** Homer Laughlin china; Cardinal glassware
- **Decorations:** please inquire about decor packages
- **Cleanup:** provided by hotel's staff

Meeting and event services

- **Audio visual and equipment:** full audio/visual productions are available through the catering department

Special services

Complement your event with a stay in one of our 109 guest rooms and suites, some featuring wood-burning fireplaces, Jacuzzi bathtubs and antique furniture.

AN EVENING OF ELEGANCE

The Alexis Hotel and Painted Table Restaurant offer intimate and elegant private dining rooms for any event or occasion. The Gallery, named for its seasonal art exhibits, features a wood-burning fireplace to ward off the winter's chill and French doors that open to spring breezes. The newly remodeled Parlor and Drawing Rooms are warm and rich with high ceilings and artful chandeliers. These two rooms adjoin to accommodate larger groups and feature a classic foyer for greeting guests.

ALJOYA

CONFERENCE CENTER at LAURELHURST

3920 N.E. 41st Street • Seattle, Washington 98105-5428
Sales Manager: Eva Bledsoe (206) 268-7000; Fax (206) 268-7001
Mon–Fri 8am–5pm • E-mail: info@aljoya.com • ***Web site: www.aljoya.com***

Capacity: 4,000+ sq. ft. of function space; 8 dedicated meeting rooms for 5–100; 30 guest rooms
Price range: rates vary with number of guests and service requested
Catering: full-service, in-house catering provided
Types of events: retreats, seminars, strategic planning sessions, and other organizational events

Availability and terms

For large groups or overnight accomodations, reserve dates one to six months in advance. However, we can usually accommodate smaller events within 24 to 48 hours' notice.

Description of services and facility

ADA: accessibility limited in some areas
Parking: ample free parking available in areas reserved for conference guests
Banquet services
- **Seating:** quality conference furnishings provided
- **Servers:** professional service staff included
- **Bar facilities:** full-service licensed bar with staff may be arranged
- **Linens, china and glassware:** provided
- **Cleanup:** please remove anything you wish to keep; we'll handle the rest
- **Decorations:** please inquire for setup time, staff support, and approval

Meeting and event services
- **Audio visual and equipment:** in-house equipment and technical staff provided

Special services

Our 30 guestrooms accommodate up to 40 individual guests. Many of the guestrooms include adjoining suites with decks and fireplaces for evening gatherings.

MINUTES FROM THE CITY, MILES FROM DISTRACTION

Aljoya Conference Center of Seattle sits on eighteen wooded acres in Laurelhurst area of Seattle, near the University of Washington campus. Just ten minutes from downtown Seattle, the Conference Center provides meeting space for up to 100 attendees in eight meeting rooms encompassing approximately 4,000 sq. ft. of space. Support facilities include 30 guestrooms, an executive dining room with full catering services, reception area and lobby, and free outdoor parking on the grounds.

In this tranquil setting, meeting, lodging and dining rooms are arranged around landscaped lawns, courtyards, walking paths, and a wildlife pond. Aljoya provides dedicated meeting facilities designed specifically for small to medium sized retreats, seminars, and strategic planning sessions.

American Kitchen

Peace Arch State Park

Washington State Parks Unique Heritage Facilities

(360) 332-8221

Web site: www.parks.wa.gov *[Click on Rental Places, then on Heritage Places]*

Capacity: 100 inside, 400 inside and outside combined
Price range: $2.52 per person per day; $50 damage deposit; please inquire about rates
Catering: client arranges own catering
Types of events: reunions, ethnic celebrations, company picnics, weddings, and receptions

Availability and terms

Reservations may be made beginning the second Monday in January for dates in that calendar year. The full fee plus a $50 damage deposit is required two weeks prior to the event. Cancellations made within two weeks of the event result in forfeiture of the damage deposit.

Description of services and facility

ADA: accessible to people in wheelchairs
Parking: ample parking nearby
Banquet services

- **Seating:** chairs for 100 indoors, with eight rectangular and eight round tables. Outdoor seating is 20 picnic tables
- **Servers and bar facilities:** caterer or client provides
- **Linens, china and serviceware:** caterer or client provides
- **Decorations:** please call to learn about possibilities and restrictions
- **Cleanup:** client is responsible for cleanup

Special services

The American Kitchen is heated and has a kitchen with a triple sink, a refrigerator, and a stove. The carpeted dining or meeting area has a fireplace (guests should take along their own firewood). A large picnic area just outside the building has 20 picnic tables and a stage with electricity.

WITH A VIEW OF THE PEACE ARCH

Vast lawns, gardens, and the magnificent Peace Arch on the Canada-United States border set the tone for any event planned at the American Kitchen. The building has all the practical amenities, and the graceful grounds that surround the facility have a grove of giant oak trees and 20,000 flowers, including hundreds of rhododendrons and azaleas throughout the park. Views include Point Roberts, Vancouver Island, and the San Juans, and there are spectacular sunsets over Semiahmoo Bay.

The Bay Pavilion

1301 Alaskan Way • Seattle, Washington 98101
(206) 623-8600 ask for Lance Fushikoshi
or Michelle Blanchard
Office Hours: Mon–Fri 8:30am–5pm by apointment only

Capacity: **Bay Pavilion Room:** up to 250 sit-down, 350 reception style; **Michelangelo's II:** up to 150 sit-down, 250 receptions style (bi-level room with deck); **Carousel Court:** 250 reception style; **Food Court:** 50–400 if combined with Carousel Court; **Whole Pier:** 1,500 reception style; **Outside at back of the pier:** 400 sit-down or 800 reception style

Price range: room charges included in catering cost; $1,200 room rental charge January through October, $2,500 November through December

Catering: full-service in-house catering provided by Bay Catering

Types of events: formal dinners to informal buffets; cocktail, retirement, or award parties, auctions, meetings, seminars, dances, and other social or business events

Availability and terms

Make reservations up to one year in advance, especially for the busy summer and holiday months. A $750 non refundable deposit is required with balance due in full prior to the event.

Description of services and facility

ADA: Carousel Court fully accessible; please inquire about other areas

Parking: adjacent lots and metered parking; metered parking is free after 6pm or on Sundays; valet or reserved parking available by prior arrangement

Banquet services

- **Seating:** all tables and chairs included in cost when using Bay Catering
- **Servers:** professional service staff dressed in black and whites with logo aprons (unless other theme attire requested) included in catering cost
- **Bar facilities:** host or no-host; please inquire about details
- **Linens, china, and serviceware:** provided with catering
- **Decorations:** we're very flexible, but please inquire; we can arrange for any rental needs
- **Cleanup:** provided with catering

Meeting and event services

- **Audio visual and equipment:** please inquire, we can arrange for any rental needs

Special services

Use Bay Catering as your caterer, and enjoy complimentary rides on our Historic Carousel!

COMPLETE WATERFRONT EXPERIENCE

Overlooking Elliot Bay, the Olympic Mountains, and Waterfront Park, The Bay Pavilion will enchant your guests with a complete waterfront experience. Enjoy the warmth of our rustic Bay Pavilion Room, or let our majestic carousel set the tone for an event to remember. When using Bay Catering we are always flexible and offer a variety of options.

See page 340 under Caterers/Food & Beverage Services.

13737-202nd Avenue N.E.
Woodinville, Washington 98072
Contact: Catering Department
(425) 883-4770
Office Hours: Mon–Fri 9am–5pm;
Saturday tours by appointment

Capacity: accommodates groups up to 400

Price range: varies according to menu selection; no room rental charge with minimum food and beverage purchase; membership is not required; catering social membership available; full cost membership not required to host an event

Catering: full-service in-house catering; customized menus

Types of events: ideal for tournaments, business events, banquets, meetings, reunions, retreats, and receptions

Availability and terms

All our banquet rooms feature panoramic views of the ninth green and reflecting lakes with illuminated fountains. The Lakeside room and adjoining terrace with canopy are ideal for summer months and can accommodate up to 400 guests. Reservations may be made up to one year in advance. We are happy to accommodate shorter notice, depending on space availability. A deposit is required to reserve your date.

Description of services and facility

ADA: wheelchair access available to all rooms

Parking: we offer ample complimentary parking

Banquet services

- **Seating:** tables and chairs provided for up to 400 people
- **Servers:** service staff included in catering cost; 20% gratuity added to final bill
- **Bar facilities:** full-service bar; compliance with all local and state liquor laws
- **Dance floor:** 30'x12' parquet dance floor; electrical outlets available
- **Linens:** linen tablecloths and napkins provided; upgrade selections available
- **China and glassware:** fine china and glassware provided
- **Cleanup:** provided by Bear Creek staff

Meeting and event services

- **Audio visual:** microphone, sound system, overhead projector, TV and VCR; additional equipment arranged upon request

EXCEPTIONAL CUISINE AND IMPECCABLE SERVICE IN A LUSH, TRANQUIL SETTING

Bear Creek Country Club was designed as a world-class facility with a golf course to rank among the region's most challenging, and a club house offering the finest in amenities, food, and recreation. Bear Creek Country Club is located just 3.5 miles north of Redmond, just minutes from Bellevue, and only 25 minutes from downtown Seattle.

See page 483 under Golf Courses.

BELL HARBOR

INTERNATIONAL

CONFERENCE CENTER

Pier 66, 2211 Alaskan Way • Seattle, Washington 98121-1604
Sales Department (206) 441-6666; Fax (206) 441-6665
Sales Dept.: Mon–Fri 8am–5pm • Event Hours: 7 days a week; 24 hour meeting room use
E-mail: info@bellharbor.org • ***Web site: www.bellharbor.org***

Capacity: 57,322 sq. ft. **Conference Center**; 16,450 sq. ft. **International Promenade**; 9,960 sq. ft. **Harbor Dining Room**; 300-seat **Bay Auditorium**; four main conference rooms with breathtaking waterfront views, six break-out rooms, and private dining room; Bell Harbor can accommodate up to 2,000 guests for receptions; Bell Street Pier rooftop plaza is available for outdoor events in the summer for up to 400 guests

Price range: Bell Harbor operates using a conference meeting package; please call for rates; banquets and receptions at Bell Harbor require a $2,500–$15,000 minimum food purchase; room fee based on food and beverage purchases

Catering: in-house, full service, executive chef on-site

Types of events: conferences, day meetings, trade shows, banquets, and receptions

Availability and terms

A 10% deposit is required to contract for space. Damage deposit may be required. Open 365 days a year.

Description of services and facility

ADA: fully accessible

Parking: covered parking available; accessed by pedestrian skybridge.

Banquet services

- **Seating:** tables and chairs provided for up to 300 in the Harbor Dining Room; 600 in the International Promenade; outdoor areas may require table and chair rental
- **Bar facilities:** Bell Harbor provides liquor, liquor liability, bar facilities and bartenders
- **Dance floor:** available in amenity package, which includes dance floor, stage, votive candles and decorative mirrors
- **Linens, napkins, china, and glassware:** provided by Bell Harbor
- **Decorations:** decorations are acceptable but must be approved by Bell Harbor staff
- **Cleanup:** provided at no extra charge

Meeting and event services

- **Audio visual:** state-of-the-art audio visual systems with built-in rear projection screens, video teleconferencing, simultaneous interpretation equipment, ISDN lines, data ports and rear projection systems
- **Equipment:** podiums, lavaliere microphones, flip chart included in conference package
- **Lodging:** assistance with guest rooms and transportation is available

11200 S.E. 6th Street • Bellevue, Washington 98004
Contact: Catering Dept. (425) 688-3382; Fax (425) 646-0184
Business Hours: 8am–5pm or by appointment
Web site: www.Bellevueclub.com

Capacity: Olympic Ballroom: 3,400 sq. ft., accommodates 250; **Suite A:** 1,744 sq. ft., 120; **Suites B & C:** 1,714 sq. ft., 60 each; **Enatai:** 392 sq. ft., 30; **Medina & Meydenbauer:** 237 sq. ft., 15; **Plaza Boardroom:** 484 sq. ft., 14

Price range: varies according to menu selection

Catering: full service in-house catering

Types of events: Bellevue Club is ideal for meetings, seminars, receptions, banquets, buffets, hors d'oeuvres, sit-down dinners, and other corporate or social events

Availability and terms

Events are scheduled up to one year in advance with a deposit; guest rooms available in blocks up to 35.

Description of services and facility

ADA: fully accessible and meets all current codes

Parking: valet and complimentary parking available

Banquet services

- **Seating:** tables and chairs provided
- **Servers:** professional staff to meet your needs
- **Bar facilities:** full service bar available
- **Dance floor:** available upon request
- **Decorations:** please inquire
- **Cleanup:** full cleanup provided by Bellevue Club

Meeting and event services

- **Audio visual and equipment:** available upon request

Special services

The Bellevue Club Hotel offers 67 award winning guest rooms. A truly four-Star, four-Diamond hotel, Bellevue Club was named the "1998 Hotel of the Year" by Small Luxury Hotels of the World. Bellevue Club Hotel is also ranked #2 in "Best in City" in Seattle, and #2 in Pacific Northwest by the 2002 Zagat Survey of Top U.S. Hotels.

IMPECCABLE SERVICE, DISTINCTIVE PRESTIGE

Special events at the Bellevue Club are remembered for their intimate scale, impeccable service, and the sheer beauty of the decor. Celebrated throughout the region, our newly refreshed banquet and meeting facilities make an ideal setting for your special event. The Olympic Ballroom is the perfect venue for gala events up to 250 and is easily divided into smaller spaces. Our experienced catering and banquet staff is fully prepared to meet and exceed your expectations.

200 University Street • Seattle, WA 98101
Troy Skubitz, Events Services Manager
(206) 215-4804; Fax (206) 215-4801
E-mail: Troy.Skubitz@benaroyahall.org
Web site: www.benaroyahall.org

Photo by Lara Swimmer

Capacity: we can accommodate small- and large-scale events; auditorium seating for up to 2,500; for meetings and receptions, from 120 to 500 seated, 225 to 1,100 standing
Price range: rates vary based on space; non-profit organizations qualify for a reduced rate
Catering: Schwartz Brothers Entertainment Services is the exclusive caterer of Benaroya Hall and has a kitchen on-site
Types of events: annual meetings, corporate presentations, holiday parties, auctions, fashion shows, wedding receptions, social events, soloist recitals, music concerts and lectures

Availability and terms

At this time, we are able to reserve dates through August 2003. A $500 deposit is required to hold a date, with the facility use fee due one month prior to the event. The remaining balance of costs is due one business day before the event.

Description of services and facility

ADA: Benaroya Hall is barrier free and meets or exceeds all criteria established by the ADA
Parking: available in the Benaroya Hall Garage and pre-paid parking vouchers may be arranged; in addition, several parking garages surround Benaroya Hall

Banquet services
- **Seating:** chairs and tables for up to 350 guests provided at no charge
- **Servers:** provided by Schwartz Brothers Entertainment Services
- **Bar facilities:** full-service bar and staff provided by Schwartz Brothers Entertainment Services with hosted or no-host options; sorry, no outside beverages allowed
- **Dance floor:** space available for optional rented dance floor
- **Linens and napkins:** ivory square linens and napkins provided at no charge; specialty linens may be arranged for a fee
- **China and glassware:** service for up to 400 available at no extra charge
- **Decorations:** free-standing decorations are allowed
- **Cleanup:** please remove anything you bring in; we will handle the rest

Meeting and event services
- **Audio and visual equipment:** lecterns, easels, wired microphones, wireless microphones, lavaliere, sound system, overhead projector, motorized projection screens, infrared sound system, and risers

Special services

Security, engineering and janitorial support are always on-site and available. Our marquee is available to advertise your event free of charge.

WORLD-CLASS

Built to astound with its architectural beauty, acoustical brilliance, and sophisticated décor, Benaroya Hall has all the necessary elements to impress your guests. Located in the heart of downtown Seattle, Benaroya Hall features 2,500- and 540-seat auditoriums, as well as an elegant lobby and other public spaces offering a panoramic view.

11211 Main Street
Bellevue, Washington 98004
(425) 455-5240 or (800) 421-8193
Fax (425) 455-0654
E-mail: kathysullivan@qwest.net
Web site: www.bestwestern.com/bellevueinnbellevuewa

BELLEVUE INN

Capacity: from 5 to 450 people
Price range: $225–$5,500 reflects range of food and beverage minimum for a variety of rooms
Catering: in-house catering, professional and friendly banquet staff
Types of events: from weddings, corporate meetings, seminars, tradeshows to large conventions

Availability and terms

Cancellations made within 7 days of the event incur full cost of event; 8–35 days prior to the event, full room rental charges apply; 36–60 days prior to the event, half the room rental charges apply.

Description of services and facility

ADA: compliant with ADA standards
Parking: up to 375 complimentary spaces 18'x20'
Banquet services
- **Seating:** 450 theater-style maximum seating; 5' tables, 8' tables, or 72" rounds
- **Servers:** full service provided by caterer
- **Bar facilities:** provided by caterer
- **Dance floor:** solid oak parquet dance floor
- **Linens and napkins:** hotel provides linens in multiple shades and colors
- **China and glassware:** hotel provides
- **Decorations:** please inquire, some restrictions apply
- **Cleanup:** provided by catering staff

Meeting and event services
- **Audio visual and equipment:** in-house audiovisual services available

Special services

DSL high speed Internet access in large ballrooms and break out rooms. Easy access for load-in and deliveries.

A MEETING PLANNER'S DREAM COME TRUE

Best Western Bellevue Inn is an ideal location for a great meeting or event. Our friendly and professional staff will give you excellent customer service to make your event run smoothly. Enjoy our 4,750 sq. ft. ballroom for your meeting with twelve-foot windows large enough to brighten any occasion.

2300 Market Street • Mount Vernon, Washington 98273
(360) 428-5678 or (800) 662-6886
Fax (360) 428-1844
E-mail: kati@cottontree.net
Web site: www.cottontree.net

Capacity: can accommodate 10 to 300 guests
Price range: $5.95 to $29.95 per person
Catering: full-service in-house catering
Types of events: corporate events, special events, retreats and conventions

Availability and terms

24 hour minimum for booking event. Cancellation notice fourteen days prior. Deposit with credit card or check due 30 days after signing contract.

Description of services and facility

ADA: fully accessible
Parking: complimentary up to 400 cars
Banquet services
- **Seating:** table and chairs provided
- **Servers:** staff included in costs
- **Bar facilities:** full service bar
- **Linens, china, and glassware:** provided by Cottontree
- **Decorations:** please inquire
- **Cleanup:** provided by staff

Meeting and event services
- **Audio visual and equipment:** please inquire for more details

IN THE HEART OF SKAGIT VALLEY

Best Western Cotton Tree Inn & Convention Center provides a full service hotel and convention center in the heart of Skagit Valley. Our service and quality are second to none. Marketplace Café & Bistro serving excellent food and drinks seven days a week with Room Service.

Leavenworth's Only
Full Service Hotel

505 Highway 2
Leavenworth, WA 98826
Reservations (800) 558-2438
Seattle (888) 353-0595
On-site (509) 548-7000
E-mail: info@icicleinn.com
Web site: www.icicleinn.com

Best Western

Icicle Inn

A Leavenworth Resort

Capacity: over 4,500 square feet of conference space in six rooms, three with mountain and pool views seating up to 250 guests, an executive boardroom, a sloped projection theater, and an outdoor barbeque lawn with mountain views

Price range: group rates depend on season and begin at $79 during the winter and include a complimentary European breakfast buffet

Catering: full catering service offered in-house

Types of events: conferences, meetings, retreats, board meetings, team building, reunions, incentive trips, adventure and activity retreats, and spousal programs

Availability and terms

Leavenworth is approximately 2.5 hours from Seattle along scenic mountain drives. We encourage early reservations; last-minute planning is based on availability.

Description of services and facility

ADA: fully accessible

Parking: ample and complimentary at the Inn; free scheduled shuttle service to downtown

Banquet services

- **Seating:** tables and chairs provided and set up to your specifications
- **Servers:** courteous and professional catering staff
- **Bar facilities:** full service bar located in restaurant, host/no-host bars for events
- **Dance floor:** available
- **Linens, napkins, china and glassware:** included in menu and conference fees
- **Decorations and cleanup:** included in menu and conference fees; special needs (rentals, extra labor) accommodated in advance for a small handling fee

Meeting and event services

- **Audio visual and equipment:** upon availability complimentary overhead and screen, TV and VCR, slide projector, flip chart easel, podum and mike

Special services

Five-acre Entertainment Park with bumper boats, miniature golf, historical train tour, remote control boats, video arcade, movie theatre, and more! Golf packaging with Kahler Glen and Desert Canyon, the #1 rated public course in Washington and special rates with Stevens and Mission Ridge ski areas. A complimentary European breakfast is served daily with view of the Cascade Mountains.

WE HAVE MORE SUNSHINE!

Sparkling clear rivers, towering pines, and lush orchards surround the Icicle Inn, providing an exciting adventure for every group. Experience interpretive hiking trails, river floats, rafting, breathtaking golf courses, two mountain Alpine and Nordic sports, miniature golf, bumper boats, replica historical train tour, sleigh rides, snowmobile tours, hayrides, barn dances, and mouth-watering barbecues... an ideal destination in Central Washington.

"Northwest Country" INNS MEMBER

BIG **PICTURE**
boutique meeting & event facility

BIG **PICTURE**

2505 First Avenue • Seattle, Washington 98121
Contact: Mark Stern or Katie Stern (206) 256-0566
E-mail: info@thebigpicture.net
Web site: www.thebigpicture.net

Capacity: **Full Venue**, including all the intriguing nooks and rooms: up to 125 guests; **Digital Theatre:** up to 110; **War Room:** up to 12; **Living Room:** up to 8

Price range: venue rental fees vary based on the time of day and day of week; we offer very flexible catering and bar options with no minimums

Catering: delicious breakfast, lunch and dinner options available

Types of events: spectacular meetings and events; multimedia presentations, seminars, team building and morale events, client entertainment, receptions, private concerts and movie screenings, birthday and anniversary parties, business & social functions

Availability and terms

We recommend reserving space in advance but will go out of our way to accommodate last minute requests. Big Picture is for guests 21 and older.

Description of services and facility

ADA: fully accessible

Parking: valet parking available

Banquet services

- **Seating:** theatre has fixed, stadium style seats; social areas offer casually arranged couches and club chairs
- **Servers:** professional and personable beverage/venue staff; caterer provides food service staff
- **Bar facilities:** full beverage service on-site, special orders accepted; hosted/non-hosted events
- **Dance floor:** our video DJ's will keep you moving
- **Linens and napkins:** provided by caterer
- **China and glassware:** provided by Big Picture
- **Decorations:** we specialize in helping to create themed events
- **Clean up:** all clean up provided by Big Picture

Meeting and event services

- **Audio visual and equipment:** state-of-the-art digital projection system capable of showcasing laptop content (PowerPoint), DVD, VHS, Satellite, Beta SP, Mini DV; jawdropping 12-speaker Dolby 5.1 sound system, DSL lines, whiteboards, flipcharts, markers; any A/V request can be accommodated

BOUTIQUE MEETINGS AND EVENTS

The only boutique meeting and event facility in Seattle, Big Picture was built as an alternative to generic event facilities. Enjoy our sophisticated social areas, plush furnishings, comfortable ambiance and versatile business theatre.We have yet to find another venue in the country that has had the vision to combine technology, business services and a digital theatre in a venue that feels as comfortable as your living room. Whether you are planning a meeting, social function or any event that you wish to make memorable—Big Picture provides an environment that inspires creative thinking, fun and the desire to come back for more.

Your hosts, Mark and Katie Stern.

At Madison Park
Seattle, Washington
Contact: Mike or Virginia Duppenthaler
(206) 328-2442; Fax (206) 328-2863
E-mail: mike@blueribboncooking.com
Web site: www.blueribboncooking.com

Capacity: ideal for groups of 15 to 65
Price range: cost varies per event ($65 to $110 per person)
Catering: in-house hands-on teaching experience
Types of events: corporate promotions, sales meetings, staff appreciation and team building experiences, birthday parties, bridal showers, rehearsal dinners and private parties

Availability and terms

We recommend making reservation 2–3 months in advance, but we are also able to accommodate your reservation as little as one week prior. 50% deposit required to confirm your reservation. Deposit is non-refundable but you may reschedule your event with two-week's notice.

Description of services and facility

ADA: limited access
Parking: on-street parking and private lot available in evening
Banquet services
- **Seating:** revolving cooking stations, tasting room and conversation sitting room
- **Servers:** Blue Ribbon provides
- **Bar facility:** client provides beer and wine with banquet permit; Blue Ribbon provides glassware and bar facilities
- **Linens and napkins:** Blue Ribbon provides
- **China and glassware:** provided by the facility
- **Cleanup:** full cleanup provided by Blue Ribbon

Meeting and event services
- **Audio visual and equipment:** all rental requirements to be arranged by the customer

A CULINARY SCHOOL OF NORTHWEST ENTERTAINING

Blue Ribbon Cooking School is a hands-on cooking experience designed to meet your entertainment needs. It is not a hotel or an institutional environment; instead, Virginia and Mike Duppenthaler welcome you into their beautifully restored 1907 craftsman-style home. The five teaching areas of their home offer opportunities for smaller groups to get together to develop new culinary skills and celebrate the bounty of this region's indigenous ingredients. We can arrange informative wine seminars to complement the foods. Each event can be customized to your specific requirements. We offer nothing for sale, but education, camaraderie and hands-on fun. We arrange one chef instructor for every 10 guests to handle groups effectively.

Visit our web site: *www.blueribboncooking.com*

BLUWATER BISTRO

1001 Fairview Avenue North, #1700
Seattle, Washington 98109
Contact: Elizabeth Williams (206) 447-0769
Private Dining (206) 344-4757
Fax (206) 447-6977
E-mail: elizabeth@bluwaterbistro.com
Web site: www.bluwaterbistro.com

Capacity: accommodates up to 175 guests for a reception, up to 90 for a sit-down dinner
Price range: varies according to menu selection, time of year, and number of guests
Catering: full-service in-house catering
Types of events: wedding receptions, rehearsal dinners, luncheons, brunches, cocktails and hors d'oeuvres, anniversaries, birthdays, meetings, and other special occasions

Availability and terms

We request that you reserve your room 4–6 months prior to the event; however, we can often accommodate shorter notice. A deposit confirms your reservation and is applied to the total cost.

Description of services and facility

ADA: fully accessible
Parking: complimentary valet parking
Banquet services
- **Seating:** provided for up to 90 in private dining room
- **Servers:** included with in-house catering
- **Bar facilities:** full-service; host or no-host available
- **Linens and napkins:** available upon request
- **China and glassware:** provided with catering
- **Decorations:** please inquire about our guidelines
- **Cleanup:** provided by BluWater staff

Meeting and event services
- **Audio visual and equipment:** rental service can be arranged

BEAUTIFUL VIEWS OF LAKE UNION

BluWater Bistro's elegant interior features plush booths, dark wood, and a warm fire. Upstairs, our private dining room offers expansive views of Lake Union, the Space Needle, and downtown Seattle. Furnished with a full bar, the dining room provides an ideal place to host your reception or rehearsal dinner. In the spring and summer months, enjoy an outdoor cabana bar on our lakeside patio. Whether inside or out, you and your guests will appreciate BluWater Bistro's spectacular views and impeccable service.

On the beautiful University of Washington campus
at the corner of N.E. 45th Street and 17th Avenue N.E.

Box 353010 • University of Washington • Seattle, Washington 98195-3010
(206) 221-2853
Call for an appointment or tour the museum daily until 5pm, Thursdays until 8pm.
Web site: www.burkemuseum.org

Capacity: accommodates up to 300 reception style and 130 seated; outdoor settings increase total capacity to 1,000
Price range: $400–$1,500
Catering: choose from our list of preferred caterers
Types of events: receptions, business events, holiday parties, fundraisers and anniversary or retirement parties

Availability and terms

Available evenings only. A 50% deposit is required to reserve your date.

Description of services and facility

ADA: fully accessible
Parking: available next to the museum
Banquet services
- **Seating:** 80 chairs and six 6' rectangular tables available
- **Servers:** provided by caterer
- **Bar facilities:** provided by caterer; banquet permit required
- **Dance floor:** wood floor in Burke Room
- **Linens, china and glassware:** provided by caterer or client
- **Decorations:** please inquire
- **Cleanup:** please remove everything you bring in; caterers and Burke staff will do the rest

Meeting and event services
- **Audio visual equipment:** available at no extra charge

DRAMATIC AND SPACIOUS SETTING

Treat your guests to a special evening in a uniquely Seattle atmosphere. Whether gazing at real dinosaurs or admiring original Northwest Coast Art, your guests will be impressed by the Burke's all-new permanent exhibits. Our expanded lobby features a spectacular 40-foot case of dazzling treasures from sparkling gems to Pacific Rim masks—a perfect backdrop for your special event. Let our staff help you create a truly memorable evening.

Canlis Restaurant

2576 Aurora Avenue North • Seattle, WA 98109
Contact: Private Dining (206) 298-9550
Web site: www.canlis.com

Capacity: Executive Room: 15–30, Penthouse: 35–90, Caché: 2–4
Price range: $55–$75 per person food average before tax and gratuity; beverages and special arrangements not included in price
Catering: full service in-house catering provided
Types of events: board dinners, award dinners, retirement dinners and corporate entertainment

Availability and terms

Private Dining rooms are reserved on a space available basis. We recommend early planning for the popular months and the holiday season. Deposits for both the Executive Room and Penthouse are $500.

Description of services and facility

ADA: fully accessible on the main floor and Executive room; 16 stairs to the Penthouse
Parking: valet parking only
Banquet services

- **Seating:** all furnishings provided by Canlis
- **Servers:** a professional staff included in the costs
- **Bar facilities:** full bar and award winning wine cellar
- **China and glassware:** elegance from Frette Napkins to Corby Hall silver
- **Decorations:** please inquire; nothing that will damage the facility
- **Clean up:** provided by Canlis

Special services

Canlis will gladly take care of any special arrangements your party may require and will coordinate all outside services for you.

ALMOST 50 YEARS OF EXPERIENCE

Canlis Restaurant has been part of, and trusted by the Seattle professional community for nearly 50 years. Known for spectacular views of Lake Union and the Cascade Mountains, outstanding service, and equally impressive food, Canlis is proud to present those strengths into the foundation of our private dining program. The Executive Dining Room, which seats 15–30 guests, is a delightful space with windows facing east and north and also has a fireplace for perfect ambiance. Our larger room called the Penthouse begins seating at 35 guests and has the capacity of up to 90 for a sit-down dinner. The third room is the Caché, seating 2–4 guests for private dinner meetings. Our menus are generous with options and the planning is very simple. Allow us to become part of your company event and in turn, we will help you carry the responsibilities that come with planning a party.

Photography by Christophoto

Featuring ***The Lakeside***
2501 North Northlake Way
Seattle, Washington

Contact: Elisabeth Hebrant or Laura Daley
(206) 632-2200; Fax (206) 545-2137
Business Hours: Mon–Fri 8:30am–5:30pm or by appointment • ***Web site: www.caterarts.com***

Capacity: unique open facility consists of two view levels—**Upper Level:** 1,280 sq. ft., up to 100 seated; **Lower Level:** 1,190 sq. ft., up to 80 seated; 250 for receptions using entire facility; waterfront patio offers an additional 800 sq. ft.

Price range: varies depending on time of day and day of the week

Catering: full-service in-house catering

Types of events: all day business meetings, corporate breakfasts, lunches and dinners, holiday parties, rehearsal dinners, weddings and receptions, bar and bat mitzvahs

Availability and terms

Reservations accepted up to one year in advance; due to high demand, a deposit consisting of full rental fee is required before your date can be confirmed. Please inquire about special corporate rates.

Description of services and facility

ADA: Accessible on lower level

Parking: complimentary lot for up to 30 cars; free street parking is available; valet can be arranged for an additional fee

Banquet services

- **Seating:** tables and chairs provided
- **Service staff:** highly trained and professional service staff
- **Bar facilities:** full-service host or no-host bar service available
- **Dance floor:** hardwood floors on lower level are ideal for dancing
- **Linens and napkins:** ivory linen included; additional colors may be rented
- **China and glassware:** included; additional patterns may be rented
- **Decorations:** please inquire
- **Clean-up:** please remove any items you bring in and leave the rest to us!

Meeting and event services

- **Audio visual:** wireless microphone available with deposit
- **Equipment:** podium included in room rental; all other items rented upon request

SPECTACULAR VIEWS OF THE SEATTLE SKYLINE

The Lakeside re-opened in the summer of 1997 after extensive remodeling. It now offers a warm and contemporary setting in which to enjoy spectacular views of the Seattle skyline. Natural wood finishes complement the subtle palette of colors used throughout the facility. French doors open onto the spacious waterfront patio and private dock. Award-winning Chef/Owner Peter Neal has a talent for creating a masterpiece with each event. In addition to planning your menu, our experienced sales staff will assist with rental items, cakes, floral, decor and entertainment, and will provide you with a detailed cost proposal. **Please see our ad on page 344 under "Caterers."**

"Seductively gorgeous." John Hinterberger, *The Seattle Times*

THE CENTRE AT NORPOINT

4818 Nassau Avenue N.E. • Tacoma, Washington 98422
Contact: Rental Coordinator (253) 591-5504 or (253) 661-3289
Business Hours: Mon–Fri 8am–5pm
Web site: www.tacomaparks.com

Capacity: 250 banquet; 300 reception
Price range: $28 to $129/hour depending on room size; $129 to $1,032 for ten hours
Types of events: reunions, meetings, business banquets, weddings, receptions, anniversaries

Availability and terms

The Centre at Norpoint has four rooms available, accommodating 30 to 300 people. Reservations are accepted up to one year in advance. Full payment is required upon reservation. Cancellation must be received in writing 61 days prior to your event to receive a 50% refund.

Description of services and facility

ADA: fully accessible
Parking: 250 free parking spaces
Banquet services

- **Seating:** 270 chairs, 30 round banquet tables, 10 buffet tables
- **Servers:** caterer to provide
- **Bar facilities:** caterer can provide liquor, bartender, and banquet license to serve liquor
- **Dance floor:** accommodates 150 people; electrical outlets available
- **Linens:** available for rent
- **China and glassware:** available for rent
- **Decorations:** decorating time included in rental fee (freestanding only)
- **Cleanup:** contract with The Centre cleaning staff

Special services

Changing rooms available for rent. Staff person will remain on site during your event. Outdoor wedding accommodations available.

THE CENTRE AT NORPOINT

The Centre at Norpoint has an open-beam structure with beautiful hardwood floors and large outdoor patios. The facility is located in Northeast Tacoma, convenient to nearby Federal Way.

A facility of Metro Parks Tacoma.

Century Ballroom

915 East Pine Street • Seattle Washington 98122
(206) 324-7263
Office Hours: Mon–Fri 11am–6pm
E-mail: centuryb@aol.com
Web site: www.centuryballroom.com

Capacity: 300 reception style includes 50 on balcony; 225 seated dinners
Price range: hourly to $1,500 day rate
Catering: in-house catering available for breakfasts, luncheons, meetings and events for up to 100 people; outside caterers welcome
Types of events: business meetings, seminars, cocktail parties, buffets, luncheons, receptions

Availability and terms

Call for availability.

Description of services and facility

ADA: accessible
Parking: on street, paylot within one block
Banquet services
- **Seating:** 85 banquet chairs and 225 folding chairs available
- **Servers:** bar staff provided by Century; servers provided by off-site caterers
- **Bar facilities:** full bar available; all bar services provided by Century
- **Dance floor:** 2,000 sq. ft.
- **Linens, napkins, china and glassware:** provided by caterer
- **Decorations:** please inquire about our requirements
- **Cleanup:** restore to original condition or hire Century staff to clean

Special services

Staff person is provided for every event. Bands, DJs and A/V equipment can be arranged through Century.

Elegantly restored 1908 ballroom
with balcony, stage and 2,000 sq. ft. dance floor.

2207 N.E. Bel-Red Rd. • Redmond, WA 98052
(425) 455-9999; Fax (425) 646-2722
Business Hours: Mon–Thu 10am–10pm,
Fri–Sat 10am–11pm, Sun 12noon–7pm
E-mail: info@champskarting.com
Web site: www.champskarting.com

Capacity: accommodates up to 250 guests
Price range: varies according to services required; please inquire about our individual and group packages
Catering: Champs offers an in-house gourmet café, as well as partnerships with select caterers
Types of events: ideal for birthdays and holiday parties, teambuilding events, meetings and seminars, bachelor or bachelorette parties, and other special occasions

Availability and terms

Reservations are required. Let us make your event memorable with a package to include kart racing and trophies, or rent the conference room separately. A 50% deposit is required to secure your date. We accept all major credit cards.

Description of services and facility

ADA: fully accessible
Parking: complimentary on-site parking is provided
Banquet services
- **Seating:** Champs features upscale European furniture and finishes; seats up to 200
- **Servers:** provided by Champs and chosen caterer
- **Bar facilities:** Champs is equipped to serve beer and wine
- **Linens and napkins:** furnished by caterer and/or Champs
- **Decorations:** helium balloons are provided; additional decorations are permitted, but please remove everything you bring in
- **Cleanup:** $30–$75 clean up fee for outside catering

Meeting and event services
- **Audio visual and equipment:** Champs is equipped with 12 TV monitors, a big-screen TV, and a complete sound system; additional audio visual equipment is available upon request

Special services

Our staff will gladly assist in the planning of your special event.

REAL RACING, REAL FUN! WASHINGTON STATE'S PREMIER INDOOR ENTERTAINMENT CENTER

Champs Karting is one of fewer than five entertainment centers in the U.S. to feature high-tech electric pro-karts. Our state-of-the-art equipment offers both responsive speed and a smooth, safe ride. Champs' experienced staff will assist you in creating and coordinating the group event that best meets your objectives. Our unique venue and professional expertise ensures that your special event will make a lasting impression on your guests. Whether you want to come race, play pool, test your skills in our Video Arcade, or kick back with a beer and watch the game—Champs is the ideal choice.

The Claremont Hotel

Seattle's favorite classic hotel

2000 Fourth Avenue at Virginia
Seattle, Washington 98121
Contact: Sales Office
(206) 694-7255 or (800) 448-8601
Fax (206) 443-1420
Office Hours: Mon–Fri 9am–5pm
E-mail: sales@claremonthotel.com
Web site: www.claremonthotel.com

Capacity: Ballroom: main floor 1,600 sq. ft., gallery 1,400 sq. ft., accommodates 100 for banquets, (200 with gallery); Virginia Room: 1,350 sq. ft., up to 100 for receptions, 90 classroom style; rooms together 250 reception; Gallery Conference Room for up to 50; Breakout rooms available for 14 to 20 classroom style, 20 to 50 theatre style

Price range: varies according to time and use

Catering: catering services available exclusively through The Claremont Hotel

Types of events: business meetings, seminars, conferences, reunions, holiday parties, anniversaries or gala

Availability and terms

Located in the absolute heart of downtown Seattle, this classic European-style hotel features high ceilings, gracious rooms, with marble, terrazzo, terra cotta, and brass accents. A deposit is required.

Description of services and facility

Parking: adjacent parking lots; event valet parking and 24-hour parking for hotel guests available

Banquet services

- **Seating:** tables and chairs provided
- **Servers:** professional service staff included in catering costs
- **Bar facilities:** complete bar facilities and service available
- **China, linens and napkins:** china and glassware provided
- **Cleanup:** handled by catering staff

Meeting and event services

- **Audio visual:** in-house A/V company can provide for any of your needs
- **Equipment:** podium, overhead projectors, flip charts available
- **Concierge services:** available

Special services

Your guests will enjoy our 120 spacious rooms, most of which are suites. All guest rooms have plush robes, hair dryers, irons and ironing boards and complete Aveda amenities. Enjoy a complimentary morning newspaper. For the business traveler, each room has a desk, dual line telephone with DID (direct inward dial) line, modem hookup and voice mail. Copy services and in-room fax machines upon request.

SEATTLE'S FAVORITE CLASSIC HOTEL

The Claremont Hotel has completed a major renovation making it one of the Northwest's finest venues for receptions and banquets. The centerpiece of the hotel is an intimate and elegant two-story ballroom with mezzanine. Adjacent to the Ballroom is the Virginia Room, a gracious setting with abundant natural light and a long cherry-wood bar. Used separately or together, these two rooms are ideal for all kinds of events.

For more information about our guest accommodations, see page 32.

COLUMBIA TOWER CLUB

701 Fifth Avenue, 75th & 76th Floors • Seattle, Washington 98104
Contact: Private Event Department (206) 622-2010

Capacity: seated events for 2 to 250; standing receptions to 500 maximum
Price range: breakfast $12–$15, lunch $25–$35, dinners $50, and receptions $35–$55 per person; full beverage service additional
Catering: full-service in-house catering provided
Types of events: ideal for business or social receptions, sit-down breakfasts, luncheons or dinners, all-day meetings, presentations, product launches

Availability and terms

The Columbia Tower Club offers twelve private rooms to meet your entertaining and business needs. A deposit is required to reserve your date with the estimated balance due prior to the event. The Club is available to members and their sponsored guests.

Description of services and facility

ADA: fully accessible
Parking: on-premise parking garage available; rates upon request
Banquet services
- **Seating:** tables and chairs for up to 200; additional charges may appy for larger groups
- **Servers:** fully trained professional staff to meet your needs
- **Bar facilities:** full-service bar and staff; host or no-host events
- **Dance floor:** available at no additional charge
- **Linens and napkins:** linen floor-length tablecloths and napkins provided
- **China and glassware:** fine bone china with gold and black accents, sterling silver flatware and Riedel stemware provided
- **Decorations:** please inquire; bud vases with fresh flowers, votive candles and custom table runners provided at no additional charge
- **Cleanup:** included at no charge

Meeting and event services
- **Audio visual and equipment:** video conferencing, T1 lines, LCD projectors, phone conferencing, automatic drop screens; arrangements can be made to meet all of your high-tech needs

Special services

Featuring superb Northwest Cuisine and an award winning wine list, the Columbia Tower Club offers flawless service and many thoughtful amenities for groups of 2–500.

THE CLUB WITH A VIEW ALL ITS OWN

Welcome to the Northwest's Premier Private Club with panoramic views of the Olympic and Cascade Mountains, Puget Sound, Lake Washington, Downtown Seattle, Downtown Bellevue, Mercer Island and Mt. Rainier. Offering three spacious and beautifully appointed dining rooms, a library and seven elegant private dining rooms, the Columbia Tower Club can accommodate your every entertaining and business need.

14030-145th Street
Woodinville, Washington 98072
(425) 488-2776, (800) 488-2347
Fax (425) 488-3460
Office Hours: Mon–Fri 8am–5pm
Web site: www.columbiawinery.com

Capacity: Woodburne Room: seats 24 theatre-style and 24 banquet style; **Milestone Room or Cellarmaster Room:** each seats 120 guests theatre-style and 80 guests at round tables; combined, they become the **Columbia Room** which seats 250 theatre-style and up to 200 at round tables

Price range: varies according to the particular room, day, and time

Catering: exclusive caterer is Schwartz Brothers Catering

Types of events: formal or informal sit-down dinners, buffets, cocktails and hors d'oeuvres; banquets and receptions, reunions, anniversaries, or any other special event

Availability and terms

With three distinctively different rooms, it is best to call for information on availability. Advance bookings may be necessary depending on the time of year.

Description of services and facility

ADA: complies with all ADA requirements

Parking: complimentary parking is provided for up to 140 vehicles

Banquet services

- **Seating:** all tables and chairs are provided to meet your event needs
- **Servers:** our professional and friendly serving staff is provided by Schwartz Brothers Catering
- **Bar facilities:** supplied through Schwartz Brothers Catering
- **Dance floor:** available on request
- **Linens and napkins:** available through Columbia Winery and Schwartz Brothers Catering
- **China and glassware:** fine china and glassware provided through Schwartz Brothers Catering
- **Decorations:** please inquire
- **Cleanup:** provided courtesy of Columbia Winery and Schwartz Brothers Catering

Meeting and event services

- **Audio visual and equipment:** podiums, flip charts, microphones, and more; we are happy to coordinate all your A/V needs

Special services

The professional staff of Columbia Winery and Schwartz Brothers Catering can assist you with all your planning needs. From arrangements for music and entertainment to flowers or audio visual equipment, we'll handle as many of the details as needed.

NESTLED IN THE BEAUTIFUL SAMMAMISH VALLEY

Located in a landmark Woodinville Victorian mansion, Columbia Winery is only 30 minutes from Seattle and 15 minutes from Bellevue. As Washington's first premium winery, Columbia Winery offers the Northwest's most unique event venue. Please call for more information and to set an appointment to tour our facilities.

AMPHITRYON, INC.

Court In The Square

401 Second Avenue South, #100
Seattle, Washington 98104
Contact: Robert Payne
(206) 467-5533
Office Hours: Mon–Fri 9am–5pm

Capacity: Atrium: 300 people; private meeting rooms are also available
Price range: prices will vary, all services are customized to your needs
Catering: full-service in-house provided by Amphitryon Specialty Catering
Types of events: hors d'oeuvre receptions to full-service dinners, business meetings, conferences, presentations, and special events; we'll develop and tailor our space and services to meet the needs of our clients

Availability and terms

Atrium reservations should be made from six months to one year in advance. We are happy to accommodate shorter notice if space is available. Meeting rooms usually require one week's notice.

Description of services and facility

ADA: completely accessible
Parking: parking adjacent to facility, validation and valet service available
Banquet services
- **Seating:** tables and chairs are provided to meet your specific needs
- **Servers:** service staff is included in the catering costs
- **Bar facilities:** full bar service and bartenders provided as needed; host or no-host functions; all alcoholic beverages provided by Amphitryon Specialty Catering
- **Linens and napkins:** linen tablecloths and napkins in assorted colors
- **China and glassware:** all china, glassware, and utensils are provided
- **Decorations:** inform us of your plans; no damage to the facility
- **Cleanup:** included in catering costs

Meeting and event services
- **Audio visual and equipment:** arrangements for any of your needs

Special services

We're happy to assist you with coordinating all your event planning needs. We are able to provide you with a wide range of specialty services, or we will be happy to refer you to additional businesses and services. We'll handle as little or as much as you specify! Menu selection is flexible, and we pride ourselves on custom food preparation.

COURT IN THE SQUARE GIVES YOU A LOCATION AS UNIQUE AS YOUR CELEBRATION

At Court In The Square, each event is considered individually. This way our staff can develop and provide personal touches especially for your event. The courtyard's elegant old world atmosphere allows for anything from a casual garden style to formal elegance.

1113-6th Avenue • Seattle, Washington 98101-3048
Catering Office (206) 464-1980, (800) 521-2762
Mon–Fri 7am–6pm; Sat by appointment
E-mail: Crowneplaza@crowneplazaseattle.com
Web site: www.crowneplaza.com

Capacity: Evergreen Ballroom: 4,200 sq. ft.; up to 350, **Tented Outdoor Pavilion:** up to 120, third-floor **Yosemite/McKinley/Crater Lake:** rooms with city skyline view, up to 120
Price range: prices are affordable; vary according to menu selections
Catering: full-service, in-house catering provided
Types of events: sit-down functions; buffets, cocktails and hors d'oeuvres, barbeques; meetings, seminars, conferences, conventions, special events

Availability and terms

Groups from 10 to 400 can gather comfortably in space that fits the function and the mood. Reservations up to one year in advance. Deposit required; varies depending on size of function.

Description of services and facility

ADA: Crowne Plaza Seattle meets standards for ADA accessibility
Parking: valet parking; limited availability; self-parking nearby
Banquet services
- **Seating:** tables and chairs for up to 350 provided
- **Servers:** professional service staff included in catering costs
- **Bar facilities:** full-service bar, bartender, and beverages provided; host/no-host
- **Dance floor:** portable dance floors available to meet your needs
- **Linens, china and glassware:** linens, fine china, and glassware provided
- **Decorations:** nothing that will damage the facility; please inquire
- **Cleanup:** please remove anything you bring in; we'll handle the rest

Meeting and event services
- **Complete satellite teleconferencing**
- **High speed internet access** available in all guest and meeting rooms
- **Audio visual:** our in-house A/V company can accommodate all your needs
- **Equipment:** podium, risers, easels and flipcharts provided

Special services

415 guest rooms, 28 executive suites, and 3 large suites. Newly renovated Club floors offer dual phone lines, concierge lounge, complimentary continental breakfast, hors d'oeuvres and more. On-site Health Club with sauna, whirlpool, and exercise room. Photocopies, FAX, teleconferencing, dry cleaning; foreign currency accepted.

SAMPLE SEATTLE AT ITS FINEST

Breathtaking mountains, spectacular water and cityscapes, located in the heart of downtown Seattle. You'll enjoy it all at the Crowne Plaza—a place with a meeting culture all its own.

CUTTERS

BAYHOUSE

2001 Western Ave. • Seattle, WA 98121
Contact: John O'Brien
(206) 448-4884; Fax (206) 727-2194
Hours: 11am–11pm, seven days a week
Web site: www.cuttersbayhouse.com

Capacity: the Bayroom accommodates 80 sit-down, 100 reception
Price range: varies seasonally; miminum food and beverage requirements
Catering: in-house catering
Types of events: ideal setting for business meetings, anniversaries, birthday parties, rehearsal dinners

Availability and terms

Cutters requests a minimum of two weeks' notice, with entree counts required 36 hours prior to your event. A $150 room charge applies to evening events, $75 for luncheons. Cancellation requires 48 hours' notice.

Description of services and facility

ADA: fully accessible
Parking: underground parking validated for discount
Banquet services

- **Seating:** tables and chairs provided to capacity
- **Servers:** professional service staff provided
- **Bar facilities:** no bar fees for hosted bar; $75 no-host charge
- **Dance floor:** none provided
- **Linens and napkins:** included in the rental cost
- **China and glassware:** provided
- **Cleanup:** Cutters cleans up at no addtional charge
- **Decorations:** nothing that will cause damage; requires Cutters' approval

Meeting and event services

- **Audio visual and equipment:** in-house company available

Special services

Cutters is committed to offering guests the freshest seasonal food available, as well as outstanding service. Whether you're hosting a holiday party or a business lunch, let us take care of everything so you can relax and enjoy all that Cutters has to offer. From selecting menus and wine to choosing a florist, we're here to take care of all your needs.

THE BEAUTY OF SEATTLE SURROUNDS YOU

Located next to Historic Pike Place Market, Cutters offers a truly unique view of the Northwest. Guests enjoy panoramic views of the Olympic Mountains, Elliott Bay and the Port of Seattle. For over fifteen years, we have been known for our hospitality, engaging service and exceptional food.

2001-4th Avenue • Seattle, Washington 98121
(206) 682-4142; Fax (206) 467-0568
E-mail: privatedining@tomdouglas.com
Web site: www.tomdouglas.com

Capacity: can accommodate up to 50 guests
Price range: varies according to selection; please inquire
Catering: full-service in-house catering
Types of events: corporate meetings, rehearsal dinners, weddings, private parties

Availability and terms

Reservations are available year-round and should be made as early as possible.

Description of services and facility

ADA: fully accessible
Parking: valet parking available
Banquet services
- **Seating:** table and chairs provided
- **Servers:** staff included in costs
- **Bar facilities:** full service bar
- **Linens, china, and glassware:** provided by Dahlia Lounge
- **Cleanup:** provided by staff
- **Decorations:** client may provide; or we can coordinate

Meeting and event services
- **Audio visual and equipment:** client provides, or we can coordinate rentals

Special services

We are happy to assist you with all your event planning needs; menu planning, special wine dinners, and seasonal menus.

SPECTACULAR PRIVATE DINING IN THE HEART OF THE CITY

The Dahlia Lounge offers the best in Northwest regional cuisine in a warm and comfortable private dining room. Award winning chef and owner Tom Douglas and his talented crew offer seasonal and creative menus for your private party needs. An extensive wine list, special menu planning and outstanding service are the hallmarks of this fine dinning restaurant in the heart of Seattle.

Bellevue Place • Leschi Marina • South Lake Union

Contact: Manager of Private Dining
(425) 462-4662
E-mail: danielsbellevue@schwartzbros.com

Capacity: **Bellevue Place:** groups up to 100; **Leschi Marina:** groups from 10 to 18; **South Lake Union:** groups up to 36 or daytime events up to 200
Price range: prices vary based on menu and services requested
Catering: complete in-house, award-winning services from Daniel's Broiler
Types of events: ideal for board dinners, executive meetings, intimate dinners, banquets, cocktail parties, receptions holiday parties and any other social or business occasions

Availability and terms

Private Dining Rooms are reserved on a space available basis. We recommend early planning for the holiday season.

Description of services and facility

ADA: completely accessible
Parking: valet parking and validated parking
Banquet services
- **Servers:** professional, attentive staff to meet your every need
- **Dance floor:** gladly provided
- **Linens, napkins, china and glassware:** all provided at no charge
- **Decorations:** Daniel's elegance and breathtaking views

Special services

Daniel's will gladly accommodate any special arrangements.

DANIEL'S AT YOUR SERVICE

A unique point of view! All three Daniel's Broilers offer the most sensational windows on the Northwest of any steakhouse in the region. Treat your guests to the breathtaking panoramic view from 21 flights up in Bellevue Place...or historic Leschi Marina on Lake Washington...or South Lake Union with its seaplanes, sailboats and marine activity.

The Daniel's experience embraces more than just Prime steaks, spectacular views and impeccable service. Our Private Dining Manager works with you every step of the way, paying attention to all the details to ensure a successful and memorable event. Enjoy award-winning entrées including USDA Prime steaks, Australian lobster, free-range chicken and the finest Northwest seafood. Daniel's Broiler, one of America's great steakhouses.

THE DOME ROOM

Presented Exclusively
by
Tony's Events & Catering

The Arctic Building
700 Third Avenue
Seattle, Washington 98104
Contact: Customer Service
(206) 328-2195
E-mail: tonybutz@aol.com

Capacity: 6,500 sq. ft.; accommodates up to 350 reception-style; 250 for seated functions
Price range: $910 + tax Sunday–Friday; $1,210 + tax for Saturdays
Catering: choose from a lovely range of custom created menus; other catering options are also available
Types of events: wedding ceremonies and receptions, corporate galas, bar and bat mitzvahs, anniversaries, retirement parties, etc.

Availability and terms

Room fee covers up to 8 hours access; bookings accepted up to 16 months in advance.

Description of services and facility

ADA: fully accessible
Parking: adjacent to building
Banquet services
- **Seating:** twenty-five 60" rounds; eight 6'–8' banquet rectangle tables
- **Servers:** banquet captain-coordinator and full professional wait staff included with your custom catering package
- **Bar facilities:** bring your own alcohol with a temporary banquet permit
- **Dance floor:** 15'x15' dance floor $350; 18'x18' dance floor $500
- **Linens, napkins, china and glassware:** all included in your catering package
- **Decorations:** to protect the architectural integrity of room nothing can be affixed to walls or suspended from stained glass dome
- **Cleanup:** included in your package

Meeting and event services
- **Audio visual and equipment:** we will take care of all your A/V needs

Special services

Tony's offers full event planning services to make your special day truly memorable

IT'S THAT BEAUTIFUL

Gorgeous antique backlit stained glass dome creates dramatic backdrop for truly elegant events. The Dome Room is now managed by Tony's Events & Catering—a company made of people who truly love their work. We will help you create the event of your dreams.

For more information on Tony's Events & Catering,
please see page 369 under Catering/Food & Beverage Services.

16500 Southcenter Parkway • Seattle, Washington 98188
Contact: Sales and Catering Office (206) 575-8220; Fax (206) 575-4743
Office Hours: Mon–Fri 8am–5pm; or by appointment
Web site: www.doubletreehotels.com

Capacity: up to 550 banquet style and 700 for receptions; 11 conference rooms plus 4 conference suites
Price range: varies based on menu and meeting room size
Catering: full-service in-house catering provided; custom menus available
Types of events: from cocktail parties to wedding receptions and social events to business meetings, Doubletree Guest Suites is the perfect host for any event

Description of services and facility

ADA: in compliance with ADA requirements
Parking: ample complimentary parking on-premise
Banquet services

- **Seating:** ample tables and chairs provided to meet your event requirements
- **Servers:** professional service staff included in catering costs
- **Bar facilities:** full-service bar, bartenders; Doubletree provides all alcoholic and non-alcoholic beverages; policies per WSLCB
- **Dance floor:** portable dance floor available on request
- **Linens and napkins:** provided with your event; special colors available at additional charge
- **China and glassware:** fine china and glassware provided
- **Decorations:** you may provide, with our approval, or we can assist you
- **Cleanup:** we'll handle all the cleanup for you

Meeting and event services

- **Audio visual and equipment:** full-service, in-house audio visual department

Special services

221 spacious two-room suites built around a newly renovated lobby. Each suite features in-room coffee, refrigerator, wet bar, iron, voice mail and daily newspaper.

SWEET DREAMS FROM DOUBLETREE

Our experienced staff, outstanding cuisine and beautiful facilities combine to ensure memorable and special events. And our freshly baked Doubletree Chocolate Chip cookies will make you feel at home. When you choose Doubletree Guest Suites to be your host, you will enjoy sweet dreams knowing we'll handle all the details with care.

 Please let this business know that you heard about them from the Bravo! Event Resource Guide.

300-112th Avenue S.E. • Bellevue, Washington 98004
Contact: Catering Office (425) 455-1300; Fax (425) 450-4119

Capacity: **Evergreen Ballroom:** 9652 sq. ft., up to 1,200; **Bellefield:** 2,356 sq. ft, up to 200; **Fairweather:** 2,432 sq. ft, up to 200; **Idylwood:** 2,432 sq. ft., up to 200; **King County East:** 2,736 sq. ft., up to 200; **Factoria:** 1,144 sq. ft., up to 80; **Lakehills:** 960 sq. ft., up to 60; **Marymoor:** 2,356 sq. ft, up to 200; **Newport:** 1147 sq. ft., up to 80; **Crossroads:** 816 sq. ft., up to 50; **Boardrooms:** 450 sq. ft., up to 20 each; **Exhibit Hall:** 35,000 sq. ft.; **Velato's**, with floor-to-ceiling atrium windows and seating for 175, is now available for social events and meetings
Price range: varies according to menu selections
Catering: full-service, in-house catering
Types of events: receptions, formal sit-down dinners, cocktails and hors d'oeuvres, meetings, seminars, conferences, conventions, and trade shows

Availability and terms

In addition to our 35,000 sq. ft. Exhibit Hall, the Doubletree Bellevue features over 17,000 sq.ft. of event space including our 9,652 sq. ft. Ballroom. Reservations may be made up to 12 months in advance based on space availability. A nonrefundable deposit will reserve your date.

Description of services and facility

ADA: all areas of the Doubletree Bellevue are fully accessible
Parking: complimentary self-parking
Banquet services
- **Seating:** tables and chairs provided
- **Servers:** experienced, professional service staff included in catering costs
- **Bar facilities:** full-service bar, bartender, and beverages available
- **Dance floor:** portable dance floors and ample electrical hook-ups available
- **Linens and napkins:** linens in a variety of colors provided
- **China and glassware:** assorted china and glassware provided
- **Decorations:** we're very flexible; nothing that will damage the facility
- **Cleanup:** please remove anything you bring in; we'll handle the rest

Meeting and event services
- **Audio visual:** in-house A/V department can take care of all your needs
- **Equipment:** podium, staging, and easels available
- **Phones:** Analog and T-1 lines available

THE IDEAL LOCATION FOR YOUR NEXT MEETING OR EVENT

The experienced staff at the Doubletree Bellevue prides itself on creating memorable events. Your catering manager will work with you and the Executive Chef to customize a menu that best suits your needs. All the details of your event will be checked and rechecked to ensure everything is just right. Throughout your event you can rest assured that the outstanding service will always complement the high quality food and beverage for which the Doubletree Bellevue is known.

Now part of Hilton Hotel Corporation and honoring the HHilton Honors Program.

DoubleTree Hotel™

SEATTLE AIRPORT

18740 Pacific Highway South • Seattle, Washington 98188
(206) 433-1881; Fax (206) 901-5902

Capacity: Grand Ballroom: 13,600 sq.ft. accommodates from 150 to 1,500; **Northwest Ballroom:** 6,250 sq. ft. accommodates from 100 to 450; two 2,100 sq.ft. rooms that will accommodate up to 200 each; 17 breakout rooms that will accommodate up to 90 each; **Maxi's Ballroom Top of the Tower:** 4,000 sq. ft. accommodates from 25 to 250

Price range: menu prices vary according to menu selection; we are happy to create custom packages

Catering: full-service, in-house catering

Types of events: full-service corporate meetings, conferences or conventions; intimate gatherings, weddings and gala events

Availability and terms

Space may be reserved up to one year in advance. Reservations should be made as early as possible to ensure availability. Dates are often available on short-term notice.

Description of services and facility

ADA: facilities are completely accessible

Parking: 1,000 parking spaces; please inquire about rates; valet parking available

Banquet services

- **Tables, chairs and dance floor:** provided at no additional charge
- **Servers:** serving staff and on-site event management included in catering costs
- **Linens, china and glassware:** choice of colors; white china, silver flatware, classic stemware provided
- **Decorations:** please inquire about guidelines
- **Cleanup:** provided by hotel staff at no additional charge

Meeting and event services

- **Audio visual:** in-house A/V company can accommodate all of your needs
- **Equipment:** podiums, risers, easels provided

Overnight accommodations

Special group rates available; deluxe guest room and luxury suites available.

WE WELCOME YOU WITH FRIENDLY SERVICE

Adjacent to Seattle-Tacoma International Airport, we are near shopping, major businesses, Mt. Rainier and Seattle's many attractions. We offer all the amenities of a first-class hotel including two restaurants, two lounges, concierge, fitness facilities and 24-hour complimentary airport shuttle service. Complete meeting facilities include 30 separate rooms totaling 39,000 square feet. Professional conference and catering specialists will take care of everything, whether you're planning for 10 or 2,000 guests.

Whether you visit for business or pleasure we welcome you with friendly service and Doubletree's signature Chocolate Chip Cookies.

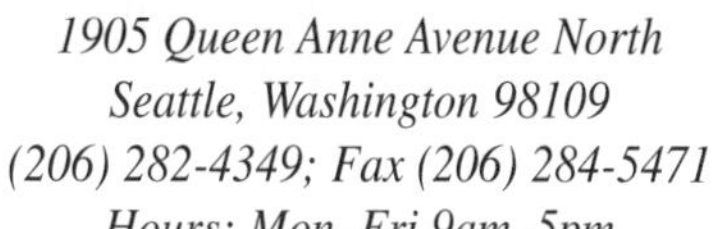

1905 Queen Anne Avenue North
Seattle, Washington 98109
(206) 282-4349; Fax (206) 284-5471
Hours: Mon–Fri 9am–5pm
E-mail: info@drachen.org
Web site: www.drachen.org

Capacity: from 80 to 100 guests
Price range: $75 per hour, with a minimum of 3 hours
Catering: client arranges own catering
Types of events: corporate meetings, lectures, receptions, and workshops

Availability and terms

Make reservations up to three weeks in advance. With a three-hour minimum. Cancellation requires one-week's notice in advance. A deposit of $200 along with a $100 liquor deposit is required.

Description of services and facility

ADA: fully accessible
Parking: ample on street parking; off-site parking lot rental available
Banquet services
- **Seating:** room seats 80 at tables; 100 auditorium-style
- **Servers:** caterer or client provides
- **Bar facilities:** client provides liquor permit
- **Kitchen/pantry:** stove, oven, dishwasher, microwave, refrigerator/freezer
- **Linens, china, glassware and silverware:** caterer or client provides
- **Decorations:** some limitations may apply; please inquire about our guidelines
- **Cleanup:** please remove anything you bring in

Meeting and event services
- **Audio visual and equipment:** screens only

A BEAUTIFUL ROOM FOR ANY OCCASION

Located in the heart of Seattle, in the urban neighborhood of Queen Anne. The Drachen Foundation offers a unique meeting and reception room, perfect for any occasion. The building is easily accessible and close to Queen Anne businesses.

DUMAS BAY CENTRE

3200 S.W. Dash Point Road
Federal Way, Washington 98023
Contact: Dumas Bay Centre
(253) 835-2000; Fax (253) 835-2010
Web site: www.ci.fed-way.wa.us *• Office Hours: Mon–Fri 8am–5pm*

Capacity: banquet room up to 98; meeting rooms for conferences to break into smaller groups; theater available for larger groups up to 250
Price range: prices vary according to event size and hours; please call
Catering: in-house caterer available
Types of events: overnight and weekend retreats, banquets, meetings, seminars, reunions, conferences, holiday parties, social or business gatherings, weddings and receptions, performing arts or threatrical performances, video presentations

Availability and terms

In addition to overnight accommodations for up to 80, the Dumas Bay Centre has four banquet rooms, as well as smaller meeting rooms. Make reservations as soon as possible. Minimum rental period is three hours. A 50% deposit and 100% damage deposit are required at the time of application with the balance due 45 working days prior to event. Call for prices on overnight packages.

Description of services and facility

ADA: fully complies with ADA requirements
Banquet services
- **Seating:** tables and chairs provided for indoor use
- **Servers:** caterer provides
- **Bar facilities:** bar service set-up with in-house caterer only
- **Linens, china and glassware:** available through caterer
- **Decorations:** nothing that will damage the facility, equipment or furniture; decorating time is included in the rental time; renter is responsible for set-up
- **Cleanup:** renter is responsible for cleanup

Meeting and event services
- **Audio visual and equipment:** TV, VCR; other A/V or equipment needs

Special services

- Meeting rooms available for conferences to break into smaller work groups.
- Overnight accommodations are available to groups of 12 or more (up to 80).

ENJOY OUR LUSH, SECLUDED GROUNDS AND VIEW OF PUGET SOUND AND THE OLYMPICS

Located on the water's edge on over 12 acres of manicured lawns and gardens, the Dumas Bay Centre is ideal for social or work gatherings. This former monastery features well-kept banquet and guest rooms with expansive views and is centrally located between Seattle and Tacoma, close to the SeaTac Airport.

See page 105 under Banquet, Getaway & Retreat Sites.

 Please let this business know that you heard about them from the Bravo! Event Resource Guide.

6205 Corson Avenue South • Seattle, Washington 98108
Contact: Todd L. Solemsaas (206) 762-5203
Office Hours: Mon–Fri 11am–7pm; evenings and weekends by appointment

Capacity: 13,000 square feet; up to 999 capacity banquet or reception style
Price range: please call for current prices
Catering: full-service, in-house catering
Types of events: banquets, receptions, reunions, meetings, seminars, special events, trade shows, company parties

Availability and terms

Rooms available for rental seven days a week. Reservations accepted up to one year advance. Deposit required to reserve date and is refundable if date can be re-booked.

Description of services and facility

ADA: all areas fully accessible
Parking: ample complimentary parking
Banquet services
- **Seating:** tables and chairs provided
- **Servers:** professional service staff available for catered functions
- **Bar facilities:** complete bar facilities and bartenders available; client provides all alcoholic beverages; banquet permit required
- **Dance floor:** hardwood floors that can accommodate up to 500 guests
- **Linens:** variety of tablecloth and napkin colors for an additional charge
- **China and glassware:** available to suit every occasion
- **Decorations:** please inquire; nothing that will damage the facility
- **Cleanup:** renter handles, or can contract with hall for $20 per hour

Meeting and event services
- **Audio visual and equipment:** we can arrange for any of your needs
- **Trade shows:** facility layout accommodates up to 63-8'x10' booths

Special services

Let us put our staff to work for you. We treat each function individually to ensure its success. We are happy to make all the arrangements for live bands or disc jockeys as well as all the other services to make your event complete.

WE'LL HELP PRESENT YOUR BEST IMAGE

Your event is sure to succeed at Eagles Aerie #1. We offer one of the largest facilities in Seattle. Our three large, modern rooms offer climate control, functional lighting, and high quality hardwood floors, and they can be rented individually or combined into one large room. From "economy" to "elegant," we'll help you present your best image. (Eagles Aerie #1 is easily accessible from downtown Seattle and SeaTac Airport with easy freeway access.)

COUNTRY CLUB

20414-121st Avenue S.E.
Snohomish, Washington 98296
Contact: Lisa Burke
(206) 362-3000, ext. 238
Office Hours: Mon–Sat, 9am–5pm
E-mail: lisa.burke@echofallsgolf.com
Web site: www.echofallsgolf.com

Capacity: the Lake Room is ideal for hosting events from 50 to 200 guests
Price range: room rental rates vary seasonally and with catering purchase
Catering: customized menu planning with full-service, in-house catering
Types of events: a perfect venue for golf tournaments, holiday parties, association luncheons, corporate retreats, class reunions, and weddings

Availability and terms

Reservations are available year-round and should be made as early as possible. A non-refundable 20% deposit secures your event date.

Description of services and facility

ADA: all areas are fully accessible
Parking: ample complimentary parking adjacent to the facility
Banquet services

- **Seating:** round tables and banquet chairs set up per you specifications
- **Servers:** professional servers led by a Banquet Captain provided; a 20% gratuity is applicable to food and hosted beverages
- **Bar facilities:** full-service bar for hosted or no-host events
- **Dance floor:** hardwood dance floor included; DJ's and bands are welcome
- **Linens and napkins:** white or ivory table linens with matching or colored napkins included
- **China and glassware:** white china table settings and glassware provided
- **Cleanup:** provided by the Echo Falls Staff
- **Decorations:** mirrors and votive candles provided for each table; exquisite buffet displays set in our Grand Boardroom; please inquire about your specific decorating ideas

Special services

Our spacious banquet room features a cozy fireplace, a private outdoor patio, an elegant foyer, and a separate room for the buffet.

PRIVACY AND CALM WITHIN YOUR REACH

An easy drive from either Bellevue or Seattle, Echo Falls rests elegantly in the Pacific Northwest Countryside. A sparkling lake, cascading waterfalls, and the rolling greens of the golf course greet you as you approach our beautiful Tudor Clubhouse. Wrapped with oak-trimmed windows, the Lake Room provides a uniquely elegant venue for your special event. Overlooking an impressive island green, it offers a scenic backdrop that will enhance any occasion.

As our premier 18-hole golf course is open to the public year-round, consider adding a round of golf as part of your event's activities. The professional staff at Echo Falls would be pleased to orchestrate an outing for players of all abilities.

THE EDGEWATER
A NOBLE HOUSE HOTEL

2411 Alaskan Way • Pier 67 • Seattle, Washington 98121-1398
(206) 728-7000 or 1-888-316-4449; Fax (206) 448-0255
Director of Sales & Marketing: Jodi Forslund
E-mail: jforslund@edgewaterhotel.com
Web site: www.noblehousehotels.com

Capacity: several unique meeting rooms accommodate from 10 to 200
Price range: varies with date, time, and menu selection
Catering: full-service, in-house catering provided
Types of events: retreats, business meetings, corporate dinners, parties, and all other functions

Availability and terms
We recommend that you reserve your space as early as possible, but we will accept reservations on short notice if space is available.

Description of services and facility
ADA: fully accessible
Parking: valet
Banquet services
- **Seating:** tables and chairs provided at no additional cost
- **Servers:** catering costs include a professionally trained staff
- **Bar facilities:** full-service bar in either host or no-host arrangement
- **Dance floor:** large, hardwood dance floor available; complimentary
- **Linens and napkins:** white linens provided at no additional cost; specialty options also available
- **China and glassware:** white china setting and stemware provided at no additional cost
- **Decorations:** votive candles, fresh-cut flowers, bud vases, and tile mirrors are complimentary; additional decorations can be arranged

Meeting and event services
- **Audio visual and equipment:** professional audio/visual equipment available upon request

Special services
Professional event coordinators assist with all details necessary to ensure a successful event.

BREATHTAKING VIEWS AND NEWLY RESTORED ELEGANCE
Experience the true essence of Pacific Northwest events at Seattle's only waterfront lodge. Rooms of warmth and comfort with fireplaces, pine furnishings, plush comforters and large windows that capture the rugged beauty of Puget Sound or the excitement of downtown.

Perced above the blue waters of Elliott Bay our new restaurant, *Six Seven,* features outdoor waterfront dining and sushi bar with influences of Northwest and Asian cuisine. An unrivaled location, breathtaking views, water view meeting rooms and a warm and friendly staff ensure a unique and inspiring event.

See page 33 under Accommodations.

EDMONDS FLORAL CONFERENCE CENTRE

~ Refreshingly Different ~

201 Fourth Avenue North • Edmonds, WA 98020
(425) 640-1808; Fax (425) 640-1024
Office Hours: Mon–Fri 9am–5pm
E-mail: efcc@edcc.edu
Web site: www.edcc.edu/centre

Capacity: **Chrysanthemum Room:** up to 350; **Rhododendron Room:** up to 60; **Orchid Room:** up to 80, or can be used as two separate rooms for up to 40 each
Price range: daily rates vary according to room size, please inquire
Catering: use our preferred list of caterers, or outside caterers welcome; spacious, well-equipped kitchen available
Types of events: business meetings, retreats, seminars, training, conferences, exhibits, strategic planning sessions, product introductions, employee recognition events, banquets, luncheons, dinners, receptions, reunions and private parties

Availability and terms

Reservations should be made as soon as possible. Deposit required at time of reservation.

Description of services and facility

ADA: fully accessible; ADA compliant
Parking: complimentary on-site and nearby
Banquet services
- **Seating:** tables and chairs provided for all events and set up per your unique specifications
- **Servers:** provided by caterer
- **Bar facilities:** provided by caterer
- **Linens:** available through Edmonds Floral Conference Centre
- **China and glassware:** provided by caterer
- **Decorations:** it would be our pleasure to discuss your ideas and needs
- **Cleanup:** please remove anything you bring in

Meeting and event services
- **Audio visual/technical support:** the Centre features a broad array of services; please inquire
- **Equipment:** extensive selection of presentation equipment available upon request
- **Lodging:** assistance with guest rooms and transportation is available

PREMIERE CONFERENCE CENTER IN A UNIQUE SETTING

The Edmonds Floral Conference Centre is a new, innovative meeting venue located just minutes north of downtown Seattle. Here you'll find gracious, flexible spaces, thoughtful amenities and a solid commitment to meet the specific needs of you and your guests.

Nestled amidst the picturesque seaside community of Edmonds, the facility has high vaulted ceilings and is flooded with natural light throughout. The Centre features a wide range of creative meeting room options—away from the hustle and bustle—free from distractions. Beachfront parks, galleries, restaurants, shops and lodging are within easy walking distance.

We welcome the opportunity of co-creating an exceptional, productive event. We will listen to your needs...very carefully. Please call to arrange a personalized tour. Perhaps we have something here you might not find anywhere else.

You can count on us to come through for you... on every detail.

El Gaucho

Seattle's Steakhouse

2505 First Avenue
Seattle, Washington 98121
(206) 728-1337
Fax (206) 728-4477
privatedining @elgaucho.com
www.elgaucho.com

Capacity: 6 to 200 for buffet receptions, sit-down dinners, luncheons and private events; four beautiful private dining rooms
Price range: please call for current pricing for your custom-designed menus
Catering: custom, full-service in-house catering
Types of events: ideal for corporate and social occasions, receptions, dinners, buffets, birthdays, anniversaries, weddings, rehearsal dinners, celebrations of all types

Availability and terms

Please call the Private Dining office at (206) 728-9593 for details regarding your custom designed event.

Description of services and facility

ADA: fully accessible
Parking: valet parking is available at our front door, ample additional parking on-street and at nearby lots
Banquet services
- **Seating:** 10 to 200; arrangements vary according to rooms
- **Servers:** all servers and support staff provided by El Gaucho
- **Bar facilities:** full-service bar; we provide all beverages, bartenders and servers
- **Dance floor:** available for rental upon request
- **Linens and napkins:** linens and napkins provided; specialty linen available for rental upon request
- **China and glassware:** fine china and stemware provided
- **Decorations:** we will be happy to discuss your exact desires for your event

Meeting and event services
- **Audio visual and equipment:** available for rental upon request

Special services

Our experienced event planners will assist you with attentive and detailed service for your event arrangements.

DINING WITH A LEGENDARY CLASSIC!

"Capturing the Glory of the Past—Burnishing it with Contemporary Style and Verve"

El Gaucho is an event. El Gaucho features 28-day Dry Aged CERTIFIED ANGUS BEEF® Prime, chops, ribs, poultry dishes and fresh seafood, all prepared to perfection over an open bed of glowing coals. Dazzling tableside preparations of salads, specialty items, flaming swords of shish kabobs, flambé desserts are the order of the day. Full bar, award winning wine list, nightly entertainment, intimate and popular Cigar Lounge.

721 Pine Street • Seattle, Washington 98101
Contact: Tev Marchettoni (206) 774-1234; Fax (206) 625-1221
Hours: Mon–Fri 8am–5:30pm, weekends and evenings by appointment
E-mail: tmarchet@seaghpo.hyatt.com • ***Web site: www.hyatt.com***

Capacity: 25,000 sq. ft. of meeting space to accommodate up to 600 people; available space includes two ballrooms, permanent theater, breakout rooms, board rooms, and hospitality suites
Price range: prices vary according to menu selections and service needs
Catering: full-service, in-house catering; Kosher service available
Types of events: corporate meetings, conferences, galas, auctions, sit-down dinners, breakfasts, luncheons, receptions, weddings, and other special events

Availability and terms

Please inquire with Elliott Grand Hyatt's Sales office to confirm availability and receive complete details about terms.

Description of services and facility

ADA: all facilities are fully accessible
Parking: valet and self-parking both available
Banquet services
- **Seating:** tables and chairs included
- **Servers:** professional staff provided by Elliott Grand Hyatt
- **Bar facilities:** full-service host and no-host bars provided by Elliott Grand Hyatt
- **Dance floor:** various sizes available
- **Linens, china and glassware:** all included with facility rental
- **Cleanup:** provided by Elliott Grand Hyatt's banquet staff
- **Decorations:** some limitations may apply; please inquire about our guidelines

Meeting and event services
- **Audio visual and technology:** built-in video conferencing, high resolution rear-projection displays, single point audio/video control system, internet access with ethernet
- **Equipment:** on-site audio visual company provides all necessary equipment

Special services

Overnight accommodations: 425 deluxe guest rooms, suites, and Regency Club guest rooms; group rates available.

UNEQUALED LUXURY, UNMISTAKABLY SEATTLE

Elliott Grand Hyatt is a one-of-a-kind property featuring 425 high-tech guest rooms and suites, and over 25,000 sq. ft. of meeting space. Designed to reflect the natural beauty and simple elegance that is unique to the Northwest, the location is superb; adjacent to the Washington State Convention and Trade Center and within walking distance to the city's most desirable shops and entertainment. We offer high-speed network connections and power outlets at every seat in our theater, and the ability to download material from presentations. We're Seattle's most tech-ready hotel...just ask the digital concierge in your room-and then use it to order tomorrow's breakfast. The restaurant showcases the talents of an award-winning chef and features a wine cellar dining room.

EMBASSY SUITES

HOTEL®

BELLEVUE

3225-158th Avenue S.E.
Bellevue, Washington 98008
Contact: Betsy DeLay, Director of Catering
(425) 644-2500, ext. 612; Fax (425) 865-8065
Office Hours: Mon–Fri 8am–5pm
E-mail: SEABL@aol.com • ***Web site: www.winhotel.com***

Capacity: Embassy Ballroom: 4,716 square feet; up to 360 for sit-down dinners; up to 500 for meetings or conferences; an additional 3,500 sq. ft. of flexible function and event space
Price range: lunches $15–$20; dinners $19–$38; custom menu tailoring available
Catering: in-house full-service
Types of events: business meetings, conferences, small conventions; sit down banquets, cocktail and hors d'oeuvres, retirement parties, wedding receptions, rehearsal dinners, wedding ceremonies in the Atrium (on Sundays only, 11am to 2pm) and more!

Availability and terms

Meetings or conventions, short term or up to one year in advance depending on space availability. For wedding receptions, reservations are taken up to one year in advance with 25% deposit to reserve space on a definite basis.

Description of services and facility

ADA: wheelchair access; hearing and sight impaired; special needs approved
Parking: complimentary parking on site
Banquet services

- **Seating:** tables and chairs provided
- **Servers:** highly experienced and trained
- **Bar facilities:** host or no-host bar available
- **Dance floor:** portable dance floor available
- **Linens and napkins:** available in a variety of accent colors at no extra cost
- **China and glassware:** ivory china provided
- **Decorations:** centerpieces available at no extra cost
- **Cleanup:** banquet staff handles all reasonable cleanup

Meeting and event services

- **Audio visual:** unlimited A/V services available including high-speed internet connection
- **Equipment:** podiums, microphones, flip charts, screens, and easels available

Special services

Two-room suites with coffee maker, refrigerator, two TVs, two phones, on-demand movies, Nintendo, high-speed internet connection, room service, full complimentary breakfast and nightly manager's reception, indoor pool, work-out room, and a six-story tropical atrium are always enjoyed by every Embassy Suites guest.

WE GUARANTEE YOU'LL MEET WITH SUCCESS!

EMBASSY SUITES HOTEL®

Seattle - North/Lynnwood

20610-44th Ave. West • Lynnwood, Washington 98036
(425) 775-2500, Reservations (800) EMBASSY
Fax (425) 774-0485
E-mail: sealw_ds@hilton.com • ***Web site: www.embassysuites.com***

Capacity: three ballrooms accommodate groups of 10–400 banquet style, 40–450 reception style
Price range: based on menu selection
Catering: full service, in-house catering
Types of events: business meetings, seminars, trade shows, wedding ceremonies and receptions, reunions, full-service sit-down luncheons and dinners, buffets from simple to elegant; Atrium cocktail and hors d'oeuvres receptions

Availability and terms

Subject to availability; make reservations up to one year in advance. A 50% deposit or credit card number reserves your date.

Description of services and facility

ADA: all areas are fully accessible
Parking: ample complimentary parking available
Banquet services

- **Seating:** tables and chairs provided for up to 450 guests
- **Servers:** highly experienced staff included in the catering costs; 18% service charge added to all food and beverage
- **Bar facilities:** full bar service and staff available for hosted or no-host events
- **Dance floor:** large parquet floor available at no extra charge
- **Linens:** white linen tablecloths and napkins
- **China and glassware:** white china and stemmed glassware
- **Decorations:** please inquire about themes; please no staples, tacks, nails or double-stick tape
- **Cleanup:** provided by Embassy Suites Hotel staff

Meeting and event services

- **Audio visual and equipment:** available upon request; high speed Internet in all meeting areas

Special services

Our professional staff will be happy to assist you in planning all aspects of your event from choosing the perfect menu to ensuring that every detail is complete. Complimentary full cooked-to-order breakfast, complimentary cocktails and light snacks.

Guest Suites: Our 240 luxury suites feature a living room and separate master bedroom offering all the comforts of home—high speed Internet, iron and ironing board, hair dryer, microwave, refrigerator and coffee maker. Please inquire about group rates.

SUITE PERFECTION

At Embassy Suites, whether you meet in one of our fully equipped meeting rooms, host a luncheon in our atrium, or convene in a conference suite, you'll always enjoy quality accommodations and a responsive, efficient staff.

Hilton HHonors Meeting Planner Program

AT&T **AT&T Communications available in every room.**

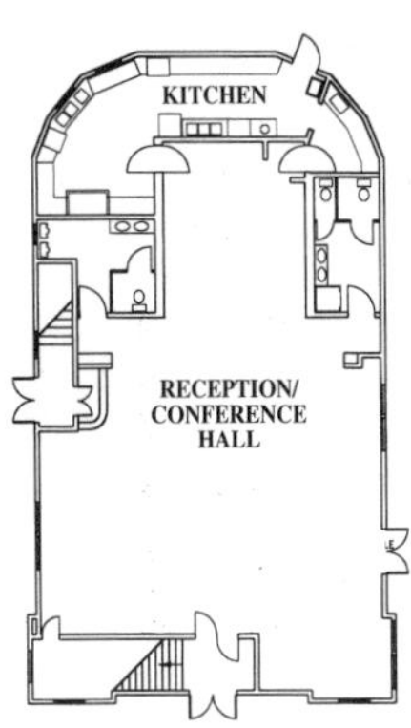

Conference Hall

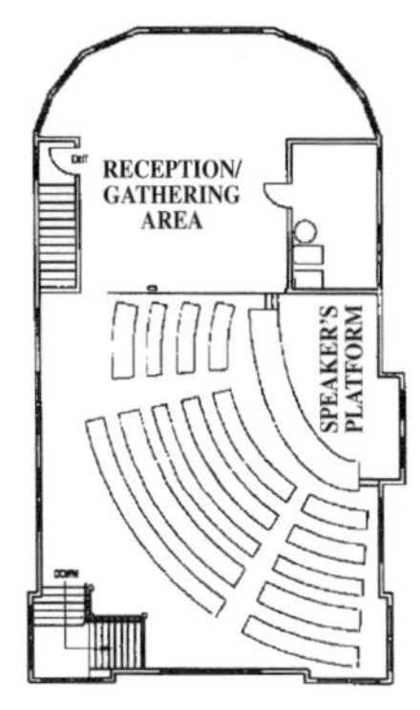

Speaker's Hall

Emerald Center

At the Emerald Chapel

6556-24th Avenue N.W. • Ballard
(206) 789-2964; Fax (206) 297-5938 • Business Office Hours: 8am–5pm
Web site: www.emeraldchapel.com

Capacity: 175 Speakers Hall theatre-style; 225 Conference Hall reception-style; 100 sit-down dinner; 75 garden courtyard
Price range: please inquire; varies according to event and day of the week
Catering: select from our preferred caterers list
Types of events: retreats, business and association meetings, corporate dinners, receptions, family events, seminars

Availability and terms

We recommend reserving your date early to ensure availability.

Description of services and facility

ADA: yes
Parking: on street; inquire regarding options
Banquet services

- **Seating:** tables and chairs provided
- **Servers:** provided by caterer
- **Bar facilities:** provided by caterer or client
- **Dance floor:** hall floor suitable for dancing
- **Linens, napkins, china and glassware:** provided by caterer
- **Decorations:** tastefully decorated hall with works from local artists requires little enhancement; please inquire regarding special requests and parameters
- **Cleanup:** provided by caterer

Meeting and event services

- **Audio visual and equipment:** excellent in-house PA, Sound System and CD changer; please inquire about our video systems

Special Services

We would be pleased to provide assistance with your event planning.

HISTORIC NORTHWEST JEWEL– A PREMIER MEETING FACILITY

We'll have to start meeting like this! Your events and meetings deserve to be held in a special setting. The Emerald Center is a unique, picturesque facility featuring stained glass lecture hall, stylish conference hall, full catering facilities and a beautiful garden courtyard.

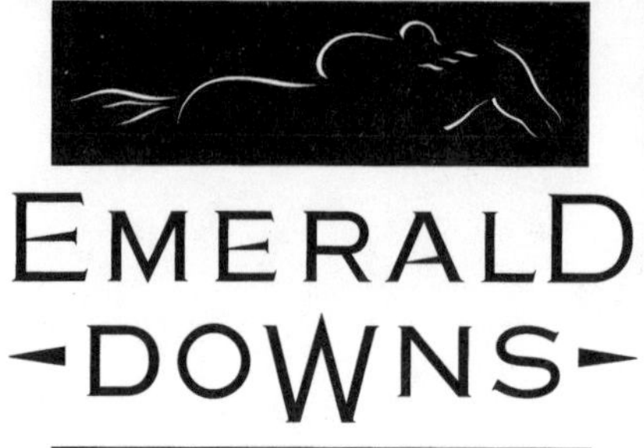

2300 Emerald Downs Drive • Auburn, Washington 98001
(253) 288-7700; Fax (253) 288-7710 • ***Web site: www.emeralddowns.com***

Capacity: 20–500 dinners, receptions, meetings; 75–1,000 picnics
Price range: varies according to type of event and menu selection
Catering: full-service, in-house catering
Types of events: Day-at-the-Races parties, dinner-dances, receptions, reunions, trade shows, breakfast/lunch meetings, auctions, proms, holiday parties

Availability and terms

Open year-round; call for date availability; 20% deposit to confirm reservation.

Description of services and facility

ADA: fully accessible
Parking: ample free parking; valet parking at an additional charge
Banquet services
- **Seating:** tables and chairs provided
- **Servers:** professional and friendly staff provided by Emerald Downs
- **Bar facilities:** full-service, hosted or no-host bar service; bartender and tableside service included in most packages
- **Dance floor:** each room has an appropriate sized dance floor with proper electrical hookups
- **Linens:** included for evening events
- **China and glassware:** house china and glassware provided
- **Decorations:** votive candles provided; inquire about restrictions
- **Cleanup:** provided by Emerald Downs

Meeting and event services
- **Audio visual:** extensive in-house audio-visual department
- **Equipment:** microphone and podium provided; additional equipment available by request; additional charges may apply

A COMPLETE EVENT FACILITY

Mount Rainier sets the backdrop for this magnificent facility. Conveniently located midway between Seattle and Tacoma, Emerald Downs is the perfect location for a variety of events.

For your next corporate picnic, staff party or family reunion, make it unique by adding the excitement of Thoroughbred racing. Whether you choose the elegance and privacy of our Triple Crown Suites, a delicious buffet in the Emerald or View Room, or a Box Lunch or BBQ Buffet in the Paddock Park, our Day-at-the-Races parties assure everyone leaves a winner.

Emerald Downs offers the freshest, finest menus and quality service in a state-of-the-art facility for day and evening events. Make your next event even more special by adding our mock racing package. Open year-round for dinner dances, auctions, breakfast/lunch meetings or trade shows—you name the event and we can do it! Our in-house audio-visual department can work with you to give your program extra impact. All of your needs will be taken care of at Emerald Downs!

See page 52 under Attractions & Activities.

EMERALD QUEEN
EQC
CASINO & NIGHT CLUB

2102 Alexander Avenue
Tacoma, Washington 98421
(888) 831-7655
E-mail: Robbynn_hoff@emeraldqueen.com
Web site: www.emeraldqueen.com

Capacity: **The Bridge Nightclub** can accommodate from 10–300 guests; **3rd Deck** can accommodate 300–500 guests; **Showroom** can accommodate 500–1,800 guests
Price range: no room fee; price varies according to event and menu selection
Catering: full service, in-house catering
Types of events: everything from small business meetings on our beautiful boat to full conventions and trade shows in our brand new entertainment pavilion

Availability and terms

We recommend that you reserve your space early, but will try to accommodate reservations on short notice.

Description of services and facility

ADA: yes
Parking: yes
Banquet services
- **Seating:** tables and chairs provided; various arrangements are possible
- **Servers:** professional and courteous service staff
- **Bar facilities:** full beverage service available
- **Dance floor:** yes
- **Linens, napkins, china and glassware:** provided by Emerald Queen
- **Cleanup:** provided by Emerald Queen

Special services

Group discounts, site tours, full service catering, shuttle services.

FROM SMALL MEETINGS TO FULL CONVENTIONS AND TRADE SHOWS...

The Emerald Queen can accommodate everything from small business meetings on our beautiful boat to full conventions and trade shows in our brand new entertainment pavilion. We can also provide a state of the art sound system, complete food service, transportation (depending upon size) and the space is free based upon availability.

See page 53 under Attractions & Activities.

Enzian Inn

590 Highway 2
Leavenworth, Washington 98826
Group Sales (509) 548-5269
Toll free (800) 223-8511
Fax (509) 548-9319
E-mail: enzgrps@rah.net
Web site: www.enzianinn.com

Capacity: 5,706 sq. ft. meeting space to 225; additional 3,334 sq. ft. for banquets up to 250
Price range: prices vary; please call for current pricing information
Catering: in-house catering provided
Types of events: corporate retreats, conferences, conventions, banquets, board meetings, seminars, receptions, team-building

Availability and terms

We suggest that you make reservations as early as possible, to ensure the best availability. A deposit and signed contract are required.

Description of services and facility

ADA: fully accessible
Parking: ample complimentary parking provided
Banquet services
- **Seating:** all tables and chairs provided at no additional cost
- **Servers:** all service staff provided by Enzian Inn
- **Bar facilities:** client with license or licensed bartender provides permit and all alcoholic beverages
- **Dance floor:** available for a nominal set-up fee
- **Linens, napkins, china and glassware:** provided at no additional charge
- **Decorations:** must be pre-approved; decorating must be done during rental hours
- **Cleanup:** client responsible for removing decorations; Enzian staff handles the rest

Meeting and event services
- **Audio visual and equipment:** full range of equipment available, if reserved

Accommodations and special services

104 guest rooms, including VIP fireplace and spa suites; please call for prices. Indoor/outdoor pool/spa, exercise room. Enzian Falls, our 18-hole championship putting course is located directly across the street from Enzian Inn. Let us help you plan a team-building event or lighthearted group tournament. Featuring natural bent grass greens and a walk-under waterfall, the course offers views of the river, mountains, and grazing goats.

OLD-WORLD CHARM & GRACIOUS HOSPITALITY

Located in beautiful Leavenworth, Enzian Inn brings gracious hospitality and old-world charm to the Cascade foothills. We invite you to enjoy the elegance of authentic Austrian furnishings and relax under our cozy down comforters. Guests awaken to our famous complimentary breakfast buffet served in our fourth-floor solarium and accompanied by an Alpenhorn serenade; views of surrounding mountains and the Bavarian Village complete the charming ambiance. Our fitness room and racquetball court provide an ideal way to begin your day's activities. Indoor and outdoor pools and hot tubs offer a refreshing way to complete the day's business or pleasure. We look forward to hosting your next special event or retreat.

See page 106 under Banquet, Getaway & Retreat Sites.

©Experience Music Project. Photo by Lara Swimmer

EXPERIENCE ***MUSIC*** PROJECT™
325-5th Avenue N. (at the Seattle Center)
Seattle, Washington 98109
Contact: Facility Sales
(206) 770-2700; Fax (206) 770-2727
E-mail: facilityuse@emplive.com
Web site: www.emplive.com

Capacity: 300 guests for a seated meal; 700 served reception-style in EMP's Sky Church and Main Lobby; a Museum Buyout allows up to 1,500 guests exclusive access to the entire museum

Price range: please inquire; rates vary according to event type, size of group, time and day of week required

Catering: work with EMP catering to create a custom menu for your event

Types of events: receptions, holiday parties, banquets, sit-down dinners, concerts, private performances, meetings, lectures, workshops, fashion shows, or other types of social or corporate event

Availability and terms

Reservations can be made in advance. A deposit and Facility Use Agreement are required to reserve your date.

Description of services and facility

ADA: fully accessible

Parking: 3,500 convenient pay parking spaces within walking distance; valet parking available

Banquet services

- **Seating:** tables and chairs provided
- **Servers:** provided by EMP
- **Bar facilities:** provided by EMP
- **Linens, china and glassware:** provided by EMP
- **Dance floor:** available
- **Decorations:** please inquire
- **Cleanup:** provided by EMP at no extra charge; special decorations must be removed immediately following the event

Meeting and event services

- **Audio visual and equipment:** state-of-the-art, technologically advanced equipment; extremely flexible creative capabilities for light and sound

Special services

Our event staff is happy to coordinate, design, and execute your event needs; please inquire for details and pricing.

DISTINGUISH YOUR EVENT

The moment your guests arrive at Experience Music Project, they'll know they're in for something very different! The museum, located at the base of the Space Needle on the Seattle Center campus, is built from a colorful, swoopy design created by world-renowned architect Frank O. Gehry. Both the building and its unparalleled collection of music-related artifacts have made EMP one of the most popular Seattle destinations for locals and city visitors alike. There are multiple event spaces within EMP, each with a distinct personality, perfect for hosting everything from private meetings and parties to lectures and receptions.

F.X. McRORY'S

419 Occidental Avenue South, #602
Seattle, Washington 98104
(206) 623-4800
Fax (206) 613-3105
E-mail: gm4mcrorys@aol.com
Web site: www.fxmcrorys.com

Capacity: three dining rooms can be reserved to seat 40, 60, or 110; all three will accommodate 300 reception style; you can also reserve a section or all of the lively Whiskey Bar which holds up to 200

Price range: no added costs, select a custom menu using McRory's regular restaurant menu prices

Catering: off-premise catering available

Types of events: perfect spot for pre-game events, cigar dinners, bachelor parties, rehearsal dinners, meetings, receptions, anniversaries, birthdays, going-away parties or any type of corporate or private entertaining; we welcome large groups on short notice

Availability and terms

Banquet space can be reserved with a minimal deposit. There is no surcharge for large parties.

Description of services and facility

ADA: complies with all ADA requirements

Parking: ample parking available

Banquet services

- **Seating:** square or rectangular tables, set-up to meet your needs
- **Servers:** one per each 20 guests
- **Bar facilities:** full service bar, host or no host; liquor, beer, wine, and/or no alcohol
- **Linens and napkins:** table linens and napkins can be provided in your choice of colors
- **Decorations:** the restaurant is beautifully appointed with double tall ceilings, brass chandeliers and vintage artwork; the Whiskey Bar features over 50 feet of the world's largest collection of Bourbons; made famous by artist LeRoy Neiman, his original F.X. McRory's Whiskey Bar painting valued at $100,000.00 hangs prominently on the north wall of the bar

Special services

We will be happy to provide personalized menus at guests' place settings; acknowledging your special event, these become keepsakes for the guest of honor.

MORE THAN 20 YEARS OF EXCELLENCE

F.X. McRory's commitment to quality and excellence is famous throughout the Northwest. Our slow roasted prime rib, alder-smoked salmon, and fresh shellfish will enhance informal gatherings and corporate meetings alike. Conveniently located in Pioneer Square.

A Grand Affaire at *The Fairview Club*

Personal–Flexible–Professional

2022 Boren Avenue
Seattle, Washington 98121
(206) 623-9003; Fax (206) 623-3315
E-mail: monica@thefairviewclub.com
Web site: www.thefairviewclub.com

Capacity: 4,500 sq. ft.; accommodates up to 350 seated; 450 reception style
Price range: facility rental varies from $800–$2,000; catering prices vary according to menu; minimums may apply
Catering: in-house, full service catering provided by A Grand Affaire
Types of events: meetings, seminars, trade shows, reunions, holiday parties, retirement receptions, weddings, fund raisers and auctions; breakfast, lunch, hors d'oeuvres and dinners

Availability and terms

We offer day or evening rentals seven days a week. A $500 deposit plus your facility rental reserves your date. Reservations are accepted up to one year in advance. We are also happy to accommodate you on short notice.

Description of services and facility

ADA: The Fairview Club is fully handicapped accessible
Parking: ample, low-cost parking in adjacent lots; reserved or valet parking can be arranged
Banquet services

- **Seating:** 60" round tables and taupe chairs are included with facility rental
- **Servers:** service staff provided with catering service
- **Bar facilities:** renters may bring own alcoholic beverages to be served with no corkage fee; glassware, soft drinks, mineral water, condiments for bar and bartenders included with beverage service; no-host bar service available
- **Linens:** cloth napkins and table linens included with catering services; specialty linens available
- **China and glassware:** bone china, polished silver and water glasses included with catering
- **Decorations:** requires little decoration; free-standing decorations are welcome
- **Cleanup:** provided by The Fairview Club staff

Meeting and event services

- **Audio visual and equipment:** built-in sound and PA system with podium and microphone; we can accommodate your complete A/V requirements on a rental basis

Special services

- Flexible bar service with no corkage fee
- No-host bar catering options
- Complete audio-visual rentals
- All-inclusive meeting packages
- Event coordination
- Great referrals
- Full service off-premise catering

CONSIDER YOUR HIGHEST EXPECTATIONS SURPASSED

The Fairview Club echoes of an earlier age—marble floors, hand-painted ceiling murals, Corinthian columns, a Chickering piano, and fireplace sitting area with antique fainting couch. The historic exterior will charm you, the interior will delight you, and the prices will prove surprisingly affordable. Simply put, The Fairview Club is a refreshing choice when you desire a remarkable event.

See page 337 under Catering/Food & Beverage Services.

7300 Fun Center Way • Tukwila, Washington 98188
(425) 228-7300; Fax (425) 228-7400
Open 365 days a year; Business Hours: 11am–11pm winter; 9am–12am summer
E-mail: tamarrah@fun-center.com
Web site: www.fun-center.com

Capacity: amusement park, 2,500 people; Bullwinkle's dining room, 300 people
Price range: $9–$28 per person
Catering: in-house
Types of events: corporate picnics, holiday parties, graduation parties, employee incentives, birthday parties, family reunions

Availability and terms

First come, first served. Reservations available during all operating hours. After-hour packages also are available. Deposits are required.

Description of services and facility

ADA: yes
Parking: 300 spaces
Banquet services
- **Seating:** indoor, 300
- **Servers:** provided
- **Linens and napkins:** specialty linens and napkins upon request
- **China and glassware:** specialty servingware upon request
- **Decorations:** upon request
- **Cleanup:** provided

Meeting and event services
- **Audio visual and equipment:** arrangements upon request
- **Corporate meeting room:** available; 30 capacity

ENTERTAINMENT FOR ALL AGES

This amazing 8-acre amusement park is located in the city of Tukwila (I-405, Exit 1). The Family Fun Center and Bullwinkle's Restaurant provide a fun and clean atmosphere, safe attractions, great food and entertainment for all ages. Attractions include miniature golf, go karts, bumper boats, batting cages, Lazer X-treme, Kidopolis (indoor, soft play), rock wall, arcade and a golf driving range.

See page 54 under Attractions & Activities.

2234 First Avenue • Seattle, Washington 98121
Contact: Amy Lemaire (206) 728-8595; Fax (206) 728-1551
Office Hours: Mon–Fri 9am–3:30pm
Web site: www.flyingfishseattle.com

Capacity: up to 40 for sit-down lunches or dinners; up to 70 for cocktail parties or receptions
Price range: $800 minimum credited toward food and beverage
Catering: full-service in-house catering by noted chef/owner, Christine Keff
Types of events: private dinners, wine tastings, cooking classes, cocktail parties, receptions, business luncheons or dinners

Availability and terms

Reservations may be made up to one year in advance. We are happy to accommodate shorter notice depending on availability. We require a $800 minimum/deposit to reserve your date.

Description of services and facility

ADA: restaurant and private banquet room are fully accessible
Parking: ample parking adjacent to facility for nominal fee
Banquet services

- **Seating:** private banquet room includes tables and chairs for up to 40
- **Servers:** courteous professional wait-staff included in catering cost
- **Bar facilities:** host or no-host full-service bar facilities available
- **Linens and napkins:** white linens provided; other colors available upon request
- **China and glassware:** fine china and crystal stemware provided
- **Decorations:** please inquire; nothing that will damage the facility
- **Cleanup:** please remove anything you bring in, we'll handle the rest

Meeting and event services

- **Audio visual and equipment:** we will be happy to coordinate any of your A/V and equipment needs with prior arrangements

A SEATTLE FAVORITE

Flying Fish, a favorite among Seattleites, is located in the urban center of Belltown. Nationally acclaimed chef/owner Christine Keff lends an innovative, imaginative touch to Northwest seafood. Consistency and quality in food and service promise to make your event a memorable one.

FORT WORDEN STATE PARK CONFERENCE CENTER

Fort Worden State Park

Washington State Parks
Unique Heritage Facilities

200 Battery Way • Port Townsend, WA 98368
(360) 344-4400; Fax (360) 385-7248
Web site: www.olympus.net/ftworden/confer.html

Capacity: two dozen meeting rooms for 12–280 people; lecture space for up to 325; dormitories for 32–365; and 33 Victorian houses for 2–23; a total of 33 units with a total capacity of 250

Price range: meeting rooms from $30–$180; a pavilion for 1,200 is $800; chapel for $100; and Victorian house rates range from $107–$375 a night

Catering: all catering is through Fort Worden's in-house caterer, Community Enterprises of Port Townsend; some catered meals are mandatory with overnight conference group accommodations; to reach the caterer, call (360) 344-4441 or (800) 890-9952, TDD (360) 379-9385

Types of events: large and small business conferences, workshops, youth camps, company picnics, weddings, family reunions, vacation groups, and retreats

Availability and terms

For day use you can make reservations 90 days in advance. For overnight stays for groups of 32 or more, reservations may be made up to two years in advance. Reservations for 2002 are being taken now. Deposits are charged to secure dates, and refunds vary; fees are charged for cancellations.

Description of services and facility

ADA: most day use buildings are accessible

Parking: ample parking for overnight stays; limited parking for day use

Banquet services

- **Seating:** all meeting rooms have chairs and tables
- **Servers:** see catering section above
- **Dance floors:** available in several buildings
- **Linens and napkins:** dining linens provided with catering; bed linens for overnight rentals provided in Victorian houses, optional in dormitories
- **China and glassware:** provided by caterers for conferences; cooking and eating utensils provided by Fort Worden in Victorian House rentals
- **Decorations:** please inquire about possibilities and restrictions
- **Cleanup:** client is responsible for light cleanup

Meeting and event services

- **Audio visual and equipment:** podiums, public address systems, easels, blackboards, pull-down projection screens, TVs, and VCRs may be available

Special services

We'll help you select a combination of meeting rooms and catering services to suit your needs. Make your event special with a stay in a Victorian house, complete with linen service and modern conveniences.

PLAN YOUR MEETING IN A HISTORIC SETTING

History is the main attraction at Fort Worden State Park Conference Center, set high on a wooded bluff overlooking the entrance to Puget Sound. The 1902-vintage Fort offers a beautiful setting, with the old-fashioned ambiance of Officers' Row Victorian houses, gun batteries, museums and gardens, as well as the galleries, restaurants and historic waterfront of nearby Port Townsend. Mix and match lodgings and services to suit your group's needs.

15221 International Boulevard • SeaTac, Washington 98188
(where Highway 99 meets 154th Street, just north of Sea-Tac Airport)
(206) 988-4888; Fax (206) 988-6166
E-mail: guestservices@funsters.com
Web site: www.funsters.com

Capacity: 30–750 people
Price range: varies according to menu selection
Catering: provided by Funsters
Types of events: parties, celebrations, promotions, demotions, weddings, divorces, arrivals, departures, reunions, meetings, staff incentive and sports events

Availability and terms

We can accommodate short notice. Deposit required to reserve your date. Room fee waived with minimum food and beverage ordered.

Description of services and facility

ADA: yes
Parking: free parking with valet Wednesday through Sunday; free shuttle
Banquet services
- **Seating:** arranged according to your needs
- **Servers:** attentive and friendly servers provided
- **Bar facilities:** full service bar, liquor, beer, wine, champagne and non-alcoholic choices
- **Dance floor:** yes
- **Linens, napkins, china and glassware:** provided by Funsters
- **Decorations:** please inquire
- **Cleanup:** provided by Funsters

Meeting and event services
- **Audio visual and equipment:** in-house, large screen TVs, 65 TVs, great A/V

Special services

Full stage for live production shows. Free shuttle service for your entire group.

GAMER'S PARADISE WITH A STAGE FOR LIVE PRODUCTION SHOWS!

We're the Northwest's newest, most electrifying place to play: A gamer's paradise with casino card games. A sports bar with wall-to-wall TVs. An arcade with electronic games for kids of all ages. The Great Room features a full stage for live production shows. The Wow Café menu has hundreds of choices including steakburgers, salads, noodle and rice dishes. The Liberty Bar offers everything from fruit and veggie smoothies to creative cocktails.

7619 Country Club Drive
Arlington, Washington 98223
Contact: Kathy Blumenstein
(360) 435-6713; Fax (360) 435-4769
Office Hours: Mon–Fri 11am–9pm;
evenings and weekends by appointment

Capacity: 1,450 sq. ft.: up to 180 seated indoors; up to 250 with outdoor patios
Price range: varies according to size of group, menu selection
Catering: full service in-house catering
Types of events: receptions, banquets, meetings, seminars, anniversaries, parties, golf tournaments and more

Availability and terms

Reservations should be made up to one year in advance, especially for summer months and the holiday season. We are happy to accommodate shorter notice depending on space availability. A $750 deposit will reserve your date.

Descriptions of services and facility

ADA: fully complies with all ADA requirements
Parking: complimentary parking
Banquet services
- **Seating:** tables and chairs for up to 180 people
- **Servers:** service staff included in catering cost: 18% service charge
- **Bar facilities:** host or no host bar; compliance with all local and state liquor laws
- **Dance floor:** available in banquet room; ample electrical hookups
- **Linens and napkins:** color linens available
- **Decorations:** please inquire about specific ideas
- **Cleanup:** provided by Gleneagle

Meeting and event services
- **Audio visual and equipment:** we are happy to arrange for anything you need

Special services

The staff at Gleneagle will be happy to assist you with your event planning to make sure your day is a special one.

RELAX AND ENJOY YOUR DAY

Enjoy our newly remodeled banquet facility and beautifully landscaped patio area overlooking the golf course. Our courteous and professional staff looks forward to helping with all of our clients needs.

 Please let this business know that you heard about them from the Bravo! Event Resource Guide.

14040 Interurban Avenue South
Tukwila, Washington 98168
Contact: Greg Bakamis
(206) 244-5400; Fax (206) 244-4542
E-mail: info@grandcentralcasinos.net
Web site: www.grandcentralcasinos.net

Capacity: up to 225 people
Price range: varies according to day and time of the event; please call for current price list
Catering: full service in house
Type of events: ideal for corporate meetings, seminars, concerts, reunions, weddings, anniversaries, birthdays, breakfast, brunch, lunch, and dinner

Availability and terms

Reservations can be made up to one year in advance or as close as one week, depending on availability. A deposit is required to secure your date.

Description of services and facility

ADA: fully complies with ADA requirements
Parking: up to 125
Banquet services

- **Seating:** variety of table sizes comfortable padded chairs
- **Servers:** staff included in catering costs, plus service charge
- **Bar facilities:** full Service bar and bartenders, policies per WSLCB and Grand Central Casino management
- **Dance floor:** yes
- **Stage:** yes
- **Linens and napkins:** variety of colors
- **China and glassware:** provided
- **Cleanup:** provided by Grand Central Casino staff; special decorations and personal supplies must be removed immediately following the event

Meeting and event services

- **Audio visual and equipment:** full array of audio visual equipment

PERSONALIZED ATTENTION

The Grand Central Casino offers personalized attention to every detail of your event and customized menu and event planning. We can arrange for floral arrangements, ice carvings, decorations, live entertainment, equipment and photographers. We are centrally located near Sea Tac Airport and numerous local quality hotels. 10 minutes to Seattle, 20 minutes to Bellevue, at the crossroad of I-405 and I-5.

We are able to accommodate groups from formal to casual, from as small as 25 to as large as 250.

Greenwood Square

8420 Greenwood Avenue North • Seattle, Washington 98103
Call **The Upper Crust Catering** *at (206) 783-1826; Fax (206) 783-1672*
Office Hours: Mon–Fri 8:30am–5:30pm
Web site: www.greenwoodsquare.com

Capacity: up to 175 for receptions or 125 for sit-down dinners
Price range: please inquire; rates vary depending on day of week and time needed
Catering: in-house caterer—The Upper Crust Catering, creators of extraordinary events
Types of events: banquets, receptions, business meetings, seminars, retreats, reunions, formal sit-down dinners or casual banquets, or any other type of business or social event

Availability and terms

This charming historic room, located on the second floor of Greenwood Square offers Seattle an enchanting new site for private parties, banquets, meetings, and events. Available weekdays, evenings and weekends. A 55% deposit will reserve your date with the balance due 30-days prior to your event.

Description of services and facility

Parking: ample street parking adjacent to the facility
Banquet services

- **Seating:** tables and chairs for up to 125 provided
- **Servers:** courteous professional wait-staff included in catering cost
- **Bar facilities:** featuring a beautiful 20' built-in mahogony bar
- **Dance floor:** the facility features a hardwood dance floor
- **Linens and napkins:** included in catering cost; specialty colors available at additional charge
- **China and glassware:** included in catering cost
- **Decorations:** please inquire; nothing that will damage this historic facility
- **Cleanup:** please remove anything you bring in, we'll handle the rest

Meeting and event services

- **Audio visual and equipment:** we will be happy to coordinate your A/V or equipment needs

Special services

The Upper Crust's in-house coordinator is on-hand to assist you in all aspects of the planning process. We pride ourselves in offering our clients superb meals and amenities plus unsurpassed service.

CLASSIC 1926 BUILDING

This classic 1926 building with vaulted ceilings and beautiful picture windows is a perfect setting for any event. It features a hardwood dance floor, built in bar and an ambiance all its own. Centrally located in Historical Greenwood, it is easily accessible from surrounding Puget Sound areas.

THE HALL AT FAUNTLEROY

• TUXEDOS 'N TENNIS SHOES CATERING, INC. •

9131 California Avenue S.W. • Seattle, Washington 98136
Co-Owners: David Haggerty or David Meckstroth
Event Coordinators: Linn Caine or Jude Lofton
(206) 932-1059; Fax (206) 937-6508
Catering Office Hours: Mon–Fri 9am–5pm; please call for an appointment
E-mail: tuxedosntennisshoes@msn.com

Capacity: **Emerald Room**–3,500 sq. ft., up to 275 guests reception style, 260 guests sit-down dinner; **Vashon Room**–2,850 sq. ft., up to 200 guests reception style, 170 guests sit-down dinner; additional outdoor areas available for 300+ (seasonal); entire facility capacity of 500+
Price range: prices vary according to your menu and service needs
Catering: full-service, in-house catering by Tuxedos 'n Tennis Shoes Catering, Inc.
Types of events: corporate events, reunions, seminars, or other social and business occasions

Availability and terms

We suggest making your reservation as early as possible. A $400 deposit will reserve your date.

Description of services and facility

Parking: ample complimentary parking provided
Banquet services
- **Seating:** tables and chairs are provided
- **Bar facilities:** client provides alcoholic beverages and banquet permit
- **Linens:** white linen tablecloths; specialty colors available upon request
- **China and glassware:** china and glassware suitable to the occasion provided
- **Dance floor:** The Hall at Fauntleroy's floors are ideal for dancing
- **Decorations:** please inquire; nothing that will damage the facility
- **Cleanup:** please remove anything you bring in; we'll handle the rest

Meeting and event services
- **Audio visual and equipment:** may be arranged through Fauntleroy or provided by client

Special services

When you book your event at The Hall at Fauntleroy, you're hiring an experienced team of professionals. Tuxedos 'n Tennis Shoes will handle as much or as little as you want, from referring you to additional services to arranging everything for you.

A WEST SEATTLE TREASURE OFFERING CHARACTER & CHARM

Located in West Seattle's historic Fauntleroy School House, we offer two unique spaces for client's use. **The Emerald Room** features an elegant foyer, beautiful brick interior and expansive floor-to-ceiling windows overlooking an ivy-covered ravine. **The Vashon Room** offers a spacious interior with soaring ceilings, period style architectural details, carpeted floors and built-in dance floor. The adjacent Garden Courtyard features a manicured lawn, a colorful perennial border and an expansive view of the Olympics and Puget Sound.

See page 370 under Caterers/Food & Beverage Services.

(private membership club)

801 Second Avenue • 17th Floor, Norton Bldg.
Seattle, Washington 98104
Contact: Catering Office (206) 623-3532
Fax (206) 623-0686
Catering Department Hours:
Mon–Fri 9am–5pm; Sat by appointment
Web site: www.harborclubs.org

Capacity: 275 guests for seated dinners, 150 seated luncheons, 450 receptions
Price range: dinners and receptions from $40 per person, lunch from $25 (food & beverage)
Catering: we offer timely or traditional Northwest fare through our in-house catering
Types of events: executive meetings to intimate dinners to lavish cocktail receptions

Description of services and facility

ADA: The Harbor Club-Seattle is fully accessible
Parking: available, including our building garage after 6pm weekdays for evening events
Banquet services
- **Servers:** professional, attentive staff to meet your every need
- **Linens, china and glassware:** linens and beautiful gold inlay Harbor Club crested china provided
- **Decorations:** with its recent renovation and spectacular views, the club requires little enhancement

Meeting and event services
- **Audio visual:** TV/VCR, overheads, slide projectors, screens
- **Equipment:** podium, microphones, white boards, flip charts and more

Membership: contact the catering department for information on becoming a member; The Harbor Club is a private club for use by members and their guests only

Special services

The Harbor Club-Seattle offers eight exquisitely furnished private rooms for meetings and events—and every room has a view! For special occasions day or night, the entire Club may be reserved by any member to accommodate parties of up to 450 persons.

SPECTACULAR VIEW AND ELEGANT SETTING!

For three decades there's been a place where Seattle's business and civic leaders have gathered to dine and share the spectacular views. The Harbor Club now boasts a second location in Bellevue atop the Rainier Plaza Building. Both Clubs are a quiet refuge—elegantly private, yet supremely inviting—where you can enjoy sweeping water and mountain views. Atop the Norton Building, above Elliott Bay and the city streets, The Harbor Club-Seattle is the place where achievements and hospitality naturally come together.

777-108th Avenue, N.E. • Rainier Plaza Bldg.,
25th Floor • Bellevue, Washington 98004
Contact: Catering Office (425) 990-1050
Fax (425) 990-1587
Catering Department Hours:
Mon–Fri 9am–5pm; Sat by appointment
Web site: www.harborclubs.org

(private membership club)

Capacity: 225 for sit-down dinners, 450 for receptions
Price range: dinners and receptions range from $40 per person, and lunch from $25 (food and beverage)
Catering: food and beverage must be provided by The Harbor Club-Bellevue
Types of events: sit-down dinners, receptions, retreats, auctions and holiday office parties

Description of services and facility

ADA: The Harbor Club-Bellevue is fully accessible
Parking: ample, underground parking
Banquet services
- **Seating:** dramatic sweeping views from every room
- **Servers:** professional attentive staff to meet your every need
- **Linens, china and glassware:** linens, white china and stemmed glassware provided at no charge
- **Decorations:** The Harbor Club-Bellevue is simply spectacular

Meeting and event services
- **Audio visual:** TV/VCR, overheads, slide projectors, screens
- **Equipment:** podium, microphones, white boards, flip charts and more

Membership: contact the catering department for information on becoming a member; The Harbor Club is a private club for use by members and their guests only

Special services

The newly-renovated Harbor Club-Bellevue offers tastefully appointed private rooms. For special occasions day or night, the entire Club may be reserved by any member to accommodate parties of up to 350.

SPECTACULAR VIEW AND ELEGANT SETTING!

Located on the 25th floor atop the Rainier Pacific Plaza Building in downtown Bellevue, The Harbor Club-Bellevue provides a sweeping panoramic view of the Cascade and Olympic mountains, Lake Washington and the Seattle skyline.Designed to meet the business and social requirements of its membership or sponsored clientele, the club includes a variety of elegantly appointed rooms to meet your needs. The Harbor Club-Bellevue continues and expands the tradition of elegance, impeccable service and unsurpassed cuisine that is the hallmark of The Harbor Club.

Harbor Creek Lodge

Located just minutes from Gig Harbor
Call ***The Upper Crust Catering***
(206) 783-1826; Fax (206) 783-1672
Office Hours: Mon–Fri 8:30am–5:30pm
Web site: www.harborcreeklodge.com

Capacity: up to 300 for indoor events; up to 500 outdoors
Price range: please inquire; rates vary depending on day of week and time needed
Catering: in-house caterer—The Upper Crust Catering, creators of extraordinary events
Types of events: banquets, cocktail and hor d'oeuvres, sit-down dinners, holiday parties, day retreats, seminars, reunions, anniversaries, weddings, proms, graduations or any other social event

Availability and terms

Available weekdays, evenings and weekends for a five-hour time block. Additional hours are available. A 55% deposit will reserve your date with the balance due 30-days prior to your event.

Description of services and facility

Parking: ample parking provided
Banquet services

- **Seating:** tables and chairs for all indoor events provided
- **Servers:** courteous professional wait-staff included in catering cost
- **Bar facilities:** host or no-host full-service bar facilities provided by The Upper Crust
- **Dance floor:** the facility features hardwood floors that are ideal for dancing
- **Linens and napkins:** provided by The Upper Crust; specialty linens available
- **China and glassware:** provided by The Upper Crust
- **Cleanup:** please remove anything you bring in, we'll handle the rest
- **Decorations:** please inquire; nothing that will damage the facility

Meeting and event services

- **Audio visual and equipment:** we are happy to accommodate your A/V or equipment needs

HARBOR CREEK LODGE IS A BREATHTAKING ESTATE WHERE PRIVACY AND ELEGANCE IS EVERYTHING!

Harbor Creek Lodge is located just a few short miles from Gig Harbor, this private estate offers a perfect party or event site for 300 inside and 500 outside, beautifully landscaped grounds, and 18 acres of privacy. This Northwest lodge was built in 1979 as a private estate with a romantic charm and elegance all its own. The lodge features vaulted ceilings, beautiful bay windows and large flowing decks with a spectacular view of the grounds.

 Please let this business know that you heard about them from the Bravo! Event Resource Guide.

Seafood Restaurant

1200 Westlake Avenue North
Seattle, Washington 98109
(206) 270-8815

Distinctive Catering

At the Harborside Restaurant.

Capacity: room capacities range from a view space for 150 seated or reception for 200 on the Lake Union level to 100 seated with a view of the Seattle skyline; or a cozy room for 40 seated with a fireplace

Price range: prices vary based on menu selection; menus are priced per person and are subject to 18% service charge and sales tax

Catering: in-house catering only

Types of events: ideal for corporate entertaining, all-day seminars, other social or business occasions, and wedding receptions, rehearsal dinners

Availability and terms

A non-refundable deposit of $200 for daytime functions and $500 for evening functions (with the exception of holiday parties) is required with the catering contract to confirm the date. The balance is due the day of the event. All deposits are deducted from the final bill.

Description of services and facility

ADA: yes

Parking: on-site parking; please inquire regarding validation

Banquet services

- **Seating:** tables and chairs provided
- **Servers:** all service staff included
- **Bar facilities:** full-service hosted or cash bar available; all beverages provided by caterer
- **Dance floor:** please inquire regarding arrangements
- **Linens, napkins, china and glassware:** provided
- **Decorations:** please inquire about our policy
- **Cleanup:** client responsible for own items; all else provided

Special services

In addition to menu consultation and budget planning, our professional staff can assist you with specialty linens, entertainment, floral display, rental upgrades or other full-service planning needs.

- **Additional Catering Venue:** McCormick & Schmick's Catering is the exclusive caterer at the Museum of Flight.
- **Off-premise Catering:** McCormick & Schmick's Catering can provide our distinctive service by catering at the location of your choice.

A TRADITION OF EXCELLENCE

McCormick & Schmick's catered events are executed with the same commitment to quality and distinctive service you have enjoyed in our restaurants for nearly 30 years.

See page 259 under Caterers/Food & Beverage Services.

195 N.E. Gilman Boulevard
Issaquah, Washington 98027
(206) 689-7311

Please call for appointment
E-mail: hedges@schwartzbroscatering.com

Capacity: unique facility ideal for 12 to 110 guests
Price range: prices vary according to event and custom menu selection
Catering: exclusive catering provided by Schwartz Brothers Catering
Types of events: cocktail and hors d-oevre receptions, holiday parties, community events, corporate dinners, birthday parties, weddings, receptions, rehearsal dinners or full-service sit-down dinners for private or professional functions

Availability and terms

Hedges Cellars offers two distinctive rooms to accommodate functions from 12 to 110. Reservations should be made as early as possible to ensure availability

Description of services and facility

ADA: completely accessible
Parking: unlimited complimentary parking
Banquet services

- **Seating:** chairs and tables provided
- **Servers:** professional and friendly service staff
- **Bar facilities:** full-service bar and bartenders provided
- **Dance floor:** floor is ideal for dancing
- **Linens, napkins, china and glassware:** china, glassware, linen tablecloths and napkins provided
- **Decorations:** setting requires little decoration, but we are happy to accommodate any specific requests
- **Cleanup:** provided by Schwartz Brothers Catering

Special services

Experience the commitment to quality and signature service of Schwartz Brothers Catering. We are happy to customize a menu to your specific needs as well as assist you in organizing every detail of your event to reflect your individual style. From food & beverage service to floral design, you work with one person—the right person—who makes it all happen.

EXPERIENCE THE EXCELLENCE!

Tucked away in nearby Issaquah, Hedges Cellars can host a myriad of social events and business meetings in an elegant, unique and peaceful atmosphere. Whether in the intimate Executive Dining Room or inviting Barrel Room, we are the perfect choice to host your next event.

Seattle

Sixth and University
Seattle, Washington 98101
Contact: Kitty Kuhnly (206) 624-0500
Office Hours: Mon–Fri 8:30am–5pm

Capacity: ideal for groups of 10 up to 350 people
Price range: varies according to menu selection
Catering: full-service in-house catering
Types of events: sit-down breakfasts, lunches or dinners; buffets, theme events, cocktail and hors d'oeuvres; meetings, seminars, conferences or any other type of business or social events

Availability and terms

We have the Pacific Ballroom or The Top of the Hilton available for your event in addition to a variety of smaller rooms ideal for meetings, seminars, conferences or as break-out rooms. These rooms can be reserved at any time, based on availability. A deposit is required upon reservation.

Description of services and facility

ADA: fully accessible
Parking: $8 to $15 per vehicle in on-site garage
Banquet services

- **Seating:** all tables and chairs provided and setup to meet your event specifications
- **Servers:** all wait staff and personnel are provided by Hilton
- **Bar facilities:** full-service bar provided; liquor, bartender, and liquor liability provided by Hilton
- **Dance floor:** dance floor accommodates up to 350; electrical outlets available
- **Linens and napkins:** white tablecloths and napkins; assortment of colored linens at additional cost
- **China and glassware:** white china and glassware to suit occasion
- **Decorations:** please inquire; varies on the physical limitations of hotel
- **Cleanup:** provided by Hilton

Meeting and event services

- **Audio visual and equipment:** we're happy to arrange for any of your A/V needs

Special services

The Seattle Hilton offers 237 guest rooms and three suites to accommodate a variety of sized groups. Room amenities include 24-hour room service, irons, ironing boards, hairdryers, coffee makers, mini bars, voice mail for guest rooms, and two phones with data ports in each room.

PANORAMIC VIEW

The Seattle Hilton, towering 29 floors, offers guests a commanding view of Seattle's city lights, the Space Needle, distant mountain ranges, and Puget Sound. Lobby level rooms, accommodating 10 to 350 guests, are available for banquets and events. At the Seattle Hilton, we tailor events to meet your needs.

SEATTLE AIRPORT & CONFERENCE CENTER

17620 Pacific Highway South • Seattle, Washington 98188-4001
Contact: Sales & Catering
(206) 244-4800; Fax (206) 248-4495
Web site: www.seattleairport.hilton.com

Capacity: 38,000 square feet; 26 separate conference rooms and event space; **Emerald Ballroom:** up to 900 banquet style or 1,200 for receptions

Price range: conference meeting packages available; charges vary according to type of event; please call for rates

Catering: services provided by Hilton Seattle Airport and Conference Center

Types of events: conferences, conventions, trade shows, consumer shows, banquets, receptions, meetings, seminars, retreats, or any other type of business or social event

Availability and terms

Terms and conditions vary with each event. A deposit is required at the time of booking an event.

Description of services and facility

ADA: fully accessible to wheelchairs, and meets or exceeds all ADA requirements

Parking: enclosed parking available in conference center

Banquet services

- **Seating:** all tables and chairs provided to meet your event requirements
- **Servers:** friendly, courteous, professional staff included in all packages
- **Bar facilities:** hosted or no-host bars provided by hotel
- **Dance floor:** three available
- **Linens and napkins:** all linens provided; upgrade selection available
- **China and glassware:** fine china, glassware, and serviceware provided
- **Decorations:** you are welcome to add your own personal touch; please inquire
- **Cleanup:** please remove anything you bring in, we'll handle the rest

Meeting and event services

- **Audio visual:** on-site audio visual provider with complete state-of-the-art systems
- **Equipment:** overhead, slide projector, flipchart and whiteboard included in conference meeting packages

Special services

Our newly renovated facility will offer 400 deluxe guest rooms and suites, indoor pool and spa, state-of-the-art fitness center, and all-new restaurant and bar for you and your guests comfort. Our team of professionals is dedicated to providing you with superior service from beginning to end.

STATE-OF-THE-ART FACILITY SECOND TO NONE!

Hilton Seattle Airport & Conference Center is the only facility of its kind in the area. Our $58 million renovation and expansion, due for completion in January 2001, will be one of the most extensive in Hilton history. Accredited by the International Association of Conference Centers, the Hilton will feature 38,000 sq. ft. of conference space, 26 individual conference rooms and the 11,000 sq. ft. Emerald Ballroom.

19621 International Boulevard • Seattle, Washington 98188
(206) 824-3200
Fax (206) 824-0233
E-mail: sales@ehotelconcepts.com

Capacity: up to 90 people
Catering: we provide a list of preferred caterers but always welcome clients choice
Types of events: meetings, seminars, small weddings; especially suited to seminars and training programs that run three days or longer

Availability and terms

We are extremely flexible and can work with last minute arrangements.

Description of services and facility

ADA: fully ADA compliant
Parking: free!
Banquet services
- **Servers:** outside caterer
- **Bar facilities:** client or caterer provides own
- **Dance floor:** available through our outside vendor
- **Linens and napkins:** hotel provides; white, wheat, maroon and green
- **China and glassware:** caterer/client
- **Decorations:** none
- **Cleanup:** caterer and hotel staff work together; fees may apply

Special services

Meet in comfort, stay in luxury, hotel provides full suites with kitchens and kitchenettes.

PEOPLE LEARN MORE WHEN THEY ARE COMFORTABLE

Why cram them into typical hotel rooms for a week when they can have suites? And finally, a hotel that invites you to use the caterer of your choice and gives you rooms, not rules.

THE HOLLYWOOD SCHOOLHOUSE

14810 N.E. 145th Street • Woodinville, Washington 98072
Contact: Lori Reeder or Jennifer Diamond (425) 481-7925
Business Hours: Mon–Fri 9am–5pm; please call for appointment
E-mail: info@hollywoodschoolhouse.com
Web site: www.hollywoodschoolhouse.com

Capacity: **Atrium and Museum:** 2,300 sq. ft., accommodates 8 to 100 guests; **Grand Ballroom:** 4,000 sq. ft., accommodates 30 to 300 guests; **The Showroom:** 3,000 sq. ft., accommodates 15 to 100 guests
Price range: $250 to $450 on weekdays and weeknights; $1,300 to $2,500 on weekends
Catering: provided by The Collectors Cafe; Executive Chef & General Manager Hal Sapadin
Types of events: parties, retreats, business meetings, seminars, retirement parties, and more

Availability and terms

Reservation accepted up to 18 months in advance. Weekday and weekend rentals are priced in 8-hour blocks.

Description of services and facility

ADA: facility complies with all ADA requirements
Parking: ample complimentary parking
Banquet services

- **Seating:** 250 chairs, 18 round tables and 20 six-foot tables are available for your use
- **Servers:** caterer provides
- **Bar facilities:** 1800's mirrored antique bar; banquet permit required; caterer will serve alcohol brought in by hosting party, no-host bar caterers available; alcohol to be purchased through Hollywood Schoolhouse
- **Dance floor:** our hardwood floors are ideal for dancing
- **Linens, napkins, china and glassware:** caterer provides
- **Decorations:** no tape or nails on walls and no tape on floors please
- **Cleanup:** caterer is responsible; cleanup time included in rental time

Meeting and event services

- **Audio visual:** coordinated through Schoolhouse; some rentals may be involved

"THE MOST CHARMING EVENT FACILITY ON THE EASTSIDE"

Built in 1912, the Hollywood Schoolhouse is located in the picturesque Woodinville Valley, nearby the winery and brewery industries and several recreational golf facilities. Lovingly restored to its turn-of-the-century style and charm, the antique ambiance of the Schoolhouse makes the perfect site for your next event. And our relaxed, informal atmosphere and total privacy make meeting productivity extremely successful. No matter what the occasion the Hollywood Schoolhouse is sure to charm your guests.

One Bellwether Way • Bellingham, WA 98225
(360) 392-3100 or (877) 411-1200
Fax (360) 392-3101
Web site: www.hotelbellwether.com

HOTEL BELLWETHER
ON BELLINGHAM BAY

Capacity: up to 350 seated, up to 700 reception; includes our Bayview Terrace on the waterfront and our Bellwether Ballroom with spectacular views of Bellingham Bay
Price range: varies according to group size and menu selection
Catering: full-service in-house catering by Harborside Bistro
Types of events: meetings, retreats, seminars, conferences, receptions, banquets, reunions, ballroom and terrace weddings, holiday parties and more

Availability and terms

We recommend reserving your date as soon as possible. Reservations confirmed one year in advance with deposit.

Description of services and facility

ADA: fully accessible as well as guest rooms
Parking: secured underground parking and public parking
Banquet services
- **Seating:** tables and chairs provided
- **Servers:** professional service staff provided
- **Bar facilities:** full service; host or no host; bartenders
- **Dance floor:** permanent dance floor in ballroom
- **Linens and napkins:** white linens and napkins are provided
- **China and glassware:** all provided
- **Decorations:** please inquire for guidelines
- **Cleanup:** handled by our staff

Meeting and event services
- **Audio visual and equipment:** in-house screen; microphone; rental service is available

Special services

Fleet of two yachts for guest charters. 100% Smoke Free Hotel. Terrace canopy available.

SUBTLE CHARM, CONTEMPORARY COMFORTS

Nestled in a quaint cove on Bellingham Bay, Hotel Bellwether offers the subtle charms of a European Inn along with the contemporary comforts today's guests require. Whether you are planning a corporate brainstorming retreat or a magical waterside wedding, Hotel Bellwether offers unique meeting and event space along with assistance from a talented staff to help you attain your vision of perfection. The unrivaled atmosphere and decadent catering options are sure to please you and your guests.

HYAK LODGE

Washington State Parks
Unique Heritage Facilities

370 Keechelus Boat Launch Road
Snoqualmie Pass, Washington 98068
Reservations (360) 902-8600, Tours (425) 434-5955
Web site: www.parks.wa.gov/hyaklodge
[Click on Rental Places, then on Heritage Places]

Capacity: 34 overnight guest rooms; **Dining Room:** 50; large **Multi-Use Meeting Room on main floor:** 100 theatre-style or 60 with table-and chair-seating; a comfortable **Recreation Room** features a stone fireplace, pool table and large-screen TV
Price range: guest rooms start at $45 per room
Catering: all catering is through a private concessionaire; call (425) 434-5960 for information
Types of events: business meetings, seminars and retreats; family reunions

Availability and terms

Reservations may be made 12 months in advance to rent the entire facility and nine months in advance to rent half the facility. Those wishing to rent the minimum of eight rooms may make reservations three months in advance. For day uses, such as meetings or day-long retreats, reservations may be made one month in advance. Deposits are charged to secure dates.

Description of services and facility

ADA: main floor fully accessible
Parking: limited parking at the Lodge; carpooling is encouraged
Banquet services
- **Seating:** dining room–50; multi-use room–100 theatre-style or 60 at tables
- **Servers:** coordinated through private concessionaire
- **Linens, china and glassware:** coordinated through private concessionaire
- **Cleanup:** please remove personal items

Meeting and event services
- **Audio visual and equipment:** multi-use room is equipped with A/V equipment

Overnight accommodations

Hyak Lodge offers a total of 34 rooms: six rooms with bunk beds and 28 rooms with full bed. Reservation minimums depending on season. Sleeping rooms on main and second floors; spacious segregated bath/shower rooms on each floor.

HAVE YOUR NEXT RETREAT IN A GREAT LOCATION

Hyak Lodge is the perfect location for business retreats, family reunions and vacation groups wishing to enjoy the great variety of recreational opportunities nearby. Hyak is at the top of Snoqualmie Pass just off U.S. Interstate 90, 45 miles east of Seattle. The lodge, with all amenities, is in close proximity to four downhill ski areas and eight Sno-Parks. Welcomed activities in Sno-Parks include cross country skiing, snowmobiling, snow shoeing and dog sledding. During the summer months, there's fishing and boating on nearby Lake Keechelus and hiking, biking, and horseback riding on the John Wayne Pioneer Trail. This trail, part of the rail trails program, is the old Milwaukee Railroad, which runs about 60 miles from North Bend to Thorp. A public swimming beach and day-use picnic area are located at Lake Easton State Park.

900 Bellevue Way N.E. • Bellevue, WA 98004
Contact: Catering Office
(425) 462-1234; Fax (425) 698-4281
E-mail: sales@bellepo.hyatt.com
Web site: www.bellevue.hyatt.com

Capacity: **Grand Ballroom:** 5,850 sq. ft., up to 440 people banquet-style; **Regency Ballroom:** 2,090 sq. ft., up to 140 banquet-style; **Wintergarden:** 4,500 sq. ft., 250 people banquet-style; **Eques Restaurant:** evening events only, 1,856 sq. ft., up to 90 people banquet-style; **Event Rooms:** up to 1,000 sq. ft., up to 60 people banquet-style
Price range: prices vary according to menu selection
Catering: full-service in-house catering; off-premise catering available
Types of events: formal sit-down dinners, cocktails and hors d'oeuvres; banquets; conventions, conferences and business meetings; we are able to accommodate any type of event

Availability and terms

The Hyatt Regency Bellevue has a total of 17,000 square feet of meeting space including two elegant ballrooms, nine smaller function rooms, a 4,500-square-foot atrium, and Eques Restaurant, our new and unique evening venue which can accommodate up to 100 guests. Rooms should be reserved early, but we will make every effort possible to accommodate reservations on short notice.

Description of services and facility

ADA: fully complies with all ADA requirements
Parking: 1,500 underground spaces; 3 hours of complimentary self parking; valet parking available
Banquet services
- **Seating:** tables and chairs provided
- **Servers:** professional service staff provided for all functions
- **Bar facilities:** full-service bar; host/no-host; all beverages provided by hotel
- **Linens:** a variety of linen tablecloths and napkins that match decor
- **China and glassware:** all china and glassware provided
- **Dance floor:** available in ballrooms; ample electrical hookups
- **Decorations:** we're flexible to your requests; rooms available for early decorating
- **Cleanup:** Hyatt Regency Bellevue handles at no extra charge

Meeting and event services
- **Audio visual:** full-service audio visual company in-house

PROVIDING QUALITY FOOD AND SERVICE

At the Hyatt Regency Bellevue, each event is custom designed to fit your needs and budget. Our professional and courteous catering staff will work with you every step of the way to create your ideal event. We're flexible to your special needs and requests and are there to assist you throughout the planning stage as well as during your event.

1933-5th Avenue • Seattle, Washington 98101
(206) 441-6330; Fax (206) 441-7037
E-mail: bulrich@icongrill.net
Web site: www.icongrill.net

Capacity: accommodates up to 22 guests
Price range: varies according to day and time of event and menu selections
Catering: full service in-house catering
Types of events: sit-down luncheons or dinners, cocktail receptions, all day meetings and rehearsal dinners

Availability and terms

Reservations are available year round and should be made as early as possible. Last minute reservations can be accommodated upon availability. Non-refundable deposits are required to reserve dates.

Description of services and facility

ADA: fully accessible
Parking: available at various pay lots near restaurant in addition to off-street parking
Banquet services
- **Seating:** Unique banquet table and chairs for up to 22 guests provided
- **Servers:** professional and courteous staff provided by *icon* Grill
- **Bar facilities:** full bar, exceptional wine list
- **Linens, napkins, china and glassware:** marble table with white linen napkins provided
- **Decorations:** please inquire, nothing that will damage the facility
- **Cleanup:** leave it up to us

Special services

Pre-packaged office meals and party platters to go!

AN OASIS IN CITY DINING

Located in the heart of downtown Seattle with easy access from most major hotels, *icon* Grill boasts a landmark look with contemporary innovation and alluring style. The décor includes traditional elements such as fine marbles, French ribboned linens, dozens of table lamps, and beautiful glass blown chandeliers, creating a relaxed escape from the ordinary. Comforting without being boring, the menu showcases the highest quality ingredients in a sophisticated yet simple manner. Critics say, "In Short: Downtown Seattle restaurants don't get much more visually or culinarily interesting than *icon* Grill."

360-923-1075 ❀ 5900 Troon Lane SE ❀ Olympia, WA 98501 ❀ Fax 360-923-9037

Contact: Catering Sales Manager

Capacity: our boardroom and banquet rooms accommodate groups from 10 to 500
Price range: prices vary according to menu selection and date
Catering: full service in-house catering provided exclusively by our culinary team
Types of events: seminars, holiday parties, auctions, business meetings, rehearsal dinners, weddings, receptions, anniversary parties, reunions, and golf tournaments, informal and formal gatherings, cocktail parties, buffets, theme dinners, hors d'oeuvres, seated dinners and trade shows

Availability and terms

A $1,000 non-refundable deposit will reserve your date. We recommend that you reserve rooms early, but will make every attempt to accommodate reservations on short notice.

Description of services and facility

ADA: fully accessible

Parking: our large, well-lit secured parking area is complimentary

Banquet services

- **Seating:** table and chairs provided
- **Servers:** all menu prices include our friendly, courteous, and professionally trained service staff
- **Bar facilities:** full service bars available; hosted/no host; we provide liquor and public liquor license; professional staff fully trained on all applicable State laws
- **Dance floor:** dance floor and piano available
- **Linens:** white linen tablecloths and napkins included; special colors ordered at additional cost
- **China and serviceware:** white china, stemware, and flatware provided
- **Decorations:** please, do not bring anything that will damage the facility
- **Cleanup:** full cleanup is provided by Indian Summer

Meeting and event services

- **Audio visual:** available at competitive rates: big screen TV, VCR, 22" TV, overhead and slide projectors, dedicated computer lines, 7'x7' screen, flip charts and markers, easels
- **Equipment:** available at competitive rates: risers, podium, and microphones

Special services

With prior arrangements, our professional staff is available to assist our clients in decorating for your special event.

THE SOUTH SOUND'S MOST DRAMATIC VIEW

Elegant wine hues, lush greens, and highlights of yellow come together to form a spectacular natural wetlands area framed by a majestic grove of old oak trees. This peaceful, exquisite backdrop is just one of the many reasons why Indian Summer is the South Sound's premiere facility for special events. Our dramatic scenery, custom menus, and professional staff will make planning your event effortless. Every event is tailored to our client's needs and specifications to ensure that it is everything you imagined!

3211-56th Street N.W.
Gig Harbor, Washington 98335
(253) 858-1111
Fax (253) 851-5402
Web site: www.innatgigharbor.com

Capacity: six attractive meeting and banquet rooms are available for groups from 10 to 250
Price range: varies according to menu selection; no room rental charge with minimum food and beverage purchase
Catering: custom menus can be provided
Types of events: corporate meetings and retreats, conventions, seminars, reunions, wedding and anniversaries, holiday parties—all types of events

Availability and terms

Make reservations up to 2 years in advance. A deposit and signed contract are required.

Description of services and facility

ADA: all areas are fully accessible
Parking: complimentary parking provided
Banquet services

- **Seating:** tables and chairs provided
- **Servers:** highly experienced staff provided
- **Bar facilities:** host or no-host bar available
- **Dance floor:** portable dance floor available
- **Linens and napkins:** white or green available
- **China and glassware:** fine china and glassware provided
- **Decorations:** centerpieces available at no extra charge
- **Cleanup:** provided by the Inn at Gig Harbor staff

Meeting and event services

- **Audio visual:** unlimited A/V services available, including teleconferencing equipment
- **Equipment:** high speed internet access available in ballroom; podiums, microphones, flip charts, screens and easels available

CASUAL ELEGANCE AT AN AFFORDABLE PRICE

64 beautiful guestrooms, including fireplace or Jacuzzi suites, come fully equipped with coffee makers, irons and boards, and two-line phones with dataports. Complimentary continental breakfast included. Massage studio, exercise room, outdoor spa, gift shop, enterprise car rental and hourly airport shuttle. Let our professional sales staff assist you in planning your next event. We offer personalized attention to every aspect of your event.

ISSAQUAH COMMUNITY CENTER

S.E. Bush Street and 1st Avenue South • Issaquah, Washington 98027
Contact: Jean Sillers (425) 837-3321; Fax (425) 837-3319
E-mail: jeans@ci.issaquah.wa.us

Capacity: multipurpose area: 14,400 square feet; up to 1,000 guests; meeting rooms accommodate 30 to 50 guests; floor plan and pictures provided upon request
Price range: varies according to event type; please call for rates and options
Catering: select the off-premise caterer of your choice, or ask us for recommendations
Types of events: corporate dinners and receptions, trade shows, auctions, parties and athletic events

Availability and terms

Available weekends. Specific dates and times upon request. Reservations are accepted up to one year in advance.

Description of services and facility

ADA: complies with all ADA regulations
Parking: ample complimentary parking adjacent to the facility
Banquet services

- **Seating:** round tables and chairs for 400 are available
- **Bar facilities:** client provides bartender, alcoholic beverages and banquet permit
- **Dance floor:** 36'x36' wooden dance floor available
- **Portable stage:** 12'x16' can be placed as needed
- **Linens, china and glassware:** selected and provided by client
- **Decorations:** we are flexible and would be happy to review the client's plan

Meeting and event services

- **Audio visual and equipment:** overhead and slide projectors, in-house sound system
- **Trade shows:** 14,400 square feet of unobstructed space make this an ideal location for trade shows

Special services

Large, covered deck provides views of the Issaquah Alps. Second floor built-in seating provides gallery opportunity for 300 guests to enjoy watching main-floor activities.

NEWLY-CONSTRUCTED, SPACIOUS EASTSIDE FACILITY

The Issaquah Community Center is a new 33,000-square-foot facility on the Eastside that is ideal for events requiring large, unobstructed, open space. Features expansive windows, wooden beams, carpet and tiled lobby. Perfect for catered dinner/dances, conventions and trade shows.

On the water front at Pier 54 • Seattle, Washington 98104
Contact: Nancy Bogue, Banquet Director
(206) 587-6500; Fax (206) 624-4895
Mon–Fri 9am–5pm or by appointment
E-mail: nancy@keepclam.com • ***Web site: www.ivars.net***

Capacity: **Restaurant:** 475; **Spirit of the Bay Room:** 50 (private); **Proclamation Room:** 45 (private); **Upper Terrace:** 110 (semi-private)
Price range: prices vary according to menu
Catering: full-service in-house catering
Types of events: business meetings, corporate entertaining, rehearsal dinners, wedding receptions, sit-down lunches, dinners, cocktail and hors d'oeuvres buffets, and special events

Availability and terms

Reservations accepted up to 18 months in advance. We are able to accommodate guests on short notice if space is available.

Description of services and facility

ADA: yes
Parking: ample street parking adjacent to the restaurant
Banquet services
- **Seating:** tables, chairs, and layout to meet your needs
- **Servers:** servers provided according to your group size
- **Bar facilities:** full-service bar; cocktail service provided
- **Linens and napkins:** linen tablecloths and napkins provided at no charge
- **China and glassware:** provided by Ivar's
- **Decorations:** early decorating with prior arrangements
- **Cleanup:** provided by Ivar's

Meeting and event services
- **Audio visual and equipment:** we're happy to arrange for any of your A/V or equipment needs

Special services

We would be delighted to assist you in coordinating all your event-planning needs. Our goal is to make your event a success and to make you shine!

A NORTHWEST TRADITION SINCE 1938

Ivar's Acres of Clams on Pier 54, a Northwest favorite since 1938, is located in the heart of Seattle's bustling waterfront. Resembling a long ship's galley, accented with deep rich mahogany woods and maritime colors, the restaurant lends a nautical ambiance to a seaside setting. Enhanced with skylights, our Spirit of the Bay room sits at the water's edge with windows which run its entire length, allowing guests to watch the ferry boats and fireboats drift by. Ivar's Acres of Clams is conveniently located next to the State Ferry Terminal and within easy walking distance of all downtown locations.

 Please let this business know that you heard about them from the Bravo! Event Resource Guide.

401 N.E. Northlake Way • Seattle, Washington 98105
Contact: Nancy Bogue, Banquet Director
(206) 587-6500; Fax (206) 624-4895
Mon–Fri 9am–5pm or by appointment
E-mail: nancy@keepclam.com • ***Web site: www.ivars.net***

Capacity: **Restaurant:** 425; **Potlach Room:** 100 (private); **Makah:** 25 (private); **Muckleshoot:** 65 (semi-private); **Lake Union Barge:** 140 (private); **Waterfront Deck:** 65 (private)
Price range: prices vary according to menu
Catering: full-service in-house catering
Types of events: business meetings, corporate entertaining, rehearsal dinners, wedding receptions, sit-down lunches, dinners, cocktail and hors d'oeuvres buffets, and special events

Availability and terms

Reservations accepted up to 18 months in advance. We are able to accommodate guests on short notice if space is available.

Description of services and facility

ADA: yes
Parking: free parking at restaurant and across the street
Boat ramp: docking free of charge
Banquet services

- **Seating:** tables, chairs, and layout to meet your needs
- **Servers:** servers provided according to your group size
- **Bar facilities:** full-service bar; cocktail service provided
- **Linens and napkins:** linen tablecloths and napkins provided at no charge
- **China and glassware:** provided by Ivar's
- **Decorations:** early decorating with prior arrangements
- **Cleanup:** provided by Ivar's

Meeting and event services

- **Audio visual and equipment:** we're happy to arrange for any of your A/V or equipment needs

Special services

We would be delighted to assist you in coordinating all your event-planning needs. Our goal is to make your event a success and to make you shine!

AUTHENTIC LONGHOUSE ON THE SHORE OF LAKE UNION

Ivar's Salmon House, on the north shore of Lake Union, is Seattle's most unique and impressive banquet venue. Expansive windows overlooking Lake Union provide an unsurpassed panoramic view of the Seattle cityscape, where guests may watch yachts, sail boats, and kayaks as they traverse this spectacular setting. Built in 1971, the Salmon House was constructed entirely from local materials to resemble a Northwest Native American Longhouse and is enhanced with historical Native American artifacts. Voted Seattle's "Best Salmon," our seafood is cooked to perfection over an open alderwood fire and served in a warm, welcoming atmosphere.

THE JERRY M. BROCKEY CENTER

at South Seattle Community College

6000-16th Avenue S.W. • Seattle, Washington 98106

Contact: Bob Sullivan (206) 768-6613

Capacity: 40 to 350 for sit-down dinner; 50 to 250 for buffet; 50 to 350 class room and up to 700 theater style

Price range: price varies on types of events and menu selection

Catering: full service in house catering

Types of events: meetings, seminars, workshops, lectures, auctions, receptions and banquets

Availability and terms

The Jerry M. Brockey Center offers three different areas to meet your needs. We recommend reserving your date at least a year out, however we can accommodate events with as little as one week notice. The room rental is due 90 days prior to the event date and is non-refundable. All events are produced in collaboration with the Culinary Arts training programs.

Description of services and facility

ADA: all facilities fully accessible

Parking: complimentary parking

Banquet services

- **Seating:** all tables and chairs provided
- **Servers:** courteous professional staff to meet your needs
- **Bar facilities:** alcohol provided by guest, bartender provided and required
- **Dance floor:** must be rented by guest
- **Linens and napkins:** white tablecloths and napkins provided for all formal events
- **China and glassware:** provided by the facility
- **Decorations:** please inquire about early access and decoration limitations
- **Cleanup:** provided by the facility

Meeting and event services

- **Audio visual and equipment:** built-in stage, sound system and microphone are provided with the room; video projection and teleconferencing arrangements are available with advance notice

Special services

Floral design and pastry programs on campus.

WEST SEATTLE FACILITY NOW AVAILABLE FOR YOUR SPECIAL EVENT

The Brockey Center at South Seattle Community College, offers a modern facility in an attractive suburban campus setting. Organizations and individuals have expressed their high level of satisfaction with the superior level of food, service and planning assistance for their event held at the center. We can provide many special services such as satellite teleconferencing and customized décor at a reasonable price. You are encouraged to visit our facility and discuss with us how we can enhance your event and meet your specific needs.

SEATTLE
731 Westlake Avenue North
Seattle, Washington 98109
Contact: Chris Weaver (206) 223-0300

TACOMA
1114 Broadway Plaza
Tacoma, Washington 98402
Contact: Jeff Weinkauf (253) 572-0300

Capacity: groups from 20 to 1,000 people
Price range: hors d'oeuvres starting at $10 per person; dinner buffets starting at $15 per person
Catering: in-house complete catering. Menu packages and custom menus available
Types of events: monthly meetings, holiday parties, staff-incentive parties, team-building tournaments, seminars, reunions, and receptions

Availability and terms

A deposit and signed reservation agreement are required to secure your date.

Description of services and facility

ADA: complies with all ADA requirements
Banquet services

- **Servers:** service staff based upon event size; standard 18% (10 to 99 people), 20% (100+ people) will be added
- **Bar facilities:** bartender provided (no additional charge); premium well-drinks, beer, wine, champagne, and full range of nonalcoholic
- **Linens and napkins:** cloth tablecloths and napkins in limited colors
- **China and glassware:** white china and stemmed glassware
- **Decorations:** no tacks and tape on wallpaper or mahogany trim; no confetti
- **Cleanup:** cleanup is provided by Jillian's
- **Restrictions:** Jillian's requests proper attire be worn

Special services

Each event is tailored to the specific needs of the host. No "packages" to which the host must conform. House Pro available to run tournaments, give informal group lessons, and help the fun along.

WE ARE MORE THAN JUST A BANQUET FACILITY!

Jillian's creates the perfect setting for parties and get-togethers by providing an active, upscale event atmosphere that encourages interaction and camaraderie. Guests experience total entertainment and enjoyment playing pool, the latest in electronic simulation games, ping pong and darts. Your guests can relax in our exclusive private party room or converse in our bar and Sports Café.

See page 56 under Attractions & Activities.

Kaspar's

KASPAR'S RESTAURANT
19 West Harrison Street
Seattle, Washington 98119
(206) 298-0123; Fax (206) 298-0146
E-mail: catering@kaspars.com
Web site: www.kaspars.com

Capacity: accommodates 10 to 250 seated, up to 300 standing
Price range: varies according to menu; no rental fees apply when food and beverage minimum is met
Catering: in-house, full-service catering
Types of events: ideal for business meetings, company events, socials, holiday parties, receptions, and other special occasions

Availability and terms

Kaspar's is available any day of the week, whether you wish to reserve the entire restaurant or one of several flexible rooms. No rental fees apply when a food and beverage minimum is met.

Description of services and facility

ADA: all facilities are fully accessible
Parking: self-parking available at no charge; valet parking can be arranged
Banquet services
- **Seating:** tables and chairs provided by Kaspar's
- **Servers:** attentive and professional staff provided
- **Bar facilities:** full bar available
- **Dance floor:** available in the fireside room
- **Linens and napkins:** provided by Kaspar's at no additional charge
- **China and glassware:** all serviceware provided by Kaspar's
- **Decorations:** little decoration required, but anything can be arranged
- **Cleanup:** included at no additional charge

Meeting and event services
- **Audio visual and equipment:** Kaspar's will assist with any necessary rentals

Special services

Kaspar's will cater off-premise events, both indoors and out. We provide all set-up and clean-up, and will gladly comply with the regulations of your chosen facility.

CONSISTENTLY MEMORABLE NORTHWEST CUISINE

Kaspar's is consistently rated among Seattle's top restaurants by Zagat, the James Beard Foundation, and many national publications. Your guests will appreciate our celebrated creativity, culinary skill, and dedication to their dining experience. We invite you to enjoy our award-winning cuisine and impeccable service at your next special event.

THE BANQUET HALL
at The Weyerhaeuser King County Aquatic Center

650 S.W. Campus Drive • Federal Way, Washington
(206) 296-4444 or (800) 325-6165, ext. 64444

Capacity: 400 theater-style; 300 banquet style
Price range: varies according to day and time of event; please call for current price list
Catering: select the off-premise caterer of your choice; kitchen available
Type of events: ideal for corporate meetings, seminars, reunions and other special gatherings

Availability and terms

Reservations are accepted up to 11 months in advance. Please call for availability and deposit requirements.

Description of services and facility

ADA: fully complies with ADA requirements
Amenities: fully carpeted and air conditioned
Parking: paved parking available for up to 200 cars, adjacent lot for 168 cars
Banquet services

- **Seating:** tables and chairs for 320
- **Servers:** caterer to provide
- **Bar facilities:** alcoholic beverages allowed on premises, must have banquet permit
- **Linens, china and glassware:** caterer to provide
- **Decorations:** few limitations; decorating time included in time of rental
- **Cleanup:** must remove anything you bring in; we will handle the rest, caterer to leave kitchen as they found it

Meeting and event services

- **Audio visual and equipment:** overhead projector, screen, TV/VCR's, podium and PA system

SOUTH KING COUNTY'S BEST KEPT SECRET

The Banquet Hall is adjacent to the King County Aquatic Center. It is a beautiful structure with an outdoor patio suitable for wedding ceremonies, barbecues or additional seating for your event. Our skylighted lobby offers a dramatic setting for artwork displays, silent auctions, and vendor booths or as a prefunction area. Our grand hall can be used as one large room or divided into two smaller rooms. All rooms have easy access to the caterers' kitchen. Our location in South Federal Way is ideal for day retreats, receptions, conferences and corporate meetings.

KING OSCAR MOTEL & CONVENTION CENTER

8820 South Hosmer
Tacoma, Washington 98444
(253) 539-1153
Fax (253) 536-3116
Office Hours: Mon–Fri 8:30am–5pm
E-mail: sales@koscar.net
Web site: www.koscar.net

Capacity: accommodates events from 10 to 700 guests
Price range: $175–$800
Catering: client selects caterer; a list of preferred caterers is available; client may provide own food
Types of events: corporate meetings, seminars, conferences, receptions, retreats, weddings, fund raisers, banquets, training sessions, and other special events

Availability and terms

A deposit and confirmed number of guests must be submitted at least three business days prior to the event. We require at least 24 hours' notice for cancellation.

Description of services and facility

ADA: fully accessible; all banquet space and restrooms on first floor
Parking: available for at least 260 cars
Banquet services
- **Seating:** round and rectangular tables, chairs are provided to accommodate 300 guests theatre-style, or 450 for a reception
- **Servers:** provided by catering company
- **Bar facilities:** caterer or client provides; client responsible for all permits
- **Dance floor:** none provided, but rental can be arranged
- **Linens and napkins:** white linens included; client may provide others
- **China and glassware:** provided by caterer or client
- **Cleanup:** caterer or client responsible; King Oscar will provide for a fee
- **Decorations:** no restrictions, but please inquire

Meeting and event services
- **Audio visual and equipment:** microphone, podium, screen, and projector available in-house; other rentals can be arranged

Special services

Professional meeting and event planners are on staff to make preparing for your event as stress-free as possible.

DYNAMIC NEW FACILITY FOR MEETINGS AND EVENTS

With convenient access to I-5, the King Oscar Convention Center offers 5,000 sq. ft. of new space for meetings, receptions, and other special events. We can accommodate a large number of overnight guests in our 221 comfortable rooms and 12 elegant suites; an indoor pool and a Jacuzzi are also available. Our professional, friendly staff looks forward to making your next event a success.

Seattle at Harbor Steps
Bellevue at Park 140

Sales Office: 2445-140th Ave. N.E. • Ste. B-100 (at Park 140) • Bellevue, WA 98005-1879
Contacts: Janet Harbold or Tom Edgar
(206) 654-6040, (425) 562-1292 or Toll Free (877) KINGSTAD • Hours: 8am–5pm

---

Capacity: seven meeting rooms at Bellevue/Park 140 site with a total of 11,000 sq. ft. and six meeting rooms at Seattle/Harbor Steps site with a total of 8,000 sq. ft.
Price range: varies by event size and menu selection; complete meeting packages available
Catering: full-service catering
Types of events: meetings, seminars, retreats, small conferences, luncheons and dinners

Availability and terms
Kingstad Meeting Centers in Seattle and Bellevue offer professionally appointed meeting rooms for up to 50 people. A 25% non-refundable deposit secures your date. Payment in full is due the day of your event. For your convenience, please inquire about direct-billing applications.

Description of services and facility
ADA: fully accessible
Parking: free on-site parking in Bellevue at Park 140; paid parking in Seattle at Harbor Steps
Banquet services
- **Seating:** tables and chairs provided with various seating arrangements offered
- **Servers:** accommodating, uniformed service staff provided
- **Bar facilities:** alcoholic beverages allowed
- **Dance floor:** available on request
- **Linens:** tablecloths and napkins with accent colors available at no extra charge
- **China and glassware:** ivory-colored china and assorted glassware
- **Cleanup:** professional service staff provide cleanup services at no extra charge
- **Decorations:** silk flower arrangements provided

Meeting and event services
- **Audio visual and equipment:** unlimited services available, including webconferencing, videoconferencing, video projectors and high speed data access

Special services
All Kingstad Meeting Centers have on-site business centers. Services include complimentary courtesy phones, data ports for Internet access, copying, faxing and other concierge services.

THE CONTEMPORARY WAY TO MEET
Kingstad Meeting Centers offer full-service, premiere meeting facilities to corporate businesses, providing a simple yet comprehensive pricing structure and booking process; state-of-the-art equipment; clean and well lighted meeting spaces; friendly and professional staff and superb food and beverage products. We will help make your meetings as productive as possible.

KNIGHTS OF COLUMBUS

722 East Union Street • Seattle, Washington 98122
(206) 325-3410

Capacity: Colonial Ballroom accommodates up to 250 banquet guests
Price range: please inquire, varies with season and use
Catering: licensed caterer; client's choice; referrals available
Types of events: weddings, parties, fundraisers, meetings, classes, exhibits

Availability and terms

Reservations accepted up to one year in advance. Room deposit due at signing of contract. Rental balance due seven days prior to event.

Description of services and facility

ADA: fully accessible, meets all ADA requirements
Parking: conveniently located adjacent to either side of the building
Banquet services

- **Seating:** tables and chairs provided for seating up to 250 guests; various layouts possible
- **Servers:** provided through caterer or client
- **Bar facilities:** mobile bar unit available; banquet permit required
- **Dance floor:** 3,000 sq. ft. maple wood floor; any portion available for dancing; carpeted platform with microphone outlet and podium at front of hall
- **Linens, napkins, china and glassware:** available through caterer or various rental companies; referrals available
- **Decorations:** nothing to be attached to walls or ceilings; no confetti, grains or similar materials permitted in the facility
- **Cleanup:** facility to be returned to its original condition prior to client's activity

Special services

The parking facilities adjacent to the building may be purchased for your event. Please inquire.

FIRST HILL GEM

An elegantly remodeled 3,000 square foot private facility for your special event. Kitchen is fully appointed for catered events including guest tables and chairs. A mobile bar is available at no additional cost. This smoke-free environment is wheelchair accessible including elevator with parking adjacent to the building and is conveniently located to major downtown hotels. Furnished lobby accommodates smaller functions of up to 40 guests.

Lake Union Café

3119 Eastlake Avenue East • Seattle, Washington 98102
Contact: Victoria Haberman (206) 568-1258
Office Hours: Mon–Fri 10am–6pm, or by appointment
Web site: www.lakeunioncafe.com

Capacity: Lake Union Café accommodates up to 350 guests
Catering: full-service, in-house catering provided
Price range: varies according to menu selection and number of guests
Types of events: dinners, receptions, meetings and seminars, weddings, anniversaries, parties, retreats, Bar and Bat Mitzvahs, and other social and corporate events

Availability and terms

A minimum $1,000 deposit is requested. Typically the Café is reserved for four hours, with an additional hour included for set-up.

Description of services and facility

ADA: fully accessible
Parking: secure private lot, with additional on-street parking
Banquet services
- **Seating:** tables and chairs are provided for 275
- **Servers:** professionally, friendly service staff provided
- **Bar facilities:** complete bar facilities and service available upon your request
- **Dance floor:** large dance floor available
- **Linens and napkins:** Lake Union Café provides cream and black linens and napkins
- **China and glassware:** house china, silverware, and glasses provided
- **Cleanup:** we take care of all cleanup and setup
- **Decorations:** oil table lamps available upon request; no rice or confetti, please

Meeting and event services
- **Audio visual and equipment:** microphone, grand piano, and sound system available

Special services

Our special event director and chef will gladly help you plan your event.

PACIFIC RIM DINING IN ART DECO ELEGANCE

Seattle's most famous pedestal clock again welcomes guests to the newly refurbished Lake Union Café, now open exclusively for private parties and special events. The Café offers fine Northwest and Pacific Rim dining in an elaborate Art Deco atmosphere. The Café's interior features handcrafted copper ceilings, mahogany revolving doors, an antique cane pulley fan system, and a large, sky-lit dance floor. We invite you to enjoy our Atrium's beautiful view of the sun setting over Lake Union, or to relax at the elegant marble bar with your favorite beverage. Private tours are available by appointment.

Lake Union Crew

Where Teamwork is Everything

11 East Allison Street • Seattle, Washington 98102
Contact: Rome Ventura (206) 860-4199; Fax (206) 860-7826
Open: Mon–Fri 9am–8:30pm; Sat–Sun by appointment
E-mail: raventura@aol.com • ***Web site: www.lakeunioncrew.com***

Capacity: upper level "Great Room" with fireplace seats 140 banquet style; approx. 1,900 sq. ft. plus balcony; lecture/video format seats 60; conference room seats 12; seminar seating for 48
Price range: $500–$1,000 dockside, or $3,000 underway
Catering: we offer a preferred list
Types of events: banquets, receptions, meetings, seminars, lectures, parties, company off-site meetings, team building adventures, which include learning to row an eight-oared shell!

Availability and terms

Reservations made up to one year in advance and short term if available. 50% deposit confirms reservation, balance due 30 days before event.

Description of services and facility

ADA: no; staff can assist if needed
Parking: on-site and nearby location
Banquet services
- **Seating:** ten 6' tables, 140 padded chairs; round tables by rental
- **Servers, linens and china:** provided by caterer
- **Dance floor:** by rental from party supplier
- **Decorations:** removable tape; open to anything that will not damage surfaces
- **Cleanup:** provided by caterer, $75 restock and cleaning fee; $200 refundable damage deposit

Meeting and event services
- **Audio visual:** excellent audio system; DJs love it—or shuffle your own CDs; VCR with 32" screen
- **Equipment:** microphone with stand, easels, white boards

Special services

We strive to make your event an experience your guests will remember for years to come! Welcome them to one of Seattle's most spectacular water venues.

ONE OF SEATTLE'S FINEST

Moored on Lake Union, this venue provides an interesting backdrop to any special event. Surrounded by watercraft of all kinds and Seattle's spectacular skyline, your guests will be delighted and entertained all day long. Excellent for off-site meetings too. See detailed description of our rowing adventure in the Team Building section of this publication. Call or e-mail anytime for a tour.

 Please let this business know that you heard about them from the Bravo! Event Resource Guide.

Lake Washington Rowing Club

Represented by Marcia Evans, Northwest Events & Parties

910 North Northlake Way • Seattle, Washington 98103
(206) 524-4918
Web site: www.lakewashingtonrowing.com

Capacity: Banquet Room: up to 150 guests; **Boardroom:** up to 14 seated guests
Price range: weekdays range from $100-$500; weekends begin at $900
Catering: please call for information
Types of events: an ideal location for corporate meetings, seminars, weddings and receptions, rehearsal dinners, reunions, anniversaries, banquets and other special events

Availability and terms

Reservations for weekend events should be made two to six months in advance, however, for weekend events during the summer and holiday season reservations should be made as early as possible to ensure availability. A $200 damage deposit and one half of the rental fee reserves your date with the balance due four weeks prior to your event.

Description of services and facility

ADA: Lake Washington Rowing Club is fully accessible
Parking: ample parking adjacent to facility for evening functions; parking lot available one block away for daytime functions; please inquire about valet services
Banquet services

- **Seating:** chairs and a selection of table sizes included in rental fee
- **Servers:** provided by caterer
- **Bar facilities:** renter or caterer provides all liquor and banquet permits
- **Dance floor:** included in facility rental
- **Linens, napkins, china and glassware:** provided by caterer or renter
- **Decorations:** please inquire; no tacks, tape, staples or anything that will damage the facility
- **Cleanup:** please remove all food, serviceware and decorations

CLASSIC ELEGANCE ON LAKE UNION'S NORTH SHORE

Lake Washington Rowing Club is located at the North end of Lake Union, just 10 minutes from downtown Seattle. Completed in October 1995, this stylish boathouse has both traditional and contemporary features. Rowing shells rest in bays on the ground floor, awaiting the next dawn's rowing practice. The second floor features comfortable, well-proportioned event spaces with unequaled views of Lake Union, Downtown Seattle, and majestic Mount Rainier. Reflecting the Club's dedication to the classic sport of rowing, these handsome surroundings offer a unique and elegant locale for your celebration.

22500 S.E. 248th Street • Maple Valley, WA
(206) 296-4298 or (800) 325-6165, x 4298
Office Hours: Mon–Fri 10am–4pm

Capacity: **Reception Areas:** 6,456 sq. ft.; up to 250 people
Price range: varies according to day and time of event; please call for current price list
Catering: select the off-premise caterer of your choice; kitchen available
Types of events: with both indoor and outdoor facilities, Lake Wilderness Center is ideal for corporate meetings, seminars, concerts, reunions, or any other special occasion or business event

Availability and terms

Reservations are accepted up to one year in advance with a security/damage deposit. Deposits are nonrefundable if the event is canceled. Liability insurance is required and is available through King County. Rental hours include the time needed for decorating, setup and cleanup.

Description of services and facility

ADA: fully complies with ADA requirements
Parking: paved parking available for 76 cars; additional overflow parking adjacent to building
Banquet services
- **Seating:** tables and chairs for 250
- **Servers:** caterer to provide
- **Bar facilities:** alcoholic beverages allowed on premises upon special request
- **Linens, china and glassware:** caterer to provide
- **Decorations:** please inquire about specific ideas; no staples, tacks, or nails; use of tape must be approved
- **Cleanup:** client's responsibility

Meeting and event services
- **Audio visual:** overhead projector and screen and TV/VCR
- **Equipment:** portable PA, blackboard, dry erase board and podium

PANORAMIC VIEW

Lake Wilderness Center is located on the panoramic shores of Lake Wilderness in Maple Valley with a breathtaking view of Mount Rainier. The center's original character has been preserved, including the magnificent 33-foot Native American totem pole carved by noted artist Dudley Carter. This tranquil setting is ideal for day retreats, conferences, corporate meetings, and inspirational activities; only 30 minutes from SeaTac International Airport.

25400 Witte Road S.E.
Maple Valley, Washington 98038
Contact: Kim Northam
Office (425) 432-8038
Office Hours: Mon–Fri 11am–9pm:
Evenings and weekends by appointment

Capacity: 1,450 sq. ft.: up to 225 seated indoors; up to 400 with outdoor patios
Price range: varies according to size of group, menu selection
Catering: full service in-house catering
Types of events: receptions, banquets, meetings, seminars, anniversaries, parties, golf tournaments and more

Availability and terms

Reservations should be made up to one year in advance, especially for summer months and the holiday season. We are happy to accommodate shorter notice depending on space availability. A $750 deposit will reserve your date.

Description of services and facility

ADA: fully complies with all ADA requirements
Parking: complimentary parking
Banquet services

- **Seating:** tables and chairs for up to 200 people
- **Servers:** service staff included in catering cost: 18% service charge
- **Bar facilities:** host or no host bar; compliance with all local and state liquor laws
- **Dance floor:** available in banquet room; ample electrical hookups
- **Linens and napkins:** color linens available for an additional charge
- **Cleanup:** provided by Lake Wilderness
- **Decorations:** please inquire about specific ideas

Meeting and event services

- **Audio visual and equipment:** we are happy to arrange for anything you need

Special services

The staff at Lake Wilderness will be happy to assist you with your event planning to make sure your day is a special one.

RELAX AND ENJOY YOUR DAY

Enjoy our newly remodeled banquet facility and beautifully landscaped patio area overlooking the golf course and lush surroundings of scenic Maple Valley. Our courteous and professional staff looks forward to helping with all of our clients needs.

LAKEWOLD GARDENS

LAKEWOLD GARDENS

(Nonprofit public estate garden)

12317 Gravelly Lake Drive S.W. • Lakewood, Washington 98499
Contact: Event Coordinator (253) 584-4106; Fax (253) 584-3021
Business Hours: Mon–Fri 8:30am–4:30pm
Web site: www.lakewold.org

Capacity: estate with gardens up to 500+ during spring and summer months; banquet rooms accommodate up to 150; several meeting rooms of various sizes for up to 75

Price range: varies according to room selection, time of day/year, and length of rental; damage/cleaning deposit required

Catering: we offer an approved caterers list to select from

Types of events: meetings, seminars, retreats, training sessions, fund raisers, recitals, receptions, banquets, anniversaries, reunions, and other special occasions

Availability and terms

Lakewold Gardens accepts reservations up to 18 months in advance. A 50% nonrefundable deposit will reserve your date.

Description of services and facility

ADA: handicap accessible; ramps and restrooms

Parking: parking for up to 100 people; valet parking required if over 100

Banquet services

- **Seating:** caterer provides
- **Servers:** caterer provides
- **Bar facilities:** client provides all alcoholic beverages; caterer provides staff; Washington State banquet permit required
- **Dance floor:** accommodates from 40 to 50 guests; ample electrical hookups
- **Linens, china and serviceware:** caterer provides
- **Decorations:** please inquire; nothing that will damage the facility or grounds
- **Cleanup:** must return to original condition; custodial fee for additional cleanup

Meeting and event services

- **Audio visual and equipment:** available on advance notice at an additional charge

ENJOY ONE OF AMERICA'S PREMIER ESTATE GARDENS

This beautiful Georgian style house is located on the shores of Gravelly Lake, just 10 miles south of Tacoma. Surrounded by 10-acres of gardens, this is the ideal location for quiet meetings for 35 or large gatherings up to 500. The beautiful brick walk along the parterre gardens with reflecting pool and gazebo provide a remarkable visual experience. The wisteria covered verandah and spacious glass sunroom overlooking Gravelly Lake are ideal for receptions, recitals and parties. Step back into an age of elegance, beauty and grace at Lakewold Gardens.

LORD HILL FARMS

Snohomish, Washington 98290
(360) 568-1780
Shown by appointment only
Web site: www.lordhillevents.com

Capacity: up to 800 indoors; up to 5,000 outdoors
Price range: varies according to the type of event; please call for a brochure and price list
Catering: full-service catering from our Carnation Restaurant, using the best quality meats, vegetables, fruits, and salads; use of our in-house catering service is preferred
Types of events: indoor and outdoor facilities for corporate picnics, Christmas and Holiday parties, seminars, board meetings, weddings, receptions, and much more

Availability and terms

All bookings are encouraged as early as possible. Lord Hill Farms features a two-story facility that can easily accommodate a wedding and reception or party. Our ceremony room will accommodate 50 to 450 guests. The reception area will accommodate up to 500 guests. Our outdoor grounds will easily accommodate any conceivable number of guests. A non-refundable deposit is required to hold your date.

Description of services and facility

Parking: ample complimentary parking available; parking managed by Lord Hill staff
Banquet services

- **Seating:** ample round and banquet tables, chairs, and pews; setup handled by Lord Hill staff
- **Servers:** included with catering charges
- **Bar facilities:** beer, wine and champagne service by previous arrangement
- **Dance floor:** located in reception area with raised stage
- **Linens, china and glassware:** linens available on rental basis or through caterer
- **Cleanup:** price varies depending on type of event and cleanup required
- **Decorations:** indoor facility is well decorated; outdoor grounds feature beautiful flowers and landscaping; further decorations available; please inquire

Meeting and event services

- **Equipment and staging:** sound system and stage provided in banquet facility upper floor; stage and large dance floor located downstairs; small commercial kitchen downstairs; portable stage available to rent for outdoor events; all picnic sites include recreational facilities

Special services

Our staff is experienced in picnic, party and wedding planning. We're your one-stop event resource! We handle all corporate functions for Lord Hill Farms as well as Remlinger Farms.

FOR ALL OF YOUR SPECIAL EVENT NEEDS

Lord Hill Farms offers a breathtaking view of the Cascade Mountains and the Snohomish Valley. We're located on a 450-acre farm, just 35-miles northeast of the Seattle-Bellevue metropolitan area. We offer both indoor and outdoor facilities to accommodate all of your event needs. Our Remlinger Farms location offers several picnic sites as well. Our facilities take you and your guests away from the bustle and stress of modern city life and spoil you in rustic elegance that will capture your hearts and create memories that will last for a lifetime.

1111 Fairview Ave. North • Seattle, WA 98109
Contact: Event Coordinator
Seattle (206) 264-0400
Eastside (425) 486-4072
Fax (206) 264-9445
Office Hours: Mon–Fri 9am–5pm
E-mail: lowell-hunt@email.msn.com
Web site: www.Lowell-Hunt.com

Capacity: dining room accommodates up to 130; water-view deck accommodates up to 240
Price range: room rental $350–$1,400, depending on day and time
Catering: in-house catering only; full-service off-premise catering also available
Types of events: seated or buffet meals, cocktail receptions, weddings, holiday parties, company meetings, special events

Availability and terms

A refundable security/damage deposit and a nonrefundable rental deposit reserve your date and are applied to your total event fee. We require half of your total estimated cost thirty days prior to your event.

Description of services and facility

ADA: fully accessible
Parking: valet parking can be reserved in the adjacent pay lot by prior arrangement
Banquet services

- **Seating:** tables and chairs for 130 guests are included in the rental price
- **Servers:** professional service staff and bartenders are available
- **Bar facilities:** all beverage service will be handled by the caterer in accordance with current WSLCB policies
- **Dance floor:** can be arranged
- **Linens and napkins:** can be arranged
- **China and glassware:** included in the rental cost
- **Cleanup:** full cleanup provided by the Lowell-Hunt staff
- **Decorations:** please inquire about our guidelines—nothing that will damage the facility

Meeting and event services

- **Audio visual and equipment:** can be arranged according to your needs

Special services

Florals and table decorations are available. Cakes and desserts created by our in-house pastry chef. We will happily assist you with any additional arrangements for your special event.

EXQUISITE CUISINE ON THE WATERFRONT

With a commanding view of Lake Union's beautiful waterfront, Lowell-Hunt continues to be Pacific Northwest's premier catering service. Serving exquisite cuisine to the region's most prominent organizations, we pride ourselves on our celebrated attention to detail.

4050 Maple Valley Highway
Renton, Washington 98058
Contact: Catering (425) 235-5044
Office Hours: Mon–Fri 9am–5pm;
Saturdays by appointment

Capacity: 4,000 sq. ft. of banquet space; 10 to 270 seated; 325 reception style
Price range: varies according to size of party and menu selections
Catering: full-service, in-house catering provided
Types of events: sit-down breakfasts, lunches, or dinners; buffets, cocktails and hors d'oeuvres, barbecues; special events, golf tournaments

Availability and terms

Overlooking the fountain of the 9th hole at the Maplewood Golf Course is 4,000 square feet of banquet space. The facility is set up so it can accommodate one large room that holds up to 270 guests sit-down or 325 reception style. The space can also be arranged into four individual rooms that hold up to 70 guests each for sit-down functions or 80 guests for receptions. A deposit is required to reserve your date and is applied to the final bill.

Description of services and facility

ADA: newly renovated building is fully accessible
Parking: ample complimentary parking provided
Banquet services
- **Seating:** tables and chairs for up to 325 provided
- **Servers:** professional service staff is included in catering costs
- **Bar facilities:** bar, bartender, and beverages provided; host/no-host
- **Dance floor:** accommodates up to 100; ample electrical hook-ups provided
- **Linens and napkins:** linens, tablecloths and napkins provided
- **China and glassware:** white china; wine and glassware provided
- **Decorations:** please inquire about early access and decoration limitations
- **Cleanup:** please remove anything you bring in; we'll handle the rest

Meeting and event services
- **Audio visual:** all A/V equipment to meet your needs is available
- **Equipment:** podium, risers, staging, and more are available

Special services

In addition to custom menus, we offer personalized attention to every aspect of your event. Our sales staff will happily arrange for company golf tournaments.

OVERLOOKING THE FOUNTAIN OF THE 9TH HOLE AT MAPLEWOOD GOLF COURSE

Maplewood Greens is the perfect spot for banquets, meetings, company golf parties, or any other special event. All of the rooms open to a beautifully landscaped outdoor patio. The professional staff at Maplewood Greens can arrange a truly memorable day of golf for your group, and we'll be happy to assist you in planning your event from start to finish.

Marina Club at Shilshole Bay

Special Events Catering
7001 Seaview Avenue N.W.
Seattle, Washington 98117
(206) 706-0257
Business Hours:
Call for an appointment
Web site: www.special-events.net

Capacity: up to 400 seated or 450 reception style
Price range: rental of the Club for a five-hour period is $1,500 for Saturdays, $1,200 for any other time; please inquire for December rates
Catering: exclusive, full-service catering provided by Special Events Catering
Types of events: meetings, receptions, hors d'oeuvre buffets, sit-down dinners, appreciation brunches, dinner buffets, high school reunions, senior proms, and fund raising auctions

Availability and terms

The Marina Club at Shilshole Bay may be reserved up to two years in advance. Reception times available on Saturdays are 12pm to 5pm or 7pm to 12am. Reservations should be made as early as possible to ensure availability. Dates are often available on short term notice. A non-refundable deposit is required to reserve your date.

Description of services and facility

ADA: complies with ADA requirements
Parking: complimentary parking available
Banquet services
- **Seating:** tables and chairs provided by Special Events Catering
- **Servers:** professional service staff and on-site event management provided by Special Events Catering
- **Bar facilities:** full-service bar provided by Special Events Catering
- **Dance floor:** 21'x21' portable dance floor provided by Special Events Catering
- **Linens, china and serviceware:** provided by Special Events Catering
- **Decorations:** provided by client
- **Cleanup:** provided by Special Events Catering

Meeting and event services
- **Audio visual and equipment:** equipment can be arranged directly by client or Special Events Catering can assist with arrangements

Special services

Our experienced catering staff is available to assist you in planning your event at our facility or venue of your choice.

THE MARINA CLUB AT SHILSHOLE BAY

Located at Seattle's scenic Shilshole Bay Marina, this unique waterfront facility offers unsurpassed views of the Marina, Puget Sound and the Olympic Mountains. Your guests can enjoy gorgeous evening sunsets and delight in the perpetual boating activity. In addition, the facility offers complimentary parking and can arrange for a marina moorage.

THE MARINE VIEW BANQUET CENTER

(formerly Everett Yacht Club)

Special Events Catering

404-14th Street (14th Street Dock)
Everett, Washington 98201
(425) 258-1604
Business Hours: Call for an appointment
Web site: www.special-events.net

Capacity: **Olympic Room:** 4,700 sq. ft., accommodates up to 350 people; **Port Gardner Room:** 3,600 sq. ft., accommodates up to 250 people; **Northwest Room:** 1,740 sq. ft., accommodates up to 100 people

Price range: Olympic/Port Gardner from $1,000 to $1,200; Northwest from $450 to $750; entire facility from $2,200 to $3,500; December rates will apply

Catering: exclusive, full-service catering provided by Special Events Catering

Types of events: meetings, seminars, retreats, auctions, reunions; banquets, rehearsal dinners, weddings, receptions and proms

Availability and terms

The Marine View Banquet Center offers four rooms to accommodate your needs. Reception times available on Saturdays are 12pm to 5pm or 7pm to 12am. Reservations should be made as early as possible to ensure availability. Dates are often available on short-term notice. A non-refundable deposit is required to reserve your date.

Description of services and facility

ADA: complies with ADA requirements

Parking: we offer ample complimentary parking

Banquet services

- **Seating:** tables and chairs provided by Special Events Catering
- **Servers:** professional service staff and on-site event management provided by Special Events Catering
- **Bar facilities:** full-service bar provided by Special Events Catering
- **Dance floor:** portable dance floor provided by Special Events Catering
- **Linens, china and serviceware:** provided by Special Events Catering
- **Cleanup:** provided by Special Events Catering
- **Decorations:** provided by client

Meeting and event services

- **Audio visual and equipment:** we are happy to coordinate any of your A/V and equipment needs with advance notice and for an additional charge

Special services

Our experienced catering staff is available to assist you in planning your event at our facility or venue of your choice.

STUNNING BAYSIDE SETTING

This stunning bayside setting with its panoramic views of the marina, Olympic Mountains, and island-studded Port Gardner Bay is ideal for your wedding, meeting, or banquet. The Marine View Banquet Center is the only waterfront public-use facility in the City of Everett.

405 Olive Way • Seattle, Washington 98101
(206) 382-6991 • Hours: Mon–Fri 9am–5pm
E-mail: afoster@mayflowerpark.com
Web site: www.mayflowerpark.com

Capacity: six attractive meeting and banquet rooms including the Fireside Room with its fireplace and intimate setting are available for groups from 10 to 200

Price range: prices will vary according to menu selection and space requirements

Catering: full-service in-house catering

Types of events: meetings, conventions, cocktails and hors d'oeuvres, buffets, breakfasts, luncheons, formal sit-down dinners, rehearsal dinners and weddings

Availability and terms

We recommend as much advance notice as possible, but reservations can be made on short notice if space is available. A deposit is required to reserve your date.

Description of services and facility

ADA: fully accessible

Parking: valet parking available; please inquire for prices

Banquet services

- **Seating:** ample tables and chairs provided to meet your needs
- **Servers:** professional staff included in catering costs
- **Bar facilities:** full service; host or no-host; bartenders, liquor, and liquor liability provided by Mayflower Park
- **Dance floor:** available for rent on request
- **Linens and napkins:** linen tablecloths and napkins provided: specialty colors available on request for an additional charge
- **China and glassware:** white china with gold rim; assorted stemware provided
- **Decorations:** please inquire; nothing that will damage the facility
- **Cleanup:** provided by the Mayflower Park staff at no additional charge

Meeting and event services

- **Audio visual:** in-house A/V company that can accommodate any of your needs
- **Equipment:** podiums and screens provided

Special services

Our friendly and professional staff is trained to meet your every need. Flowers and votive candles are provided for all functions with food service. The Mayflower Park Hotel also offers 171 beautifully appointed guest rooms and suites.

INDIVIDUAL ATTENTION AND OLD WORLD CHARM

Built in 1927, this historic building has been beautifully restored. Crystal chandeliers, lofty ceilings, antiques, stained glass windows, and fresh flowers contribute to the feeling of old world charm. The Mayflower Park Hotel is the perfect place for smaller groups where personalized care and attention are required.

THE INN - APARTMENTS℠

THE MEDITERRANEAN INN

425 Queen Anne Avenue North • Seattle, Washington 98109
(206) 428-4700 or Toll-free (866) 425-4700
Fax (206) 428-4699
E-mail: innaptsglenn@hotmail.com

Capacity: **Boardroom** seats 12 boardroom style; **Meeting Room** accommodates 16 classroom and 20 for a reception
Price range: please call for rates
Catering: use the caterer of your choice
Types of events: business meetings, seminars, receptions, luncheons, dinners, and receptions

Availability and terms

Please call for availability and deposit requirements

Description of services and facility

ADA: facility is fully accessible
Parking: hotel parking available; charges vary
Banquet services

- **Seating:** table and chairs provided at no additional charge
- **Servers:** to be provided by the caterer of your choice
- **Bar facilities:** no bar, banquet permit required if alcoholic beverages are to be sold
- **Linens and napkins:** to be provided by caterer
- **China and glassware:** to be provided by caterer
- **Decorations:** please inquire, nothing that will damage the facility
- **Cleanup:** caterer and renter to remove all event related items, our staff will handle the rest

Meeting and event services

- **Audio visual and equipment:** all meeting rooms are wired for High-speed Internet and have data ports; additional audio visual and meeting equipment to be provided by client

SEATTLE'S NEWEST HOTEL

The Mediterranean Inn is located in the vibrant Queen Anne neighborhood adjacent to the Key Arena and Space Needle. Your guests will enjoy our beautifully decorated hotel within walking distance of restaurants and shopping. Take a break from your meeting to enjoy our roof top deck with sweeping views of downtown Seattle and Elliott Bay.

See page 35 under Accommodations.

THE
MONTE VILLA FARMHOUSE

3300 Monte Villa Parkway Bothell, Washington 98021

Contact:
Dave Richards or Dana Arnim
(425) 485-6115
Office Hours: Mon–Fri 9am–5pm
E-mail: dave@montevilla.com
Web site: www.montevilla.com

Photo: Bonjour

Photo: Christophoto

Capacity: Ballroom: 850 sq. ft.; up to 120 guests theatre style; **Living Room:** 600 sq. ft.; up to 60 guests theatre style; total sq. ft. of all 3 floors, including break-out rooms, basement meeting room with bar, and offices; approximately 5,600 sq. ft.

Price range: call for full range of weekend and weekday prices or see our web site

Catering: selection of preferred caterers; outside caterers allowed with fee

Types of events: receptions, banquets, meetings, company parties and special events

Availability and terms

The entire house and gardens are rented on the weekends for two six-hour time periods per day. Individual rooms or the entire main floor may be rented on weekdays and evenings. A variety of payment terms are available.

Description of services and facility

ADA: entire main floor is accessible including path to garden

Parking: ample free parking

Banquet services

- **Seating:** tables and chairs for 180, utilizing entire house; 120 maximum, theatre-style, in one room
- **Servers:** provided by caterer or client
- **Bar facilities:** serving stations provided; service, liquor, and liability by caterer or client
- **Dance floor:** 400 sq. ft. dance floor with bandstand; ample electricity
- **Linens, china and glassware:** provided by caterer or client
- **Decorations:** no staples, nails, or tapes; fixed hooks provided
- **Cleanup:** client removes all food and decorations

Meeting and event services

- **Audio visual:** overhead projector with screen, built-in riser/bandstand, flip charts and podium available at no extra charge; additional equipment available for rent
- **Equipment:** built-in sound system for background music

BEAUTIFUL AND HISTORIC FARMHOUSE

Located in Bothell, the Monte Villa Dairy Farm has been lovingly enhanced and enlarged. The farmhouse has hardwood floors, three fireplaces, a formal living room, ballroom, dining room, sun porch, and both bride's and groom's suites for preparations. A secluded patio and an event garden, complete with fountains and a trellis arch for outdoor ceremonies, make the Farmhouse an elegant and charming setting for both social and business occasions. Please check our web site for more information, photos, special offers, and new items.

NOW OPEN on site: GIFTS AT MONTE VILLA.

7108 Lakewood Drive S.W.
Tacoma, Washington 98467
(253) 473-7516
Web site: www.tacomaparks.com

Capacity: October–March up to 200; April–September up to 100
Price range: $7.50 to $17.95 per plate plus tax and gratuity; $25 per hour room charge, 3-hour minimum
Catering: full-service in-house catering and beverage service
Types of events: rehearsal dinners, small weddings and receptions; banquets; barbecues, business meetings, lunches or dinners, golf tournaments, and more

Availability and terms

Make reservations three to four weeks in advance.

Description of services and facility

ADA: fully accessible
Parking: ample free parking
Banquet services

- **Seating:** can accommodate various-size groups; banquet room seats up to 65
- **Servers:** professional servers included in catering costs
- **Bar facilities:** full-service bar; all bartenders and servers provided by Mulligans
- **China and glassware:** white china and assorted glassware provided
- **Decorations:** no staples or nails; nothing that will damage the facility
- **Cleanup:** please remove anything you bring in

Special services

At Mulligans, we are flexible to meet your needs. We can cater a barbecue on the patio, coordinate an early morning or lunch meeting, or assist you in planning a wedding reception or a full banquet.

WE IMPRESS TACOMA'S MOST CRITICAL AUDIENCE EVERY DAY!

Mulligans restaurant and full-service lounge are set on Tacoma's popular, 27-hole Meadow Park Golf Course. Our private meeting and banquet facility provides a unique setting for all kinds of social or corporate events. From intimate wedding receptions or rehearsal dinners, to birthday parties, corporate meetings and banquets, the staff at Mulligans is here to assist you with all your planning needs.

A facility of Metro Parks Tacoma.

9404 E. Marginal Way S. • Seattle, WA 98108
Contact: Special Events Department
(206) 764-5706; Fax (206) 764-5707
Business Hours: please call for an appointment
Event Hours: 7 days a week, 7am–midnight
Web site: www.museumofflight.org

Capacity: 113,000 square feet of event space; large and small spaces can accommodate 10–2,500 guests

Price range: prices vary according to space, from $7 per person to $15,000 for 2,500 guests

Catering: exclusive catering provided by McCormick & Schmick's Catering

Types of events: sit-down or buffet dining, cocktail parties, business meetings, trade shows; weddings and receptions, all social occasions

Availability and terms

Please make reservations as early as possible. A 50% nonrefundable deposit is required, with the balance due one week prior to the event.

Description of services and facility

ADA: fully complies with ADA requirements

Parking: ample complimentary parking

Banquet services

- **Servers, bar facilities, seating, linens and china:** provided by McCormick & Schmick's Catering
- **Dance floor:** please discuss rental needs with catering sales representative
- **Decorations:** please contact Special Events Department for regulations
- **Cleanup:** please remove anything you bring in; catering and museum staff will handle the rest

Meeting and event services

- **Audio visual:** standard A/V package provided for no fee; please contact the Special Events Department for your audio visual needs
- **Equipment:** podiums, microphones, VCRs, monitors, data projector, slide projectors, screens, satellite downlink; other equipment available

Special services

Because we are located on Boeing Field, guests may fly directly to the Museum for their event.

WHERE EVENTS TAKE FLIGHT

The Museum of Flight, one of Seattle's most spectacular attractions, is a unique setting for your next special event. Located on Boeing Field only minutes from downtown, the seven-acre complex features the historic Red Barn, original home of The Boeing Company, and the ultra-modern Great Gallery. The Museum and its seven distinctly different spaces provide dramatic backdrops for special events, from small meetings to large receptions of up to several thousand people. In addition to enjoying a memorable function, guests may also explore the Museum's galleries, view a film in the William M. Allen Theater or browse in the Museum Store.

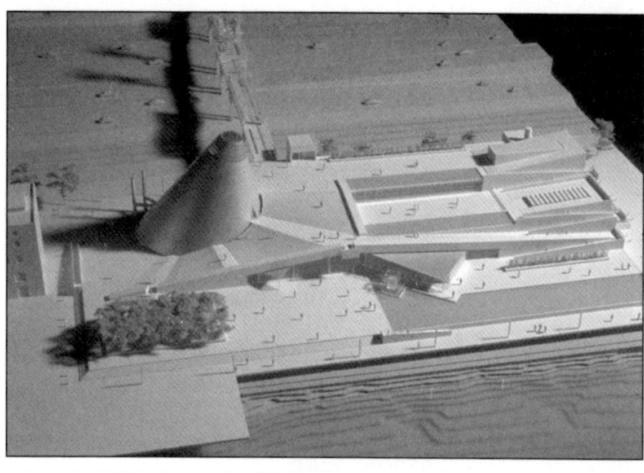

Tacoma, Washington USA
(253) 396-1768, ext. 2148
Fax (253) 396-1769
www.museumofglass.org

Capacity: Grand Hall: 280 sit-down, up to 1,000 standing; **Theater:** seats 180; **Hot Shop:** seats 140; **Main Level Plaza:** 200 sit-down, up to 650 standing; **Central Level Plaza:** 200 sit-down, up to 700 standing; **Rooftop Plaza:** 340 sit-down, up to 900 standing
Price range: varies by venue and the date of event
Catering: a list of preferred caterers and preferred rentals is available
Types of events: corporate events, receptions, presentations, rehearsal dinners, ceremonies, birthdays, anniversaries, weddings, and other celebrations

Availability and terms

Opening in July. Non-refundable deposit required to reserve a date. Balance due four weeks prior to event. Please call for availability.

Description of services and facility

ADA: full accessibility
Parking: underground parking; client responsible for making necessary parking arrangements
Banquet services
- **Seating:** provided and arranged through caterer
- **Servers:** service staff provided by caterer
- **Bar facilities:** please contact event coordinator
- **Linens, napkins, china and glassware:** provided by caterer
- **Decorations:** must be approved in advance by Museum
- **Cleanup:** provided by client and caterer

Special services

The Museum offers a premier contemporary art setting for special events. Whether an intimate party for 30 or a larger event for 2,500—The Museum can accommodate you, from private docent-led tours through the expansive galleries or glass blowing demonstrations in the Hot Shop Amphitheater. Pricing and capacity are determined by the event design. Contact the Facility Coordinator for more information.

OPENING IN JULY

The Museum of Glass is situated on the Thea Foss Waterway overlooking a public esplanade. While passers-by see a shimmering wall of glass from the roadway, guests get a markedly different view of The Museum from its entrance near the esplanade. A series of terraced plazas with reflecting pools ascend to The Museum's panoramic rooftop. At the south end of the rooftop plaza, the Grand Staircase spirals gracefully down the outside of The Museum's 90-foot-tall cone which leads to the 6,900 sq. ft. Grand Hall entrance. This spacious area, bathed in natural light, adjoins The Museum's theater, hot shop and galleries. These architectural elements provide an unparalleled atmosphere for individuals, corporations and organizations to host a special event in the context of contemporary art in the Greater Puget Sound Region.

2700–24th Avenue East • Seattle, Washington 98112
(206) 324-1126; Fax (206) 324-1346
Special Event Facilities Available 7am–Midnight
E-mail: specialevents@seattlehistory.org

Capacity: McCurdy Gallery: 3,500 sq. ft., up to 200 sit-down, 300 reception; **McEachern Auditorium/Theatre:** 373-seat professionally equipped performance and presentation space with adjacent lobby; **Clise Gallery:** 50 sit-down, 150 reception; **Founders Room:** up to 25; **1880s Gallery:** 40 sit-down, 75 reception

Price range: price varies depending on specific event requirements

Catering: choose from Museum-approved caterers; call for concession policy

Types of events: corporate/social/cultural parties, reunions, auctions, breakfast meetings, business luncheons, formal dinners, receptions, seminars, performances, shareholders meetings, film festivals and screenings

Availability and terms

We schedule events from three weeks to three years out. Available for convention overflow. Security damage deposit is required to reserve date; full event fees due three weeks prior to event.

Description of services and facility

ADA: fully accessible

Parking: ample free parking on site

Banquet services

- **Seating:** 200 folding chairs; 20-6' buffet tables; 20-60" rounds
- **Bar facilities:** client or caterer provides liquor, bartender and permit
- **Dance floor:** available through rental agency; ample electrical hookups
- **Decorations:** free standing, weighted balloons or centerpieces; votive candles allowed; no artifacts disturbed; no glitter, confetti
- **Cleanup:** facility restored to original condition; all event-related materials and garbage removed from building and grounds

Meeting and event services

- **Audio visual:** projectors: slide, overhead, 35mm and 16mm; screen: standard, 13'x20' fixed in auditorium, microphones: standard/wireless, lapel/handheld; CD player; VCR; 25" TV, cassette player
- **Equipment:** podium, easels, flip chart and PA system; please inquire for current list
- **Additional gallery access:** nominal fee; special rates for Benefactor-level MOHAI members

BRING US YOUR SPECIAL EVENT AND WE'LL HELP YOU MAKE HISTORY

Nestled in beautiful McCurdy Park on the shores of Lake Washington, the Museum of History and Industry is the perfect backdrop for your corporate, social or cultural gathering. Conveniently located, with easy freeway access from both downtown and the eastside, the museum features fascinating exhibits on the rich heritage of the Pacific Northwest. Please call (206) 324-1126 to reserve this unique setting for your upcoming event!

See page 95 under Auditoriums, Theatres & Classrooms.

NEWHOLLY

NEIGHBORHOOD CAMPUS

7054-32nd Avenue South
Seattle, Washington 98118
(206) 760-3280; Fax (206) 760-3290
Mon–Fri 8am–6pm
E-mail: newhollycampus@hollypark.com

Capacity: will accommodate groups of up to 250; suites available in a variety of sizes
Price range: priced by the hour, the day, or the evening; please inquire
Catering: chosen by client
Types of events: banquets, receptions, seminars, lectures, social and business gatherings

Availability and terms

We request that you reserve space at least three weeks in advance, and require a two-hour minimum room rental. A $250 deposit confirms your date, and fees will apply to cancellations on short notice.

Description of services and facility

ADA: fully complies with all ADA regulations
Parking: ample off-street parking provided
Banquet services
- **Seating:** chairs and 60" round tables provided
- **Servers:** provided by caterer or client
- **Bar facilities:** client must arrange for all necessary permits
- **Dance floor:** beautiful hardwood floors, with a raised stage
- **Linens, china, and glassware:** provided by client or caterer
- **Decorations:** must be approved by New Holly management in advance
- **Cleanup:** provided by New Holly maintenance staff

Meeting and event services
- **Audio visual and equipment:** audio and video systems available upon request

SOUTH SEATTLE'S NEWEST EVENT FACILITY

The Gathering Hall is a new facility conveniently located in the New Holly Neighborhood Campus just off 32nd Avenue and South Myrtle Street in South Seattle. The facility has standing capacity for over 400, and has dinner seating for up to 200. It includes gleaming hardwood floors and a wall of windows, a kitchenette, a stage, and is great for business meetings, events, and social gatherings. Plenty of free parking is available for your guests!

15500 Six Penny Lane
Newcastle, Washington 98059
Contact: Catering Department (425) 793-5566
Business Hours: 8am–5pm or by appointment
Web site: www.newcastlegolf.com

Capacity: **St. Andrew's Ballroom:** 350 seated; **Prestwick Terrace:** 150 seated; **Muirfield Room:** 60 seated; **Boardroom:** 12 seated; **Hospitality Range Suite:** 20 seated
Price range: prices vary according to menu selection and season
Catering: full-service, in-house catering provided exclusively by our culinary team
Types of events: ideal for company retreats, seminars, employee appreciation, corporate receptions, business meetings, holiday parties, special events and golf tournaments; we can accommodate formal and informal gatherings, cocktail parties, barbecues, buffets, theme dinners, receptions, and plated dinners

Availability and terms

We recommend that you make your reservations as early as possible. However, every effort will be made to accommodate your needs on short notice. Reservations will be confirmed with the receipt of a booking fee and signed contract.

Description of services and facility

ADA: fully accessible

Parking: complimentary parking for over 400 cars in a well-lit, secure parking lot

Banquet services

- **Seating:** tables and chairs provided
- **Servers:** professionally trained, on-site service staff
- **Bar facilities:** hosted or no-host full-service bars available
- **Dance floor:** available upon request at no extra charge
- **Linens, china, and serviceware:** provided by our culinary team
- **Cleanup:** full cleanup is provided by The Golf Club at Newcastle

Meeting and event services

- **Audio visual and equipment:** all meeting rooms are wired for data transmission; a selection of audio visual and other equipment is available for your convenience

DISTINCTION AND EXCELLENCE

Enjoy a majestic mountain backdrop with breathtaking views of Seattle and Lake Washington as you unwind in the ambience of the Calcutta Grill, relax over a specialty cigar in the Northwest's premier cigar bar, The Wooly Toad, or compete in a round of golf on our beautifully-landscaped greens. Whether you are planning a sit-down banquet, a buffet, or a standing reception, The Golf Club at Newcastle is committed to the vision of providing you and your guests with an unparalleled level of service. Equipped with cozy private dining rooms, banquet facilities spacious enough for several hundred, and a classically designed garden terrace, The Golf Club at Newcastle offers elegant and unique settings for all of your celebrations and special occasions.

NILE GOLF & COUNTRY CLUB

6601-24th Street S.W.
Mountlake Terrace, Washington 98043
(425) 775-2412
Fax (425) 744-9611
E-mail: office@nileshrine.org
Web site: nileshrine.org

Capacity: **Grand Ballroom:** up to 462 receptions, 300 banquets; **Red Room:** up to 200 receptions, 95 banquets; **Potentate's Lounge:** up to 100 for banquets; **Gold Room:** up to 90 receptions, 58 banquets; **Picnic facilities:** 5 areas available

Price range: please inquire; varies with season and room reserved

Catering: As You Like It Catering, our full service in-house caterer, will provide sumptuous menus for all occasions

Types of events: banquets, receptions, meetings, seminars; breakfasts, luncheons, dinners; anniversaries, reunions, dances, holiday parties, auctions, golf tournaments, picnics

Availability and terms

Reservations accepted up to one year in advance. Rental fee and damage deposit due at signing.

- **Grand Ballroom:** showplace of the entire property; overlooks the golf course and Lake Ballinger; features cathedral ceiling, chandeliers, fireplace and spacious dance floor
- **Red Room:** adjacent to lobby; ideal for mid-sized groups, can be opened to enlarge ballroom
- **Potentate's Lounge:** overlooks the golf course, this unique room features a high, vaulted ceiling and spectacular view of the surrounding wooded grounds
- **Gold Room:** popular for smaller groups; features fireplace and scenic view of the grounds
- **Restaurant & Lounge:** open to the public daily
- **Picnic Facilities:** four areas available

Description of services and facility

ADA: fully accessible, meets all ADA requirements

Parking: ample free parking adjacent to club house

Banquet services

- **Seating:** tables and chairs provided
- **Servers:** professional service staff provided by in-house caterer, As You Like It Catering
- **Bar facilities:** fully licensed for full-service host or no-host bar service
- **Dance floor:** 30'x40' dance floor in Grand Ballroom; risers available for band or DJ
- **Linens, napkins, china and glassware:** available on site
- **Cleanup:** provided by our trained, efficient staff

Meeting and event services

- **Audio visual and equipment:** A/V equipment, easels, black boards, risers and podium available on request, for additional fee

ON THE SHORES OF LAKE BALLINGER

Located just 20 minutes from downtown Seattle, the Nile Golf & Country Club is one of the Pacific Northwest's most distinctly impressive properties. Nestled among 88-acres of tall stately firs on the shores of Lake Ballinger, this unique venue is suitable for all kinds of events, from formal banquets to informal meetings in our chateau-styled clubhouse, to golf tournaments on our 18-hole golf course, or picnics at any one of our five individual picnic areas.

See page 338 under Caterers/Food & Beverage Services
and page 546 under Picnic & Recreation Sites.

NORTHWEST TREK WILDLIFE PARK

11610 Trek Drive East
Eatonville, Washington 98328
Group sales: (360) 832-7181; Mon–Fri 8am-4:30pm
Web site: www.nwtrek.org

Capacity: **Picnic Pavilion:** 200; **Picnic Meadow:** 300; **Alder Acres:** 1,000; **Forest Theater:** 100; **Fir Bough Cafe:** 90; **Hellyer Natural History Center:** 50

Price range: please call for current prices; rental fees vary per selection and special requirements

Catering: in-house food service

Types of events: company parties, business meetings, retreats, seminars, receptions, reunions and picnics

Availability and terms

Reserve space as far in advance as possible to ensure availability. A deposit is required to reserve your space and is nonrefundable with cancellation notice less than 30 days prior to your event date.

Description of services and facility

ADA: all exhibits and facilities are wheelchair accessible

Parking: ample complimentary parking

Banquet services

- **Seating:** depends on client's needs
- **Servers:** friendly, professional staff included in event and catering costs
- **Bar facilities:** rental party provides necessary permits to serve liquor (after hours functions only)
- **Decorations:** all decorations must be pre-approved
- **Cleanup:** fees included in event costs; excessive cleanup may require extra charge

Meeting and event services

- **Audio visual:** available, please inquire

Special services

Our mission is the exhibition and conservation of native Northwest wildlife. Your group will enjoy our spectacular setting along with the special activities Trek offers. Each event is customized to meet your needs.

NORTHWEST TREK—It's wild!

Venture into the "wild" aboard comfortable trams at one of the nation's most unique wildlife parks. Northwest Trek features 600 acres of native plants and animals. Excitement, adventure and education are a part of every visit and sure to thrill your group. You'll find that Trek is the "wildest" location you have ever held an event or business meeting. Come see our grizzlies, cougar, bison and more!

See page 58 under Attractions & Activities.

 Please let this business know that you heard about them from the Bravo! Event Resource Guide.

©Don Wilson, Port of Seattle

ODYSSEY

The Maritime Discovery Center

Pier 66, 2211 Alaskan Way • Seattle, Washington 98121-1604
Contact: Catering Sales Department (206) 441-6666; Fax (206) 441-6665
Catering Department Hours: Mon–Fri 8:30am–5pm
E-mail: info@bellharbor.org • ***Web site: www.bellharbor.org*** *or* ***www.ody.org***

Capacity: 20,000 sq. ft. of waterfront Gallery and Mezzanine space including four main exhibit areas and over 50 interactive exhibits; Odyssey can accommodate up to 500 guests for private receptions

Price range: Odyssey group admission fee varies; please contact catering department; food and beverage purchase required

Catering: catering provided by Bell Harbor International Conference Center; executive chef on-site

Availability and terms

Food and beverage purchase required. Group admission fee is applicable; please contact catering department. A 10% deposit is required to contract for space.

Description of services and facility

ADA: fully accessible

Parking: covered parking available, accessed by pedestrian skybridge

Banquet services

- **Seating:** tables and chairs provided by Bell Harbor International Conference Center
- **Servers:** staff included in catering costs
- **Bar facilities:** Bell Harbor provides liquor, liquor liability, bar facilities, and bartenders
- **Dance floor:** contact catering department for available sizes and pricing
- **Linens, napkins, china, and glassware:** provided by Bell Harbor
- **Decorations:** decorations are acceptable but must be approved by Bell Harbor staff
- **Cleanup:** available at no extra charge

Special services

Bell Harbor event staff is available to assist in planning all aspects of your event (valet parking, live entertainment, themed events, and holiday parties). On-site Odyssey staff provided for guided tours. Early access for decorating is available on case-by-case basis.

WATERFRONT LOCATION WITH INTERACTIVE EXHIBITS

Located on Seattle's exciting downtown waterfront, Odyssey, The Maritime Discovery Center offers a unique extravaganza of interactive exhibits for groups to enjoy. Perfect for convention and business receptions up to 500 guests, or 2,000 if combined with Bell Harbor International Conference Center located directly above.

OVERLAKE SQUARE
CONFERENCE CENTER

Managed by Avid Events, Inc.

14625 N.E. 24th Street
Bellevue, Washington 98007
(425) 882-9097, ext. 2; Fax (425) 882-1312
E-mail: sales@avidevents.com

Capacity: accommodates up to 325
Price range: varies according to date, time and event type
Catering: select from our preferred list or in house catering
Types of events: corporate special events, meetings or private events

Availability and terms
Reservations can be made year round for day, evening or weekend events. A non-refundable deposit is required to reserve venue.

Description of services and facility
ADA: complies with ADA regulations
Parking: ample free parking available
Banquet services
- **Seating:** ample tables and chairs provided
- **Servers:** caterer will provide
- **Bar facilities:** assistance provided
- **Dance floor:** available for rent
- **Linens, napkins, china and glassware:** provided by caterer
- **Decorations:** please inquire about our policies
- **Cleanup:** caterer and venue staff will provide

Meeting and event services
- **Audio visual and equipment:** available for rent

Special services
Theme décor and more are available for rent.

THE NEWEST EASTSIDE VENUE
Conveniently located just off Highway 520 in Bellevue is a brand new event facility, Overlake Square. High ceilings, open floor plan, tasteful décor and free parking will help in making any event a success.

PACIFIC SCIENCE CENTER

200 Second Avenue North
Seattle, Washington 98109-4895
Contact: Cindy Messey
(206) 443-2899
Fax (206) 443-3631
E-mail: clmessey@pacsci.org
Web site: www.pacsci.org

Capacity: over 100,000 sq. ft.; can accommodate up to 4,500 guests
Price range: wide variety of packages available; please call for more information
Catering: please call for information
Types of events: corporate events, wedding receptions, pre and post convention gatherings, bar/bat mitzvahs and holiday parties; limited meeting space available

Availability and terms

A variety of rooms are available to meet your specific needs. We require a standard deposit of 50% of the minimum guaranteed fee due upon receipt of facility use agreement.

Description of services and facility

ADA: Pacific Science Center is fully accessible
Parking: several parking lots are conveniently located around the facility; please call for additional information

Banquet services

- **Servers:** caterer provides
- **Bar facilities:** caterer provides; no red wine inside the facility
- **Linens, napkins, china and glassware:** caterer provides
- **Decorations:** helium balloons are not allowed inside the facility

Meeting and event services

- **Audio visual and equipment:** one microphone and podium included in facility rental fee

Special services

IMAX® movies and laser shows are fun and unique additions to any event or party. Clients may also arrange an exclusive private show as the event itself. The new Boeing **IMAX®** Theater presents the clearest quality movie experience on a screen 60 feet high and 80 feet wide. Laser shows feature digital images and colorful laser lights choreographed to music.

ENJOY THE FUN IN THE HEART OF SEATTLE

Located under the arches near the Space Needle, Pacific Science Center offers an unconventional facility with fun and entertainment built into one site. Hands-on exhibits such as virtual reality basketball, robotic dinosaurs, Tropical Butterfly House, dynamic science demonstrations and out-of-this-world astronomy shows offer something fun for everyone. Professional and friendly staff customize each event to meet your priorities. Buildings provide access to our courtyard with stunning views of the fountains, pools and the Seattle skyline.

IMAX is a registered trademark of Imax Corporation.

See page 59 under Attractions & Activities.

PALISADE

Elliott Bay Marina
2601 W. Marina Place • Seattle, Washington 98199
Contact: Laura Adams (206) 285-5865
Office Hours: Mon–Fri 9am–5pm
or call for an appointment

Capacity: Orchid Room: 2,300 sq. ft., up to 125 sit-down, 175 for receptions; with access to open deck area; **Magnolia Room:** 800 sq. ft., up to 50 sit-down, and 75 for receptions; **Entire Restaurant:** up to 400 guests reception-style

Price range: varies according to menu selections; please inquire

Catering: full-service in-house catering provided

Types of events: business or social events; cocktail and hors d'oeuvres, sit-down luncheons or dinners, buffets; banquets, meetings or seminars

Availability and terms

We recommend you make your reservations up to one year in advance, especially for the popular summer months and holiday season. A rental fee is required to confirm your date. Palisade will close the restaurant on Saturday afternoons to accommodate private events for up to 400 guests reception-style.

Description of services and facility

ADA: fully accessible

Parking: ample complimentary parking, complimentary valet parking for evenings

Banquet services

- **Seating:** ample tables and chairs provided
- **Servers:** professional service staff included in catering costs
- **Bar facilities:** full-service host/no-host bar available
- **Dance floor:** available in the Orchid Room
- **Linens and napkins:** provided in a variety of colors
- **China and glassware:** restaurant china and all glassware provided
- **Decorations:** please inquire; nothing that will damage the facility
- **Cleanup:** we'll handle it for you

Meeting and event services

- **Audio visual and equipment:** available through our in-house A/V company

Special services

Palisade will provide you with the attentive and detailed service that will make your event worry free. From rental equipment to flowers or ice sculptures, we are happy to coordinate all outside services for you.

OVERLOOKING THE ELLIOTT BAY MARINA

If you are looking for one of the best views in Seattle combined with superb dining and impeccable service, Palisade is the place for you. Located at Elliott Bay Marina, just minutes from downtown Seattle, Palisade offers spectacular views of the Marina, the Downtown Seattle skyline, and Mount Rainier.

THE
PARAMOUNT
EST. 1928
SEATTLE, WASHINGTON

911 Pine Street
Seattle, Washington 98101
Contact: Jason Ferguson
(206) 467-5510, ext. 150
Fax (206) 682-4837

E-mail: jasonf@theparamount.com • ***Web Site: www.theparamount.com***

Capacity: elegantly hosts groups of 100 to 2,500
Price range: rates vary according to time of day and day of the week; please inquire
Catering: select the caterer of your choice from our preferred list
Types of events: receptions, luncheons, formal sit-down dinners, pre- and post-convention gatherings, holiday parties, meetings, private performances, trade shows, or any other type of social or corporate event

Availability and terms

The excitingly new, yet elegantly appointed Paramount Ballroom is the ideal venue for all kinds of business or social events. A deposit of 50% of the rental fee confirms your date, with the balance due 30 days prior to your event.

Description of services and facility

ADA: The Paramount is in full compliance with the ADA theatre standards
Parking: convenient pay lots and parking garages nearby, plus street parking
Banquet services

- **Seating:** tables, chairs and linens arranged according to your event needs
- **Servers:** caterer provides
- **Bar facilities:** full bar service provided by The Paramount
- **Dance floor:** several areas within the theatre are sure to meet your dance floor needs
- **Serviceware:** caterer provides all china and serviceware

Meeting and event services

- **Audio visual and equipment:** the theatre features a video system that projects events on monitors throughout the venue; we are happy to coordinate any additional A/V or equipment needs

Special services

Host an intimate pre-function reception or treat your keynote speaker or celebrity to the comforts of our state-of-the-art "star" dressing room with fireplace and jacuzzi.

WHERE DID ALL THE SEATS GO?

They're still here...we've just tucked them under the floor.

The convertible floor technology we installed transforms The Paramount's auditorium into a stunning ballroom. The historic landmark's inspiring architecture and elegant surroundings create a one-of-a-kind environment, perfect for groups of 100 to 2,500. Call us about staging your next event at The Paramount, a refreshingly different event atmosphere.

See page 96 under Auditoriums, Theatres & Classrooms.

Pickering Barn

S.E. 56th Street and 10th Avenue N.W. • Issaquah, Washington
Contact: City of Issaquah Parks and Recreation Department
(425) 837-3321; Fax (425) 837-3319
By appointment only
E-mail: PickeringFarm@ci.issaquah.wa.us

Capacity: accommodates up to 400 guests
Price range: varies according to the type of event
Catering: select an off-premise caterer of your choice, or ask for recommendations
Types of events: receptions, retirement parties, day retreats, fundraisers, birthdays and anniversaries, corporate special events, music festivals

Availability and terms

A non-refundable deposit and signed contract are required to confirm your reservation.

Description of services and facility

ADA: complies with all ADA regulations
Parking: ample complimentary parking provided
Banquet services

- **Seating:** chairs and round tables provided by Pickering Barn
- **Servers:** service staff provided by caterer
- **Bar facilities:** caterer or client arrange for all beverage service and the requisite banquet permit
- **Dance floor:** Pickering Barn offers hardwood floor in The Hay Barn that is ideal for dancing
- **Linens, china and serviceware:** provided by caterer
- **Decorations:** we are flexible and happy to review a client's plan
- **Cleanup:** do-it-yourself or arranged depending on the client's needs

Special services

The Pickering Barn offers event planners and coordinators a wide range of options; the facility includes a catering support area, a portable stage, and two private classrooms.

HISTORIC ISSAQUAH BARN RESTORED

Originally built in the nineteenth century, Pickering Barn has been beautifully restored and fully equipped to make today's events a success. Expansive windows and a high, vaulted ceiling give our state-of-the-art facility a sense of openness that your guests will appreciate.

25625 East Plateau Drive • Sammamish, Washington 98074
(425) 868-6063; Fax (425) 836-4421
Office Hours: Mon–Fri 8:30am–5:30pm

Capacity: **Club Suite:** 25 to 30; **Fairway Suite:** 20; **Alder Room:** 230; and **outdoor tent and lawn:** 200 seated or 300 reception style
Price range: rates vary according to menu selections and season
Catering: full-service in-house catering provided by our exclusive culinary team
Types of events: weddings, receptions, rehearsal dinners, golf tournaments, business meetings, seminars, retreats, breakfast, lunch, dinner, appetizer buffets, private parties, and more...

Availability and terms

A 50% deposit of the estimated food and beverage costs is required to reserve your date. We recommend booking early, but always attempt to accommodate reservations on short notice.

Description of services and facility

ADA: fully accessible
Parking: complimentary parking provided
Banquet services

- **Seating:** table and chairs provided
- **Servers:** friendly, courteous, and professionally trained service staff
- **Bar facilities:** full-service bars available; hosted/no-host; we provide the liquor and public liquor license; professional staff is fully trained on all applicable State laws
- **Dance floor:** dance floor available
- **Linens and napkins:** white linen tablecloths and napkins
- **China and glassware:** white china, stemware, and flatware provided
- **Cleanup:** full cleanup is provided by The Plateau Club
- **Decorations:** please inquire

Meeting and event services

- **Audio visual and equipment:** podium, easels, microphone and additional equipment available on request; special board room with permanent conference table for 12

Special services

The Plateau Club makes planning easy. Our on-staff event planner will assist you with referrals to other services or help plan an exciting golf tournament.

AN EXCEPTIONAL LOCATION

Completed in 1999, The Plateau Club features floor length windows offering beautiful views looking over the 220 acre championship golf course greens and fairways, or out into the wooded plateau surroundings. Contemporary and elegantly appointed, The Plateau Club offers an exceptional location for your special event.

32305 N.E. 8th Street
Carnation, Washington 98014
Contact: Birgit or Larry Lindvig
(425) 333-6770; Fax (425) 333-6799
E-mail: birgitr@seanet.com
Web site: www.pleasanthillestate.com

Capacity: 3.5 acres featuring a barn which accommodates 150 guests indoors and 250 outdoors
Price range: varies with season and day of the week
Catering: a list of preferred caterers is available
Types of events: weddings, receptions, anniversaries, bar mitzvahs, birthdays, seminars, board retreats

Availability and terms

Pleasant Hill Estate makes itself available year-round in blocks of 6 or 8 hours. Reservations are required, and a $500 deposit secures your date. This deposit includes a $250 damage deposit refunded within two weeks after your event, provided that no damage to the facility occurs. One half of the total deposit remains refundable until six months prior to the event.

Description of services and facility

Parking: available for 100 cars; valet service included in site rental

Banquet services

- **Seating:** twelve 60" round tables, two 56" cake tables, and eight rectangular tables included
- **Bar facilities:** client must obtain banquet permit; bartenders available for a fee
- **Dance floor:** space available in the barn for dancing
- **Linens:** white tablecloths provided for existing tables
- **China:** provided by caterer
- **Decorations:** no limitations in the barn; please no additional decoration in the main house
- **Cleanup:** garbage and decorations must be removed

Special services

Hosts Birgit and Larry Lindvig can assist you with event coordination or planning; their extensive knowledge of floral design and wines are at your service. Candelabras, arches, and table decorations are available to rent for a nominal fee.

ACCOMMODATING ELEGANCE WITHIN EASY REACH

Enclosed in ivy-covered walls, Pleasant Hill Estate's 3.5 acre grounds offer many romantic and picturesque settings for an outdoor celebration. A beautifully refurbished barn accommodates indoor receptions or weddings; four sets of French doors extend your reception to spacious patios. The charming 1915 farmhouse features a dining room with a deck overlooking a rose garden and gazebo. A grand staircase descending from the bridal dressing chambers enhances the elegance of the center hall. Pleasant Hill prides itself on an old-fashioned, attentive hospitality that strives to accommodate these beautiful facilities to your personal tastes and style. We invite you to visit our grounds and observe the beauty we offer within easy reach of Seattle and the Eastside.

POINT DEFIANCE LODGE

(in Point Defiance Park)

5400 North Pearl St. • Tacoma, Washington 98407
Contact: Facility Coordinator (253) 305-1010
Business Hours: Tue–Fri 8:30am–4:30pm
Web site: www.tacomaparks.com

Capacity: up to 75 people standing; 55 people seated
Price range: please call for rates
Types of events: banquets, meetings, special events, reunions, weddings and receptions

Availability and terms

The Lodge has a full veranda and seven rooms to accommodate up to 100 people. Reservations accepted up to one year in advance. Full rental fee required to secure date. Cancellations must be received in writing 60 days prior to your event to receive a 50% refund. All events are required to dismiss by midnight. A refundable damage deposit is required.

Description of services and facility

ADA: fully accessible
Parking: 20 parking spaces available; additional parking nearby
Banquet services

- **Seating:** 55 chairs, 7 folding tables (6'x3')
- **Servers:** caterer to provide
- **Bar facilities:** caterer can provide liquor, bartender and banquet license to serve liquor
- **Linens and napkins:** provided by caterer
- **China and glassware:** provided by caterer
- **Decorations:** no staples, nails, or duct tape; decorating time included in rental time
- **Cleanup:** renter responsible for cleaning or making arrangements for cleaning

Special services

Staff person remains on site during your event, but staff not responsible for decorating or cleanup.

A HANDSOME 1899 RUSTIC-STYLE BUILDING

Located near the Rose Gardens in Point Defiance Park, the lodge is a handsome 1899 rustic-style building. Wood paneling, beamed ceilings and a wrap-around veranda provide a gracious and private setting in a lushly landscaped park.

A facility of Metro Parks Tacoma.

POINT DEFIANCE PAGODA

(in Point Defiance Park)

5400 N. Pearl Street • Tacoma, WA 98407
Contact: Facility Coordinator
(253) 305-1010
Business Hours: Tue–Fri 8:30am–4:30pm
Web site: www.tacomaparks.com

Capacity: 200 people standing; 100 people seated
Price range: please call for rates
Types of events: banquets, seminars, family gatherings, weddings, receptions

Availability and terms

Reservations are accepted up to one year in advance. Full rental fee is required to secure your event date. Cancellation must be received in writing 60 days prior to your event to receive a 50% refund. A refundable damage deposit is required.

Description of services and facility

ADA: fully accessible
Parking: free parking for 75 cars around building; more parking nearby; no valet parking
Banquet services

- **Seating:** 100 chairs; 15 folding tables (8'x3')
- **Servers:** provided by caterer
- **Bar facilities:** caterer can provide liquor, bartender, and banquet permit to serve liquor
- **Linens and napkins:** provided by caterer
- **China and glassware:** provided by caterer
- **Decorations:** no nails, staples, or duct tape; decorating time included in rental time
- **Cleanup:** applicant must provide cleanup

Special services

Staff person remains on site during your event, but staff not responsible for decorating or cleanup.

GORGEOUS JAPANESE GARDEN SETTING

A focal point of Point Defiance Park's Japanese Garden, the 1914 Pagoda is a replica of a 17th century Japanese lodge. The gardens surrounding the Pagoda feature pools, a picturesque footbridge, cherry trees, azaleas and rhododendrons.

A facility of Metro Parks Tacoma.

Point Defiance Zoo & Aquarium

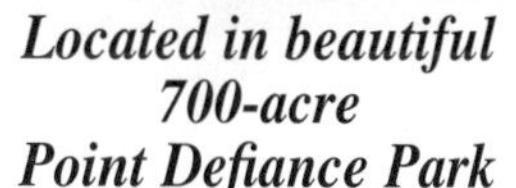

Located in beautiful 700-acre Point Defiance Park

5400 N. Pearl Street • Tacoma, Washington 98407
Phone (253) 404-3643; Fax (253) 591-5448
Office Hours: Mon–Fri 8am–5pm • ***Web site: www.pdza.org***

Capacity: accommodates groups of 25 to 250 for banquets or 25 to 1,000 for picnics

Price range: varies depending on food and beverage selections, room or site selection, and time of day; Zoo and Aquarium admission charged only for events held during Zoo hours

Catering: our full service, in-house professional catering staff is dedicated to creating a delectable dining extravaganza for your event

Types of events: all types of social or corporate events; meetings, reunions, birthdays or holiday parties, picnics, weddings, receptions, banquets; breakfast, lunch or dinner

Availability and terms

Reservations are booked in four-hour time increments. A $200 deposit is required on booking with the balance due the day of the event.

Description of services and facility

ADA: all grounds and facilities are fully accessible

Parking: ample complimentary parking provided

Banquet services

- **Seating:** indoor or outdoor; sit-down or stand-up receptions; some tenting for outdoor events provided
- **Servers:** attentive wait-staff is professionally attired; all service staff included in catering charges
- **Bar facilities:** client may supply own alcoholic beverages; banquet permit required; corkage fee applies
- **Linens, china and glassware:** fees may apply depending on your requirements
- **Decorations:** please inquire, nothing that will damage the facility
- **Cleanup:** included in facility rental fees

Meeting and event services

- **Audio visual and equipment:** A/V or equipment needs available upon request

Special services

Ask about including a behind-the-scenes tour of the Zoo and Aquarium in your event. Point Defiance Zoo & Aquarium offers the opportunity for guests to get up close and personal with the animals and their keepers.

DINE WITH THE SHARKS OR BARBECUE ON THE LAWN

With the broad blue expanse of Puget Sound as a backdrop, Point Defiance Zoo & Aquarium is not only a top American zoo, but among the most beautiful. The exotic sights and sounds combined with superb cuisine and impeccable service ensure that you and your group will have a festive and memorable event!

See page 547 under Picnic & Recreational Sites, and page 61 under Attractions & Activities.

3014 Third Avenue North
Seattle, Washington 98109
Contact: Richard Malia
Restaurant (206) 284-3000
Fax (206) 284-4768
Hours: Mon–Fri 11:30am–12am; Sat 5pm–12am; Sun 5pm–12am

Capacity: features two private dining rooms overlooking the ship canal; one room accommodates up to 25 for sit-down dinners, and the other up to 40 for sit-down dinners or 50 for cocktail receptions; please inquire about reserving the main dining room or the entire restaurant
Price range: prices vary according to menu selections
Catering: full service in-house catering provided
Types of events: receptions, banquets, parties; cocktail and hor d'oeuvres, buffets or sit-down luncheons or dinners, weddings, rehearsal dinners

Availability and terms

The entire restaurant, seating 200+, is available Saturdays and Sundays during the day for weddings and receptions. Ideal for rehearsal dinners or smaller banquets, Ponti is one of Seattle's most popular restaurants. Reservations for our private dining areas should be made as early as possible. A $250 deposit will reserve your date with the balance due the day of the event.

Description of services and facility

ADA: fully accessible
Parking: parking adjacent to the facility; valet service provided
Banquet services

- **Seating:** all tables and chairs provided
- **Servers:** professional service staff included in catering costs
- **Bar facilities:** full service bar; host or no-host
- **Linens and napkins:** tablecloths and napkins that complement the decor provided
- **China and glassware:** restaurant china and glassware provided
- **Decorations:** please inquire about any special decorations you would like to bring in; nothing that will damage the facility
- **Cleanup:** remove anything you bring in, we'll handle the rest

Special services

Let Ponti's staff help design a memorable custom menu from selections of our award winning Fusion cuisine. We're also happy to refer you to additional services like florists or ice sculptures.

ELEGANT ITALIAN-STYLE VILLA OVERLOOKING THE LAKE WASHINGTON SHIP CANAL

Located on the southwest side of the Fremont Bridge overlooking the Lake Washington Ship Canal, Ponti provides guests with spectacular views of Seattle's busiest waterway. Our entry courtyard and fountain, massive fireplace in the bar, intimate dinning areas with segmented outdoor patio access, and 180 degree views combined with our award-winning Asian Fusion cuisine ensure you and your guest will have an entertaining and palate pleasing dining experience to be remembered.

SOME OF OUR AWARDS INCLUDE: Best Seafood Award '94, '95 and '96. Best Northwest Cuisine '94 and '95. *Gourmet Magazine* "Top Table" Award, October '96. "Spectacular fusion of Northwest Bounty, European Techniques, Bistro Informality, Mediterranean sensibility and Pacific Rim Pizzazz."

1201 First Avenue South • Seattle, Washington 98134
(206) 682-8322, ext. 323
Fax (206) 682-8420
E-mail: wsimeona@PyramidBrew.com
Web site: www.PyramidBrew.com

Capacity: **Alehouse:** up to 400; **Retail Mezzanine:** up to 70 for sit-down functions; **VIP Room:** up to 40 for meetings; **Executive Room:** up to 60; **combined rooms:** up to 115 reception style
Price range: varies according to date, time and menu selected; please inquire
Catering: Pyramid Alehouse provides complete in-house catering services
Types of events: business or social events, sit-down luncheons or dinners, rehearsal dinners, buffets, beer and appetizer receptions, brewery tours and tastings, or Brewmaster dinners

Availability and terms

Our mezzanine levels and large party dining areas are available for your private use. Minimum food and beverage purchase required. Pyramid Alehouse welcomes children of all ages.

Description of services and facility

ADA: fully accessible

Parking: ample complimentary parking in front of and behind the Pyramid Alehouse

Banquet services

- **Seating:** table and chairs provided
- **Servers:** professional service staff is included in catering cost
- **Bar facilities:** the Pyramid Alehouse provides all beverages
- **Linens and napkins:** all styles and colors available for an additional fee
- **China and glassware:** provided by the Pyramid Alehouse
- **Cleanup:** please remove anything you bring in; the Pyramid staff will do the rest
- **Decorations:** please inquire; nothing that will damage the facility

Meeting and event services

- **Audio visual and equipment:** audio/visual equipment available for an additional fee

Special services

Pyramid Alehouse will provide you with attentive and detailed service that will make your event worry free. Please inquire about tours of our Brewery, the home of Seattle's Pyramid Ales—brewing craft beers since 1984.

LOCATED DIRECTLY ACROSS THE STREET FROM SAFECO FIELD, HOME OF THE SEATTLE MARINERS. VISIT OUR BEER GARDEN PRIOR TO THE GAME!

The Pyramid Alehouse not only offers a great dining experience, but has also become Seattle's game day destination; please visit our beer garden prior to the game. From award-winning handcrafted beers, renowned for their distinctive styles, to traditional "Pub Grub," the Pyramid Alehouse makes a tasting adventure out of every dining experience or event.

290 Southcenter Mall • Seattle, Washington 98188
(206) 248-8882; Fax (206) 248-2026
Hours: Mon–Thu 11am–9:30pm;
Fri–Sat 11am–10pm; Sun 11am–9pm
Web site: www.rainforestcafe.com

Capacity: up to 325 seated; 600 for cocktails
Price range: varies according to group size and menu selection
Catering: in-house catering
Types of events: birthday celebrations, reunions, corporate award dinners, holiday parties, graduation night celebrations, office parties

Availability and terms

Groups of 20 or more should reserve two weeks in advance; buyouts reserve one month in advance. Deposits required for groups of 30 or more.

Description of services and facility

ADA: fully accessible
Parking: complimentary parking is available in mall parking lot
Banquet services
- **Seating:** tables and chairs provided and arranged to fit your needs
- **Servers:** professional service staff provided
- **Bar facilities:** full service
- **Linens and napkins:** paper dinner and beverage napkins provided
- **China and glassware:** all provided
- **Decorations:** unique atmosphere; please inquire
- **Cleanup:** handled by our staff

Meeting and event services
- **Audio visual and equipment:** client provides own

Special services

You will receive special attention and service in planning your special event. Customized and personalized menus are available.

A WILD PLACE TO SHOP AND EAT®

Escape into a tropical adventure with exotic ambiance that makes an ideal setting for client entertainment, employee rewards, theme events, new product introductions, holiday parties, birthday celebrations, reunions and more! Rainforest Cafe's® professional event staff will handle every detail from special menus to entertainment, linen, floral arrangements and gifts. Order from an assortment of our signature menu items with Caribbean, Mexican and Asian influences and our wide array of exotic drinks. Complete your journey in our Retail Village, which is overflowing with souvenirs of your adventure: adult and children's clothing, bath and body products, plush animals and many other items.

RAY'S BOATHOUSE CATERING
6049 Seaview Avenue N.W.
Seattle, Washington 98107
(206) 789-6309
Fax (206) 781-1960
Office Hours: Mon–Fri, 9am–5pm
E-mail: rayscatering@rays.com • ***Web site: www.rays.com***

Capacity: **The Northwest Room** accommodates 64 for seated meals and 80 for receptions (up to 120 in the summer with canopied deck); **The Top Deck Room** accommodates 32 for seated meals and up to 50 for receptions
Price range: varies according to menu selection
Catering: full-service in-house and off-premise catering
Types of events: seated and buffet meals, cocktail receptions, company meetings and special events, wedding receptions, rehearsal dinners, birthdays, anniversaries

Availability and terms

The Northwest Room is available year-round, and The Top Deck Room is available October–March. Room rental fee waived when minimum food and beverage order requirement is met. A $500 deposit is required to reserve date for private dining rooms. A 50% deposit is required for off-premise catering. Deposit is refundable up to 90 days prior to the event.

Description of services and facility

ADA: fully accessible
Parking: complimentary valet service (evening events) and free on-site parking
Banquet services

- **Seating:** tables and chairs provided
- **Servers:** staffing is based on menu selection and guest count
- **Bar facilities:** full-service bar and bartender available
- **Dance floor:** available for a fee
- **Linens, china and serviceware:** cloth napkins and tablecloths, china, flatware and glassware provided
- **Decorations:** Ray's provides fresh flowers and votive candles for guest tables
- **Cleanup:** provided by Ray's Boathouse

Meeting and event services

- **Audio visual and equipment:** Ray's coordinates audio-visual equipment and accessories, phone/modem access, flip charts and rentals.

Special services

Ray's Catering will exceed your expectations. Whether you are planning an intimate dinner for 20, an all-day meeting for 40, or a wedding in the park for 400, our focus is to provide you with a successful event.

"VISITING SEATTLE WITHOUT DINING AT RAY'S WOULD BE LIKE VISITING PARIS AND MISSING THE EIFFEL TOWER." —*The New York Times*

Located on picturesque Shilshole Bay just north of the Ballard Locks, Ray's Boathouse is famous for its world-class cuisine and spectacular view of Puget Sound and the Olympic Mountains. Voted one of the Top 10 most romantic restaurants in the world by *Town & Country Magazine,* it is a favorite place for meetings and retreats, holiday parties, rehearsal dinners, weddings, birthdays, and anniversaries. A Seattle original for over 28 years, there's no better place to show your guests the best of the Northwest!

For menus and information, visit our web site at *www.rays.com*
or e-mail us at *rayscatering@rays.com*

14300 N.E. 145th Street
Woodinville, Washington 98072
Contact: Teresa Do (425) 483-3232, ext. 222
Fax (425) 481-4010
Web site: www.redhook.com

Capacity: **Weatherman's Room:** 3,800 sq. ft., up to 200 guests; **Tour Gallery:** 1,300 sq. ft., up to 50 guests; **Redhook Bowl:** outdoor amphitheatre, up to 300 guests; **Riverside Picnic Area:** up to 125 guests

Price range: $200 to $400 weekday; $350 to $800 weekends; Redhook Bowl: $500; Picnic Area: $175

Catering: use our in-house catering service or choose from our list of approved caterers

Types of events: corporate functions, holiday parties, reunions, receptions, auctions, picnics, or any professional or social gathering

Availability and terms

We suggest making reservations as soon as possible for best date availability. A signed contract and a $400 room deposit will reserve your date.

Description of services and facility

ADA: facilities are completely accessible

Parking: complimentary on-site parking available

Banquet services

- **Seating:** tables and chairs provided for 175; caterer responsible for room setup
- **Servers:** all food service personnel to be provided by caterer
- **Bar facilities:** bartenders, beer, wine, and non-alcoholic beverages provided by Redhook
- **Dance floor:** 15' x 9'
- **Linens, china and serviceware:** provided by caterer
- **Decorations:** room requires minimal decorations
- **Cleanup:** caterer responsible for cleanup

Meeting and event services

- **Audio visual and equipment:** can be arranged; please inquire

Special services

Plant tours, picnic grounds, banquet rooms, Redhook store, Forecasters Brew Pub & Beer Garden, Redhook Bowl (amphitheater), and special events (Haul Ash Bike Ride, Street Dance, Outdoor Moonlight Cinema, etc.).

Be sure to visit the Trolleyman Pub at our Seattle location where we've be pouring world class ales since 1982. For more information, call: (206) 548-8000.

LOCATED IN PICTURESQUE WOODINVILLE

Redhook offers guests an opportunity to celebrate social occasions in a working brewery. Banquet rooms are located adjacent to our brewhouse so visitors can get an up-close view of how our famous ales are made. Group and private brewery tours are available. Please contact us to book your next Redhook experience.

222 Yale Avenue North • Seattle, Washington 98109
(206) 223-1944 or Toll-free (888) 873-1938; Fax (206) 223-1407
Business/Office Hours: Mon–Fri 10am–9pm, Sat 10am–7pm, Sun 11am–6pm
E-mail: seattle@rei.com • ***Web site: www.rei.com/storelocator/seattle***

Capacity: **Casey Schwabland Conference Hall:** up to 250; **North Side only:** 28–120 depending on set-up; **South Side only:** 24–80 depending on set-up
Price range: please inquire about our all-day or half-day rates
Catering: international cuisine provided by World Wrapps; outside caterers welcome with a cleaning deposit
Types of events: meetings, seminars, workshops, training, retreats, lectures, film, and more

Availability and terms

Make reservations up to one year in advance, especially for evenings and weekends. We are happy to accommodate reservations on shorter notice depending on space availability. A 50% deposit is required at time of reservation; your deposit is refundable with 30 days notice of cancellation.

Description of services and facility

ADA: yes
Parking: FREE covered garage parking
Banquet services
- **Seating:** all tables and chairs provided
- **Servers:** provided by the caterer of your choice
- **Bar facilities:** no alcoholic beverages may be consumed on REI property
- **Linens and napkins:** provided by client or caterer
- **China and glassware:** provided by client or caterer
- **Decorations:** please inquire; nothing that will damage the facility
- **Cleanup:** please remove anything you bring in; we will handle the rest

Meeting and event services
- **Audio visual and equipment:** microphones, large projection screens, overhead projector, VHS video projector, slide projector, TV/VHS monitor on cart, podium, easels/ flipcharts (digital projector available for rent)

Special services

The professional staff at REI will assist you with all your planning needs so you can enjoy yourself. We can provide ideas on adventure presentations for meetings.

EXPERIENCE REI...YOUR OUTDOOR ADVENTURE INSIDE!

We offer beautiful spacious meeting rooms with panoramic views of Seattle along with full audio-visual equipment to make your meeting or event successful and memorable. Don't forget about REI's Pinnacle towering 65 feet high, one of the tallest freestanding indoor climbing structures in the world. Now it is available for rent and makes for a great team building experience! Please call for more information and to set an appointment to tour our facilities.

See page 475 under Games & Team Building Activities.

RENAISSANCE. MADISON HOTEL

515 Madison Street • Seattle, WA 98104
Contact: Catering Office (206) 583-0300
Office Hours: Mon–Fri 8am–5pm
Web site: www.RenaissanceHotels.com

Capacity: Courtyard Ballroom: up to 450 for sit-down dinners or up to 600 for receptions; **Visions** on 28th floor: up to 100 guests; 11 additional smaller meeting rooms also available
Price range: prices vary depending on menu selections and service needs
Catering: full-service in-house catering provided; kosher service available
Types of events: corporate meetings, seminars, or conventions; seated or buffet breakfasts, lunches, or dinners; receptions, weddings, bar and bat mitzvahs

Availability and terms

The Madison has 15 different rooms available to accommodate your meeting or entertaining needs. Please call for availability and deposit requirements.

Description of services and facility

ADA: all facilities fully accessible
Parking: hotel parking available; charges vary
Banquet services
- **Seating:** tables and chairs are provided at no additional charge
- **Servers:** courteous professional staff to meet your needs
- **Bar facilities:** full-service bar and staff; host or no-host events
- **Dance floor:** large dance floor available at no extra charge
- **Linens and napkins:** white linens provided; specialty colors available for a nominal fee
- **China and glassware:** white china, silver flatware and classic stemware provided
- **Decorations:** please inquire; we can create designs to meet your needs
- **Cleanup:** please remove anything you bring in; we will handle the rest

Meeting and event services
- **Audio visual:** in-house A/V company can accommodate all your needs
- **Equipment:** podium, easels, and stage provided

Special services

In addition to the Courtyard Ballroom, Visions, and our eleven other banquet and meeting rooms, the Renaissance Madison Hotel offers 553 spacious guest rooms including 85 corner and 3 luxury suites. In addition to complimentary coffee and newspaper delivered to your door each morning, and rooftop Italian dining at Prego, guest services include: Club Floor; Full-service business center; Indoor pool and Health Club; and Hair salon.

For your banquet, meeting or convention, our professional catering staff will assist you with everything from room design and menu planning, to flowers, specialty decorations, entertainment, staging and audio visual needs.

THE PERFECT LOCATION FOR YOUR NEXT MEETING OR EVENT

The Renaissance Madison Hotel is consistently rated one of Seattle's best hotels. Our award winning chef and catering staff as well as our concierge and business center personnel are dedicated to making your function a truly memorable and successful event.

City of Renton

COMMUNITY CENTER

1715 Maple Valley Highway • Renton, Washington 98055
(425) 430-6700; Fax (425) 430-6701
Business Hours: Mon–Fri 9am–5pm; Banquet Hours: Fri & Sat until 1am, Sun until 12am

Capacity: a variety of rooms available for groups from 30 to 800; banquet room: up to 300 seated; divided into three (3) sections, up to 100 each; three (3) meeting rooms for 40 each; double gym for groups up to 800

Price range: hourly rates for meeting room events range from $15 to $75 per hour; event prices range from $500 to $900 based on a 10-hour block of time

Catering: no in-house catering available, outside caterers welcome; full-kitchen available

Types of events: meetings, seminars, company or holiday parties, retreats, reunions, conventions, trade shows, banquets, birthdays, anniversaries, weddings, receptions and more...

Availability and terms

The City of Renton Community Center offers a variety of rooms that are flexible to fit your needs. Six individual meeting rooms are available, or space can be configured into one banquet room for up to 300, with three meeting rooms for break-out sessions. Reservations are accepted up to one year in advance. A $200 damage deposit is required. Weekend dates are available in 10-hour blocks of time. A minimum three-hour reservation is required for weekdays.

Description of services and facility

ADA: fully accessible

Parking: complimentary parking for up to 300 cars

Banquet services

- **Seating:** all tables and chairs provided
- **Servers:** to be provided by caterer of your choice
- **Bar facilities:** no bar; banquet permit required if alcoholic beverages are to be sold
- **Dance floor:** built-in dance floor in banquet room
- **Linens:** caterer or renter provides
- **China and glassware:** equipment provided to seat and serve 250 people banquet-style
- **Decorations:** we will be happy to discuss your decorating needs
- **Cleanup:** renter responsible for all cleanup; cleanup time included in rental time

Meeting and event services

- **Audio visual and equipment:** podium, overhead projector, slide projector, microphones, 12'x12' projection screen; staging and other incidental equipment available

Special services

The Community Center offers a full kitchen facility for outside caterer's use. A staff person remains on-site during your event. Hotel accommodations are located within walking distance.

ON THE BANKS OF THE CEDAR RIVER

Conveniently located just off I-405 on the banks of the Cedar River, the Renton Community Center provides an ideal location for receptions and business meetings. Classrooms, large meeting rooms, and a banquet facility (with full kitchen) are available to accommodate a variety of needs from theatre-style seating to banquet-style dining. Additionally, a double gym is available to provide seating for up to 800 people, as well as a 310-seat auditorium for lectures or presentations. Our fully trained staff will see to all your needs from start to finish.

See page 93 under Auditoriums and Theatres.

RESORT

Inn Spa Golf Marina Real Estate

SEMIAHMOO

9565 Semiahmoo Parkway
Blaine, Washington 98230
(360) 318-2000 or (800) 770-7992
Fax (360) 318-5490
Web site: www.semiahmoo.com

Capacity: over 20,000 sq. ft. of newly renovated banquet facilities offer a variety of options that include: exterior view of surrounding bay and Puget Sound, two flexible ballrooms, a tiered theatre, a 7,200 sq. ft. exhibit hall, executive boardroom, two meeting parlors, outdoor tented pavilion along the water, outdoor terrace and function area, two golf clubhouses; 186 guestrooms and 12 suites, many with a waterview and fireplaces

Price range: prices vary depending on menu selection and service needs

Catering: in-house, full service catering provided

Types of events: sit-down or buffet, brunch, lunch, or dinner; ceremonies, receptions, rehearsal dinners, reunions, retreats, parties, or any other types of social event

Availability and terms

We suggest you make your reservations as soon as possible, especially for summer and holiday events; however, we will attempt to accommodate your needs on short notice if possible.

Description of services and facility

ADA: fully accessible and meets current codes

Parking: ample complimentary parking on-site

Banquet services

- **Seating:** table, chairs and patio furniture provided
- **Servers:** courteous, professional staff to meet your needs
- **Bar facilities:** full-service bar and complete wine list
- **Linens and napkins:** provided; please inquire about special color requests
- **China and glassware:** silver, china and classic stemware included in menu prices
- **Cleanup:** please remove anything you bring in; we'll handle the rest
- **Decorations:** we will be happy to discuss personalized decorations to augment our special setting

Special services

Consider one of our two championship golf courses, miles of hiking and biking trails or our spa and fitness center for additional activities for your guests. Our professional event staff is available to assist you in coordinating a truly memorable and first-class event that you and your guests will remember for years to come.

SPECTACULAR WATERFRONT RESORT WITH FIRST-CLASS SERVICE

Nestled on a 1,100-acre natural wildlife preserve just two hours north of Seattle and 45 minutes south of Vancouver, B.C., our AAA Four-Diamond resort is a member of Preferred Hotels and Resorts Worldwide. The waterfront location and expansive meeting and banquet space is ideal for intimate gatherings, larger guest receptions, corporate meetings and events.

The beautiful setting, luxurious guest accommodations, first-class banquet and dining facilities and gracious staff are all reasons that Resort Semiahmoo is Washington's premier waterfront destination and is ranked as "One of the Best Places to Stay in the Whole World" by *Condé Nast Traveler* Gold List.

1250 First Avenue South
Seattle, Washington 98134
Contact: Jennifer Mojo
(206) 346-4228
Fax (206) 346-4250
E-mail: jmojo@seattlemariners.com
Web site: www.seattlemariners.com

Capacity: 10 to 47,000; we can accommodate different sized events; our spaces include the **Bullpen Market** (outdoors and field view), **Diamond Club Lounge**, **Group Suites** (field view), **Hit it Here Café** (field view and outdoor/indoor), **Lookout landing** (outdoor), **Outside Corner Patio** (outdoor), **Press Box** (field view), **Terrace Club Lounges** (field view)

Price range: prices vary according to the type of event, call for current rate information or check out our web site at ***www.seattlemariners.com***

Catering: full-service in-house catering by Masterpiece Creations, customized menus, and chef samplings available

Types of events: banquets, bar/bat mitzvahs, proms, graduations, corporate meetings, fund raisers, weddings, receptions, rehearsal dinners, and other social or business events

Availability and terms

Availability may be limited during baseball season (April–October). We recommend booking your event as early as possible. Standard deposit amounts will apply to each event.

Description of services and facility

ADA: fully accessible

Parking: SAFECO Field Garage located on Atlantic Street (2,000 spaces)

Banquet services

- **Seating:** table and chairs provided and arranged to your specifications; rates vary
- **Servers:** staff included in catering costs
- **Bar facilities:** full service hosted or cash bar available in Diamond Club Lounge, Hit it Here Café, and Terrace Club Lounges
- **Linens, china, and glassware:** provided
- **Decorations:** please inquire; no helium balloons allowed in the facility
- **Cleanup:** please remove everything you bring in; our caterers will do the rest

Meeting and event services

- **Audio visual:** full A/V services available for an additional fee
- **Equipment:** scoreboards, matrix board, and cameras available for an additional fee
- **Group tours:** available for an additional fee
- **Moose appearances:** available for an additional fee

THE HOME OF WINNING EVENTS

From the fun and casual atmosphere of the Bullpen Market to the elegant intimacy of the Diamond Club Lounge, SAFECO Field has a setting for any event. Against a backdrop of America's favorite pastime, your guests will be treated to a unique Seattle experience. You can dine on traditional ballpark fare, elaborate seafood platters, or create your own menu ideas. Whatever your event needs SAFECO Field will exceed your expectations and help you produce a winning event.

SAINT EDWARD GRAND DINING HALL

Saint Edward State Park

Washington State Parks Unique Heritage Facilities

14445 Juanita Drive N.E. • Kenmore, Washington 98028
(425) 823-2992
***Web site: www.parks.wa.gov** [Click on Rental Places, then Heritage Places]*

Capacity: up to 50
Price range: $249.47 for up to 50 people; rental period is four hours
Catering: client arranges own catering
Types of event: meetings, reunions, weddings, and receptions

Availability and terms

Reservations may be made 11 months in advance. The full fee is required up front to reserve your date. Cancellations with a full refund may be made at least 60 days in advance of reservation date.

Description of services and facility

ADA: not accessible to wheelchairs
Parking: limited parking adjacent to the hall
Banquet services

- **Seating:** chairs and tables for 50
- **Servers and bar service:** caterer or client provides
- **Dance floor:** yes; small performance riser is available
- **Linens and napkins:** caterer or client provides
- **China and glassware:** caterer or client provides
- **Decorations:** please inquire about possibilities and restrictions
- **Cleanup:** client is responsible for cleanup

Special services

Saint Edward Grand Dining Hall lends charm to any event, with its tall, arched-glass windows and views of well-maintained grounds outside. It has a kitchen space with refrigeration, water and electricity, and restrooms. There are no cooking appliances.

PLAN YOUR GRAND DAY IN THIS ROOM WITH A VIEW

Washington State Parks and Recreation Commission has a variety of historic and unique places available for the public to rent for daytime events and some for overnight use. One of these unique places is the Saint Edward Grand Dining Hall, with its graceful windows overlooking the verdant grounds of Saint Edward State Park on Lake Washington.

The Grand Dining Hall has a great atmosphere for meetings and other events. The Hall was built in 1931 by the Seattle Catholic Diocese, to be used as a seminary by the Sulpician (educational) Order of priests. In 1977, the Diocese sold the grounds and facility to the State of Washington. The charming garden alcove known as The Grotto, situated near the Grand Dining Hall, may be rented as well.

6501 Railroad Avenue S.E.
Snoqualmie, Washington 98033
Contact: Bonny Hawley
(425) 831-6598; Fax (425) 888-9634
Office Hours: Daily 8:30am–5:30pm
Web site: www.salishlodge.com

Capacity: five rooms, including the Ballroom, accommodate up to 150 guests for sit-down functions; up to 150 for receptions; outdoor events for up to 200 people
Price range: vary depending on menu selections
Catering: full-service in-house catering provided by Salish Lodge
Types of events: a terrific choice for banquets or receptions, meetings, seminars or all-day retreats, holiday parties; breakfasts, luncheons or dinners; buffet or sit-down

Availability and terms

Unquestionably one of Washington state's most spectacular locations, Salish Lodge & Spa offers an ideal location for a truly memorable event. A deposit is required to reserve your date and reservations should be made as early as possible.

Description of services and facility

ADA: fully accessible
Parking: valet parking provided
Banquet services
- **Seating:** all tables and chairs for up to 150 guests provided
- **Servers:** courteous professional staff will take care of all your event needs
- **Bar facilities:** full-service bar facilities; host or no-host functions
- **Dance floor:** available on request
- **Linens and napkins:** a variety of options are available
- **China and glassware:** all china and stemware provided
- **Cleanup:** provided by Salish Lodge's professional staff
- **Decorations:** custom flowers and decorations available

Meeting and event services
- **Audio visual and equipment:** we are happy to accommodate any of your A/V needs

Overnight accommodations

Salish Lodge & Spa features 91 luxury guest rooms and suites available for your out-of-town guests or wedding party. Honeymoon Packages available.

PERCHED ON THE EDGE OF SNOQUALMIE FALLS

Long a destination site for travelers from around the world, this spectacular location is a magical setting for banquets, meetings, retreats, or any other type of business or social event. As a Four Diamond lodge, Salish Lodge & Spa provides the finest dining, exceptional service and attention to detail. Located 30 minutes from downtown Seattle.

ON ALKI BEACH

1936 Harbor Avenue S.W.
Seattle, Washington 98126
Banquets & Catering (206) 937-1085
Office Hours: Mon–Fri 9am–5pm
Web site: www.saltys.com

Capacity: **Skyline Ballroom/Admiral Stateroom:** 3,816 sq. ft; 300 reception, 225 seated; **Alki Room:** 1,670 sq. ft; 120 reception, 100 seated; **Duwamish Room:** 1,390 sq. ft; 90 reception, 70 seated; **Admiral Stateroom:** 756 sq. ft; 40 reception, 36 seated; **outside deck** is available from the Skyline Ballroom, Alki Room, and Duwamish Room; **outside patio** is also available—please inquire

Price range: varies according to time, size, and menu selection

Catering: full-service, in-house catering; off-premise catering also available

Types of events: company meetings, sit-down dinners, luncheons or brunches, cocktails and hors d'oeuvres, or other special events

Availability and terms

Reserve your room six months to one year prior to the event; however, we can accommodate shorter notice. A deposit is required to reserve your date. Room fees are waived with a minimum of food and beverage ordered.

Description of services and facility

ADA: fully complies with ADA requirements

Parking: ample free parking; complimentary valet parking Friday and Saturday nights

Banquet services

- **Seating:** tables and chairs are provided
- **Servers:** staff included in the catering costs
- **Bar facilities:** full-service bar provided; host/no-host; liquor, beer, and wine
- **Linens:** linen tablecloths and napkins; colors available upon request
- **China and glassware:** restaurant silver, china, and glassware available
- **Decorations:** early decorating available
- **Cleanup:** handled by Salty's staff

Meeting and event services

- **Audio visual and equipment:** overhead, slide projector and screen available

Special services

Our catering associates work closely with you to ensure your event's success. We're experienced in working with a variety of different themes and will be happy to refer you to other services.

THE BEST VIEW OF SEATTLE IN SEATTLE

Located on Elliott Bay, Salty's on Alki offers a spectacular view of the Seattle skyline! Experience warm hospitality and exceptional Northwest cuisine from our waterfront banquet rooms, outside decks and patio. We are conveniently located eight minutes from downtown. Salty's is the perfect setting for both large and intimate groups.

See page 366 under Caterers/Food & Beverage Services
and page 574 under Restaurants.

 Please let this business know that you heard about them from the Bravo! Event Resource Guide.

SCOTTISH RITE MASONIC CENTER

1155 Broadway East
Seattle, Washington 98102
Contact:
Chris Williams or Brian Lorton
(206) 324-3330
Fax (206) 324-3332
Business Hours:
Mon–Fri 7am–4pm;
evenings and weekends by appointment

Capacity: up to 500 depending upon type of function
Price range: varies according to rooms used—$60 to $1,000; we offer per-hour rental to accommodate morning functions
Catering: the caterer of your choice or choose from a list of caterers familiar with our facility
Types of events: seminars, weddings, special or corporate events, forums, meetings, fund raisers, trade shows, performances, reunions, receptions, banquets

Availability and terms

The Scottish Rite Masonic Center offers meeting and banquet rooms to accommodate 10 to 500 people depending upon event. Reservations are accepted two years in advance. We are happy to accommodate short notice rentals if space is available. We will hold reservations for seven days after which we require a deposit with balance due prior to the event.

Description of services and facility

ADA: wheelchair accessible to all rooms
Parking: complimentary on-site parking
Banquet services

- **Seating:** tables and chairs available–arranged with you to fit your needs
- **Servers:** provided by you or your caterer
- **Bar facilities:** beer, wine, champagne with license provided by you or your caterer
- **Linens and napkins:** provided by you or your caterer (we have vinyl covering for smaller functions at no extra cost)
- **China:** china and flatware for 350 available or you or your caterer may provide
- **Decorations:** please inquire about guidelines
- **Cleanup:** by arrangement with our staff

Meeting and event services

- **Audio visual and equipment:** all rooms have a PA system which is included in your rental; 12' screen, slide projector, available on request

Special services

A member of our staff will always be available during your function. We have wine glasses and table lamps available for an additional charge.

OFFERING YOU FLEXIBILITY

From a list of caterers to a variety of setup designs, your creative ideas for events are endless. We are happy to work with you to ensure all rental arrangements will suit your needs.

the seattle aquarium

1483 Alaskan Way, Pier 59
Seattle, Washington 98101
Aquarium Scheduler (206) 386-4314
Office Hours: Mon–Fr`i 8am–5pm
Web site: www.seattleaquarium.org

Capacity: up to 600 people or more depending on type of event
Price range: starts at $400/$1,600 (exhibit space); auditorium and board room also available
Catering: select from our list of approved caterers
Types of events: corporate functions and meetings, weddings, receptions, proms, reunions, bar and bat mitzvahs, birthday parties, auctions, and celebrations of all occasions

Availability and terms

The entire Aquarium can be rented from 6:30pm to 1am every evening of the week from Labor Day to Memorial Day. From Memorial Day to Labor Day, The Aquarium is available from 8:30pm to 1am. A rental application should be completed at least four weeks prior to the event. A deposit ($100 for Exhibit Space or $50 Auditorium or Board Room) is required to confirm the date and is not refundable. The remaining base fees are due four weeks before the event. The deposit will be applied to the final bill.

Description of services and facility

ADA: accessible
Parking: street parking, pay lots and garages available
Banquet services

- **Seating:** limited tables are provided; up to 100 stacking chairs available
- **Servers:** provided by caterers; rental staff provided by The Aquarium
- **Bar facilities:** client or caterer provides liquor; caterers can provide bartender; liquor permit must be provided by caterer or submitted with application by client
- **Dance floor:** available through rental agency; ample electrical hookups
- **Linens, china and glassware:** available through caterer or provide your own
- **Decorations:** please inquire
- **Cleanup:** client provides; if cleanup extends past 2am, there is an extra charge

Meeting and event services

- **Audio visual and equipment:** projection screen (for auditorium rental only)

Special services

The Aquarium rental staff is available to assist with your event planning. In addition to tables and chairs, The Aquarium can provide a coat rack (holds up to 50 coats). Your group can enjoy a film on The Eruption of Mt. St. Helens or other subjects at the IMAXDome Theater located next to The Aquarium. Call (206) 622-1869 for theater rental information.

PARTY WITH THE "STARS!"

Sea stars, that is—and more than 380 other species of sea life. From the Underwater Dome to the Pacific Coral Reef, The Aquarium offers an affordable one-of-a-kind setting for your event. Call today and let us help you plan an unforgettable evening in another world. The Seattle Aquarium is a division of the Seattle Department of Parks and Recreation. The prices quoted above are subject to change. Call for more information.

100 University Street
Seattle, Washington 98101
Contact: John Ferguson
(206) 654-3140

Capacity: up to 500 guests for receptions
Price range: room rentals run from $50 to $3,000
Catering: catering provided by the Sheraton Seattle Hotel & Towers exclusively
Types of events: corporate events, weddings or receptions; meetings and other gatherings can be held in the auditorium, lecture hall, or board room

Availability and terms

The Seattle Art Museum offers six different areas to meet your needs. We recommend reserving your date as soon as possible; however, we can accommodate events with as little as two-weeks notice. A deposit is required to reserve your date with the balance due three days before the event.

Description of services and facility

ADA: completely accessible
Parking: several lots adjacent to facility; valet parking can be arranged
Banquet services
- **Seating:** up to 200 chairs, fourteen 5' round tables, and eight 6' rectangular tables provided
- **Servers:** all service staff provided by the Sheraton Seattle Hotel & Towers
- **Bar facilities:** all beverage service provided by the Sheraton Seattle Hotel & Towers
- **Dance floor:** museum floors are ideal for dancing
- **Linens, china, and glassware:** included in catering costs
- **Decorations:** only free-standing decorations allowed
- **Cleanup:** please remove anything you bring in; extra charge for cleaning if any additional cleaning is required

Meeting and event services
- **Audio visual and equipment:** available on request

SEATTLE'S PREMIERE DOWNTOWN ATTRACTION

The Seattle Art Museum displays some of the finest collections of art available for public viewing anywhere. The Museum also presents exciting opportunities to hold special events in a one-of-a-kind environment. A variety of stunning spaces are available, including an auditorium, board room, lecture hall, private dining room, and magnificent grand stairway and mezzanine. The Sheraton Seattle Hotel & Towers provides exclusive catering and can accommodate a wide range of events, from intimate gatherings to gala celebrations.

Find out how our convenient downtown location, singular atmosphere and creative catering can make your next event a masterpiece.

SEATTLE ASIAN ART MUSEUM

Located On Capitol Hill in Volunteer Park
1400 East Prospect
Seattle, Washington 98112
Contact: John Ferguson (206) 654-3140

Capacity: up to 200 guests for receptions
Price range: room rentals run from $200 to $2,000
Catering: your choice of caterers from our approved caterers list
Types of events: corporate events or weddings and receptions; meetings and other gatherings can be held in the auditorium or activities room

Availability and terms

The Seattle Asian Art Museum offers four different areas to meet your needs. We recommend reserving your date as soon as possible; however, we can accommodate events with as little as two-weeks notice. A deposit is required to reserve your date with the balance due three days before the event.

Description of services and facility

ADA: completely accessible
Parking: complimentary parking in front of the Museum; valet parking can be arranged
Banquet services

- **Seating:** up to 140 chairs, fourteen 5′ round tables, and eight 6′ rectangular tables provided
- **Servers:** all service staff provided by caterer from our approved caterers list
- **Bar facilities:** caterer provides
- **Dance floor:** space available for optional rented dance floor
- **Linens, china and glassware:** caterer provides
- **Cleanup:** please remove anything you bring in; extra charge for cleaning if any additional cleaning is required
- **Decorations:** only free-standing decorations allowed

Meeting and event services

- **Audio visual and equipment:** available upon request

A MEMORABLE BACKDROP FOR ANY OCCASION

Make your next event something really special. Hold it at the Seattle Asian Art Museum located on Capital Hill in Volunteer Park. Built in 1933, this distinctive facility features a superb collection of Chinese, Indian, Japanese, Korean and Southeast Asian works of art and will make a memorable backdrop for your next special event.

5701 Sixth Avenue South
Seattle, Washington 98108
(206) 689-7300
Please call for appointment
E-mail: sdc@schwartzbroscatering.com

Schwartz Brothers CATERING AT

SEATTLE DESIGN CENTER

Capacity: unique open facility ideal for 50 to 700 guests
Price range: prices vary according to event and custom menu selection; call for current menus
Catering: catering services provided, including floral services
Types of events: cocktail and hors d'oeuvre receptions, luncheons, reunions, holiday parties, bar and bat mitzvahs, community events, corporate affairs, seminars, weddings or full-service sit-down dinners for private or professional functions

Availability and terms

The Seattle Design Center offers three different venues to accommodate functions from 50 to 700. Reservations should be made as early as possible to ensure availability

Description of services and facility

ADA: completely accessible
Parking: unlimited free parking
Banquet services

- **Seating:** chairs and tables provided
- **Servers:** professional and friendly service staff
- **Bar facilities:** full-service bar and bartenders provided; Schwartz Brothers Catering arranges all alcoholic and non-alcoholic beverages
- **Dance floor:** oak parquet floors; ample electrical hookup
- **Linens, napkins, china and glassware:** china, glassware, linen tablecloths and napkins in assorted color provided
- **Decorations:** setting requires little decoration, but we are happy to accommodate any specific requests
- **Cleanup:** provided by Schwartz Brothers Catering

Special services

Schwartz Brothers Catering is committed to ensuring your wedding is memorable. We are happy to customize a menu to your specific needs as well as assist you in organizaing every single detail of your event. From food & beverage service to props, flowers, music, decorations, A/V equipment, espresso service, photographers, even invitations, you work with one person—the right person—who makes it all happen.

WHERE CREATIVE CELEBRATIONS COME ALIVE!

Seattle Design Center provides a unique setting where guests experience an unforgettable event. From hors d'oeuvre receptions to elegant buffets and sit-down dinners, we turn your special occaision into a celebration, your event into a sensation.

155 Mercer Street
Seattle, Washington 98109
Contact: Michael Betts, Rental Manager
(206) 443-2210; Fax (206) 443-2379
Office Hours: Mon–Fri 9am–6pm
E-mail: michaelb@seattlerep.org
Web site: www.seattlerep.org

Capacity: 90,000 square feet of Performance, Meeting and Lobby space accommodating up to 1,100
Price range: please call to discuss options available to your group or event
Catering: in-house catering is not available; recommendations are available upon request
Types of events: performances, annual meetings, conferences, seminars (5–850 people), weddings, social/corporate/specialty parties; if you can imagine it, we can present it

Availability and terms

A variety of performance spaces, meeting rooms and reception spaces are available. The Seattle Rep's seasonal hiatus is May through mid-September. Please call to inquire about your specific date. First consideration is always given to Seattle Repertory Theatre's own season.

Description of services and facility

ADA: all facilities fully accessible for both attendees and performers
Parking: several parking lots are conveniently located around the facility
Banquet services

- **Seating:** both theatres provide seating for your performance/meeting; **Bagley Wright Theatre** seats 856; **The Leo Kreielsheimer** seats 286; **Smaller venues** are also available; **Lobby** seats up to 350 for sit down dinner (tables and chairs must be provided by caterer)
- **Bar Facilities:** caterer provides; red wine negotiable
- **Decorations:** all on a case by case basis
- **Cleanup:** caterer to provide cleanup

Meeting and event services

- **Audio visual and equipment:** microphones and podium available for use; other technical needs can be acquired for each event
- **Events representative:** a staff member is provided to oversee each event

Special services

We offer discounted tickets for groups of ten or more people. Senior and youth groups save over 60% on tickets when they attend as a group. Theatre tickets are an excellent fund raiser. Non-profit organizations can purchase tickets at a deeply discounted rate and re-sell or auction them to supporters for their full value. With a group ticket purchase, we offer free space rental for a pre-show reception or silent auction when available.

SPECTACULAR EVENTS AT SEATTLE REPERTORY THEATRE

See a show or put on your own show (convention, dinner, etc.) at The Rep, the Northwest's only Tony® Award-Winning Theatre. The Rep now boasts two stages, a glassed-in rotunda, and a spacious lobby, all located on the grounds of the beautiful Seattle Center.

 Please let this business know that you heard about them from the Bravo! Event Resource Guide.

Sheraton Seattle

HOTEL & TOWERS

1400 Sixth Avenue
Seattle, Washington 98101
Contact: Catering Department
(206) 389-5735
Catering Office Hours: Mon–Fri 8am–5pm
Web site: www.sheraton.com/seattle

Capacity: 20 to 1,400 seated; up to 2,400 for receptions; **Grand Ballroom:** elegantly appointed, accommodates 150 to 1,400; **Metropolitan Ballroom:** accommodates 100 to 360; **Cirrus Room:** located on 35th floor with a spectacular view of downtown Seattle, this room features Venetian chandeliers, and Italian marble foyer, accommodates 75 to 250; **Fullers Premiere Private Dining:** personalized events in an artful setting, accommodates 15 to 150
Price range: prices vary according to menu; we are happy to create custom packages
Catering: full-service, in-house catering; Kosher or off-premise available
Types of events: formal sit-down dinners, buffet, cocktail and hors d'oeuvre receptions, rehearsal dinners, reunions and luncheons

Availability and terms

All in-house facilities can be reserved. Certain restrictions apply for reservations. Please call your catering sales manager for details.

Description of services and facility

ADA: all facilities are fully accessible
Parking: on a space available basis in hotel garage for a nominal charge
Banquet services

- **Seating:** tables and chairs provided at no extra cost
- **Servers:** serving staff and on-site event management included in catering costs
- **Bar facilities:** full-service bar and staff; hosted or no-host events
- **Dance floor:** provided at no extra cost
- **Linens and napkins:** white and beige tablecloths; several colors of linen napkins available
- **China and glassware:** white china, silver flatware, classic stemware provided
- **Decorations:** floral/design staff on-site; let our staff customize each arrangement to fit your theme and budget

Overnight accommodations: special group rates available; deluxe guest rooms

OFF-PREMISE CATERING SERVICES

We are the exclusive caterer at the Seattle Art Museum and first option caterer at the Seattle Asian Art Museum. We have extensive experience catering at locations such as Act Theater, Pacific Science Center, The Paramount and other venues.

When it comes to the memorable occasions of life, let us add the special touches that reflect your personal style. Our catering experts can create an exquisite event for a multitude or a cozy, intimate gathering. Just for you. Just your style.

Call our catering department at (206) 389-5735

Shilshole Bay Beach Club

Special Events Catering
6413 Seaview Avenue N.W.
Seattle, Washington 98107
(206) 706-0257
Business Hours:
Call for an appointment
Web site: www.special-events.net

Capacity: South Room: 2,850 sq. ft. accommodate up to 150 seated or 200 reception style; **North Room:** 4,700 sq. ft. accommodate up to 250 seated or 300 reception style; **Entire Facility:** up to 450 seated or 500 reception style

Price range: South Room: $1,200 Saturday, $950 any other time; North Room: $1,400 Saturday, $1,100 any other time; please inquire for December rates

Catering: exclusive, full-service catering provided by Special Events Catering

Types of events: ideal for meetings, cocktails and hors d'oeuvres, sit-down dinners, buffets, luncheons or brunches, high school reunions, senior proms, and fund-raising auctions

Availability and terms

The Shilshole Bay Beach Club may be reserved up to two years in advance. Reception times available on Saturdays are 12pm to 5pm or 7pm to 12am. Reservations should be made as early as possible to ensure availability. Dates are often available on short term notice. A non-refundable deposit is required to reserve your date.

Description of services and facility

ADA: complies with ADA requirements

Parking: 200 complimentary parking spaces available

Banquet services

- **Seating:** tables and chairs provided by Special Events Catering
- **Servers:** professional service staff and on-site event management provided by Special Events Catering
- **Bar facilities:** full-service bar provided by Special Events Catering
- **Dance floor:** large area available for dancing
- **Linens, china and serviceware:** provided by Special Events Catering
- **Decorations:** provided by client
- **Cleanup:** provided by Special Events Catering

Meeting and event services

- **Audio visual:** equipment can be arranged by client or Special Events Catering can assist with arrangements

Special services

Our experienced catering staff is available to assist you in planning your event at our facility or venue of your choice.

SPECTACULAR WATERFRONT SITE

Located along Seattle's scenic Shilshole Bay, this elegant waterfront event facility offers superb views of Puget Sound and the Olympic Mountains from every room. Your guests can enjoy cool breezes and evening sunsets from one of the tiered outdoor terraces right at the water's edge.

5984 North Darrk Lane • Bow, Washington 98232
*(877) 2-SKAGIT or (877) 275-2448 • **Web site: www.theskagit.com***

Capacity: 460-seat Pacific Showroom, 460-seat Northwest Ballroom, 6 meeting rooms
Price range: varies according to room and menu selections
Catering: full-service in-house catering
Types of events: corporate meetings, retreats, conventions, trade shows, private gatherings, specialty theme parties, weddings

Availability and terms

The Skagit consists of 26,075 square feet of gaming, 103 deluxe rooms including 29 luxurious suites as well as 14,000 square feet of meeting/conference space for groups of various size. Reservations may be confirmed three months in advance. A 50% deposit with signed contract confirms your date.

Description of services and facility

ADA: fully accessible
Parking: ample free parking available
Amenities: luxury hotel, Las Vegas-style Casino, indoor heated pool and spa, fitness center, newly expanded convention center

Banquet services
- **Seating:** all seating layouts available
- **Servers:** provided by The Skagit
- **Bar facilities:** full service bar
- **Dance floor:** available upon request
- **Linens, napkins, china, and glassware:** provided by The Skagit
- **Decorations:** client may provide, or The Skagit can provide all decorations as well as assistance with theme parties
- **Cleanup:** provided by The Skagit

Meeting and event services
- **Audio visual and equipment:** all in-house please inquire

RETREAT, MEET, STAY AND PLAY... THE SKAGIT HAS IT.

At The Skagit work and play are interchangeable. Set in the glorious atmosphere of the Pacific Northwest's Skagit Valley, The Skagit combines the grace and elegance of a four star resort with the energy and excitement of a real Las Vegas style casino. Offering 103 deluxe guest rooms, 29 luxurious suites, a Casino with more than 600 slot machines, table games, three restaurants, live entertainment, and fully appointed conference rooms. Not to mention our new indoor pool with retractable roof, hot tub, sauna, fitness center, sundeck and a spacious 450-seat showroom/ballroom. Coming soon, a spectacular par 72, 18-hole golf course. The Skagit offers all the amenities to make any event perfect.

Skansonia Ferryboat

2505 N. Northlake Way • Seattle, Washington 98103
Contact: Tamara (206) 545-9109
Business Hours: Mon–Fri 10am–6pm • E-mail: skansonia@aol.com
Web site: www.skansonia.com

Capacity: seated up to 300; standing up to 400
Price range: varies depending upon menu selection, time and size of event
Catering: full-service, waterfront catering facility
Types of events: corporate and social; fine dining to summer barbecues; all-day seminars, retreats, trade shows, theme parties, casino nights, weddings

Availability and terms

Skansonia offers a large dining area, reception area, upstairs salon, and grand view balcony. Reservations are for four-hour periods, with one extra hour for setup. A $600 nonrefundable deposit is required. With 90-day notice an event may be postponed.

Description of services and facility

ADA: fully accessible
Parking: ample free parking
Banquet services

- **Seating:** tables and chairs provided
- **Servers:** professional and friendly serving staff
- **Bar facilities:** full bar set-up with friendly, professional bartenders
- **Dance floor:** large dance floor included in cost with electrical outlets
- **Linens and napkins:** cloth tablecloths and napkins on all tables for dinners; quality paper napkins for receptions; special requests available for additional charge
- **China and glassware:** house china and glassware provided
- **Decorations:** free standing decorations only; please, no votive candles

Special services

Enjoy a full NW experience. Taste the NW Native American Indian BBQ salmon or smoked seafood products. Drink the local coffee brews, microbrews and wines. Or, if you want to escape, we can bring you Jamaican "jerk" chicken from the islands, paella from Spain and dim sum from China. Let Skansonia bring the entire NW experience together in one evening.

MOORED ON LAKE UNION

The Skansonia is a retired 1928 Washington State Ferry now available for private parties and receptions. This 164' ferry is moored on the north shore of Lake Union and has an incredible view of the city skyline, Lake Union, and the UW. During the winter, you'll be cozy and warm with forced-air heating and two fireplaces; in the summer, you'll be cool from the breeze when you open the huge bay doors at either end of the ferry.

SLEEPING LADY

7375 Icicle Road • Leavenworth, WA 98826
Contact: Michael Molohon
(800) 574-2123; Fax (509) 548-6312
E-mail: info@sleepinglady.com
Web site: www.sleepinglady.com

Sleeping Lady is a mountain conference retreat located on 67 woodland acres beside Icicle Creek

---

Capacity: 10 meeting spaces, from 352 to 2,020 square feet, accommodate up to 200
Price range: $91 to $202 per person per night, includes lodging, three gourmet buffet meals, meeting space, beverage breaks, A/V equipment and general meeting supplies; day conference rates available
Catering: full service, in-house catering provided
Types of events: conferences, meetings, corporate retreats, board meetings, team building programs, reunions, receptions, holiday dinners, and parties

Availability and terms

Year-round conference center and mountain retreat; deposit required.

Description of services and facility

ADA: fully accessible
Parking: complimentary parking
Banquet services
- **Seating:** all tables and comfortable chairs provided and set up to meet your needs
- **Servers:** courteous, well-trained and experienced professional staff
- **Bar facilities:** beer, wine and spirits; host or no-host events; Grotto bar
- **Dance floor:** space available for dancing
- **Linens and china:** tablecloths and china included in costs

Meeting and event services
- **Audio visual and equipment:** state-of-the-art equipment included in room rate

Special services

Our experienced event planners will assist you throughout the conference planning process. Sleeping Lady's exceptional customer service inspires most groups to book their next event with us before they check out! Ask about our complimentary winter charter transportation for groups.

A CONFERENCE EXPERIENCE THAT ENHANCES COMMUNICATION AND ENCOURAGES CREATIVE THINKING

Sleeping Lady, a mountain conference retreat, is designed for professional and personal renewal. We offer advanced electronic conference support in a casual meeting environment. Feast on the freshest of good foods, sleep in down-fluffed comfort, stroll our woodland trails, work out in the fitness room, arrange for a massage. Outdoor recreation at Sleeping Lady includes hiking, cycling, cross-country skiing, and snowshoeing. Enjoy nature walks, birdwatching, and stargazing led by our staff naturalist. Golf, whitewater rafting, horseback riding, and downhill skiing are available nearby.

The Chinese Room at Smith Tower

506 Second Avenue, 35th Floor
Seattle, Washington 98104
Contact: Erin Mitchell,
Hospitality Director
(206) 622-3131
Fax (206) 622-9357
Office Hours: Mon–Fri 7am-4pm
View by Appointment Only
E-mail: erinm@smithtower.com • ***Web site: www.chineseroom.com***

Capacity: The Chinese Room can accommodate as many as 99 people in a reception style atmosphere and can comfortably seat 70 for a dinner setting

Price range: reasonable rates; please call

Catering: The Smith Tower offers a variety of exceptional, full service caterers who specialize in a broad range of culinary selections

Types of events: special events, formal or informal dinners, weddings and receptions, rehearsal dinners, business and corporate meetings, bar and bat mitzvahs as well as seminars

Availability and terms

You will want to make reservations well in advance, especially during peak seasons, though short notice bookings are possible depending on availability. Deposit required.

Description of services and facility

ADA: fully accessible

Parking: valet parking can be arranged; pay lots nearby; on and off-street parking

Banquet services

- **Seating:** all tables and chairs provided by The Chinese Room
- **Servers:** to be provided by caterer
- **Bar facilities:** client or caterer provides all alcoholic beverages; banquet permit required
- **Dance floor:** large black marble dance floor included in cost
- **Linens, china and glassware:** provided by caterer
- **Decorations:** nothing that will damage the facility; no birdseed, rice, confetti or popcorn
- **Cleanup:** caterer and Smith Tower responsible for cleaning arrangements

Meeting and event services

- **Audio visual and equipment:** arrangements can be made for any of your audio visual needs

Special services

We are happy to assist you with additional arrangements for your special event.

THE LEGENDARY CHINESE ROOM AND OBSERVATORY

High atop the historic 1914 Smith Tower, this newly remodeled and elegant room offers a spectacular 360 degree view of Mt. Rainier, Puget Sound, and the full grandeur of the Olympic and Cascade mountain ranges. In the evening, the Smith Tower provides a magnificent view of the Seattle city lights. The original ornate copper and brass elevators in the building are still operated by hand. The Chinese Room is decorated in 17th century works of art and furniture made of imported Chinese blackwood, intricately carved by hand. The ceiling panels recite the history of Washington, Alaska and Seattle in Chinese characters. A main attraction of the Chinese Room is the 'Wishing Chair,' a gift from the Empress of China. Legend has it that an unmarried woman sitting in the chair and wishes to be married will be a bride within a year's time.

36005 S.E. Ridge Street • Snoqualmie, WA 98065
Contact: Catering Department
(425) 396-6000 • E-mail: www.tpcsr.com
Web site: tpcsnoqualmieridge.com

Capacity: **Grand Ballroom:** up to 300 for a seated affair; up to 450 reception style; **View Ridge:** 120 seated; **Twin Peaks:** 80 seated; **Glacier Peak:** 100 seated; **Cascadia Foyer:** 50 seated
Price range: prices vary depending on menu selection and day of week
Catering: custom, full-service in-house catering
Types of events: corporate parties, business meetings and retreats, golf tournaments, sit-down dinners, luncheons, breakfasts, bar and bat mitzvahs, holiday parties, auctions, weddings and receptions

Availability and terms

This truly magnificent facility offers four private rooms that can be combined to create a Grand Ballroom. We suggest you make your reservation as early as possible to ensure booking availability. A booking fee and signed reservation agreement is required to reserve your date.

Description of services and facility

ADA: fully accessible
Parking: complimentary parking; additional valet parking can be arranged
Banquet services
- **Seating:** all necessary tables and chairs provided at no extra cost
- **Servers:** professional, attentive staff to meet your every need
- **Bar facilities:** provided by Snoqualmie Ridge Golf Club
- **Dance floor:** portable dance floors available
- **Linens and napkins:** linens and napkins provided; specialty linens available upon request
- **China and glassware:** fine china and stemware provided
- **Decorations:** we will be happy to discuss your ideas and needs

Meeting and event services
- **Audio visual and equipment:** we can arrange to accommodate any of your needs

Special services

In the finest tradition of private clubs, we offer world class hospitality and impeccable service. Our signature menus and lavish food presentations denote the characteristics of a prominent event facility. Allow our professional staff to assist you in making your event memorable.

CREATED FOR NORTHWEST TRADITIONS

Surrounded by the majestic beauty of nature sits the Snoqualmie Ridge Golf Club. A place where dreams come true and traditions continue. Our banquet facility is rich in details, featuring Craftsman style furnishings, state-of-the-art audio equipment and Country Club comfort. What awaits you is elegance and luxury, and a staff trained to accommodate the most discriminating palate. Perfection, only 20 minutes from Bellevue.

SORRENTO HOTEL

900 Madison Street • Seattle, Washington 98104-9742
Contact: Director of Catering (206) 622-6400 or (800) 426-1265; Fax (206) 343-6159
Office Hours: Mon–Sat 9am–5pm • E-mail: mail@hotelsorrento.com
Web site: www.hotelsorrento.com

Capacity: three rooms combined will accommodate up to 200 people; **Penthouse Suite:** U-shape 15, theatre 40, classroom 16, reception 60, banquet 40; **Top of the Town:** U-shape 32, theatre 80, classroom 44, reception 120, banquet 80; **Sorrento Room:** theatre 25, classroom 16, reception 45, banquet 24

Price range: varies according to menu selection

Catering: full-service in-house catering

Types of events: banquets, luncheons, buffet, cocktails and hors d'oeuvres; rehearsal dinners, business meetings and seminars; graciously elegant atmosphere for any special event

Availability and terms

We suggest you make your reservations as soon as possible, especially for summer and holiday events. The Sorrento always tries to accommodate every customer's needs, so reservations can be made on shorter notice if space is available.

Description of services and facility

ADA: all facilities are fully accessible

Parking: valet parking available

Banquet services

- **Seating:** up to 80 people for a sit-down dinner; arrangements vary according to room
- **Servers:** all servers and support staff available through hotel
- **Bar facilities:** full-service bar; we provide all beverages, bartenders, and servers
- **Dance floor:** available for rent upon request
- **Linens and napkins:** white linens with white skirting
- **China and glassware:** silver, china, and glassware provided by hotel
- **Decorations:** we will be happy to discuss your ideas and needs
- **Cleanup:** handled by the Sorrento staff

Meeting and event services

- **Audio visual and equipment:** available upon request

Special services

Town Car and limousine services available.

ELEGANCE AND SERVICE AT ITS FINEST

European charm and personalized service are renowned at the elegant Sorrento Hotel. Each banquet room has a different city view, each unique in design and ambiance.

SOUTH PARK COMMUNITY CENTER

4851 S. Tacoma Way • Tacoma, WA 98409
Contact: Center Supervisor
(253) 591-5299
Business Hours: Mon–Thurs 8am–8pm; Fri 8am–5pm; Sat 9am–2pm
Web site: www.tacomaparks.com

Capacity: two rooms; 325 and 225 people
Price range: please call for rates
Types of events: banquets, meetings, reunions, weddings, receptions

Availability and terms

South Park Community Center has two rental halls. Six-month advance reservation advised. Full rental fee required to reserve your date. Cancellations must be received in writing 60 days prior to your event to receive a 50% refund. A refundable damage deposit is required 15 days prior to rental date.

Description of services and facility

ADA: fully accessible
Parking: ample free parking
Banquet services

- **Seating:** 650 chairs; 30 rectangular, 8 eight-foot, 40 round tables
- **Servers:** provided by caterer
- **Bar facilities:** caterer provides liquor, bartender, and banquet license to serve liquor
- **Dance floor:** accommodates up to 325 people; electrical outlets available
- **Linens and napkins:** provided by caterer
- **China and glassware:** provided by caterer
- **Decorations:** no staples, nails, or duct tape; decorating time included in rental time; candles in enclosed containers only
- **Cleanup:** renter to clean

Special services

The Community Center offers kitchen facility for outside caterer's use. A staff person will remain on site during your event.

PARK SETTING

Featuring an excellent dance floor, the recently remodeled South Park Community Center is located in an attractively landscaped park. The adjacent rose garden and gazebo make a charming backdrop for weddings.

A facility of Metro Parks Tacoma.

Located at Seattle Center • Entrance at Broad and John Streets
Sales Office: 203-6th Avenue North • Seattle, Washington 98109
(206) 905-2180, (800) 964-7695; Fax (206) 905-2107
E-mail: skyline@spaceneedle.com • ***Web site: www.spaceneedle.com***

SKYLINE™

Capacity: 3,755 sq. ft.; 20 to 350 people; additional space available on the Observation Deck (seasonal), at Seattle Center and Pacific Science Center

Price range: please call for current prices; custom-designed menus; elevator ride is included

Catering: full-service catering at the Space Needle and off-premise

Types of events: business meetings, seminars, receptions, breakfast, brunch, lunch or dinner, buffets, birthdays, anniversaries, etc.

Availability and terms

The newly remodeled 100-ft. SkyLine Level has private rooms that can be used individually or in combination to host up to 350 guests. Reservations taken up to one year in advance or as close as one week, depending on availability. A deposit is required to reserve your date. Prepayment required.

Description of services and facility

ADA: fully complies with ADA requirements

Parking: valet parking on a first-come, first-served cash basis; ask about additional parking and monorail

Banquet services

- **Seating:** variety of table sizes; comfortable padded chairs, perimeter seating ledge
- **Servers:** staff included in catering costs, plus service charges
- **Bar facilities:** full-service bar, bartenders; Space Needle provides all beverages; policies per W.S.L.C.B. and Space Needle management
- **Dance floor:** brand new granite dance floor
- **Linens, napkins, china and glassware:** provided; classic china and silver service available
- **Cleanup:** provided by the Space Needle at no extra charge; special decorations and supplies must be removed immediately following the event

Meeting and event services

- **Audio visual and equipment:** full array of audio visual equipment available

Special services

The Space Needle catering team offers personalized attention to every detail of your event and customized menu planning. We can also arrange for added touches like floral arrangements, ice carvings, decorations, entertainment, and photographers.

THE SKYLINE LEVEL

Our unmatched views and freshly prepared Northwest cuisine will assure a unique and unforgettable event.

See page 63 under Attractions & Activities.

Please let this business know that you heard about them from the Bravo! Event Resource Guide.

SPIRIT MOUNTAIN
CASINO

P.O. Box 39 • Grand Ronde, OR 97347
Contact: Group Sales (800) 760-7977
Business Hours: Mon–Fri 8am–5pm
Casino Hours: 24 hours
E-mail: groupsales@spiritmtn.com
Web site: www.spiritmountain.com

Capacity: Rogue River Room: 2,500 square-foot room that divides into two equal sections, up to 200 banquet-style or 250 theater-style; **Kalapuya Room:** 2,200 square-foot room that divides into two sections, up to 160 banquet-style or 225 theater-style

Price range: room is complimentary with a $150 minimum food and beverage purchase

Catering: full-service, in-house

Types of events: meetings, seminars, conventions, luncheons, dinners, receptions, parties, weddings, corporate functions

Availability and terms

Contact Group Sales at (800) 760-7977. Online RFP available at ***www.spiritmountain.com***.

Description of services and facility

ADA: fully complies

Parking: ample free parking, including complimentary valet service

Banquet services

- **Seating:** maximum seating capacity is 250 theater-style in the Rogue River Room; other seating styles available for both rooms
- **Servers:** provided
- **Stage/dance floor:** complimentary with advance notice
- **Linens, napkins, china and glassware:** provided
- **Decorations:** allowed with prior approval
- **Cleanup:** provided

Meeting services

- **Audio visual and equipment:** overhead, slide projector, LCD projector, TV, VCR, flip charts, podium, cordless hand-held and lavaliere microphones

Entertainment: At Oregon's most popular attraction, you'll find 1,500 slots machines, blackjack, poker, roulette, craps, Pai Gow and Let It Ride poker, Keno, a Big 6 Wheel, off-track betting, and an 850-seat bingo hall which also hosts live headline entertainment. Live weekend entertainment is featured in the Summit View Lounge. The 5,200 sq. ft. non-smoking casino features all the games and slots found in the regular casino in a non-smoking environment.

Dining: Legends restaurant features Northwest cuisine. Coyote's Buffet presents a rotating menu with over 300 dishes. Other options include the Summit View, a casual dining experience; Rock Creek Court featuring an American Grill, a New York-style deli and traditional Asian Cuisine; and Spirit Mountain Café, proudly brewing Starbucks® Coffee.

Lodging: Spirit Mountain Lodge has 100 guest rooms and suites featuring Northwest-style furnishings and original cultural art. A hospitality suite to accommodate up to 15 people is also available. Group rates available.

We're located about an hour from Portland and a half hour from Salem.
Groups may be eligible for free luxury motorcoach transportation.

the
STIMSON-GREEN
mansion

1204 Minor Avenue • Seattle, WA 98101
(206) 624-0474; Fax (206) 624-9596
Business Hours: Mon–Fri 10am–4pm
Facility shown by appointment
E-mail: sgm@stimsongreen.com
Web site: www.stimsongreen.com

Capacity: up to 200 for buffet receptions; 48 for sit-down dinners, luncheons and seminars
Price range: varies according to event and menu selection; please call for current rates
Catering: custom, in-house catering
Types of events: receptions, seminars, banquets, holiday parties, sit-down dinners/lunches

Availability and terms

Reservations are accepted up to one year in advance. A deposit is required to hold your date. Time periods available: Corporate meetings/seminars: Tuesday–Friday (8am–6pm). Receptions: Tuesday–Friday (6pm–11pm); Saturday–Sunday (11:30am–5pm and 6pm–11pm).

Description of services and facility

Parking: available; please inquire about rates
Banquet services

- **Seating:** upholstered chairs and tables provided
- **Servers:** service staff provided; 20% gratuity applied to catering charges
- **Bar facilities:** client provides alcoholic beverages with a banquet permit; Stimson-Green provides bartenders, stemware and nonalcoholic beverages
- **Linens and napkins:** white tablecloths, napkins and runners provided
- **China and glassware:** Royal Doulton china and appropriate glassware provided
- **Decorations:** the mansion is a very unique and ornate backdrop; little embellishment is needed
- **Cleanup:** provided by Stimson-Green service staff

Facility

This turn-of-the-century home exhibits an excellent flow for entertaining. Each of our "function" rooms, as well as the grand staircase, opens to an ornate, oversized central hall. **Exterior:** classic English Tudor; **Library:** medieval-style fireplace, piano, detailed hardwoods; **Parlor:** Neo-Classic with Greco-Roman friezes covering the walls and ceiling; **Dining Room:** Italian Renaissance with gleaming sycamore paneling and Italian tile fireplace; **Veranda:** covered porch enclosed and heated during the winter months.

Special services

The Stimson-Green Mansion is a unique location for corporate seminars, retreats and receptions. The atmosphere is an elegant and refreshing change from the more standard meeting facilities. Your guests will enjoy the delicious custom catering by our Executive Chef and Sous Chef. Make use of the many diverse rooms available for receptions, group presentations or breakout spaces.

THE PRIDE OF FIRST HILL

Make your next company party or meeting a memorable one at the Stimson-Green Mansion! Our professional staff look forward to helping you make every detail of your event a success.

A DESIGNATED STATE AND NATIONAL HISTORIC SITE — 100 YEARS OLD IN 2001

(206) 325-3926

STUDIO catering

1406-10th Avenue, Second Floor • Seattle, Washington 98122
Contact: Kit Vannocker (206) 325-3926
E-mail: studio7000@qwest.net • ***Web site: www.studio7000.com***

Capacity: three studios offering 1,200 to 8,600 sq. ft.; events from 50 to 375 guests
Price range: $85 to $150 per guest inclusive; facility, parking, catering, bar, cleaning fee; price defined by event requirements and menu selections
Catering: full service on-site offered by Studio Catering's Executive Chef Brenda Neuweiler-Casas
Types of events: ideal for any type of social or business event

Availability and terms

Tour facility and reserve space up to 10 months prior to event. Your $1,000 non-refundable deposit and signed contract will hold your date.

Description of services and facility

ADA: fully accessible

Parking: reserved parking lots, street parking and valet available

Banquet services

- **Seating:** tables and chairs included
- **Servers:** some of Seattle's finest service staff provided
- **Bar facilities:** full service bar ranging from beer and wine to premium liquor
- **Dance floor:** yes
- **Linens, napkins, china and glassware:** standard selections included
- **Decorations:** please inquire for guidelines
- **Cleanup:** cleaning fee included; remove decorations you provide; no confetti, please

Meeting and event services

- **Audio visual and equipment:** we can coordinate your needs; ample power for DJs, band

Special services

Studio 7000 is a full service intimate facility offering extraordinary on site catering and one-on-one guest service. We specialize in innovative menus and fresh foods from around the world. We offer theme design, floral, entertainment and more. Our single mission is to provide unparalled service in an attempt to eliminate to event planning hassles.

TRENDY LOFT SYTLE URBAN SETTING ON CAPITOL HILL

Seattle's Studio 7000 is quickly becoming "the place" to hold an event of any type. From fashion shows to weddings! Located in historic Capitol Hill, our top floor location offers a private setting unlike hotels or other banquet facilities. The space boasts brilliant southwestern exposure making it light and airy for daytime events, while evening functions have sparkling views of downtown Seattle and the Space Needle. Our unique floor design, 14' ceilings with exposed beams, pine planked floors and sweeping windows give you a truly downtown "gallery feel."

STUDIO (o)ne sixteen

116 Elliott Avenue West
Seattle, Washington 98109
(206) 860-7449
Fax (206) 860-7488
Proprietors: Rocky Salskov & Mike Seidl
E-mail: dena@ravishingradish.com
Web site: www.studioonesixteen.com

Capacity: up to 100 for sit-down events, up to 203 for reception/cocktails events

Price range: $550 Mon–Thu, $600 Fri & Sun, $800 Sat; price includes eight hours (must include setup/cleanup); extra hours available for additional fee

Catering: full-service catering and event planning by Ravishing Radish Catering; at Ravishing Radish Catering, food is art

Types of events: ideal for wedding receptions, corporate functions, meetings, seminars, team building events, dances, rehearsal dinners

Availability and terms

$250 deposit and signed contract will reserve the event date. Balance is due 30 days prior to event. Please call for additional information.

Description of services and facility

Parking: limited street parking available; convenient parking garage available across the street

Banquet services

- **Seating:** tables and chairs available
- **Servers:** serving staff provided by caterer
- **Bar facilities:** banquet license required
- **Dance floor:** existing floor suitable for dancing
- **Linens, napkins, china and glassware:** coordinated by caterer
- **Decorations:** provided by client; early access for decorating available
- **Cleanup:** provided by caterer

A UNIQUE VENUE IN DOWNTOWN SEATTLE

With 3,600 square feet of stylish artist's studio, Studio One Sixteen is the perfect location for your next event. The Studio's urban feel along with its wood-beamed ceilings make it a truly unique venue in centrally located downtown Seattle.

For a photo tour and further information,
please visit our website at
www.studioonesixteen.com

Sun Mountain Lodge

P.O. Box 1000
Winthrop, Washington 98862
(800) 572-0493
Seattle Office: Lisa Adair
(425) 487-6638; Fax (425) 487-1278
E-mail: smtnsale@methow.com
Web site: www.sunmountainlodge.com

Capacity: 384 to 2,112 square feet of event space accommodating groups up to 200
Price range: prices vary depending on food and beverage selections
Catering: provided by Sun Mountain Lodge's award winning restaurant
Types of events: corporate retreats, conferences, meetings, team building, outdoor events; banquets, receptions, weddings, rehearsal dinners, and more

Availability and terms

This popular Northwest resort accepts reservations up to five to ten years in advance (shorter notice available depending on space availability; room rates not confirmed until one year out). A $500–$1,000 deposit is required on booking with the balance due 90 days prior to arrival.

Description of services and facility

ADA: fully accessible
Parking: ample complimentary parking adjacent to Lodge
Banquet services

- **Seating:** all tables, chairs and/or patio furniture provided and set up to meet your needs
- **Servers:** professional service staff included in catering costs
- **Bar facilities:** full service bar; host or no-host; cocktail stroller also available
- **Dance floor:** available at additional charge
- **Linens, china and glassware:** included in catering costs
- **Decorations:** please inquire; nothing that will damage the facility
- **Cleanup:** handled by Sun Mountain Lodge

Meeting and event services

- **Audio visual and equipment:** podium, microphones, easels, flipcharts, overhead and slide projectors provided; we'll be happy to coordinate any additional A/V needs

Special services

Let our experienced event staff design non-traditional group or team building activities for your retreat, conference, or event.

DELUXE RESORT SET ON 3,000 PRIVATE ACRES OF MAGNIFICENT WILDERNESS

Sun Mountain Lodge has won distinguished interior design awards for creating space that meets your highest expectations. 115 guestrooms featuring beautiful rustic furniture with bedspreads and decor handcrafted by local artisans. Many rooms feature fireplaces and jetted tubs. Several of our meeting rooms offer the spectacular backdrop of the entire Methow Valley and during breaks, your group can wander out to a courtyard and recharge on fresh mountain air. Sunny 300 days a year, Sun Mountain offers a year-around playground with mountain biking, horseback riding, cross-country skiing, heli-skiing, ice skating, fly fishing and miles of hiking trails. Complete spa services available. Team building has never been so fun! Ask about our non-traditional group activities designed to celebrate the uniqueness of our surroundings. Scheduled air service is just 90 minutes away in Wenatchee or take the 170 mile scenic route by car from Seattle.

THE TACOMA NATURE CENTER

1919 S. Tyler Street • Tacoma, WA 98405
Contact: Center Staff
(253) 591-6439; Fax (253) 593-4152
Business Hours:
Mar–Oct: M–F 8am–5pm, Sat 10am–4pm
Nov: Tue–Fri 8am–5pm, Sat 10am–3pm
Dec: Tue–Fri 8am–4pm, Sat 10am–3pm
Jan–Feb: Tue–Fri 8am–5pm, Sat 10am–4pm
Web site: www.tacomaparks.com

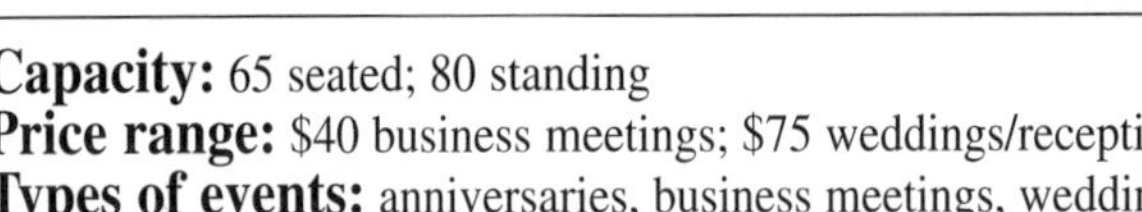
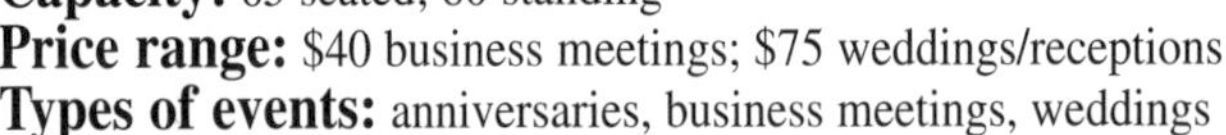

Capacity: 65 seated; 80 standing
Price range: $40 business meetings; $75 weddings/receptions
Types of events: anniversaries, business meetings, weddings

Availability and terms

The Tacoma Nature Center auditorium is one of the most unique facilities available. It's southern wall of windows slides open to reveal the beauty of the natural preserve. It can accommodate up to 80 people with a two-hour minimum rental time. A deposit is required to secure reservation. A $220 refundable damage deposit is also required. Cancellations must be received 14 days prior to your event to receive a full refund.

Description of services and facility

ADA: fully accessible
Parking: free parking for up to 50 cars
Banquet services

- **Seating:** 90 chairs, 18 folding tables
- **Servers:** caterer to provide
- **Bar facilities:** caterer to provide
- **Linens and napkins:** caterer to provide
- **China and glassware:** caterer to provide
- **Decorations:** masking tape only, no pins; decorating time included in rental time
- **Cleanup:** renter to clean

Special services

In addition to the auditorium, a scenic outdoor area is also available for weddings. Staff person on site during event.

BEAUTIFUL WOODED SETTING

The Tacoma Nature Center is a 54-acre, wooded, urban nature preserve. It is ideally suited for small receptions, meetings and business retreats. Full audio-visual support is available at no additional charge.

A facility of Metro Parks Tacoma.

The Vault at The Tacoma Rhodes Center

949 Market Street, Suite 542 • Tacoma, Washington 98402
(253) 597-4141; Fax (253) 597-3606
E-mail: robinnest2000@cs.com • ***Web site: www.vaultcatering.com***

Capacity: accommodates from 15 to 700
Price range: please inquire; room rental rates vary from $75 to $900
Catering: full-service in-house catering, exclusively by The Vault Catering
Types of events: conferences, trade shows, fundraisers, receptions, holiday parties, reunions, weddings, rehearsal dinners, banquets and receptions

Availability and terms

You can reserve The Tacoma Rhodes Center up to six months in advance. There is a four-hour minimum time block. A 50% deposit with the signed contract will reserve your date. Cancellations require a 180-day written notice.

Description of services and facility

ADA: fully accessible
Parking: 300 to 500 space available in parking garage adjacent to The Tacoma Rhodes Center
Banquet services

- **Seating:** tables and chairs provided
- **Servers:** professional service staff provided by The Vault Catering
- **Bar facilities:** fully licensed for full-service host or no-host bar service
- **Dance floor:** available for rent
- **Linens, napkins, china and glassware:** available for rent
- **Decorations:** please inquire; nothing that will damage the facility
- **Cleanup:** please remove any decorations you bring in; we'll handle the rest

Meeting and event services

- **Audio visual and equipment:** rental costs include use of A/V equipment including television, VCR, stereo, projectors, screens, easels and other conveniences as well as access to business services including in-room telephone, voice messaging and fax service

Special services

The Vault Catering provides you with a personal event planner on-site at The Tacoma Rhodes Center to assist you with all your planning needs.

THE TACOMA RHODES CENTER IS ALIVE WITH ACTIVITY

Formerly the home of the UPS law school, the newly renovated Tacoma Rhodes Center features a dramatic five-story atrium capped with a huge skylight that drenches the interior space with light. Elevators take off from the Broadway lobby atrium area and rise to the fifth floor conference center. Once again, this beautiful center bustles with activity and life making it a centerpiece of downtown Tacoma.

Tacoma Union Station

1717 Pacific Ave., Room #2448 • Tacoma, WA 98402
Contact: Rotunda Rental Coordinator
(253) 863-5173, ext. 223
Fax (253) 863-2040 • Office Hours: by appointment

Capacity: accommodates up to 1,200 reception style and 800 seated, utilizing all three floors; also ideal for smaller functions using the Rotunda level alone

Price range: $700 to $1,200 ($200 per hour for event and $100 per hour for setup and cleanup); additional security charges apply for groups of over 400 people

Catering: client is to provide all catering services; a 10'x20' catering area is available adjacent to the rotunda main floor with counter, sink, and a small ice machine; garbage cans, coat racks (150 capacity) and minimal cleaning tools provided

Types of events: Union Station is ideal for award ceremonies, retirement banquets, company parties and holiday functions, receptions, dinners, reunions, banquets, weddings, dances, and any other type of private, social, or business event

Availability and terms

Union Station is available for weekend and holiday functions, or on weeknights after 5:30pm. A 25% nonrefundable deposit will secure your date with the balance due 30 days prior to your event.

Description of services and facility

ADA: fully accessible from the main entrance on Pacific Avenue

Parking: on-street parking, with limited parking just north of the building

Banquet services

- **Seating:** caterer and client provide all tables and chairs
- **Servers:** provided by you or your caterer
- **Bar facilities:** caterer provides all beverage service
- **Dancing and sound levels:** the Rotunda's original marble floors are ideal for dancing and no other flooring is needed; due to the nature of the Rotunda, we require that music levels be at or below 85 decibels
- **Decorations:** please inquire; no taping, tacking, or other forms of decorations that will damage the facility; also, no helium balloons or large candle displays
- **Cleanup:** please remove all the decorations you bring in and remove trash

Meeting and event services

- **Audio visual and equipment:** client provides all A/V and equipment for events

WORLD CLASS FACILITY, SPECTACULAR VIEW

We are pleased to offer one of the most unique settings in the Northwest to hold your event. Currently a public art display by the famed local glass artist Dale Chihuly resides in the Union Station. We are not only a beautiful building, but are a world class facility offering a mixture of history, art, local flavor and some of the most spectacular views of the surrounding areas. Please contact the Rotunda Coordinator with questions and/or to make an appointment. Currently we are booking one year in advance for summer and fall dates. Please call early to reserve your date.

& TEMPLE T THEATRE

47 St. Helens Avenue
Tacoma, Washington 98402
Please call (253) 272-2042
Fax (253) 272-3793
Business Hours: Mon–Fri 8:30am–5:30pm

Capacity: **Roof Garden:** 2,450 sq. ft., up to 180; **Plaza Grand Ballroom:** 7,924 sq. ft., up to 800; **Corinthian:** 3,660 sq. ft., up to 300; **Gothic Ballroom:** 3,280 sq. ft., up to 300; **Mt. Adams Hall:** 1,254 sq. ft., up to 85; **Mt. Bachelor Hall:** 1,200 sq. ft., up to 85; **Ionic Ballroom:** 1,457 sq. ft., up to 90; **Doric Hall:** 1,339 sq. ft., up to 85; **Rainier:** 1,679 sq. ft., up to 90; **Board Room:** 633 sq. ft., up to 35; **Temple Theatre Ballroom:** 8,000 sq. ft. up to 1,500 theatre-style, 750 for receptions, or 400 classroom-style

Price range: $275 to $2,000

Catering: full-service in-house catering; off premise catering also available

Types of events: corporate events, seminars, trade shows and, conventions

Availability and terms

We have ten unique banquet ballrooms in our historic building. TLCC also has a 1,300-seat, full-production theatre. We can accommodate trade shows and large seminars. Each room represents the historic look and feel of the 1926 era. A deposit is required upon reservation. Flexible cancellation policy.

Description of services and facility

Parking: on-site parking plus free parking in area; valet parking available

Banquet services

- **Seating:** tables and chairs provided
- **Servers:** fully trained staff provided
- **Bar facilities:** full hosted or no-host services available
- **Linens and napkins:** tablecloths and napkins available in assorted colors
- **China and glassware:** variety of china and glassware available
- **Dance floor:** dance floors for 60 to 500 people; electrical outlets available
- **Decorations:** no nails, tacks, or staples; table decorations available
- **Cleanup:** provided by TLCC

Meeting and event services

- **Audio visual:** TLCC has a complete A/V rental department
- **Equipment:** slides, overhead, TVs, VCRs, flip charts, and more

Special services

Some rooms include spectacular views and decks. We are a perfect site for large groups, meetings, and conventions. Each room is private and elegant.

WE HAVE JUST THE RIGHT ROOM FOR YOU

The Landmark Convention Center offers exceptional meeting spaces, both large and small. Our full service catering department is unmatched in both quality and value. Conveniently located with easy freeway access in downtown Tacoma. Free parking available in our parking lot. A professional audio and visual rental department with trained technicians is available for each event. Finally, our in house production team will assist with the planning and implementing of your special event.

Tibbetts Creek Manor

(750 Renton-Issaquah Road)
Mail to: P.O. Box 1307
Issaquah, Washington 98027-1307
Contact: Events Manager
(425) 837-3366
Business Hours:
Mon–Thu 8:30am–12:30pm; Fri 8:30am–noon
E-mail: Tibbetts@ci.issaquah.wa.us

Capacity: up to 120 sit-down dinner, 150 standing reception style
Price range: January–July, September–December: $1,250/$1,300; August: $1,350/$1,450/$1,300; 6-hour time block; Seminar Rate: $300 Monday–Friday 8am–5pm only; Hourly: $100 per hour; Breakout rooms (upstairs): $25 each (all prices subject to rental increase 1/1/2002)
Catering: all caterers must be health certified with business license; caterer use fee: $50–$100
Types of events: seminars, meetings, anniversaries, retirements, picnics

Availability and terms

A nonrefundable deposit of $300, or 50% of fees, is required upon signing of contract to secure your date. Reservations are taken one year in advance. Events held downstairs with two additional breakout rooms upstairs. Weekend events in six-hour increments only; cancellations must be made 60 days in advance. No refund of nonrefundable deposit; no transfers/exchanges.

Description of services and facility

ADA: front entrance (south side) ADA ramp to deck; wheelchair access through front door
Parking: parking for 75 cars (two lots); no valet parking allowed

Banquet services

- **Servers:** staff provided by your caterer
- **Bar facilities:** liquor provided by client or caterer; banquet permit at Washington State liquor store; dispensed by caterer only (no red wine or beer kegs)
- **Dance floor:** available; limited electrical
- **Linens and napkins:** through caterer or rental agency
- **China and glassware:** through caterer or rental agency
- **Decorations:** nothing affixed to walls; no confetti/sprinkles; table decorations provided by client or florist
- **Cleanup:** caterer to clean all items noted on the Checklist; additional labor for our staff assistance deducted from the damage deposit; Client Checklist signed

Meeting and event services

- **Audio visual and equipment:** overhead and screen included in rental; 20'x40' canopy on outside deck

AMBIANCE AND ELEGANCE

Tibbetts Creek Manor is a unique rental facility sitting on three acres and offering ambiance combined with interior elegance. A recently finished two-month renovation has enlarged the Manor's meeting space; Sun Room/Great Room have now become one room. The Manor is a year-round facility. Note: Internal remodel will occur September 17, 2001 through November 7, 2001.

Tillicum Village
On Blake Island

Sharing Northwest Traditions

Located on beautiful Blake Island, just 8 miles from Seattle's Central Waterfront

2992 S.W. Avalon Way
Seattle, Washington 98126
(206) 933-8600
or (800) 426-1205
E-mail: mail@tillicumvillage.com
Web site: www.tillicumvillage.com

Under lease operated in conjunction with Washington State Parks and Recreation Commission.

Capacity: **Longhouse** accommodates over 850 guests; small **Conference Room** accommodates 60 standing or 40 seated for board meetings, retreats or small receptions
Price range: $65.00 inclusive per adult; please call to inquire about other rates
Catering: full-service in-house catering provided
Types of events: corporate, convention or social events; retreats, picnics, or meetings

Availability and terms

Reservations should be made as soon as possible. A $500 deposit is required at the time of booking. An additional deposit may be required depending on the size of the group.

Description of services and facility

ADA: fully accessible
Access: by charter vessel, float plane, or private vessel
Banquet services
- **Seating:** all tables and chairs are provided
- **Servers:** fully trained professional staff included in catering cost
- **Bar facilities:** private label wine; beer
- **Linens and napkins:** paper provided; specialty linens can be arranged for an additional fee
- **China and glassware:** individually designed fish plates provided; china can be arranged for
- **Decorations:** the Native American and Northwest decor requires little or no enhancement
- **Cleanup:** additional charges will apply if more than standard cleanup is required

Meeting and event services
- **Audio visual and equipment:** podium, microphone provided; other equipment can be rented

Special services

Tillicum Village is a truly unique Northwest experience which encompasses personalized attention to every detail of your event. We can arrange for added touches to enhance your experience such as entertainment, hosted bar, hor d'oeuvres reception, and more.

ENJOY THE PEACEFUL ISLAND SETTING WITH PRISTINE FORESTS THAT SURROUND TILLICUM VILLAGE

Tillicum Village is the essence of the Northwest with an authentic Native American longhouse, curved paths, award-winning salmon, spellbinding entertainment, plus a narrated harbor tour enroute to your event. This is a perfect setting with a professional staff to assist you with special requests. (Tillicum Village is under lease, and operated in conjunction with Washington State Parks and Recreation Commission.)

TITLOW LODGE COMMUNITY CENTER

8425-6th Avenue • Tacoma, WA 98465
Contact: Center Supervisor
(253) 591-5297
Business Hours: Mon–Fri 8:30am–5pm
Web site: www.tacomaparks.com

Capacity: 200 people standing; 140 seated
Price range: please call for rates
Types of events: parties, business banquets, meetings, reunions, weddings, receptions, anniversaries

Availability and terms

Titlow Lodge has one large hall and two smaller rooms for meetings. Reservations of three months in advance are recommended. Two-hour minimum reservation is required. Cancellation must be received in writing 60 days prior to your event to receive a 50% refund. A refundable damage deposit is required.

Description of services and facility

ADA: fully accessible
Parking: 100 free parking spaces
Banquet services

- **Seating:** tables and chairs for 140 people
- **Servers:** caterer to provide
- **Bar facilities:** caterer can provide liquor, bartender, and banquet license to serve liquor
- **Dance floor:** hardwood floors; electrical outlets available
- **Linens and napkins:** provided by caterer
- **China and glassware:** provided by caterer
- **Decorations:** hooks available on wall and ceiling; no tape on walls or floors, please; decorating and cleanup time included in rental time; candles in enclosed containers only
- **Cleanup:** renter to clean

Special services

A staff person will remain on the premises throughout your event.

PARK SETTING WITH BEACH ACCESS

Titlow Lodge is a recently refurbished Craftsman-style former hotel, built in 1911 near the Tacoma Narrows in the city's west end. The quaint lodge is located in a 49-acre park with beach access.

A facility of Metro Parks Tacoma.

93 Pike Street, Suite 307 • Seattle, Washington 98101 • (206) 447-9994
Web site: www.thetopofthemarket.com

Capacity: can accommodate groups from 10 up to 150
Price range: call for a full range of weekday and weekend prices
Catering: please select from our list of preferred caterers
Types of events: an ideal location for wedding ceremonies and receptions, rehearsal dinners, seminars, meetings, retreats, reunions, holiday parties and any special occasion

Availability and terms

Separately or combined, the Elliott Bay Room and the Atrium Room will accommodate a wide variety of social events. We recommend making reservations as early as possible during the holiday and wedding seasons, however, we are happy to accommodate shorter notice if space is available. Please inquire for rental prices and payment schedules.

Description of services and facility

ADA: wheelchair stair lift
Parking: Easy parking...Under the Market Skybridge on Western Avenue; special parking accommodations are easily arranged.

Banquet services
- **Seating:** chairs and a selection of table styles included in rental fee
- **Servers:** provided by caterer
- **Bar facilities:** renter or caterer provides all liquor and banquet permits
- **Dance floor:** overlooking Seattle's harbor, the Elliott Bay Room's hardwood floor is the perfect place for dancing and DJ set-up
- **Linens, napkins, china and glassware:** provided by the caterer or client
- **Decorations:** please inquire; Special services available for decorating needs
- **Cleanup:** arranged according to the nature of the event

Meeting and event services
- **Audio visual:** overhead projectors, slide projectors, screens, TV monitors, VCRs, easel white boards and flip charts, microphones, sound system and data ports
- **Equipment:** table top and standing podiums, rolling AV carts; galvanized tubs for iced-drink service, round, rectangular, and classroom size tables.

Special services

Special event services are available to offer you assistance with all your coordinating and planning needs to ensure that your special occasion at the Top of the Market is the perfect location to host your next event. We offer our guests a convenient location, as well as a magnificent view of Seattle's waterfront. Please call to arrange for a private tour of our unique setting.

VIEW OF ELLIOT BAY

Located in the heart of historic Pike Place Market, the Top of the Market is the perfect location to host your next event. We offer our guests a convenient location, as well as a magnificent view of Seattle's waterfront. Please call to arrange for a private tour of our unique setting.

1119 Eighth Avenue (at Seneca)
Seattle, Washington 98101
(206) 652-4255; Fax (206) 652-5858
E-mail: info@townhallseattle.org
Web site: www.townhallseattle.org

Capacity: historic Town Hall in the downtown Seattle area offers four event spaces: **The Great Hall** seats 900 for concerts and lectures; **Seneca Space** and the **Lobby** seat 375 and 350, respectively, or up to 800 for receptions—both can be divided into break-out spaces; **Board Room** accommodates 25 seated, or 50 for receptions

Price range: varies according to space rented; discounts for non-profits; please call for rates

Catering: select from our excellent list of preferred caterers, other caterers are acceptable, but require a minimal service fee

Types of events: meetings, seminars, weddings, auctions, performances, lectures, retreats, dinners, conferences, media presentations, and other special events

Availability and terms

A refundable security deposit is required to secure your date, with the full rental amount due no later than 14 days prior to your event.

Description of services and facility

ADA: fully accessible entry, navigation, and bathrooms

Parking: ample commercial parking available around building, and within one block

Banquet services

- **Seating:** we provide 20–60" round tables, 30 banquet tables, chairs for 200
- **Servers:** may be arranged through caterer
- **Bar facilities:** client or caterer provides liquor, bartender and all necessary permits
- **Dance floor:** required for Seneca Space; please call to inquire
- **Linens, china and glassware:** provided through your caterer
- **Cleanup:** please remove anything you bring into the building
- **Decorations:** please discuss your needs with Town Hall staff

Meeting and event services

- **Audio visual and equipment:** Town Hall provides in-house sound and theater lights, podium, overhead and slide projectors, screens

HISTORIC ELEGANCE IN THE HEART OF SEATTLE

Town Hall is a historic three-level 1922 building in Roman Revival style, suitable for cultural, social, business and community events. The stately furnishings remain intact, including the Great Hall's stained glass windows, soaring arches and dome, the six-columned portico entrance, and the Lobby's original art glass fixtures. The Lobby, recently renovated, can be used for dining, meetings, receptions, and partitioned break-out areas. Seneca Space offers the same options within a more contemporary decor. Town Hall is conveniently located one block from I-5 in the downtown area, close to the Convention Center, major hotels, and theaters. Our staff looks forward to helping you plan your next event at Town Hall!

Trattoria Grazie

2301 North 30th • Tacoma, Washington 98403
Contact: Thomas Day
(253) 627-0231; Fax (253) 627-4729
Business Hours: 11am–2am

Capacity: accommodates up to 250 people
Price range: varies according to party size and menu
Catering: full service, in-house catering provided by Trattoria Grazie, off-premise catering also available
Types of events: ideal for rehearsal dinners, weddings and receptions, banquets, special events, cocktails and hors d'oeurves, buffets, sit-down luncheons and dinners

Availability and terms

We recommend making reservations as soon as possible. A $150 deposit will reserve your date with the balance due the day of the event.

Description of services and facility

ADA: fully accessible
Parking: ample complimentary parking provided
Banquet services

- **Seating:** tables and chairs provided and arranged to meet your needs
- **Servers:** professional service staff provided
- **Bar facilities:** full service bar provided, host or no-host functions; Trattoria Grazie will provide all liquor, beer, or wine.
- **Linens:** table linens and napkins are provided
- **China and glassware:** fine china, silver and glassware provided
- **Decorations:** this elegant setting requires little decoration; however, guests are welcome to decorate to their liking; please, nothing that will damage the facility
- **Cleanup:** provided by Trattoria Grazie

Special services

To ensure your event is a success, our professional staff will walk you through the complete set-up and menu preparation process.

VOTED MOST ROMANTIC RESTAURANT IN PUGET SOUND!

Overlooking Commencement Bay in charming Old Town Tacoma, this elegant establishment consists of a two-story Victorian building with period fixtures and furnishings. Our Old World ambiance and sumptuous cuisine have created a loyal following in the Pacific Northwest. Celebrate the good life with Trattoria Grazie!

TUKWILA COMMUNITY CENTER

12424-42nd Avenue South
Tukwila, Washington 98168
(206) 768-2822; Fax (206) 768-0524
Mon–Fri 8am–7pm
Web site: www.ci.tukwila.wa.us

Capacity: **Gymnasium:** 650 for banquets, 1,200 for exhibits; **Banquet Hall:** 200 for banquets, 350 for exhibits; **Social Hall:** 100 for banquets, 250 for exhibits; **smaller meeting rooms** are also available

Price range: please call for current rates

Catering: preferred caterer list available, or use your own caterer

Types of events: trade shows, conferences, meetings, weddings, receptions, reunions, anniversaries, and other special occasions

Availability and terms

50% of the rental fees are due at the time of application; the balance and a deposit are due one month prior to the event. Tukwila residents may reserve space up to 12 months in advance. Non-Residents may reserve space up to 11 months in advance. Large trade shows and conferences may reserve space up to 24 months in advance.

Description of services and facility

ADA: fully accessible

Parking: complimentary parking provided for 300 cars

Banquet services

- **Seating:** tables and chairs provided
- **Servers:** provided by your chosen caterer
- **Bar facilities:** bar in social hall only; alcohol allowed by permission of the Community Center; some events may require a banquet permit
- **Dance floor:** hardwood floors in banquet hall and social hall
- **Linens, napkins, china and glassware:** caterer or renter provides
- **Decorations:** please inquire; nothing that will damage the facility
- **Cleanup:** responsibility of the client

Meeting and event services

- **Audio visual and equipment:** portable PA, overhead, TV/VCR, stage, and podium

Special services

A large grassy area overlooking the river may be reserved for outdoor ceremonies. An adjacent picnic shelter, softball field and soccer field may also be reserved.

A PERFECT PLACE FOR A PERFECT EVENT

Located on the scenic Duwamish River, the Tukwila Community Center offers breathtaking views of Mt. Rainier. A spectacular 48,000 sq. ft. facility, it features a variety of banquet and meeting rooms in a classic décor that will suit the needs of your special event. Elegant hardwood floors and expansive windows create the perfect atmosphere for any occasion. Whether you are planning a trade show, your wedding and reception, or a family reunion, our beautiful facility has an array of amenities to offer you.

1100-5th Avenue
Seattle, Washington 98101
Contact: Gillian Baumann (206) 623-1066
E-mail: gillian.baumann@tulio.com
Web site: www.hotelvintagepark.com

Capacity: up to 60 people for sit-down events; up to 100 people for reception/cocktail buffet
Price range: prices vary depending on menu selection and service options
Catering: full-service, in-house catering
Types of events: breakfast, lunch, dinner, receptions—events of all types

Availability and terms

For your next special event Tulio Ristorante's private dining facility is available seven days a week. A deposit is required to ensure your reservation.

Description of services and facility

ADA: fully complies with ADA requirements; access through the Hotel Vintage Park
Parking: limited valet parking available; ample pay lots available close by; side-street parking also available

Banquet services

- **Seating:** existing tables and chairs are arranged to accommodate your event
- **Servers:** service staff is included in in-house catering costs
- **Bar facilities:** full bar, extensive award-winning wine list
- **Linens and napkins:** white linens provided
- **China and glassware:** china and glassware provided
- **Cleanup:** included in in-house catering

Meeting and event services

- **Audio visual and equipment:** available upon request

Special services

All audio visual services can be arranged through an outside company. Complete your special event with accommodations for guests at the adjacent Hotel Vintage Park.

SUPERB FOOD, GREAT SERVICE, INTIMATE ATMOSPHERE IN DOWNTOWN SEATTLE

Enter the antique revolving doors of Seattle's Tulio Ristorante and you'll discover the sounds and aromas of a bustling Italian trattoria. Dine downstairs and enjoy a busy scene and theatre kitchen in action, or relish the warm ambiance and privacy of the upstairs dining room.

For nine years, Chef Walter Pisano has wowed guests with his refined hand on traditional Italian dishes. At Tulio, baked breads, gelatos, granitas and desserts are all made fresh daily. Specialties include such creations as traditional baccala with a Venetian twist; house-made salmon ravioli; linguini with plump local mussels; and marinated Washington lamb sirloin.

Our fine service, excellent cuisine and welcoming atmosphere have made Tulio one of Seattle's favorite dining spots.

Tony's

EVENTS & CATERING

At Tyee Yacht Club

3229 Fairview Avenue East
Seattle, Washington 98102
(206) 328-2195; Fax (206) 328-2754
Web site: www.tonyscatering.com

"You should see your next event from our point of view!"

Capacity: up to 200 reception style; up to 160 for sit-down dinners
Price range: prices vary according to menu selection
Catering: provided exclusively by Tony's; off-premise catering services also available
Types of events: hors'doeuvres to sit-down menus; formal to informal; banquets and receptions, meetings, parties, proms, reunions or any other business or social event

Availability and terms

The Tyee Yacht Club features hardwood floors, brass accents and a spacious covered deck create the perfect setting for elegant affairs. Make reservations as early as possible. Deposit required with balance due prior to event.

Description of services and facility

ADA: fully accessible
Parking: complimentary parking provided in our Club lot located just one-block away
Banquet services

- **Seating:** tables and chairs provided
- **Servers:** trained professionals to meet your needs
- **Bar facilities:** bar service available; client provides all liquor and banquet permit
- **Dance floor:** Club features hardwood floors; sound system and microphone provided
- **Linens and napkins:** your choice of linen colors for a minimal fee
- **China and glassware:** fine china and stemmed glassware included in catering cost
- **Decorations:** please inquire; nothing that will damage facility
- **Cleanup:** please remove anything you bring in; we'll handle the rest

Meeting and event services

- **Audio visual and equipment:** we will be happy to arrange for any of your needs

Special services

Your personal event planner will help you explore a world of options that await you, from informal hors d'oeuvres buffets to lavish theme parties to formal sit-down dinners. Please know that every event is completely customized to meet your precise needs, tastes and budget.

WE HELP MAKE MEMORABLE EVENTS

Your catering options in Seattle have just taken a delicious turn for the better. Better food, better service, better pricing and better ideas for creating the special event of your dreams.

As a full-service caterer, Tony's is pleased to offer you its beautiful Lake Union facility, the Tyee Yacht Club. Located on the north end of Lake Union just one block off Eastlake, the Tyee Yacht Club is priced to offer you a truly affordable piece of the lake.

Arriving by boat? Because the Tyee Yacht Club rests on the water's edge with adjoining spacious boat dock, feel free to arrive by yacht, or let us rent one for you.

See page 369 under Caterers/Food & Beverage Services.

4th Avenue South & South Jackson • Seattle, Washington 98104
(206) 706-0257
Office Hours: Please call for an appointment or tour

Capacity: up to 550 seated and 700 reception-style
Price range: $4,500 rental charge for five hours
Catering: select from our list of exclusive caterers
Types of events: business meetings, seminars, reunions, dances, banquets and receptions

Availability and terms

The Seattle Union Station is available for rental on Friday evenings, Saturday and Sunday all day. Dates are often available on short-term notice. A non-refundable deposit is required to reserve your date.

Description of services and facility

ADA: complies with ADA requirements
Parking: available in adjacent pay lots; valet parking available at an additional charge
Banquet services
- **Seating:** various set-up styles available; tables and chairs provided by caterer
- **Servers:** provided by preferred caterer
- **Bar facilities:** provided by preferred caterer
- **Dance floor:** Union Station's marble floors are ideal for dancing
- **Linens and napkins:** provided by caterer
- **China and glassware:** provided by caterer
- **Cleanup:** provided by caterer
- **Decorations:** please inquire; no balloons, no tape or nails on walls or floors or anything that will damage this historic facility

Meeting and event services
- **Audio visual and equipment:** handled by client from our preferred vendor list

ONE-OF-A-KIND NATIONAL LANDMARK

Completely restored, recreating its original historic charm. This national landmark train station's architectural details include a spectacular black and white mosaic tile floor with over 400 lights glittering from its 55-foot vaulted ceiling. The Seattle Union Station's grandeur ambiance is unique in the downtown Seattle area.

1025 Pacific Avenue • Tacoma, WA 98402
Contact: Marnie Jackson
(253) 572-2933; Fax (253) 572-0515
Office Hours: Mon–Fri 9am–5pm
Web site: www.vaultcatering.com

Capacity: accommodates from 6 to 300
Price range: please inquire; varies according to menu selections
Catering: full-service in-house catering; competitively priced to suit every mood and budget
Types of events: meetings, seminars, retreats, board meetings, reunions; formal or informal banquets and receptions; ideal for any type of social or business event

Availability and terms

Ballroom: for evening or weekend functions, our main floor ballroom accommodates up to 200; **Balcony:** Ballroom functions have the opportunity to expand to our balcony, creating a quiet overlook from which your guests can view your entire function: **The Vault** provides a unique, convenient site. Guests enter this downstairs hideaway through the original 10′ high, solid steel vault door; **Conference Room:** accommodates groups up to 80 and includes access to all on-site business conveniences and built-in bar; **Executive Board Room:** features classic board room conference table and is ideal for groups up to 10; **Luxury Suite:** features an intimate living-room setting with adjoining multi-purpose conference room. Reserve The Vault up to nine months in advance. A $100 deposit with the signed contract will reserve your date.

Description of services and facility

ADA: fully accessible
Parking: convenient street or lot parking adjacent to facility
Banquet services

- **Seating:** tables and chairs provided
- **Servers:** professional service staff included in catering costs
- **Bar facilities:** full-service host or no-host bar available
- **Linens, china and glassware:** included in the catering costs
- **Cleanup:** please remove any thing you bring in
- **Decorations:** nothing that will damage the facility

Meeting and event services

- **Audio visual and equipment:** rental costs include use of A/V equipment including television, VCR, stereo, projectors, screens, easels and other conveniences as well as access to business services including in-room telephone, voice messaging and fax services

LOCATED IN THE HEART OF DOWNTOWN TACOMA

Whether for a shareholders meeting of 150 or informal planning retreats for 10, The Vault can accommodate your next meeting or conference in a luxurious atmosphere with every business convenience you'll need right at your fingertips.

Facility use packages can be individually tailored to your meeting needs, with space rental by the hour or full-day room use and catering plans developed to your specifications.

See page 374 under Catering/Food & Beverage Services.

The TOP FLOOR at The Vault

1025 Pacific Avenue • Tacoma, Washington 98402
Contact: Marnie Jackson
(253) 572-2933; Fax (253) 572-0515
Office Hours: Mon–Fri 9am–5pm
Web site: www.vaultcatering.com

Capacity: accommodates up to 200
Price range: please inquire; varies according to event
Catering: full-service in-house catering; competitively priced to suit every mood and budget
Types of events: business functions like seminars or retreats, and board meetings; reunions, weddings, receptions, or formal or informal banquets

Availability and terms

You can reserve The Vault's Top Floor up to nine months in advance. A $100 deposit with the signed contract will reserve your date.

Description of services and facility

ADA: fully accessible
Parking: street or lot parking adjacent to facility
Banquet services

- **Seating:** tables and chairs provided
- **Servers:** professional service staff included in catering costs
- **Bar facilities:** full-service host or no-host bar available
- **Linens, china and glassware:** included in the catering costs
- **Decorations:** please inquire; nothing that will damage the facility
- **Cleanup:** please remove any decorations you bring in

Meeting and event services

- **Audio visual and equipment:** rental costs include use of A/V equipment including television, VCR, stereo, projectors, screens, easels and other conveniences as well as access to business services including in-room telephone, voice messaging and fax service

LOCATED IN THE HEART OF DOWNTOWN TACOMA

The Vault's new Seventeenth Floor in the penthouse of the Washington Mutual Building is a towering addition to our selection of facilities. The room's tall windows open up an attention-grabbing panoramic view of downtown Tacoma, Mt. Rainier, and the city's marinas.

The building's classic style has been complemented by a thorough refurbishing including new window dressings, floor coverings, and lighting.

At The Vault, even the top of Tacoma is versatile. The room can be arranged for sit-down banquets or in an open fashion for dancing and cocktail parties. The Vault can accommodate any appetite with its vast menu, featuring light hors d'oeuvres like bacon-wrapped scallops, artistically extensive brunch buffets, and conversation-starting meals of hand-carved prime rib with all the trimmings.

See page 374 under Catering/Food & Beverage Services.

VERRAZANO'S

28835 Pacific Highway S. • Federal Way, WA 98003
Contact: Banquet Coordinator
(253) 946-4122; Fax (253) 946-1405
Business Hours: 11am–2am daily

Capacity: private rooms for 15–300
Price range: varies according to party size and menu selections
Catering: full-service, in-house catering provided by Verrazano's; off-premise catering also available
Types of events: ideal for receptions, banquets, business meetings, or any other kind of special event; cocktail and hors d'oeuvres, buffets, sit-down luncheons, or dinners

Availability and terms

We recommend that you make your reservation as soon as possible. A $200 deposit will reserve your date with the balance due the day of the event.

Description of services and facility

ADA: fully accessible
Parking: ample complimentary parking provided
Banquet services

- **Seating:** tables and chairs provided and arranged to meet your needs
- **Servers:** professional service staff provided
- **Bar facilities:** full-service bar provided; host or no-host functions: Verrazano's provides all liquor, beer, or wine
- **Linens and napkins:** table linens and napkins are provided
- **China and glassware:** fine china, silver, and glassware provided
- **Decorations:** this elegant setting requires little decoration; however, guests are welcome to decorate to their liking; please, nothing that will damage the facility
- **Cleanup:** cleanup is provided by Verrazano's service staff

Meeting and event services

- **Audio visual:** please provide any A/V equipment you will need
- **Equipment:** podium and stage available for your use

Special services

To ensure your event is a success, our professional staff will walk you through the complete set-up and menu preparation process.

OVERLOOKING THE PUGET SOUND

Verrazano's is a newly refurbished two-story gourmet restaurant that overlooks the Puget Sound and features a spectacular view of the majestic Olympic Mountains. Verrazano's also boasts some of the largest outside dining decks in the Southend!

SEATTLE

1112 Fourth Avenue • Seattle, Washington 98101
(206) 264-6150; Fax (206) 264-6001
Office Hours: Mon–Fri 8am–5pm or by appointment
E-mail: wseattle.sales@whotels.com
Web site: www.whotels.com

Capacity: up to 350 seated, or 500 reception-style; our Great Room is 4,500 sq. ft.; studios #1–#8 range from 500 to 1,500 sq. ft. and accommodate up to 140 theatre-style
Price range: varies according to menu selection
Catering: full-service, in-house catering
Types of events: corporate meetings, conferences, receptions, banquets, weddings, rehearsal dinners, and other special events

Availability and terms

We encourage reservations as soon as possible. Call us to confirm availability and terms.

Description of services and facility

ADA: fully accessible
Parking: valet parking available
Banquet services
- **Seating:** tables and chairs provided
- **Servers:** all service provided by W Seattle
- **Bar facilities:** full-service bar; bar packages customized
- **Dance floor:** hardwood dance floor and staging available
- **Linens and napkins:** cream, black, or khaki napkins provided
- **China and glassware:** all china, stemware, and silver provided
- **Decorations:** please inquire
- **Cleanup:** handled by W Seattle staff

Meeting and event services
- **Audio visual and equipment:** full-service audio visual is available in-house

Special services

W Seattle offers 426 deluxe guestrooms and suites with our W signature bed. Enjoy the luxury of our 250 thread count linens, goose down pillows, and a cloud-like comforter while you tap into the outside world via our high-speed internet access. High tech with high touch.

DESIGNED FOR COMFORT WITH A SOPHISTICATED SENSE OF STYLE

The W Seattle Hotel offers a variety of meeting and event spaces to meet the needs of any organization. Enhanced by our state-of-the-art technology and award-winning culinary team, a special event at the W is certain to be a memorable success. Our dramatic décor featuring floor-to-ceiling windows sets the stage for your event and makes a lasting impression on your guests.

WASHINGTON ATHLETIC CLUB

1325 Sixth Avenue • Seattle, Washington 98101
Contact: Catering Department (206) 464-3050; Fax (206) 464-3052
Office Hours: Mon–Fri 8am–5pm, Saturday by appointment
E-mail: catering@wac.net • ***Web site: www.wac.net***

Capacity: 16 banquet rooms seating 6 to 350, varies by type of event
Price range: varies with room and menu selection
Catering: professional full-service, in-house catering only, including in-house bakery
Types of events: seated or buffet dining for breakfast, lunch and dinner; business meetings, retreats, cocktail parties, wedding receptions, family gatherings and other social or business occasions

Availability and terms

Private club requiring membership. Non-members may be sponsored by a member. Banquet rooms should be reserved early for best availability. Contract and deposit is required to confirm reservation for most rooms.

Description of services and facility

ADA: complies with all ADA requirements
Parking: available in the WAC parking garage as well as several other garages in immediate area, and validation provided for seated dinners after 5pm

Banquet services

- **Seating:** tables and chairs are provided to meet your specific needs
- **Servers:** professional, friendly service staff provided for all functions
- **Bar facilities:** full-service and host/no-host bars with all beverages provided by the WAC
- **Dance floor:** available at no charge
- **Linens, napkins, china:** bone china on white linen provided
- **Decorations:** individual table flowers with mirrors and votives provided

Meeting and event services

- **Audio visual and equipment:** complimentary easels, movie screens, podiums, platforms; all meeting rooms equipped with dedicated DSL; other audio-visual equipment available upon request for a minimal charge

PROVIDING DISTINCTIVE SERVICE FOR OVER 70 YEARS...

Our professional catering representatives are happy to assist you in planning all aspects of your event. After enjoying scrumptious pastries from the club's bakery, you can plan to have one of our certified Fitness Instructors visit for a 15-minute "corporate stretch." The WAC offers 113 elegantly appointed hotel rooms at the Inn at the WAC to members and their guests. Overnight guests enjoy free local phone calls and local paper, as well as access to premier athletic facilities.

 Please let this business know that you heard about them from the Bravo! Event Resource Guide.

WASHINGTON STATE HISTORY MUSEUM

1911 Pacific Avenue • Tacoma, Washington 98402
Contact: Amice Barreras or JoAnn Puccia (253) 798-5895, or Gary Larson (253) 798-5893; Fax (253) 272-9518
Business Hours: Mon–Fri 10am–5pm • ***Web site: www.wshs.org***

Capacity: accommodates up to 350 for indoor events or 350 outdoor settings
Price range: varies; depends on type of event and space needed; catering/rental packages available
Catering: full-service in-house catering provided by The Vault Catering Company
Types of events: receptions, meetings, conventions, reunions and corporate events

Availability and terms

- **Grand Lobby:** spectacular space featuring a huge arched ceiling with balconies above; reception space for 140, up to 350 if combined with the Mezzanine and Odlin Lobby
- **Ben B. Cheney Mezzanine:** overlooks the lobby, Museum Store and the Grand Lobby; reception space for 140 people or banquets for 120
- **Odlin Lobby:** domed ceiling and balconies overlooking the Grand Lobby and Mezzanine below completes our three-tiered public spaces; space for 70 people reception style or 40 for banquets
- **Peter Simpson Boardroom:** located on the 5th floor, the room has sweeping views of the Thea Foss waterway and Cascade Mountains; banquets for 24, reception style for 40; a lovely room for small corporate meetings, receptions or retreats
- **Outdoor Plaza:** ideal for receptions during summer months; surrounded by views of the waterway and the classic brick arches of the Museum and the adjacent Union Station
- **Outdoor Boeing Amphitheater:** located adjacent to the Plaza, the Amphitheater is well suited for entertainment, presentations or banquets; the graduated levels seat up to 250
- **Auditorium:** seats 215; *see page 98 for information about our Auditorium*

Many dates are presently available on short notice. A 25% non-refundable deposit required at booking with balance due two weeks prior to the event. A $300 refundable damage deposit required.

Description of services and facility

ADA: fully accessible
Parking: nominal fee in adjacent lots
Banquet services

- **Seating:** 20 round tables, 18 rectangular tables and 215 chairs provided at no additional cost
- **Servers and beverage service:** provided by The Vault Catering Company
- **Dance floor:** the Grand Lobby or Outdoor Plaza/Amphitheater are ideal for dances
- **Linens, china and serviceware:** provided by The Vault Catering Company
- **Decorations:** please inquire
- **Cleanup:** please remove all decorations

Meeting and event services

- **Audio visual and equipment:** wide range of A/V equipment available at no charge

Special services

The rental includes an on-site Event Coordinator, security and open exhibits for viewing.

ELEGANT AND UNIQUE INDOOR AND OUTDOOR SETTINGS

The Washington State History Museum opened in 1996 and is the most elegant and unique venue in Tacoma for receptions, banquets, performances, and private or business functions.

625-116th Avenue N.E.
Bellevue, Washington 98004
(425) 455-9444; Fax (425) 646-0229
Business/Office Hours:
Mon–Fri 7:30am–5:30pm
E-mail: sales@westcoastbellevue.com
Web site : www.westcoasthotels.com

Capacity: ballroom can accommodate up to 250 guests, buffet-style or sit-down dinner
Price range: varies according to menu selection
Catering: full service, in-house catering
Types of events: full service corporate meetings, receptions, formal sit-down dinners, cocktails, hors d'oeuvres, seminar, conferences or conventions, weddings, anniversaries or any other type of social event

Availability and terms

Reservations may be made up to a year in advance to ensure availability. Dates are often available on a short-term notice.

Description of services and facility

ADA: fully accessible
Parking: complimentary parking, on-site
Banquet services
- **Seating:** tables and chairs provided
- **Servers:** experienced, professional and courteous staff included in costs
- **Bar facilities:** full service bar and bartender
- **Dance floor:** available
- **Linens and napkins:** available in variety of colors at no extra cost
- **China and glassware:** all china and glassware provided
- **Decorations:** mirrors and votives at no additional cost; please inquire
- **Cleanup:** provided by hotel staff at no extra cost

Meeting and event services
- **Audio visual and equipment:** able to arrange any of your audio visual needs; please inquire for details and pricing

Special services

Special group rates available for overnight accommodations.

BEST KEPT SECRET IN BELLEVUE

Located in the heart of Downtown Bellevue, come and experience the generous hospitality and delicious Pacific Northwest Cuisine. From stylish to a more relaxed event, our staff will provide you with an experience you will never forget.

WESTCOAST GRAND HOTEL
ON FIFTH AVENUE

1415 Fifth Avenue • Seattle, Washington 98101
Contact: Tamara Hall (206) 971-8069 or (206) 971-8030; Fax (206) 971-8101
Office Hours: Mon–Fri 8am–6pm; please call for an appointment
E-mail: tamara.hall@westcoasthotels.com
Web site: www.westcoasthotels.com

Capacity: Emerald Ballroom: 8,900 square feet; accommodates from 120 to 630 in three dividable sections; five other meeting rooms: accommodate groups from 15 to 120; ask about our Terrace Garden and patio for Sunday receptions, capacity 190
Price range: prices vary according to group requirements and menu selection
Catering: full-service, in-house catering
Types of events: full-service corporate meetings, conferences and conventions; from an intimate reception in our luxury suite to gala dinners; Kosher events welcomed

Availability and terms

West Coast Grand Hotel on Fifth Avenue offers eight event rooms; featuring our Emerald Ballroom, accommodating from 120 to 630 guests. Other event rooms accommodate from 15 to 120 guests. Reservations may be confirmed three months in advance. Certain restrictions apply for reservations more than three months in advance; however, dates are often available. A 25% deposit with signed contract confirms your date.

Description of services and facility

ADA: all facilities are fully accessible
Parking: space available basis in hotel garage at hourly rates; special rates for overnight guests, valet and self-park

Banquet services
- **Seating:** tables and chairs provided at no additional cost
- **Servers:** serving staff and on-site event management included in catering costs
- **Bar facilities:** full-service bar with staff; hosted and no-host events
- **Linens:** several colors available; other colors available at nominal charge
- **China and glassware:** traditional white china, classic stemware provided
- **Decorations:** please inquire; nothing that will damage the facility
- **Cleanup:** provided by hotel staff at no additional cost

Meeting and event services
- **Audio visual:** our in-house A/V company can accommodate all your needs
- **Equipment:** podium, staging, easels provided
- **Wireless Internet**

CREATING A NEW TRADITION

WestCoast Grand Hotel on Fifth Avenue is situated in the heart of Seattle's most vibrant downtown neighborhood. Unique facilities with a Northwest flair—the hotel features 297 guest rooms, nine executive suites and one luxury suite, with spectacular views of Puget Sound and the Seattle city skyline, honor bars, in-room coffee and coffee makers, hair dryers, dataport phones, aerobic fitness center. Our hotel is surrounded by 10 million square feet of upscale shopping, restaurants and business headquarters and is within easy walking distance of many Seattle attractions, including Pike Place Market and the Waterfront…the perfect setting for your guests and colleagues to feel comfortable and welcome!

1900 Fifth Avenue • Seattle, Washington 98101
Contact: Jason Tyler, Director of Catering
Main Catering Number: (206) 727-5833
Business Hours: Mon–Fri 8am–5pm, Saturday by appointment
E-mail: jason.tyler@westin.com • ***Web site: www.westin.com***

Capacity: the largest hotel ballroom in the Pacific Northwest—**Grand Ballroom** is 18,000 sq.ft. and seats 2,120 theatre-style; **Cascade Ballroom** is 5,200 sq.ft. and seats 550 theatre-style; **Suites** overlook the Puget Sound, lakes and surrounding mountain ranges
Price range: varies according to event and menu selection
Catering: full service, in-house catering
Types of events: seminars, luncheons, auctions, buffets, sit-down dinners, corporate and special events

Availability and terms

Catering reservations are accepted up to one year in advance and based on space availability. It is suggested that arrangements be made as soon as possible especially for the holiday season and summertime.

Description of services and facility

ADA: fully accessible
Parking: valet parking available; additional parking is available in The Westin Seattle garage
Banquet services

- **Seating:** tables and chairs provided
- **Servers:** Westin's professionally trained staff services every event
- **Bar facilities:** full-service bar; the hotel will provide all beverages, bartenders, and servers
- **Dance floor:** available upon request
- **Linens:** white, black and creme/vanilla are included
- **China:** silver, china and glassware provided by the hotel
- **Decorations:** we will be happy to discuss decorations with you on a personal basis
- **Cleanup:** handled by The Westin Seattle staff

Meeting and event services

- **Audio visual:** provided at additional charge by Presentation Services, our in-house A/V company
- **Equipment:** podium and risers are provided by the hotel at no charge

FIRST CLASS VENUE

Every event is customized with menus created to fit your individual budget and theme. Our goal is to develop a partnership while planning your function to ensure the success of your event. All of our event space was completely re-designed in 1998 providing you with a first class venue. Guests wishing to stay with us will enjoy downtown Seattle's only hotel with 360 degree views of Puget Sound, Lake Union and the Cascade Mountain ranges. Located in the heart of downtown Seattle we have easy access from all areas of the city.

THE WESTIN SALISHAN

LODGE & GOLF RESORT

Gleneden Beach, Oregon

7760 Highway 101 North • Gleneden Beach, Oregon 97388
Contact: Group Sales
(800) 890-9316; Fax (503) 764-3510
Web site: www.salishan.com

Capacity: 14,000 square feet of flexible meeting space for groups of 5 to 500
Price range: price varies depending on event
Catering: full-service in-house catering
Types of events: conferences, receptions, banquets, catered functions

Availability and terms

Reservations are recommended six months to one year in advance.

Description of services and facility

ADA: yes
Parking: plenty of parking available
Banquet services

- **Seating:** tables and chairs provided for up to 600
- **Servers:** one server per 25 guests
- **Bar facilities:** full-service in-house bar
- **Dance floor:** 400-square-foot dance floor available
- **Linens and napkins:** a variety of colors are available at no charge
- **China and glassware:** china and crystal available
- **Cleanup:** provided at no charge

Meeting and event services

- **Audio visual and equipment:** full service available; podiums, easels and risers available at no charge

Special services

The Westin Salishan Lodge features 205 oversized guest rooms with fireplaces, private balconies, forest or bay views; golf course, golf links, tennis courts, Westin Kids Club, and putting course.

EXPERIENCE YEAR-ROUND ATTRACTIONS OF THE OREGON COAST

The Westin Salishan Lodge and Golf Resort offers conference groups, individuals, couples and families a unique opportunity to experience the year round attractions and activities of the Oregon coast. Recreational activities include Oregon coast eco tours, hiking, beach combing, shopping at the local factory stores and marketplace, classic tours of the nationally renown wine cellar, wine tasting, horseback riding, tennis, golf, massages and storm watching. In addition to two unique on-site restaurants, Salishan is located within a seven mile radius of over 60 restaurants.

willowsLODGE

14580 N.E. 145th Street • Woodinville, Washington 98072
Contact: Catering Department
(425) 424-3900, Toll-free (877) 424-3930
Fax (425) 424-2585
Office Hours: Mon–Fri 8:30am–5:30pm, or by appointment
E-mail: mail-@willowslodge.com
Web site: www.willowslodge.com

Capacity: several distinct, flexible rooms can accommodate from 10 to 150
Price range: varies with date, time, and menu selection
Catering: full-service, in-house catering provided
Types of events: retreats, business meetings, corporate dinners, parties, and all other functions

Availability and terms

We recommend that you reserve your space early, but will try to accommodate reservations on short notice.

Description of services and facility

ADA: Willows Lodge fully complies with all ADA requirements
Parking: complimentary parking
Banquet services

- **Seating:** tables and chairs provided; various arrangements are possible
- **Servers:** professional and courteous service staff included in catering costs
- **Bar facilities:** full beverage service available; all service and beverages provided by Willows Lodge
- **Dance floor:** portable dance floor available
- **Linens and napkins:** beautiful tabletops, linens, and napkins provided
- **China and glassware:** provided by Willows Lodge with all food and beverage service
- **Decorations:** we would be happy to discuss your needs; please inquire
- **Cleanup:** all cleanup provided by the Willows Lodge staff

Meeting and event services

- **Audio visual and equipment:** wired for business; built in screens, high-speed Internet access, and full audio visual rentals available

Special services

In addition to over 3,500 square feet of event space, Willows Lodge offers 88 beautifully appointed luxury guest rooms.

A NORTHWEST CELEBRATION OF THE SENSES

Events at Willows Lodge are remembered for their ease of planning, excellent cuisine, and a perfect setting along the Sammamish River. Easily accessible from Interstate 405, Willows Lodge offers an exceptional venue in the heart of Western Washington's wine country. Our staff looks forward to hosting your next meeting, banquet, or other special event.

GRAND BALLROOM

4710 University Way N.E.
Seattle, Washington 98105
Contact: Lora Kingsley
(206) 524-0450; Fax (206) 524-0040
Business Hours: Wed–Sun
E-mail: arwen@wilsonian.com • ***Web site: www.wilsonian.com***

Capacity: 247 reception style, 150 seated; 2,450 square feet
Price range: very reasonable daily rates available
Catering: select your own; list of suggestions available
Types of events: meetings, seminars, continuing education classes, cocktail parties, buffets, luncheons, company special events

Availability and terms

You'll want to make reservations well in advance, though short notice bookings are possible depending on availability. Deposit required.

Description of services and facility

ADA: ballroom is fully accessible
Parking: special rates available in nearby lots
Banquet services
- **Seating:** tables and chairs provided
- **Servers:** provided by caterer
- **Bar facilities:** client provides banquet license
- **Dance floor:** spring-supported oak dance floor
- **Electrical:** ample electrical outlets available
- **Linens:** provided by caterer
- **China:** provided by caterer
- **Decorations:** please inquire about decorating possibilities and parameters
- **Cleanup:** please remove anything you bring in; we'll handle the rest

Meeting and event services
- **Audio visual:** new sound system, wireless microphone
- **Equipment:** podium, stage

Special services

We are happy to assist you with additional arrangements for your meeting or special event.

ADD CLASS TO YOUR CORPORATE MEETING OR EVENT

Give your meeting, seminar or special event an extraordinary setting in our beautifully restored 1923 Grand Ballroom. The wall of leaded Tiffany glass windows, the varnished spring supported oak dance floor, the handsome fireplace and the grand piano are set off by elegant lighting, which can be adjusted for either meeting or reception purposes.

WOODMARK HOTEL

on Lake Washington

1200 Carillon Point
Kirkland, Washington 98033
Contact: Catering Department
(425) 827-1986; Fax (425) 803-5586
Office Hours: Mon–Fri 8am–5pm
or call for an appointment
E-mail: mail@thewoodmark.com
Web site: www.thewoodmark.com

Capacity: receptions to 120; increases to 225 in the summer; **Marina Room:** 2,450 sq. ft.; up to 120; summer patio add 30; **Lake Washington Ballroom:** 1,500 sq. ft.; 150; seated 120; classroom 80; **Olympic Terrace:** 1,800 sq. ft.; up to 200; seated 180; **Luxury Executive Board Rooms:** up to 20; **Woodmark Suite:** 900 sq. ft.; up to 30

Price range: room rental fees negotiable; minimums apply according to size and date of event

Types of events: conferences, executive meetings and retreats, receptions, formal and casual dinners, al fresco dining with outdoor grill, weddings and bar/bat mitzvahs

Availability and terms

Events confirmed up to one year in advance with deposit. Groups may reserve up to 30 guest rooms. Olympic Terrace available spring through fall.

Description of services and facility

ADA: meets all current codes

Parking: valet service and ample parking at minimal fee

Banquet services

- **Seating:** tables, chairs, patio furniture and dance floor at no additional fee
- **Servers:** professional, attentive service staff to meet all your needs
- **Bar facilities:** full-service bar and complete wine list, special order items available
- **Linens, china and glassware:** included in all menu prices
- **Decorations:** small accents to enhance our lakeside view of the mountains and sunsets are recommended; please inquire about setup times and deliveries

Meeting and event services

- **Audio visual:** on-site AV service company with technical support as required

A JEWEL OF A SITE

Recognizing your need for flawless planning and execution of meetings and special events, The Woodmark Hotel devotes particular attention to conference settings and service. Our unique function rooms adapt to any occasion from private high-profile board meetings to festive al fresco receptions. The lakefront Olympic Terrace with its dramatic canopy is the premier destination for grand occasions and events. Our creative cuisine accents freshness and imaginative flavors.

2200 Alaskan Way, Suite 410 • Seattle, WA 98121
(206) 956-4590; Fax (206) 374-0410
E-mail: info@wtcseattle.com
Web site: www.wtcseattle.com

WORLD TRADE CENTER
SEATTLE

Capacity: up to 80 for sit-down dinners; up to 120 for receptions
Price range: speak to sales manager for pricing, room rentals and F&B minimums
Catering: full-service in-house catering featuring international cuisine
Types of events: rehearsal dinners, receptions, banquets, cocktail and hor d'oeuvres parties, or business meetings and functions

Availability and terms

As the newest addition to the Seattle waterfront, the World Trade Center Seattle opened October 1998. This spectacular facility is available for evening or weekend functions. A 10% deposit is required with payment in full due prior to the event.

Description of services and facility

ADA: fully accessible

Parking: ample on-site parking; valet parking available with prior arrangement

Banquet services
- **Seating:** tables and chairs, staging for band or DJ and decorative buffets provided
- **Servers:** professional service staff and bartender included in catering costs
- **Bar facilities:** full-service host or no-host bar available
- **Linens, china and glassware:** included in the catering costs; bud vases and votives also included
- **Decorations:** please inquire; nothing that will damage the facility is allowed
- **Cleanup:** please remove any decorations you bring in

Meeting and event services
- **Audio visual and equipment:** we will be happy to arrange for any of your a/v needs

Special services

The World Trade Center Seattle offers a world class setting and impeccable service. Our event staff is available to assist in planning all aspects of your event (special menus, decorations, valet parking, entertainment, themed events and more). Early access for decorating is available at 4pm; earlier depending on availability.

SEATTLE'S NEWEST WATERFRONT VENUE

The World Trade Center is Seattle's newest waterfront venue featuring fabulous views of Elliott Bay showcased by floor to ceiling windows, refined furnishings, and elegant decor. Available evenings and weekends for private functions, this spectacular facility promises to be a new jewel in the crown of the Emerald City!

YALE STREET LANDING

EVENT AND CONFERENCE CENTER

1001 Fairview Ave. N. • Seattle, WA 98109
(206) 344-4757; Fax (206) 447-6977
Office Hours: Mon–Fri 9am–5pm,
Please call for an appointment
E-mail: elizabeth@bluwaterbistro.com
Web site: www.bluwaterbistro.com

Capacity: Alexander Room: our rooms accommodate from 10 to 300

Price range: prices will vary depending on space used, time of day and season

Catering: our exclusive caterer offers a full range of options; we'll work with you to create a menu that complements your specific needs and budgets; whether you want a formal sit-down dinner, an exquisite buffet, or an elegant hors d'oeuvres reception, you will enjoy superior cuisine carefully prepared and presented with style

Types of events: business meetings, conferences, banquets, sit-down dinners, buffets, cocktails and hors d'oeuvres, wedding receptions, and more

Availability and terms

Yale Street Landing offers two rooms. Reservations should be made as early as possible to ensure availability.

Description of services and facility

ADA: access and facilities available

Parking: parking lots nearby; valet parking available

Banquet services

- **Seating:** tables and chairs provided
- **Servers:** friendly, professional service staff included in catering costs
- **Bar facilities:** full service bar on-site
- **Dance floor:** 18'x18' dance floor available
- **Linens, china and glassware:** included in catering costs
- **Decorations:** discuss your thoughts with our event coordinator, or we'd be happy to share our ideas
- **Cleanup:** provided by Yale Street Landing

Meeting and event services

- **Audio visual:** 10'x10' built-in screen; state-of-the-art A/V equipment
- **Equipment:** podium, microphones, and more; we'll arrange for any additional A/V needs

SEATTLE'S PREMIER EVENT FACILITY

Located at the south end of Lake Union just minutes away from downtown Seattle, Yale Street Landing features stellar views of the Space Needle, Lake Union and the city skyline. This 3,200-square-foot facility sits atop the Yale Street Landing Marina and offers 12' floor-to-ceiling, lake-view windows as well as a balcony overlooking the lake and park-like setting. Your guests are sure to enjoy this waterfront plaza facility.

YARROW BAY GRILL

a worldly feast for the senses

1270 Carillon Point • Kirkland, WA 98033
Contact: Vicki McLellan (425) 889-7497
Office Hours: Mon–Fri 9am–6pm,
please call for an appointment
E-mail: vmclellan@ybgrill.com
Web site: www.ybgrill.com

Capacity: Yarrow Bay Grill's Bayshore Room can accommodate from 10 to 100 guests
Price range: prices vary according to menu selections
Catering: full-service in-house catering; off-premise catering also available
Types of events: business meetings or seminars, sit-down dinners, buffets or hors d'oeuvres

Availability and terms

Bayshore Room: Center stage of Carillon Point, this elegant room is just steps from Lake Washington. An impressive floor-to-ceiling glass wall overlooks the marina, and a private patio suggests unlimited possibilities.

Reservations can be made up to one year in advance, especially for summer months and the holiday season. A $500 deposit is requested to reserve your date.

Description of services and facility

ADA: fully complies with ADA requirements
Parking: guest parking and valet service available
Banquet services

- **Seating:** provided and arranged to accommodate your needs
- **Servers:** professional staff provides impeccable but unobtrusive service
- **Bar facilities:** full bar services and staff are provided
- **Linens and napkins:** colors that complement the room decor
- **China and glassware:** white china and all glassware provided
- **Decorations:** please inquire; subject to approval; nothing that will damage the facility
- **Cleanup:** Yarrow Bay Grill handles all clean up

Meeting and event services

- **Audio visual and equipment:** we'll rent to meet client's needs; please inquire
- **DSL line:** please inquire

Special services

Let our Chef dazzle you with a unique custom menu. Allow us to coordinate all the details: flowers, music, and more. Exciting theme parties are our specialty. Enjoy selecting your favorite wine from our award-winning list.

SERVING THE BEST THE WORLD HAS TO OFFER...

From our gracious service to our innovative menus, it's clear that our first priority is quality. The Bayshore Room captures the panoramic view of Lake Washington.

NOTES

Cakes & Specialty Desserts

❖❖❖

HELPFUL HINTS

Theme Desserts: The variety of desserts now available are limited only by your imagination. They are not only delicious, but have also become works of art. These new "custom" desserts can be created in the form of:

- Ships or boats
- Scale models of your corporate headquarters or even an entire city
- Company logos
- Musical instruments from pianos to cellos
- Cornucopias
- Animals
- Book, catalogue or magazine covers
- And more

Ordering: If you are planning on having a specialty dessert for your event, be sure to meet with the baker as soon as possible. These desserts are very time consuming to make, so you need to be on the bakery's schedule well in advance of your event so they can complete your order to your specifications.

Serving instructions: Be sure to get instructions on how to cut and serve your specialty dessert. You don't want to destroy this edible work of art with the first slice. Also check with the banquet facility; they will often provide a professional server for this purpose.

Specialty Candies: Chocolates or candies with your company logo or a special message like "thank you" stamped on them make great favors, thank-yous, or acknowledgments for event attendees or can be used as a client appreciation gift. Candies can also be designed in a variety of sizes and shapes.

"You Won't Believe It's A Cake!"

Redmond, Washington
(425) 869-2992
Fax (425) 869-0651
Web site: www.mikesamazingcakes.com

We at Mike's Amazing Cakes have worked very hard to build a reputation as the most customized and creative cake company in the country. Whether it is a simple 6" round or a scale model of your home, we put the best ingredients and all of our talent into each cake we make.

The facts...

- Our office hours are Tuesday–Saturday, with consultations and tasting available by appointment only.
- We will do any style and type of design from traditional to unusual.
- We can help you design a cake incorporating anything from the design on the bodice of your wedding gown to the architectural details of your reception site.
- We have a portfolio containing hundreds of photographs for you to review as well as cake samples available during consultations.
- Our wedding cake prices begin at $1.90 per serving, which includes a standard finish and most of our flavors and fillings.
- Occasion cake prices, including sculptures, are based on cake size and design.

Accomplishments...

- 1996 Grand Prize Winner of the Domaine Carneros National Wedding Cake Competition
- Best Dessert—Issaquah Salmon Days, 1996
- Showcased at the 1996 San Diego Presidential Debates
- Featured in "The Perfect Wedding," "Weddings for Dummies," "Bride's Magazine," "Modern Bride," "The Robb Report," "The National Enquirer," "The Seattle Times," "The Seattle Post Intelligencer," "The Journal American," "Palm Beach Illustrated," "National Public Radio," "The Wall Street Journa.," "Seattle Bride," KOMO, KIRO, and KING.

NOTES

Catering/ Food & Beverage Services

❖❖❖

CATERING/FOOD AND BEVERAGE SERVICES

HELPFUL HINTS

- **Liquor laws and liability:** With today's strict liquor laws, it's always advisable to check into who assumes the liability for any alcoholic beverage service. Although the event facility and/or the caterer may carry liability insurance, the host or coordinator of the function may still be considered liable. Make sure all parties involved with the event are properly insured, and consult with an insurance agent to make sure you have appropriate coverage for yourself.
- **Banquet permits:** In Washington, functions with private hosted bars featuring hard alcohol, beer, and wine are required to have a Washington State Liquor Control Board (WSLCB) Banquet Permit. Many banquet sites are already registered with the State to serve alcoholic beverages, while others are not. If your banquet site requires you to purchase a liability waiver or banquet permit for the day, do it! It's for your protection. Remember that only WSLCB licensed food and beverage establishments can provide no-host bars. For more information, call the WSLCB at (206) 464-6094. *(Banquet Permits can be obtained one week in advance of your function at any Washington State Liquor Store.)*
- **Hotels and off-premise licenses:** Most hotels do not have off-premise liquor licenses, and their on-site licenses do not apply to events held on other properties. When planning an event at another site, make sure to obtain a one-time only license for any off-premise event.
- **Private hosted bars:** If you are serving hard liquor (alcohol other than beer or wine) at a hosted bar, you should consider having a state-licensed bartender.

  If you have a no-host bar where money changes hands, the law requires that you have a server with a permit from the WSLCB showing the completion of alcohol-server education.
- **Advantages of hiring professional beverage servers:** Beverage or catering service companies provide professionally trained staff who can handle complete bar services at your event. They take care of the purchasing, bar set-up and clean-up, serving, and liability. It may be worth the extra cost to ensure that the bar will be handled in a professional and legal manner. These people are trained to detect if someone should not be served more, or if someone is underage. This service also allows you to enjoy the event without worrying about your guests.
- **Beverages in bulk or case discount:** How do you get a good selection of beverages on a budget? Distributors, wine shops, and some stores offer variety and savings when you purchase in bulk. In some instances, unused beverages may be returned for a refund.
- **Control liquor and keep consumption costs down:** Have a no-host bar. Shorten the cocktail reception by 15 minutes. Serve beer, wine, water, and soft drinks only; eliminate hard liquor from hosted receptions. Avoid serving salty foods (pretzels, peanuts, etc.) during hosted bars. Instruct caterers or waiters to uncork wine bottles only as needed. As a healthy alternative, offer a juice bar or an espresso bar.

Contact: Greg Garrison
(206) 545-7771; Fax (206) 545-7818
Web site: www.allamericancatering.com

LIQUOR CATERING & BEVERAGE SERVICE

The Puget Sound's premier beverage caterer

All American Catering is the areas only exclusive beverage caterer. We specialize in bar service and liquor catering. Let our expertise in this area help with your next special event.

Hosted or no-host bars available

With our hosted bar service, a tab is kept and the host is billed for all beverages consumed. With our no-host bar, guests pay for their own drinks. Choose the option most appropriate for your occasion.

Great selection of beer, wine and spirit

Our draft and bottled beer selection includes domestic, import, and northwest microbrews. We also feature the finest house and premium wines, available by the glass or by the bottle. For mixed drinks, we offer a house or premium well, liqueurs, cognacs, and specialty cocktails.

Professional bartenders

Your bar will be staffed with experienced and courteous bartenders. Every bartender is fully licensed and certified by the Washington State Liquor Control Board. Your guests will appreciate their impeccable service.

Fully licensed and insured

We provide all of the necessary licenses for your bar service. All American Catering also carries liquor liability insurance.

Complete service

All American Catering provides everything you'll need for your bar service. This includes professional bartenders, glassware or plastic tumblers, ice, soft drinks, bar mixers, beer draft systems, condiments, beverage napkins, set-up and clean-up. So sit back, relax, and enjoy your special event. All American Catering has your bar service covered.

For more information, please call Greg Garrison.
(206) 545-7771

aristocrat's catering
alcohol & beverage

Dennis and Lydia Mascarinas

14342 Ashworth Avenue North • Seattle, Washington 98133
206-786-2561 or 206-793-6437
aristocratscatering.com

At aristocrat's catering, we handle the work for you. We will accommodate all your beverage needs, from the alcohol, mixers, sodas, juices, glasses to the beverage servers.

Customize your function

We offer you a wide range of affordable options for your special occasion. Choose from a "hosted bar" or a "no-host bar." For a completely easy, no-fuss function, consider our popular all-inclusive "pre-paid" packages.

We will be happy to assist you with any queries or questions.

Professional staff

We provide friendly, professional, qualified bartenders for your function. All staff is licensed by the Washington State Liquor Control Board (WSLCB), and will hold all necessary licenses.

Variations and special requests

We will attempt to accommodate any requests or special needs you may have. Please feel free to discuss your ideas with us. We cater any function—weddings, special occasions, corporate events and parties.

P.O. Box 46954
Seattle, WA 98146
Contact: Janet Lickey
(206) 248-2290; Fax (206) 243-8760
Web site: www.pourgirls.com

• LIQUID CATERERS WITH SPIRIT •

Pour Girls & Some Guys provides...

Bartending services for your business functions, social events, holiday parties, birthdays, anniversaries, and wedding receptions. We have licensed professional bartenders and servers to pour mixed drinks, or beer, wine, and champagne for you and your guests.

- Licensed Personnel With WSLCB Class 12 Mixologist Permits
- Professionally Attired In Black And White

We come with...

A minimum of two bartenders who can serve up to 200 people; a third bartender is added for larger groups. This ensures you get the best service and attention to detail!

We save you money!

Because the client provides all beverages, there are no markups or corkage fees. You select and purchase the beverages you want served, have them delivered to the site, and then Pour Girls handles the rest! We arrive one to one-and-a-half hours prior to the event, set up the bar and ice down the beverages so that everything is ready as your first guest arrives.

- We are happy to consult with you on beverage quantities and varieties, as well as any rental equipment you may require.
- Your bar is customized to fit your tastes.
- When you purchase the beverages yourself, you can save money by taking advantage of case discounts.
- And, towards the end of the event, we don't open a lot of extra bottles, so that in many instances, you can return any unopened bottles or cases.

Experience

Pour Girls has been serving the Pacific Northwest since 1995. Our professional staff of experienced bartenders and servers arrive on-time, in professional attire, and with a great attitude.

Cost and terms

- Beer, wine, and champagne service: $47/hour, which covers two servers; for each additional server, add $25/hour.
- Mixed drinks plus beer, wine and champagne service: $57/hour, which covers two servers; for each additional server, add $25/hour.
- One server is provided for events hosting fewer than 100 guests, for beer, wine and champagne, at a rate of $30/hour.

A $25.00 travel fee may apply. There is a minimum of four hours per booking, which starts one hour prior to the starting time of the event. This is done to make sure that your bar is ready as your guests arrive and that everyone receives impeccable service. We recommend that our services be reserved 40 to 60 days prior to your event, however, we always try to accommodate last minute bookings. A 50% deposit is required to reserve your date with the balance due at the time of service. Corporate accounts with billing are welcome. Gratuities are gratefully accepted.

8309 S.E. 57th Street • Mercer Island, Washington 98040
Phone & Fax (206) 232-2692
Pager (206) 648-4829

THE TOTAL ESPRESSO EXPERIENCE CATERED TO ANY EVENT

Whether you're planning a large convention, an office social event, or a special family occasion, your guests will appreciate our hand-roasted, Italian-style coffees. We offer on-site lattes, mochas, cappuccinos, americanos, and hot chocolate. Italian sodas are also served in a wide variety of flavors. COFFEES a la CART caters delicious beverages to all types of events throughout the Puget Sound region:

- Corporate Meetings
- Tradeshows
- Surprise Parties
- Office Events
- Club Meetings
- Weddings
- Conventions
- Business Seminars
- Bar/Bat Mitzvahs
- Family Gatherings
- Birthdays
- Anniversaries
- Retirement Parties
- Church Functions
- Open Houses
- Picnics
- School Functions
- Fund-raisers

Our beans are hand-roasted to precise specifications that ensure a satisfying taste in the tradition of Europe's mild, full-bodied coffees. We prepare each cup to your individual preference.

Polished and professional

COFFEES a la CART provides a fully stocked espresso cart, complete with a specially trained Barista, and the supplies that best complement your special event. Our Baristas typically dress in a tuxedo shirt, but can adjust their attire to fit the formality or themes of your event. We use only state-of-the-art equipment.

SUPERB SERVICE & UNFORGETTABLE COFFEE

COFFEES a la CART offers over six years of experience working with event planners and organizations in the Seattle area. We also offer kosher service. Please call for our reasonable prices and other information.

ESPRESSO ZITA!

On Site Catering of Espresso

9452-114th Avenue N.E.
Kirkland, Washington 98033
Contact: Zita Gustin
(425) 803-0651
E-Mail: zita@espresso-cater.com
Web site: www.espresso-cater.com

ESPRESSO CATERING FOR YOUR CELEBRATION

Since 1992, we have been bringing the "golden" delight of espresso and the good feelings that go along with it to many events throughout the Greater Seattle and Puget Sound area. Our portfolio of events include:

- Employee Training Sessions
- Board Meetings
- Trade Seminars
- Corporate Merger Kickoffs
- Corporate Picnics
- Weddings
- Monthly Employee Appreciation
- Farewell Gatherings including Funerals
- Customer Appreciation
- Grand Openings
- Marketing Blitz Kickoffs
- Commercial/Residential Open House
- Corporate/Private Holiday Parties
- Corporate/Private Cruises
- Bar or Bat Mitzvahs

Cost and terms…

Our base price for two hours of service for groups of 100 or less starts at $275 plus tax. Prices will vary for events with more guests or longer serving times—please call for a price quote on your particular needs. A nonrefundable deposit of $100 is required to hold your date and time frame. The balance is due one week prior to your event. We now accept VISA, MasterCard, and American Express for your convenience. Prices subject to change.

PLEASE VISIT OUR WEB SITE FOR MORE INFORMATION

www.espresso-cater.com

Espresso Catering Service

6615 Marine View Drive
Edmonds, Washington 98026
(425) 743-4671; Fax (425) 787-8973
E-mail: creativeconcpt@cs.com

Seattle-Style Espresso Service
Catered To Your Event

Delight your guests or employees with our delicious specialty drinks and gourmet brews. Our premium coffee is always ground fresh on-site from the finest beans to ensure you with the most wonderful cup of coffee. All Baristas are knowledgeable, professional and friendly. Our unique manual style machines are the most powerful in the catering industry and have a reputation for putting out the most flavorful espresso. We have been serving the Puget Sound area since 1987 and are fully licensed and insured. Whether your event is large or small, indoors or out, let us provide an elegant touch with our on-site espresso catering service.

Beverage Service

All services include a fully staffed espresso bar. Hot and iced espresso drinks, hot chocolate, a variety of Tazzo tea, Yerba Maté, (a unique tea beverage brewed through the espresso machine), Chai tea, and Italian Sodas. We provide all cups, lids, stir sticks, flavors, whipped cream, Equal, S&L, sugar, vanilla, chocolate, cinnamon and nutmeg toppings. We offer 2%, nonfat and soymilk.

Set-up equipment

Our carts are portable, attractive and fully self-contained. We fit through standard doorways and elevators. All we need is access to a standard 110-volt outlet, or if your event is outdoors or no power is available, we have our own generator and canopies.

Cost and terms

Our base price for one and one half hours of unlimited drink service and up to seventy-five guests starts at $225.00 plus tax. Please call for a price quote on your event. We can fax or mail you a brochure with menu upon request.

Espresso is our passion, and we want it to be yours too!

HELPFUL HINTS

Food and beverages contribute significantly to the success of an event. In addition to breakfast (full or continental), lunch or dinner, food and beverage functions can include theme events, receptions, cocktail parties, and refreshment breaks. At any event or meeting, the food often has a lasting impression on your attendees. Whether it was too cold, not enough, or absolutely great, you will hear about it. Include regional or local specialties as often as possible for a memorable touch. Be health conscious and try to offer a variety of foods that are nutritionally balanced and colorful. Avoid heavy sauces, and plan a light lunch to keep attendees alert!

Menu selection and the weather: Be certain that your menu selections will withstand your event's anticipated weather. Avoid hot or heavy meals on muggy and humid days. High humidity may also wilt potato chips, cut cheeses, and similar foods. On hot days extra care should be taken to protect easily spoiled foods. Be especially careful with mayonnaise-based items, raw shellfish, and the like. For summer meetings or events, and especially hot days, don't serve alcohol. Shade tables with umbrellas, and provide lots of water, juices, and fresh fruit.

You are NOT limited to printed menu options. Either give the food and beverage providers a budget from which to generate options, or give them an idea of what you want and ask them to determine the cost.

It is important not to run out of food. Some attendees will have one plate at a buffet, and others will go back for thirds. Customize your menu and quantities based on the types of attendees. Ask your caterer's opinion as to whether served portions or banquet style better suits your event.

Meal Guarantees: Facilities usually require a "guarantee" for the number of guests that will need to be served at each meal function. The guarantee is usually required at least 48 hours in advance of the event. After the guarantee has been given, the facility will allow you to increase the numbers but not to decrease them.

Catering Guidelines: Ask the caterers what their guidelines are—and how they figure them. How do they provide for extra people? Some may automatically figure for 10% extra, which will be added to your final bill. Get several estimates if you are using an outside caterer—the price, portions, and what is or isn't included may vary for the same menu. Make sure the prices quoted will be valid the day of your event, or have the caterers commit to a percentage cap that can't be increased. For example, the price of beef may rise, but the caterer would guarantee quoted beef prices within 10%.

What a caterer supplies: Caterers can generally supply serviceware, flatware, dishes, cups, and table linens. They also normally provide servers, bartenders, and clean-up crew. Be sure to check what items and services are included.

Delivery of food: If the caterer delivers the food, ask that it be transported in warmers and coolers to ensure that it stays at the appropriate temperature.

Saving Dollars: Order bottled beverages served by consumption; at the end of the event count the empty bottles to make certain you are charged the correct amount. Avoid labor intensive foods. Replace a full breakfast with a continental breakfast; it won't be as heavy, and people can snack throughout the meeting.

Beverage Conversion: One gallon coffee=20–8 oz. cups. One bottle of wine=5–6 oz. glasses. One full-size beer keg=15 gallons, or 200–10 oz. or 160–12 oz. glasses.

IMPORTANT NOTE: Do not leave food out for long periods of time unless hot food is in chafing dishes and cold food is on ice.

3901-7th Avenue South • Seattle, Washington 98108
(206) 244-5100; Fax (206) 433-5148
Office Hours: Mon–Fri 8am–5pm
Web site: www.briazz.com

Food That's Always Fresh Fast And Fabulous!

A New Style of Dining

Whether you visit a Briazz café or prefer to have our gourmet fare delivered, Briazz redefines the breakfast and lunch experience. Featuring sumptuous sandwiches and lively salads—all made fresh daily and ready to eat when you are.

Starting with freshly baked breads, the freshest produce, choice meats, and a tantalizing array of flavors, our sandwiches and salads are winning rave reviews from critics and customers alike.

The Lunchtime Meeting Solution

Looking for the perfect solution for the in-office lunch meeting? Go no further. Briazz offers a wide assortment of Box Lunches and Catering Platters to meet your needs. Prepared fresh daily, we have something to please even the most particular palate. All of our fabulous box lunches include: Sandwich or salad entrée, gourmet snack, fresh fruit cup, freshly baked dessert and natural spring water.

Briazz Box Lunches Feature:

- No Minimum Delivery. We deliver 1–2,000 box lunches!
- Same Business Day Box Lunch orders accepted until 9:30 am (Mon–Fri).
- We deliver Hot Soup! Served ready to eat, it's the perfect accompaniment with any sandwich or salad.
- Free Delivery to downtown Seattle, Bellevue and Redmond. Minimum service fee to other areas.
- Weekend and home delivery available.
- Gift Certificates available.
- Catering options available. Please see our ad under "Caterers" or visit our web site at ***www.briazz.com***.
- We accept all major credit cards. Corporate House Accounts available.

Ordering from Briazz is a breeze!

Please call us at (206) 244-5100 or visit us on the web at ***www.briazz.com***. We offer free delivery to downtown Seattle, Bellevue and Redmond locations with no minimum order.

Please call us at (206) 244-5100 or visit us on the web at *www.briazz.com*.

We are passionate about great food!

See page 341 under Catering/Food & Beverage Services.

1625 West Dravus Street • Seattle, Washington
Contact: Steve Holmquist (206) 283-9030
Web site: www.pandasia.com

Types of menus

High-quality Asian and innovative, Asian-inspired cuisine. Appetizers, salads, soups, entrees, vegetarian and customized menus. We make our own chow mein noodles, pot sticker dumplings, Asian raviolis, mu shu pancakes, sauces, and dressings. Only the freshest ingredients are used. Check out our web site: ***www.pandasia.com*** for menu ideas, or visit our restaurant.

Specialty

Order our *FLASH BUFFET* for luncheon meetings: *"A hot luncheon buffet at a box-lunch price."* The unique *FLASH BUFFET* warmers are portable, thermal containers. Our driver will set up your buffet and have it ready to serve within minutes of delivery.

Other Catering Specialties

- We also offer full service catering with formal food presentations for weddings, holiday parties, receptions, corporate meetings, and other special occasions.
- We offer individual and group hot box lunches with ***FREE DELIVERY***.

Experience

Owner Steve Holmquist has over 30 years of experience in restaurant catering. His extensive background ranges from managing at the original El Gaucho restaurant to opening Seattle's first Asian delivery restaurant in 1986. Under his leadership, Pandasia, which he opened as Panda's in 1989, offers you a friendly and experienced staff, eager to take the worry out of planning an event.

Pandasia was voted best take-out by readers of *The Seattle Weekly* and *Seattle Magazine*, and has been listed in *Seattle's Best Places* and *Seattle Cheap Eats*.

Services

No attendant is necessary for our *FLASH BUFFET*. For full-service catering events, set-up and buffet attendants are generally included; additional servers and bartenders are available at an hourly charge. We can provide beverages, dishes, glassware, linens, tables, and chairs. We can also assist with special items such as flowers, ice sculptures, decorations, entertainers, etc.

Cost

Pandasia is known for quality and value. Each catering event is customized and cost is determined by the menu and services chosen. Prices of sample menus and services may be viewed on our web site: ***www.pandasia.com***.

EXCEPTIONAL EVENTS AT A MOMENT'S NOTICE

Pandasia has offered innovative, high quality cuisine and experience since 1989. Our friendly and professional staff makes party and event planning easy.

Call Pandasia today at (206) 283-9030
for your next catering event.

See page 361 under Catering/Food & Beverage Services.

A Friend in the Kitchen Catering

906 East Lake Sammamish Parkway N.E.
Redmond, Washington 98053
Contact: Steve Baldwin, Chef or Laura Gonzalez, Sales
(425) 868-5948
E-mail: laura@afriendinthekitchen.com
Web site: www.afriendinthekitchen.com

The philosophy of A Friend in the Kitchen is
To combine flavors and food with a unique atmosphere!

Experience trendy catering

A Friend in the Kitchen Catering uses only the freshest seasonal Northwest ingredients, enhanced by culinary techniques of international origin! Our Chef Steve Baldwin obtained his culinary skills in the East Coast working in Hotels and Restaurants, and perfected his skills under a Master Chef in Washington State. He has accrued over fifteen years of cooking experience and expertise.

A variety of menus and concepts

We offer a vast array of menus including…

- Private in-home catering
- Complete buffets
- Corporate Events
- Extensive hors d'oeuvres
- Breakfast, Lunch and Dinner
- Box Lunches
- Assorted party trays
- Theme Buffets–Caribbean, Western, Safari, Mexican, etc.

Full service and consulting

We offer experienced and trained wait staff, bartenders and on-site chefs. Also, in the planning stage of your event we can offer rentals, referrals and advice towards your event requirements.

Cost and terms

A $500.00 non-refundable deposit is required to hold your day. A 50% non-refundable event deposit is due three weeks prior to the event! The remaining amount is due on the event day. Your personal check, money order, Visa, Mastercard or American Express will be accepted.

A Friend in the Kitchen Catering looks forward
to serving your very special event!

Robb & Monica Newby, Owners
2022 Boren Avenue • Seattle
Phone (206) 957-0037
Fax (206) 623-3315
www.agrandaffaire.com

We specialize in Classical Preparations with Elegant Presentation ...to make each event A Grand Affaire

---

We are experienced in catering to all occassions...

- Weddings
- Rehearsal Dinners
- Commitment Ceremonies
- High Tea Bridal & Baby Showers
- Day After Wedding Brunches
- Bar & Bat Mitzvahs
- Quinceneras
- Birthdays
- Anniversaries
- Reunions
- Corporate Celebrations
- Outdoor Picnics & BBQ
- Meetings & Seminars
- Association Luncheons
- Fantastic Theme Parties

As your full-service caterer we will help you...

- locate the perfect venue for your event
- design your own ideal menu to create a signature feast
- coordinate tents, linens, tables, chairs, china, silver, glassware, décor, etc.
- reflect your unique signature with special touches utilizing our recommended vendors

Though our cuisine is classical in style, we customize each menu to reflect the cultural diversity of our guests. Our catering options feature...

- prices ranging from an average of $17.00 to $32.00 per person
- all kitchen and service staff with delivery and complete set-up included in menus
- elegant & lush buffet décor with specialty linens, candelabras, fresh fruits, and flowers
- ethnic cuisine: Asian, Latin, Caribbean, Italian, Greek, Indian, French, Creole, etc.
- a dizzying array of choices to create the perfect menu for you and your guests
- licensed bartenders to serve your own alcoholic and/or non-alcoholic beverages
- detailed cost proposals to assist you in planning and comparing

Experience and personal service beyond compare...
is what we, as owners and operators at A Grand Affaire offer you. We have been the exclusive caterer and managing entity at The Fairview Club for over four years, and will bring the same elegance and grandeur to your affaire, wherever it may be. Our sincere caring for you and your special occasion provide that personal touch which will ensure that you have an exquisite affaire and a rewarding experience. —***Robb & Monica Newby, owners***

With splendor, style and great taste an event becomes...A Grand Affaire

See page 189 under Banquet, Meeting & Event Sites.

Seattle Office: 9400 Roosevelt Way N.E. • Seattle, Washington 98115
(206) 523-9570; Fax (206) 524-4792

***Mountlake Terrace Office:** Located at The Nile Golf & Country Club*
6601-244th Street S.W. • Mountlake Terrace, Washington 98043
(425) 775-2412; FAX (425) 744-5622

E-mail: asyoulikeit@qwest.com • ***Web site: www.cateringasyoulikeit.com***

"McBride Construction has held their Holiday Party at the Nile for forty years and have always been pleased. This year, our experience with As You Like It Catering was the best ever! The presentation, taste and attentive service were superb."

—Christy Burnett, Office Manager, McBride Construction

"You and your crew did a fantastic job...with style!"

—Katrina R. Lande, Marine Administration Specialist, Port of Seattle

"Thank you, thank you, thank you...!"

—Lori A. Owens, Assistant to the Chairman, Shurgard Storage Centers, Inc.

"It is the food that makes a party distinctive and exceptional. We really appreciate your beautiful presentation, courteous service, and expert help in putting together a perfect menu."

—Denise Sparhawk, Director of Human Resources, Salt Mine Creative, Inc.

Our Services Include:

- Professional service staff
- Full Bar Service
- Artistic Wedding Cakes
- Exquisite Floral Arrangements
- Imaginative Custom Decorations
- Antique to Elegant Serving Pieces
- Classy Corporate Meetings
- All-Day Conferences
- Business Grand Openings
- Large and Small Cocktail Receptions
- Carefree Cruises

Our Menus Feature:

- Sophisticated or casual Hors d'Oeuvres
- Elegant Dinner Buffets
- Formal Sit-Down Dinners
- Sumptuous Pasta Bars
- Gracious Garden Parties
- Get-Down Picnics and Barbecues

As You Like It Catering is proud to offer one of Seattle's finest venues for special events. Nestled among 88 acres of tall stately fir trees on the shores of Lake Ballinger, just 20 minutes north of downtown Seattle, the Nile Golf & Country Club is ideal for parties of 30 to 450. Golf tournaments, picnics, barbecues, team building, reunions, auctions, seminars or meetings and retreats...we can accommodate your every event need.

See page 243 under Banquet, Meeting & Event Sites
or page 546 under Picnic & Recreation Sites.

Catering Office: 1801 East Marion Street • Seattle, Washington 98122
Baci Café: 15th Avenue N.E./N.E. 41st Street • Seattle (Henry Art Gallery, UW Campus)
(206) 323-6986; Fax (206) 324-9150
Web site: www.bacicatering.com

"We create elegant and visually exciting foods at competitive prices, handled with confidence and ease, so our clients feel like guests at their own events!"

SPECIALTIES

Elegant Handcrafted Foods using Local, Fresh, Organic Ingredients whenever possible
Delectable Desserts & Pastries created by our Pastry Chef Karen Duggan Jenkins
Corporate & Private Events ~ Weddings ~ Expertise in handling Large Events
Fully Customized Event Planning to meet your Personal Preferences & Budget Parameters
Complimentary Consultation & Menu Tasting

MENUS

Hors d'oeuvre Receptions ~ Plated and Buffet Dinners ~ Themed Events
International Cuisine ~ Northwest Buffets ~ Exceptional Vegetarian Fare ~ Holiday Parties
Buffet Luncheons ~ Continental or Buffet-style Breakfasts
Corporate Boxed Lunches ~ Picnics
Let Chef Karen Jurgensen create an elegant custom menu for you!

FACILITIES

Exclusive Caterer at the Henry Art Gallery ~ Visit our Baci Café
Preferred Caterer at many fine venues in and around the Seattle area, including:
The Paramount Theatre, Seattle Center and The Smith Tower Chinese Room

RAVES

"Unbelievably perfect." ~ S.A., Banana Republic

"WOW ~ what a fabulous party! The food, as usual, was superb..."
~ M.S., Reception for 200

13401 Alaskan Way • Seattle, Washington 98101
(206) 623-8600 ask for Lance Fushikoshi or Michelle Blanchard
Office Hours: Mon–Fri 8:30am–5pm by apointment only
E-mail: lancef@p57.com or jacquesb@p57.com

Types of Menus and Our Specialties

We provide a variety of different theme events with elaborate decor included. Our most prized corporate event we offer is "The Taste of the Neighborhoods" which features a variety of food stations each representing a different Seattle neighborhood. We'll assist you in creating a menu and party tailored to meet your specific taste, theme, and style.

Cost

Buffet Dinner Menus start at $25 per person for 100 guests or more. A $750 non-refundable deposit confirms the date. Ask about our Olympic Beverage Package!

Experience

Bay Catering has provided excellent service for all types of great events for over ten years!

Services

We are happy to assist you with all aspects of your event including entertainment, floral arrangements, photographers, and any rentals. Our full time pastry chef can prepare wonderful cookies and cakes for that special day! Bay Catering is a licensed full service banquet and catering facility.

Food Preparation

At Bay Catering our food is exquisitely prepared with the freshest ingredients by Executive Chef Steve Giacommini formerly of Ray's Boathouse. We feature local seafood and seasonal fruits, vegetables, and Northwest favorites!

Service Staff

Our service staff is professionally trained with years of experience in the hospitality industry. With them working for you, your event will run smoothly and you will be able to just sit back and enjoy yourself!

WHAT MAKES US UNIQUE

The Bay Pavilion is known for its unique waterfront setting in the heart of the Historic Downtown Waterfront District. Surrounded by so much history, we bring you innovative, prestigious, and punctual service to ensure that your experience here will be a memorable one as we continue to make history...

See page 144 under Banquet, Meeting & Event Sites.

3901-7th Avenue South • Seattle, Washington 98108
(206) 244-5100; Fax (206) 433-5148
Office Hours: Mon–Fri 8am–5pm
Web site: www.briazz.com

Food That's Always Fresh Fast And Fabulous!

A New Style of Dining

Whether you visit a Briazz café or prefer to have our gourmet fare delivered, Briazz redefines the breakfast and lunch experience. Featuring sumptuous sandwiches, lively salads and hot soups—all made fresh daily and ready to eat when you are.

Starting with freshly baked breads choice meats, the freshest produce and a tantalizing array of flavors, our sandwiches and salads are winning rave reviews from critics and customers alike.

Everything you need for a successful lunch

Looking for the perfect solution for the in-office lunch meeting? Go no further. Briazz offers a wide assortment of Box Lunches and Catering Platters to meet your needs. Prepared fresh daily, we have something to please even the most particular palate.

Catering Features:

- Catering options available for groups from 5–1,000.
- Catering orders for groups of 5–75 need only 24 hours notice. Please call in advance for larger groups.
- Free Delivery to downtown Seattle, Bellevue and Redmond. Minimum service fee to other areas.
- Hot Soup! Served ready to eat, it's the perfect accompaniment with our sandwich platters or salad bowls.
- Variety of sizes on both our sandwich platters and salad bowls. You design the menu you want!
- Breakfast platters with freshly baked muffins and bagels.
- Incredible array of freshly baked desserts and a bountiful selection of party pleasers.
- Frequent menu updates to give you an even greater menu variety.
- We accept all major credit cards. Corporate House Accounts available.
- Box Lunches available. Please see our ad under "Box Lunches" or visit our web site at ***www.briazz.com***.

Ordering from Briazz is a breeze!

Please call us at (206) 244-5100 or visit us on the web at ***www.briazz.com***. We offer free delivery to downtown Seattle, Bellevue and Redmond locations with no minimum order.

We are passionate about great food!

See page 334 under Box Lunches, Catering/Food & Beverage Services.

33710-9th Avenue South, Suite 16 • Federal Way, Washington 98003
Contact: Amy Hatcher

(253) 927-4489 Toll free (888) 927-0927 Fax (253) 927-2786

E-mail: john@cafepacific.com • ***Web site: www.cafepacific.com***

Let Café Pacific Catering Attend To All Of Your Food & Beverage Needs!

We can handle any size:

- Corporate Meeting
- Picnic or Barbecue
- Box Lunches
- Open House
- Office Function
- In-home Dinner
- Class/Family Reunion
- Party
- Grand Opening
- Anniversary
- Wedding
- Convention

We are experienced in event planning and can assist you with:

- Full-Service Sit-Down Dinners
- Linens & Centerpieces for Guest Tables
- Music, Entertainment
- Custom, Personalized Menus
- Tables, Chairs, Tenting
- China, Silver, Glassware
- Decorations, Themes, Ice Carvings
- Event Planning, Facility Location

Important facts about Café Pacific Catering, Inc.:

- In operation since 1989
- Fully insured
- Licensed for all alcoholic beverage service
- Seattle/King county Department of Public Health approved and regularly inspected kitchen
- All Federal, State & City licenses
- Fully trained, professional service staff covered by workman's compensation

Creative • Professional • Competitive
Scrumptious Menus • Fun & Hassle-Free • Certified Chef

Café Pacific Catering is privately owned and operated so all aspects of your event are professionally and carefully attended to down to the smallest detail.

Contact Amy Hatcher for a no-obligation, complimentary consultation, or to simply request our full line of printed menus.

Puget Sound's Best Value

(206) 343-8646 or (425) 646-8646

www.larrysmarkets.com

With a variety of box lunches and catering platters to suit every taste and preference, Catering by Larry's Markets can make even the most routine business meetings appetizing.

From continental breakfasts to savory sandwiches, salads and premium boxed meals and complete buffets. Catering by Larry's Markets delivers delicious made-to-order meals direct to your offices or off-premise meeting. And because it's Catering by Larry's Markets, you're assured of quality cuisine that's fresh, delicious and tastefully presented.

- **Caterer of choice** for hundreds of Seattle's top corporations, cultural institutions and non-profit foundations.
- **Ultimate Box Lunches** for quick and convenient meals that always satisfy. Extensive menu selections to fit any budget.
- **Perfect Picnics** make planning a breeze! For groups of 100 to 1,000+, we're available to grill on site.
- **Ala Carte and Seasonal Fresh Sheets** will make your decision easier. Signature appetizers, market entrees and plenty of sweet treats!
- **Gift Baskets** are great for promotions, incentives, thank-you's and arriving guests. We offer the best mix of local flavor.

When it has to be good value, great tasting and on-time, it has to be *Catering by Larry's Markets.* Call today

(206) 343-8646 or (425) 646-8646

www.larrysmarkets.com

2501 N. Northlake Way • Seattle, WA
Contact: Elisabeth Hebrant
or Laura Daley
(206) 632-2200; Fax (206) 545-2137
Business Hours: Mon–Fri
8:30am–5:30pm or by appointment
Web site: www.caterarts.com

Experience and Specialty

Classically trained at La Becasse in Glen Arbor, MI, Chef/Owner Peter Neal went on to prepare cuisine for some of Seattle's finest restaurants, including Metropolitan Grill, The Brooklyn and Tulio Ristorante. After four years as Nordstrom Catering's Head Chef, Neal established CaterArts to express his acclaimed creative style.

Menus, Costs and Terms

We design our menus to highlight the freshest seasonal items available in the Pacific Northwest. Our experienced sales staff will consult with you to customize a menu that is appropriate for your particular event. Our detailed proposals spell out every cost associated with your event such as food, beverage, rental items, service staff, floral and entertainment. Once our proposal has been accepted, we require a 50% deposit of estimated charges to hold the date with the remainder due one week prior to your event.

Our Place or Yours

We are proud to offer our new facility on the north shore of Lake Union, The Lakeside. This event facility offers panoramic views of the Seattle skyline, hardwood floors, natural lighting and French doors which open onto the spacious waterfront patio and private dock. The Lakeside consists of two view levels and will accommodate up to 250 reception style when using the entire facility. We are also happy to cater at the location of your choice. Our off-premise food and beverage minimum ranges from $800–$2,500 depending on the date.

Service Equipment and Personnel

We can supply all the necessary rental items such as tables, chairs, china, linen, glassware, silver service, tenting, espresso carts and anything else you may need.

Beverage Service: Host and no host bars available.

Service Staff: We pride ourselves in providing the highest level of service in the industry. Staffing is charged at $15–$25 per hour based on job requirement and is calculated on a portal-to-portal basis. We will gladly quote you a staffing estimate once menu, timing and guest count are established.

"From an intimate gathering, to a grand affair for four hundred guests, CaterArts never misses a beat. Their attention to detail, superb menus, and exemplary service continues to set them apart from other companies in the industry." —Jeanne Berry, RealTime Productions

See page 157 under Banquet, Meeting & Event Sites.

 Please let this business know that you heard about them from the Bravo! Event Resource Guide.

20302-10th Drive S.E. • Bothell, Washington 98012
Contact: Michael or Kemberli Greco
(425) 482-2716
E-mail: chefinseattle@msn.com • Web site: www.chileheadcatering.com

---

Menus and specialties

Chilehead Catering offers a wide range of catering services, from casual backyard barbecues to formal wedding banquets. Our specialties range from Southwestern Smoked Beef Brisket to Oysters Rockefeller. We can cater a complete Caribbean Feast or a Candlelit five-course dinner for two.

A tradition of customized, personal service

Chilehead Catering grew out of our desire to work more closely with our clients than a restaurant setting usually allows. As caterers, we appreciate the opportunity to discuss everything from the menu to small details, and to customize the meal according to your guests' tastes and preferences.

Exceptional barbecue for your company picnic

Chilehead offers exceptional barbecue, ideal for company picnics and other special events. Whether you prefer charcoal, propane, wood fire, or smoking pit barbecue, count on Chilehead to provide the best cuts, season them with the finest spices, and create the most flavorful barbecue:

- Tender Smoked Beef Brisket
- North Carolina Pulled Pork
- The All American
- Northwest Salmon Feast
- Pork Spareribs or Babybacks

Hot food delivery and boxed lunches

We will deliver hot entrées to your business, a cost-effective and delicious lunch program for your employees. We also provide a variety of boxed lunches featuring traditional and specialty sandwiches.

Cost and terms

A 50% deposit reserves our services. Our professional staffing is priced separately from our menu, but included in your total cost. Please inquire about the latest pricing information.

FLAVORS OF THE SOUTHWEST AND THE WORLD

Chilehead offers a delicious combination of fine food, catering expertise, and attentive service. Our menu offers authentic Southwestern cuisine as well as fresh seafood from the Puget Sound region, all served with a generous selection of favorite sides and appetizers. We create the feast that makes your vision a reality.

Chilehead Catering also features a full list of delicious vegetarian items and complete meals.

the City Catering Company

4520-50th Avenue South
Seattle, Washington 98119
(206) 721-0334
E-mail: weddings@citycateringcompany.com
Web site: www.citycateringcompany.com

What's happening at The City Catering Company?

We're rolling up our sleeves and getting back to the basics of matching good food to good friends. The key is in the details, and we have plenty of experience helping clients iron out those details. You might say its our forte. Whether it's a formal dinner party to impress your most important client or a down-home barbeque for your whole company, we've seen it before, and we'll make the day unforgettable.

Our claim:

Challenge us, and we'll work hard to pull off a truly impressive event. And as locals, our staff has both the knowledge and the expertise to back that claim. Chef Paul Coile brings years of experience in some of Seattle's finest downtown restaurants, where he came to appreciate the mix of the eclectic and traditional that distinguishes Seattle cuisine. The City Catering Company emphasizes using only fresh, local ingredients. Our menus capture the rustic integrity of the Pacific Northwest while also allowing for the wide range of tastes our clientele should expect from a full-service caterer.

A final, simple ethic:

To give you choices, to serve you well.

Dedicated to excellence in creative cuisine and unparalleled service

407 North 36th • Seattle, Washington 98103
(206) 547-3131; Fax (206) 223-2066
Web site: www.classiccateringnw.com

Classic Catering specializes in the fresh, flavorful dishes that have made Northwest cuisine world renown. Our culinary team will delight you with their savory selections, imaginatively prepared and artfully presented. Whether you're planning a festive buffet, elegant sit-down dinner, theme party or casual picnic, you'll be impressed with our commitment to excellence.

Menus

Our menus feature the freshest and finest ingredients available including prime beef, local seafood, seasonal fruit, market fresh vegetables and our own unique specialties. We pride ourselves in creating a menu that complements your style and accommodates your budget.

Show Stopping Signature Salmon Bake

Fresh King Salmon presented in the traditional Indian Style. Whole sides are basted with citrus lemon butter and baked over an open alderwood flame. It is the perfect alternative to the ordinary summer picnic. Just one simple call and we can bring this unique, show stopping barbeque to the location of your choice or even, your company parking lot. Ideal for groups of 100–3,000.

Beverages

Full-service beverage service is available. You may host all or part of the beverage service or your guests may purchase their own.

First class service

Our friendly gracious staff is trained to recognize and respond to your needs. Every individual is dedicated to exceeding your expectations. Our reputation for excellence is the cornerstone of our unparalleled service.

Site recommendation

We have secured preferred status at some of Seattle's premier venues. Let us help you find the perfect location for your next event.

Special services

Classic Catering can design the perfect blend of food, beverages and enhancements to make your event uniquely your own. We have preferred relationships with many local vendors that can help make your event complete including rentals, entertainers, DJ's, florists and more. From start to finish, we'll handle as much or as little as you want.

(425) 455-1742; Fax (425) 454-2023
E-mail: cosmocat1@peoplepc.com
www.cosmopolitancatering.com

Well-Seasoned & Flavorful Experience

With over 30-years of combined Catering Industry experience—from hotels, resorts, restaurants and private clubs—owners Max and Debra Popejoy are a husband and wife catering team from Hawaii who moved to Seattle in 1992. Max was born with a passion for food, especially the multi-cultural foods he grew up with in Hawaii. Debra has an attention to detail and excellence, and plans each event with enthusiasm and flair.

Zesty Fresh Flavors from Around the World ✦ Cosmopolitan Cuisine

Your personal chef will create and blend zesty fresh flavors from around the world in the location of your choice. Unique combinations of multi-cultural foods are creatively presented to feast your eyes, as well as your taste buds. "Cosmo blending" of flavors, color, and texture will enhance your occasion. Artistically presented food displays are a favorite feature of our service, and is a regular compliment of all our clients. The extra step, and the attention to detail set us apart from the rest. Our menus are custom designed to meet your taste and budget needs—and if you wish—stretch your culinary experience.

Support Services & Professional Catering Staff

We can assist with all your event details with creative suggestions and ideas from our experience with hundreds of events. We are a Preferred Caterer at several premier facilities, and we can recommend a location that best fits your special occasion. Wait staff are experienced and trained, and are appropriately attired. Culinary staff are passionate about food, and our flavors and presentation are a reflection of their commitment. Our service has a touch of warm Hawaiian hospitality, and our corporate culture is a sweet "Aloha Spirit" that is contagious!

Cosmo Custom-Designed Events

- Corporate Events
- Social Events
- Holiday Parties
- Company Picnics
- Cooking Classes
- Chinese Family-Style Dinners
- Global Cuisine
- Barbecues
- Personal Chef Service
- Vegetarian Menus
- Authentic Hawaiian Luaus
- Bento Box Lunches
- Dim Sum
- Sushi
- Noodles

Cosmo Policy

Our menu prices are per person and do not include labor, linen or rental items. We require a 50% non-refundable deposit to confirm your date.

Contact Cosmopolitan Catering
for your global culinary tour!
(425) 455-1742

CULINARY ART *inc.*

6100 Fourth Avenue South • Seattle, Washington 98108
(206) 768-0677
E-mail: catering@culinaryart.com
Web site: www.culinaryart.com

Menus

Culinary Art, Inc. has developed a full range of breakfast, luncheon, and dinner menus. Our hors d'oeuvre buffets are noted for their beautiful presentation. We will be happy to send you a full brochure packet which includes mouth-watering descriptions of our most popular menu items. After a brief consultation, we can prepare custom menus to fit your taste, theme and budget.

Box Lunches

We have also created an exceptional box lunch menu that offers a wide variety of choices. Our "Portfolio Picnics" lunches come with freshly prepared sandwiches or salads, fruit, beverage, and our signature espresso dessert bar—all packed in our classic box and delivered to your location.

Services

We understand that a successful catered event requires more than excellent food; let us help with all of the other details. We can make arrangements for all necessary rentals, staffing, and bartending, as well as beautiful floral and display items. We accept VISA and MasterCard for your convenience. Corporate accounts are also available.

Pricing

Prices vary based on menu selection and other requirements. Deposits are required in most cases, with the balance due upon completion of the event. We prepare a detailed proposal for each event so there are no last-minute surprises.

Please feel free to call us with any questions you might have.
We look forward to working with you soon!

CULINARY ART *inc.*

Bellevue, Washington
(425) 467-8129
E-mail: designperfecttoo@msn.com
Web site: www.designperfecttoo.com

**Same Great Food . . .
Only Our Look Has Changed**

Experience

The chefs at Design Perfect, Inc. bring with them twenty-five years of expertise in preparing creative, original menus. Executive Chef Mark Carter perfected the art of garde manger at the Seattle Yacht Club, Bellevue Club Hotel and Bellevue Red Lion before deciding to open his own catering service. He enjoys using uncommon herbs and unique ingredients to create his own new and exciting "traditional Northwest" cuisine.

Corporate events

Design Perfect, Inc. knows that corporations today are changing the way they show appreciation to their employees and how they conduct business meetings. If you want to make an impact on prospective clients or just want to thank employees for a job well done, Design Perfect, Inc. is sure to impress.

Presentation

Crystal, antique silver, and imported linen are attractively displayed to enhance the visual appeal of your buffet. Every buffet includes a complimentary centerpiece, and fresh floral arrangements are available by request.

**Our staff is committed to perfection
in taste, ingredients, presentation,
and originality.**

Visit our new web site for an online proposal!
www.designperfecttoo.com

**See page 397 under Decorations, Themes & Props
and page 504 under Meeting & Event Planners.**

3131 East Madison
Suite 101
Seattle, Washington 98112
(206) 324-3663
Fax (206) 324-0619
E-mail: nwcatering@attglobal.net

Quality First

The Famous Northwest Catering Company is a premier Seattle area caterer with over 20 years experience. We pride ourselves on the quality and freshness of our foods. All of our items are tastefully presented on beautifully garnished trays, platters, and baskets. Each of us at Northwest Catering is dedicated to making your event a success with our outstanding service and delicious food.

Complete Catering Services

Our full-service off-premise catering company can assist you with all aspects of your event. We would be happy to help you with site selection, entertainment, bar service, valet parking, floral arrangements, and any rental equipment that you will need. Our full-time pastry chef is Cordon Bleu trained and also makes beautiful, memorable wedding cakes. For less formal events we offer a large selection of boxed lunches, with free delivery of 10 or more in Seattle.

Customized Menus

We believe that each event we cater is unique, therefore we provide customized menus for your specific needs. We would be happy to meet with you to create your perfect menu. Whether you are hosting an intimate dinner party or a large reception, you will receive our individual attention to every detail.

Professional Catering Staff

All of our wait staff are trained, highly professional individuals. Their traditional black and white attire and special attention to detail will ensure the festive atmosphere that you desire. Let our staff take care of everything from start to finish so that you can enjoy your own party.

Make your next event your best event!
Please give us a call today.
(206) 324-FOOD

Catering

Passionate About Great Food!

3520 Genesee Street S.W. • Seattle, Washington 98126
Owners: B.J. Duft and Jens Dressler
(206) 937-5740; Fax (206) 937-5974
Office Hours: Mon–Fri 8:30am–4:30pm
E-mail: fieldtofeast@qwest.net • ***Web site: www.citysearch.fieldtofeast.com***

Menus

Our Pacific Northwest region produces endless varieties of fresh and delicious ingredients, so we have built our mission around delivering that bounty to our customers through creative and evolving menus of high-quality products. We choose to support regional growers, from the San Juan Islands to the Wenatchee Valley, and pride ourselves on creating recipes that highlight the flavors and characteristics of each locale. A fresh combination of abundant herbs, local delicacies and culinary imagination has resulted in a unique and exciting interpretation of Northwest regional cuisine—from Field To Feast!

We Have Menus For Your Special Occasions:

Breakfast • Luncheon • Box Luncheons • Appetizers • Dinner

Guarantees and Guest Count

A 50% non-refundable deposit is required to confirm your event on our catering calendar. The balance will be due with final invoicing on or before the day of the event. A guaranteed guest count is due five business days prior to your event although increases in the guest count may be requested up to 24 hours in advance.

Pricing

Our proposals reflect menu, equipment and staffing requirements based on your budget and specifics to your event. We can provide and/or coordinate china, flatware, tables, chairs, linens, floral arrangements and décor. At Field To Feast we believe that service staff is just as important as out food and presentation. Our professionally trained and caring staff will assist you with any aspect of your event from planning to on-site set-up, service and clean-up. Rates are as follows:

- On-Site Chef & Event Lead: $30 per hour
- On-Site Assistant Chef: $25 per hour
- Bar & Food Server: $25 per hour

Estimated service time is calculated door-to-door with a four-hour minimum guarantee. If your event should require service staff, an 18% service fee will be added to your invoice. Should your event not require service staff, we will gladly provide delivery, set-up and pick-up for a nominal fee and the gratuity will be left to the client's discretion. Some venues charge an additional fee which will passed on to the client.

We accept Visa, MasterCard & American Express
Products and prices subject to change

Grand Central Bakery can effortlessly cater your office meetings and events.

Exceptional Food

We offer full gourmet lunch, breakfast pastry and party menus. We are happy to serve your lunch on beautiful buffet style platters or as sack lunches. Our breakfast menu has a full line of delicious, fresh pastries as well as fresh fruit, Torrefazione Italia coffee, tea, juice and more. A full selection of sweet and savory platters is available for your party or event.

Service

We always work with our customers to provide them with worry-free, professional service. Delivery service is available Monday through Friday to downtown Seattle at no charge. Pick-up service is available at or Pioneer Square location Monday through Saturday.

Our Mission

In the big scheme of things...we focus on one of the small things—in creating delicious foods from wonderful ingredients. We pour our daily efforts, concerns and pride into creating foods that satisfy our desire—and yours, we hope—to eat and serve something delicious, comforting and elemental.

• Specializing In Corporate Events •

722-17th Avenue East • Seattle, Washington 98112
(206) 328-2500
Web site: www.greatfeasts.com

Menus that surprise and delight on any occasion

Great Feasts is a full-service catering company specializing in custom designed events. Renowned for our ability to create an abundant, eye-catching and palate pleasing menu, we will also work to fit your budget. Our menus draw from ethnic cuisines around the world, from classical to contemporary.

Sample "Great Feasts"

Client Recognition Dinner:

Smoked Salmon Ribbon on Pepper Toast
Mixed Seasonal Greens with Pear, Roquefort & Candied Walnuts
Poached Halibut with Citrus Butter Sauce
Tenderloin Medallions with Cabernet Glaze
Warm Onion & Potato Gratin
Fresh Yakima Asparagus

Gala Open House:

Orange & Roasted Garlic Shrimp Skewers
Goat Cheese & Watercress Canapé
Ginger-Scallion Chicken Spears
Prosciutto-Gruyere Pinwheels
Grilled Miso Salmon Satay
Caviar Toast

Pacific Rim Feast:

Southeast Asia Crispy Shrimp Salad Rolls
Grilled Beef Satays with Fiery Peanut Sauce
Seared Chicken in Red Curry Coconut Cream
Seven Vegetable Stir-Fry with Soba Noodles
Sake-Marinated Grilled Salmon
Sesame Noodle Salad

Staff Appreciation Lunch:

Linguine with Scallion Sauce & Sautéed Shrimp
Moroccan Chicken with Lemon, Olives & Saffron Rice
Great Feasts Caesar Salad
Tropical Fruit Salad w/ Honey-Thyme Glaze
Chocolate Decadence Cake

Call Great Feasts Today!
Imagine the possibilities and let us do the rest!

We take pride in being creative, punctual and flexible in this unique service industry. So sit back and enjoy the compliments as we ensure a successful event for you and a wonderful time for your guests.

GREAT FEASTS
For Exceptional Custom Catering

Joanie's Catering

3416 S.W. Webster Street
Seattle, Washington 98126
(206) 938-9890
Fax (206) 764-9041
Email: joanieclare@attbi.com
Web site: www.joaniescatering.com

Distinctive Creations That Stir The Soul

Chef Joan Allen, owner, has been a life long resident of the Puget Sound area. She began her career in the food service industry in the Pike Place Market in 1975. Graduate of the Culinary Arts program at South Seattle Community College in 1981. She started working in the catering business in 1980 and has many years of restaurant & hotel chef experience, most recently as Executive Chef of Tuxedos N' Tennis Shoes catering company (1995–2000). She has extensive knowledge of ethnic, regional and classical cooking for two to two thousand!

We offer full service catering for any size...

- Wedding
- Reception
- Barbecue
- Anniversary
- High Tea
- Bar/Bat Mitzvah
- Holiday Party
- Gallery Opening
- Theatrical/Backstage
- Private Party
- Commitment Ceremony
- Business Gathering
- Plated Sit Down Dinner
- Banquet
- Company Picnic

The uncommonly delicious...

Offerings on our menus are selected with a great deal of care. Unique ethnic feasts, down home American food and classic cuisine are prepared with seasonally fresh ingredients from the Pacific Northwest in our fully licensed, commercial kitchen.

Exciting flavors, artful presentation, attention to details, experienced professional service staff and an organized, well executed plan frees you from worry, allowing you to relax and enjoy yourself!

Services

We offer free cousultation and custom menu planning tailored to your tastes and budget to ensure that no details are overlooked.

Costs and terms

Menu prices are determined on a per person basis. Service staff, floral arrangements, rentals and beverage services provided at an additional charge. 50% deposit of the estimated charge secures that date with the balance due the day of event.

Ours Is A Labor Of Love

Julia's Catering

4401 Wallingford Avenue North
Seattle, Washington 98103
(206) 334-0516
Fax (206) 633-5208

Classically beautiful, timeless elegance.

Julia's Restaurant is proud to introduce our new, full-service catering department, specializing in custom designed events. By combining the freshest seasonal ingredients with an eye for detail, we can create a memorable and worry-free event for you.

Types of menus and specialties

Our menus draw from Northwest, ethnic, vegetarian and vegan cuisine from classical to contemporary. We can create a custom tailored menu to suit your style, budget and theme. For catering a small dinner party with friends, an office luncheon or a wedding reception at your place or ours, together we can plan a unique experience.

Cost and terms

Price is determined on your final menu selections and number of guests. Full service staff, rentals, tax and gratuity are additional. A deposit will confirm your date and payment-in-full is requested the day of the event.

Complete catering services

- Coordinate equipment rentals
- Custom-created menus
- Various service styles—buffet, passed and seated
- Professional service staff, chefs and bartenders
- Wide range of events,from picnics to corporate functions, holiday parties to small family dinners

Special services and equipment

Julia's catering department offers menu consultation, rental arrangements and full service staff. In house events at both Julia's of Wallingford and Julia's of Issaquah restaurants are limited to certain days and times. Please call Daniele Mosher at (206) 334-0516 for a free consultation.

 Please let this business know that you heard about them from the Bravo! Event Resource Guide.

Kaspar's

19 West Harrison Street • Seattle, Washington 98119
Contact: Catering (206) 298-0123; Fax (206) 298-0146
E-mail: catering@kaspars.com
Web site: www.kaspars.com

IMPRESSIVE

Only the very best chefs can truly impress their dinner guests, and few of them can do so time after time. Chef Kaspar Donier is one whose creativity, culinary skill, and dedication to his guests have earned repeated praise.

Kaspar's Catering and Banquet Services are similarly unique—it would be difficult to find a comparable caterer if you wish to host a memorable dining experience for your guests. Kaspar's attention to detail and courteous, experienced staff will give you total confidence...along with the freedom to enjoy your event. And the food—naturally—will be remarkable.

Contemporary Northwest Cuisine...for groups large or small, casual or formal, buffet or sit-down, our place or yours. Select from our menus, or let us customize one for you.

Experience... Chef Kaspar Donier has been creating memorable meals in Seattle for over 12 years. Combine this with an experienced team of event specialists and you've got an unbeatable combination.

Service... Kaspar's provides full-bar service, tables, chairs, and linens for events in our restaurant and elegantly appointed private dining rooms. And we'll gladly assist you with these arrangements and more for off-site events. All equipment necessary for the attractive presentation of your menu is provided, and we're pleased to offer assistance in arranging for decorations, entertainment or audio-visual equipment.

Servers... Professional servers and bartenders will be attired in black and white unless otherwise requested. We provide all setup and cleanup and we comply with the regulations of any chosen facility.

Costs... Most menus are priced per person. A deposit will confirm your date and payment in full is requested the day of the event.

Please call on us
to cater your next event—
at our place or yours!

635 C Street S.W. • Auburn, Washington 98001
(253) 804-9600; Fax (253) 804-5493 • E-mail: auburn@longhornbarbecue.com
Visit us on the WEB! www.longhornbarbecue.com

You Round Up the Guests, We'll Do the Rest!

Who is Longhorn Barbecue?

Your source for the best darn barbecue you ever tasted.

The Longhorn Barbecue originated in Houston, Texas in 1946. After 10 years in the "pistol packin' city," the brothers decided to move out to the Great Northwest. Since coming to Spokane from Texas, the brothers have captured the hearts of Spokane diners with excellent "Texas Southern Pit Style Barbecue." In 1997, the Longhorn headed west to Auburn, Washington. Now folks can enjoy our specialties on both sides of the mountains. Pardnur, this is REAL pit barbecue because the meats are smoked on the pits by a combination of apple, cherry, alder, and birch woods. Whether it's a company function or a family event, when the Longhorn "Chuck Wagon" rolls up, the feed bag is on.

Please consider Longhorn Barbecue for your

Summer Picnic! • Holiday Party! • Business Meeting or Recognition Event! • Wedding!

Our specialty is Barbecue, however, we now offer new menus featuring Northwest favorites—Salmon and Prime Rib, Homestyle Tradition—Turkey and Pot Roast, Mexican Fiesta and Zesty Italian.

Competitive Prices on a per person basis. Menu prices range from $6.95–$16.95. All catering is served buffet style and "No one leaves hungry!" Call today so we can fax or mail you our menus. Be sure to ask for our Seasonal Special! Discounts for parties of 300 or more.

Raves from our clients:

"Your professionalism, congeniality, and efficiency came through as a class act. You took care of every detail, leaving nothing to chance. Your truck and equipment were immaculate."

—B.L. & S.N., Costco Wholesale

"You played an important role in our overall success by helping to plan the layout, quickly delivering the food to the large crowd, and providing a truly outstanding meal. We were also very impressed with the professional attitude and integrity that all of you demonstrated in your work."

—T.J., Boeing Company

Bravo! Bonus:
Say you found us in *Bravo! Resource Guide* and come in for a complimentary tour of our kitchen and samples!

9404 East Marginal Way South • Seattle, Washington 98108
(206) 762-4418; Fax (206) 767-1827
Web site: www.mccormickandschmicks.com

Catering at the Museum of Flight or the Venue of your Choice Anywhere in Western Washington

MEETINGS • CORPORATE EVENTS • HOLIDAY PARTIES • OPEN HOUSES
PRODUCT LAUNCHES • PICNICS • RECEPTIONS • FORMAL DINNERS

Our cuisine

- Unique blend of classic and contemporary cuisine
- Fresh ingredients featuring Northwest products
- Custom menus or event packages

Our services

- Event coordination including specialty linens, entertainment, floral and other rentals
- The highest quality customer service
- Attention to detail throughout

Our beverages

- Hot or cold, traditional or exotic, alcoholic or non
- Yours or ours, cash or hosted, we are fully licensed and have an extensive selection of spirits, wines and beers

Our experience

- 25 years of hospitality and tradition
- Currently operating 30 restaurants and 5 catering divisions throughout the country

OUR COMMITMENT

To share with our clients 25 years of McCormick & Schmick's tradition and hospitality!

Moveable Feast

CUSTOM CATERING

Cindy & Mark Langmas
(360) 474-0113
Web site: www.moveablefeastcatering.com

Moveable Feast Catering has a great selection of delicious foods!

Northwest Favorites Sample Menu

San Juan Salmon—mesquite grilled with olive oil then topped with a tomato-basil relish.

Stuffed Salmon Bake—Dungeness crab and bay shrimp with cream cheese and fresh herbs.

Champagne Chicken—grilled tender chicken breasts with mushrooms and onions in a creamy champagne sauce.

London Broil—marinated for three days then mesquite grilled to order and served with hot horseradish.

Cornish Game Hens—baked tender with apricot and whiskey sauce.

Trayed Hors d'oeurves—Gorgonzola Grapes, Crab Tarts, Smoked Salmon Flowers, Italian Sausage Mushrooms and many more

We also offer:

- Baked or Boxed Lunches
- Outdoor Barbecues
- Appetizer Buffets
- Luncheon and Dinner Buffets

For your convenience Bone China Plates & Silverware are included with most of our menus. Also included are Buffet Table Linens & Drop Cloths, Color Coordination & Candelabra

"Moveable Feast made our wedding reception everything we dreamed it could be, and more!"
—Alyson & Steve Douglas

"Your food and presentation is excellent! Our friends are still raving about the stuffed salmon. Wow!"

"What a wonderful experience it is to dine with friends, worry free. Thank you for every last bite."
—Beverly & Skip Steffens

"We dub you The culinary magicians of the Northwest, with pleasure and thanks."
—The Andersons

"Our first time hiring a caterer, and we got the best. Your love for the job show through in the wonderful way you work togther, and in the delicious food. Thank you, Moveable Feast Catering."
—Corel & Shan Hoel

1625 West Dravus Street • Seattle, Washington
Contact: Steve Holmquist (206) 283-9030
Web site: www.pandasia.com

Types of menus

High-quality Asian and innovative, Asian-inspired cuisine. Appetizers, salads, soups, entrees, vegetarian and customized menus. We make our own chow mein noodles, pot sticker dumplings, Asian raviolis, mu shu pancakes, sauces, and dressings. Only the freshest ingredients are used. Check out our web site: ***www.pandasia.com*** for menu ideas, or visit our restaurant.

Specialty

Order our *FLASH BUFFET* for luncheon meetings: *"A hot luncheon buffet at a box lunch price."* The unique *FLASH BUFFET* warmers are portable, thermal containers. Our driver will set up your buffet and have it ready to serve within minutes of delivery.

Other Catering Specialties

- We also offer full service catering with formal food presentations for weddings, holiday parties, receptions, corporate meetings, and other special occasions.
- We offer individual and group hot box lunches with ***FREE DELIVERY***.

Experience

Owner Steve Holmquist has over 30 years of experience in restaurant catering. His extensive background ranges from managing at the original El Gaucho restaurant to opening Seattle's first Asian delivery restaurant in 1986. Under his leadership, Pandasia, which he opened as Panda's in 1989, offers you a friendly and experienced staff, eager to take the worry out of planning an event.

Pandasia was voted best take-out by readers of *The Seattle Weekly* and *Seattle Magazine*, and has been listed in *Seattle's Best Places* and *Seattle Cheap Eats*.

Services

No attendant is necessary for our *FLASH BUFFET*. For full-service catering events, set-up and buffet attendants are generally included; additional servers and bartenders are available at an hourly charge. We can provide beverages, dishes, glassware, linens, tables, and chairs. We can also assist with special items such as flowers, ice sculptures, decorations, entertainers, etc.

Cost

Pandasia is known for quality and value. Each catering event is customized and cost is determined by the menu and services chosen. Prices of sample menus and services may be viewed on our web site: ***www.pandasia.com***.

EXCEPTIONAL EVENTS AT A MOMENT'S NOTICE

Pandasia has offered innovative, high quality cuisine and experience since 1989. Our friendly and professional staff makes party and event planning easy.

Call Pandasia today at (206) 283-9030
for your next catering event.

CATERER FOR DIXIE'S BBQ

CATERING OFFICE: *3113 Portland Avenue East • Tacoma, Washington 98404*
Contact: Catering Manager (253) 472-6595; Fax (253) 472-5277
Office Hours: Mon–Fri 9am–5pm

Web site: www.portersplace.com

PORTER'S PLACE RESTAURANT: *(253) 472-0291 • Hours: Tue–Sat 11am–7pm*

Make Your Event Something Everyone Will Enjoy The Best Southern Style Barbecue in the Pacific Northwest!

Porter's Place specializes in lip-smacking, finger-licking good and not-so-traditional spicy Southern Style barbecue. It's perfect for those people who want their rehearsal dinner, wedding reception, or any other private function to bring out the best in people and just be down right fun! Some of our favorites include:

- Barbecued Chicken
- Barbecued Ribs
- Barbecued Beef Brisket
- Boneless Pork Ribs
- Smoked Turkey
- Butter Baked Hams
- Hamburgers
- Hot Dogs
- Baked Beans
- Mashed Potatoes
- Red Garlic Potatoes
- Fresh Vegetable Platters
- Fruit Tray
- Brownies
- Ice Cream

All you can eat...

Everyone always has a big appetite when it comes to Porter's Place barbecue! That's why our pricing is based on the size of the event instead of single servings so that everyone leaves with a smile on their face having had all they can eat!

We'll handle all the details...

Barbecue is our family tradition, so we serve it with Southern Style hospitality and graciousness. We'll set up and decorate the buffet table, provide centerpieces and decorations, then serve your guests a memorable meal that will keep them talking and coming back for more. As a full-service caterer, Porter's Place provides all:

- Dishes
- Linens and Skirting
- Decorations
- Glassware
- Serving Attendants
- Theme Decor

At Porter's Place, we give new meaning to the word "The Man"

Hot and spicy, but smooth and tasty...that's "The Man!" Created years ago in the owner's of Porter's Place's mother's kitchen and a favorite served for years in the family owned restaurant, Dixie's BBQ, our hot and spicy barbecue sauce has become a regional favorite of barbecue fans. It comes with every event and is something you have to taste to truly understand the full barbecue experience.

Come Meet "THE MAN" at Safeco Field and Husky Stadium

Come experience the best Southern Style BBQ in the Pacific Northwest at Safeco Field. Porter's Place is now serving ½ LB. BBQ Chicken, Pork and Beef sandwiches at the BullPen Market in Centerfield. Open three hours before game time, you can eat great BBQ and watch the action from the open air, centerfield concourse. Husky Stadium opens two hours before game time.

 Please let this business know that you heard about them from the Bravo! Event Resource Guide.

Pyramid Catering

The Secret to throwing a great party!

300 Third Avenue West
Seattle, Washington 98119
(206) 691-9918
Fax (206) 352-4063
E-mail: events@pyramidcatering.com
Web site: www.pyramidcatering.com

Why should you choose Pyramid Catering?

Delicious food!

We offer you and your guests a world of menu possibilities featuring hand-picked foods from Seattle's Pike Place Market. Executive Chef Benjamin Jablonsky will gladly customize the perfect menu to complement your taste and budget, showcasing his fresh Contemporary Northwest style. Our buffets are beautifully presented using a myriad of unique serving pieces, including colored marble, silver platters, mirrors, baskets and blown glass—all decorated. Our seated meals are skillfully designed with the care and passion that you would expect from the finest restaurants.

Gracious service! Personal, Flexible, Professional.

We are there from beginning to end, ensuring that all of your expectations are fulfilled. We can handle all of the details of your event, from finding the perfect venue to host your event to suggesting a wine that best complements your menu. Our tuxedo-attired service staff are drawn from the area's finest hotels and restaurants; they have embraced our "guest first" approach and the warm, friendly service that Pyramid Catering is known for.

Competitive pricing!

We will gladly send you a customized proposal itemizing all the costs involved, in order to assist you in planning and comparing. We offer monthly menu tastings, no cake cutting fees, and no corkage fees. A $750 deposit will secure your date on our calendar. Our flexible pricing allows us the opportunity to provide many types of catering, from business luncheons to festive holiday galas.

The Perfect Location!

We are proud to offer our catering services at the area's premiere event facilities. Whether you're looking for **Waterviews**, **Mansions**, **Garden Settings**, or **Yachts**, we can assist you in locating your ideal event site. With over 50 possible venues designed for capacities from 30 to 500, we're sure to accommodate most any style and taste.

Types of Events

Holiday Parties • Corporate Affairs
Meetings & Seminars • Fund Raisers & Auctions • Birthdays & Celebrations

". . . the presentation was outstanding . . ."
". . . the best food we ever had at a catered event . . ."
". . . you give new meaning to full-service catering . . ."

In Seattle at 801-26th Avenue East • Seattle, Washington 98112
Contact: Kerry Jean Francois (206) 860-7449
Business Hours: Mon–Fri 9am–5pm
Web site: www.RavishingRadish.com

FOOD IS ART

Since 1993

Ravishing Radish Catering has specialized in friendly service and artful presentation. Our menus showcase the Northwest's freshest ingredients and are always imaginative.

Menus

From festive holiday parties to simply delicious boxed lunches, our event planners are here to help make your event a success.

- ***Grand Openings*** with hors d'oeuvres of local favorites like our soy ginger salmon skewers...
- ***Company Picnics*** with our chef preparing food fresh from the grill and our always memorable build-your-own strawberry shortcake…
- ***Festive Holiday Buffets*** full of eye-catching dishes, uniquely presented on antique platters and accented with evergreen boughs and fresh cranberries…
- ***Elegant Seated Dinners*** complemented with impeccable service and attention to every detail...
- ***Boxed Lunches:*** Choose from our extensive menu or ask us about our customized boxed lunches for your next special event.

Terms

Prices are based on a per-person food cost, any necessary rental items (china, flatware, linens, etc.), and service staff or delivery fee.

A 25% non-refundable deposit will secure your date and is applied to your balance. Full payment is due upon completion of event. Corporate accounts are available. Mastercard/ Visa accepted.

Let our passion for creating extraordinary food help you in planning your next culinary adventure...

RAY'S BOATHOUSE CATERING

6049 Seaview Avenue N.W.
Seattle, Washington 98107-2690
(206) 789-6309; Fax (206) 781-1960
Office Hours: Mon–Fri, 9am–5pm
E-mail: rayscatering@rays.com
Web site: www.rays.com

A Seattle Original for over 28 years

Ray's Boathouse has been serving Seattle the quintessential Northwest experience since 1973. Ray's Catering brings the restaurant's legendary quality and service to your event. Our goal at Ray's Catering is to exceed our guests' expectations in food, service, and quality. We strive to make every event pleasurable—both to plan and to attend.

Menus

We provide only the freshest, highest quality products prepared in our own kitchen. Our chefs have extensive culinary backgrounds and a palatable passion for food. Ray's is capable of executing menus ranging from simple buffets and hors d'oeuvre receptions to custom multi-course plated dinners, backyard barbecues and theme parties. Pre-designed buffet packages for brunch, lunch, and dinner make planning a snap. We can custom design a menu for your event. Our menu changes seasonally to take advantage of the best products available locally.

Experience

Ray's Catering has extensive experience in executing events for parties of any size. Ray's Catering has catered events at Seattle's Woodland Park Zoo, the Arboretum, Kingstad Meeting Centers, Chateau Ste. Michelle, the Issaquah Community Center, the Edmonds Floral Conference Center, Argosy tour boats, the Matchmaker yacht, wineries, mansions, parks, private homes and yachts. We are a preferred caterer for A Contemporary Theatre, Town Hall, the Paramount Theatre, and Redhook Brewery.

Services and rentals

Our event planners visit your event site to coordinate menus and wine selection, rentals and audio-visual equipment, logistics and seating. We offer referrals for entertainment, décor, and photography. Our professional servers provide exceptional service and hospitality so that you can relax and enjoy your guests. Events are priced according to menus and services selected. We can send a customized proposal of estimated costs.

Terms

A 50% deposit is required to confirm the catering contract. The balance is due five business days prior to the function. Any adjustments are payable the day of the event.

Whether you are hosting a rehearsal dinner in one of our private dining rooms, an all-day meeting at the office, or a full-scale bash at one of Seattle's fabulous reception sites, there's no better way to show your guests the best of the Northwest!

See page 259 under Banquet, Meeting & Event Sites.

ON ALKI BEACH

1936 Harbor Avenue S.W.
Seattle, Washington 98126
Contact: Banquets and Catering
(206) 937-1085
Office Hours: Mon–Fri 9am–5pm
Web site: www.saltys.com

Salty's Caters to Your Taste Buds. Your Place or Ours.

If your group can't come to Salty's on Alki Beach, we'll come to your place. You can count on Salty's to deliver a perfectly catered affair, with all the gourmet touches that have made Salty's the most popular "seefood" restaurant in Seattle. Salty's is known for world-class cuisine, Northwest seafood prepared with exceptional flair, and flawless service.

Menus

Choose from extensive menus or let Salty's work with you to accommodate any special needs. Beverages include hosted or cash bar with an extensive wine list, liqueurs, microbrews and liquors.

Equipment

We can assist you in selecting rental items necessary for your event, including tables, chairs, glassware, dishware, linens and silver, flower displays and entertainment. We'll work with you whatever your needs.

Services

Salty's will exceed your expectations. We'll supply the services you need for your event or help you find the right services.

Costs

Events are priced according to menus and services required. Just call us and we'll accommodate your needs. A deposit of 50% is applied to the final billing.

Recommendation

"I wouldn't hesitate to recommend Salty's for any event. The support from Salty's is stress-free and leaves me more time." —Lois Roberts, Boeing Propulsion Systems

See page 268 under Banquet, Meeting & Event Sites
and page 574 under Restaurants.

SPIRIT OF WASHINGTON CATERING

P.O. Box 835 • Renton, Washington 98057
Contact: Marni Ness
(425) 277-8408; Fax (425) 277-8839
Web site: www.spiritofwashingtoncatering.com

Spirit of Washington Catering

A Northwest favorite since 1992, the Spirit of Washington Dinner Train proudly introduces its new division, Spirit of Washington Catering.

Bringing food and beverage service of the highest quality in taste and appearance to your selected location. We are available for sit-down events or buffet service. Prices vary based on menu selection and your event's size. To accommodate many budgets, Spirit of Washington Catering offers pick-up service, delivery, or full on-site staffing. We provide service staff on an hourly basis, charged portal-to-portal with a four-hour minimum. Rates include pulling equipment, travel, setup, the actual event, clean up and return.

We would be happy to incorporate theme menus into your invitations and décor. We also welcome the opportunity to highlight seasonal items from the Northwest in your menu.

Policies

- **Deposit/Payment:** To confirm your event, a signed Catering Agreement must be returned with 50% of the estimated event balance; the balance is due 3 days prior to your event.
- **Cancellation:** Deposits are refundable up to 30 days prior to your event. Fees imposed by your facility or other contractors will be deducted from the deposit before the refund is mailed. Refunds requested within 30 days of the function may be applied to another event. Less than 72 hours' notice will result in a full charge for all items listed on the Catering Agreement.
- **Menu:** Prices and menu may be guaranteed 30 days prior to your event. All menus must be confirmed 2 weeks prior to your event. We serve two entrees at seated functions. Exact counts of each entree will be due three days prior to your function; place cards must be supplied to denote menu choices.

TOTAL EVENT PACKAGING

As part of our commitment to service, we can provide total event coordination. This includes rentals of linens, china, glassware, flatware, tables, chairs, tenting, music, photography, dance floors, entertainment, audio visual, and floral. Event packages or custom designed menus can also be included. We can help choose a location for your event; some menu items may need to be adjusted to complement the characteristics of certain venues. If you have questions, please contact our sales office.

6743-48th Avenue S.W.
Seattle, Washington 98136
(206) 715-4748
E-mail: andreweigenrauch@cs.com
Web site: www.crepecatering.com

A FEAST FOR THE SENSES!

Specializing in made to order Sweet and Savory Crêpes

We are passionate about this fresh and interactive culinary treat usually reserved for the streets of Paris. Our crêpes are made with batters that are spread delectably thin on our authentic Breton hot plates with the mesmerizing turn of a small wooden rake. They become a heady canvas, both crispy and soft, on which we create a balance of simplicity and refinement. You can choose from our twenty-five delicious sweet or savory fillings and sauces to give your guests an experience their palates will not soon forget!

A few selections from our menu...

- ***Served in a sweet crêpe...***
  "Crêpe Suzette"—Curacao orange sauce and Grand Marnier Flambé
  White Chocolate Mousse with fresh raspberries and raspberry coulis
- ***Served in a savory buckwheat galette...***
  Prosciutto, Emmental Swiss, bechamel sauce, and spinach
  Scallops and mushrooms sautéed with a hint of cognac in a créme fraîche sauce

Professional and reasonable service

Choose from our complimentary menu including salad, hors d'oeuvres, beverages and wine bar; sweet and savory crêpes are versatile enough to be satisfying for any meal from breakfast through dessert. We are also happy to accompany another caterer. Our staff is at your service to plan and execute truly special events from 10–1,000 guests.

Receptions	**Employee Appreciation**	**Mimosa Brunches**
Weddings	**Indoors or Outdoors**	**Private Parties**

"I received numerous, unsolicited compliments about the flavors of your crêpes, your friendly service and the long hours you put in to ensure the success of your visits. I would recommend you without hesitation."
—Robin Mogenson, *Amazon.com*

Tony's
EVENTS & CATERING

3229 Fairview Avenue East
Seattle, Washington 98102
Contact: Tony Butz
(206) 328-2195
Fax (206) 328-2754
Web site: www.tonyscatering.com

We Haven't Forgotten That Catering Is A Verb

At Tony's, we work tirelessly to create the right menu, the right atmosphere and the right price—all designed to exceed your precise expectations. Box lunches, theme menus, gourmet dessert buffets, formal sit-down dinners—whatever your next event calls for, your catering options in Seattle have just take a delicious turn for the better.

Excellence Guaranteed

At Tony's Events & Catering, we offer better food, better service, better pricing and better ideas for creating the special event of your dreams.

Your personal event planner will help you explore a world of options that await you, from informal hors d'oeuvres buffets to lavish theme parties to formal sit-down dinners. Please know that every event is completely customized to meet your precise needs, tastes, and budget.

Your Place Or One Of Ours...

As a full-service caterer, Tony's is pleased to provide impeccable food and service at the site of your choice, or one of ours.

- **Tyee Yacht Club**
  Tony's is pleased to present a truly affordable piece of the lake, the Tyee Yacht Club. This charming facility, situated on the shores of Lake Union just one block off Eastlake, can host special events from 20 to 200. We had you in mind during our recent remodel; easy-on-the-eyes neutral tones, refinished hardwood floors, soft lighting, a covered deck, dock, and a spectacular water view.

- **Capitol Hill Mansions, Eastside Wineries or Classic Riverboats**
  Tony's can assist you with additional sites including historic Capitol Hill mansions, Eastside wineries, or classic Riverboats. For more information, simply call (206) 328-2195.

See pages 169 and 302 under Banquet, Meeting & Event Sites.

Tuxedos 'n Tennis Shoes Catering

9131 California Avenue S.W. • Seattle, WA 98136
Co-Owners: David Haggerty or David Meckstroth
Event Coordinators: Linn Caine or Jude Lofton
(206) 932-1059; Fax (206) 937-6508
Office Hours: Mon–Fri 9am–4pm;
Please call for an appointment
E-mail:tuxedosntennisshoes@msn.com

Types of menus and specialties

Tuxedos 'n Tennis Shoes Catering takes great pride in the creation of delicious, beautifully presented menus. We utilize only the freshest of ingredients, taking advantage of the region's finest seafood, produce and specialty goods, and preparing them with imagination and flair. From elegant hors d'oeuvres to elaborate dinners, our classically trained chef will create a menu that is reflective of your specific style and taste.

Cost

Prices vary according to party size and menu selection. Rather than assigning pre-set menus to your event, we will consult with you to design a menu that fits your budget and exceeds your expectations.

Experience

Tuxedos 'n Tennis Shoes Catering has operated in the Seattle area since 1985. Trained in Seattle's finest restaurants, we bring a wealth of knowledge and expertise to each event. We will gladly provide references upon request.

Special services and equipment

As a full-service caterer, we can provide as much help as you require in planning your function. We offer wonderful referrals for entertainment, floral services, ice sculptures, specialty cakes, photographers, specialty linens and rental equipment. In addition to the above services, we are also available to coordinate your site location, whether at our own banquet facility "The Hall at Fauntleroy," or at any number of unique locations throughout the greater Seattle area.

Service staff

Our staff is drawn from Seattle's finest hotels and restaurants and is known for the courteous, professional service. The depth and variety of our experience in the service field ensures that you and your guests will be royally treated—right down to the last cup of coffee!

A TRADITION OF EXCEPTIONAL FOOD AND OUTSTANDING SERVICE

We are a full-service catering company emphasizing a fun, dynamic and "worry free" approach to professional event planning and guest services. We invite you to enjoy a free consultation at our kitchen and banquet facility in the Fauntleroy area of West Seattle. There you can discuss the details of your event, tour our facility and meet with our staff to plan the specific services required to make your party a memorable success!

See page 197 under Banquet, Meeting & Event Sites.

15815 S.E. 37th Street • Bellevue, Washington 98006
(425) 641-5400; Fax (425) 641-5800
E-mail: twelvebaskets@msn.com
Web site: www.twelvebasketscatering.com

Deliciously Distinctive Catering for Every Budget!

Since 1976 Twelve Baskets Catering has specialized in serving both large and small corporate accounts as well as families, schools and churches. We have an outstanding reputation in the Greater Seattle Area for our diverse menu, exceptional service standards and, of course, our fabulous food. We have years of expertise providing exceptional food and service for all kinds of events from a small, intimate gourmet dinner for 20 or 30 to elaborate wedding buffets for 300 or 400 and company picnics for thousands.

Menus

Our complete menu includes Northwest favorites like Salmon and Beef Tenderloin, Standards from the kitchens of our well known restaurants such as Chicken Dijon, as well as International cuisine and Hors d'oeuvre and Holiday Buffet Packages and a corporate lunch and box lunch program. Our pricing is mid-range and the foundation for our food presentation is still, as always, the acquisition of the finest quality ingredients and emphasis on creativity. All of our menus and prices can be seen on-line at our website ***www.twelvebasketscatering.com*** as well as pictures of some of our buffet and menu presentations. Click on the hyperlink "view our creations" at the bottom of our home page.

Services

Twelve Baskets Catering can provide hot food prepared in our kitchens to any venue as well as cook on-site for barbeques or breakfasts and intimate dinners. All food prices include the serving dishes and serving utensils. Event Planning Services and Buffet decorations are complimentary in most cases. **Additional Catering Items:** We also provide the following services at additional charge: Linen, Paper goods, Full China service, Eating Utensils, Glassware, Tables, Chairs, Elaborate Theme Décor, Complete Serving, Set-up and Clean-up and Licensed Bartending services.

Terms

Our food is sold on a per person basis with generous portions. Delivery, Service and Rental Items are additional and minimum purchases for catering begin at $75.00 for the Eastgate area and increase for greater distances. There is a 10-person minimum for most menu items. $100.00 non-refundable deposit secures the event date for larger events. Contact us for the full terms for our catering. All Major credit cards are accepted.

"Thank you for providing good food and excellent service.
We look forward to next year!" —SGC, Inc.

"...the food was wonderful (not to mention gorgeous!) and
was exactly as I'd imagined it would be (or better!)." —Nancy Brower

"Amazing! Especially the Apple Pie! Why isn't everyone
using these guys!" —Microsoft Internal Administrative Memo

LET TWELVE BASKETS CATERING MAKE
YOUR NEXT EVENT THE MOST MEMORABLE!

Uncle Roy's Catering

6532 Phinney Avenue North
Seattle, Washington 98103-5234
Phone/Fax (206) 706-1874
Email: uncleroys@worldnet.att.net

"Just Like Mom Used to Make, Only Better!"

Uncle Roy's specializes in home-cooked meals made from only the finest and freshest ingredients. Most of our menu selections and all our baking is done from scratch.

Choose from:

- **Cold hors d'oeuvres:** mini scones & muffins, sun-dried tomato & fresh basil canapés, deviled eggs, cheese tortellini skewers, garlic marinated mushrooms, shrimp cocktail, cocktail bagels with smoked salmon cream cheese
- **Hot hors d'oeuvres:** buffalo wings, spanakopita, scallops wrapped in bacon, stuffed mushrooms, pot stickers, rumaki, chicken satay skewers, mini potato latkes with sour cream & applesauce
- **Lunch & Dinner Suggestions:** lasagna—vegetarian, seafood, with meatballs; Chicken Pot Pie, Deli Platters, Salmon, Beef Stroganoff, Quiche, Entree-sized cold salads—chef's, spinach, Caesar, Greek and more
- **Homemade Desserts:** all butter cookies, many varieties of brownies, nanaimo bars, lemon bars, fruit crisps, chocolate dipped strawberries
- **Cakes & Pies:** apple, pecan, pumpkin, seasonal fruits, carrot cake, chocolate fudge cake, cheese cakes, poppy seed cake, coffee cakes

We also cater box lunches & continental breakfasts: Please give us 24 hours notice (minimum order 6) and we can deliver just about anywhere from South Seattle to the North End—including the Eastside. Box lunches include sandwiches &/or entree salads, beverage, chips, dessert, fresh fruit and all paper goods—in a white paper sack (less waste!) Please give us plenty of advance notice and we can customize your order.

Experience: Roy Chase is a graduate of the Culinary Institute of America ('76) in Hyde Park, New York with diverse experience in the food service industry.

Special diets: We can accommodate most special diets—vegetarian, low sodium, kosher-style, low fat, dairy free. We can always come up with something special to suit your needs.

Affordable: Call for menu or we can do a proposal for your next event. We are a full service caterer. We can provide all paper goods, rentals, servers, clean up crew.

Terms: 50% deposit in advance, payment in full upon completion of job, unless other arrangements have been made. Washington State sales tax will be added. Gratuity not included.

"Thank you very much for choosing us for your next event!"

—Roy A. Chase, chef/owner

Creators of Extraordinary Events; EST 1983

8420 Greenwood Avenue North
Seattle, Washington 98103
(206) 783-1826; Fax (206) 783-1672
Office Hours: Mon–Fri 8:30am–5:30pm
or by appointment
E-mail: info@theuppercrustcatering.com
Web site: www.theuppercrustcatering.com

Create An Unforgettable Event

From custom designed menus to elegant presentations, The Upper Crust Catering will make your event something you and your guests will remember forever. Attention to detail and creativity, coupled with over 18 years of experience, are what make your events so extraordinary. Allow The Upper Crust Catering to help you in planning your event from the facility to the perfect linens. The Upper Crust Catering will make your event a complete success.

Creative Specialty Menus

Our renowned chef, Donald Platt, and his team of culinary professionals create all our specialties using the best ingredients possible, from locally made pastas and Northwest basics to imported oils and cheeses. Our goal is to carefully work with you to create a menu specific to your tastes and needs, whether you would like an elegant, themed or simple menu.

Special Services

We specialize in weddings, receptions, bar/bat mitzvahs, holiday parties, special promotions, fundraisers, boat cruises, grand openings, picnics, and open houses. Our experienced event planners will handle all the details from facility rentals to floral bouquets to ensure that you will be able to relax knowing that your event will be professionally attended to at every level.

Premier Locations

The Upper Crust Catering offers several exclusive venues in the Puget Sound area or will go to your location. Let our experienced event planners help to find your perfect location, whether in our own classic facilities, **Greenwood Square** and **Harbor Creek Lodge**, or our affiliates ARGOSY Cruises, Seattle Aquarium, Town Hall, Knights of Columbus, Tibbets Creek Manor, Red Hook Brewery, or Corinthian Yacht Club, just to name a few.

FOR MORE INFORMATION
ON OUR FACILITIES...

See pages 196 and 200 under Banquet, Meeting & Event Sites.

©Photos by Craig O'Brien

1025 Pacific Avenue
Tacoma, Washington 98402
Contact: Marnie Jackson
(253) 572-2933
Office Hours: Mon–Fri 9am–5pm
Web site: www.vaultcatering.com

• Fresh ingredients and expert preparation are our hallmark •

Fresh ingredients and expert preparation are the hallmark of our fine catering department. The Vault offers a broad menu for both on- and off-site catering services. Whether for a luncheon, banquet or reception at our location or the location of your choice, our catering experts can help you plan the perfect menu for your event.

We develop menus to fit every taste and budget

We are extremely proud of our menu selections and party presentations. Our culinary team is experienced in developing menus to fit every taste and budget. Following is a sampling of some of the more popular items we do:

- **Hors d'oeuvres:** Chicken skewers in peanut sauce, assorted international cheese displays, cascading vegetable selections, rounds of baked brie cheese, hot crab and artichoke dip, and bacon wrapped scallops
- **Entrees:** Poached salmon, chef-carved baron of beef, smoked salmon fettucine, or chilled seafood medley
- **Desserts:** Delicious assortment of cookies, cheesecakes, pies or petit fours
- **Beverages:** Extensive wine selection; fully stocked bar service featuring premium liquors, liqueurs and ports; gourmet coffee, tea and assorted soft drinks

We can coordinate as much or as little as you want

Whether you just want all your food and beverage selections delivered to your location or you need everything from tables and chairs to china and linens, The Vault catering professionals will coordinate all the arrangements.

Special occasions call for a special company!
Whether you're planning for 10 or 400,
the catering experts at The Vault will
make your next event a memorable one!

For information about our banquet facilities, see pages 291, 304 and 305.

 Please let this business know that you heard about them from the Bravo! Event Resource Guide.

SINCE 1972

3238 N.E. 45th Street
Seattle, WA 98105
(206) 523-2560; Fax (206) 524-3886
Office Hours: Mon–Fri 9am–5pm or by appointment
Web site: www.thewedgecatering.com

Recognized for excellence

- Recommended as one of Seattle's select party professionals by *Entertaining for Business*
- Consistently voted one of "Seattle's Best Places"

Complete catering services

- From simple boxed lunches to full-service events
- All types of events; picnics and barbecues, corporate functions, receptions, holiday parties, breakfasts, lunches and dinners
- All service styles available: seated, buffet and passed
- Specializing in events from 50–500 guests
- Professional serving staff, bartenders and chefs
- Approved at many famous Seattle event facilities
- Provide assistance with other event details such as invitations, decor, music and entertainment
- Coordinate equipment rentals
- Assorted beverages available
- Custom menus created just for you
- WEDDINGS: formal sit-down, casual buffet or hors d'oeuvres only

Freshly prepared gourmet foods

- Our food is flavorful, healthy and beautifully presented
- Popular menus frequently include ethnic cuisines as well as all-American comfort foods
- We accommodate your special dietary requirements

Information to help you plan

- We have experienced, creative event planners who listen carefully to your specific needs
- We furnish information that will help you make the best choices for your event
- We provide you with excellent planning guidelines and accurate estimates

NOTES

Convention & Exhibition Facilities

HELPFUL HINTS

Coordinating a trade show is a large task. Your facility coordinator will be your partner for several months. Make sure that you have good communication with your facility and coordinator.

It is important for you to find out in the beginning whether the facility can meet your needs. Here is a list of the information that you should get from the facility in advance of booking your trade show:

- Complete floor plan (entrances, loading dock, improvements, etc.)
- Exhibition floor space (total square footage)
- Heights of ceilings (lighting)
- Does the facility meet ADA (Americans with Disabilities Act) requirements?
- Are meeting and banquet rooms available? How far from exhibit space?
- Are there accessible loading and unloading areas?
- Limitations that exhibitors need to be aware of (weight, loading area dimensions, etc.)
- Are there freight elevators and ramps (how many floors to exhibit space, size of elevator, weight limitations)?
- Are there elevators, stairs, and escalators (location, and how many)?
- Are there storage facilities available (if so, cost)?
- What are the insurance requirements?
- Cost of facility (deposit, and terms of payment)
- What services are available? Who is recommended? What are union requirements (labor rates of electricians, carpenters, decorators, security etc.)?
- Additional expenses (telephones, parking, fax machine, press room, utilities, computers, typewriters, show management, desk/office, storage, etc.)
- What are regulations concerning: licenses, liability, fire, building codes, alcohol, cleanup, etc.
- Exhibitors information: shipping address, check-in and checkout procedures, earliest setup time, latest takedown time, inspection dates and times, etc.
- Types of admission: open/free of charge, badge, charge, etc.
- Key contact for security, theft reporting, off-hour contact

Exhibit Professionals: This is a rapidly growing industry. There are many professional companies that can help you accomplish your tasks. Exposition service contractors can provide all the services listed here, or you can develop your own team of experts. Exhibit services include: furniture, floor coverings, accessories, pipe and drape, utilities, floor plans, signage, audio visual equipment, staffing, flower/ plant rentals, cleaning service, security services, exhibit design and construction, lighting, sound, communications, photographic services, business service centers, postal packing services, and consulting.

HELPFUL HINTS

Market Analysis: Your success with exhibitors will be based on bringing together the right buyers and sellers. If you have had a show before, it is best to survey the attendees to analyze the type of attendee you are attracting. Sample questions include: How did you hear about the show? What is your age? Will you use the products or services presented at the show? What did you like or dislike about the show?

Site Selection:

- How much exhibit space is available?
- How many exhibits will fit?
- How accessible is the space for load-in and load-out?
- Are professional decorators available? Needed?

Exhibits are becoming a more integral part of meetings and conventions. This is often due to the revenue they bring to a meeting from exhibitors' fees. The exhibit program complements the convention and as much time should be spent planning the exhibit portion as the other vital parts of a meeting.

Exhibitor Promotion: Be sure the exhibitors have as much information as they need about your attendees, as well as what needs the exhibitors can expect from the attendees. Also, be sure the exhibitors have all of the detailed information: the size of the booth, the layout of the booths, the exhibit hours, the color of pipe and drape, the booth inclusions, available utilities, and advertising that is available and/or provided.

Communicate often: Exhibitors need to be kept up to date with highlights of the program, list of exhibitors, numbers of attendees. They will also need an exhibitor packet that will give them details on all the official contractors they may order through. For example, forms to order flowers, tables, crate storage, shipping, electricity, etc.

Attendance Promotions: You are obligated to deliver visitors to the exhibitors. You may use direct mail, advertising in newspapers, television, newsletters, and magazines. Be sure to include the name of the event, date, time, location, description of products displayed, fees (if any), and any special attractions.

On-Site: Prepare an operations manual. This will include the exact details of how you plan to run the exhibit portion (including the times, dates, location) and who is responsible for what.

Evaluations and Follow-up: A simple questionnaire to gather timely information from your exhibitors will be worth a lot as a planning tool. Find out how the exhibitors did and how you can improve the event for the next time.

BELL HARBOR INTERNATIONAL CONFERENCE CENTER

Pier 66, 2211 Alaskan Way • Seattle, Washington 98121-1604
Contact: Sales Department (206) 441-6666; Fax (206) 441-6665
Sales Department Hours: Mon–Fri 8am–5pm
Event Hours: 7 days a week; 24-hour meeting room use
E-mail: info@bellharbor.org • ***Web site: www.bellharbor.org***

Capacity: 57,322 sq. ft. **Conference Center**; 16,450 sq. ft. **International Promenade**; 9,960 sq. ft. **Harbor Dining Room**; 300-seat **Bay Auditorium**; four main conference rooms with breathtaking waterfront views, six break-out rooms, and private dining room; Bell Harbor can accommodate up to 2,000 guests for receptions; Bell Street Pier rooftop plaza is available for outdoor events in the summer for up to 400 guests

Price range: Bell Harbor operates using a conference meeting package; please call for rates; banquets and receptions require a $2,500–$15,000 minimum food purchase

Catering: in-house, full service, executive chef on-site

Types of events: conferences, day meetings, trade shows, banquets, and receptions

Availability and terms

A 10% deposit is required to contract for space. Damage deposit may be required. Open 365 days a year.

Description of services and facility

ADA: fully accessible

Parking: covered parking available; accessed by pedestrian skybridge

Banquet services

- **Seating:** tables and chairs provided for up to 300 in the Harbor Dining Room; 600 in the International Promenade; outdoor areas may require table and chair rental
- **Bar facilities:** Bell Harbor provides liquor, liquor liability; bar facilities and bartenders
- **Dance floor:** available in amenity package, which includes dance floor, stage, votive candles, and decorative mirrors
- **Linens, napkins and china:** provided by Bell Harbor
- **Decorations:** decorations are acceptable but must be approved by Bell Harbor
- **Cleanup:** provided at no extra charge

Meeting and event services

- **Audio visual:** state-of-the-art audio-visual systems with built-in rear projection screens, video teleconferencing, simultaneous interpretation equipment, ISDN lines, data ports, T1 line, and rear projection systems
- **Equipment:** podiums, lavaliere microphones, flip charts included in conference package
- **Lodging:** assistance with guest rooms and transportation is available

BELL HARBOR INTERNATIONAL CONFERENCE CENTER ROOM SPECIFICATIONS

ROOM	Square feet	Approx. Dimens.	Ceiling Height	Theater	Classroom	U-Shape	Conference
Bay Auditorium	6,048	72 x 84	10′–14′	—	300	—	—
Sound	1,800	40 x 45	9′–18′	160	84	44	36
Cove	1,092	28 x 39	9′–18′	70	48	32	34
Marina	980	28 x 35	9′–18′	60	40	32	28
Pacific Board Room	858	26 x 33	9′	48	32	24	22
Coastal Room	224	14 x 16	9′	12	—	—	10
Channel	196	14 x 14	9′	10	—	—	8
Seaway	160	10 x 16	9′	10	—	—	8
Pierside	196	14 x 14	9′	12	—	—	12
Port	272	16 x 17	9′	12	—	—	12
Waterway	160	10 x 16	9′	10	—	—	8

ROOM	Square feet	Approx. Dimens.	Ceiling Height	Banquet	Reception
Harbor Dining Room	3,876	51 x 76	12′–15′	300	500
Inlet	588	21 x 28	10′–14′	40	45
International Promenade	9,000	variable	variable	600	1,000
Prefunction Lobby	9,000	variable	—	—	400
Outdoor Terrace	4,000	variable	—	—	100
Bell Harbor & Odyssey Combined	77,987	variable	—	—	2,000
Odyssey Contemporary Maritime Museum *(partially shown)*	20,665	variable	variable	100	500

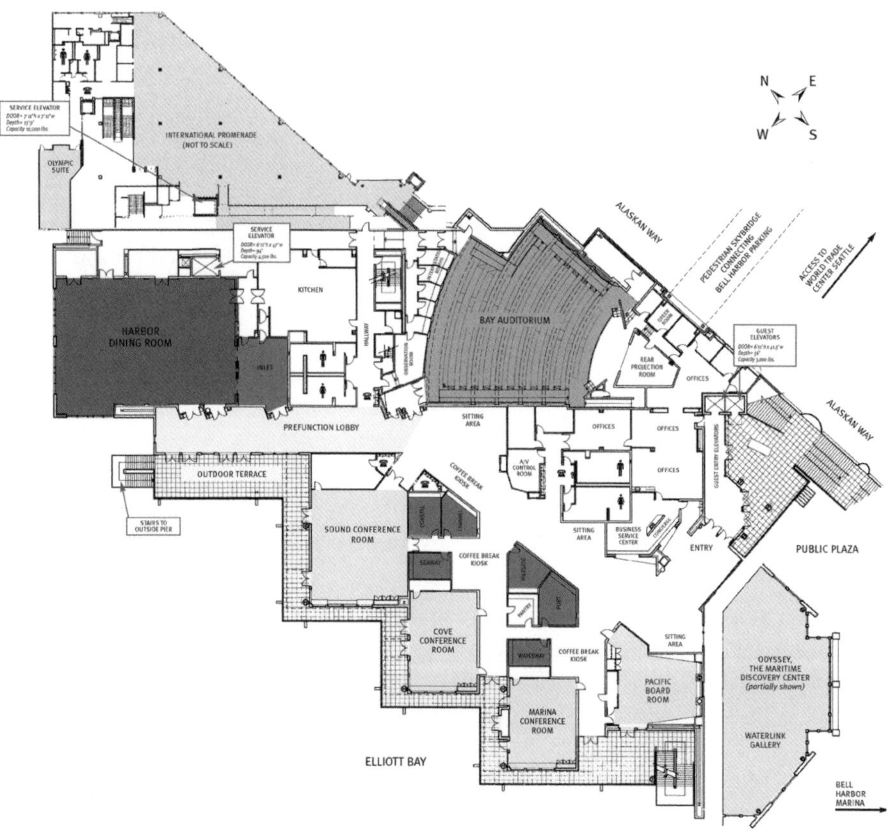

MEYDENBAUER CENTER

11100 N.E. Sixth Street
Bellevue, Washington 98004
Contact: Guest Services Department
(425) 637-1020; Fax (425) 637-0166
Office Hours: Mon–Fri 8am–5pm
E-mail: sales@meydenbauer.com
Web site: www.meydenbauer.com

Capacity: the Eastside's largest meeting and banquet facility; **Exhibit Hall:** 36,000 sq. ft.; divisible into two sections of 18,000 sq. ft. each with a 30-ft. ceiling; **Meeting Rooms:** 12,000 total sq. ft. divisible into nine individual rooms and can be combined to 1,000 to 6,000 sq. ft. each—ceiling height is 16 ft. in all meeting rooms; **Theater:** a 410-seat performing arts theater that is technically suited for artistic performances as well as seminars

Price range: price is determined by event and specific menu

Catering: nationally recognized for excellent catering services; full-service catering is provided exclusively by Meydenbauer Center Catering Department; you may select from our extensive menu items or work with our Executive Chef to create a custom menu to suit your needs; in addition, a rental credit is applied to your banquet rooms that will reduce or waive any room rental charges

Types of events: conventions, trade shows, meetings, banquets, receptions, theatrical performances and consumer shows; the Eastside's most versatile facility

Availability and terms

Please contact the Guest Services Department for date availability. Terms and conditions vary with each event. A deposit is required at the time of booking to confirm your date. Final guarantee is required 72 hours prior to the event.

Description of services and facility

ADA: Meydenbauer Center is fully accessible

Parking: underground parking garage with 440 spaces; parking is $2 the first hour and $1 each hour thereafter; overflow parking near-by at similar rates

Banquet services

- **Seating and servers:** provided as needed
- **Bar facilities:** host or no host; all servers and beverages provided
- **Linens, napkins, china and glassware:** variety of linens, special colors at an additional charge, silver coffee service, ivory china and stemmed glassware
- **Dance floor:** available upon request
- **Decorations:** attractively set buffet lines and coffee stations, table lamps on mirrored bases and your choice of napkin folds; floral arrangements, ice carvings, themed decor available at an additional charge
- **Cleanup:** all cleanup is handled by Meydenbauer Center

Meeting and event services

- **Audio visual and telecommunications:** overhead and slide projectors, screens, LCD panels and other equipment upon request; available telecommunications services include DSL, ISDN and T-1 lines

MEYDENBAUER CENTER

Meydenbauer Center is a full-service convention center located in downtown Bellevue. The Center offers an artful blend of inspired architecture, functional space and inviting atmosphere that's unmatched in the Pacific Northwest. Meydenbauer Center is designed for and around people…to ensure your group receives the professional attention and impeccable service necessary for a successful event.

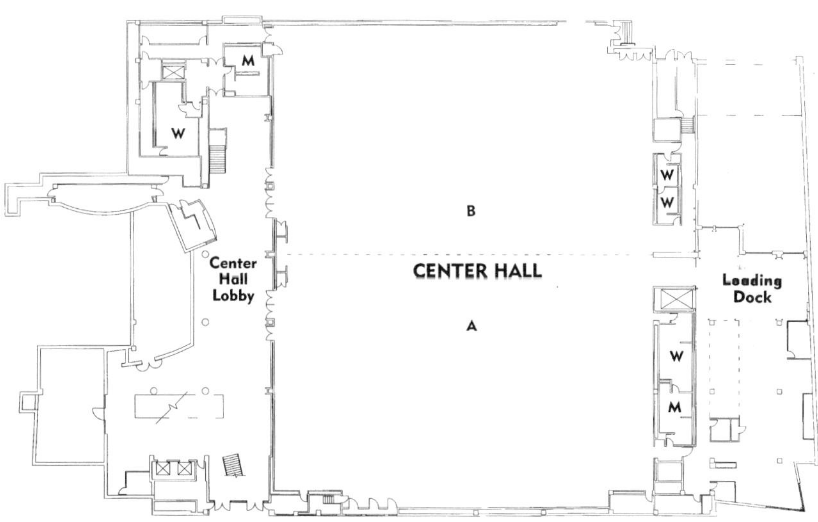

EXHIBIT HALL LEVEL

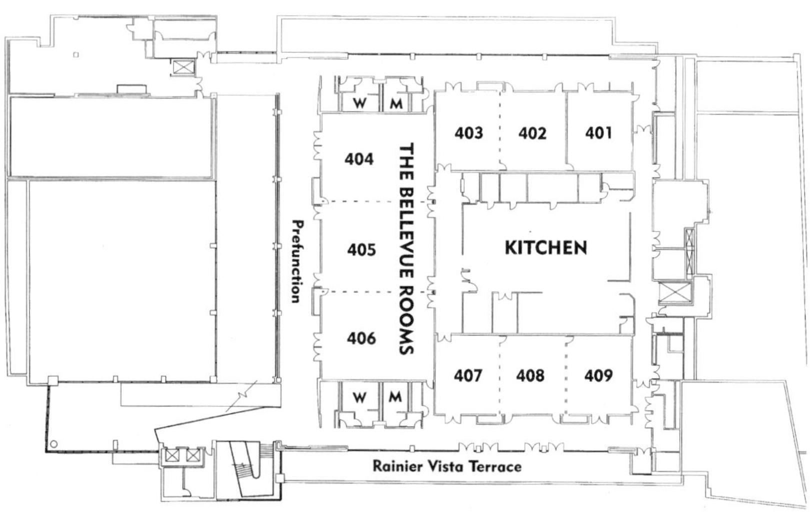

MEETING ROOM LEVEL

800 Convention Place
Seattle, Washington 98101
Contact: Susan Newcomb
(206) 694-5111
Fax (206) 694-5398
Office Hours: Mon–Fri 8am–5pm
E-mail: sales@wsctc.com
Web site: www.wsctc.com

Capacity: **Individual Meeting Rooms:** 56 meeting rooms vary from an executive boardroom for 12 to a presentation room for 1,000. Many are flexible in design with multiple combinations for large groups or more intimate events; **Ballrooms:** five ballrooms accommodate groups from 300 to 2,600 guests for formal banquets or presentations, the ballrooms also double as light trade show space; **Exhibit Halls:** six exhibit halls combine for a total of 205,700 square feet of exhibit space, with a ceiling height of 25′, accommodating up to 972 10'x10' booths

Price range: pricing determined by actual space used

Catering: winner of the coveted 1997 NACE award for "Best On-Premise Catered Event of the Year;" seasonal Northwest foods are highlighted with flair by our professional culinary staff committed to the highest standards of quality and service; menus are tailored to your group's special needs and tastes

Types of events: banquets, conferences, meetings, seminars, social events, conventions, trade shows and consumer shows

Availability and terms

Terms and conditions vary with each event. A deposit is required at the time of booking an event, with additional payments scheduled for full payment prior to the commencement of the event.

Description of services and facility

ADA: fully accessible to wheelchairs, and meets or exceeds all ADA requirements

Parking: enclosed parking garage has over 1,600 parking stalls with direct access into the facility.

Banquet services

- **Dance floor:** 30'x30' dance floors available
- **Decorations:** you are welcome to add your own personal touch with customized decor for exhibits, booths and special themes

Meeting and event services

- **Audio visual and equipment:** services can be provided by an on-site audio visual provider, with complete state-of-the-art systems.

Special services

A public Galleria filled with art and exhibits delights visitors. Retail shops and services are conveniently located inside the facility.

WASHINGTON STATE CONVENTION AND TRADE CENTER

Our team of professional staff is dedicated to providing superior service to each guest. The combination of quality service and superb facilities ensures great success for your next event at the Washington State Convention and Trade Center.

6E
6C
6B
6A
Kitchen
610
605
618
617
619
(6F)
616
620
615
M
W
611
612
614
613
609
606
(6D)
608
607
W
M
604
603
602
601
M
W
West Lobby
East Lobby
South Lobby (Below)
Galleria (Below)

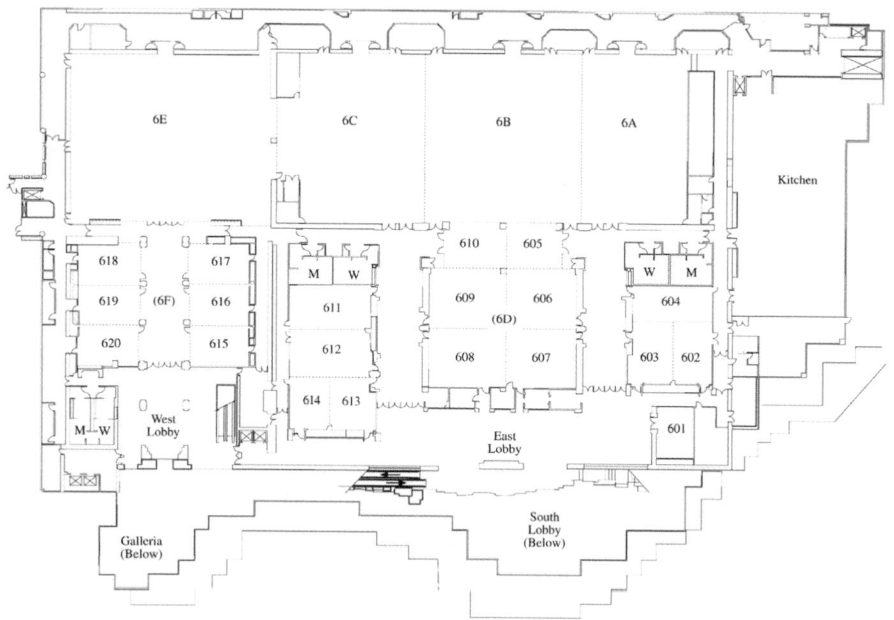

Level 6 Meeting Rooms

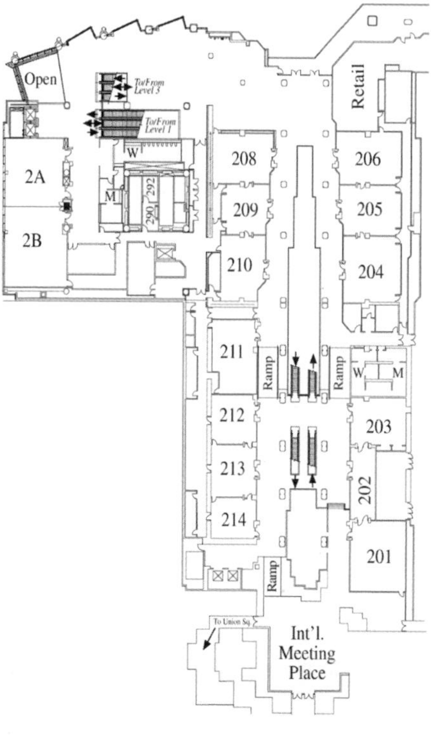

Open
To/From Level 3
To/From Level 1
Retail
2A
2B
W
M
292
290
208
209
210
206
205
204
211
Ramp
Ramp
W
M
212
213
214
203
202
201
Ramp
To Union Sq.
Int'l. Meeting Place

Open
To/From Level 2
To/From Level 4
Public Parking
3A
3B
W
M
392
390
307
308
309
310
306
305
304
303
Galleria
302
301
IMP Below

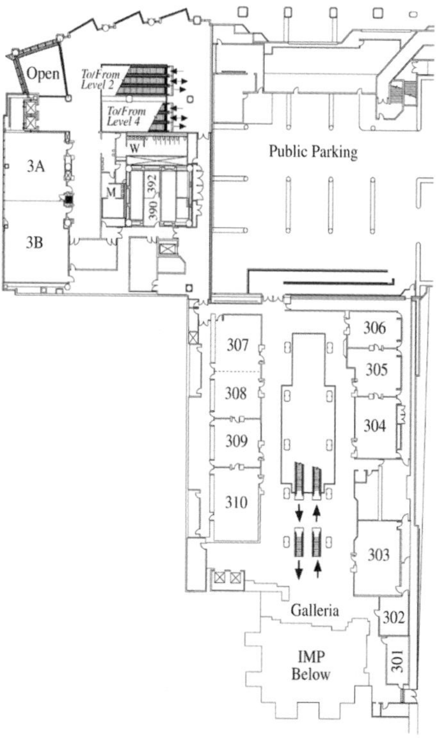

Level 2 Meeting Rooms

Level 3 Meeting Rooms

Washington State Stadium & Exhibition Center

1000 Occidental Ave. S. • Seattle, WA 98104
Contact: Steve Eckerson, Director of Marketing
(206) 381-7575; Fax (206) 381-7557
Web site: www.stadiumexcenter.com

Capacity: **Main Hall:** 165,370 usable sq. ft. for up to 868 booths; **East Hall:** 90,185 usable sq. ft. for up to 460 booths; **Concourse Level:** 36,860 usable sq. ft. for up to 120 booths; **Stadium North Hall** (to be completed in 2002): 60,730 usable sq. ft. for up to 300 booths; **Stadium Club Level & Restaurant** (to be completed July, 2002): 62,605 usable sq. ft.
Price range: please inquire; prices will vary according to space requirements
Catering and concessions: on-site food service handled by Aramark
Types of events: conventions, exhibitions, trade shows, banquets, receptions, concerts, sporting events, or consumer shows

Availability and terms

Reservations for trade shows and exhibitions are scheduled up to five years in advance. A deposit is required on booking.

Description of services and facility

ADA: fully accessible; meets or exceeds all ADA requirements
Restrooms: twice the minimum number of bathrooms required by code
Parking: Exhibition Center parking garage accommodates more than 2,000 vehicles; additional parking available at Union Station, Seattle Mariners' SAFECO Field, and surrounding lots
Exhibition services

- **Access:** multiple entrances make the Stadium Exhibition Center accessible to both vehicles and pedestrians
- **Loading bays:** multiple loading bays, adjacent parking areas, and direct drive access onto the exhibit floor simplify freight handling
- **Clearance:** Main Exhibit Hall: 40'; Swing Space: 20'; Concourse Level: 15'
- **Utilities:** 30' floor utility box module for communications, power, and drainage; compressed air and water utility box located in 90' columns

YOUR PLACE FOR SPACE!

WSSEC offers an outstanding environment for nearly any event experience. Adjoining historic Pioneer Square in Seattle's South of Downtown District (SODO), visitors converge on an impressive urban sports and exhibition complex unlike any in the world. The combined 525,000 total gross sq. ft. make the WSSEC the largest facility in the Pacific Northwest. Exhibitors will appreciate practical conveniences such as multiple loading bays and direct drive-on access points. In addition to easy freeway access and ample parking, the WSSEC is near bus, train, and ferry service. Visitors will also enjoy a rich variety of downtown accommodations and entertainment within blocks of the facility. With ample area for both intimate gatherings and the city's most extravagant large-scale functions, the WSSEC provides the perfect environment for your next event.

 Please let this business know that you heard about them from the Bravo! Event Resource Guide.

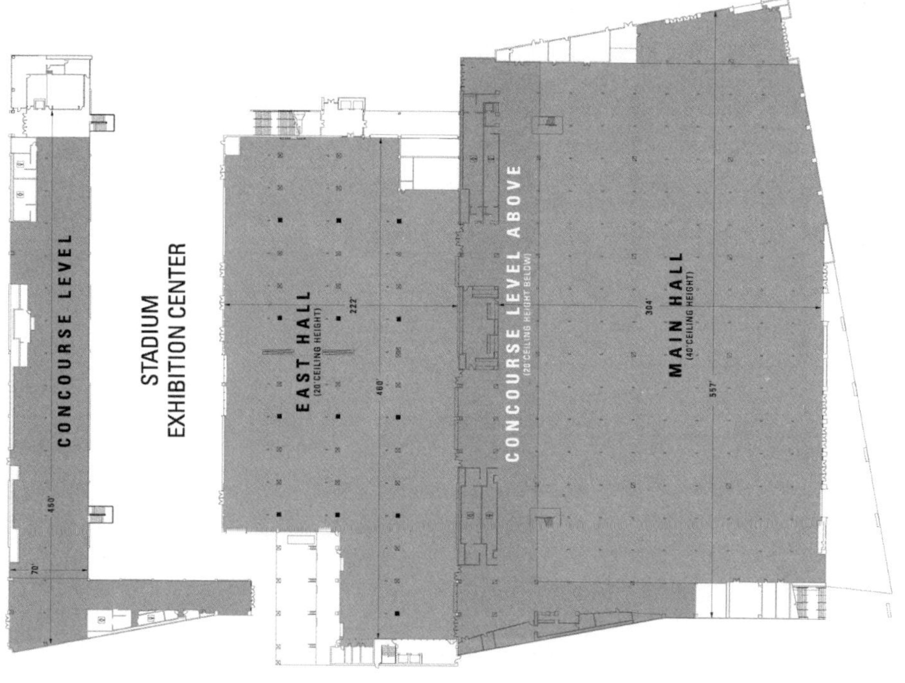
STADIUM
EXHIBITION CENTER
CONCOURSE LEVEL
EAST HALL
(20' CEILING HEIGHT)
CONCOURSE LEVEL ABOVE
(20' CEILING HEIGHT BELOW)
MAIN HALL
(40' CEILING HEIGHT)
450'
70'
460'
222'
304'
557'

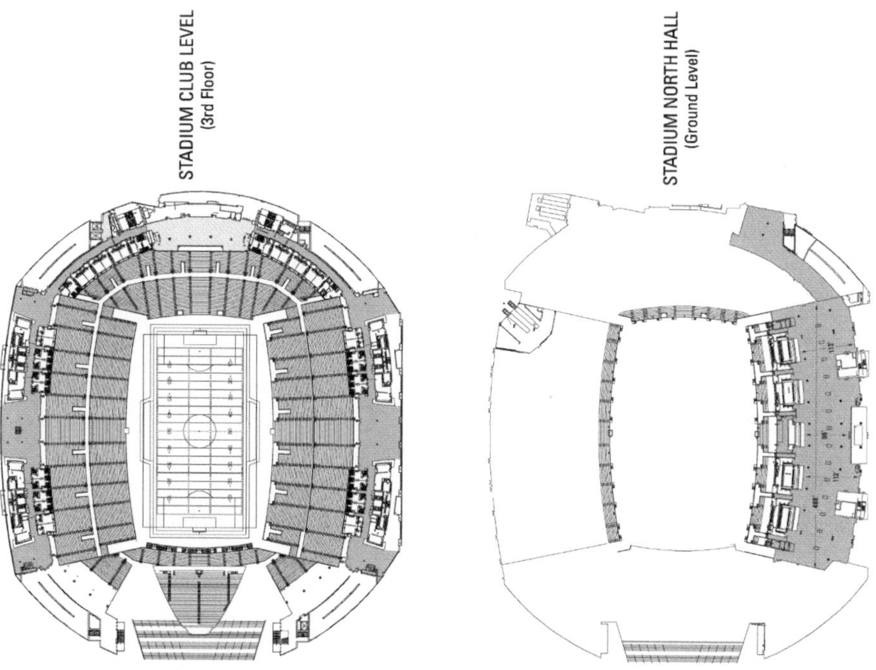
STADIUM CLUB LEVEL
(3rd Floor)
STADIUM NORTH HALL
(Ground Level)

NOTES

Convention & Exhibition Services

❖❖❖

CONVENTION AND EXHIBITION SERVICES

HELPFUL HINTS

Trade shows are often an important part of a convention or meeting and need to be carefully planned. The help of experts in designing your exhibit space is always advisable. Convention services decorators can assist with everything from producing a floor plan and complying with local fire regulations to providing furniture, carpet, electricity and trash cans for your exhibitors. They can also work with a trade show coordinator in producing reasonable time schedules for set up and tear down, dealing with local restrictions or union regulations and consulting on other matters that can affect the success of your exhibitors.

For most trade shows you will require booths delineated with pipe and drape. You will need to decide on the size of each exhibit booth (8' x 10' or 10' x 10' are most common). To determine how much space will be needed for an exhibition, the following calculation is useful. Take the total number of exhibit booths you wish to have, multiply by the square feet of each booth and multiply by 2 to get the total square feet you will need for a typical trade show. (For example: If you intend to have 85 booths at 10 square feet each, 85 x 10 = 850 x 2 = 1,700 total square feet needed.) This estimate allows room for wide aisles and ample space for attendees to move between trade show exhibitors.

Utilizing convention services professionals can make your life much easier. In addition to pipe and drape, furniture and carpet, they will prepare a room diagram of your show, signage for each booth, and may offer such extras as easels, plant rentals, audio visual equipment and lighting. The company will prepare and send a packet to all your trade show exhibitors from which they can request electricity, furniture, carpeting or other special services. Some exhibitor services also take full charge of receiving crates of exhibit materials, getting them to the site, then re-packing the crate and shipping the materials back to you. If your organization does trade shows around the country, it may contract to use the same company in each location in order to have consistent service.

4060 Lind S.W. • Renton, Washington 98055
(425) 251-6565; Fax (425) 251-9878
Web site: www.gesexpo.com

GES Exposition Services is the Leading Trade Show and Event Marketing Company in North America

Headquartered in Las Vegas, GES has offices in 36 major trade show and event cities in the US and Canada.

GES Provides Multiple Innovative and Comprehensive Services

- Event Planning–Trade Shows, Corporate & Special Events
- Exhibit Systems–Rental & Custom Design
- Exhibit Labor–Installation & Dismantling
- Decorating
- Furniture Rental
- Graphics & Design
- Custom Floor Plans
- Temporary Electrical Systems, Service & Lighting
- Complete Freight, Logistics & Drayage Services
- Interactive Website Solution for Trade Shows & Events

Our Discernible Differences are:

Our People • Leading Edge Technology
Continuous Process Improvement Culture • Innovative Services

Because of our discernible differences, and the multiple services we provide, we attract clients from a wide variety of industries and businesses of all sizes including corporations, associations, show management companies as well as the individuals who exhibit at trade shows.

We Stage The World's Most Recognized Trade Shows and Events

COMDEX, Consumer Electronics Show, Super Show, PGA Show, National Restaurant Show, National Association of Broadcasters, Food Marketing Institute, PC Expo, E3, Western Shoe, MacroMedia, Networld + Interop, MAGIC, The 1984 and 1996 Olympics, Democratic National Convention, Holiday Hospitality, World Cup Soccer, JavaOne, Walgreens, GM Mexico, Sun Micro Systems, MLB, All Star FanFest, Indy FanFest, NFL Players Party and PGA World Championship

Our Commitment To You

In today's global marketplace, GES will partner with you to bring together all of the elements needed for the success of your trade show or event - all within one company.

Put The Power of One to Work for You...

ONE TEAM, ONE COMPANY, ONE GOAL —YOUR SUCCESS!

GES. *At Your Service!*[sm]

The Northwest's Premium Choice for Convention, Trade Show & Special Event Services

12614 Interurban Avenue South • Seattle, Washington 98168
(206) 431-1010; Fax (206) 431-2643
E-mail: greg@triumphevents.com

Triumph Events Network, Inc. is a Northwest Company Dedicated to Providing World-Class Service to its Clients

Mission Statement:

We are dedicated to providing our customers with an outstanding trade show or event experience by applying the highest standards of quality to our products and services. We are committed to the idea that our customers are the reason we are in business.

What We Offer:

- Event Planning and Coordination
- Furniture Rentals
- Modular and Custom Display Rentals
- Rigging
- Custom Graphics and Signage
- Production of Floor-plans
- Installation and Dismantling of Exhibits
- Freight Handling and Logistics
- Special Events Services
- Electrical Services
- Largest Selection of Velour Drape in Seattle

Why We Shine:

- We offer outstanding, personalized customer service—regardless of how large or small your event.
- Our equipment is all state-of-the-art, well-maintained, and professional in appearance.
- We are 100% locally owned and managed.
- We hire only the finest people available for ALL our positions, and recognize that our outstanding staff is the key to our success.

Whether your event is a 20-booth hotel show, a 1,000-booth trade show, or a special event with unique requirements, Triumph Events Network, Inc. will provide you with superb service and outstanding equipment.

Decorations, Themes & Props

DECORATIONS, THEMES AND PROPS

HELPFUL HINTS

Why use a theme? It provides interest and coherence for the attendees. Planning is more efficient with a theme, creating an automatically organized process. In addition, the key to a successful event is audience participation. The more involved people become in the event they are attending, the more likely they are to enjoy themselves and remember the experience. Attendees may not remember the name of the keynote speaker, but they will remember the "Wacky Olympics" special event!

When is a theme appropriate? Anytime. When done properly, themes can be used to enhance a business meeting, client appreciation, awards event, and even reunions.

How is a theme chosen? Define the goals of your event first; what you want to accomplish with the event, who is attending, and what you want them to take away with them. Then, you can decide what theme options may work.

Creative brainstorming: Producing a new idea that ties in with the event can be a great challenge. An effective way of coming up with new and innovative ideas is to work with a group of people to draw synergy out of fun, and to build cooperative teamwork to produce ideas and solutions. Find a meeting space free of distraction—phones, foot traffic, etc. A storyboard can be helpful in this meeting so that all ideas can be captured with an open-mind. Some of the smallest ideas can turn into the best campaigns.

Make sure it is the right theme or concept: The best ideas can end up a failure unless the details of the theme and campaign are thought out. Ask specific questions like: Does it fit within the organization's image? Will it offend any of our customers or employees, or conflict with our products? Is it one people will remember? Is the message clear, or lost within the creative? Is it an idea to be proud of and put in the portfolio?

Are theme events expensive? They don't have to be. Some of your theme ideas can be accomplished with a small budget if you and your committee are willing to spend the time. However, a much better use of your time and money may be to use a meeting planner, prop, professional decorator or entertainment company.

Decorating tips for theme events: Consider three to four main areas of the facility for theme props. Main focus areas can include the entryway to the event, stage, dance floor, guest tables, or food and beverage stations, to name a few.

Check-out props and displays: A visit to the prop shop or decorator will allow you the opportunity to see the quality, size, and color of the design ideas and available props. While at the studio, ask to see their portfolio to view actual designs used at various events and browse to see what other props or displays they have. This trip may awaken an idea several months later for a future project.

Theme ideas for your next event:

- Casino Night
- M•A•S•H
- Cruise Ship
- Mexican Fiesta
- Western/ Wild West
- International Themes
- Fabulous 50s
- The Jazz Club
- Around the World
- Treasure/Scavenger Hunt
- Winter Wonderland
- Tropical Island
- Underwater
- Tropical Rain Forest
- Circus! Circus!
- Hawaiian Luau
- The Great Northwest
- State Fair
- Chinese New Year
- Toy Chest
- Murder and Mystery
- South of the Border
- African Jungle
- Mardi Gras
- Medieval Castle
- Nautical
- Great Gatsby Party
- Super Bowl
- Beach Party
- Haunted Halloween

Balloon Tunnel

Company Logo Replica

Gingerbread House

Around The Sound Balloons

Contact: Wendy Hubbard, Certified Balloon Artist
(425) 402-9686
E-mail: balloondecor@msn.com
Web site: www.aroundthesoundballoons.com

Creative and Classic Balloon Decorating

Rely on proven professionals to create the perfect expression for your event. Our Certified Balloon Artist has completed a comprehensive certification program and has years of experience creating professional balloon décor.

Custom designed balloon décor is our distinction. Our team of experts can create an atmosphere that's elegant and sophisticated or fanciful and fun. We have the vision to transform your event into a festive celebration by creating:

- Majestic dance floor canopies
- Showstopping logo replicas
- Enchanting entryway arches, tunnels and columns
- Unique buffet and table centerpieces
- Unforgettable larger-than-life sculptures

Complimentary Consultations are available at the site of your event. Our Certified Balloon Artist will meet with you and help you plan unforgettable décor within your budget. Trust the proven expertise of balloon professionals.

When the décor looks good, you look good!

Call the balloon decorating professionals today at (425) 402-9686

Pepsi's 100th Birthday

Mardi Gras

Cinema Grand Opening

Contact: Dan or Jenny Bender, CBAs
(253) 566-0201
Fax (253) 566-3151
E-mail: info@balloonmasters.com
Web site: www.BALLOONMASTERS.com

PUGET SOUND'S PREMIER CHOICE FOR DECORATING EXCELLENCE

Visualize the dramatic effect of:
- Entryway Mural and Arch Designs
- Spectacular Stage Presentations
- Dance Floor and Room Canopies
- Custom Logo Murals and Banners

Experience the excitement of:
- Exploding Balloons and Walls
- Confetti and Streamer Canons
- Balloon Drops and Releases
- Unbelievable Sculptures

ENHANCE your design choices with motion lighting, rotators, fabrics, silks and special signage.

CUSTOMIZE any type of theme or special event with your choice of balloon styles and colors.

COMPLETE DÉCOR PACKAGES created for excitement, high impact, and exceptional value.

THEME DÉCOR with **ORIGINALITY!**

Certified Balloon Artists
Professional balloon art and design is an emerging, creative means of event and theme decor. Experienced, artistic designers are a must. Balloon Masters is the only Northwest company to offer five Certified Balloon Artists on staff. They are proven professionals dedicated to excellence in balloon design, display and event décor.

Consultations
Complimentary consultations are offered both on-site and at our design studio. One of our CBAs will meet and tour the facility with you to develop a décor plan, or welcome you to our design studio to view a large selection of portfolio pictures of various types of events.

Balloon Master's designs are regularly featured in five world wide publications
Excellent special event, trade show, corporate and private references available

COMPARE PORTFOLIOS...SEE THE DIFFERENCE!

FROM CLASSIC BALLOON DÉCOR, TO UNIQUE IDEAS BEYOND BOUQUETS, RELY ON PROFESSIONALS!

CALL TODAY FOR A COMPLIMENTARY PROPOSAL
(253) 566-0201

Bellevue, Washington • (425) 467-8129
E-mail: designperfecttoo@msn.com
Web site: www.designperfecttoo.com

Same Great Décor . . .
Only Our Look Has Changed !!

Design Perfect: Your event décor and design resource.

Without question, décor is one of the essential elements that contributes to the success of your event. Along with the menu and the entertainment, the visual environment created at your event will be captured in your guests' memories.

A full-service production corporation, Design Perfect, Inc. offers consultation, design, fabrication, and event production management. We respond promptly and professionally to clients' requests for any size event or specific event décor need. We offer décor for corporate events, holiday theme parties, weddings, trade shows, picnics, ethnic themes, and other special occasions.

Although Design Perfect, Inc. has hundreds of event décor theme props in stock and readily available, we pride ourselves on our ability to create custom décor that brings your imagination to life. We endeavor to create the unusual and innovative. The Design Perfect, Inc. design and décor team will expertly coordinate every facet of your organization's event from start to finish. We coordinate, plan, and design events with just the right ambiance.

Visit our new web site for an online proposal!
www.designperfecttoo.com

See page 350 under Catering/Food & Beverage Services
and page 504 under Meeting & Event Planners.

PJ Hummel and Company, Inc.

The Art of Event Production & Décor

405 South Sheridan • Tacoma, Washington 98403
Contact: PJ Hummel
253-272-6605 or toll-free at 1-888-382-6605
E-mail: pj@pjhummel.com
Web site: www.pjhummel.com

Award Winning Event Design & Décor

PJ Hummel & Company, Inc. is an award winning, full service, event design and décor company. We develop, create, and produce themed décor for corporate events, tradeshows, banquets, award ceremonies, holiday celebrations, and other special events.

We are recognized for...

- 15,600 square-foot warehouse of authentic props
- Complete in-house design studio
- Unique and unusual event themes
- Custom floral design and plant rental
- Lighting and specil effects packages
- Custom linens and centerpiece options
- Themed entertainment
- Photo ops
- Staging
- And much, much more!

Visit our *NEW* website at *www.pjhummel.com*
for a detailed look at our themes and services.

5406 North Albina Avenue • Portland, Oregon 97217
(877) 650-9519; Fax (503) 283-3651
Please call for an appointment
info@propshop.com • ***www.propshop.com***

Creative Environments for Every Event

Our team assists you with the development of your theme and transforms it into a full design concept. Custom-designed backdrops, scenery, lighting and our award-winning staff are elements we use to make your event a unique success.

Full Service Event Decorating, Design and Production

Our internationally recognized team of designers and decorators create your vision using our extensive inventory or custom-designed scenery for your special event. We coordinate each phase of your event, including site inspection, design, fabrication, delivery, setup and take down.

- **Corporate Events**
  Awards Ceremony, Customer Appreciation, Anniversary Celebration, Holiday Party, Sales Kickoff, Team Building, Strategic Planning, Open House, Ground Breaking and New Product Launch
- **Conventions**
  Welcome Ceremony, Opening Night Party, Interactive Seminar, Sponsor Party, Awards Ceremony, Closing Night Gala
- **Trade Shows**
  Theme Decorations, Interactive Booth Design and Fabrication, Special Product Incorporation
- **Non-Profit Events**
  Auction, Fund-Raiser, Open House
- **Festivals and Picnics**
  Company Picnics, Outdoor Festivals, Holiday Celebrations, Sporting Events

A few of our more popular themes are: Survivor, Mardi Gras, Roaring 20s, Hollywood, Tropical, Western, Circus, Tuscany, 60s, 70s and Futuristic.

Association Memberships:

Chamber
MPI • SCVB
ACEP Board • CVBWCO • POVA

See page 476 under Games & Team Building Activities.

Robinson Designs & Events

Artists • Designers • Fabricators

22833 Bothell-Everett Highway, Suite 102, #1118
Bothell, Washington 98021
Contact: Scott or Jan Robinson
(425) 821-1127; Fax (425) 483-8552
E-mail: events@robinsondesigns.com
Web site: www.robinsondesigns.com

Over 30 years of total environment theme parties, hand painted scenery, props, trees, waterfalls, eye-catching centerpieces and sculptures...

In-house fabrication allows us to meet the challenge of finding or creating that "extra touch" or grand finale that turns a wonderful event into a spectacular one. Scott Robinson is an artist with a degree in theatre set design, and background in many facets of theatre, film and television. Scott's artistic talent is complemented by Jan's skill in event and theme design, sculptures, water elements, and European floral design. Their talent together is in creating special touches in design and set decoration to surprise and delight clients and their guests.

Partial list of themes:

- Pacific Northwest
- Native American
- Asian
- Mardis Gras
- Undersea
- Confetti cannons
- Pike Place Market
- Tropical/Jungle
- Wizard of Oz or Emerald City
- Baseball
- Forties, Fifties to Sixties
- Seasonal
- Klondike
- Outer Space and Planets
- Morocco or Indiana Jones
- Titanic
- Circus
- Spiritual / Religious
- Custom themes welcome...

Types of events:

- Corporate Theme Parties
- Grand Openings
- Conventions
- Art Commissions
- Conferences
- Trade Shows and Exhibits

Partial list of clients:

Alaska Airlines, Auction of Washington Wines: "Circle of Care," Bellevue Art Museum, Seattle Aquarium, Microsoft, Sprint PCS, Pacific Northwest Arts Fair, Disney, Bellevue Club, Sammamish Club, Bear Creek Country Club, Swedish Hospital, Providence Hospital, event planners, theatres, television, and many more...

300 Third Avenue West • Seattle, Washington 98119
(206) 957-0091; Fax (206) 352-4063
E-mail: julie@vangardevents.com
Web site: www.vangardevents.com

---

vanguard: n. the leading position in a movement or trend.

Our approach to décor incorporates both the image of the company (or individual), as well as the direction you wish the event to take. We capture that spirit whether we are producing a corporate holiday party, an elegant and sophisticated executive dinner, or an anniversary celebrating your company's past, present, and future. This approach to ambient design is only possible because of our careful attention to the latest trends and colors.

Many of our designs are researched to their origins, and we incorporate tradition into all of our designs that reflect the past. While some companies continually reproduce the same themed event, we create unique, custom events for our clients that have an eye towards the future and choose to be tasteful in their vision of entertaining.

Our close association with professional event planners from lighting, catering, graphic design, and entertainment companies allows us the resources to design entire theme concepts that are seamless and smooth. Style, sophistication, drama and trend-setting are very important to us and we truly enjoy the challenge of discovering the unique characteristics of our clients and reproducing them in our designs.

For an event that is truly a reflection of your vision, please visit our web site at ***www.vangardevents.com***, and share in the memories of just a few of the events we have produced.

Julie Hale: designer

WINTERGARDEN DESIGN

9121-151st Avenue N.E. • Redmond, Washington 98052
(425) 869-9415; Fax (425) 881-5009
Web site: www.wintergardendesign.com

Wintergarden Design is a...

Full service event design and production company. We create, produce and install décor for banquets, awards ceremonies, trade shows, holiday celebrations, and other special events. We service all Eastside and Seattle hotels, conference centers, and event facilities.

We are...

Recognized as the place to go for quality production, delivered on time and on budget. We provide:

- Scenery
- Lighting
- Entertainment
- Florals
- Staging
- Audio Visual Services

Wintergarden maintains a vast inventory to create themed environments at reasonable costs, and serves events of all sizes.

The proof is in our portfolio. Please give us a call.

Entertainers & Performers

❖❖❖

ACappella-Go!

Singing great songs for your special event!

Exclusively Represented by

ENTCO International, Inc.

(425) 670-0888; Fax (425) 670-0777

Web site: www.ENTCO.com

A cappella: *vocal music without accompaniment*
Go!: *to move, to be or act in harmony*

Why ACappella-Go!

ACappella-Go! has a reputation for bringing first-class, family entertainment to corporate, individual, and public events for a reasonable fee with minimal set-up and technical support. Easy for you and more enjoyment for your guests.

Kathy, SuzAnne and Ginger have been performing together since 1995 for festivals, fairs, corporate events, private parties, clubs and cruise ships. They have produced two CDs, won numerous awards at Northwest a cappella competitions and have been the opening act for famous performers, including Roberta Flack.

ACappella-Go! is perfect for most events

- **Versatile:** The trio will perform on stage, or stroll among your guests. They are effective in any venue. Minimum one-hour booking, but the length of their performance is also based entirely on your schedule and needs.
- **Self-contained:** They have no instruments; they bring a compact sound system that can operate on batteries—so outside venues can be served with equal ease.
- **Special themes:** ACappella-Go! has several theme shows, including an appropriately costumed Holiday show.

Partial Song List

- Sing, Sing, Sing
- Heebie Jeebie Blues
- Sentimental Journey
- Lullaby of Broadway
- Mr. Sandman
- In the Mood
- One Fine Day
- Baby, I'm Yours
- All I Have to Do is Dream
- Chapel of Love
- Blue Skies
- Etc., Etc., Etc.

What People are saying about ACappella-Go!

"You made (the sponsor's) day a total success as well as thrilled the 'Out to Lunch' audience. I look forward to having you back again year after year. Thanks!"

—Erika Snyder, Downtown Seattle Association

"...the compliments continue to be expressed...Thank you for giving us a first-class show."

—Margaret Krows, Queen City Yacht Club

All photos © SHOTSnow

Kyra Stewart
(425) 747-9881
E-mail: info@aMasquerade.com
Web site: www.aMasquerade.com

Bring your theme to life, one cameo appearance at a time.

Costumes bring theme events to life, but most people don't really want to wear a costume throughout an entire event. *Cameo-to-Go* gives attendees a chance to step back in time, celebrate the season, travel around the world, or discover an alter ego, then peel it all off after capturing the moment on film. They keep a commemorative souvenir photo showcasing your theme in a fun way, yet don't have to hassle with wearing a costume as they enjoy the rest of your event.

We also offer standard costume rentals if you'd like to dress greeters or staff to set the mood of your theme event; and retail accessories if you'd like to present masks or other costume related items as gifts.

Specialty

Attendees entertain themselves as they dive into the theme of your event donning hats, wigs, accessories, costumes and props to take a commemorative souvenir photo. Interactive fun dressing each other, hamming it up for the camera and laughing at the new looks.

Fees and Terms

Fee for *Cameo-to-Go* service includes customized assortment of rental costumes and accessories, interactive display rack with mirror, delivery, set-up, and wardrobe assistant staff to help guests get into character for their photos. Does not include photography services. We recommend SHOTS***now***, offering digital photographs printed on-site for your attendees to take with them.

A sampling of companies who have enjoyed Cameo-to-Go theme dress-up photostations on-site at their events:

- Microsoft
- Northwest Composites
- Action Events
- Bill Pierre Enterprises
- Sandusky Radio
- Vulcan

Cameo-to-Go **Dress-up Theme Photo Station to entertain your guests.**

See page 559 under Rental Services.

An ESP Experience

"Intuitive Presentations Tailored To Your Needs"

Lance Campbell
(206) 682-0653
E-mail: Mind1flow@aol.com
Web site: www.AnESPExperience.com

Two presentation styles that create fun and intrigue!

★ **Mind Reading:** This is a fun and interactive show that is presented to the entire group at once. It's a dramatic program infused with humor. When you book this presentation you will not only witness extraordinary things, but experience them.

★ **Numerology Readings:** Using the numbers in a persons birth date, I will reveal insights about their inner self as well as their potential. After each one on one reading, the individual is given their chart to take as a souvenir. This enhances the fun as people wander about comparing charts. This presentation fits easily into any situation.

Varied Venues

I have performed in theaters and hotels, on boats, trains and television. So I am certain that I can create a presentation that will work just right for you.

Varied Audiences

Groups ranging from 9 to 500 people. Ages from teens to seniors.

Surpassed Their Expectations...

Hilton Hotels
Eaton Corporation
Insurance Advocates
G&J USA Publishing
D.A. Zuluaga Construction, Inc.
Washington Education Association

Over the years I have performed at various functions throughout the Northwest, bringing something unique to each event. I look forward to doing the same for you!

To guarantee a successful event, contact:

Lance Campbell / An ESP Experience
(206) 682-0653
E-mail: Mind1flow@aol.com

Chip Pemberton

COMEDY HYPNOSIS

(206) 624-0333

www.comedyhypnotists.net

A talented stage performer, Chip Pemberton will amaze and amuse your guests with his skillful hypnotism and his keen sense of humor. Available to meet your entertainment needs throughout the greater Puget Sound area, Chip's performances add memorable fun to:

Corporate Events

Private Parties

Holiday Parties

Graduations

Each show contains three major elements of entertainment: One—volunteers from the audience become the stars of the show; Two—the mystery of hypnotism; and Three—lots of funny and interesting skits for the hypnotics to do.

Qualifications:

• 20 years of experience as a Comedy Performer •

• Bachelor of Fine Arts in Acting •

• Certified Hypnotherapist Training •

Represented by:

Comedy Entertainment

also providing comedians

Please call (206) 624-0333 for more information.

Firetruck Slide

Train Bouncer with music/light system

Tsunami Double Chute Slide

Call for a free brochure
Seattle (206) 763-3236 or (800) 763-3236
or visit our ***Web Site: www.clownsunlimited.com***

Over 45,000 Events Since 1981

Serving the Puget Sound area since 1981, Clowns Unlimited has provided quality entertainment and games for parties, picnics, promotions and more. We are a tradition for many families and companies as we continue to delight and amaze children and adults.

Entertainers

- Clowns
- Balloonists
- Magicians
- Jugglers
- Facepainters
- Santa Claus
- Airbrush Facepainting
- Seasonal Characters
- DJ's/Sound Systems
- Kid's Karaoke

Interactive Games and Attractions

- Aquatic Adventure
- Ball Pond
- Beanie Typhoon
- ***Assorted Bouncers***
  - Blue Dog
  - Castle
  - Clown
  - Choo Choo Train
  - Dinosaur
  - Elephant
  - Gorilla
  - Lion
  - Race Car
  - Spaceman
  - Bouncy Boxing
- Bungee Run
- Bungee Bull
- Cameron the Caterpillar
- Carnival Games
- Crocodile Slide and Hide
- Dance Dance Revolution
- Dunk Tanks
- Equalizer Bungee Challenge
- Go Karts
- Gyrotron
- Human Spheres
- IronMan Obstacle Course
- Joust
- Krazy Karts
- Lazer Tag
- Mobile Circus Train
- Monster Trucks
- Mutiny on the Bouncer
- Pony Rides
- Puffer the Train
- Robo Surfer
- Rockem Sockem
- Rocky Mountain Climber
- ***Slides***
  - 25 ft. Slide
  - 40 ft. Slide
  - 50 ft. Slide
  - Firetruck Slide
  - Rocket Turbo Slide
  - TotTitanic Slide
  - Tsunami Double Chute Slide
- Spin Art
- Submarine
- Sumo Wrestling
- Team Challenge
- Toddler Play Area
- Twin Spin Thrill Ride
- Twister
- Velcro Wall

"They are always on the cutting edge of cool and are extremely dependable."
—Christine Beatty, Microsoft

"They show consistency in timeliness, quality service and courtesy. They are professionals!"
—Jason Jones, Remlinger Farms

Professional Entertainers • Top Quality • Best Prices
Satisfaction Guaranteed • Fully Insured • Trained Staff

PAUL BLAIR
Hula-Hoop Stuntman

1-800-726-5836
E-mail: dizzyhips@onebox.com
Web site: www.DizzyHips.com

Dizzy Hips is Paul Blair, *aka* "Shazam! The Hula-Hoop Stuntman." He has orbited the planet and performed in 17 countries. Paul Blair is the original "gyronautical explorer" and statesman for retro-third grade fun and exercise. With the help of Hula-hoops, ("the other Social Lubricant") he entertains any audience and gets any group "jumpin'" and "twirlin.'" Paul Blair holds Guinness Book world records in four categories.

SHOWS

- **PAUL BLAIR – HULA-HOOP STUNTMAN Comedy Shows**
  A variety of crowd-pleasing acts to fit any event. Ranging from 4–30 minutes. *"He's the Jackie Chan of Hula-Hoops doing Buster Keaton-style comedy."*
- **GYROPELVIDELICS® Light and/or Fire Spectacle!**
  "Whirling, cosmic eye candy gyronautica."

PARTIES

- **DIZZY HIPS CIRCUS® Group Games, Lessons and Show!**
  Get the wiggles out at a corporate event, school or wedding, etc. This is fun for all ages. Can't Hoop? Don't be shy! Paul is a master at teaching and with his specially designed handcrafted hoops he can teach anyone in just a few minutes! Presented in a variety of themes. Temporary tattoos, and/or face painting available.
- **DODGE-BALL RETURNS!—"Big Kid-style!"**
  This is a great "anti-chair" activity. Get ready to rumble! All the action without the pain, we use state-of-the-art soft-skin dodge-balls.
- **HAND-CRAFTED HULA-HOOPS "Dizzy Hips® and Hip Candy® Hula-Hoops**
  Best quality, resilient hula-hoops on the market. Fire hoops and breakdown, portable hula-hoops. Available in black light, holographic, plain, and unique color designs. They come in a wide variety of sizes. Bulk order discounts. We ship anywhere!

Public safety and fun is Dizzy Hips Circus top priority. Be rest assured, these shows and activities are insured for public liability (in excess of 2million dollars).

Contact Paul Blair–Hula-Hoop Stuntman at 1-800-726-5836

by e-mail at *dizzyhips@onebox.com*

or visit his web site at *www.DizzyHips.com*

Geoffrey Ronning

"The Northwest's Most Popular Corporate Variety Entertainer"

(425) 712-1976 or (888) 545-5256
Fax (425) 672-6826
E-mail: geoffr@gte.net
Web site: www.mrhypnosis.com

Novel, Interactive Comedy Entertainment!

Two Program Options:

- **The Comedy Mindreading Magic Show:** Geoffrey Ronning's unique mindreading magic for sophisticated corporate audiences. Suitable for on-site events. Fully self contained, fast paced, non-stop laughs.
- **The Corporate Comedy Hypnosis Show:** The Geoffrey "Mr. Hypnosis" Ronning Comedy Hypnosis Show. 60 or 90 minute formats. Your audience stars in this incredible, funny, unique and novel show. Fully self contained.

Proven Program

Geoffrey has helped hundreds of groups make their events a success: groups like Microsoft, Asymetrix, WSU, Washington Beer & Wine Wholesalers Association, Harrahs Hotel, Comp USA, Swedish Hospital, Doubletree Hotel, International Association of Firefighters, plus hundreds more. Now let him help you.

Engage a Celebrity Entertainer

You or your employees have probably seen Geoffrey on television, in the newspaper or heard him on the radio. Recently he has appeared on KOMO TV4, Northwest Afternoon, KVI 570AM, KISW 99.9FM, The Kent and Allen Show, KPLZ, Star 101.5FM and KUBE 93FM.

Free Helpful Booklet: 10 Steps to a Successful Corporate Event

How to plan, organize, and execute a successful event. Call to request this free, helpful booklet.

Corporate Clients Rave!

"The Funniest Show they ever saw!" —Terri Mooney, Kitsap County Fire District

"Our group thoroughly enjoyed your program!" —Steve L. Severin, Deloitte & Touche

"Amazing – Fun – Entertaining!" —Margaret Degroot, H&R Block, Inc.

"I have organized our Parties for nine years and have never had such an enthusiastic response from the guests. Everyone had a great time, including the owners of the company!" —Debbie deBoer, Miles Sand & Gravel Company

"Thank you for an outstanding performance! We had a tremendous response to your dynamic and hilarious show. Our guests expressed their enjoyment and amazement at your talent, and our foresight to retain you! —Lianna S. Collinge, Tacoma Executive Association

For full promotional packet, video, and date inquiries, call the number above or your favorite event planner.

 Please let this business know that you heard about them from the Bravo! Event Resource Guide.

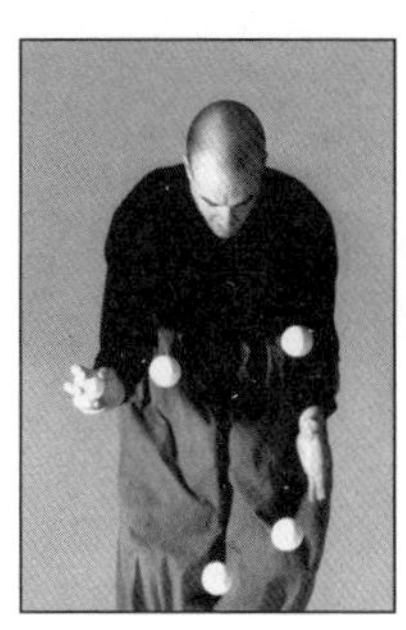

P.O. Box 31012 • Seattle, Washington 98103
(206) 528-5500 or (888) 664-4904; Fax (206) 527-3078
E-mail: bookings@gregbennick.com
Web site: www.gregbennick.com

Juggler — Unicyclist — Comedian — Emcee

Greg Bennick is the most versatile entertainer in the Pacific Northwest. Able to perform stage shows, strolling, or appear as a Master of Ceremonies, Greg is an interactive comedian who blends an incredible variety of skills with a thorough knowledge of the corporate marketplace. Read on to discover more about the Pacific Northwest's best "corporate comedic strategist."

Client specific...

Whether riding a six foot unicycle or juggling seven balls, Greg makes sure that his comedy and overall delivery are interwoven with the initiatives and messages that the client wants conveyed. Greg meets with all clients in advance of the event, preferably onsite, in order to understand completely what the purchaser has in mind.

Corporate "safe"...

Always tasteful, Greg's humor is crafted with corporate audiences in mind. His dynamic stage presence and amazing skills have been a hit with Microsoft, Boeing, Timex, Sheraton Hotels, State Farm Insurance, Planet Hollywood, Remington, Nike, AT&T, Pfizer, FAO Schwartz, Nintendo, and hundreds of others since 1983.

Always professional...

Greg Bennick is committed to providing quality entertainment. His shows are backed by a $2,000,000 insurance policy. Meeting planners will find working with Greg to be a breeze. His show is entirely self contained and includes a full sound system. He is always willing to go the extra distance to ensure a successful event.

Proven success!

"Our 300 attendees were thoroughly entertained by your performance, as evidenced by the STANDING OVATION at the conclusion of your show!"

—Steven L. Sanderson, United Way of America

Call for a full promotional packet, references, or to reserve dates.

Ho, Ho, Ho & Co

"The Memorable Santa Claus"™

Michael Baldwin

2212 Queen Anne Avenue North
Seattle, Washington 98109
(206) 282-8338

E-mail: sleighboy@paladinpacific.com

"A right jolly old elf,"

My heartfelt portrayal of Santa Claus brings the joy and magic of Christmas to your business holiday function, personal party or Christmas Eve visit to the kids!

"And he looked like a peddler just opening his pack."

No expense was spared to achieve exactly the right Holiday look! My Santa suit is a unique blend of traditional and contemporary in a deep red silk velvet. It's trimmed in white lamb's wool and finished with a real leather belt, boots with jingling sleigh bells and a green velvet Santa bag. An alternative look is the traditional, billowy sleeved, white cotton shirt with a festive vest of forest green velvet trimmed in a wonderful red, green and gold pattern—with the red pants and black boots.

"His eyes how they twinkled! His dimples how merry!"

With warmth, a joyous yet professional attitude, flowing real beard and great costumes I bring magic to your holiday event. A dramatic entrance, handing out gifts with jolly flair, a joyful reading for the kids of "The Night Before Christmas"—use your imagination, anything is possible at Christmas!

"He spoke not a word, but went straight to his work,"

- Artful Catering
- Immunex
- Easter Seal Society
- KING TV's Jeff Renner & Family
- Fred Hutch Holiday Gala
- Microsoft
- Fred Hutch Santa Breakfasts
- Nordstrom's–Seattle
- Four Seasons Hotel
- QA Helpline Benefit

Don't Wait . . .
Call Early for Best Date and Current Rate!

1025 N.W. Gilman Boulevard
Issaquah, Washington 98027
(425) 427-2444
E-mail: info@illusionz.com
Web site: www.illusionz.com

EXPERIENCE THE MAGIC!
EXPERIENCE THE FUN!

Steffan Soule...

is a seasoned professional with an extensive body of work. While performing his world class magic shows for the adult and family audience, Steffan's sense of mystery and enchantment has made him one of the hottest corporate acts on the national scene today. Now, as magic director for two magic theatres and star of the longest running magic show in the Northwest, Mysterian, he can bring you more magic than ever before.

Steffan Soule in Mysterian

The largest, most spectacular magic show from here to Las Vegas plays every weekend and by special request for private events. The reviewers say the show is like nothing you have ever seen before—a *"definite must see."* Mysterian is *"like a well-scripted Disney movie"* with *"big, eye popping magic carried out with dramatic panache." "A mind-blowing, big effects magic show with spectacular, world-class grand illusions."* The magic will leave you breathless with wonder. Your imagination will never be the same! Come experience the thrill of elaborate original illusions that have become Soule's signature crowd-pleasers. (Performed in the 200+ seat magic theatre.)

Experience Magic

Sophisticated Close-Up Magic performed in our specially designed 30-seat, close-up magic theatre. Intimate sleight of hand performed right before your eyes. "Experience Magic" is performed for the public every weekend and any time for private groups.

Birthday Party Magic Shows

A magic show created for young audiences and performed as an addition to any of our incredible birthday party packages. Performed in our special close-up magic theatre.

Corporate and Special Events

Your CEO appears from your Logo as it flies through the air. Your award recipients are highlighted as they participate in interactive magic effects on stage. Steffan weaves themes and business concepts into his magic to illustrate even the most complicated ideas. Seven different magic shows to choose from with endless variations.

Magic for the corporate and family audience.

See page 55 under Attractions & Activities.

WE'D KILL FOR YOUR BUSINESS

CALL ENTCO INTERNATIONAL
(425) 670-0888
Toll Free: (800) 803-0298; Fax (425) 670-0777
E-mail: ENTCO.com
Web site: www.ENTCO.com

She was a cold blooded killer with a pair of icy blues and a heart to match. Now that @#*! cop wants to know why she talked to you all evening. So does your wife.

"Our faces hurt from laughing so much."

Pardon me, is that a knife in your back?

"The president of our association kept asking how we're going to top IT'S A MYSTERY...Well, I honestly don't think we can..."

As soon as I heard the gun, I knew it meant trouble; but who could have imagined this?

"...the entire crew were highly professional, courteous, articulate, incredibly funny, and creative beyond belief."

I'm Detective Richard Sheridan. Don't call me Dick.

"...remarked that this was the most unforgettable and fun event they have ever attended!"

Isn't that Mike's favorite golf club next to the body?

"...the best entertainment we have ever had at a company Christmas party."

JOLENE

Interactive Fun Specialist

vm: 206.470.0595
ph: 425.489.1073
jo@funspecialist.com
www.funspecialist.com

Customized Entertainment

ORIGINAL! FUN! VERSATILE!

JOLENE THE FUN SPECIALIST is a professional and experienced entertainer who energizes events with her unique talents. She is focused on fostering positive human interaction. We know that smiling and laughing are contagious; Jolene gets the ball rolling. She raises spirits, breaks the ice and gets people talking, moving and interacting before they know it. Her creativity and humor captures people's attention and brings everyone together. Jolene's knowledge of people, theater and sign language allow her to communicate in many ways.

REJUVENATE YOUR MEETINGS, CONFERENCES AND EVENTS...

Could your events have more impact if they were more fun? Bring personality and enthusiasm to your event. Get people involved in different and creative ways.

EVENTS...

- Team Building Sessions
- Orientation & Retreats
- Exhibits & Trade Shows
- Fundraisers & Auctions
- Weddings & Anniversaries
- Family & Children's Events

JOLENE THE FUN SPECIALIST'S TANGIBLE TALENTS...

- Team Building
- Ice Breakers
- Balloon Artistry
- Master of Ceremonies
- Face Painting
- Spontaneous Amusement
- Swing Dancing
- Line Dancing
- Calligraphic Banners

CUSTOMIZE YOUR EVENT...

Jolene is a Fun Consultant who will produce a fun package of her skills to fit your needs.

CLIENTS INCLUDE...

Microsoft, Nordstrom, Washington Mutual, State Farm Insurance, Gene Juarez, KLSY 92.5, Pepsi Cola, Starbuck's Coffee, Seattle Hilton, Goodwill, Voice Stream, Pacific Science Center, Corporate Express, Perkins Coie, and many others.

Featured in *The Seattle Times, Seattle Post-Intelligencer, Eastside Journal,*
on KING-5 TV, Q13 News, KIRO-7 TV and other major media.
See TV Interviews, Video Clips, Pictures and Descriptions at ***www.funspecialist.com***

KAREN CORNELL

(425) 673-1930

or

(800) 421-1682

E-mail: karencornell@angelwood.com

Web site: www.angelwood.com

HAVING A PARTY?
MAKE YOUR CORPORATE EVENT STAND OUT!

Using numerology and a conventional deck of cards, Karen Cornell is able to answer questions about life with amazing clarity and accuracy. The cards and numerology work well together, as numerology tells things in larger blocks of time and gives an over-view or plan for your life, while the cards focus on what is happening right now and for the next few months.

During each reading, Karen will discuss your current "personal year" and will draw two spreads of cards to focus on events in your life for the next three months.

Parties and events

Karen tailors herself to your event's needs. By doing five to ten minute mini-readings for your guests, Karen keeps things moving while being entertaining and informative. All she requires is a card-sized table with two chairs.

Terms

Karen charges an affordable rate of $125.00 per hour, with a two-hour minimum. Travel outside the Seattle area is extra, and payment is due in full the night of the event.

A student of metaphysics for 35 years

Karen has been associated with the A.R.E. (Edgar Cayce Foundation) and studied with Jan Weiss. She is currently the hostess for the "Psychic Northwest" television show, and is heard on local radio stations taking call-ins and discussing psychic abilities.

Call Today To Schedule Your Event

(425) 673-1930 or (800) 421-1682

The Art of Lip Print Reading

by

Jilly Eddy

(206) 937-6510

Let your Lip Prints do the talking!

Entertain in unique style with Lipsology: The art of assessing personality characteristics and energy levels based on the shapes, lines, marks and color of an individual's lip prints.

Your lip prints are like chapters of a book, each one telling more about your story. Your lip prints reveal things like: Are you creative and artistic? Do you need a vacation? Do you have champagne and caviar tastes? Jilly has been entertaining with Lipsology at private parties and corporate events since 1996. Her engaging, energetic, enthusiasm gets everyone involved. They all want to know what she sees in their lip prints. Her skill and accuracy are amazing!

Lipsology will captivate your guests at any event:
Birthdays, Anniversaries, Grad Nights, Reunions, Grand Openings, Bat and Bar Mitzvahs, Corporate Events, Trade Shows, Weddings, Showers, Picnics, Teas and Holiday Parties.

Featured in widely distributed publications:
The Chicago Tribune, The Florida Sun, Los Angeles Times, The New York Times, Seattle Post-Intelligencer, The Seattle Times and *Women's World.*

She's also presented her skills on television:
Crook & Chase, Northwest Cable News, Panel Talk and Northwest Afternoon.

Word of mouth:

> *"Jilly is the most unique entertainer in the Northwest. She combines life affirming insights with humor to delight your guests."*
>
> —Patty Belik, Owner, A Class Act Event Planning
>
> *"Jilly does a phenomenal job...people learn about themselves and have a great time doing it!"* —Jane Hummer, Owner, Mangetout Catering

Contact Jilly at (206) 937-6510
and schedule entertainment your guests
will be talking about for a long time.

The Magic And Comedy of Bruce Meyers

(800) 430-5779
E-mail: mystifier@msn.com
Web site:
www.brucemeyersmagic.com

Maximizing audience enjoyment

Bruce Meyers is dedicated to capturing the imagination of his audience. His magic astounds and baffles in uniquely comical performances celebrated throughout the Pacific Northwest. Meyers developed his astonishing routines through thousands of live performances; conventional tricks vanish into his original magic. Interactive by design and great fun for all, his performances feature voluntary audience participation, always handled with courtesy, respect and safety.

Illusions and intrigue

Bruce Meyers' routines incorporate everything from card waterfalls to graceful birds and rabbits. With the legendary Standing Rope of India and mysterious lights from nowhere, Meyers performs magic as it was meant to be.

A few of our mystified clients...

- Boeing Company
- Hanjin Shipping
- Retired Agents of The FBI
- American President Lines
- Eagle Productions
- Cargolux Airlines
- Dairy Farmers of Washington
- Burn Children Recovery Foundation
- Clinitech
- Franssen Motors
- Bax Global
- Data I/O

Fully equipped to astonish

We can turn any common banquet room into a theater. We offer one-hour standup performances featuring a cabaret-style delivery and full stage productions. Our own standup stage is available, as well as curtains, lights, and a sound system.

Always mindful of the details, we also carry $1,000,000 worth of liability insurance. After all, Bruce has over 30 years of experience up his sleeve.

"You were fabulous...I am getting compliments every day. We have not laughed this hard since we were kids."
—Penny Lee Gurschmidt, President, Penny Lee Trucking, Inc.

"We all thoroughly enjoyed your show...[If] 'laughter is the best medicine,' we certainly had our share...I'll call you again for another event!"
—Val McDonough, Executive Assistant, Foothills Toyota

Tim & Eirien Hart

For Mid-sized Multitudes or Under Your Nose

(425) 806-8734
E-mail: hartmagic@w-link.net

The award-winning Magic of Tim & Eirien Hart always brings lots of surprises and laughter to your event. Their playful personalities add to the fun, along with impossible effects and plenty of audience interaction.

ENTERTAIN YOUR WHOLE GROUP AT ONCE

Stage or Platform

Tim & Eirien use the larger effects and illusions, along with volunteers from the audience, to answer these and other important questions:

- Are computer games 1,000 years old?
- Do dragons really exist?
- Where does the other sock go?

MORE INTIMATE MAGIC

Strolling

Tim walks through your event creating Magic with everyday objects like coins, matchboxes, cards and borrowed dollar bills. Magic literally in your hands and under your nose!

SPECIAL EVENTS

Are you planning a theme? Introducing a product at a trade show? Having a grand opening? Tim & Eirien can tailor their Magic to fit **YOU**.

Professionals since 1982—their clients include: Boeing, Piper Jaffray, Microsoft, Seafirst Trust, Edward Jones, Seattle Mariners, Zurich International, the Oyster Olympics, Cascade Controls, Siemens Ultrasound, Harza Engineering, BankAmerica.

"For the second year in a row I received many compliments on your act. the membership always enjoys having you perform. I look forward to doing it again next year."
Mark Trinder–Overlake Country Club

"Thank you so much for the terrific performance you gave at our graduation ceremony. Your magic crossed all boundaries with our international students and allowed them to relax, laugh and have fun." Cathy Braun–Bellevue Community College

The Art of Henna Painting

2211 N.W. Market Street
Seattle, Washington 98107
(206) 782-7314

PARTIES!

Add the timeless art of henna painting to your next party!

It's a beautiful, painless and temporary tattoo that last about two weeks. Tell your clients, employees and friends that you appreciate them by including us at your next holiday party, summer picnic or get together.

They can choose from traditional Indian or tattoo style designs, i.e., suns, dragons, crosses, symbols, roses, butterflies...we can also custom create tattoos around your company logo.

Companies who have enjoyed us at their celebrations include...

Starbucks, Microsoft, Paul Allen Private Parties, EMP Grand Opening, Borden Chemicals, The United Way and *The Seattle Times*. We also participate in a large number of festivals in the Puget Sound area such as the Bite of Seattle, Bumbershoot, Folk Life and WOMAD USA.

Krysteen Lomonaco, who owns and operates Mehndi Madness Inc., has spent years studying and perfecting this age old form of artistic expression. She has traveled extensively to fine-tune her creative ability of providing timeless works of art on her clients' bodies throughout the Pacific Northwest. Krysteen believes Henna and the art it creates not only beautifies the body but rejuvenates the spirit of both those who create it and those who are adorned by it.

We use only natural henna that stains a beautiful, brown/red color. If you've never heard of Mehndi Madness or Henna tattoos, now is the time to find out!

Rates

For one artist: $125 per hour with a 2-hour minimum. Additional artist: $25 per hour.

Photos and Additional Information sent at your request.

Please call (206) 782-7314

Thank you,

Krysteen Lomonaco, President

Robots4Fun

Leading Edge Entertainment

(425) 766-6666; Fax (208) 687-2863
E-mail: ken@robots4fun.com • ***Web site: www.robots4fun.com***

They talk, they walk, they'll even hand out your company literature!

Meet Ernie and his friends. These state-of-the-art robots each have different capabilities and appeal making them adaptable to a variety of events. All have full motion to move and roam and play your selection of music.

Promotional Robot performances

Our favorite thing to do is to perform at events and parties. Over the last nineteen years, we have appeared at over 1,000 tradeshows, conventions, or other types of events in 6 countries and 49 states.

- **All Occasion Parties:** Ernie and his pals love to party and are available for birthday or themed private parties, bar mitzvahs, open houses, corporate events, or as an airport greeter.
- **Sales Promotion:** Let Ernie increase your sales power by advertising for you in public locations!
- **Corporate Events:** Give your customers or employees something to remember. Have Ernie or one of our other robots welcome everyone as they enter and then maybe even join them on the dance floor!
- **Conventions and Expos:** Entire conventions have been designed around Ernie and the gang. There is no better way to attract attention to your booth and company than a talking robot! Ernie even has a monitor for PowerPoint presentations customized to your requirements.

An affordable way to get people's attention!

$150 per hour includes professional operator/showman and robot. Day rate is $850 plus travel expenses, if applicable.

Check out our web site and meet the gang at:
www.robots4fun.com

Rod Long

Clean Comedy

It's never out of style!

Exclusively Represented by
ENTCO International, Inc.
(425) 670-0888
Fax (425) 670-0777
Web site: www.ENTCO.com

Comedian – Master of Ceremonies

Clever & Topical
with a sporting attitude

Trivial Pursuit "Roast" Master

for those !!th Birthdays, Bachelor(ette) Parties
and other "Gotcha"
kinds of occasions.

ROD LONG

Always customizes his material to suit your program or function.

**THE IDEAL MAN
WHEN FUN & GAMES
ARE A MUST!**

REFERENCES

Seattle Times • Everett Herald • Microsoft • Boeing
Seattle Seahawks • Super Sonics • Seattle Mariners
Ken Griffey Jr. • Charles Barkley
My Mom

Exclusive Representation

ENTCO International
Web site: www.ENTCO.com

(425) 670-0888
Fax (425) 670-0777

Seattle Celebrity Look-Alike

or contact Neil Morris (206) 786-6996 • E-mail: neilm@entco.com

---

The largest roster of Look-Alike talent in the Northwest.

Wow and amaze party guests with your close *Celebrity* friends.

Need a "GOTCHA!" for some office buddies?

Fulfill a fantasy for that special someone.

Let your imagination take over...it is more fun than the real thing!

Parties • Receptions • Meetings • Birthdays

Any resemblance to actual persons living or dead

is

DELIBERATE

Sheila Lyon

Psychic Entertainer

Palm Reader & Much More!

P.O. Box 4681
Rolling Bay, Washington 98061
(206) 713-8506
Web site: www.speakeasy.org/sheila

Photo by Thor Radford

Company functions • Annual meetings • Icebreakers
House parties • Bridal showers • Picnics

Make your next occasion a hit with the sparkling personality and divinatory talents of well-known fortuneteller Sheila Lyon. Everyone, regardless of age or sex, social or economic status, is curious to catch a glimpse of what the future may hold. Sheila's fabulous icebreaker act enchants and captivates all audiences.

A veritable Pied Piper of entertainment, Sheila injects life into any gathering as she circulates among your guests, reads minds, tells fortunes, and spins a magical web of captivating stories. Her act is sophisticated enough for large corporate social occasions, yet personal enough for small dinner parties.

"You were the best guest we've had in weeks!" —Johnny Seattle, KQBZ 100.7 FM

"Thank you so much for sharing your thoughts on 'the Fascination of Divination' at our board retreat last week. You were superb! The laughter and camaraderie were infectious!" —Kris Tiernan, Executive Assistant, Valley Medical Center

"The Boeing Company is very pleased with the exceptional entertainment you provided..." —Maryann DiPasquale, Corporate Meeting Planner

Here are just a few of the people for whom Sheila has cast her spell:

- Microsoft
- Sheraton Seattle Hotel
- Union Bay Clothing
- Seattle Community College
- The Boeing Company
- Redhook Brewery
- The Seattle Mariners
- The Westin Hotel
- Edgewater Hotel
- *Cosmo Girl* Magazine
- AEI Music
- Nordstroms

Sheila Lyon is one of America's foremost psychic entertainers. A lifelong student of parapsychology and the divinatory arts, Sheila captivates audiences everywhere with her special blend of warmth, humor, showmanship, and audience involvement. She has been featured in a *Reader's Digest World Video* on mysticism, and in such magazines as *National Geographic Travel, Seattle, Metropolitan Living,* and *Endless Vacation.* Sheila is co-owner of The Magic Shop in Seattle's historic Pike Place Market, where she also conducts ghost tours.

 Please let this business know that you heard about them from the Bravo! Event Resource Guide.

TOM "*Huf*" HOFSTEDT

Exclusive Representation
ENTCO International, Inc.
(425) 670-0888
Fax (425) 670-0777
Web site: www.entco.com

FASTEST PEN in the WORLD!

Creates 40+ caricatures per hour.

Over 1,000,000 (THAT'S A MILLION!) **Caricatures**

It's the *entertainment highlight* of any gathering.

The overhead projector shows Huf's lightning pen capturing a pleasing likeness. A cartoon body is added acting out the person's hobby, sport or occupation.

Why buy a gift or party favor when they have a "Huf"

1962 Seattle World's Fair

Six years at Disneyland

12 years at International Marketplace in Honolulu

20 years "Doing the Puyallup"

Notes

Entertainment Consultants

❖❖❖

HELPFUL HINTS

Entertainment: More and more people are deciding to have entertainment at their events. Entertainment breaks the ice and gets your guests mingling. Entertainment can be anything from a band or DJ to an artist recording the event on canvas as it happens, or a strolling magician entertaining guests with his tricks.

Setup requirements: The formality, facility, and size of your event will determine the type of music or entertainment that is appropriate. Be very specific about getting the space and setup requirements for your entertainers so that you can accurately relay the information to your event coordinator and facility.

Contracts: Any time you book any form of entertainment, be sure to get a contract that covers exactly what you are expecting the entertainers to do. Be clear about the times you want them to perform, and how you want them to interact with your guests.

Entertainment consultants: Your event is not the time to try out unproved talent. An entertainment consultant can be a big asset to your event planning team. They work with musicians and entertainers on a regular basis so they are familiar with the full spectrum of services available for your event. They are also able to book either local or national talent, depending on what you are looking for. Some of the variety of services available include:

- Bands
- Vocalists
- Comedians
- Magicians
- Psychics
- Disc Jockeys
- Speakers
- Caricaturists
- Mimes
- Masters of Ceremony
- Individual Musicians
- Clowns
- Jugglers
- Hypnotists
- Ventriloquists

Event design and coordination: Most entertainment consultants are able to design and orchestrate theme parties and events. From booking the talent to coordinating props or equipment, they can handle as much or as little as you want.

Be sure to ask about a "Green Room": Sometimes entertainers require a dressing room, a place to rest and/or wait for their performance.

A Amoré Events & Entertainment, LLC

206-241-8070

or 888-94-AMORE

Web site: www.seattledj.com

"Providing Entertainment to the Great Northwest and Beyond"

A Amoré Events and Entertainment, LLC, is hardly new; we have been providing services for over 7 years! We have access to many artists and entertainers that you're familiar with, as well as many great entertainers that you have never been introduced to. We don't have an "exclusive entertainment policy," so we offer an open door to entertainers who want to be part of your corporate event.

Live Music Entertainment

Dance R&B–Doctor Funk, Society's Child, Shades, Real to Reel, Ready Made Family
Top 40 Variety–Nitecrew, Chain Reaction, The Players
Motown & Party Rock–The Sensations, The 57's, The Edsels
Retro Specialty Dance–The Hit Connections, Spandex Ballet, 80 Something, Afrodisiacs
Reggae & Caribbean–Rude Boy, Soca Fiesta, Alex Duncan & the Good Vibes
Jazz & Blues–May Palmer, Smooth Groove, Michael Hershman, Moonlily
String Quartet–Northwest String Quartet, Evergreen String Quartet, Swan String Quartet
À Capella–Curfew
And much more!!! *Not enough space to name all the Great Entertainment available.*

National Entertainers

A Amoré Events and Entertainment, LLC works with many national agencies that can bring some of the top names in entertainment to your special event!

Other Entertainment Ideas

Murder Mystery Show
Strolling Magicians
Stage Magicians
Impersonators
Improv. Comedian Show
Casino Parties
Digital Photography
Mafia Family Night
Alien Abduction Night
Game Shows
Customized Comedy Shows
Employee Academy Awards
Glow Parties
Lighted Marquee Boards
Clowns/Balloon Artists
Caricature Artists
Sumo Wrestler
Velcro Wall
Psychics/Fortune Tellers
Jugglers
Stage lighting

Audio/Visual Rentals Available

Interactive Disc Jockeys and Emcees

We are also well known for our Interactive Entertainment Disc Jockeys. We do everything from providing basic disc jockey services to entertaining your guests with interactive games, group dances, and crowd-pleasing sound effects. Professional, state-of-the-art sound systems and the most up-to-date and complete music libraries available ensure quality audio for your event.

Ask about our Glow Products

Nothing quite makes a party like Glow Products, for adults as well as children! We have a full line of "Chemical Shake and Break Jewelry," everything from necklaces, bracelets, and pendants, to name badge and glow sticks! Please ask us how to make your party a "Bright Idea."

Video and Photo Needs

We have been in the business of helping people; we are not afraid to refer you to Photographers, Florists, Decorators, and Videographers! We have worked with some of the best professionals and have a wide selection of people who want to work for you.

Andy Mirkovich Productions

Entertainment, Meetings, and Events

11811 N.E. First Street, Suite A-302
Bellevue, Washington 98005-3033
Contact: Margaret or J.P. Perugini
(425) 454-4817; Fax (425) 646-2988
E-mail: info@mirkprod.com
Web site: www.mirkprod.com

Andy Mirkovich Productions provides Entertainment, Event and Meeting Management Services, allowing clients to remain focused on their core business while taking advantage of AMP's competencies in these fields of expertise. Andy Mirkovich Productions is recognized as the Pacific Northwest's premier resource for Entertainment, Meeting and Event Planning Services. Our 37 years of experience has given us the opportunity to work with thousands of National and International Clients, planning and producing their special events and providing all the entertainment required to complete their program and create a memorable affair.

Entertainment and Meeting Planning Services

A few of our Local Attractions include...

- **Antowaine & Groove Masters** (Variety, R&B, Dance Band)
- **The Main Attraction** (a Capella & Variety R&B Dance Band)
- **Afrodisiacs**; **Nitecrew**; **Summer Girls**; **Blue Moon Howlers** (Top 40, Retro, Contemporary Rock)
- **The Islanders**; **Flambeau**; **Panduo** (Steel Drum Bands)
- **Dudley Manlove Quartet** (Cocktail Band)
- **Bobby Medina & The Red Hot Band** (Great Variety Dance Band in the Style of the Big Band)
- **Theresa Carnovale & City Life** (Variety Dance Combo)
- **Andy O, Calypso Blue** (Reggae, Calypso—Fun Party Bands)
- **Jr. Cadillac**, **Marvellas** (Party Rock & Roll—50s/60s)
- **Doug Zangar** (Background to Jazz to Variety Dance)
- **The Dickens Carolers** (A 24-year Northwest Holiday Tradition)

Exciting National Acts—A show stopper for your next event

- **Earth Wind & Fire**
- **Jan & Dean**
- **Colin Raye**
- **Bruce Hornsby**
- **BTO**
- **Crystal Gail**
- **Heart**
- **War**
- **Natalie Cole**
- **Loretta Lynne**
- **Manhattan Transfer**
- **Edie Money**
- **Temptations**
- **Trisha Yearwood**

Interactive Entertainment

- Game Shows
- Clowns
- Human Bowling
- Casinos
- Moon Walks
- Sumo Wrestlers
- Gyrotrons
- Velcro Crawl
- Monster Trucks
- Climbing Rock
- Dunk Tanks

Alternative Entertainment Suggestions

- Strolling Musicians
- Caricature Artists
- Game Shows
- Emcee
- Psychics
- Keynote Speakers
- Magicians
- Comedians
- Mystery Dinners
- Jugglers
- Mimes
- Casino Night
- Santa
- DJs

Entertainment/ Bands

HELPFUL HINTS

Deciding on a band: Every band should have a music list available for you to review. This will be helpful in deciding on a band. You may want to ask if the band is currently playing somewhere, and then you can listen to their music live and observe their stage presence before you make a final decision.

Reserving a band: Reserve a band or orchestra for your event immediately, especially if the date of your affair falls during peak party seasons like Christmas or New Year's. Popular bands and orchestras are often reserved up to a year in advance.

Written contract: It is advisable to get a written contract stating exactly what you have agreed upon: date, number of hours, the total cost, and so on.

Setup requirements: The formality, facility, and size of your event will determine the type of music that is appropriate. Inquire about whether the site can accommodate dancing and has the area necessary for the musicians to set up and perform. Be very specific about getting the space and electrical requirements from the band so that you can accurately relay the information to your contact person at the facility.

Cutoff hours: When you make all the final arrangements with your facility, be sure to ask if they have any specified time limitations for music. Some facilities require that music be stopped as early as 10pm for the comfort of neighboring homes, businesses, or other guests.

Background music and dancing music: Remember when reserving your music that the first hour of your event is a time for introductions and mingling with guests. If your band begins playing immediately, you'll want to make sure that the music is background-type music that doesn't overwhelm and interfere with conversations. The band can be instructed or signaled to pick up the pace of the music for dancing at a certain time.

NOTE: Make sure your contract is sound, and that your event won't be bumped for a larger engagement. A deposit is usually required.

Leader Dick Coolen

Dick Coolen's Swing Orchestra

A 2- to 18-Piece Band

For Booking Information or Promotional Material

Contact: Dick Coolen Music
P.O. Box 4031 • S. Colby, WA 98384-0031
(360) 769-8415

Information and Song Samples on the web at: ***www.coolen.com***

Music and entertainment for your event

- Solo Piano
- Duos
- Variety Combos
- Jazz
- Latin
- Classic Rock-N-Roll
- Variety Music
- Custom Show

Big Band Swing

- 15,000 song selections
- Request Your Favorites

Dick Coolen's Swing Orchestra...

performs extensively throughout the Northwest as a 2- to 18-piece dance or show band, playing arrangements of the timeless bands like: Glenn Miller, Tommy Dorsey, Count Basie, Les Brown, Duke Ellington, and many more. The band also plays some rock-n-roll to fill out a variety menu. The smaller combos play jazz and Latin arrangements of Cole Porter, Gershwin, Jerome Kern, and others. Piano, vocal, classical guitar and trumpet are also available for weddings or fill in background prior to dancing.

Dick Coolen's Swing Orchestra presents the most loved dance music of the 30's, 40's, and 50's from the great Big Bands

The 18-piece ensemble brings the music and memories of the big bands alive performing the original arrangements of yesterday with the top jazz players of today!

"...fantastic. A real big band sound that sparkles..."

—Michael D. Summers, Classic Sound

"...entertaining and exciting...outstanding evening..."

—Thelma I. Channon, Canterwood Country Club

Dancing and entertaining...

go hand in hand with Sentimental Journey. Lush ballads, Latin rhythms, fast-paced swing... Just a few of the more popular numbers from the band include:

- In The Mood
- Tea For Two
- Moonlight Serenade
- Sweet Georgia Brown
- Green Eyes
- Blue Moon
- Begin the Beguine
- All Of Me
- Chattanooga Choo Choo
- Tangerine
- Jump, Jive & Wail
- Georgia On My Mind
- Sentimental Journey
- String of Pearls
- Opus One
- Stardust
- Pennsylvania 6-5000
- New York, New York
- Satin Doll
- It Had To Be You
- Take The "A" Train
- Moonlight In Vermont
- Misty
- Sing Sing

The list of timeless hits goes on and on...
Just let us know your favorites!

Dix Delux

Exclusively Represented by
ENTCO International, Inc.
(425) 670-0888
Fax (425) 670-0777
Web site: www.ENTCO.com

DIX DELUX...Classic rock delivered with a smile

One of the Northwest's most seasoned party bands, the members of Dix delux are a very tightly knit group of musicians who continue to win audiences each time they plug in and play! For nearly two decades (these guys can't be that old, can they?) Dix Delux have been bringing their little monkey show to any venue that has the foresight to call them!

The following is a partial list of the various establishments where Dix Delux has recently created their special brand of good times and fun:

Seattle Tennis Club
Riley's Pub–Mukilteo
Mill Creek Café
Seafair Torchlight Parade
Rainier Club–Seattle
Carillon Point–Kirkland
Winthrop Palace
Emerald Downs
Argosy Cruise Lines
Bite of Seattle
Taste of Edmonds
Seattle International Raceway
Red Lion Hotel–Bellevue
Seattle Golf & Country Club
Seattle Yacht Club
Olympic Four Seasons
The Westin Hotel
Seattle Sheraton
Taste of Tacoma
Sahalee Country Club
Salmon Days–Issaquah
The (Late) Kingdome

DIX DELUX'S non-stop barrage of hit after classic hit includes:

Memphis
Mama Don't Dance
Honey Don't
That's Allright Mama / Mystery Train
Stand By Me
Sweet Home Alabama
Wonderful Tonite
Honky Tonk Woman
Brown Sugar
Money
Johnny B. Goode / Roll Over Beethoven / Jailhouse Rock / Hound Dog
Under My Thumb
We Gotta Get Outta This Place
Sunshine Of Your Love
You Really Got Me
Born To Be Wild
Before You Accuse Me
Bring It On Home
Love The One You're With
Margaritaville
Ain't No Sunshine
Kansas City
Takin' Care of Business
Can't Get Enough
R.O.C.K. In the U.S.A.
Pretty Woman
Allright Now
Sharp Dressed Man
Saw Her Standing There
A Little Help From My Friends
Twist & Shout
Back In The U.S.S.R.

DJ & Photographer available on request.

Downtown Sound—Swing, Latin, and Light Rhythm & Blues

Contacts: Jim Sisko (206) 579-5192 • E-mail: jimsisko@juno.com
Kelley Johnson (206) 323-6304 • E-mail: kelley@speakeasy.org

When the music counts

Whether you're planning an intimate gathering or a grand affair, you can count on the utmost quality and professionalism of The Downtown Sound. Our sextet features tight arrangements, a stellar horn section and the divine singing of Ms. Kelley Johnson. Specializing in swing, Latin, and light rhythm and blues, we offer a wide selection of popular tunes with hip jazz stylings. Our music is fun, sophisticated and always danceable.

Setting the mood

Since music is a matter of personal taste, we're happy to work with you to create the perfect mood for your event. The Downtown Sound provides smooth, elegant background music and vocals that gently simmer till it's time to dance, when we can break into a lively swing, salsa or funky jump blues.

About town and around the globe

The Downtown Sound is composed of six of Puget Sound's most in-demand session players who have performed together extensively both as a group and as solo artists in festivals and clubs from Canada to France to Asia, including appearances at Jazz Alley, New York's Birdland and Carnegie Hall. Collectively our resume includes performances with the Glenn Miller Orchestra, Manhattan Transfer, Seattle Symphony, Seattle Repertory Jazz Orchestra, Woody Herman Orchestra, Kingston Trio, Natalie Cole, Ernestine Anderson and Steely Dan saxophonist Pete Christlieb.

> *"The Downtown Sound played for us at an important corporate party this summer. They kept the entire boat swinging for hours and were only eclipsed when the Blue Angels flew overhead."* —Marcia Evans, Northwest Events & Parties

CALL FOR A FREE SONG LIST,
FREE DEMO CD & PRICE QUOTE

L. J. Porter

and

The Vampin' Ho's

Contact: L.J. Porter
(425) 865-8996
*Fax (425) 865-8996, *51*
Web site: www.LJPorter.com

Soulful and Sassy

Ms. Porter traces her singing roots to her grandfather's church in a little town in Louisiana. Before the Rev. Paree Porter, the congregation, and God Almighty, a very young L.J. would use her sweet sound of soul to bring inspiration—and the house would be rock'n! Those very important roots are part of L.J.'s expression, along with her soulful voice and bountiful rousing sound.

Gospel launched

Gospel launched the career that would have L.J. singing as a founding member of one of the Northwest's hottest acts, "The Seattle Women of R&B." With these ladies, L.J. has had the pleasure of opening for the likes of **B.B. King**, **Booker T and the MG's**, **Roy Orbison**, **Mary Wells**, and **Charlie Musslewhite**, to name a few.

Always moving...

L.J.'s love of R&B, her gutsy style, and the no-holds-barred playful rapport she has with her audiences has created a faithful following of peers and fans alike. L.J. is a woman who uses all of her natural gifts to provide a sometimes sweet, sometimes sad, occasionally nasty, but always moving vocal experience. When her voice caresses your ear, you have the feeling of a real good time, with good people, listening to good music!

Combined with the backup of The Vampin' Ho's...

You'd expect a powerhouse like L.J. Porter to have nothing short of raw energy backing her vocals. So what, you may ask yourself, goes well with that "blue flame moonshine?" DYNAMITE!!!

The Vampin' Ho's supply the rock-solid foundation for Ms. Porter's smooth, hot grooves. Imagine James Brown colliding with B.B. King and you've got the high-octane, soulful sounds of the Ho's. Comprised of former members of Burgandy Express, Sly Stone, and the Almost Live Band, the Vampin' Ho's step to the stage with "in-your-face, let it all hang-out" sound.

L.J. Porter, a woman who's going places...

"The Diva's" first-released CD, "Rollercoaster" showcases the artist's vocal abilities that are best described as "Blue Flame Moonshine"—a sound that goes down smooth and finished warm with a kick! This first project was presented at the Midem Asia music conference in Hong Kong, May 1997, and is currently being considered for international distribution. L.J. has also caught the interest of several major independent recording labels.

You've got to experience this heat yourself,
but don't say we didn't warn you!
Performing at Experience Music Project
New CD "Blue" Just Released • 600 Stations Nationwide

 Please let this business know that you heard about them from the Bravo! Event Resource Guide.

RainbowConnection
Music

Contact: Barry Gordon
(206) 764-9495
E-mail: mrjaz@home.com
Web site: www.rainbowconnectionmusic.com

The RainbowConnection Party Orchestra

You Deserve The Best

Your wedding represents the culmination of two spirits and styles. The choices you make today while planning your celebration will create the magic that you will share for a lifetime. The RainbowConnection knows about magic. They come from one of the most magical and romantic rooms in the country, the Rainbow Room in New York. A place where music stirs the soul and lingers in the heart.

The RainbowConnection has played together for 14 years, the past 6 years in Seattle. Their New York background and demanding client base along with years of experience makes them one of he finest orchestras in the Northwest. The RainbowConnection will make your party fun. Think fun, think PARTY!

A Repertoire That Says It All!

Barry Gordon and the RainbowConnection play more than music. They bring a New York savvy that lights up any room. Their repertoire is amazingly diverse, from Chopin to Shania Twain and a whole lot more:

Big Band	**Rumbas**	**Disco**	**Sinatra**
Swing	**Cha Cha**	**Standards/Jazz**	**Cahn**
40's Medley	**Country Pop**	**Motown**	**Gershwin**
50's/60's/70's/80's	**Merangue**	**Top 40**	**Harold Arlen**

SMOOTH GROOVE PRODUCTIONS

Live Musical Entertainment for Any and All Occasions

5202-218th St. S.W. • Mountlake Terrace, WA 98043
(425) 775-9269; Fax (425) 778-9439
Contact: E. Emmanuel del Casal
E-mail: emman@smoothgroove.net
Web site: www.smoothgroove.net

The proper ambience for any special occasion. Whether your celebration calls for an elegant light jazz performance, an energetic dance set, or both, the *Smooth Groove Band* offers reliable, first class musicianship that will impress your guests and give you peace of mind. When it comes to live musical entertainment and production, the *Smooth Groove Band* is the name to call on for the utmost in providing the proper ambience and touch to that special occasion.

Proven musical expertise. Veteran musicians Steve Nowak and Emmanuel del Casal are the frontmen for *Smooth Groove's* ensembles, which usually range in size from solo acts to sextets and above. A guitarist and vocalist, Steve has performed and recorded with many major artists and continues to compose and teach. A bass player and composer, Emmanuel has taken his musical skill to audiences worldwide, and is no stranger in the recording studio.

We don't miss a beat. Thoughtfully selected live music adds as much to a memorable experience as the food catered for a special event. Our versatility and expertise ensure high quality entertainment that complements your celebration. We look forward to adding our touch of live musical elegance to the noteworthy occasions in your life. **FREE CONSULTATION.**

Entertainment/ Disc Jockeys

❖❖❖

HELPFUL HINTS

Deciding on a disc jockey: Meet with disc jockeys in person, and make sure the person you meet is the one you are hiring for your event. Ask to see the equipment and portfolios or presentations of their shows so you know what to expect. If they do more than one show per day, check to make sure they have the appropriate equipment setups for two or more shows. The disc jockey should be able to provide you with a list of music available so that you can pre-select favorites you want played. Be sure there is a good mix of music so that people of all ages can enjoy and participate.

Written contract: It is advisable to get a written contract stating exactly what you have agreed upon: date, number of hours, types of equipment, who will be doing the show, the total cost, what is included, and so on.

Emcee: Ask whether your disc jockey can act as the emcee at your event. This will help the event flow smoothly. Give your emcee a list of special guests' names and see to it he/she can pronounce them.

Volume of music: Discuss the selection of music you would like with your disc jockey, as well as the volume at which it should be played. Keep the volume of music low for the first hour of your event, allowing guests to mingle and ensuring that the sound level is comfortable for older guests. Then when the dancing begins, the volume can be increased.

Setup requirements: Inquire about whether the site can accommodate dancing. Find out whether your disc jockey needs early access to the room and what the space and electrical requirements are. Make sure your facility contact knows about these needs and that they can be met.

Cutoff hours: When you make all the final arrangements with your facility, be sure to ask if they have any specified time limitations for music. Some facilities require that music be stopped as early as 10pm for the comfort of neighboring homes, businesses, or other guests.

Special effects and requests: Most disc jockeys are glad to play special songs if they are requested. Also inquire about any special effects they can supply, such as lighting, strobes, mirror balls, and fog.

Serving the Northwest for Over 20 Years!

425•277•1777

E-mail: bestshow@msn.com

www.action-entertainment.com

ENTERTAINMENT • INFLATABLES • LOCATION • CATERING
"For Something Different"

Our commitment...

is to redefine and build working relationships and to facilitate personal development in a party environment.

We create *unforgettable* corporate events, including holiday parties, picnics, employee appreciations, conventions, weddings and many more.

Featuring

Music and Dancing

Creative programming of all styles and eras
on a state-of-the-art digital sound system

Events and Games

"We get everyone involved."
Over 25 innovative events and game shows designed for total audience participation

We get results. . .

These fun activities break down barriers, enhance communication
and build team spirit through laughter and action.

With A Action Entertainment your corporate event will be the best ever!

A few of our satisfied clients. . .

- Microsoft
- Alaska Airlines
- McDonalds Corporation
- AAA of Washington
- Costco
- Phil Smart Mercedes
- Starbucks
- AT&T
- IBM
- Space Needle
- Bally Total Fitness
- JC Penney
- EMP
- Baugh Construction
- Verizon
- Four Seasons
- Boeing
- Kinkos

Book Early • (425) 277-1777 • Fax (425) 277-0922
E-mail: bestshow@msn.com
Web site: www.action-entertainment.com

See page 462 under Games & Team Building and page 499 under Meeting & Event Planners.

A Sound Celebration

Contact: Erin Sweeney
(425) 277-6672
Fax (425) 430-8487

A party can end up as just conversation, but an event is the etching of memories. The difference can be the correct selection of a professional music company or random chance.

A Sound Celebration carefully listens to your desires and offers suggestions that will enhance and individualize your affair.

Types of music

The music selection is entirely up to you, choosing from our extensive library consisting of Big Band, Rock and Roll, Country, R & B and Top 40. Your DJ will work with you, making sure all your music needs are met.

Demo

Consultations are always encouraged, so that you can personally meet with your DJ before your event, making sure you feel completely assured that he understands your needs.

Experience

All our DJs have years of experience and conduct themselves professionally at all times. We can provide many references from satisfied clients and facilities at your request, like the Woodmark Hotel, Hotel Edgewater, The Golf Club at Newcastle, Columbia Tower Club, Harbor Club, Museum of Flight as well as many corporate event planners.

Equipment

All of our equipment is encased so that no unsightly wires and cords are exposed. We play off both professional CD and mini discs and always have back-up equipment on hand.

MORE THAN JUST GOOD MUSIC

- **Professional DJs in Tuxedos**
- **Wide Variety of Music for All Ages and Occasions**
- **Your Requests Always Played**
- **Professional Sound Equipment**
- **Wireless Microphones for Toasts and Announcements**
- **Free Consultations**

(800) 874-4533 or (425) 822-2073
Web site: www.letsdanceentertainment.com

CORPORATE AND SPECIAL EVENT ENTERTAINMENT

You name it we play it

- Top 40
- Country
- 50s & 60s
- Big Band
- 70s & 80s
- Your favorite music

Fun DJs

- YMCA
- Conga Line
- Limbo
- Line Teachers Available
- Macarena
- Games

Just a few of the companies who use our services

Boeing, A T & T, GTE, Microsoft, Southwest Airlines, Alaska Airlines, F.B.I., Regence Blue Shield, COSTCO, Weyerhaeuser, and Home Base.

Premier facilities that recommend Let's Dance Entertainment

The Space Needle, The Woodmark Hotel, Salty's, Bellevue and Washington Athletic Club, Four Seasons Olympic, Monte Villa Farmhouse, Tibbetts Creek Manor, The Harbor Club, Ray's Boathouse, Hollywood Schoolhouse, Rosario Resort, Clise Mansion, Robinswood House, Embassy Suites, and many more.

Complete Video Production,
Big Screen Video Projectors
and Sound Systems Available
Web site: *www.letsdanceentertainment.com*

CALL
(800) 874-4533
(425) 822-2073

puget sounds premier service
dj service one customer at a time

(206) 381-8944
E-mail: dj@pugetsounds-dj.com
Web site: www.pugetsounds-dj.com

The success of your event is our first priority!

We are committed to your success and peace of mind from the beginning. Even before you reserve our services, our Consultant-DJ will plan a free, no-obligation consultation to discuss your needs.

Puget Sounds DJ Service has built a reputation for affordable and highly personalized entertainment services throughout the Pacific Northwest. We take pride in being accessible and personable.

Our mission:

We provide the highest quality customer service by maintaining the personal contact that we develop with each and every one of our clients. Puget Sounds is a DJ Service that will listen courteously to your concerns and meet your needs with the most professional solutions. You have a vision for your event, and we are here to serve you.

We offer assistance and referrals.

Our Consultant can help you plan all your event's activities and announcements. We can refer you to our preferred vendors, but we are also pleased to work other professionals you choose.

All music is digitally enhanced, on compact disc, and programmed to your exact specifications. Our archive contains music from the 1940's, the latest hits, and everything in-between.

Puget Sounds DJ service is a company that celebrates
our diverse Pacific Northwest Community.
We maintain a consistent insurance policy of $1,000,000 to protect our clients.
We specialize in multi-cultural events.

Puget Sounds DJ Service:
"Premier Service One Customer at a Time...Period!"

Corporate Parties & Events • Public School Dances
Private Parties • Cultural Events

Contact: Robert O'Shaughnessy
(253) 876-0720 or (800) 266-8649, ext. 3
Fax (253) 856-0678
Web site: www.thesound-factory.com

Washington's cure for the common disc jockey

When only the best entertainment will do, choose The Sound Factory to provide unforgettable music and fun for your special event. We offer the proven experience and professional equipment that bring excitement to school events, parties, and other special occasions.

We specialize in youth events

The Sound Factory is dedicated to creating a fun, safe, and above all a different kind of dance. Our DJs specialize in school dances, birthday parties, college parties, senior graduation parties, and any other event related to the youth market. In fact, we are the only professional mobile disc jockey company in Washington that specializes in youth events.

High quality, professional audio and lighting equipment

We offer a wide variety of concert, club, and effect lighting, including the most powerful black lights available. In fact, we are the only DJ company that can provide a true Laser Light Show. Our one-of-a-kind visual effect show remains unmatched in the Pacific Northwest.

Experienced DJs focused on the music

Not only do we provide the best mix of music around, we also mix it ourselves. Many of our DJs spend their summers as resident DJs in some of the Seattle area's hottest clubs. We have visited many of the nation's best clubs, and we want to bring their exciting atmosphere to your next event. Some DJs try to be photographers or videographers, but we focus our expertise on the music.

Find out for yourself why we are fast becoming Washington State's favorite mobile disc jockey company.

For booking information,
please call (253) 856-0720 or (800) 266-8649, ext. 3
or e-mail us at *robert@thesound-factory.com*

www.thesound-factory.com
A Zesty Productions Company

Your Music Your Way!

ROCK R&B

Contact: Brian Dale
(425) 771-1167 or (800) 360-WAVE (9283)
Web site: www.wavelinkmusic.com

• Holiday Parties • Theme Parties • Auctions • Anniversary Parties
• Birthday Parties • Team Building Events • Business Meetings
• Company Picnics • Cruises • Indoor/Outdoor Events

The Northwest's most complete Mobile Disc Jockey Service, Wave Link Music features dependable, experienced, and professional DJs who offer personal, friendly service at competitive rates. Established in 1982 and incorporated in 1989, we have the experience to provide outstanding entertainment for any event. Whether it's a wild and crazy theme party, a formal holiday dinner party, or a casual summer picnic, indoors or outdoors, on land or at sea, our talented DJs will create a memorable event for you and your guests.

"Your Music, Your Way!": we guarantee your satisfaction

To ensure that your event meets your expectations, you consult with your DJ well in advance of your event to discuss music selections and other details. We are happy to help with suggestions, but we will definitely do things the way you would like them done.

We offer a complete Digital Music Library with musical styles ranging from the 20's and 30's to today's Top-40. We have music of all kinds to meet your needs, from R&B and Alternative to Country, Latin, and Techno. Your favorites are sure to be available, whether from the 50's and 60's, the 80's and 90's, or the Disco era. Our DJs program your selections, but also take requests from your guests throughout the event.

We use the finest professional equipment

All of our systems feature top-of-the-line Pro-Audio Sound Reinforcement, digital turntables (not just ordinary home stereo CD players), and wireless microphones at no extra charge. Everything is encased and skirted to conceal the wiring. We provide a small lighting package for additional atmosphere at no additional charge. We will also arrange for special lighting requests, limited only by your imagination.

CALL TODAY FOR A QUOTE ON YOUR NEXT EVENT
(425) 771-1167 or (800) 360-WAVE (9283)

A Zesty Productions Company

Notes

Entertainment/ Musicians & Vocalists

❖❖❖

ENTERTAINMENT/MUSICIANS AND VOCALISTS

HELPFUL HINTS

Live music sets the stage: Live music adds to any event. Depending on the size and formality of your event, you can choose to have the soft background music of an individual pianist or string quartet, or make a pronouncement with trumpeters or a brass quartet, even bagpipes.

Setup requirements: The formality, facility and size of your event will determine the type of music that is appropriate. Be very specific about getting the space and electrical requirements from your musicians so you can accurately relay the information to your contact person at the facility.

Be creative with your selection of music: Selecting your music can be a lot of fun. If you can't decide what you want, talk with some of the musicians or entertainment consultants, listen to their demo tapes and review their song lists. Musicians and entertainment consultants can be very helpful and will gladly offer ideas and suggestions to make your event unique.

Contracts: Any time you book any form of entertainment, be sure to get a contract that covers exactly what you are expecting them to do. Be clear about the times you want them to perform, and how you want them to interact with your guests.

Note: Before you make arrangements for all kinds of music and entertainment, be sure to check with your facility about any restrictions (like cut-off times) they may have.

PIANO/SMALL COMBOS

CLAYTON MURRAY

(206) 367-5759

E-mail: claytone@foxinternet.com

Web site: web3.foxinternet.com/claytone

Style

My styles include Jazz, Ragtime, Ballads, Latin, Broadway, Pop and Classical. I have a demo CD or cassette available.

Experience

I have been performing professionally for the past 25 years both here in the Pacific Northwest and internationally. My wide range of musical experience enables me to handle varying requirements.

Solo piano or combo

In addition to solo piano, I have several combinations of other instruments I perform with ranging from duo, trio and quartet to dance combos. I own a portable keyboard for locations without a piano.

FRIENDLY AND PROFESSIONAL

I always work with my clients to provide them with worry-free, professional service, and I do my best to ensure that their special event is a success.

MUSICAL ELEGANCE FOR SPECIAL OCCASIONS

(206) 783-9493

E-mail: harp4u@worldnet.att.net

Web site: www.harp4u.com

On that Special Occasion, you want the right music to set the mood, create a lovely ambiance, and treat your guests to subtle, sophisticated, sublime entertainment that will highlight your celebration.

Harp provides that ambiance...indoors or outside...classical to romantic...traditional to Broadway...popular to ethnic...it will add elegance and charm to your party.

Various instruments in combination with the harp can enhance the setting. Flute, cello or violin may be added to form a full yet mellow ensemble.

Our recording, "Wedding Music," was voted Best Instrumental Album of the Year.

For more information, please call:
Susi Hussong (206) 783-9493

Cynthia Rice Kuni

Harpist

(206) 789-5091

E-mail: cynthiakuni@yahoo.com

- **EXPERIENCED:** public performer in the Puget Sound area since 1987. Principal harpist for the Northwest Symphony Orchestra since 1994.
- **ECLECTIC:** playing a wide variety of musical styles to appeal to a broad audience.
- **AFFORDABLE:** competitive rates that include travel within the greater Seattle area.
- **RELIABLE:** all work is backed by a written contract, no surprise costs.
- **PROFESSIONAL:** "I arrive early, take minimal breaks, and always present a positive attitude."

2002 Prices

Background music is billed at $150 for the first hour, $100 per hour thereafter. (Wedding ceremony music is not covered under this pricing structure.) Travel outside the greater Seattle area is $30 and up (please call for an exact travel rate). Non-refundable deposit of $50 to hold your event date; balance due on date of performance.

DAVID PAUL MESLER

Pianist • Vocalist • Bandleader

(206) 528-7464

E mail: dpmesler@aol.com • ***Web site: www.davidpaulmesler.com***

Critic's Choice: *The Seattle Times, The Seattle P-I, The Seattle Weekly*
Ensembles: The Dave Mesler Group (jazz), Trio Presto (classical)

Experience

David is an award-winning pianist and vocalist with 20 years experience helping people make their special occasions memorable. He has performed for a wide variety of politicians, corporations, celebrities and business leaders—including President Bill Clinton, Vice President Al Gore, Governor Gary Locke, Steven Spielberg, Elizabeth Taylor, Paul Newman, Harrison Ford and Bill Gates—and has played at most of the reception sites in the greater Northwest.

Style

An accomplished musician, David is as comfortable playing Mozart and Beethoven as Gershwin, Sinatra, Elvis, The Beatles or Rodgers and Hammerstein. His specialties include jazz, swing, big band, classical, early rock and roll, showtunes and standards.

A Sampling of Venues and Clients

Benaroya Hall • Canlis • Columbia Tower Club • Columbia Winery • Four Seasons Olympic • The Golf Club at Newcastle • The Harbor Club • Microsoft • Palisade • The Ruins • Safeco Field • Seattle Art Museum • Seattle Repertory Theater • Seattle Tennis Club • Seattle Yacht Club • Sheraton Seattle • The Skansonia • Smith Tower • Sorrento Hotel • Space Needle • Ste. Michelle Winery • United Way • University of Washington • Washington Athletic Club • Washington Mutual Tower • Washington State Convention Center • Westin Hotel and Towers

Solo or Combos

David is the pianist and bandleader for two highly acclaimed ensembles: The Dave Mesler Group (jazz) and Trio Presto (classical). David is also available to perform as a solo pianist or pianist-vocalist, and regularly puts together tailor-made duos, trios, quartets and beyond to help create just the right musical atmosphere for your event.

Please contact for a price list and FREE demo tape.
David travels with a full-size portable keyboard if needed.

L. J. Porter

and

The Vampin' Ho's

Contact: L.J. Porter
(425) 865-8996
*Fax (425) 865-8996, *51*
Web site: www.LJPorter.com

Soulful and Sassy

Ms. Porter traces her singing roots to her grandfather's church in a little town in Louisiana. Before the Rev. Paree Porter, the congregation, and God Almighty, a very young L.J. would use her sweet sound of soul to bring inspiration—and the house would be rock'n! Those very important roots are part of L.J.'s expression, along with her soulful voice and bountiful rousing sound.

Gospel launched

Gospel launched the career that would have L.J. singing as a founding member of one of the Northwest's hottest acts, "The Seattle Women of R&B." With these ladies, L.J. has had the pleasure of opening for the likes of **B.B. King**, **Booker T and the MG's**, **Roy Orbison**, **Mary Wells**, and **Charlie Musslewhite**, to name a few.

Always moving...

L.J.'s love of R&B, her gutsy style, and the no-holds-barred playful rapport she has with her audiences has created a faithful following of peers and fans alike. L.J. is a woman who uses all of her natural gifts to provide a sometimes sweet, sometimes sad, occasionally nasty, but always moving vocal experience. When her voice caresses your ear, you have the feeling of a real good time, with good people, listening to good music!

Combined with the backup of The Vampin' Ho's...

You'd expect a powerhouse like L.J. Porter to have nothing short of raw energy backing her vocals. So what, you may ask yourself, goes well with that "blue flame moonshine?" DYNAMITE!!!

The Vampin' Ho's supply the rock-solid foundation for Ms. Porter's smooth, hot grooves. Imagine James Brown colliding with B.B. King and you've got the high-octane, soulful sounds of the Ho's. Comprised of former members of Burgandy Express, Sly Stone, and the Almost Live Band, the Vampin' Ho's step to the stage with "in-your-face, let it all hang-out" sound.

L.J. Porter, a woman who's going places...

"The Diva's" first-released CD, "Rollercoaster" showcases the artist's vocal abilities that are best described as "Blue Flame Moonshine"—a sound that goes down smooth and finished warm with a kick! This first project was presented at the Midem Asia music conference in Hong Kong, May 1997, and is currently being considered for international distribution. L.J. has also caught the interest of several major independent recording labels.

You've got to experience this heat yourself,
but don't say we didn't warn you!
Performing at Experience Music Project
New CD "Blue" Just Released • 600 Stations Nationwide

Sandra Locklear

Represented by

(206) 439-8519
E-mail: thundereyeSL@netscape.net

Seattle's Premier
Pianist • Singer • Bandleader

"Sandra brought class, spirit, and artistic inspiration to our event . . ."
—David Syre, CEO, Trillium Corporation

Remarkably versatile

A seasoned entertainer who plays to the crowd, Sandra plays and sings solo, or with her combo backup band. Pairing a rich alto voice with jazz piano stylings and drawing from a tremendous repertoire, she performs jazz standards and Broadway show tunes, popular and classical music, folk and blues She recently released her debut CD of original compositions, ***"Goddess Rising,"*** available at ***Amazon.com*** and at selected outlets.

Experienced and educated

With two decades' worth of experience, Sandra's dynamic career includes regional and overseas tours. She received her two degrees in music Phi Beta Kappa and Magna Cum Laude. Locally, Sandra entertains at private parties and corporate events, for Microsoft, Olympic Four Seasons and Sheraton Hotels, the Seattle Trade Center and the Washington State Convention and Trade Center, the Space Needle, the Rainier Club and other prominent venues.

At fees you can afford

Sandra works with her clients to establish an affordable price. Costs vary depending on the size of the musical group (solo, duo, trio, etc.) and whether or not a piano is provided on-site. She provides a state-of-the-art piano and sound equipment if necessary. Total reliability by an experienced professional is Sandra's guarantee.

What people are saying . . .

"She has a vibrant, warm personality that mixes well with a crowd . . ."
—Dayna Chambers, Georgia Department Industry, Trade & Tourism

"I was impressed that she took the time to come by in advance to get familiar with the instrument and the environment. She also asked for information to help her make the most appropriate choices from her extensive repertoire." —Jennifer James, Author

"We were impressed because she directed her songs and music to the audience, and there was something for everyone. She plays and sings beautifully, and we highly recommend her."
—George Finney, Executive Secretary, Washington Land Title Association

SMOOTH GROOVE PRODUCTIONS

Live Musical Entertainment for Any and All Occasions

5202-218th St. S.W. • Mountlake Terrace, WA 98043
(425) 775-9269; Fax (425) 778-9439
Contact: E. Emmanuel del Casal
E-mail: emman@smoothgroove.net
Web site: www.smoothgroove.net

The proper ambience for any special occasion. Whether your celebration calls for an elegant light jazz performance, an energetic dance set, or both, the *Smooth Groove Band* offers reliable, first class musicianship that will impress your guests and give you peace of mind. When it comes to live musical entertainment and production, the *Smooth Groove Band* is the name to call on for the utmost in providing the proper ambience and touch to that special occasion.

Proven musical expertise. Veteran musicians Steve Nowak and Emmanuel del Casal are the frontmen for *Smooth Groove's* ensembles, which usually range in size from solo acts to sextets and above. A guitarist and vocalist, Steve has performed and recorded with many major artists and continues to compose and teach. A bass player and composer, Emmanuel has taken his musical skill to audiences worldwide, and is no stranger in the recording studio.

We don't miss a beat. Thoughtfully selected live music adds as much to a memorable experience as the food catered for a special event. Our versatility and expertise ensure high quality entertainment that complements your celebration. We look forward to adding our touch of live musical elegance to the noteworthy occasions in your life. **FREE CONSULTATION.**

THE SYLVAN STRING QUARTET

Music for Special Occasions

(206) 524-2911
Web Site: www.sylvanquartet.com

Types of music

The Sylvan String Quartet performs a variety of music suitable for your corporate event. From baroque and classical to popular music, the quartet offers a varied repertoire that ensures a memorable musical experience for you and your guests. A free consultation is included to help you select the music most suitable for your event.

Experience

This established quartet has a well-earned reputation for dependability, and a willingness to work with their clients to create a music program for banquets, corporate events, holiday parties, business openings, and receptions.

Whatever the event, the Sylvan String Quartet promises to enhance your special occasion with its unique flair.

Call (206) 524-2911 to request a demo tape and free consultation.

TYRONE HEADE

HIGHLAND BAGPIPE
SCOTTISH SMALL PIPE

Contact: Tyrone Heade (206) 285-4989
Web site: www.bagpipe-entertainment.com

Grand, majestic music

The grand music of the Highland Bagpipe or the soft timbre of the Small Chamber Pipe bring majesty to great celebrations. Lively and spirited jigs and reels, distinctive marches, and the noble power of ancient classical music offer a wide variety of musical expressions to set the ambiance for your event.

Experience

Tyrone Heade is the Resident Cathedral Piper for both St. James Cathedral and St. Mark's Episcopal Cathedral in Seattle. Tyrone performs full-time throughout Western Washington, and he and his students have won numerous awards in competitive piping throughout Washington, Oregon and British Columbia. As a voting member of the National Academy of Recording Arts & Sciences, Tyrone's performances have been broadcast on regional television and radio and his musical talents appear regularly on commercial recordings.

Solo or ensemble performances available

All performances are tailored to your specific desires. Tyrone is also Pipe Sergeant of Seattle's award-winning Elliott Bay Pipe Band, and leads Seattle's only Scottish acoustic ensemble, Iona Abbey, featuring small pipes, cello, fiddle, guitar and bodhran. Event price varies for location and duration.

(206) 527-1922
Web site: www.windstrings.com

Creating a warm and elegant atmosphere

With over 12 years of professional experience, the Windstrings ensemble specializes in providing elegant music for banquets, weddings, receptions, and other private events. All members hold music degrees, and perform regularly as a trio featuring flute, violin, and cello.

Windstrings has enchanted audiences all over the world with performances in Japan, South America and Europe. They offer an extensive repertoire ranging from classical to popular. We are happy to work with you to select the music that will best complement your ideal special event.

Demo tape available
(206) 527-1922

NOTES

Games & Team Building Activities

❖❖❖

GAMES AND TEAM BUILDING ACTIVITIES

HELPFUL HINTS

Why use a theme and audience participative entertainment? A theme provides interest and coherence for the attendees. Planning is more efficient with a theme, creating an automatically organized process. In addition, the key to successful events is audience participation. The more involved people become in the event they are attending, the more likely they are to enjoy themselves and remember the experience. Attendees may not remember the name of the keynote speaker, but they will remember the "Wacky Olympics" special event!

When is a theme appropriate? Anytime you have an event. When done properly, themes can be used to enhance a business meeting, client appreciation, awards event, and even reunions.

How is a theme chosen? Define the goals of your event first, what you want to accomplish with the event, who is attending, and what you want them to take away with them. Then you can decide what theme options may work. Brainstorming with a committee or colleague can be a big help .

Are theme events expensive? They don't have to be. It depends on your budget. Some of your theme ideas can be accomplished with a small budget if you and your committee are willing to spend the time. However, a much better use of your time and money may be to use a meeting planner, prop, or entertainment company.

Decorating tips for theme events: Consider three to four main areas of the facility for theme props. Main focus areas can include the entryway to the event, stage, guest tables, beverage and food stations, to name a few.

Interactive and Theme ideas for your next event:

- Casino Night
- Murder and Mystery
- Tropical Island
- Cruise Ship
- African Jungle
- Tropical Rain Forest
- Western/ Wild West
- Medieval Castle
- Hawaiian Luau
- Fabulous 50s
- Great Gatsby Party
- Winter Wonderland
- M•A•S•H
- South of the Border
- Underwater
- Mexican Fiesta
- Mardi Gras
- Circus! Circus!
- International Themes
- Nautical
- The Great Northwest

4310 South 300th Street • Auburn, Washington 98001
Contact: Bob Newell
Phone (253) 946-1230; Fax (253) 946-1230; Pager (206) 955-6228
Web site: www.see21forfun.com

Don't Gamble With Your Next Party,
Make A Sure Bet...

No one loses, everyone has a great time!

21 For Fun (Casino Parties) is an exciting way to liven up your next company function. As a traveling casino, we come to the site of your choice and put together an event where nobody loses and everybody has a great time!

Transform any function into an EVENT!

Our professional, experienced and courteous staff will help make your casino night a hit! We provide the chips, dice, cards and dealers, plus the games like:
- Craps
- Roulette
- Blackjack
- Pai-Gow Poker

Ideal for:

- Employee Incentives
- Client Goodwill
- Reunions
- Holiday Parties
- Graduation Parties
- Fund Raisers
- Or, Any Reason For A Celebration

Affordably priced...

We're affordably priced to fit any party budget. Booking dates are limited, so call now for a free estimate!

Don't Gamble With Your Next Party...
Make A Sure Bet With
21 For Fun (Casino Parties)

A Action Entertainment and EVENT PLANNING

Produced by David Lersten

Serving the Northwest for Over 20 Years!

425•277•1777

For your best company picnic ever!

Our commitment . . .

is to redefine and build working relationships, and to facilitate personal development in a party environment. We create *unforgettable* **Picnics**, **Team Building**, and **Mini Olympics**

Music and Karaoke

Creative programming of your favorite summertime hits on a state-of-the-art digital sound system.

Team Building Events Package Includes:

- Master of Ceremonies
- Music on Digital Mini-Disc System
- Fun Line & Popular Dance Instruction
- Wild Wet Roulette
- Mondo Hula Hoop
- Team Earth Ball Challenge
- Hop till You Drop
- Water Cannon Wars OR Sumo Wrestling
- Coordinators
- Tug-o'-War
- Hula Mania
- Water Grenade Toss
- Caribbean Limbo
- Whistling Rocket Toss
- Giant Jump

Many other entertainment options are available, including inflatables for children and adults.

We get results . . .

These fun activities break down barriers, enhance communication, and build team spirit through laughter and interaction. With A Action Entertainment, your corporate event will be the best ever!

A few of our satisfied clients . . .

- Microsoft
- Alaska Airlines
- McDonalds Corporation
- AAA of Washington
- Costco
- Phil Smart Mercedes
- Starbucks
- AT&T Wireless
- IBM
- Space Needle
- Bally Total Fitness
- JC Penney
- EMP
- Baugh Construction
- Verizon
- Four Seasons
- Boeing
- Kinkos

Book Early (425) 277-1777 • Fax (425) 277-0922
E-mail: bestshow@msn.com
Web site: www.action-entertainment.com

See page 441 under Entertainment/Disc Jockeys and page 499 under Meeting & Event Planners.

Preferred Vendor of Microsoft

Contact: Kristin Berry
(800) 981-7469
Fax (360) 419-3151
E-mail: info@actionevent.com
Web site: www.actionevent.com

Entertainment Party Package

Action Events has developed an innovative party package that works with every age group. The overwhelming success we have had with our entertainment package is largely due to our extremely high-energy staff who gets everyone involved and working together. The music is chosen to specifically correspond with the activities your group has requested for your event. Don't lift a finger—just your phone, and let a professional take all the stress out of planning your next interactive event.

- Master of Ceremonies
- Klucker Kilometer
- Limbo
- Whip It
- Hula Hoops
- Super Soakers
- Music and Crystal Clear Mini-Disc System
- Team Skiing
- Balloon Race
- Balloon/Ball Run
- Tricycle and Wagon Races
- Tug-o-War
- Hot Potato
- Off With Your Head
- Egg/Spoon
- Dizzy Race
- Chubby Bunny

Includes 4 hours of music with up to 2 hours of party games

Full-Service Event Planning

We are party professionals specializing in spectacular high-quality events including:

- Corporate Events
- Company Picnics
- Entertainment
- Conventions
- Holiday Parties
- Team Olympics
- Company Meetings
- Themed Events
- And more…

Our Clients aren't Just Satisfied, they RAVE about Our Services!

"I cannot express enough how much I enjoyed working with your staff. They pulled off a party for 3,500 people in only a couple of weeks time. Their energy, professionalism, and creative planning will continue to catapult your business to success."—Microsoft

"We've been holding our company picnics for 13 years and I can honestly say that Action Events organized the greatest event we ever had. People at work are still talking about it. I can't begin to tell you how nice it was to just enjoy the picnic instead of worrying about setting up, cleaning, cooking, and making sure everyone was having a good time. We are anxiously waiting to see what surprises Action Events has in store for our Christmas party."—Costco

Don't Lift A Finger—Just The Phone (800) 981-SHOW (7469)

At Madison Park
Seattle, Washington
Contact: Mike or Virginia Duppenthaler
(206) 328-2442; Fax (206) 328-2863
E-mail: mike@blueribboncooking.com
Web site: www.blueribboncooking.com

A Gastronomic Team Building Experience

Welcome to Blue Ribbon Cooking School. A small private cooking school designed by husband and wife team Virginia and Mike Duppenthaler. Virginia and Mike host a one of a kind hands on cooking experience in their beautifully restored 1907 craftsman-style home. The School offers a unique opportunity for companies and organizations to build stronger working relationships in an atmosphere that is intimate as well as challenging and stimulating.

Virginia brings her 26 years of experience and love of cooking together creating educational programs that help develop camaraderie and team work. The teaching area of their home is divided into 2 to 5 different cooking stations. One group maybe exploring the philosophy of regional barbecuing, while another group develops skills in classic French cuisine, while another group gathers around the pastry table. And, if that was not enough, you may find yourself working side by side with one of Seattle's local guest chefs, learning their trade secrets.

In the end, when the aprons come off, everyone gathers to indulge for a moment, review their accomplishments and compliment their efforts as a team.

Some of our clients who find this exciting...

Arthur Andersen, Accenture, Avanade, Avenue A, Costco Wholesale, Forest Pharmaceuticals, Merck, Microsoft, Microsoft Press, N2H2, Perkins Coie, Point B, Soft Resources, Timber Product Resources, Totem Ocean Trailer Express, Table Top Company, Travelocity.com, Washington Dental Services

Our services

Virginia and Mike offer their home any day or evening of the week on a limited basis. Evening sessions usually run from 6:30pm to 9:30pm. Lunch sessions run from 11:30am to 2:30pm. Costs vary per event ($65 to $110 per person).

Blue Ribbon Cooking School is located on the corner of Madison Street at McGilvra Boulevard East in Madison Park, just 10 minutes from downtown Seattle.

Our school offers nothing for sale, but education, camaraderie and hands-on fun.

Visit our Web Site for Background Information

www.blueribboncooking.com

Firetruck Slide

Train Bouncer with music/light system

Tsunami Double Chute Slide

Call for a free brochure
Seattle (206) 763-3236 or (800) 763-3236
or visit our ***Web Site: www.clownsunlimited.com***

Over 45,000 Events Since 1981

Serving the Puget Sound area since 1981, Clowns Unlimited has provided quality entertainment and games for parties, picnics, promotions and more. We are a tradition for many families and companies as we continue to delight and amaze children and adults.

Entertainers

- Clowns
- Magicians
- Facepainters
- Airbrush Facepainting
- DJ's/Sound Systems
- Balloonists
- Jugglers
- Santa Claus
- Seasonal Characters
- Kid's Karaoke

Interactive Games and Attractions

- Aquatic Adventure
- Ball Pond
- Beanie Typhoon
- ***Assorted Bouncers***
  - Blue Dog
  - Castle
  - Clown
  - Choo Choo Train
  - Dinosaur
  - Elephant
  - Gorilla
  - Lion
  - Race Car
  - Spaceman
  - Bouncy Boxing
- Bungee Run
- Bungee Bull
- Cameron the Caterpillar
- Carnival Games
- Crocodile Slide and Hide
- Dance Dance Revolution
- Dunk Tanks
- Equalizer Bungee Challenge
- Go Karts
- Gyrotron
- Human Spheres
- IronMan Obstacle Course
- Joust
- Krazy Karts
- Lazer Tag
- Mobile Circus Train
- Monster Trucks
- Mutiny on the Bouncer
- Pony Rides
- Puffer the Train
- Robo Surfer
- Rockem Sockem
- Rocky Mountain Climber
- ***Slides***
  - 25 ft. Slide
  - 40 ft. Slide
  - 50 ft. Slide
  - Firetruck Slide
  - Rocket Turbo Slide
  - TotTitanic Slide
  - Tsunami Double Chute Slide
- Spin Art
- Submarine
- Sumo Wrestling
- Team Challenge
- Toddler Play Area
- Twin Spin Thrill Ride
- Twister
- Velcro Wall

"They are always on the cutting edge of cool and are extremely dependable."
—Christine Beatty, Microsoft

"They show consistency in timeliness, quality service and courtesy. They are professionals!"
—Jason Jones, Remlinger Farms

Professional Entertainers • Top Quality • Best Prices
Satisfaction Guaranteed • Fully Insured • Trained Staff

13817 Short School Road
Snohomish, Washington 98290
Contact: Judy Craven
(360) 568-2601; Fax (360) 568-9001
E-mail: vistafarm@aol.com
Web site: www.cravenfarm.com

A place to be creative and productive

Craven Farm offers a casual setting for meetings, retreats, team building seminars, and workshops, away from the distractions of the city and your normal routine. Our 2,400 sq. ft. barn will comfortably seat 125 to 150 people. With the doors open, seating can extend onto two acres of picnic grounds that accommodate many more. Ample on-site parking is provided at no charge.

Food and banquet services

- Catering provided by the outside caterer of your choice
- On-site staff available for hire
- Beer and wine permitted with proper permits
- Some kitchen facilities provided

Picnics and recreation

Craven Farm is an ideal site for your next picnic. We have outdoor tables with benches that allow you and your guests to enjoy the great out-of-doors. Our picturesque setting is surrounded by beautiful farmland. You're welcome to take a stroll down the lane between the fields of growing crops and enjoy the peaceful serenity of the Farm.

Outdoor activities include volleyball, baseball, and horseshoes.

Availability, price range and terms

The barn is available from May through September. Prices vary according to the day and time of your event; please inquire. A deposit is required to reserve your date, with the balance due two weeks prior to the event. The client is responsible for providing any liability insurance.

ENJOY COUNTRY CHARM AT THE FARM

Craven Farm offers you a country setting that will captivate you and your guests. The open fields surrounding the farm, along with a view of the Cascades, provide a peaceful country setting perfect for work or play. Come experience the farm for team building, a work session, or to brainstorm. You will enjoy the farm's relaxed atmosphere and thoughtful hospitality.

See page 541 under Picnic & Recreation Sites.

Bringing True Nation-Wide Team Building To You!

BRINGING THE LATEST IN TEAM BUILDING TO YOU!

Themed Team Builders

Themed Team Builders provide entertainment, changing individual and group behavior, as well as influencing the way people think about each other and the world. Perfect for groups needing a team-oriented experience, they also make fantastic rewards programs, relationship builders, and morale boosters. Catering to groups of 10–1,000 and up, Themed Team Builders can be experienced inside or outside!

Choose from a variety of themes, including Survivor, Bootcamp, School Daze, Destination Resort Challenge, and the Yakima Valley Wine Challenge.

Custom designed to develop team thinking, these programs offer modules emphasizing both physical and mental challenges.

Morale Boosters

Our Morale Boosters are custom-designed for every event to best meet your needs. Take a sampling of high adrenaline games, stimulating intellectual challenges, scoring towers, heart thumping music and lighting, and you come close to imagining the excitement and energy at our Morale Boosters! Throw in live video, prizes, and event MC's and you've got a recipe for high energy success!

Working as individuals, everybody gains points for their team, whether they win or lose! Points just for participating are vital to encourage full-participation energy!

Table Top Olympics

Table Top Olympics were designed to meet the needs of groups meeting for any kind of table-oriented function, such as dinners, lectures, seminar, or whatever! Custom-built packages for every event feature both intellectual and physical challenges, all within the constrains of a table-top environment. If you need "ice breakers," look no further! We have designed sets of "Olympic"—type games designed to encourage full participation, communication, and fun!

Creative Playing cares about purposeful recreation—team building with an emphasis on corporate culture, competition, cooperation, adrenaline, and good old-fashioned fun! Stand out from the corporate crowd with our team builders designed with you in mind. Stimulate team spirit and corporate wellness with Creative Playing.

ELWAY RESEARCH, INC.

7107 Greenwood Avenue North
Seattle, Washington 98103
Contact: Jone Howard
(206) 264-1500
Fax (206) 264-0301
E-mail: jone@elwayresearch.com

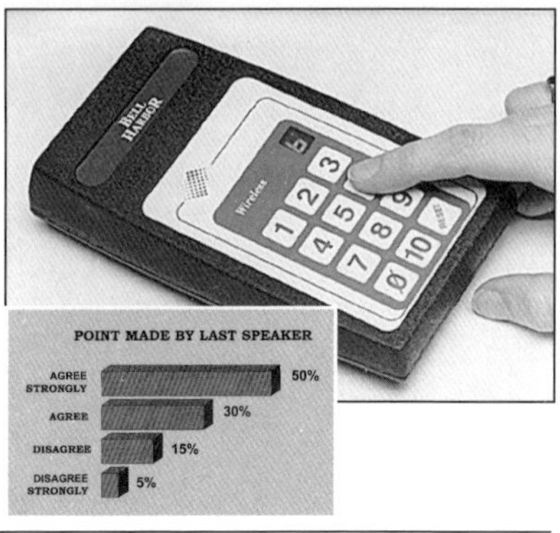

Conduct Meetings That Are Fun And Productive With Electronic Polling

With EGIS, the Electronic Group Interaction System, each meeting participant is able to instantly respond to material being presented through an individual keypad. Participants responses are continuously recorded on the systems computer. Results can be projected for viewing by all participants or displayed to meeting organizers on a monitor in a separate room. The data are saved—available for statistical analysis.

- **Anonymous response and instantaneous display of group responses** means more productive meetings.
- **EGIS keeps the process moving and on task.** As participants register their opinions, tabulated results are displayed to the group for further consideration.
- **Diverging opinions are revealed.** One group's answers can be instantly compared with another's, and/or with information gathered from a source outside the meeting.
- **Everyone participates, equally and continuously.** Because participants register their responses anonymously, they are included equally—without regard to verbal skills, language barriers, or willingness to speak up in a meeting.

Enable Participants To:

- Remain actively engaged in the meeting.
- Feel motivated to participate.
- Stay continuously involved.

Enable Meeting Organizers To:

- Measure participant attitudes on key questions.
- Monitor response as the meeting takes place.
- Direct/re-direct based on participant response.
- Get information to the right people.
- Enhance team building.

Instant Surveys: What do participants think about?

- Important issues?
- The points the speaker just made?
- The future of the organization?
- A question from the floor?
- The topic of the next speaker?

Move To Consensus:

- Participants see how their views match those of the group.
- Questions can be re-formulated as the discussion evolves.

Question On The Fly:

- Questions can be added as quickly as you can type.
- Results are displayed in 5 seconds!

Vote:

- EGIS tallies and reports votes instantly.

Elway Research offers a complete range of meeting services:

- Equipment Rental
- Meeting Facilitation
- Question Design
- Hard Copy Charts
- Polling Facilitation
- Data Analysis & Report

CALL FOR A FREE CONSULTATION ON YOUR NEXT MEETING!

FUN RENTALS

4072-148th Avenue N.E.
Redmond, Washington 98052
Contact: Susan Smith
(425) 702-3700
Web site: www.funrent.com

We Deliver Fun for Any Occasion!

Family Fun

At Fun Rentals, we specialize in providing high quality equipment and games for children, adults and families. We deliver individualized service to create unique experiences for any event.

Exciting Inflatable Bouncers

- Tall Tigers
- Jungle
- Fantasy Castle
- Fire Station
- Outer Space
- Russian Castle
- Circus
- Ghost Castle
- NASCAR
- Clown
- Basic Bounce
- Always new ones

Amazing Inflatable Activities

- Obstacle Courses
- Slides
- Ball Pond Houses
- Boxing
- Joust
- Caterpillar Crawl

Specialty Amusement

- 9 Hole Mini-Golf
- Hi-Striker
- Over 70 Carnival Games
- Skeeball
- Arcade Sports Games
- Speed Pitch
- Hose Hockey
- Golf Billiards
- Dunk Tank & Splash Tank
- Spin Art
- Replica Fire Truck
- Air Hockey/Foosball

Special Services

- Wholesale Prizes
- Food Concessions
- Retail Prize Store
- Indoor Space for Winter Parties

Original Games & Characters

- Treasure Hunts
- Scavenger Hunts
- Costumed Characters
- Field Games
- Indoor Party Games
- Balloon Artists
- Clowns
- Face Painters
- Magicians

Our Commitment

We love to make children of ALL ages happy! We bring flexibility and creativity to our personalized services. Free delivery and a 100% Guarantee of Fun. Insured.

Visit our Web Site at *www.funrent.com*

PORTABLE
Miniature Golf Rental Service

32345-20th Place S.W. • Federal Way, Washington 98023
Contact: Pam Taylor
Office (253) 661-1640; Fax (253) 661-7915
E-mail: golftogo@hotmail.com
Web site: www.minigolftogo.com

Putt Putt in Your Office,
at a Party or Event!

We bring miniature golf to your location or special event

All inclusive 9-hole or 18-hole event packages include delivery and setup, putters, balls, scorecards and pencils.

Our standard rates are $625 for 9-holes and $1,050 for 18-holes. These rates include:
- Delivery/set-up
- A manager for 3 hours of play time
- Standard score cards with pencils
- Putters and balls
- Break down

Golf To Go…is a real crowd pleaser for all participants, golfer or not! We'll provide the tournament play organization with a staff game manager. We help you every putt of the way!

Golf To Go…is ideal for in-office gatherings, company picnics, sales meetings, trade show, corporate events, etc. Sets up inside or outside.

Rates and Discounts

- Half-day rental package of 9 holes—$625
- Half-day rental package of 18 holes—$1,050
- 10% discount for three or more confirmed bookings
- 5% discount for pre-paying, in full, 30 days or more in advance
- Custom rentals available

Call for more information
Golf To Go
(253) 661-1640
or
1-800-369-7448

www.minigolftogo.com

Puget Sound Leader in Indoor Karting

2105 Frank Albert Road
Fife, Washington 98424
(253) 922-7722
Open Daily 11am–11pm
Web site: www.grandprixraceway.com

Racers Start Your Engines...

Your group, perhaps for the first time in their lives, will be in the driver's seat of a real racing go kart, on a real race track. Our Honda powered Zip karts can reach 40 mph (which feels more like 100 mph riding only an inch off the ground!). The GRAND PRIX pit crew will outfit your drivers with everything for the event, from racing coveralls, full coverage helmet, gloves and safety briefing to trophies and awards at a podium ceremony. Think of the excellent photo opportunities!

This is an excellent and fast paced opportunity for client entertainment, employee rewards, product launches, fundraisers, company parties and team building. A state-of-the-art computerized timing system can provide each driver with a personalized race certificate showing race times accurate to 1/1000th of a second. It times each kart every lap around our 1/5 mile circuit and shows split times and driver positions. The race report can be viewed from the comfort of our Drivers Lounge on monitors. We also offer a meeting room so you can attend to business and then let the fun begin.

Averaging about $60.00 per participant, all of our group packages include five practice laps and winner recognition at a podium ceremony.

GRAND PRIX: Ideal for groups of 25 or more. Race grid positions will be chosen at random for three 20-lap races—points will be allocated according to finishing positions. The top three point earners will receive trophies at a podium ceremony.

INDY ENDURANCE TEAM RACE: The drivers are split into teams and issued a kart to be used for the entire event. Following each driver's 5-lap practice sessions, the teams are gridded up to start the 2-hour times race. The AMB timing system keeps positions, split times and lap times on all karts at all times. When the driver changes take place each team's kart enters the track at the same interval that the previous driver earned.

Besides a day of racing you will not soon forget, your party has the option of catered meals or the use of our snack bar. Also on the premises is a gift shop featuring motorsports memorabilia, licensed products, clothing, souvenirs and a game room.

If your group is seeking a real adrenaline rush, please feel free to inquire about our outdoor racing opportunities in the Rotax Max! This is a 125cc water-cooled engine with centrifugal clutch and electric start that tops out at 90 mph! 28-horsepower of exciting racing action! visit or web site for details.

LET THE GOOD TIMES ROLL!

WE'D KILL FOR YOUR BUSINESS

CALL ENTCO INTERNATIONAL
(425) 670-0888

Toll Free: (800) 803-0298; Fax (425) 670-0777

E-mail: ENTCO.com

Web site: www.ENTCO.com

She was a cold blooded killer with a pair of icy blues and a heart to match. Now that @#*! cop wants to know why she talked to you all evening. So does your wife.

"Our faces hurt from laughing so much."

Pardon me, is that a knife in your back?

"The president of our association kept asking how we're going to top IT'S A MYSTERY...Well, I honestly don't think we can..."

As soon as I heard the gun, I knew it meant trouble; but who could have imagined this?

"...the entire crew were highly professional, courteous, articulate, incredibly funny, and creative beyond belief."

I'm Detective Richard Sheridan. Don't call me Dick.

"...remarked that this was the most unforgettable and fun event they have ever attended!"

Isn't that Mike's favorite golf club next to the body?

"...the best entertainment we have ever had at a company Christmas party."

 Please let this business know that you heard about them from the Bravo! Event Resource Guide.

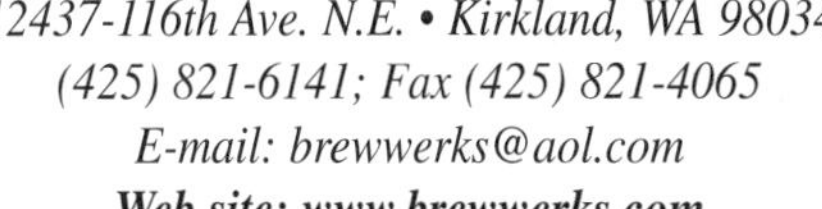
12437-116th Ave. N.E. • Kirkland, WA 98034
(425) 821-6141; Fax (425) 821-4065
E-mail: brewwerks@aol.com
Web site: www.brewwerks.com

NORTHWEST
BREWWERKS

Looking For Something Different?
Let Us Help Make Your Next Event Unique!

What we are

We are a gold medal winning microbrewery, a pub, an U-brew and a restaurant. We have six brew kettles, each a scaled down version of a microbrewery. You just select from any of our 65 recipes (or create your own) and our knowledgeable, helpful staff will help you every step of the way—no experience necessary. In about two hours your brewing process will be complete. Your beer goes into our fermentation room for one week, then into the cold room for another week. Your group then returns after 2 weeks for a second party to bottle and enjoy their beer!

Party while you work together

We help you "brew up" a team-building activity, a company celebration or an out-of-the ordinary event for clients. Everyone leaves with a sense of accomplishment and professionally self-brewed beer, wine or cider follows in a few short weeks. You get two parties—one during brewing and one during bottling! We have hosted parties for product launches, promotions, team incentives, retirements—you name it!

- We can accommodate parties of up to 60 brewers and "advisors"
- Or you can buy beer from us for a special function or occasion

If I host my event there, what do I need to bring?

Just bring people looking for a fun time doing something different—simple as that!

What else do you provide?

We have our award-winning Hole In The Wall Barbecue on-site. Our smokers slow cook our meats (pork, beef, chicken, turkey, bratwurst) to perfection. We have our own chili, cornbread, beans, potato salad, ceasar salad and much more. Have special needs? We will work with you to provide for all participants. And, of course, we have our own beers on tap—12 beers, cider and rootbeer.

Satisfied companies include:

Boeing, AT&T, Microsoft, Bank & Office Interiors, Puget Sound Energy, U.S. Coast Guard, Kaiser Aluminum, Glaxo & Wyeth Ayerst Pharmaceuticals, Verizon Wireless, Drugstore.com, ImageX.com, Anderson Consulting, Targeted Genetics and many more...

We make it easy for you to be successful. We will work with you on special needs—just ask!
Packages for all group sizes and budgets—schedule your party soon!
Contact Ward or Jill Taylor
For more information, our beer recipe list and full BBQ menu, go to *www.brewwerks.com*
Celebrating our 5th year of making your group function a memorable one!

Survivor Series©

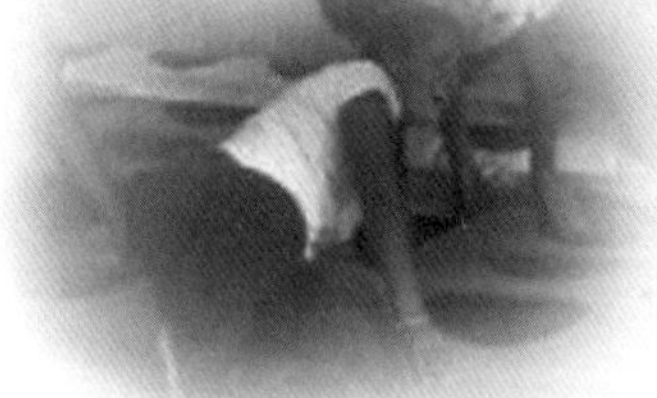

Contact: Mark Thibodeau

(360) 438-2211 or (800) 853-5867

Web site: www.partyoutfitters.com

Complete Party & Picnic Packages

You relax. We handle the details!

Site Selection • Catering • Entertainment • Games • Themes

Featuring over 100 games.

Big fun for all . . .

- Velcro Wall
- Human Spheres
- Golf Driving Challenge
- Hurling High Ball
- Wacky Trikes
- 28 ft. Inflatable Rocky Mountain Climber
- Speed Pitch
- Titanic Adventure Challenge
- Gladiator Jousting
- Big Time Bouncy Boxing
- Hoop'n It Up Basketball
- Human Gyroscope
- Inflatable Obstacle Course
- Miniature Golf
- 22' & 26' Tall Inflatable Slides
- Rodeo Roper
- Bungee Bull Ride
- Batting Cage
- Bungee Run
- Off With Your Head
- Sumo Wrestling
- Laser Tag
- Human Foosball
- NASCAN Sprinters
- Millennium Challenge

Especially for kids

- Ellie the Elephant
- Noah's Ark Bouncer
- Choo Choo Express Train
- Dalmatian Bouncer
- Moonjumps
- Giraffe Bouncer
- Cameron the Caterpillar
- Ball Pond
- Splativity
- Purple Dragon
- Winston the Whale

We're the Experts!

Party Outfitters specializes in providing fun, interactive games for special events including: team building, company picnics, trade shows, graduation parties, holiday parties and promotions. When quality, dependability, safety and experience count, hire the pros at Party Outfitters.

Customer Comments

"I would like to compliment your staff on doing an excellent job for our Senior All Night party. They arrived early, were very polite and courteous." —Beverly F., Mossyrock, WA

"Your staff were prompt and helpful. Their presence was very reassuring that nothing would go wrong...thank you for making it so easy for me to plan an enjoyable day in the sun!" —Kelly B., Portland, OR

DELIVERED • INSURED • STAFFED

Call for a FREE fun-filled 36-page catalog and RESERVE EARLY:

(360) 438-2211, (800) 853-5867

Visit our on-line catalog at *www.partyoutfitters.com/*

222 Yale Avenue North • Seattle, Washington 98109
(206) 223-1944 or Toll-free (888) 873-1938
Fax (206) 223-1407
Business/Office Hours: Mon–Fri 10am–9pm, Sat 10am–7pm, Sun 11am–6pm
E-mail: seattle@rei.com
Web site: www.rei.com/storelocator/seattle

GET OUTSIDE YOURSELF!

Treat your guests to a hands-on adventure in one of Seattle's best-known landmarks. The REI flagship store is home to one of the world's tallest freestanding indoor climbing structures and our expert belay staff can guide climbers of all levels through an exhilarating trip to the summit. All routes, novice to extremely challenging, lead to a spectacular 360-degree view of the city. A terrific individual or team activity that can be a great introduction to the sport of rock climbing. All equipment is provided.

Group Rental Information

Monday, Wednesday and Friday: 8am–10am; Tuesdays: 10am–9pm

- Your 2-hour reserved time includes safety talks, and preparing participants with shoes and harnesses.
- A maximum of 15 climbers are permitted during each 2-hour group session.
- Costs—Corporate Rate: $300 per 2-hour session; Non-Profit Rate: $150 per 2-hour session.
- $75 non-refundable fee is required at time of reservation.

Individual Climb Information:

Sign-ups begin when the store opens. Pinnacle is closed on Tuesdays for Group Reservations.

- Cost—REI members: $3 per climb; Non-members: $8 per climb.

Location! Location! Location!

- Walking distance to hotels, restaurants, & downtown shopping
- FREE covered Parking Garage
- Easy I-5 access
- Restaurant located in store

EXPERIENCE REI...YOUR OUTDOOR ADVENTURE INSIDE!

REI is an internationally renowned outdoor retailer dedicated to inspiring, educating and outfitting our customers for their adventures! Don't forget about REI's beautiful spacious meeting rooms with panoramic views of Seattle along with full audio-visual equipment to make your meeting or event successful and memorable. Please call for more information and to set an appointment to tour our facilities.

See page 261 under Banquet, Meeting & Event Sites.

5406 North Albina Avenue • Portland, Oregon 97217
(877) 650-9519; Fax (503) 283-3651
Please call for an appointment
info@propshop.com • ***www.propshop.com***

Team Building

The need for organizational interplay has increased and our specially trained coaches, custom designed and equipped games and challenges set the stage for different departments and their members to enjoy working and playing together.

Organizational Development

Our nationally recognized facilitator, Thomas Jones, Ph.D., shares his extensive knowledge and experience in organizational development, strategic planning, leadership development and crisis management with your group. From a few hour seminars, to a week-long retreat Dr. Jones and our staff will incorporate teaching with a "creative learning environment" using elements including, color, sound, smell and scenery.

Team Building:

- Team Rallies
- Inter-Department Challenges
- Problem Solving Competitions

Organizational Development:

- Leadership Development
- Strategic Planning
- Crisis Management
- Problems Solving Techniques

Benefits:

- Team Spirit
- Clear Focus and Direction
- Company Unity
- Increased Productivity

Association Memberships:
Chamber
MPI • SCVB
ACEP Board • CVBWCO • POVA

See page 399 under Decorations, Themes & Props.

Casino Parties and D.J. Entertainment

8916-122nd Avenue N.E.
Kirkland, Washington 98033
(425) 822-0711
(866) 780-0457

The "Bright Light City" is now here in the "Emerald City"

Vegas Nites

The most exciting casino party in the Northwest, is the only company in the state of Washington that is produced and managed by an experienced Las Vegas team.

Dealers

Our dealers are friendly, trained professionals who will answer your questions in a manner that is easy to understand.

Tables

Our table games are brand new and designed to Las Vegas specifications. Vegas Nites will make your gaming experience as authentic as playing in a real casino.

Our Games:

- Blackjack
- Roulette
- Pai Gow Poker
- Craps
- Let it Ride
- Celebrity Tables
- Big Six Wheel

The door has been opened with recent changes in the law...Vegas Nites is now able to provide Casino Party games for non-profit fundraisers.

Casino parties have become a big hit in the Northwest. Now you can customize your casino event for corporate dates, private parties and now fundraisers.

Call for details to make your fundraiser a night to remember!
We will customize your casino party at any location!

206.938.0569 or 888.915-8555
Fax 206.937-8470
Web site: www.casinoforfun.net

It's Your Deal!

The excitement of Las Vegas-style gaming is a sure bet for the success of your next event. We offer complete or customized packages, with event consultation and organization.

Games Include:

- Craps
- Red Dog
- Roulette
- Poker
- Blackjack
- Big Six Wheel
- High/Low
- Caribbean Stud Poker
- Video Horseracing
- Pai Gow
- Let It Ride
- Casino War

Personalize Your Casino Event

West Coast Casino Parties can customize printed casino chips, Las Vegas-style playing cards or add your logo to the gaming equipment.

For the complete Las Vegas experience we'll provide live entertainment including:

- Lounge Acts
- Caricaturists
- Impersonators
- A Dynamic Hypnotist Show
- An A Capella Singing Group
- "Night at the Improv" style Comedy Show
- Magic Show with one-on-one walk around magician

Add variety to your casino event...as West Coast also offers:

- Disc Jockey, Auctioneer and Emcee Services
- Peddle Powered Monster Trucks
- Video Olympics on a big screen
- Pseudo Sumo Suits
- Miniature Golf
- Velcro Maze
- Gyrotron
- Karaoke

WEST COAST IS YOUR ANSWER
WITH FUN ALTERNATIVES FOR ANY EVENT:

• Conventions • Parties • Fund Raisers • Social Events
• Class Reunions • Company Parties • Hospitality Suites
• Holiday Parties • Wedding Receptions

FOR MORE INFORMATION CALL 206.938.0569
OR TOLL-FREE 888.915.8555

www.casinoforfun.net

E-mail: rudy@wcent.com

 Please let this business know that you heard about them from the Bravo! Event Resource Guide.

CASINO PARTIES
GAME SHOWS
AND MORE

Phone (206) 241-4777 or (800) 330-4777
Fax (206) 241-6956
Web site: www.wildbills.com

Wild Bill's provides the finest in exciting interactive entertainment for:

Fund Raisers • Company Parties • Reunions • Conventions • Grad Nights
Client Appreciation Parties • Holiday Parties • Picnics • Private Parties

Everyone has a great time at a Wild Bill's Party because we get them involved in the action. Whether you envision an intimate setting or a lavish extravaganza, you can leave the details to us. Just tell us where and when, and we'll do the rest.

Casino Parties

Since 1982, Wild Bill's has provided authentic casino parties, known to event planners nationwide as the most popular form of corporate entertainment. Your guests wager with Wild Bill's Bucks at games like blackjack, craps, and roulette, all hosted by our friendly, professional dealers. It's all in fun, with no real gambling.

Game Shows

It's an hour of high energy, fast-paced Hollywood-style entertainment, where your guests are contestants in some of the wildest and zaniest games we could think up. We supply all the bells, buzzers, and a professional emcee. Great for team-building or reinforcing educational programs.

Video Horse Racing

Your event site becomes a casino "sportsbook lounge" complete with big-screen TV programs, betting slips, and personnel. Guests wager with Wild Bill's Bucks on eight exciting races from some of America's most famous tracks.

Comedy Hypnosis

Our professional hypnotist will convince even the most skeptical of the power of hypnosis as he casts his spell over members of the audience...with hilarious results!

Also available . . .

Micro Reality Stock Car Racing, Inflatable Games, DJs, and more!

Member: National Association of Casino & Theme Party Operators,
National Association of Catering Executives, and Meeting Professionals International

Notes

Golf Courses

❖❖❖

ORGANIZING A GOLF TOURNAMENT

Planning a golf tournament is a fun way to raise dollars. Golf is also a recreational sport that can promote team building. There are many forms of golf activities:

- Retreat break
- Fund raiser
- Reunions
- Team building
- Employee motivation
- or pure recreation

There are fun forms of golf for even those with little experience. Scramble golf is where a team of four all play the same ball—each gets a chance to hit. This is a fun, fast way for a large group of experienced and not so experienced golfers to have fun! During hot summer months, try to book golf tournaments early in the morning or late in the day.

The following pages feature a variety of golf courses.

ADMINISTRATION/GOAL SETTING

- Planning, objectives, action plan, budget setting
- Event planning, layout of event
- Tournament calendar
- Mailing list, timelines, committee assignments
- Logo design, brochure design
- Sponsorship packages, sales
- Signage, prizes, auction
- Award Ceremony

COMMITTEE FUNCTIONS/ A GOOD WORKING COMMITTEE IS A MUST

- Securing local clubs for the tournaments
- Developing a calendar for planning the event
- Establishing and obtaining prizes
- Planning additional fund-raising activities, such as auctions and raffles
- Solicitation of sponsors and "thank you's" after the tournament is held
- Arranging publicity and promotion participation
- Provisions for proper records, including accounting, contestant entries, etc.
- Notifying the committees of all meetings

SPONSORSHIP DEVELOPMENT

- Design packages
- Solicitation, sales, contact list
- Pro/Am packages

SUB-COMMITTEES

- Sponsorship committee: secures sponsors
- Publicity committee: news releases, media exposure
- Prize committee: set and obtain tournament prizes and tee gifts

VOLUNTEERS

- Contact charities to help with parties, day of event registration, etc.

FORMAT FOR DAYS OF PLAY

- Sponsor contests, putting contest, hole-in-ones
- Layout signage
- Tournament play, format of day's play
- Catering services
- Awards, auction

13737-202nd Avenue N.E.
Woodinville, Washington 98072
Contact: Catering Department
(425) 883-4770
Office Hours: Mon–Fri 9am–5pm;
Saturday tours by appointment

ONE OF THE REGION'S MOST CHALLENGING GOLF COURSES

Bear Creek Country Club is a world-class facility complemented by an 18 hole golf course that ranks among the region's most challenging. The club house offers the finest in amenities, food and beverage and service. The club is located 3.5 miles north of Redmond, just minutes from Bellevue and only 25 minutes from downtown Seattle.

• Holes: 18 • Length: 6,422 yards • Par: 72 • Slope 130 •

PGA Golf Professionals

Our golf professionals are available to help you plan your entire event from 18 holes of golf to driving or putting competitions. Pre-tournament clinics are available.

Pro shop

Our fully-stocked pro shop includes:

- **Apparel:** select from men's and women's golf apparel by Ashworth, Polo, Descente, Cutter & Buck, Haley, Tail
- **Equipment:** Titleist, Ping, Spalding, Cobra, Callaway; we also offer custom fitting
- **Accessories:** Foot Joy shoes, Belding golf bags, towels, hats, gloves, golf balls, tees and more

Additional services

- Tournament scoring by our staff professionals
- Driving range, practice chipping and putting greens
- Rental clubs including Callaway Big Bertha irons and woods
- A full fleet of power carts
- Gift certificates

Banquet and event facilities

Our banquet facilities accommodate groups up to 400 and feature panoramic views of the ninth green and reflecting lakes with illuminated fountains. Bear Creek Country Club offers full-service, in-house catering with customized menus.

Availability and terms

Tournaments are booked up to one year in advance. A $3,000 deposit is required. For banquet facilities, reservations may be made up to a year in advance, but we are happy to accommodate shorter notice, depending on space availability.

See page 145 under Banquet, Meeting & Event Sites.

MAPLEWOOD GOLF COURSE

4050 Maple Valley Highway • Renton, Washington
Contact: Catering
(425) 235-5044; Fax (425) 235-0937
Hours: Mon–Fri 9am–5pm, Saturdays by appointment

18 HOLES THAT WILL TEST GOLFERS OF ANY LEVEL

Maplewood Golf Course offers a wide variety of holes which will test golfers of any level. The front side features water on seven of its nine holes, and the backside will challenge even the straightest drives with its tight, tree-lined fairways. Enhancing this scenic course is the elegant Maplewood Greens, a full service catering, meeting, and event facility specializing in custom menus to compliment any function.

• LENGTH: 5,816 YARDS • PAR: 72

PGA Golf Professionals

Our experienced professionals are on hand to facilitate your golfing adventure from start to finish. Maplewood Golf Course gives personalized attention to every aspect of your tournament or event.

Pro Shop

- A fine selection of quality equipment, apparel, and accessories
- Golf Carts available for an additional fee

Availability and tournament information

A deposit is required and is refundable up to six months in advance of the scheduled event date. Tournament play costs $27 per guest, which includes green fees, tournament setup fees, and a $4.00 merchandise allowance at our Pro Shop. Please contact Maplewood Golf Course for further information.

Additional services

- Putting contests
- Corporate team building events
- Driving range privileges

Banquet and event facilities

Maplewood Greens is the perfect setting for any occasion from the all day business seminar and meeting to a formal corporate dinner featuring our full service in-house catering. Maplewood Greens offers a picturesque 4,000 square foot ballroom which will accommodate more than 300 guests. This spacious facility may also be divided into four separate rooms to host a smaller guest list. Each room extends onto an outdoor patio overlooking a magnificent fountain on the 9th hole. An outdoor cathedral tent is available in addition to the four banquet rooms.

THE PERFECT SETTING FOR YOUR SPECIAL EVENT

Maplewood Greens commands a breathtaking view of the beautifully landscaped Maplewood Golf Course, the perfect setting for your special event. Our new banquet and meeting facility exudes all the charm and elegance of an exclusive country club while remaining readily available to serve you and your guests.

See page 231 under Banquet, Meeting & Event Sites.

7108 Lakewood Drive West Street
Tacoma, Washington 98467
Contact: Gerry Mehlert
(253) 473-3033; Fax (253) 471-9266
Hours: Dawn to Dusk
Web site: www.tacomaparks.com

Meadow Park Golf Course offers 27 Holes of golfing enjoyment:

• a challenging **71-par, 18-hole** championship course of **6,093 yards** •

• an executive **29-par, 9-hole** course of **1,475 yards** •

Lined with magnificent fir and oak trees, Meadow Park offers a challenging yet relatively flat golf course. Suitable for players of any experience or ability and dry in the winter, Meadow Park welcomes individual players, large groups, and tournaments.

Tee times are available up to one week in advance.

Special Meadow Park features:

- **Lessons** are available for groups and individuals
- **Driving range:** partially covered with 35 stations
- **Pro shop:** fully equipped for all your golfing needs
- **Restaurant:** Mulligans offers a full menu to players on the 18-hole course; juice, pop, and beer are also available while playing
- **Chipping area**
- **Practice putting greens**

Tournaments, availability and terms

Meadow Park provides partial and full-service tournament operations. Weekday and weekend shotgun starts are available. We recommend that you schedule tournaments well in advance; reservations may be made as early as January 2nd of the calendar year. Please call for further information.

Banquet and special event facilities

Meadow Park provides in-house catering through Mulligans restaurant and lounge. Mulligans banquet room accommodates up to 65 guests, but larger groups may be accommodated using the restaurant, lounge, patio, and tents. Our catered meals range from hamburger barbecues to sit-down dinners.

Please call for information or reservations:
(253) 473-3033

ARLINGTON

Gleneagle Golf Club — 7619 Country Club Dr., Arlington WA 98223 *See page 194*
(360) 435-6713, Fax (360) 435-4769

AUBURN

Auburn Golf Course — 29630 S.E. Green River Road, Auburn WA 98092
(253) 833-2350

Jade Greens Public Golf Course — 18330 S.E. Lake Holm Road, Auburn WA 98092
(253) 931-8562

BELLEVUE

Bellevue Municipal Golf Course — 5500 140th N.E., Bellevue WA 98005
(425) 452-7250, Fax (425) 869-3857

BELLINGHAM

Belleingham Golf & Country Club — 3729 Meridian St., Bellingham WA 98225
(360) 733-5381 or (360) 733-3450

Lake Padden Golf Course — 4882 Samish Way, Bellingham WA 98226
(360) 738-7400

Sudden Valley Golf & Country Club — 2145 Lake Whatcom Blvd., Bellingham WA 98226
(360) 734-6435

BLAINE

Semi-Ah-Moo Golf & Country Club — 8720 Semiahmoo Parkway, Blaine WA 98230
(360) 371-7005

BOTHELL

Wayne Public Golf Course — 16721 96th Avenue N.E., Bothell WA 98011
(425) 485-6237 or (425) 486-4714

BREMERTON

Gold Mountain Public Golf Club — 7263 West Belfair Valley Road, Bremerton WA 98312
(360) 415-5432 or (206) 464-1175, Fax (360) 415-6880

Kitsap Golf & Country Club — 3885 NW Golf Hill Rd., Bremerton WA 98312
(360) 373-5101 or (360) 377-0166

Rolling Hills Golf Course — 2485 N.E. McWilliams Rd., Bremerton WA 98311
(360) 479-1212

BURLINGTON

Avalon Golf Course — 19345 Kelleher Road, Burlington WA 98233
(360) 757-1900 or (800) 624-0202, Fax (360) 757-2555

CARNATION

Carnation Golf Course — 1810 W. Snoqualmie River Rd. N.E., Carnation WA 98014
(206) 583-0314, Fax (425) 333-6103

ENUMCLAW

Enumclaw Golf Course — 45220 288th S.E., Enumclaw WA 98022
(360) 825-2827

FALL CITY

Snoqualmie Falls Golf Course — 35109 S.E. Fish Hatchery Road, Fall City WA 98024
(425) 222-5244

Tall Chief Public Golf Course — 1313 W. Snoqualmie River Road S.E., Fall City WA 98024
(425) 222-5911

Twin Rivers Golf Course — 4446 Preston-Fall City Road S.E., Fall City WA 98024
(425) 222-7575

FEDERAL WAY

Christy's Golf Range — 37712 28th Avenue S., Federal Way WA 98003
(253) 927-0644

FREELAND

Holmes Harbor Golf Course — 5023 Harbor Hills Drive, Freeland WA 98249
(360) 331-2363

GIG HARBOR

Gig Harbor Golf Club — 6909 Artondale Drive N.W., Gig Harbor WA 98335
(253) 851-2378 or (253) 851-2428

Madronna Links Golf Course — 3604 22nd Avenue N.W., Gig Harbor WA 98335
(253) 851-5193

KENT

Meridian Valley Golf & Country Club — 24830 136th Ave. S.E., Kent WA 98042
(253) 631-3131

Riverbend Golf Complex — 2019 W. Meeker, Kent WA 98032
(253) 854-3673

LYNNWOOD

Lynnwood Municipal Golf — 20200 68th Avenue W, Lynnwood WA 98036
(425) 672-4653

MAPLE VALLEY

Elk Run Golf Course — 22500 S.E. 275th Pl., Maple Valley WA 98038
(425) 432-8800 or (800) 244-8631 Golf Course, Fax (425) 432-1907

Lake Wilderness Golf Course — 25400 Witte Rd. S.E., Maple Valley WA 98038 *See page 227*
Events (425) 432-8038 or Pro Shop (425) 432-9405

MARYSVILLE

Battle Creek Public Golf Course — 6006 Meridian Avenue N., Marysville WA 98271
(360) 659-7931 or (800) 655-7931, Fax (360) 659-3431

Cedarcrest Municipal Golf Course — 6810 87th St. N.E., Marysville WA 98270
(360) 659-3566

MOUNTLAKE TERRACE

Ballinger Lakes Golf Course — 23000 Lake View Dr., Mountlake Terrace WA 98043
(425) 775-6467

Nile Golf & Country Club — 6601-244th S.W., Mountlake Terrace WA 98043 *See pages 243 & 546*
Events (425) 775-2412 or Pro Shop (425) 776-5154
Fax (425) 744-5622

MUKILTEO

Harbour Pointe Golf Club — 11817 Harbor Pointe Blvd., Mukilteo WA 98275
(800) 233-3128 or (425) 355-6060

NEWCASTLE

The Golf Club at Newcastle — 15500 Six Penny Lane, Newcastle WA 98059 *See page 242*
(425) 793-5566

NORTH BEND

Cascade Golf Course — 14303 436th Avenue S.E., North Bend WA 98045
(425) 888-0227, Fax (425) 888-6600

OLYMPIA

Capitol City Golf Club — 5225 Yelm Hwy. S.E., Olympia WA 98513
(360) 491-5111, Fax (360) 493-6067

Delphi Golf Course — 6340 Neylon Dr. S.W., Olympia WA 98512
(360) 357-6437

Indian Summer Golf & Country Club — 5900 Troon Ln. S.E., Olympia WA 98501 *See page 211*
(360) 923-1075, Fax (360) 923-9037

ORTING

High Cedars Golf Club — 14604 149th Street Court E, Orting WA 98360
(360) 893-3171

PORT LUDLOW

Port Ludlow Golf Course — 751 Highland Drive, Port Ludlow WA 98365
(360) 437-0272

PORT ORCHARD

Horseshoe Lake Golf Course & Restaurant — 1250 S.W. Clubhouse Court, Port Orchard WA 98367
(253) 857-3326, Fax (253) 857-4352

McCormick Woods Golf Course — 5155 McCormick Woods Drive S.W., Port Orchard WA 98367
(800) 323-0130 or (360) 895-0130

PORT TOWNSEND

Chevy Chase Golf Club — 7401 Cape George Road, Port Townsend WA 98368
(800) 385-8722

PUYALLUP

Lipoma Firs Golf Course — 18615 110th Avenue E, Puyallup WA 98374
(253) 841-4396 or (800) 649-4396

Meridian Greens — 9705 136th Street E, Puyallup WA 98373
(253) 845-7504

REDMOND

Willows Run Golf Club — 10402 Willows Road N.E., Redmond WA 98052
(425) 883-1200

RENTON

Maplewood Greens — 4050 Maple Valley Hwy., Renton WA 98058 *See pages 231 & 484*
Events (425) 235-5044 or Pro Shop (425) 6800

SAMMAMISH

The Plateau Club — 25625 E. Plateau Dr., Sammamish WA 98074 *See page 251*
(425) 868-6063, Fax (425) 836-4421

SEATAC

Tyee Valley Golf Club — 2401 S. 192nd, Seatac WA 98188
(206) 878-3540

SEATTLE

Greenlake Golf Course — 5701 W. Green Lake Way N., Seattle WA 98103
(206) 632-2280

Jackson Park Golf Club — 1000 N.E. 135th, Seattle WA 98125
(206) 363-4747, Fax (206) 361-6636

Jefferson Park Golf Club — 4101 Beacon S, Seattle WA 98108
(206) 762-4513

West Seattle Golf Course — 4470-35th Ave. S.W., Seattle WA 98126
Events (206) 935-0991 or General (206) 935-5187

SEQUIM

Dungeness Golf & Country Club — 1965 Woodcock Road, Sequim WA 98382
(800) 447-6826 x. 4 or (360) 683-6344, Fax (360) 683-1709

Sunland Golf & Country Club — 109 Hilltop Drive, Sequim WA 98382
(360) 683-6800

SNOHOMISH

Echo Falls Country Club — 20414-121st Ave. S.E., Snohomish WA 98296
(206) 362-3000, x238

Snohomish Golf Club — 7805-147th Avenue S.E., Snohomish WA 98290
(360) 568-2676 or (800) 560-2676

SNOQUALMIE

Mount Si Golf Course & Driving Range — 9010 Boalch Avenue S.E., Snoqualmie WA 98065
(425) 888-1541

Snoqualmie Ridge Golf Club — 36005 S.E. Ridge St., Snoqualmie WA 98065 *See page 281*
(425) 396-6000

SPANAWAY

Classic Country Club — 4908 208th Street E., Spanaway WA 98387
(253) 847-4440, Fax (253) 846-9868

STANWOOD

Kayak Point Golf Course — 15711 Marine Dr., Stanwood WA 98292
(360) 652-9676, Fax (360) 652-3812

SUMNER

Tapp Island Golf Course — 20818 Island Park Wy. E., Sumner WA 98390
Events (253) 862-6616 or Golf (253) 862-7011, Fax (253) 862-3310

TACOMA

Allenmore Public Golf Course — 2125 S. Cedar, Tacoma WA 98405
(253) 627-7211

Brookdale Golf Course — 1802 Brookdale Road E., Tacoma WA 98445
(253) 537-4400 or (800) 281-2428, Fax (253) 537-0640

Ft. Steilacoom Golf Course — 8202 87th Avenue S.W., Tacoma WA 98498
(253) 588-0613

Highlands Golf Course — 1400 N. Highland Parkway, Tacoma WA 98406
(253) 759-3622

Lake Spanaway Golf Course — 15602 Pacific Avenue, Tacoma WA 98444
(253) 531-3660

Meadow Park Golf Course — 7108 Lakewood Dr. S.W., Tacoma WA 98467 *See page 485*
(253) 473-3033, Fax (253) 471-9266

North Shore Golf Course — 4101 North Shore Blvd. N.E., Tacoma WA 98422
(253) 927-1375 or (800) 447-1375, Fax (253) 838-5898

Pacific Lutheran University Golf Course — 754 South 124th, Tacoma WA 98444
(253) 535-7393

TUKWILA

Foster Golf Links — 13500 Interurban Avenue S., Tukwila WA 98168
(206) 242-4221

WOODINVILLE

Bear Creek Country Club — 13737-202nd Ave. N.E., Woodinville WA 98072 *See pages 145 & 483*
(425) 883-4770

Wellington Hills Golf Course — 7026-240th Street S.E., Woodinville WA 98072
(425) 485-5589

YELM

Nisqually Valley Golf Course — PO Box 5160, Yelm WA 98597
(800) 352-2645

NOTES

Ice Carvings

❖❖❖

HELPFUL HINTS

Ice Carving is a specialty art form. From the casting of the crystal clear block of ice to the careful hand carving process, each piece is individually created and unique.

- **Ice carvings make spectacular centerpieces:** Used as the centerpiece of your buffet table, an ice carving makes a dramatic visual enhancement to your room decor.
- **Select from a variety of styles:** Ice carvings come in every shape and size, from dramatic winged birds to romantic hearts, woven baskets for floral arrangements to specially carved wine baskets.
- **Ice carvings last** six to nine hours indoors and up to four hours outdoors in the sun without losing their shape.
- **Be sure you let your caterer or facility coordinator know you will be using an ice carving** so that they can plan the layout of your buffet table and place it near an electrical outlet. Ice carvings are shown at their best when lighted from underneath.
- **Have your ice carver coordinate the delivery and set-up with your caterer.** You don't want your ice carving delivered too early or too late. Your caterer is the best person to coordinate delivery times and set-up requirements.
- **Ask about having your ice carving created on-site:** Your guests will enjoy watching as your block of ice turns into a work of art.

Contact: Janson Iwakami
(425) 255-5255
Web site: www.amazingice.com

When you want your event to be extra special, an Amazing Ice Sculpture is the answer.

- The Best in Corporate Logos
- Colored Ice logos
- Cocktail Party Ice Bars
- Sushi/Seafood Ice Bars
- Ice Luges
- Wedding Sculptures
- Theme Party Sculptures
- Tabletop Centerpieces
- Ice Columns
- Sorbet Dishes
- Ice Bowls

Over 11 years of high quality standards and reasonable prices.

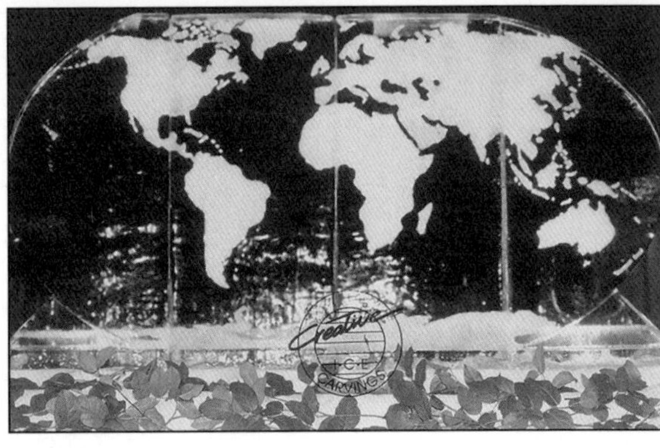

Contact: Steve Cox
(253) 941-7248
Web site: www.creativeice.com

COOL DECOR

An ice sculpture from Creative Ice Carvings is a beautifully engineered object that could be the coolest part of your event. Your guests won't believe it's ice until they touch it! Let Steve Cox, owner of Creative Ice Carvings, work his frozen magic for your special event.

Your imagination is the only limit

Display an elegant custom centerpiece at your next event. Creative Ice Carvings can recreate most corporate logos and has done logo sculptures for many Northwest businesses. Ask Steve to sculpt your team mascot or choose from a variety of his designs. For a quote, fax your idea and/or logo to (253) 941-0917.

Steve's hand-carved sculptures are seen in major hotels, fine restaurants, social clubs and other businesses in the Puget Sound area. Each sculpture is delivered and set up in a clean, waterproof backlit display.

Lingering beauty

The ice sculptures last between six and nine hours under normal conditions without losing their shape. In the sun, the sculptures look good for about four hours. Steve said he does sculptures for many outdoor events without a problem.

Special touches

Steve works with crystal clear ice he makes himself. He also can use colored lights to accent the sculpture and can match the colors of your event. For a different look, Steve will pack snow (created in the sculpting process) into the indentations. If desired, Steve can bring a chunk of ice and sculpt on site so guests can witness the cool change.

Experience

Creative Ice Carvings has been in business for 14 years. Steve does an average of 10–15 sculptures a week at corporate events, birthday parties, weddings and other occasions. The company does ice carvings full-time so they can always squeeze someone into their schedule—although a month's notice is suggested. "We're here for service and we're here to make things special," Steve says.

Creative Ice Carvings
The highest quality and service available.

Meeting & Event Planners

❖❖❖

MEETING AND EVENT PLANNERS

HELPFUL HINTS

Event planning services: Event and meeting planners can arrange as little or as much of the event as needed. How they bill for their services varies depending on the consultant or job. Some bill hourly, others by the project. Even though you are paying them for their time, they will more than pay for their services in most cases with their knowledge, experience, and contacts.

Why hire a professional event coordinator? People are often under the misconception that they can save money by doing it all themselves, when in fact it can cost more—not only monetarily, but also in time and headaches! The responsibility of planning an event, especially to a new planner, can be overwhelming. When you hire a professional planner, you hire the confidence that the event will run without any major problems. Experienced planners have tried it all, and have found what works and what doesn't. You can benefit from their experiences.

Time alone is a reason for hiring a professional: If you delegate this job to an employee, that person will make this event a priority and regular duties may get pushed aside. The fees of the professional will not come near the cost for a full-time employee's time.

Coordinator's relationships and knowledge: Established relationships with vendors allow the coordinator to get the best quality and value within budget. Vendors will go the extra mile to make sure this coordinator is pleased, because they know potential business will sprout from a successful event.

Expertise ensures a successful event: True event expertise cannot be learned from a textbook; it comes from trial and error and experience. It is better to hire the coordinator with years of experience than leaving an employee lost in the hundreds of details that will undoubtedly surround an event. Every event has its flaws, but a good coordinator handles those problems before they become serious.

Destination Management Companies (DMC): These companies are hired by conventions and out-of-state planners. They specialize in packaging group and VIP events. They can customize local "activities" to fit the planner's need.

Selecting a coordinator: Talk to different consultants before making your final decision. Find out by referral who is familiar with your type of meeting or event. Don't be afraid to ask questions or see a portfolio of their work. Ask for and check references. The person or company you select should be someone with whom you feel very comfortable professionally and personally—you will be working closely together over the next several months.

Finding a convention, banquet, or meeting site: A professional planner can be very helpful in finding a site to meet your requirements. Some planners have video tapes, photographs, and specifications for various sites. Their experience in having had an event at that site can be incredibly helpful.

IMPORTANT NOTE: Make sure you are specific about the services you will need and your budget. A planner can offer a variety of suggestions to save time, money, and energy. Be sure to read any and all contracts before signing them so there is no confusion later about who is responsible for what and how much it will cost.

Serving the Northwest for Over 20 Years!

425•277•1777

E-mail: bestshow@msn.com

Web site: www.action-entertainment.com

ENTERTAINMENT • INFLATABLES • LOCATION • CATERING
Your full event planning company!

We take the worry out of event planning.

From Company Picnics to Holiday Parties, Team Building to Graduation Parties, we'll help you plan an outstanding event that gets all the participants involved. Our team of event planning specialists will help you find the venue or site, select a caterer, coordinate interactive games, activities and entertainment, arrange for decoration and flowers, or whatever else you may need.

We cater delicious barbecue, the perfect addition to your company picnic. An event including our fun, games, and team building will work up your appetite. Count on us to satisfy your hunger for good food and quality entertainment.

We offer a wide variety of inflatables for children and adults. These popular items add fun and personality to any special event. We have something to complement the themes and spirit of any occasion.

We've been getting results for over 20 years!

The Original A Action Entertainment has been taking care of clients' needs for over 20 years. A few of our satisfied customers include:

- Microsoft
- Alaska Airlines
- McDonalds Corporation
- AAA of Washington
- Costco
- Phil Smart Mercedes
- Starbucks
- AT&T Wireless
- IBM
- Space Needle
- Bally Total Fitness
- JC Penney
- EMP
- Baugh Construction
- Verizon
- Four Seasons
- Boeing
- Kinkos

Our commitment to you . . .

is to redefine and build solid working relationships, and to facilitate personal development in a party environment. Fun activities break down barriers, enhance communication, and build team spirit through laughter and interaction. With A Action Entertainment, your corporate or school event will be the best ever!

For an unforgettable event,
call (425) 277-1777.

For more information about our Game and Team Building Activities, see page 462
For details about our Disc Jockey Services, see page 441.

Preferred Vendor of Microsoft

Contact: Kristin Berry
(800) 981-7469
Fax (360) 419-3151
E-mail: info@actionevent.com
Web site: www.actionevent.com

Full-service Event Planning

We are party professionals specializing in spectacular high-quality events including:

- Corporate Events
- Company Picnics
- Entertainment
- Preferred vendor at Microsoft and Seattle Center
- Conventions
- Holiday Parties
- Team Olympics
- Company Meetings
- Themed Events
- Entertainment Packages
- And more…

Total Event and Meeting Management

We can provide venues, caterers, entertainers, music, transportation, decorations, flowers, interactive games, casino, unique activities and entertainment. We provide services to meet your every need in order to make your event a success.

Experience

We have planned highly successful events for a variety of companies including Microsoft, Alaska Airlines, Starbuck's, Northwest Composites, Onyx Software, Carlyle Inc., US West, Wilder Construction, Harrah's Casino and Overlake Hospital.

> *"I cannot express enough how much I enjoyed working with your staff. They pulled off a party for 3,500 people in only a couple of weeks time. Their energy, professionalism, and creative planning will continue to catapult your business to success."*—Microsoft

> *"We've been holding our company picnics for 13 years and I can honestly say that Action Events organized the greatest event we ever had. People at work are still talking about it. I can't begin to tell you how nice it was to just enjoy the picnic instead of worrying about setting up, cleaning, cooking, and making sure everyone was having a good time. We are anxiously waiting to see what surprises Action Events has in store for our Christmas party."*—Costco

Winning Philosophy

Action Events' mission and number one priority is to facilitate our client's needs. This winning philosophy is what makes Action Events one of the top event planning companies in the Northwest, and a Preferred Vendor of Microsoft.

Don't Lift A Finger — Just The Phone

(800) 981-SHOW (7469)

Andy Mirkovich Productions

Entertainment, Meetings, and Events

11811 N.E. First Street, Suite A-302 • Bellevue, Washington 98005-3033
Contact: Margaret or J.P. Perugini (425) 454-4817
Fax (425) 646-2988 • E-mail: info@mirkprod.com
Web site: www.mirkprod.com

Entertainment and Meeting Planning Services

Andy Mirkovich Productions is the Northwest's Premier Meeting Planner. Andy Mirkovich Productions provides Entertainment, Event, and Meeting Management Services, allowing clients to remain focused on their core business while taking advantage of AMP's competencies in these fields of expertise. Andy Mirkovich Productions:

- Produces more meetings than any other Northwest meeting planning organization
- Is the *Senior* Entertainment Consultant in the Northwest with more than 37 years experience booking top local and National Acts **(see page 430)**
- Works with clients to develop events that create excitement and establish a signature to their function
- Has been voted Seattle Meeting Professional International 1996 Vendor of the Year
- Has been awarded the Microsoft Vendor Honor Roll Award by the Corporate Services Group for 1995, 1996 & 1997
- Has a Certified Meeting Professional on staff

Andy Mirkovich Productions will consult with you on your next event and can provide the following residual services:

- **Professional meeting planning**
- **Consultation and management**
- **Theme design and decoration**
- **Vendor coordination**
- **Catering hospitality**
- **Local, regional and celebrity entertainment**
- **Interactive entertainment**
- **Ground transportation**
- **Site/Venue selection**
- **Audio visual services**
- **Registration and signage**
- **Security**

Professional affiliations

Bellevue Chamber of Commerce; Convention Liaison Council; East King County Convention & Visitors Bureau; International Association of Fairs & Expositions; International Theatrical Agencies Association; Meeting Professionals International; National Association of Catering Executives; Oregon Fairs Association; Seattle-King County Convention & Visitors Bureau; Washington Fairs Association.

Please call us today at (425) 454-4817.

Visit our web page at *www.mirkprod.com* or e-mail at *info@mirkprod.com*

BK Classic Coordinators

(425) 385-3570
By appoinment only
bkclassic@hotmail.com

BK Classic Coordinators is a premier Event and Meeting Planning Service

BK Classic Coordinators is dedicated to assist you with planning your special event. You will receive personal attention that will ensure everything is tailored to your specific needs. We have relationships with many of the areas finest caterers, banquet facilities, hotels and transportation services. Your complete satisfaction is our primary goal.

Benefit from our experience

With over 35 years of experience between them, Rosa Beck and Kitty Kuhnly, have planned events from large New Years Eve Celebrations, Weddings, Conferences and more. By choosing BK Classics you will receive a team that is creative, thorough, able to problem solve, and adept at meeting the needs of your event.

Venues that can be planned together with you...

- Church functions
- Business meetings
- Seminars
- Banquets
- Corporate events
- Conventions
- Theme parties
- Weddings

Let us plan your next event!

With BK Classics, you can have confidence that your event will run smoothly.

 Please let this business know that you heard about them from the Bravo! Event Resource Guide.

Contact: Jennifer Monteleone, APR
(360) 563-1161 or
Toll-free (877) 591-8488
Fax (360) 563-9211
E-mail: info@coralrief.com
Web site: www.coralrief.com

Extraordinary Events Start By

Creating a unique and quirky event concept that indelibly delivers your message. That's where we come in.

Our team consists of some of the most creative and innovative event professionals in the Northwest. We're known to resourcefully manage one-of-a-kind events specifically tailored for our client's individual event challenge.

Our event services include:

- Employee Award & Recognition Programs
- Executive Leadership Retreats
- Company Parties
- Entertainment Selection
- Grand Openings
- Marketing Support
- Presentation Development
- Quirky Team Buildings
- Theme Development
- Vendor Selection & Management

Generating Kudos Every Time

Every member of our team has served in corporate marketing and event management positions, and with more than 20 years of combined experience, we know how it feels to sit in the hot seat.

We work diligently and with the utmost integrity to ensure that our clients receive rave reviews and the accolades they deserve.

"After two weeks, I am still receiving rave reviews on our employee picnic. This is quite unusual for our employees and is a testament to the incredible job you and your staff did in putting this event together. We can't wait to work with you again for our picnic next year."

—Greg, Bothell

"To the team at Coral Rief: thank you!!! I appreciate your creativity, running with the ideas we came up with and prodding me for answers to keep us on schedule. This is what makes you so successful and of course, fun to work with!! I really didn't have to do anything except for make decisions on little things, which was so nice. It was very successful, and I've gotten a number of nice compliments, to which I owe to you!"

—Sandy, Redmond

Give us a call to learn how innovatively quirky your next event can be.

Coral Rief Weddings & Special Events
Toll-free (877) 591-8488
or visit us at ***www.coralrief.com***

Bellevue, Washington
(425) 467-8129
E-mail: designperfecttoo@msn.com
Web site: www.designperfecttoo.com

Same Great Service . . .
Only Our Look Has Changed!!

Bringing the picture in your mind to life . . .

Do you have a vision of your special event, but need help pulling the details together? Too much to do, too little time? We can relieve your stress! Our full-service event planning and production company focuses on your special event so that you can continue business without interruption. We will help you bring to life that picture in your mind.

The magic that dazzles your guests . . .

We take the time to understand the needs of each client. Often, we establish long-term relationships with them. We want you to relax and enjoy your special event as much as your guests do. You should be able to join them and enjoy the compliments. Design Perfect, Inc. will make you sparkle, bring magic to your event, and simply dazzle your guests.

We can plan your special event for you . . .

Our event specialists work closely with you to orchestrate the many details that make any affair a memorable and successful event. From start to finish, we handle all aspects of planning and implementing a special occasion. We will leave your guests with something to talk about for years to come, whether it's a company picnic, trade show, private party, corporate luncheon, or product launch. An event planned by Design Perfect, Inc. will leave even the most sophisticated guests in awe!

Visit our new web site for an online proposal!
www.designperfecttoo.com

See page 350 under Catering/Food & Beverage Services and page 397 under Decorations, Themes & Props.

Bringing focus to your special events.

2629 Stonecrest Lane N.W.
Olympia, Washington 98502
(360) 867-9717; Fax (360) 438-8238
E-mail: eddy@eweventco.com
Web site: www.eweventco.com

Bringing focus to events around the Puget Sound

EW Eventco specializes in helping clients establish and carry out their event goals. We provide the expertise that allows you to produce a memorably successful event within your allocated budget. We want you to come to your event with confidence that the details have been efficiently resolved—without compromising the professionalism your company and its guests expect.

Bringing flexible expertise to your event

Although golf tournaments remain an Eventco specialty, we offer a wide variety of flexible services. We can be involved in your event to any degree that you deem appropriate. Our expertise extends to everything from site selection and entertainment to bid solicitation and contract negotiations. We will also arrange for caterers and musicians. Whether you seek comprehensive special event planning, or just a helping hand along the way, we can provide the professional services to ensure that you meet your objectives.

Taking the stress out of your event

We will transform your next meeting or event into a cost effective masterpiece, sparing you the added stress of coordinating all the details by yourself. With our professional assistance, you and your company will inspire, motivate, or excite your guests. We can sell them or impress them, but we always show them a good time. Whether you're planning a company picnic or a quarterly management meeting, our services allow you and everyone else in your organization to participate in the fun.

ESTABLISHING A NEW STANDARD

"[Thank you Eventco] for your part in making K2's annual summer picnic a success. The comments following the event have been extremely positive. Your involvement in the planning and execution of our picnic was invaluable . . . Associates at K2 have been especially complimentary about the arrangements made for 'kids activities.' Eventco's involvement . . . has established a new standard for the K2 company picnic." —Robert Moynan
Director of Human Resources
K2 Corporation

Please call for a free consultation

(360) 867-9717

P.O. Box 3427 • Redmond, Washington 98073-3427
(425) 898-1064; Fax (425) 868-8015
E-mail: service@eventsavvy.net

Event Savvy Expertise

We're comprised of professional meeting planners that strategically plan and facilitate corporate meetings, events, and incentive programs. With our experience and broad range of resources, Event Savvy can spearhead the planning and facilitation of an entire tactical program, or we can supplement the efforts of you and your staff in some key areas of your program. We respect the unique nuances of corporate cultures and meld well with our clients' situations. Our goal is to provide a user-friendly, quality program with a thorough communication process so that you have a positive experience and accomplish your objectives efficiently. Event Savvy specializes in the following types of events:

- ***Seminar Series***
- ***Ship Inaugurations***
- ***Incentive Programs***
- ***Product Launches***
- ***Team-building Events***
- ***Training Programs/Trips***
- ***Management Meetings***
- ***Employee Appreciation Events***
- ***VIP Client/Vendor Trips***
- ***Award & Dedication Ceremonies***

Event Savvy Strategy

We provide the support you need so that you enjoy your event and its successful results, while we handle the laborious details. We structure every program in a very systematic, organized fashion. Our creative abilities add a unique flair to give a fresh perspective to your event. Our comprehensive approach includes:

- **Initial Planning Phase:** Goal, Theme, and Budget development; Communication Plan development and maintenance
- **Logistical Phase:** Venue selection and negotiation; Audio/Visual, Catering, Decoration, Activities/Entertainment; Collateral Materials (i.e., brochures, gifts, invitations, etc.); RSVP Administration Process; Management Tracking Reports (i.e., attendance counts, budget)
- **Implementation Phase:** On-site Management of event
- **Follow-up Phase:** Evaluation reports, Accounting reconciliation

Event Savvy will help you to accomplish your goals and make a positive return on your investment. We invite you to give us a call with your questions. We would be happy to discuss your event planning needs and customize a proposal for you that would achieve results in a systematic, fiscally sound, effective manner.

Comprehensive services – Creative ideas – Successful results
Please contact us for a free consultation (425) 898-1064

16300-126th Avenue N.E.
Woodinville, Washington 98072
(206) 849-9770
Web site: www.nweventsuccess.com

Event Planning and Management

Event Success has over twelve years of experience in high quality events. If you would like help planning from beginning to end or if you are just looking for some assistance, Event Success is able to help you as much or as little as you need!

Event Success can provide professional meeting planning, consultation and management services by coordinating venues, caterers, entertainers, music, transportation, flowers, interactive games, casinos, audio-visual services, unique activities and entertainment. We take care of the logistics so that you can concentrate on the content and business goals.

Whatever your celebration, we can help you make your special occasion a memorable one! Our staff's creativity can transfom an idea into a theme for your special occasion no matter how large or small.

We are meeting and event professionals specializing in spectacular high quality events including:

Corporate Retreats
Holiday Parties
Entertainment
Conferences
Retirement Parties
Incentive Events
Business Meetings
Marketing Events
Convention Ancillary Events
Congratulation Celebrations
Company Picnics

Weddings
Birthdays
Anniversaries
Graduations
Showers
Holiday Parties
Family Reunions
Bar/Bat Mitzvahs
House Warmings
Children's Parties
and Much, Much More...

We provide services to meet your needs
in order to make your event a success!

See page 542 under Picnic & Recreation Sites.

Northwest Events and Parties

Specialists in Creating Memorable Occasions

4511-37th Avenue N.E. • Seattle, Washington 98105
Contacts: Marcia Evans or Portia Omdal
(206) 524-4918; Fax (206) 527-8660
E-mail: marcia@northwestevents.com or *portia@northwestevents.com*
Web site: www.northwestevents.com

Professional creativity designed to enhance your special occasion!

We provide coordination for...

Corporate parties, award banquets, or an elegant evening affair.
We also create holiday and birthday parties, anniversaries, and reunions.
...any occasion where people want to celebrate!

Northwest Events and Parties, Seattle's Premier Event Planner, is a full service coordinating company with over 10 years of experience in the Puget Sound area. Our attention to details and commitment to customer satisfaction is why we are truly specialists in creating memorable occasions.

We have carefully chosen a select group of the Northwest's finest vendors to meet any need. Our prices reflect our continual search for the highest quality of service at reasonable rates.

Our experts will help you create a memory your guests will treasure long after they leave. Let us take care of the details so you can relax and enjoy the day!

Please inquire about hosting your next event at one of our unique event facilities!

Top of the Market **in historic Pike Place Market, or**
Lake Washington Rowing Club **on Lake Union**

P.O. Box 40527 • Bellevue, Washington 98015
(425) 644-5500 or (866) 363-5500
Fax (425) 644-0691
E-mail: info@PaintItRedEvents.com
Web site: www.PaintItRedEvents.com

Puget Sound Area's Event Planning Experts

Add color to your next event with Paint It Red Event Company. We are full-service and experienced event planning experts specializing in:

- Corporate, Board and Director Retreats
- Employee Recognition Events/Parties
- Holiday Parties
- Annual, Quarterly Meetings
- Employee Enrichment Excursions
- Company Picnics
- Auctions
- Proms
- High School Graduation Parties
- And More!

We'll Make Your Event Stand Out

We offer comprehensive coordination and assistance to those involved in planning the event. Here's an overview of the services we offer:

- Consultation and Management
- Site Venue Location and Negotiation
- Catering
- Design and Decorations
- Entertainment
- Photography
- Design and Print all Promotional Materials, Invitations, and Programs
- On-Site Event Management
- Transportation Arrangements

Paint It Red Event Company is committed to providing creative, quality event planning services to our clients.

When your event has to be a success...
Paint It Red!

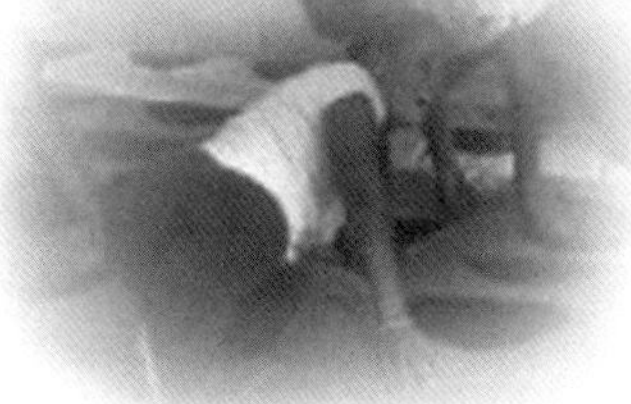

Contact: Mark Thibodeau

(360) 438-2211 or (800) 853-5867

Web site: www.partyoutfitters.com

Complete Party & Picnic Packages

You relax. We handle the details!

Site Selection • Catering • Entertainment • Games • Themes

Featuring over 100 games.

Big fun for all . . .

- Velcro Wall
- Human Spheres
- Golf Driving Challenge
- Hurling High Ball
- Wacky Trikes
- 28 ft. Inflatable Rocky Mountain Climber
- Speed Pitch
- Titanic Adventure Challenge
- Gladiator Jousting
- Big Time Bouncy Boxing
- Hoop'n It Up Basketball
- Human Gyroscope
- Inflatable Obstacle Course
- Miniature Golf
- 22' & 26' Tall Inflatable Slides
- Rodeo Roper
- Bungee Bull Ride
- Batting Cage
- Bungee Run
- Off With Your Head
- Sumo Wrestling
- Laser Tag
- Human Foosball
- NASCAN Sprinters
- Millennium Challenge

Especially for kids

- Ellie the Elephant
- Noah's Ark Bouncer
- Choo Choo Express Train
- Dalmatian Bouncer
- Moonjumps
- Giraffe Bouncer
- Cameron the Caterpillar
- Ball Pond
- Splativity
- Purple Dragon
- Winston the Whale

We're the Experts!

Party Outfitters specializes in providing fun, interactive games for special events including: team building, company picnics, trade shows, graduation parties, holiday parties and promotions. When quality, dependability, safety and experience count, hire the pros at Party Outfitters.

Customer Comments

"I would like to compliment your staff on doing an excellent job for our Senior All Night party. They arrived early, were very polite and courteous." —Beverly F., Mossyrock, WA

"Your staff were prompt and helpful. Their presence was very reassuring that nothing would go wrong...thank you for making it so easy for me to plan an enjoyable day in the sun!" —Kelly B., Portland, OR

DELIVERED • INSURED • STAFFED
Call for a FREE fun-filled 36-page catalog and RESERVE EARLY:
(360) 438-2211, (800) 853-5867
Visit our on-line catalog at *www.partyoutfitters.com/*

RED-LETTER DAY

2406-2nd Avenue West
Seattle, Washington 98119
(206) 691-9979; Fax (206) 691-5422
Contact: Kelley Moore • E-mail: kelley@red-letterday.com
Web site: www.red-letterday.com

Exceptional Events

From large corporate events and conferences to small technical training sessions, Red-Letter Day is a technology-oriented full service organization with the capability to plan and manage any or all aspects of your event worldwide. We work with you toward a common purpose, apply our expertise to your marketing objective, and create a unique event, which is implemented as a cost-effective solution.

We provide strategic consulting to develop event goals, messaging and marketing for your most successful event ever. Through our experience, we partner with our clients to manage each project from pre-conference preparation and content development to onsite management and post-conference evaluation. Throughout the project, we ensure that you meet your goals on time and on budget.

The following services are offered but not limited to:

- User Conferences
- Technology Seminars
- Product Launches
- Trade Shows
- Road Shows
- Company Meetings
- Production & Staging
- Budget Management
- Event Marketing
- Food & Entertainment
- Global Services
- Company Picnics
- Dinner Parties
- Cocktail Receptions
- Retirement Parties
- Themed Events

Red-Letter Day brings together highly talented designers, producers and vendors locally, nationally and internationally to create your virtual team. With Red-Letter Day program management blending the talents of all these contributors, we deliver an event that will meet your budget and exceed your expectations.

P.O. Box 40527 • Bellevue, Washington 98015
(425) 644-1044 or (800) 954-1044; Fax (425) 644-0691
E-mail: info@ReunionsWithClass.com
Web site: www.ReunionsWithClass.com

Full Service Reunion Planning Specialists

Reunions With Class is well known for coordinating memorable and individualized reunions throughout Western Washington. Our staff takes care of all the time consuming tasks involved in the planning process, allowing your reunion committee to concentrate on the important special touches that help make it a night to be remembered.

Reasons You'll Want Us Working For You

- **No Financial Worries**—We pay all deposits and up front costs. Our fee is included in the package price. We handle all contracts with facilities, caterers, photographers, and entertainment. We process and track reservations providing committees with up-to-date status on attendance.
- **Classmate Location**—We search for every class member using a variety of search tools. We are tenacious at locating as many classmates as possible to publicize the reunion.
- **Invitations**—We produce, print and mail the invitation and all follow-up reminder notices.
- **Our Web Site**—Classmates can view the reunion information, update their personal contact information, even make their reservation online. Committees have their own section and can view and print status reports not available to the rest of the class.
- **Keepsakes**—Classmates always enjoy browsing through their reunion Memory Book, which includes a class directory, along with photos and biographies submitted by members of the class. We can also arrange for the Class Photo, a great memento of all who shared in the fun evening.

And at the Reunion We Provide...

- On Site Event Management
- Photo Nametags
- Table Decorations
- Set Up, Check In, Tear Down

Reunions With Class will make your reunion experience a great one.
Why wear yourself out?
Let us do the work so you can have the fun!

VARLAND DESIGN

DISTINCTIVE PLANTSCAPING
EVENT & HOLIDAY DECOR

Showroom: 6150-6th Avenue • Seattle, Washington 98108
(206) 763-6884; Fax (206) 763-0864
E-mail: connie@varlanddesign.com
Web site: www.varlanddesign.com

Varland Design has been locally owned and operated since 1985.

From an Intimate Setting to High Profile and Corporate Affairs. Our award winning designers will bring to life an event to remember.

Varland Design specializes in...
Event planning, holiday décor, an extensive prop collection, lighting, interior plantscapes, silk & fresh floral design.

Please call for an on-site consultation.

Contact: Tony Kutch
(206) 391-4572
E-mail: tonyk@venture2inc.com
Web site: www.venture2inc.com

SITE RESEARCH, CONFERENCE MANAGEMENT & EVENT TECHNOLOGY CONSULTING

Venture2 leverages today's technology and yesterday's tradition of customer service so you can "Get It On"...on-time, on-budget, on-line and on-site.

Site Research

In today's economy, event planners are being continually tasked to do more work with fewer resources. That means you probably don't have the time to fully research a destination and select the best location for the best value. But, you are still expected to get a great rate and have the answer when someone asks, "Why didn't we stay there?" That's why it makes sense to work with Venture2.

AT NO COST TO YOU Venture2 will fully research a market, negotiate with the hotels and provide you with a comprehensive report, including the best possible pricing. It's an easy equation. We do the work you don't have time to do. We provide you with the absolute best rates by getting multiple hotels to bid. And, we get paid by the hotels for bringing them business.

Plus, Venture2 goes the extra mile to help you negotiate the terms of your contract. This makes the seasoned planner even more efficient and it ensures the less experienced planner doesn't get stung with unexpected resort fees and contingency clauses.

At Venture2 we are proving that when it comes to Site Research you can do even better than FREE. Leverage our service and you will also be more efficient, more comprehensive and less stressed.

Conference Management

Conference Management is more than a one-person job. Very few people are ready to tackle all of the challenges from concept to implementation. That's why the Venture2 team is structured to provide expertise where you need it. Our team can help you with your entire event or just the areas where we add value to you. Let us provide you with pricing for any or all of the following:

- **Travel & Accommodations:** Site research and negotiation; Rooming list coordination; Air transportation; Ground transportation
- **Collateral Design & Production:** Theme/Décor planning and design; Giveaways; Travel guides; Signage; AV presentation production; Website development
- **Meeting Management:** Agenda development; Online registration; Meeting room scheduling, set-up and AV; Onsite staffing; Pre- and Post-event marketing
- **Food, Beverage & Activities:** Menu planning and contract negotiation; Meal scheduling and set-up; Coordination and planning of activities; Special event and theme party planning; Event photographer scheduling

Event Technology Consulting

The Internet, Intranets, Extranets, Software...there are very few industries that can leverage these resources more than event planning. But how do you know if the dot-com you plan to use for online registration is going to be in business when your program takes place? Do you have the time to learn new software or do your own Web development? Venture2 will analyze what you need and find the right solution so you don't get stuck. We have the knowledge and experience to guide you through all the choices and protect you from making an event threatening decision.

206.938.0569
Fax 206.937.8470
Web site: www.wcent.com

We plan more high school parties than anyone

With two decades of experience, West Coast Entertainment has worked with almost every school and PTA in the state to create memories that last a lifetime. Exclusively representing many of Seattle's hottest venues, including the Columbia Tower Club and Planet Hollywood, we are well equipped to enhance the elegance of Prom or the excitement of graduation.

Flexible planning with all the extras

West Coast Entertainment makes it easy to plan a successful and memorable event. Not only do we provide a free consultation to discuss your event goals, we also feature the flexibility of a fully refundable deposit. Once you're ready to let us entertain you, insurance is included, and no damage deposit is required. West Coast Entertainment provides six complimentary chaperone tickets per 100 students, and a scholarship program is available.

"Committed to Excellence"

West Coast offers a wide variety of the finest entertainment from around the Sound. Widely known for exciting and energetic casino parties, we also have the hottest DJ's, emcees, and Laser Karaoke. Live performers are also available, everyone from comedians and impersonators to hypnotists and magicians. And whether it's Sumo Wrestling or the Gladiator Joust, no one exceeds our game expertise.

A few of our popular venues...

- Spirit of Puget Sound
- Planet Hollywood
- GameWorks
- Waterways Cruises
- Space Needle
- Bay Pavilion
- Columbia Tower Club
- Rainforest Café
- Jillian's
- Argosy Cruises

PROVEN EXPERTISE FOR ALL YOUR NEEDS

West Coast Entertainment is pleased to be celebrating over twenty years of producing high school, casino, and special entertainment events. Clients consistently praise our polished image and high quality service. Let us bring you the personal side of complete event planning, because you don't get a second chance to create lifelong memories.

FOR MORE INFORMATION CALL 206.938.0569
OR (OUTSIDE THE SEATTLE AREA) CALL 888.915.8555
Web site: www.wcent.com E-mail: dan@wcent.com

Meeting & Event Planning Organizations

❖❖❖

MEETING PROFESSIONALS INTERNATIONAL (MPI)
(972) 702-3000 National Phone
Website: www.wscmpi.org
MPI now offers its members their own on-line service, called MPINet, based on the CompuServe system. MPI's resource center will do research for members and non-members on just about any subject. MPI can also provide destination information through the Worldview program. The local chapter of MPI is a great education and networking group of local meeting planners and suppliers.
For local membership information see page 523 in this section.

AMERICAN HOTEL & MOTEL ASSOCIATION (AH&MA)
(202) 289-3100

AMERICAN SOCIETY OF ASSOCIATION EXECUTIVES (ASAE)
(202) 626-2748

AMERICAN SOCIETY OF TRAVEL AGENTS (ASTA)
(703) 739-2782

CONVENTION LIAISON COUNCIL (CLC)
(800) 725-8982

INTERNATIONAL ASSOCIATION OF CONVENTION & VISITOR BUREAUS (IACVB)
(202) 296-7888

INTERNATIONAL ASSOCIATION FOR EXPOSITION MANAGEMENT (IAEM)
(972) 458-8002

INTERNATIONAL SPECIAL EVENT SOCIETY (ISES)
(800) 688-4737

SOCIETY OF GOVERNMENT MEETING PLANNERS (SGMP)
(717) 795-7467

WASHINGTON SOCIETY OF ASSOCIATION EXECUTIVES (WSAE)
(253) 858-7037

BAINBRIDGE ISLAND/KITSAP COUNTY

Bainbridge Island
Chamber of Commerce — 590 Winslow Way E, Bainbridge Island WA 98110
(206) 842-3700

BELLINGHAM/WHATCOM & SKAGIT COUNTIES

Bellingham/Whatcom County
Chamber of Commerce — PO Box 958, Bellingham WA 98227
(360) 734-1330
La Conner Chamber of Commerce — PO Box 1610, La Conner WA 98257
(360) 466-4778

EVERETT/SNOHOMISH COUNTY

City of Snohomish
Chamber of Commerce — PO Box 135, Snohomish WA 98291
(360) 568-2526
Everett Area
Chamber of Commerce — 11400 Airport Road, Suite B, Everett WA 98204
(425) 438-1487
South Snohomish County
Chamber of Commerce — 3500-188th Street NE, Suite 490, Lynnwood WA 98037
(425) 774-0507

OCEAN SHORES/GRAYS HARBOR COUNTY

Ocean Shores
Chamber of Commerce — PO Box 382, Ocean Shores WA 98569
(360) 289-2451

OLYMPIA/THURSTON COUNTY

Olympia-Thurston County
Chamber of Commerce — PO Box 1427, Olympia WA 98507-1427
(360) 357-3362

SEATTLE/KING COUNTY

Bellevue Chamber
of Commerce — 10500 NE 8th Street, Suite 212, Bellevue WA 98004
(425) 454-2464
Capitol Hill Chamber
of Commerce — 501-19th Avenue, Seattle WA 98122-0813
(206) 323-8035
Greater Seattle
Chamber of Commerce — 1301-5th Ave., Suite 2400, Seattle WA 98101
(206) 389-7200

Southwest King County Chamber of Commerce — 16400 Southcenter Pkwy., Suite 210, Tukwila WA 98188
(206) 575-1633

Sports & Events Council — Greater Seattle Chamber of Commerce, 1301-5th Avenue, Suite 2400, Seattle WA 98101
(206) 389-7200

Vashon Island Chamber of Commerce — PO Box 1035, Vashon Island WA 98070
(206) 463-6217

TACOMA / PIERCE COUNTY

Eastern Pierce County Chamber of Commerce — PO Box 1298, Puyallup WA 98371
(253) 845-6755

Gig Harbor/Peninsula Area Chamber of Commerce — 3302 Harborview Drive. Gig Harbor WA 98332
(253) 851-6865

Lakewood Chamber of Commerce — 6122 Motor Avenue SW, Lakewood WA 98499
(253) 582-9400

Tacoma-Pierce County Chamber of Commerce — PO Box 1933, Tacoma WA 98401
(253) 627-2175

WHIDBEY ISLAND

Langley Chamber of Commerce/Whidbey Island — PO Box 403, Langley WA 98260
(360) 221-6765

YAKIMA/EASTERN WASHINGTON

Lake Chelan Chamber of Commerce — PO Box 216, Chelan WA 98816
(509) 682-3503 or (800) 424-3526

Leavenworth Chamber of Commerce — PO Box 327, Leavenworth WA 98826
(509) 548-5807

Skamania County Chamber — PO Box 1037, Stevenson WA 98648
(509) 427-8911

Yakima Chamber of Commerce — PO Box 1490, Yakima WA 98907-1490
(509) 248-2021

PUGET SOUND

Bellingham/Whatcom County
Convention & Visitors Bureau — 904 Potter Street, Bellingham WA 98226
(360) 671-3990

Bremerton Visitors & Convention Bureau — PO Box 229, 301 Pacific Avenue, Bremerton WA 98337, (360) 479-3579

East King County Convention
& Visitors Bureau — 520-112th Avenue NE, Suite 101, Bellevue WA 98004
(425) 455-1926 or (800) 252-1926

Edmonds Visitors Center — 121-5th Avenue N, Edmonds WA 98020
(425) 776-6711

Kitsap Peninsula Convention
& Visitors Bureau — PO Box 270, 2 Rainier, Port Gamble WA 98364
(360) 297-8200 or (800) 416-5615

Lewis County Tourism — 500 NW Chamber Way, Chehalis WA 98532
(360) 748-8885 or (800) 525-3323

Long Beach Peninsula Visitor Bureau — PO Box 562, Long Beach WA 98631
(360) 642-2400

North Olympic Peninsula Visitors
& Convention Bureau — 338 West First, PO Box 670, Port Angeles WA 98362
(360) 452-8552 or (800) 942-4042

Ocean Shores-Grays Harbor Visitors
& Convention Bureau — PO Box 1447, Ocean Shores WA 98569
(360) 289-4411

San Juan Islands Visitor
Information Services — PO Box 65, Lopez Island WA 98261
(360) 468-3663 or (888) 468-3701

Seattle-King County Convention
& Visitors Bureau — 520 Pike Street, Suite 1300, Seattle WA 98101
(206) 461-5800

Snohomish County
Tourism Bureau — 909 SE Everett Mall Way, Suite C-300, Everett WA 98208
(425) 348-5802 or (888) 338-0976

Tacoma/Pierce County Visitors
& Convention Bureau — 1001 Pacific Avenue, Suite 400, Tacoma WA 98402
(253) 627-2836

EASTERN WASHINGTON

Spokane Convention
& Visitors Bureau — 801 Riverside, Suite 301, Spokane WA 99201
(509) 624-1341

Tri-Cities Visitor
& Convention Bureau — 6951 W Grandridge Boulevard,
PO Box 2241, Kennewick WA 99302
(509) 735-8486 or (800) 254-5824

Wenatchee Valley Convention
& Visitors Bureau — 116 N Wenatchee Avenue, Wenatchee WA 98801 *See page 125*
(800) 572-7753

Yakima Valley Visitors & Conv. Bureau — 10 N 8th Street, Yakima WA 98901
(509) 575-3010

VANCOUVER ISLAND, CANADA

Tourism Association of Vancouver Island — 203-335 Wesley Street, Nanaimo, BC V9R 2T5 Canada
(250) 754-3500

What is NACE?

Headquartered in Louisville, Kentucky, the National Association of Catering Executives (NACE) is the only association covering all aspects of professional catering. Founded in 1958, NACE is the oldest and largest catering association in the United States. NACE provides you with a network of peers, industry news and information, education, professional development and informational resources. With 40 chapters and over 2,600 members in the United States and Canada, NACE represents hotel caterers, on-premise caterers and off-premise caterers, as well as companies providing products and services for this special market.

What are the Association's objectives?

The purpose of the National Association of Catering Executives is to raise the levels of education and professionalism among its members, creating a forum for the exchange of ideas within the catering industry. The Association keeps the membership informed of key issues pertinent to the catering industry, and encourages the practice of high standards and professional conduct of its members. NACE also provides the members with an excellent vehicle for personal career development and enhancement.

Who is eligible for membership?

There are five categories of membership in NACE:

- **Active membership** is available to anyone currently employed as a director of catering, catering manager, off-premise caterer, banquet manager or equivalent.
- **Associate membership** is available to general managers, sales managers, or any executive position of the food and beverage division of properties with banquet facilities.
- **Affiliate membership** is available to purveyors, primarily at the local level, of products and services or their firms.
- **Corporate membership** (for suppliers only) provides involvement at the chapter level for national corporations through participation of local representatives.
- **Student membership** is available to students enrolled in recognized food-service education programs.

For more information about NACE membership, call:

Pacific Northwest Chapter (Seattle)
Wendy Wojcick (206) 542-2935

Tacoma/South Sound Chapter
Geri Windecker (206) 241-4777

Party Supplies

HELPFUL HINTS

Kinds of party supplies: Be sure to stop by a party supply store for many great ideas. You will discover fun ways to decorate—from crepe paper to balloons in every color imaginable. A party supply store can help you with special themes and ideas for decorating tables, walls, ceilings, and floors!

Case or bulk discounts: Be sure to inquire about discounts when buying large quantities of items. You may want to consider renting a tank of helium so you can coordinate your own balloon decorations and save money.

Special-occasion decorations: Party shops carry a large selection of party decorations and accessories for theme events, birthdays, anniversaries, etc. Theme-coordinated decorations are very popular—matching plates, napkins, cups, invitations, plus many other accessories. Gift supplies include coordinated wrapping paper, ribbon, gift bags, tissue, cards, and more.

Balloon ideas: Balloons are a creative means of decorating and provide a dramatic visual effect. Balloon décor often is used to enhance a room and can also be used to hide flaws in walls or ceilings. From smaller tabletop, to large free-standing designs, balloons can be sculpted in any shape you desire. Classic Balloon Décor such as arches, columns and swags can be customized to your event. They will enhance entrances, stages, dance floors, guest tables and buffet tables. Balloon drops and releases are always a big hit. There are Certified Balloon Artists available to assist you in planning the designs that will best suit your event. **Note: Some facilities do not allow "helium" filled balloons.**

Colors of balloons: Balloons come in a wide variety of colors, sizes, and styles. A special theme color can be created by placing a balloon of one color inside another of a different color.

Imprinted balloons: Balloons can be imprinted with your business logo or event name and date.

Rental decorations: Rental decorations come in a variety of choices—ficus trees with twinkle lights, waterfalls, and fountains. You can create any visual effect you want with the right decorations. An underwater theme is fun with live fish in bowls on the tables as centerpieces. Netting and garland for seaweed hanging from the ceiling creates the illusion of being underwater.

Balloon Tunnel

Company Logo Replica

Gingerbread House

Around The Sound Balloons

Contact: Wendy Hubbard, Certified Balloon Artist
(425) 402-9686
E-mail: balloondecor@msn.com
Web site: www.aroundthesoundballoons.com

Creative and Classic Balloon Decorating

Rely on proven professionals to create the perfect expression for your event. Our Certified Balloon Artist has completed a comprehensive certification program and has years of experience creating professional balloon décor.

Custom designed balloon décor is our distinction. Our team of experts can create an atmosphere that's elegant and sophisticated or fanciful and fun. We have the vision to transform your event into a festive celebration by creating:

- Majestic dance floor canopies
- Showstopping logo replicas
- Enchanting entryway arches, tunnels and columns
- Unique buffet and table centerpieces
- Unforgettable larger-than-life sculptures

Complimentary Consultations are available at the site of your event. Our Certified Balloon Artist will meet with you and help you plan unforgettable décor within your budget. Trust the proven expertise of balloon professionals.

When the décor looks good, you look good!

Call the balloon decorating professionals today at (425) 402-9686

Pepsi's 100th Birthday

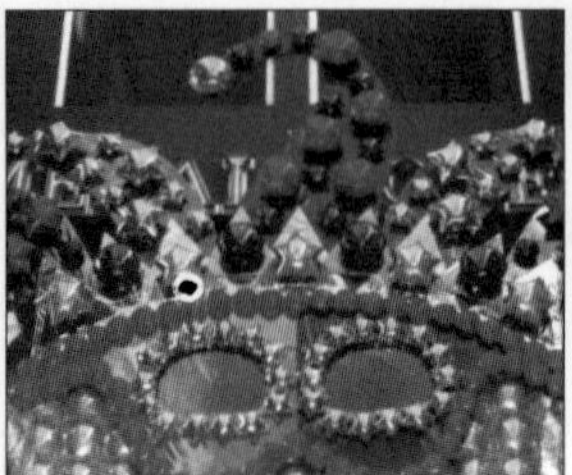
Mardi Gras

Cinema Grand Opening

Contact: Dan or Jenny Bender, CBAs
(253) 566-0201
Fax (253) 566-3151
E-mail: info@balloonmasters.com
Web site: www.BALLOONMASTERS.com

PUGET SOUND'S PREMIER CHOICE FOR DECORATING EXCELLENCE

Visualize the dramatic effect of:

- Entryway Mural and Arch Designs
- Spectacular Stage Presentations
- Dance Floor and Room Canopies
- Custom Logo Murals and Banners

Experience the excitement of:

- Exploding Balloons and Walls
- Confetti and Streamer Canons
- Balloon Drops and Releases
- Unbelievable Sculptures

ENHANCE your design choices with motion lighting, rotators, fabrics, silks and special signage.

CUSTOMIZE any type of theme or special event with your choice of balloon styles and colors.

COMPLETE DÉCOR PACKAGES created for excitement, high impact, and exceptional value.

THEME DÉCOR with **ORIGINALITY!**

Certified Balloon Artists

Professional balloon art and design is an emerging, creative means of event and theme decor. Experienced, artistic designers are a must. Balloon Masters is the only Northwest company to offer five Certified Balloon Artists on staff. They are proven professionals dedicated to excellence in balloon design, display and event décor.

Consultations

Complimentary consultations are offered both on-site and at our design studio. One of our CBAs will meet and tour the facility with you to develop a décor plan, or welcome you to our design studio to view a large selection of portfolio pictures of various types of events.

Balloon Master's designs are regularly featured in five world wide publications
Excellent special event, trade show, corporate and private references available

COMPARE PORTFOLIOS...SEE THE DIFFERENCE!

FROM CLASSIC BALLOON DÉCOR, TO UNIQUE IDEAS BEYOND BOUQUETS, RELY ON PROFESSIONALS!

CALL TODAY FOR A COMPLIMENTARY PROPOSAL

(253) 566-0201

PHOTOGRAPHERS

❖❖❖

HELPFUL HINTS

Why are photographs important? Photographs capture the results of months of hard work and are great to have on hand after an event is over. Photographs can thank a sponsor. Photographs of a grand opening or award presentations can be used in press releases after the event or for future events. Photographs can be a great keepsake and follow-up thank-you for the supporters who attend the function year after year.

Selecting a photographer: Find a photographer whose style you like. Look closely at his or her sample albums, and don't be afraid to ask for references. A contract is important to reserve the date and should confirm that the estimate given will be the actual cost. With over 250 photographers currently listed in the phone book, you want to make sure you select the best photographer to meet your specific needs.

Consulting with your photographer: When you finally select your photographer, sit down together so you can communicate what you envision your photographs will look like. Be specific about formal and candid photographs. Make sure you let the photographer know exactly what you are expecting.

Assigning a photographer's helper: Save time the day of the event by assigning someone to be the photographer's helper. Submit a list of photographic requests to both the photographer and helper one week before the event so that your helper can guide the photographer to all the right people, places, or set ups.

GONE DIGITAL!

photography by gail ann & kelley rae

***offering photographic coverage of your special event...
digital or film, we have the talent, we have the tools!
Call us for a quote when planning your next event.***

(206) 371-0585 or (206) 915-6420
Fax (206) 935-5773
E-mail: gailannphoto@aol.com or kelleyrae@aol.com
Web site: www.gailannphotography.com

**Planning a special event? Golf tournament?
Dance or reunion? Holiday party?**
We'll be there.

**Need photographic coverage of your corporate event?
Grand opening? Award presentation?**
We'll be there.

Is Santa coming? Call for date availability regarding Santa photos.
We'll be there.

**Need headshots of company employees fast?
Need images of a product for catalogs? Annual reports?**
We'd enjoy working for you. Call us to see a portfolio of work and get a price quote on your next commercial project.

Planning a charitable event?
We think it's a good thing to give back to the community...we hope you do, too. Let us show you how our philanthropic side can help you help your charity.

Executive portraits, families, kids and weddings also.
Film based images are lifetime guaranteed!

Call us...when you need it yesterday!

Photo Promotions, the Pacific Northwest's premier promotions and events photographer, has been serving customers all over the Oregon, Washington and British Columbia area since 1980.

Our friendly, courteous, professional staff is ready to provide your next event with colorful, high "studio" quality instant digital photos, as well as exciting finishing options.

Photo Promotions also has "Real" Santas, Mrs. Claus, Elves, and "Custom" Easter Bunnies available to entertain at your next event.

Take your photos home with you after your event!

- Add a fun border for a custom look (first "customized" border is free)
- Choose from a wide range of print sizes to build you own packages
- You see your photos before they're processed
- Get extra prints while you wait
- Flat rate charges begin at only $5 per sheet!
- No extra charges for group shots
- We accept VISA, MasterCard, Discover/Novus, AMEX, checks and cash
- Sepia photos (old fashion tones) also available
- Excellent references available

Holiday & Theme Parties
Bar/Bat Mitzvahs
Golf Tournaments
Fundraisers
Conventions
Graduations
Dances
Auctions
Reunions
Promotional/Celebrity Events
Tradeshows

E-mail: photo.promotions@verizon.net

Web site: www.photopromotions.com

Corporate & Special Event Photography

(425) 396-5026; Fax (425) 696-0058
E-mail: buckw@shotsnow.com
Web site: www.shotsnow.com

Digital photographs with custom borders... that your attendees take with them!

Just think, no dealing with the mail, no days on end as your attendees wait to see their photographs. Instead, your guests leave with their pictures in hand, presented with a custom border that commemorates the event name, date, and company or sponsor logo.

ShotsNow brings everything you need to the location of your choice for on-site photography and print delivery. Our professional event staff has the experience and know-how to make things run smoothly, ensuring that everyone has a good time.

• Holiday & Theme Parties

• Golf Tournaments

• Conventions • Tradeshows • Award Banquets

• Bar/Bat Mitzvahs • Celebrity Events

• Graduations • Reunions • Dances

• Auctions • Fundraisers

Cascade West Photography

Contact us via phone, fax, or email
Voice (253) 850-6007 or Toll-free 1-888-480-9122
Fax (253) 852-8421
E-mail: cwp@foxcomm.net
Web site: www.wiseimages.com

Check with us for your event imaging needs—
and wants—and desires!

Corporate events, Social events, and Fundraisers,
For distribution, publication, or personal memories.

Wherever and whenever you have a group gathered,
We will provide you with the special images
to help your people remember your event.

Digital services **Traditional film**

We shoot it if it moves...
...or if it doesn't

Cascade West Photography

Award Winning Photography Throughout the West

For business needs—
—and personal desires.

CONSTANCE OWEN PHOTOGRAPHY

Need VISUAL solutions?

imagery for the web

brochure/editorial

executive/portrait

corporate events

Greg Nystrom

PHOTOGRAPHER

1607 Dexter Avenue North, #2B
Seattle, Washington 98109
(206) 286-1452
Web site: www.gregnystrom.com

Publicity Headshots
Events, Brochures
Celebrations, Awards
Corporate Image

35mm, and medium format. Black and white, or color.
Give me a call to receive a quote.

Satisfied clients include:

- Bank of America
- Chateau Ste. Michelle
- Pilchuck Glass School
- Lucent Technologies
- Channel Corporation
- Apian Software
- Washington Defense Trial Lawyers
- Northwest Emmy Awards
- Infinity Broadcasting
- Accountants on Call
- National Wildlife Federation
- Graham & James, LLC
- Know Ware
- SASCO
- McDonald's Corporation
- Dale Carnegie Training
- Merck
- The Coxe Group
- Downtown Seattle Association
- Family Services
- Media Plus

Member, Seattle Professional Photographers Association. Think SPPA.

PAX PHOTO SERVICES

Your Event, Your Way, on Your Budget

www.SEATTLEWEDDINGPHOTO.COM

206-242-2300

PROFESSIONAL PHOTOGRAPHIC SERVICE CUSTOMIZED TO PRECISELY FIT YOUR NEEDS

HIGHEST QUALITY PHOTOGRAPHY WITH FLEXIBILITY FOR YOUR NEXT SPECIAL EVENT

No two special events are ever quite the same. Whether yours is an intimate dinner with 10 employees to celebrate a promotion, or a formal black tie fund-raiser with 1,500 guests, we won't offer another "standardized packages" so common with many photographers. Instead, our services are available on a per hour and per roll basis to provide you and your guests with photography which is well-planned, flexible, fun and stress-free.

No Venue Nor Event is Too Small or Large

Our special event photography service offers client—friendly extras:

- Pre-planning and scouting of your location prior to the event
- A complete staff of assistants
- Corporate or political events
- Weddings, Bar Mitzvahs, Bat Mitzvahs
- Parties, promotions, rollouts, retirements
- Formal events, fund-raisers
- Reunions and anniversaries
- Holiday events and celebrations
- Color or black /white, medium format or 35mm films
- Professional studio lighting for set-ups or roving camera
- Fast turn-around on processing and delivery
- Negatives, finished prints or proofs: all rights to client.

Call us today for a no-obligation consultation to discuss your special event plans.

Call 206-242-2300

now to schedule your event date or visit us on the web to veiw on-line portfolios.

See page 598 under Video Services.

The Seattle Professional Photographers Association
. . . able to meet all your corporate, social and commercial needs

Corporate Events

• Conventions • Award Banquets • Grand Openings • Product Launches • Fundraisers
• Golf Tournaments • Trade Shows • Executive Portraits • Group Portraits

Commercial/Advertising

• Brochures • Annual Reports • Catalogs • Postcards • Industrial

Social Events

• Anniversaries • Reunions • Retirement Parties/Roasts
• Holiday Parties • Weddings • Company Picnics • Bar/Bat Mitzvahs

---

- ***Gail Ann – Gone Digital***
  Digital or film, we have the talent, we have the tools!
  (206) 371-0585
  E-mail: gailannphoto@aol.com
  www.gailannphotography.com

- ***Dani Weiss Photography***
  Documentary style photography for any event.
  (206) 760-3336
  E-mail: dani@daniweissphotography.com
  www.daniweissphotography.com

- ***Heather Quintans Photography***
  (206) 297-2064
  E-mail: info@heatherphoto.com
  www.heatherphoto.com

- ***Carol Sinnott–Sinnott Photography***
  (206) 568-6645
  E-mail: Sinnottphoto@hotmail.com
  www.users.qwest.net/~sinnottphoto.net

- ***Spirit of the Day! Photography by Ted Case***
  Custom Designed Coverage at reasonable prices.
  (360) 568-3444
  E-mail: tedcase@virtual-cafe.com
  www.tedcase.com

- ***Barbara Roser Photography***
  (425) 391-9371
  E-mail: roserfstop@msn.com
  www.roserphotography.com

- ***Jeffrey Fong Photography***
  (206) 226-5444
  E-mail: jfong@foxinternet.net
  www.thinksppa.com/jeffreyfongphotography.com

- ***Andy Walthers Photography***
  Digital or traditional film imagery.
  (206) 550-2122
  E-mail: andy@walthersphotography.com
  www.walthersphotography.com

- ***Lens-Art Photo Studio***
  Quality at Reasonable Prices.
  (425) 349-1562
  E-mail: wwgrace@aol.com
  www.mukilteo.org/photography

- ***Rick Fletcher– Crowning Touch Photography***
  (253) 833-9384
  E-mail: crowningtouchphoto@hotmail.com

- ***Chris Wartes–Christophoto***
  (425) 481-8090
  E-mail: chris@christophoto-inc.com
  www.christophoto-inc.com

- ***Kim Wise–Cascade West Photography***
  We shoot it if it moves...or if it doesn't!
  (253) 850-7380 or 1-888-480-9122
  E-mail: wiseimages1@home.com
  www.wiseimages.com

Visit *www.thinksppa.com/Bravoeventguide.com*

Picnic & Recreation Sites

HELPFUL HINTS

Planning a company picnic can be easy or difficult depending on several factors: how long you have to plan, how many you are planning for, the type of activities planned, etc. Here are a few things to remember when you begin planning a company picnic:

- **Remember to book your picnic site early!** Spaces are limited, and some companies book their picnic sites up to a year in advance.
- **Confirm dates and times in writing.** Don't assume that since you had your picnic somewhere last year that the space is reserved for you this year. Examine the site to make sure it is presentable and what you need for your event.
- **Develop a committee or committees of volunteers** to help coordinate food and beverages, games and prizes, publicity and sign-ups, entertainment, etc. Get feedback from participants on how the event can be improved from previous years.
- **Be sure your contact at the site has a clear picture of what you want.** Be open to suggestions and solutions from the contacts at the site. They have experienced all sizes and types of events at their particular site and can be very helpful with what works and what doesn't.
- **Work with the experienced planners on-site** (if one is not available, then check in the "Meeting and Event Planners" section of this Guide to find one). The only way you'll find the answer to your questions is by asking someone who has been through it before. You may have never coordinated an event like this, so ask questions to figure out the best solutions. There will always be last-minute problems, such as expecting 700 people and having 1,000 show up. Experienced coordinators and planners can handle even the worst problems. DON'T PANIC! When you work with the professionals, they will not disappoint you.
- **Most importantly, don't make the picnic so complicated** that you drain your volunteers of their energy! This is supposed to be a morale-building event, not a burnout.
- **Prizes and promotions:** Don't forget to have a keepsake to take home from the picnic, like baseball hats with your company's logo, water bottles, Frisbees, etc.
- **Games and activities.** Sports-related games and activities can add excitement to your event. Employees would especially love to see the managers in the dunk tank. There are professional companies that can come and set-up games and arrange prizes listed under "Audience Participation" in this Guide.
- **Tents and pavilions.** Picnics are planned for summer fun, but you can never count on the sun to shine. A tent or pavilion at your site in case of bad weather can ensure a great event—come rain or shine.

  Important Note: Never use canvas tents treated with mineral oil for waterproofing, they are extremely flammable.
- **Food for the picnic.** Food choices for a traditional picnic include barbecued hamburgers, ribs, chicken, hot dogs and baked beans, and salads. Remember that proper refrigeration can eliminate food spoilage in heat.
- **On-site barbecue trucks.** Special barbecue caterers are using on-site barbecue trucks to store and cook the food right on site. The food is excellent and employees enjoy the event without cooking or helping with cleanup.
- **Portable lavatories:** Don't forget to provide an adequate number of portable lavatories for off-site events; one portable lavatory for every 100 attendees is typical. Be certain that they are easily located and accessible.
- **Dress code:** Be certain to communicate to your guests what kinds of attire will be appropriate for the activities you are planning. They need to know how to dress for both the terrain and the weather. Consider, for example, whether high heels would become hazardous or inconvenient at your picnic site.
- **Security:** Plan ahead for safety and security, especially in public park settings.

13817 Short School Road
Snohomish, Washington 98290
Contact: Judy Craven
(360) 568-2601; Fax (360) 568-9001
E-mail: visitafarm@aol.com
Web site: www.cravenfarm.com

Capacity: 2,400 sq. ft. barn plus two acres of lawn and picnic grounds comfortably accommodate groups of 125 to 150
Price range: please call for current rates
Catering: limited kitchen facilities available
Types of events: company picnics, barbecues, dances, family reunions, meetings, seminars, parties and more...

Availability and terms

We recommend you reserve your date as early as possible. The barn is available for events from April 1st through mid-September. A deposit is required to reserve your date with the balance due prior to the event.

Description of services and facility

Parking: ample complimentary parking provided
Liability insurance: client is responsible for providing liability coverage
Picnic and recreational services

- **Seating:** 15 picnic tables with benches
- **Activities:** a variety of games including volleyball, baseball, ping pong and horseshoes, and more are available for rent

Food and banquet services

- **Seating:** tables and chairs for the barn are available for rent
- **Beverage service:** beer and wine service allowed with WSLCB banquet permit
- **Serviceware:** provided by client
- **Decorations:** we are happy to work with you in accommodating your decorating ideas and needs; please inquire; nothing that will damage the facility
- **Cleanup:** renter's responsibility or you may hire the farm staff for $15 per hour

ENJOY COUNTRY CHARM AT THE FARM

Are you looking for a unique Country setting for your next event? Come on out to the farm! Open fields surround it, along with a Cascade view, a relaxed country atmosphere and enjoy the fresh air.

See page 466 under Games & Team Building Activities.

FOOD

GAMES

ENTERTAINMENT

LOCATIONS

& MUCH MORE

Great Picnics - Guaranteed

P.O. Box 55428
Seattle, WA 98155

(206) 363-4100
Fax (425) 670-2350

One Call Does it All

Complete Picnic Packages!

You choose the services you need from complete picnic packages to just the entertainment.

- Catering
- Locations
- Entertainment
- Clean-up
- Decorations
- Activities
- Transportation
- Security

Picnic Facilities!

We offer a wide variety of conveniently located picturesque picnic facilities—with and without the ability to serve alcohol.

- Beach Party Locations
- Private and Public Parks
- Picnic Farms
- Unique Mountain Side Retreats

Picnic Entertainment and Activities!

We feature the best entertainment and activities available anywhere. From giant slides and moon bouncers to music and games, count on us for fun!

- Clowns
- Disc Jockeys
- Face Painters
- Picnic Games
- Tattoo Artists
- Bands
- Pony Rides
- Inflatable Games
- Giant Slides
- Moon Bounces
- Go-Karts
- Climbing Mountains
- Magicians
- Hypnotists
- Volleyball
- Caricaturists

Picnic Catering!

Our specialized picnic catering includes classic and unique menus.

- BBQ Chicken & Beef
- Hot Dogs & Hamburgers
- Pacific Rim Cuisine
- Full Beverage Services
- Beer & Wine
- Complete Theme Menus
- Desserts
- Vegetarian
- Popcorn & Cotton Candy

Above All Else!
Count on us for FUN! FUN!! And, of course, more FUN!!!

See page 508 under Meeting & Event Planners.

The Farm

4301 Rivershore Rd. • Snohomish, WA 98290
Bob and Carol Krause
(425) 334-4124
Web site: www.thefarm1.com

The farm is a great place for all kinds of outdoor activities.

Capacity: 3,000 sq. ft. of covered picnic area, plus over three acres of lawn for picnics and 25 acres for recreational activities; accommodates over 500 guests
Catering: kitchen facilities available; optional on-site catering
Types of events: company picnics, reunions, barbecues, team building activities, outdoor weddings, parties, receptions, meetings

Picnic services

- **Seating:** chairs and tables for 250
- **Bar services:** beer and wine service allowed with WSLCB banquet permit; renter's responsibility
- **Amenities:** ample parking, water/power access, port-o-let facilities, hand washing stations

Attractions

- Washington State Corn Maze
- Haybarn maze and slide
- Championship putting course
- Wagon rides
- Horseshoe pit
- Softball field
- Volleyball
- Badminton
- Basketball court
- U-pick flowers

A WONDERFUL PLACE TO BE TOGETHER FOR FUN AND CELEBRATION

Located along the Snohomish River four miles west of Snohomish and within eight miles from I-5, ours is a real working farm on 125 scenic acres along the Snohomish River. The Farm is a great place for a variety of outdoor activities. It is especially suited for families and children of all ages. Home to the famous "Washington State Corn Maze" and newly completed championship putting course.

KING COUNTY PARK SYSTEM

(206) 296-4232
(800) 325-6165, ext. 4232
Web site: www.metrokc.gov/parks/

Picnic in a beautiful King County Park

Whether you're looking for an intimate spot for a picnic for two or planning a company picnic for thousands, King County Parks offers you over 200 locations.

Picnic shelters and large picnic areas can be reserved in advance

- Sites feature tables, grills and rest rooms
- Reasonable rates
- Staff to assist in site planning
- Available any day of the week
- Special features at several sites: boat moorage, fishing pier, amphitheater, pools, sport courts, ball fields, children's play areas, or interpretive trails

Reserved Sites North of I-90
Call (206) 296-2966

- Cottage Lake Park (Woodinville)
- Luther Burbank Park (Mercer Island)
- Tolt MacDonald Park (Carnation)
- Marymoor Park (Redmond)
- O.O. Denny Park (Kirkland)
- Juanita Beach (Kirkland)

Reserved Sites South of I-90
Call (206) 296-4287

- Cougar Mountain Regional Wildland Park (Newcastle)
- Dockton Park (Vashon Island)
- Five Mile Lake Park (Federal Way)
- King County Fairgrounds (Enumclaw)
- Lake Wilderness Park (Maple Valley)
- Lakewood Park (White Center)
- *Indoor Facilities call (206) 296-4298*

PACK A PICNIC AND HEAD TO A KING COUNTY PARK NEAR YOU!

Plenty of free, first come, first served picnic tables in over 50 well-maintained parks. For more information about King County Park System, facilities or events, call (206) 296-4232.

Visit our Web Site for a detailed look at each park and facility in the *King County Parks Atlas:* www.metrokc.gov/parks/

4702 South 19th Street • Tacoma, Washington 98405
Office Hours: Mon–Fri 8am–5pm
Web site: www.tacomaparks.com

• Tacoma's Scenic Parks are the Ideal Spot for Company Picnics, Parties, or Retreats! •

Metro Parks offer:

- Picnic sites at over 12 area parks.
- A swimming pool and outdoor wading pools are available for group rentals.
- Meeting space in more than a dozen community centers located throughout the city. Call (253) 305-1000 for community center rental information.

Availability and terms

Reservations can be made for picnic locations starting March 1st. For groups of 200 and more a refundable damage deposit of $200 is required. Wading pools in season and in operation are rentable. Rental fees will vary by site. For more information, please call (253) 305-1010.

ALLING PARK
South 60th & Sheridan
Approximate capacity: 50 people

FRANKLIN PARK
South 12 & Puget Sound
Approximate capacity: 50

FORT NISQUALLY
Point Defiance Park
Approximate capacity: 50 people

GIG HARBOR VIEWPOINT
Point Defiance Park
Approximate capacity: 50 people

POINT DEFIANCE MAIN AREA
Point Defiance Park
Approximate capacity: 100 people

**OWEN BEACH–
BLUE & GREEN AREAS**
Point Defiance Park
Approximate capacity: 200 people (both areas)

LINCOLN PARK
South 37th & Thompson
Approximate capacity: 200 people

MANITOU PARK
South 66th & Stevens
Approximate capacity: 50 people

TITLOW PARK HIDDEN BEACH
West end of 6th Avenue
Approximate capacity: 50 people
Weekdays rental start at 4pm to dusk
Saturday & Sunday all day till dusk

TITLOW PARK MAIN
West end of 6th Avenue
Approximate capacity: 150 people
Weekdays rental start at 4pm to dusk
Saturday & Sunday all day till dusk

**WAPATO LAKE PARK–
KIWANIS AREA**
South 72nd & Sheridan
Approximate capacity: 200 people

WAPATO LAKE PARK–MAIN AREA
South 72nd & Sheridan
Approximate capacity: 200 people

TO RESERVE YOUR LOCATION WITH A CREDIT CARD, CALL (253) 305-1010.

NILE GOLF & COUNTRY CLUB

6601-24th Street S.W. • Mountlake Terrace, Washington 98043
(425) 775-2412; Fax (425) 744-9611
E-mail: office@nileshrine.org • ***Web site: nileshrine.org***

ON THE SHORES OF LAKE BALLINGER

Located just 20 minutes from downtown Seattle, the Nile Golf & Country Club is one of the Pacific Northwest's most distinctly impressive properties. Nestled among 88-acres of tall stately firs on the shores of Lake Ballinger, this unique venue is ideal for all kinds of events.

PICNIC GROUNDS

Our Picnic Grounds boast five individual areas and have become one of the most desirable close-to-city properties for groups and corporations. Each area features its own covered cooking facilities, with water, power and charcoal grills, plus sturdy built-in picnic tables.

On-site activities:

- Public Rest Rooms and Changing Facilities
- Ample space for races, games and pickup baseball
- Children's Wading Pool
- Horseshoe Pits

Price range: $300 for groups of 75 to 100, up to $3,000 for groups of 1,001 to 1,500

Catering: As You Like It Catering, our full service in-house caterer, will prepare your picnic for 75–3,000 guests

Beverage service: all picnic clients will be charged a fee to cover the cost of providing security weh alcohol will be served; $100 per officer—1 officer for up to 150 guests, 2 officers for 150 to 300, and 3 officers for anything over 300 guests

18-HOLE GOLF COURSE

This short, but interestingly laid out 18-hole regulation course features strategically placed bunkers, trees and doglegs that create a great test for all levels of players. Reservations for tournaments are accepted after December 1st for the following year. A deposit is required on signing the contract with the balance due 10-days prior to the event.

• **Holes:** 18 • **Length:** 5,000 yards • **Par:** 68

PGA Golf Professionals: our professional staff of pros are experienced in designing tournaments for every kind of group from competitive serious golfers to those who are looking for a more relaxed but entertaining day

Pro Shop: fully stocked Pro Shop for all your golfing needs including apparel, accessories, and equipment for rent or purchase; and rental golf carts available

Additional Services: practice chipping and putting greens, private or group lessons, junior golf camps and programs

See page 243 in the Banquet, Meeting & Event Sites and page 338 under Caterers/Food & Beverage Services.

Point Defiance Zoo & Aquarium

• *Located in beautiful 700-acre Point Defiance Park* •

5400 N. Pearl Street • Tacoma, WA 98407
(253) 404-3643; Fax (253) 591-5448
Office Hours: Mon–Fri 8am–5pm
Web site: www.pdza.org

Capacity: accommodates groups of 25 to 1,000

Price range: varies depending on food and beverage selections and site selection; Zoo and Aquarium admission charged only for events held during Zoo hours

Catering: from barbecues to box lunches, our full service, in-house catering staff will accommodate all your food and beverage needs

Types of events: all types of social or corporate events; picnics, reunions, private parties, meetings, tours, weddings, receptions or banquets

Availability and terms

Reservations are booked in four-hour time increments. A $200 deposit is required on booking with the balance due the day of the event.

Description of services and facility

ADA: all grounds and facilities are fully accessible
Restrooms: close to all designated picnic areas
Parking: ample complimentary parking provided
Picnic services

- **Seating:** outdoor picnic tables and benches provided; tenting available for shelter and shade
- **Servers:** all service personnel included in catering costs
- **Beverage service:** client may supply own alcoholic beverages; banquet permit required; corkage fee applies
- **Decorations:** please inquire, nothing that will disturb the animals or damage the grounds
- **Cleanup:** included in rental fees

Special services

Ask about including a behind-the-scenes tour of the Zoo and Aquarium in your event. Point Defiance Zoo & Aquarium offers the opportunity for guests to get up close and personal with the animals and their keepers.

BARBECUE ON THE LAWN OR DINE NEXT TO THE SHARKS

With the broad blue expanse of Puget Sound as a backdrop, Point Defiance Zoo & Aquarium is not only a top American zoo, but among the most beautiful. The Zoo features areas for picnics for groups of 25 to 1,000, and our professional catering staff has a wealth of experience in designing menus (barbecues to box lunches) that will suit your event while pleasing the palate. All this combined with the exotic sights and sounds of Point Defiance Zoo & Aquarium ensures that you and your group will have a festive and memorable event!

See page 255 under Banquet, Meeting & Event Sites, and page 61 under Attractions & Activities.

Carnation, Washington 98014
Contact: Jaque Remlinger
(360) 568-1780; Fax (360) 568-6613
Web site: www.lordhillevents.com

Capacity: 100 to 20,000 people
Price range: varies according to event; please call for a brochure
Catering: we offer full-service catering out of our restaurant, using the best quality meats, vegetables, fruits, and salads
Types of events: outdoor facilities for corporate picnics, and concerts; indoor facilities for seminars, board meetings, birthdays and other parties

Availability and terms

All bookings are encouraged as early as possible. A deposit is required. Remlinger Farms features a room small enough for a board meeting or enough outdoor space to hold an event for up to 20,000 people!

Description of services and facility

Parking: ample free parking available
Picnic sites: we have five outdoor sites to choose from; all sites are private and secluded; they each include softball area and equipment, volleyball area and equipment, tetherball, horseshoes and equipment, 20 picnic tables, portable restrooms, playground

Banquet services
- **Seating:** picnic tables, banquet tables, and chairs
- **Servers:** included in package
- **Bar facilities:** we provide alcoholic beverages for an additional fee
- **Electrical:** most facilities on the premises are equipped with electricity
- **Linens, napkins, china and glassware:** available on rental basis
- **Cleanup:** let us do your dirty work!; cleanup is up to us
- **Decorations:** provided for a small fee
- **Entertainment:** we provide complete entertainment and catering event planning services

Meeting and event services
- **Audio visual and equipment:** available; please inquire

Special services

Let us take the troubles out of planning your next event. Whether it will be at our place or another facility, we can orchestrate an event to remember. There's no need to worry when planning your next event. We can help you plan your party or plan it for you.

WE ACCOMMODATE ALL YOUR NEEDS

Remlinger Farms is located in the heart of the Snoqualmie Valley, just 25 miles northeast of the Seattle-Bellevue metropolitan area. Natural settings cater to privacy for each individual event. We have hundreds of acres, peaceful rolling fields, trees, streams, ponds, and riverfront. After the event, your guests can visit our fresh produce market and take a little bit of the farm back home with them.

Shown by appointment only.

36201 Enchanted Parkway South
Federal Way, Washington 98003
(253) 661-8001
Web site: www.sixflags.com

Capacity: 100 to 15,000
Price range: prices start at $14.99 per person plus catered meal
Catering: preferred caterer is O'Callahan's Catering
Types of events: company picnics, park buyouts, group outings, themed events, youth celebrations, holiday parties

Availability and terms

Most group events can be accommodated on any regularly scheduled operating day from May 19 through Labor Day, weekends in October during FrightFest, plus December 6–31 during the popular Holiday with Lights. Deposits are not usually required and the client is usually billed after the event. Park buyouts available in off season months of March–May and September–November.

Description of services and facilities

ADA: park and some rides are accessible
Parking: $5.00 per car
Picnic and banquet services

- **Seating:** park offers six large covered pavilions that can each accommodate more than 400 guests each; client may arrange to use one or more pavilions
- **Servers:** provided by caterers; all meals served buffet-style
- **Bar facilities:** beer, wine and liquor may be provided by licensed caterer only
- **Linens, napkins, china and glassware:** available through caterer
- **Decorations:** available through park but suggested client go through independent contractor
- **Cleanup:** caterer and park responsible for cleanup

Meeting and event services

- **Audio visual and equipment:** may be rented through park or from independent contractor

OFFERS MORE TO DO THAN ALL OTHER FACILITIES IN THE AREA COMBINED

The Pacific Northwest's premier entertainment location offering seventy acres of family fun, there's something for everybody at Wild Waves and Enchanted Village. Thirty rides, a huge waterpark, great shows, shopping and dining. Six covered pavilions located in a beautiful, elevated wooded area of the Park, and great food provided by O'Callahan's.

NOTES

Presentations

❖❖❖

HELPFUL HINTS

Selecting a presentation company: The reason for an event is to communicate a message to an audience of potential buyers, employees, peers or the general public. In any situation, the message needs to be clear consistent and precise. The way to insure success is to present the message with multimedia, video, sound, lights and stage presentations. To achieve the value of success add the ingredient that creates entertainment, excitement, interactivity, direct communication and interest, which is an audio/visual presentation.

The cost of this main ingredient is usually relative to the event and should be budgeted separately from other event costs. You must know your event budget before talking to any presentation company. The way you pick a venue, caterer, designer, coordinator, multimedia/video producer, or printer is the same way you would go about hiring any professional contractor. Never feel intimidated by the terminology or possible budgetary restraints. Pick a company that has a good track record, references, examples, and one you feel comfortable around. Video and multimedia presentations are a vital ingredient to any event.

Warning: A bad presentation can have a negative effect and deliver a completely different message than intended, don't fall short of a great opportunity to capture the audience and deliver your message.

How do you go about picking a company for your next event and making sure it is a success?

- **Ask other businesses** that use multimedia or visuals if they recommend a production company, and if they have idea on an average price range.
- **Tell the people you have already contacted** for venue, catering, printing or coordination that you are interested in creating a visual presentation. They work these jobs regularly and know the best choices for production companies.
- **Make sure you have an idea or concept** before seeking out any services. You must have the same basic requests for each contractor when comparing production companies.
- **After you have identified possible companies,** ask for examples, references, and estimates for the job.
- **All companies with any experience will be able to help you** in developing concepts and organizing the technical side of your production.
- **Feel comfortable with your contact** and be sure to meet all the people working on your project. Don't be afraid to ask any question. Remember that this is your production and you are accountable for the results.

Once you choose a company remember that concept is king. Make sure the visual presentation meets your requirement for the event. Keep the message clear and simple. The music and graphics should up-hold the standards of your company. Be involved from beginning to end. Always schedule enough time for set-up and a dry run. This is the time to make necessary changes or adjustment to the technical equipment or the program. Never leave any element to chance.

Don't fall short of the opportunity to make a great impression on your audience. One of the best ways to educate, entertain and inform is through an audio/visual medium. You can take the event your planning to the next level of success. Do your homework, choose the experts, always ask questions and demand the very best within your budget and time restraints.

HELPFUL HINTS

Lights, Cameras, Music....ACTION! Coordinating a successful event is a big enough task alone, but having your attendees walk away saying, "WOW!" should be the primary goal of every meeting planner and event coordinator.

It is much more than booking a meeting space, sending out invitations, and coordinating the production. There are companies with presentation expertise, and that have access to the right equipment, who can assist in helping planners deliver that unforgettable experience.

The following is a list of information that is key to reaching, "WOW!"

- **Hiring one chief:** Hire an experienced overall coordinator. Letting one person do the lights, one person the sound, another the set design, and still another handle the multi-media presentation offers too many chances for errors. Even if different companies are supplying the different elements, appoint one overall coordinator that is responsible for the entire project.
- **Check references:** Don't just look at resumes!!! Call and check for references. Does the organization, and person, have the experience to pull off your event? What was the satisfaction level of the reference? Would they hire them again?
- **Remember that content is the most important element of a well-coordinated event.** You can have a great video presentation, an unbelievable light set-up, and incredible sound, but unless all is coordinated to marry with each other, you'll come up short on delivering an unforgettable experience.
- **Finding the right equipment:** Find the right equipment for the event. It helps to hire a presentation coordinator that has worked similar events. More importantly, find out if they have done events at the proposed facility. Having knowledge of the quirks found in a facility will avoid major hurdles the day of the event.
- **Presentations don't have to break the bank:** Go in with a pre-determined budget. There are a number of companies that provide all the services mentioned, or that have the resources to coordinate all the elements. Let the experts develop a plan for you, within your budget.
- **Hold a dry run:** Practice makes perfect! Hold a dry run before the actual event. Test lights, sound, cameras, etc. Have back up plans for any problems you may encounter.
- **Evaluate and get ready for the next event:** Hold a debriefing meeting after the event. Talk about the elements that went well, and how to improve on those that were challenging. Find out how you can improve on them for next time.

2200 Sixth Avenue, Suite 750
Seattle, Washington 98121
(206) 256-0420; Fax (206) 256-0419
E-Mail: eln@eln.com
Web site: www.eln.com

EVENT PRESENTATION SPECIALISTS

from small social gatherings to large national events

- Concept, Creative, & Production Consulting
- Full Video (multi-media) Capabilities
- Live Event Broadcasts & Webcasts
- Design, Construction, Lighting, & Sound
- Projection Systems (including large screen IMAG systems)
- Entertainment Network (booking talent)
- Satellite Services & Videoconferencing

OUR COMMITMENT TO YOU...

"I can't tell you what it means to work with people of your caliber; who you can always count on, professionally and personally."

—Kathy Haggart, Executive Director, Boys & Girls Clubs of Bellevue

"Thank you for all of your efforts in making the PONCHO Wine Auction a success. The addition of the video was tremendous."

—Robert DiPietrae & Marc Sherman, Production Chairs, PONCHO

"In the 25 years I have been with the Institute I have never witnessed such a powerful, and beautiful presentation."

—Peggy Casey, The Pacific Institute

RECENT ELN EVENT PRODUCTIONS

- Poncho Auction & Poncho Wine Auction—Seattle, WA
- Fred Hutchinson Holiday Gala—Seattle, WA
- Cystic Fibrosis Auction—Seattle, WA
- American Foundation for Suicide Prevention (live broadcast of three city event to 55 markets and a simultaneous webcast)—New York, NY
- Miami's 100th Anniversary (350,000 people at Bay Front Park)—Miami, FL
- Camp LeJune (live concert and satellite transmission to 27 cities)—LeJune, NC

Whether you are an individual, corporate planner, marketing agency, or producer, let ELN be your creative partner in providing memorable events!

Call us for a free complimentary consultation.

Rental Services

❖❖❖

HELPFUL HINTS

Rental stores carry almost everything. You'll find such things as serviceware, portable bars, arches, tents, chairs, tables, and all the tableware, dishes, glassware, and flatware you need. Many shops also carry disposable paper products and a variety of decorations. For meetings, seminars, and conventions, you will find audio visual, lighting, and sound equipment to meet your needs.

Event Rental Coordinator. Event shops can be full-service for your event needs: Decorating, coordinating the caterer, entertainment, etc. They can be a wealth of ideas and knowledge. The details and specifics often become especially tedious at the end of planning a meeting or event, so having ready assistance with the logistics and coordination can be a life-saver.

Visit a rental store while planning. It's advisable to visit a showroom for ideas and to see the types and styles of merchandise and equipment in stock. Rental stores have brochures that describe all the different items available for rent, including style, colors, sizes, and prices. Rental stores are also terrific places to obtain decorating ideas. Meet with the store's consultants and go through your event plans step-by-step. You'll find they will help you select the right items to meet your needs, as well as help determine the correct quantities. You will work very closely with the rental store you choose—make sure you feel confident in the services its staff will provide you. They will be an important extension of your staff.

Tent Rental. A tent often serves as an ideal back up location for an outdoor event, in case of unsuitable weather conditions. Many tents feature transparent vinyl siding that can be raised and lowered as needed. A tent supplier can recommend sources for any portable heating or air conditioning that you might need.

Important Note: Never use canvas tents treated with mineral oil for water-proofing, they are extremely flammable.

Tent Capacities. The following are estimated capacities for tents of typical sizes under normal conditions:

16' x 16' accommodates 45 reception, 32 buffet with seating, 24 served dinner
20' x 20' accommodates 65 reception, 56 buffet with seating, 40 served dinner
20' x 30' accommodates 100 reception, 86 buffet with seating, 60 served dinner
30' x 30' accommodates 180 reception, 124 buffet with seating, 100 served dinner
40' x 40' accommodates 350 reception, 280 buffet with seating, 240 served dinner

Choosing a Tent Site. When arranging tents with a single transparent vinyl side, consider the position of the sun during your event; if the clear portion faces due west through an evening event, the sunset may be blinding. Also, be certain that you do not pitch your tent over low or uneven ground that might accumulate water runoff.

Decide on formality and budget. Keep in mind the colors and decor of the site. Pick linens or paper products and tableware that will complement the room. Prices will vary depending on the formality you choose.

Table art has become very popular for many events. Your event theme is carried through to the tables—the linens, chair covers, dishware, and centerpiece all have a purpose. This "table art" is the newest buzz among event planners! Visit a rental, specialty linen, or chair cover company today to get lots of incredible ideas!

Deposits, delivery, and setup. Reserve your items as far in advance as possible, especially during the summer months when outdoor events are popular. A deposit will secure the order for your date. Only a certain number of tents and canopies are available, and every item is reserved on a first-come, first-served basis. There is a charge on most items for delivery, setup, and pickup. Make sure you ask in advance how much those charges are so you can include them in your budget. You can also make arrangements to pick up and return the items yourself.

Returning items. If you don't arrange delivery and pickup services with the rental company, you will want to put someone in charge of picking up and returning the rented items for you. You will be responsible and may forfeit any deposit for items that are damaged, broken, lost, or late.

Specialty event rentals. All kinds of equipment, from cellular phones and pagers to computers and specialty staging and lighting, are available for rent. Due to the sophisticated nature of this type of equipment, you may wish to work with specialized rental companies. They have the technicians on staff to maintain, set up, and operate this equipment.

Custom Chair Covers

Seattle's Original Chair Cover Rental Company

3902 West Valley Highway, Suite 400
Auburn, Washington 98001
(253) 939-7119; Fax (253) 939-0984

WE'LL TRANSFORM ALL YOUR SPECIAL EVENTS FROM SOMETHING ORDINARY... INTO SOMETHING EXTRAORDINARY!

The event professionals...

Since 1991, Custom Chair Covers has been the company party and event professionals have come to count on for extraordinary customer service and follow through, plus exceptional product. Custom Chair Covers helps you bring your ideas and party themes to life.

- Banquets
- Receptions
- Holiday Parties
- Auctions
- Reunions
- Anniversaries
- Award Parties
- Conventions
- Grand Openings
- Special Events
- Picnics
- Retirement Dinners

When every detail counts...

Let one of our event specialists show you how to pull all the elements together to create the atmosphere and decor that your guests will be sure to admire and talk about. At Custom Chair Covers, our chair covers have been designed to custom-fit a variety of different chair styles. We offer many choices of bows, sashes and tie-backs to complement and enhance your event colors and theme.

Always the "best seats in the house"...

Every guest will know just how important they are to you and feel like they've been given the "best seat in the house" when you decorate with chair covers from Custom Chair Covers.

Custom and promotional items

At Custom Chair Covers, we offer an entire division dedicated to manufacturing custom promotional items. You can duplicate your company's logo, feature the guest of honor's name, include the company motto, feature a new product being introduced, or incorporate your event name. Just use your imagination, and we'll do the rest.

- Chair Covers
- Chair Backs
- Sport Eye Glass Cover
- Head Rests
- Putter Covers
- Bike Helmets

Custom Chair Covers—Making Ordinary Chairs...
EXTRAORDINARY
For Rental or Sales Information, please call (253) 939-7119

All photos © SHOTSnow

Kyra Stewart
(425) 747-9881
E-mail: info@aMasquerade.com
Web site: www.aMasquerade.com

Rent a moment in the spotlight for your attendees.

No other costume rental company brings the shop to you, and dresses your attendees. *Cameo-to-Go* provides pure entertainment as attendees step back in time, celebrate the season, travel around the world, or discover an alter ego, then peel it all off after capturing the moment on film. They keep a commemorative souvenir photo showcasing your theme in a fun way, yet don't have to hassle with wearing a costume as they enjoy the rest of your event.

Full range of rental items available

Cameo-to-Go customized mobile wardrobe and interactive display of costumes and accessories for attendees to wear while posing for commemorative photos of your theme event.

We also offer standard costume rentals if you'd like to dress greeters or staff to set the mood of your theme event; and retail accessories if you'd like to present masks or other costume related items as gifts.

Ordering and delivery

Cameo-to-Go includes a customized assortment of rental costumes and accessories, interactive display rack with mirror, delivery, set -up, and wardrobe assistant staff to help guests get into character for their photos. Does not include photography services. We recommend SHOTS***now***, offering digital photographs printed on-site for your attendees to take with them.

See page 405 under Entertainers & Performers.

SEATTLE
6404-216th Street S.W.
Mountlake Terrace, WA 98043
(425) 640-5547

TACOMA
1325 South Tacoma Way
Tacoma, WA 98409
(253) 472-7000

Web site: www.aaparty.com

AA Party Rentals is the premier party rental company of the greater Puget Sound area and the Pacific Northwest. Whether you're planning an intimate dinner party for two, a wedding for 300, a business function for 700 or a charity event for thousands—you can depend on us to help you. ***AA Party Rentals*** will provide you with the highest quality merchandise mixed with an experienced, knowledgeable, service oriented staff. Call either of our locations to start the planning of your next event.

- CHAIRS—numerous styles including gold, silver and mahogany ballroom chairs
- TABLES—all sizes and shapes
- CHINA—twelve patterns
- CRYSTAL and GLASSWARE
- DANCE FLOORS
- STAGING
- LINENS—the largest selection in the Seattle area
- TABLETOP and WEDDING DÉCOR
- CONCESSION EQUIPMENT
- COOKING and SERVICE EQUIPMENT
- *and much more!*

AA Party Rentals is your ultimate source for **TENTING**. Tenting can add distinction and beauty to any event along with extra space. They can protect you from the elements—scorching sun or Seattle rain. We specialize in tenting of all sizes—whether it be a backyard wedding, a company picnic in the park or even an arts festival. Our tents range in size from 10'x10' to 50'x180'. Our comprehensive line of accessories completes your tented event.

- HEATERS
- LIGHTING
- SIDEWALL
- DANCE FLOOR
- TENT LINERS
- STAGING
- PORTAFLOOR
- ASTROTURF

AA Party Rentals offers complimentary on site consultations. Please call to make an appointment with one of our experts or to have a brochure mailed to you. Visit one of our showrooms or our web site to see how we can make your event a truly special event.

Seattle
(425) 640-5547

Tacoma
(253) 472-7000

Toll Free 1-800-21-TENTS
(1-800-218-3687)

www.aaparty.com

PARTY RENTS

1310 North 131st Street
Seattle, Washington 98133
(206) 362-3222 or (800) 89-Abbey;
Fax (206) 362-1322
Web site: abbeypartyrents.com

For the most fabulous event ever, you need to call us!

We will make sure that your event is the very best that your friends and associates have ever attended our party consultants will go to your home or office and assist you with all of the details free of charge. They will measure your site, determine what you need and help your party be an absolute success! For an additional charge, a consultant can be on site during your event, to provide worry-free assistance to you.

We rent...

- Tables
- Chairs
- China
- Silver
- Catering Equipment
- Chafing Dishes
- Coffeemakers
- Serving Trays

Ordering and delivery

Reservations are highly recommended so that we can guarantee item availability. We are more than happy to deliver and pick up please call our party consultants for an estimate or free consultation.

A grand time

We want you to have a wonderful time too! We care about our customers and want you to continue to depend on us for all of your party needs.

Expect the best

We are experts in our field working for us are the very best people in the industry. They know what they are doing and are dedicated to making your event a memorable one! Parties for 20 or 1,000—nothing is too small or too large for us to handle.

Trades shows/convention services

We specialize in pipe & drape, electrical & lighting. We also do draped tables, planning and consultant services for all your event needs.

We also rent dance floors, staging and our famous canopies! You have seen our canopies at the UW, SAFECO Field and The KUBE haunted house, among others. We also provide a 24 hour emergency pager number, just in case a situation arises. You can count on us to handle any emergency.

Please call for a list of our rental items.

20031 Highway 99
Lynnwood, Washington 98036
(425) 774-9666
or Toll Free (877) 939-RENT
Business Hours: Mon-Sat 8am–6pm,
Sun 9am–5pm

The Success of your day begins and ends with ABC Rentals.

Knowledgeable and Friendly Service

Being the first to arrive and the last to leave is our business. From the first phone call you make to the last champagne glass packed away we will make every effort to ensure that you receive the professional service you deserve. Our knowledgeable party consultants will work with you to arrange all the details, from choosing proper quantities and making helpful suggestions to determining set-up times, deliveries and pick-ups.

A Full Range of Rental Supplies

Arches	Glassware	Candelabras	Canopies
China	Columns	Concession	Dance Floors
Flatware	Linens	Portable Bars	Serving Equipment
Skirting	Staging	Tables & Chairs	Tents
Truck Rentals	Wedding Accessories	Centerpieces	Catering Needs

See the Difference

Wondering if a canopy will fit in your backyard? Give us a call, we have experienced staff that will meet with you at your site to give you ideas and answer any questions that you may have. It is our belief that, "seeing is believing," so whether you are selecting fine china or casual buffet ware, we offer you quality and quantity at a fair price.

Ordering and Delivery

We recommend that rental orders be placed well in advance of your wedding date. Most rentals are for a one day charge, which includes a day for pickup, a day for use, and a day for returning. Long term rates are available. Delivery is available seven (7) days a week.

COMPARE OUR PRICES

Since 1969 we have strived to provide a quality service with a quality product at a competitive price. Our experienced staff will go the extra mile and help you with your every need. Delivery is available seven days a week anywhere in Western Washington.

Please call for a complimentary catalog (425) 774-9666
or toll free 1-877-939-RENT

1523-15th Avenue West
Seattle, Washington 98119

(206) 282-1987

Web site: www.AlexanderPartyRentals.com

WHEN YOU WANT MORE THAN *"JUST ANOTHER PARTY"*— CALL ALEXANDER PARTY RENTALS!

From the simplicity of a picnic to the extravagance of a wedding, discover how our experienced consultants can assist you with all your rental needs. We offer free on-site or over the phone consultations to assist you with the sizing, decor and design of your event. At Alexander Party Rentals, we carry all your party and event needs!

Party and Event Department

- Tenting
- Tables
- Chairs
- Dance Floors
- Staging
- Wedding Supplies
- Table Linens
- Coffee Service
- Silver Service
- China
- Glassware
- Flatware
- Beverage Service
- Centerpieces
- Food Service
- Balloons
- Decorations
- Disposable Items

Commercial Food Service

- Barbecues
- Food Slicers
- Hot Plates & Burners
- Griddles
- Portable Ovens
- Steam Tables
- Stock Pots
- Cookware
- Hot Boxes
- Transit Units
- Woks
- Deep Fat Fryers

And Much More...

- Audio Visual
- Props and Decor
- Concession Machines
- Guest Rental Needs
- Free Consulting
- Quality Service

Call (206) 282-1987 for Price List

ELWAY RESEARCH, INC.

7107 Greenwood Avenue North
Seattle, Washington 98103
Contact: Jone Howard
(206) 264-1500
Fax (206) 264-0301
E-mail: jone@elwayresearch.com

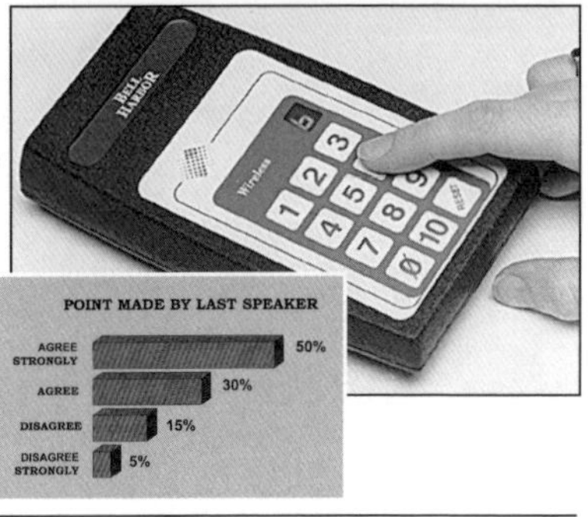

Conduct Meetings That Are Fun And Productive With Electronic Polling

With EGIS, the Electronic Group Interaction System, each meeting participant is able to instantly respond to material being presented through an individual keypad. Participants responses are continuously recorded on the systems computer. Results can be projected for viewing by all participants or displayed to meeting organizers on a monitor in a separate room. The data are saved—available for statistical analysis.

- **Anonymous response and instantaneous display of group responses** means more productive meetings.
- **EGIS keeps the process moving and on task.** As participants register their opinions, tabulated results are displayed to the group for further consideration.
- **Diverging opinions are revealed.** One group's answers can be instantly compared with another's, and/or with information gathered from a source outside the meeting.
- **Everyone participates, equally and continuously.** Because participants register their responses anonymously, they are included equally—without regard to verbal skills, language barriers, or willingness to speak up in a meeting.

Enable Participants To:

- Remain actively engaged in the meeting.
- Feel motivated to participate.
- Stay continuously involved.

Enable Meeting Organizers To:

- Measure participant attitudes on key questions.
- Monitor response as the meeting takes place.
- Direct/re-direct based on participant response.
- Get information to the right people.
- Enhance team building.

Instant Surveys: What do participants think about?

- Important issues?
- The points the speaker just made?
- The future of the organization?
- A question from the floor?
- The topic of the next speaker?

Move To Consensus:

- Participants see how their views match those of the group.
- Questions can be re-formulated as the discussion evolves.

Question On The Fly:

- Questions can be added as quickly as you can type.
- Results are displayed in 5 seconds!

Vote:

- EGIS tallies and reports votes instantly.

Elway Research offers a complete range of meeting services:

- Equipment Rental
- Meeting Facilitation
- Question Design
- Hard Copy Charts
- Polling Facilitation
- Data Analysis & Report

CALL FOR A FREE CONSULTATION ON YOUR NEXT MEETING!

www.sonsationalevents.com

BRAND NEW EQUIPMENT EVERY YEAR!

Games Available For All Ages and Needs...Call For FREE Brochures!

We offer all the standard interactive and arcade games available on the market today, as well as a full line of entertainment services including professional DJs with dynamic sound and lighting! Listed below is just a sampling of some of our more unique and exciting games.

INTERACTIVES: Batting Cage • Big Time Wrestling • Climb-n-dangle • Gladiator Dome • 4-Way Joust • Go Racers • High Ball • Human Whirl • Jacob's Ladder • Mechanical Rides—*Bull, Can, Bottle, Football, Surf Board, Snowboard* • Psycho Swing • Team Twirl • Trampoline Thing

SLIDES: Fire Truck • Mt Rainier • Titanic • Tsunami • Water Slide • Wave of Fire • Wild Rapids (inner tubing!)

BOUNCERS: Jurassic Park • Noah's Ark • Octopus Play Center • Cody the Cowboy • Monster Truck • Palm Tree • Ellie the Elephant • Thomas the Train

OBSTACLE COURSES: Adrenaline Rush • Commando Zip Line • Extreme 70' • Figure-8 • Iceberg • Kong Challenge • Search and Rescue • Seven Element • Ultimate Survivor • Vertical Jeopardy

POPULAR CHILDREN'S ITEMS: Alpine Racer • Ball Ponds • Copterland • 4-In-1 Extreme Kid's Combo • Gilligan's Adventure • Interactive Airplane • Space Carnival • Jungle Maze • Parachute Express

BILLIARDS & ARCADE GAMES: Air Hockey • Foosball • Golf Chip Challenge • Indy Video Cars • Pool • Putting Challenge • Slot Car Racing • Video Game Pods

ENTERTAINMENT: Bingo W/ MC • Clicker Game Wheel • Dance Dance Revolution • Pro DJ Packages • Game Show Mania • Reaction Attraction • Karaoke

TENTS, TABLES & CHAIRS: We offer an extensive range of wedding-quality tents from 10'x10' through 30'x50' available with sides, heaters, lighting, etc. We also have round and banquet tables and collapsible chairs.

Contact: Pat Mobley
(253) 564-7766
Fax (253) 564-7725
E-mail: pmobley@bbjlinen.com
Web site: www.bbjlinen.com

BBJ Linen is one of the premier specialty linen rental companies in the United States. It was started 18 years ago in Skokie, Illinois, a suburb of Chicago. BBJ provides fine table linen for many notable events including the Seattle Opera, Washington State Wine Auction, the Swan Ball, United Way Fundraisers, the Chicago Symphony and Lyric Opera Galas. BBJ now has showrooms in Atlanta, Chicago, Dallas, Detroit, Los Angeles, Nashville, Orlando, Phoenix, and St. Louis. In addition, the company has representatives in Milwaukee and Seattle.

BBJ's philosophy is to provide fashion forward, high quality linen, supported by strong customer service. In the last year, BBJ added over 50 new styles to its collection of over 400 patterns, which come in a variety of colors and sizes. Chair covers in white, black, ivory and navy, chiffons and a rainbow of colors in satin provide an added dimension to your special event. Chair ties; in a multitude of patterns, colors and fabrics enhance our covers. As always, BBJ is "fashion forward" in it's thinking and is able to offer you the most current selection of styles and patterns. Ask to see the latest trend in wedding and special event décor.

In addition to table linen, BBJ provides linen installation services for large events. Teams of set-up professionals go to the event site install chair covers and ties, and customize the presentation of tablecloths for more elegant, eye-catching looks.

BBJ is a certified Women's Business Enterprise and is a member of the Textile Rental Services Association, the American Rental Association, Meeting Professionals International, The National Association of Catering Executives and the International Society of Event Specialists.

CHOICE LINENS

***fancy* table linen rental**

◆

Our Showroom
111 Battery Street • Seattle, Washington 98121
(206) 728-7731; Fax (206) 448-2007
Mon, Wed, Fri 9am–5pm; Tue and Thu 9am–6pm; Sat by appointment
E-mail: info@choicelinens.com
Web site: www.choicelinens.com

Service & Style

Choice Linens provides Seattle with exquisite rental table linens which can be seen at our Belltown showroom six days a week. After almost a decade in Seattle, we have customized our linens for event venues as well as specifically for our sophisticated clientele. Our extensive inventory, which include damasks, sheer organzas, toile cottons and metallics is located here in Seattle. We are able to provide exceptional service from start to finish for your table top.

Your Resouce for the Ultimate in Tabletop Design

Choice Linens is proud to introduce the Pantry, an Event Design Gallery located adjacent to our showroom in Belltown. We have researched centerpieces, interesting silverware, unique plates as well as place card holders and silver julep cups. The Pantry showcases various styles of rental chairs and rental chair cover options are presented to go with the chairs.

Our extensive resource library is available for perusal with vignettes to give a nudge to an idea or two. Choice also offers design consulting (it is all in the details) with your style and budget in mind.

New in 2002

Choice Linens has been providing Seattle with exquisite choices enhancing the tabletops of the finest events. We work in all of the major hotels as well as many private clubs and residences. Choice Linens introduces into its line for 2002, specialty glassware, base plates, napkin rings and more.

We provide timely delivery and pick-up service. Additionally, Choice Linens in house staff is available for project management , on site event coordination and event installation.

Please visit our comprehensive website

www.choicelinens.com

We will be happy to send swatches upon request.

Linens By Alice

11222-20th Avenue South • Seattle, Washington 98168-1717
(206) 650-4334; Fax (206) 246-2566
E-mail: pat@linensbyalice.com
Web site: www.linensbyalice.com

Linens for All Occasions

Linens By Alice has been providing exceptional table linens to individuals, caterers, and event planners since 1985. We take special pride in the outstanding quality of the products and services we offer. Our attention to detail ensures that the linens each client receives will be fresh, crisp, and clean.

Selection

Our unique selection of designer fabrics, distinctive textures and extensive inventory enable us to tailor our service to you and your particular event. Our collection includes a wide variety of chiffons, crepes, damasks, prints, silks and velvets. Linens By Alice also carries an array of organzas, metallic netting, and lamés which are sure to add a dramatic dimension to any tablescape.

Style

Our creative team would be delighted to assist you in developing a linen concept for any occasion. In addition to our website, ***www.linensbyalice.com***, we have an extensive catalogue of digitized photos of our designer fabrics. We can set up a sample table in our design studio, send fabric swatches, or e-mail you a photo collection for you to view. We would be delighted to set up an on-site personal consultation for any event, at your convenience, days or evenings.

Service

Linens By Alice provides complete delivery and pick-up services. Our delivery team is prompt, reliable and knowledgeable. We also offer set-up and break-down services for those events which need that extra special attention to detail. Please feel free to contact us at (206) 650-4334 for further information or assistance. We look forward to the opportunity to work with you soon!

1-800-503-3433

www.daywireless.com

Rental Services

Day Wireless Systems specializes in the rental of wireless equipment. Whether your needs are short term or long term, whether you're equipping a legion of employees or just a few, we can design a Rental Program that's just right for you.

Renting provides numerous advantages for today's business:

- Improve your productivity and profitability
- Increase your efficiency
- Keep in touch with key personnel
- Provide greater safety on the job site

We offer Daily, Weekly or Monthly Rental of Portable Two-Way Radios, Cellular Phones, Nextel Phones, Satellite Phones and more. All available for shipment within 24-hours, and at terms to meet your budget. You can also look to Day for a complete range of accessories to make your rental products even more effective.

Rental products are ideal for:

- Construction
- Fairs
- Corporate moves
- Conventions
- Festivals
- Facility management

Please contact us at 1-800-503-3433
or visit our website at *www.daywireless.com*
for more information.

Notes

RESTAURANTS

❖❖❖

722 Pine Street • Seattle, WA 98101
(206) 467-7777; Fax (206) 467-8891
Dinner 4pm to 1am
Weekday Lunch 11am to 4pm
Breakfast daily starting at 7am
E-mail: catering@dragonfishcafe.com
Web site: www.dragonfishcafe.com

"A place for sharing."

Description of Restaurant: Pan Asian cuisine with a twist. Watch sizzling woks and handcrafted sushi rolls prepared in our open kitchen. Pachinko machines line the walls in our lively cocktail lounge which offers daily happy hour specials. The energetic ambiance is accented with an ocean water aquarium and ceramic tile mural. The café is open daily and offers two private banquet rooms seating 30 and 50 guests.

Types of cuisine: Dragonfish Asian Café presents pan Asian cuisine rooted in the traditional foods of Japan, China, Thailand, Korea and Vietnam. Our dishes are evolutionary and cross-cultural in the Pacific Rim. Try lots of things and pass them around the table. Small plates, Dim Sum, and sushi are designed for tastes or appetizers. Noodles and Sharing plates work as starters or substantial bites for two. Explore.

- **Location:** corner of 8th & Pine located in the Paramount Hotel
- **Price per person:** $25
- **ADA:** accessible
- **Parking:** self parking across the street

BRUNCH•LUNCH•DINNER•BAR•RESERVATIONS

900 Madison Street • Seattle, WA 98104
(206) 343-6158
E-mail: mail@hotelsorrento.com
Web site: www.hotelsorrento.com

Description of restaurant

Recently honored by *Gourmet* as one of the nation's best restaurants, the Hunt Club is celebrated for its intimate and elegant setting. Wooden beams and shuttered windows create a relaxing ambiance in which to enjoy our attentive service and excellent cuisine.

Type of cuisine

The Hunt Club features delicious cuisine from the Pacific Northwest and the Mediterranean.

- **Location:** inside the Sorrento Hotel on Seattle's First Hill
- **Price per person:** lunch $24–$35; dinner $50–$100
- **ADA:** fully accessible
- **Parking:** complimentary valet parking for dining patrons

BREAKFAST•BRUNCH•LUNCH•DINNER•BAR•RESERVATIONS•OUTDOOR DINING IN JULY & AUGUST

2601 West Marina Place • Seattle, Washington 98199
(206) 285-1000; Fax (206) 285-7087
Dinner: Fri 5pm–10pm; Sat 4:30pm–10pm;
Sun 4pm–9:30pm; Mon–Thu 5:30pm–9:30pm
Lunch: Mon–Sat 11:30am–2pm; Brunch: Sun 10am–2pm

Description of restaurant

Palisade Restaurant offers elegant waterfront dining. Our guests enjoy beautiful views of the marina, the mountains, and downtown Seattle. Embellished with rich koa wood accents and a glass art décor, Palisade's interior offers an unforgettable atmosphere for our superb cuisine.

Type of cuisine and specialty

Palisade serves the finest Northwest cuisine, often complemented by delicious Polynesian and Asian flavors. Our specialty dishes center around the freshest seafood and meats.

- **Location:** Elliott Bay Marina, ten minutes from downtown
- **Price per person:** lunch: $20; dinner: $45
- **ADA:** Palisade is fully accessible
- **Parking:** complimentary valet and self parking both available

BRUNCH•LUNCH•DINNER•BAR•RESERVATIONS•OUTDOOR DINING•VIEW/SCENIC

28201 Redondo Beach Drive South
Des Moines, Washington 98198
(253) 946-0636
Fax (253) 946-5099
E-mail: redondo@saltys.com
Web site: www.saltys.com

Salty's
AT REDONDO BEACH

Description of Restaurant

Built over the waters of Puget Sound in the charming village of Redondo just a short drive from Tacoma or Seattle, Salty's is famous for a fun beachfront atmosphere, small-town friendly service and impeccably prepared food. Enjoy our water views topped off by the Olympic Mountains outdoors on our seaside decks or indoors where every table has a view of the waterfront. We also accommodate private meetings, parties or events up to 100 seated.

Types of cuisine

Salty's serves Northwest cuisine featuring live Dungeness crab, local oysters and clams, wild salmon, and Prime steaks. Enjoy everything from soup and sandwiches with your favorite beverage to exquisite champagne meals in the dining room. Salty's Sunday Brunch is world famous! Chilled Dungeness crab legs, freshly shucked oysters on the half shell, prawns, salmon, plus traditional breakfast favorites such as Belgian waffles, breads, fresh fruit, custom made omelets, crepes and more.

- **Location:** from the north or south, take I-5, Exit 147; turn onto 272nd Street heading west; follow 272nd all the way to the waterfront, where you can't miss us—we're the building on the water, resting on piers
- **Price per person:** $15–$22
- **ADA:** yes
- **Parking:** adjacent lot free

BRUNCH•LUNCH•DINNER•BAR•RESERVATIONS•OUTDOOR DINING•VIEW/SCENIC

1936 Harbor Avenue S.W.
Seattle, Washington 98126
(206) 937-1600
Web site: www.saltys.com

Description of restaurant

Located on Elliott Bay, Salty's is "One of the World's Great View Restaurants," as described by a local restaurant critic. Whether dressed up or casual, guests love Salty's for fresh Northwest seafood, award-winning seaside decks and patio views. We offer lunch and dinner daily, as well as live jazz in the café. Award-winning banquets and off-premise catering are also available.

Types of cuisine

A world-class restaurant, Salty's serves Northwest cuisine featuring live Dungeness crab, local oysters and clams, salmon, and prime steaks. Readers of *Seattle Magazine* (1999) and *Seattle Weekly* (1998 and 1999) named Salty's Sunday Brunch a top prize winner of the year.

- **Location:** just ten minutes from downtown Seattle, Salty's on Alki is located in West Seattle on the waterfront of Elliott Bay
- **Price per person:** $15–$35
- **ADA:** elevator at sea level will take you to dining rooms
- **Parking:** ample free parking on-site; valet service available on weekends

BRUNCH • LUNCH • DINNER • BAR • RESERVATIONS • OUTDOOR DINING • VIEW/SCENIC

---

space needle

Located at Seattle Center • Entrance at Broad & John Streets
(206) 905-2100 or (800) 937-9582
Lunch: Mon–Fri 11am–3pm; Dinner: Mon–Thu 4:30pm–9pm,
Fri–Sat 4:30pm–10pm, Sun 4:30pm–9pm;
Brunch: Sat–Sun 9am–3pm
Web site: www.spaceneedle.com

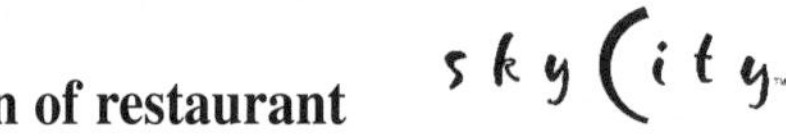

Description of restaurant

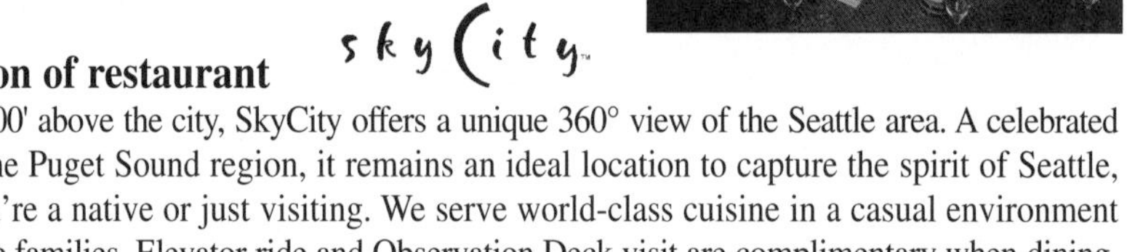

Revolving 500' above the city, SkyCity offers a unique 360° view of the Seattle area. A celebrated symbol of the Puget Sound region, it remains an ideal location to capture the spirit of Seattle, whether you're a native or just visiting. We serve world-class cuisine in a casual environment and welcome families. Elevator ride and Observation Deck visit are complimentary when dining.

Type of cuisine

SkyCity specializes in the finest Pacific Northwest cuisine. Our chefs insist on preparing our menu with the freshest available seafood, locally grown vegetables, and fine-aged meats. Nearly everything we serve originates in our own beautiful region.

- **Location:** conveniently located on the Seattle Center campus
- **Price per person:** $25–$42; elevator ride and observation deck visit are included
- **ADA:** the Space Needle is fully accessible
- **Parking:** valet parking is available at an additional charge

Speakers

❖❖❖

HELPFUL HINTS

Why a professional? Professional speakers will provide you with a depth of experience and a proven track record that can be verified by checking their references. In addition, they can customize their presentation for your group and provide previews of their work. Professionals reduce your risks. Don't take the chance of having an amateur practice at your event. You have only one chance to get it right.

Speakers can contribute to your event or meeting: A successful speaker generates excitement, motivation and boosts overall morale of the audience. The speaker and or the topic can motivate guests to attend a function.

Where to find a speaker: On the following pages you will find some of the local speakers. Other resources for speakers are: Consultants (listed in "Entertainment Consultants" section of this Guide), Speakers Bureaus, Universities and your own professional groups or peer recommendations.

Get a good reference: Observe the speaker performing live, if possible, or via an audio or video tape of a recent presentation. Talk to some of his or her recent clients and ask their opinions. If you are looking for a speaker and have no references, or are uncomfortable contacting speakers directly, consult with a reputable speakers bureau. They don't charge for their services. If you're planning an event outside the Puget Sound area, you'll find speakers bureaus listed in the yellow pages of most cities.

Agree on fees and expenses in advance: Be sure that the terms of the honorarium or speaker's fee and expenses are clearly agreed upon in advance.

Get it in writing: Advise the speaker (confirmed with a contract to be signed and returned) of the day, time, and place of the engagement. Specify if you expect the speaker to attend any function before or after the presentation, and be sure such attendance is within the parameters of the fee and the travel schedule.

Ask for the speaker's help: Request a list of audio visual or other requirements needed for the most effective presentation. If there will be handouts, clarify who is responsible for printing them. Provide the speaker with the audience profile and theme of your meeting and any other information that will help him or her relate to the audience. Request information and photos from the speaker to simplify development of your program and to utilize in promotional materials for the event.

Speaker and audio visual rehearsal: Give the speaker a chance to rehearse with the microphone and podium they will be using so they are comfortable with the placement and setup.

Back-up speaker: Plans can change, so it's always smart to keep a back-up speaker in mind, especially if you have a political figure scheduled.

VIP transportation: Having speakers, leaders, and important guests picked up at the airport is good insurance that your VIPs will arrive on time. These people are critical to the success of the event, and they deserve special treatment. Check on arrival and departure times, customs, etc. Select the best route to your destination.

Multi-media presentations: A visual presentation, whether on video, slide or projector, can be an enhancement to any program. Unless your company is equipped and accustomed to producing visual presentation materials, it is smart to seek out experts who specialize in this field.

Speakers helper: It's a good idea to assign someone to greet the speaker and show him/her the meeting room in advance of your function.

Presentations with Pizazz!

Coral Rief Communications, Inc.
Contact: Jennifer Monteleone, APR
(360) 563-1161 or Toll-free (877) 591-8488
Fax (360) 563-9211
E-mail: info@coralrief.com
Web site: www.coralrief.com

Need some assistance developing your next presentation?

Our event services include:

- Employee newsletters
- Executive briefings
- Executive retreat presentations
- Graphic design
- Key message development
- Powerpoint presentation development
- Media interview preparation and training
- Sales meeting concepts and presentation development
- Speech writing
- Team building speakers and presentations

Our Experience

With more than 20 years of combined communications experience, we can assist you in crafting the right message, perfectly packaged to generate the results you deserve.

For presentations that deliver results, give us a call:

Coral Rief Communications
Toll-free (877) 591-8488
or visit us at
www.coralrief.com

LEADERSHIP QUEST

Steve Gutzler

4580 Klahanee Drive S.E., PMB 102
Issaquah, Washington 98029
(425) 681-9871 or (206) 660-6568
E-mail: stevegutzler@hotmail.com

Steve Gutzler, the founder and president of **Leadership Quest**, a Seattle-based leadership organization, is an authentic and engaging communicator. Having traveled and spoken extensively over the past 20 years throughout the country, he has had an opportunity to interact with many accomplished individuals. It is through experiences like these that Steve has come to understand what develops and drives leaders to sustain success.

He believes strong leaders live within a context defined by **Three Key Factors:** an extraordinary mission, expressed core values and impassioned goals. He will convince you that professional excellence and career achievement need not come at the expense of a satisfying, purposeful life. In fact, inspiring others to lead and live richer lives has become Steve's leadership quest...his purpose!

An ability and willingness to tailor keynote speeches, seminars and personal coaching sessions to address the specific needs of his audience also makes Steve Gutzler relevant and fresh. He captivates listeners by speaking with passion, warmth and humor and promotes group participation through thought-provoking questions. He masterfully puts people at ease as he guides, encourages and inspires them to be all they can be. Experience Steve Gutzler's dynamic message, spontaneously delivered with heart and soul, clarity and vision.

We work closely with each client to assure that each event is targeted and current to the audience. Some of the most recent keynote addresses and seminars include:

- **"And Then Some" Attitudes...***transform & sustain impassioned attitudes*
- **Powers of an Extraordinary Mission...***conquer mission drift, clear value fuzziness; achieve bold & imposing goals*
- **"Surprise and Delight"...***provide unexpected and exceptional customer service*
- **Art of Self-Leadership...***the feeling one gets when they live out their values*
- **Leading with Significance...***develop and sustain high performance successful teams*
- **Leadership—Keeping Calm in Chaos...***the keys to focused results during turbulent times*

"People came to me for weeks to tell me what a big impact Steve made."
—Wesley Moorhead, Director of Finance, Microsoft Corporation

"I've never seen morale so high or a group coming together so quickly."
—Bill Harris, Vice President, Bernard Hodes Group

R. DAVID COUSINEAU

2142 Tenth Avenue West
Seattle Washington 98119
(206) 298-9630
E-mail: rdcousin@seattlechildrenshome.org • ***Web site: www.seattlechildrenshome.com***

A compelling speaker, R. David Cousineau offers his expertise through keynotes and trainings. His outcome-driven vision for today's organizations continues to attract both local and national attention. David has become known throughout the community as a gifted speaker developing a platform for social awareness. His talks address the unique needs of the next generation's at-risk youth, and socially responsible ways in which the business community can seek to meet these needs. Illustrating ways to eradicate socioeconomic burdens, he calls today's communities to action, and he suggests what WE can do as business people and concerned citizens to help create a better tomorrow.

Twenty-five years of experience in the non-profit sector, currently as President of Seattle Children's Home, afford Cousineau the professional expertise to address many timely issues. The following titles are representative of his extensive repertoire:

Don't Flirt in the Dark — the ingredients for leadership in life

Keep the Bug on the Mountain — the role of passion, mission and outcomes in management and business

Good Outcomes, Not Just Good Agencies — the future of non-profits in America

Living in the Shadows — three years in a homeless shelter; the secret pains of poverty

Spirituality in the Workplace — a fire within for the fire without

A River of Children — the journey of refugee children in the world—from poverty to prostitution

Going to the Dogs — effective public and corporate speaking

rdcousin@seattlechildrenshome.org

www.seattlechildrenshome.org

Stephanie A. Horton, CMP

P.O. Box 447 • Grapeview, WA 98546
(360) 275-7370; Fax (360) 275-7306
E-mail: shorton@pacificrimprotocol.com
Web site: www.pacificrimprotocol.com

"Giving your Best and Getting your Best from People"

Good manners are back! Raise a glass to successful business with local etiquette expert Stephanie Horton, CMP as your keynote speaker. Today's business people have questions—many questions—about how to conduct themselves in today's competitive business world. *High tech = high touch*, but that doesn't mean everyone appreciates a big bear hug instead of a warm handshake! From customer service to dealing with the challenges of everyday change, look to Stephanie for a new approach to motivational speaking. Give your audiences an entertaining presentation that will help them every day. And, for you? A private session on professional grooming. Call for hourly fees.

POLISHING THE APPLE: Tailored Topics for Today's Business Executives

The Power of Common Courtesy...Business Etiquette that Works!
How to Dine with Clients
Networking that Means Business...Schmooze or Lose!
Cutting Edge High-Tech Etiquette
Navigating in a Sea of Change
Who Sits at the Head of a Round Table? (Who said "team?")
What? Communicating through the Crowd
How to Start an Event Planning Business
Selling Rooms & Space with Style & Grace
Professional Server School...training for hospitality waitstaff
Customer Service Rules! The Royal Treatment
And more

www.pacificrimprotocol.com

Stephanie Horton, CMP is the instructor for
Highline Community College's
Event & Meeting Planning Certification Program.
Call today for more information.

Transportation & Valet Services

❖❖❖

HELPFUL HINTS

Airfare savings: Special negotiated airfares are available for groups of ten or more. To qualify, travelers must share a common destination and be traveling in the same time frames. Travelers need not originate from the same city.

Meeting dates and times for travelers: Planning your meeting dates and times will enable attendees to take advantage of non-refundable excursion airfares which are discounted up to 70%. Schedule meeting dismissal time so attendees can take the last afternoon/evening flight out to avoid the cost of an additional night's stay at the hotel.

Bus and coach transportation: Buses and coaches come in your basic style of school buses to luxury-Elite Motorcoaches. You'll want to determine your audience and then select the most appropriate transportation.

Livery service: There are taxi cabs, limousines, and livery service. Livery service is a luxury form of transportation without the recognition of a local cab or limousine. The driver is uniformed and highly skilled with exceptional customer service. This is a VIP form of transportation for important attendees, speakers and special guests.

Valet service: For your next event or special occasion, valet service adds that special touch. Services include: shuttle vans, lot attendants to park your guests' cars, and parking consulting services to help maximize parking space and to monitor the traffic flow. These companies should be properly insured and licensed.

Ground transportation: Get facts and figures on capacities, capabilities and types of transportation available to and from the meeting site. Talk to planners who have handled groups of your size. Select your transportation on the basis of cost, reputation, degree of service, number, condition and availability of vehicles. Motor-coaches (buses) are the most frequently used vehicle for moving groups. You may need charter buses or shuttle buses. A charter follows a pre-determined route for a specified length of time. A shuttle operates continuously on a regularly established route.

Common questions that should be asked of various transportation companies: Are there minimum rental periods? What is the bus capacity? How is dispatch done? Can disabled passengers be accommodated? Are backups available? Are buses air conditioned? What routes will be used? How comprehensive is their insurance liability? Can the price be negotiated?

VIP transportation: Pick up speakers, leaders, and guests at the airport or other locations. These people are critical to the success of your event. They deserve special treatment.

Assign staff members as official greeters, select appropriate vehicles, check arrival and departure times and potential customs or immigration problems. Select the best airport location to meet as well as the best drop-off points and the quickest route.

Don't reserve a vehicle over the phone: Go to the transportation company and inspect the vehicle you are considering renting. Be sure you are dealing with an established, reputable company. These businesses will display, or readily make available, important information like their business license and their liability insurance certificate. If you have concerns or questions, ask for references.

Be sure you get what you pay for: Make sure the limousine or bus will be clean and presentable for your event. Read the contract carefully before paying the deposit. Make sure the date, times, location, and specific vehicle are spelled out in writing.

Seattle, Washington
(206) 283-6600 or Toll Free (866) 526-6600
Fax (206) 282-8007
E-mail: bmclimo@aol.com
Web site: www.bmclimo.com

Since 1987

FOR YOUR MOST SPECIAL EVENT

We offer the Northwest's largest fleet of chauffeured *vintage* Bentleys, Rolls-Royces and other exceptional English vehicles. And at surprisingly affordable prices for some of the finest motor cars in the world.

Expertly detailed, plush leather interiors, with all accessories. Our classic, elegant and unique, one-of-a-kind, beautiful British Motor Coaches can be yours on your Event Day for a stylish and memorable ride you'll never forget. And how about a 1936 Dodge Bros. Hose Pumper Fire Engine for something really unique?

Although originally specializing in weddings, we now find ourselves in ever increasing demand for all types of corporate events: city tours; special guest luncheons and dinners; retirements; incentive awards for employees; gifts for clients, vendors, etc.

Also available—excellent ticket and transportation packages for both the Mariner and Seahawk games.

Services

All our vehicles come complete with uniformed chauffeur, an ice bucket, crystal glasses, water, cider and a complimentary jar of Grey Poupon, of course.

Cost and terms

We charge a minimum rental fee of two consecutive hours in the classics at a rate depending on the vehicle and the day of the week. Special rates are available for four hours or more and for the use of multiple cars. Corporate accounts welcomed. Major credit cards accepted. Reservation form on our web site: ***www.bmclimo.com***.

Vehicles available

- **1950 Bentley MK V1**; two available—2-passenger
- **1957 & 1962 Rolls-Royce Silver Clouds**—2-passenger
- **1963 Vanden Plas Princess**; right hand drive (RHD)—6-passenger
- **1969 Daimler Limousine** (RHD)—6-passenger
- **1967 Austin London Taxi Cab** (RHD)—4-passenger
- **New 8-passenger custom Lincoln Stretch Limousines**: black or white available
- **New Custom Executive Vans**—14-passenger
- **1936 Dodge Bros. Hose Pumper Fire Engine**
- **New Luxury Sedans**

Gray Line of Seattle

4500 West Marginal Way S.W. • Seattle, Washington 98106
(206) 624-5077 or (800) 544-0739
Fax (206) 626-5209
Business Office Hours: 8am–5pm
E-mail: info@graylineseattle.com
Web site: www.graylineofseattle.com

YOUR NORTHWEST CHARTER AND TOUR EXPERTS!

Gray Line of Seattle has the largest fleet of vans, mini-coaches and motorcoaches in the Northwest. We have more than 90 years experience as a full service motorcoach operator and have the largest ADA equipped fleet in the area. We offer a wide range of customized tours and package tours, as well as convention and meeting planning services, charter services and airport transportation.

Types of vehicles and capacities

- **MCI Renaissance**—54-passenger premium motorcoaches
- **MCI 102**—47-passenger deluxe motorcoaches
- **MCI MC-9**—47-passenger standard motorcoaches
- **Executive mini-coaches**—27-passenger
- **Mini-coaches**—24-passenger
- **23 passenger squires**
- **14 passenger vans**
- **Old Time Trolley replicas**—35-passenger

Amenities

Coaches are fully air-conditioned and have PA systems. Many have reclining seats and CD or cassette players. VCR equipped vehicles are available.

Driver experience

All drivers are fully licensed and insured. Drivers hold Commercial Drivers Licenses and go through extensive training. Not only are they professionals, they are knowledgeable, fun and friendly.

Reservations and cost

Reservations can be made on short notice depending on availability. Costs include coach and driver. Gratuities not included. Package pricing available. Please call for details.

 Please let this business know that you heard about them from the Bravo! Event Resource Guide.

811 Stewart Street • Seattle, Washington 98101
(206) 621-0271 or Toll free (800) 403-0024; Fax (206) 621-0295
Business Hours: 8am–5pm
E-mail: mklein@greyhound.com
www.greyhound.com

Your Partner in Reliable Charter Transportaation!

Pacific Northwest Coaches is the newest motorcoach operator in the Pacific Northwest. As a subsidiary of Greyhound Travel Services, we span the United States and Canada with an array of companies capable of helping you plan and execute your transportation needs. Pacific Northwest Coaches offers charter motorcoach transportation, meet-&-greet services, step-on-guide services, group sightseeing and package tours. Our goal is to create loyal customers by providing quality transportation and related services while maintaining affordable rates.

Types of Vehicles

- MCI 102DL3 55-passenger capacity
- MCI 102C3 47-passenger capacity
- MCI MC9 47-passenger capacity

Amenities

All motorcoaches have restrooms, are air conditioned and have public address systems. VCR equipped motorcoaches are available as well.

Driver Experience

All drivers hold Commercial Driver's Licenses and are insured through Pacific Northwest coaches' insurance policy. All drivers complete comprehensive safety and customer service oriented training course.

Reservations and Cost

Last minute reservations are taken on a "motorcoach" available basis. We recommend that reservations are made at least one month prior to departure date. Prices are all inclusive except for driver gratuity. Package pricing is available upon request.

800 S.W. 16th Street • Renton, Washington 98055
Corporate Office (425) 981-7070 or Reservations (425) 981-7000
Fax (425) 981-7053
Web site: www.shuttleexpress.com

Seattle's #1 Transportation Company

Shuttle Express has provided the Northwest with safe, reliable and convenient service since 1987. It's a locally owned and operated company serving the greater Seattle area including south to Tacoma and north to Everett. Shuttle Express is proud to be Seattle's premiere transportation provider

Services

Shuttle Express offers two types of exclusive services ideal for groups and conventions:

- **Express Car:** Lincoln Towncar service, with room for up to four people, will take you to your destination in comfort and style.
- **Charters:** Private van service with room enough for 7, 10 or 21 people and plenty of storage space that will take you to and from any destination of your choice.

Fleet

Our vehicles are current models, smoke free and cleaned before each shift. Our fleet is on a proactive maintenance schedule to provide a clean and safe traveling environment.

Drivers

Our drivers, over 200 of them, are professionally trained, uniformed, drug tested and have exceptional customer service skills. Shuttle Express is proud to operate in a drug free environment.

Reservations

Our reservations agents and group sales coordinators are friendly and helpful. We are available 24 hours a day, everyday. You can also place your reservation over the internet at ***www.shuttleexpress.com***.

P.O. Box 77793 • Seattle, Washington 98177
Business (206) 533-9201; Fax (206) 533-9301
Web site: www.butlervalet.com

Parking Perfection

At Butler Valet, we understand that enjoyable, hassle-free arrival and departure is an essential part of your guests' overall experience. The responsibility of caring for something as personal and valuable as an automobile is not taken lightly. Butler Valet is a family-owned and operated business founded by experienced service professionals that play a hands-on role in each and every parking event.

A Unique Approach

Unlike other valet companies, Butler Valet begins each job with a thorough event evaluation. Drawing from our years of experience, we consider event size, timing and guest flow as part of our comprehensive planning process.

No Worries

Butler Valets conducts an onsite check in advance of the event to determine the optimal staffing levels and traffic flow, and most importantly, plan for the unexpected. We are committed to delivering a superior parking experience under any circumstances.

Flawless Presentation

Our staff of parking service professionals understands the importance of positive face-to-face interaction and presentation. Each member of our team is trained to exude a sophisticated and charismatic demeanor while establishing a level of trust with your guests.

Customized Service and Pricing

Butler takes pride in being the most flexible and resourceful parking services company in the Pacific Northwest. We work within virtually any budget to find a parking solution that meets your needs.

Butler's Promise to You

- Experienced and courteous valet professionals
- Competitive pricing
- Liability insurance
- A choice of various uniforms to fit the occasion or environment
- A written agreement outlining all costs

Additional Services Available

- Shuttle Service
- Traffic Management

Bus & Motorcoach

DELTA, BC–CANADA

Quick Shuttle, Ltd. — 8730 River Road, Delta BC V4G 1B5 CANADA
(604) 940-4428 or (800) 665-2122

PORT ORCHARD

Janssen's City Tours — 1623 Woods Road E., Port Orchard WA 98366
(800) 922-5044 or (360) 871-2446, Fax (360) 871-0245

POULSBO

Majestic Charter & Tours — 16952 Clearcreek Rd. N.W., Poulsbo WA 98370
(360) 394-2102

PUYALLUP

Gazelle International State Lines — P.O. Box 38, Puyallup WA 98371
(206) 762-8983, Fax (206) 762-9047

Totem Coaches, Inc. — PO Box 38, Puyallup WA 98371
(253) 845-7291 or (800) 845-7291, Fax (253) 840-3274

SEATTLE

Airport Express — 4500 W. Marginal Way S.W., Seattle WA 98106
(206) 626-6088, Fax (206) 626-5209

Gray Line of Seattle — 4500 W. Marginal Way SW, Seattle WA 98106 *See page 584*
(206) 624-5077 or (800) 426-7532

Holland American Line/ Westours, Inc. — 300 Elliott Avenue W, Seattle WA 98119
(206) 281-3535

Laidlaw Transit, Inc. — PO Box 80627, Seattle WA 98108
(206) 764-9700, Fax (206) 767-0167

Pacific NW Coaches — 811 Stewart St., Seattle WA 98101 *See page 585*
(206) 621-0271 or (800) 403-0024

Starline Transportation — 150 S. Kenyon Street, Suite C, Seattle WA 98108
(206) 763-5817, Fax (206) 763-5819

VANCOUVER, BC–CANADA

Pacific Coach Lines, Ltd. — #210 1150 Station Street, Vancouver BC V6A 4C7 CANADA
(800) 661-1725

Limousines & Passenger Vans

BELLEVUE

American Classic Limousines — Bellevue WA
(425) 226-0123

Ashton Limousine — PO Box 123, Bellevue WA 98009
(425) 455-4008, Fax (425) 746-3046

Executive Towncar Service — 4624 148th Ave. S., Bellevue WA 98006
(206) 443-4343

Signature Towncar Service — 4624 - 148th Ave. S., Bellevue WA 98006
(206) 443-4343

KIRKLAND

Elite Limousine — 13044 Juanita Drive, Kirkland WA 98034
(425) 821-5466

OAK HARBOR

Liberty Limousine — 1875 NW Beach Rd., Oak Harbor WA 98277
(360) 675-7116

RENTON

Shuttle Express — 800 S.W. 16th St., Renton WA 98055 *See page 586*
(425) 981-7070 or (800) 487-7433

SEATTLE

A Carey Limousine Sedans & Vans Service — PO Box 88963, Seattle WA 98138
(206) 762-9432, Fax (206) 768-1607

Bayview Limousine
Services, Inc. — 22001 Pacific Hwy. S., Suite 112, Seattle WA 98198
(206) 824-6200, Fax (206) 824-9884

British Motor Coach, Inc. — Seattle WA *See page 583*
(206) 283-6600 or (866) 526-6600, Fax (206) 282-8007

First Class Limousine — PO Box 22069, Seattle WA 98122
(206) 329-5395

Seattle Limousine — PO Box 80205, Seattle WA 98108
(206) 762-3339

Washington Limousine, Inc. — 8016 Ashworth Avenue N., Seattle WA 98103
(206) 523-8000

Taxicabs

SEATTLE

Farwest Taxi — 2450 Sixth Avenue S., Seattle WA 98134
(206) 622-1717
Graytop Cabs — 74 South Hudson, Seattle WA 98134
(206) 282-8222
Orange Cab — 11621 Des Moines Memorial Drive, Seattle WA 98168
(206) 522-8800
STITA Taxi — PO Box 69774, Seattle WA 98168
(206) 246-9999
Yellow Gray Top Cabs — 74 South Hudson, Seattle WA 98134
(206) 622-6500

Air Charters

ANACORTES

West Isle Air – Anacortes — 4000 Airport Road, Anacortes WA 98221
(800) 874-4434

RENTON

Sound Flight, Inc. - Renton Airport — PO Box 812, Renton WA 98057
(425) 255-6500 or (800) 825-0722

SEATTLE

Classic Helicopter Corporation — 6505 Perimeter Road S., Seattle WA 98108
(206) 767-0515, Fax (206) 767-4018
Kenmore Air — 6321 N.E. 175th (Lk. Union & Lk. Wash. Terminals), Seattle *See page 57*
(800) 543-9595
Northwestern Executive Air — 7205 Perimeter Road S., Seattle WA 98108
(206) 767-2539 or (800) 244-7538
Seattle Seaplanes — 1325 Fairview Ave. E., Seattle WA 98102
(206) 329-9638, Fax (206) 329-9617
West Isle Air – Seattle — 7277 Perimeter Road S., Seattle WA 98108
(206) 768-1945

 Please let these businesses know that you heard about them from the Bravo! Event Resource Guide.

Tuxedos & Formal Wear

❖❖❖

TUXEDOS AND FORMAL WEAR

HELPFUL HINTS

Formal attire makes any event fun and memorable: Numerous formal wear styles are available. The formal wear shop you decide to work with can offer suggestions for styles and colors that will customize your look for any occasion. Tuxedos do not have to look rented. The thousands of styles and accessories available make everyone look original. Women look great in tuxedos, too.

Final fitting and pickup date: You must instruct each event participant to pick up his/her own tuxedo. Make sure they try on the entire outfit at the store. This will avoid the most common problem with formal wear—fit. If adjustments or replacements need to be made, they can usually be done on the spot or arrangements for substitutions can be made. Don't forget about appropriate shoes and socks.

Out-of-town guests: If some guests live out of town, the formal wear shop can supply you with measurement cards you can mail back to them. Any clothing or alterations shop should be able to do a complimentary fitting. It is imperative that gentlemen take the time to try on their entire outfit when they go to pick it up!

Group rates and discounts: Many formal wear shops offer special group rates, discounts, or rebates for black-tie or black-tie-optional events. Ask about setting up a special rate for all the guests who will attend the event or function.

Women's formal and evening attire: There are women's rental shops that carry designer formal and evening gowns for special occasions and pageants. These salons carry one-of-a-kind gowns or a limited selection so you won't bump into your gown on someone else at the same event.

Company parties: Not only will your staff look and feel great in black tie, but renting is more affordable than buying a new suit.

Auctions and benefits: Black tie makes any affair an event to remember. People enjoy having a reason to dress up. These events attract guests who don't mind paying a little extra for an unforgettable evening.

Trade shows: Formal wear adds that finishing touch to your booth or exhibit; your staff will stand out from the competition.

Awards and banquets: There is no better way to honor your esteemed guests than to dress in black tie. Whether presenting or receiving an award, when formally dressed, you are sure to enhance any accomplishment.

Costume theme parties: Tuxedos make great costumes for any theme event. Go avant garde with a black tie and blue jeans, cruise with a white dinner jacket, or stand out at a Hawaiian Luau with the Hawaiian print cummerbund and bow tie.

25 Years of Excellence

Corporate Office:
1205 S.E. Grand Avenue • Portland, Oregon 97214
Marketing: (800) 284-4889
Web site: www.mrformaltuxedos.com
29 convenient locations—
serving Puget Sound and Oregon Area

A Black Tie Event Is Unforgettable

Mr. Formal continues to bring a touch of class and sophistication to special events in the Northwest—a tradition for over 25 years. Mr. Formal offers unbeatable rates, quality, and service. With 29 locations in Oregon and Washington, tuxedo fittings and pickups are always convenient. So let Mr. Formal enhance the atmosphere at your next fund raiser or special event.

Fund Raising Opportunities

Mr. Formal proudly works with many local charities and fundraisers, offering a special rental rate with a donation back to your cause with every tuxedo rented. Mr. Formal will design, print, and deliver custom invitations or ticket inserts announcing the program for your event.

- **$10 donated back to the charity with each full-price rental.**
- **$5 donated back to the charity with each discounted rental.**
- **10% of each retail purchase for the event donated back.**

Corporate Rental Rates

✦ 12–40 persons from	**$ 60.00 per rental**
✦ 41–60	**$ 55.00**
✦ 61 +	**$ 50.00**

Tuxedos include coat, pants, shirt, jewelry and choice of matching cummerbund and tie. Shoes and vests are optional and additional. (Restrictions may apply May through June.)

Event Planning Ideas

- **Special events**—Formalwear brings a touch of class and sophistication
- **Fundraisers**—Black tie makes any affair an event to remember
- **Trade shows**—Formalwear adds that finishing touch to your booth or exhibit
- **Award banquets**—No better way to honor your esteemed guests

A Few Of Our Clients...

- St. Joseph Hospital
- Microsoft
- Cystic Fibrosis Foundation
- United Grocers
- Home Builders Association
- U.S. Bank
- Ronald McDonald House
- Yoshida Group

View our formalwear collection at *www.mrformaltuxedos.com*

Notes

Video Services

HELPFUL HINTS

Video can greatly enhance your event. Many non-profit organizations have found that incorporating video into their live auctions can increase donations for selected items three or four times what was received using still slides. The increase more than pays for the costs of producing the presentation. Trainers have found that the retention of presented materials is increased with the use of video. But how do you budget for the inclusion of a multi-media presentation? What costs are incurred for projecting the video to your audience? And how do you know you are getting a good value for the dollars you spend?

It is recommended that you go to a production company with a budget. Asking what a video costs is like asking for a house to be built, but not telling the contractor if you want a shack or a mansion.

Pricing varies from company to company: Asking for a competitive bid is like comparing apples to oranges. Some will charge less for shooting the material, but charge more for postproduction and duplications. Others will charge a competitive rate but will retain ownership of the material. If you ever want to go back to make changes with another production company, you may have difficulty getting the footage or pay an exorbitant fee. And still others will make numerous charges for additions you add to your production (like music, narration, graphics, titles, etc.). None of those scenarios take into consideration the production content. That too can alter a budget.

Here are some questions you should ask:

1) What format does the production company work with? (Beta SP or Digital is preferable and are considered broadcast standards)
2) To leverage your budget, can you simultaneously produce the project for multi-use? (Trade shows, television broadcast, web-cast, direct marketing, etc.)
3) Who owns the material? (Scripting, final master, and all shot footage.)
4) Will you receive all the shot video upon completion of the project?
5) If the production company archives the video for you, is there a charge, and can you get that footage at any time for your own personal use?
6) Do you get a master copy that you can personally get reproductions done? What are the reproduction charges if using their services?
7) What are the charges for background music?
8) What are the charges for graphics, and/or incorporating multi-media presentations (like a PowerPoint file)?
9) If using talent, what are the costs and union ramifications? Will you have to pick up annual fees for using the material? Are there limitations placed on using the video?
10) What happens if postproduction projections are underestimated? Who absorbs those costs? What about other changes to the production?

It is important to find a production company that listens. How will the production be used? If projecting the video onto large projection screens, what considerations should be made? If considering streaming the video for web-casts, does the production company have experience in providing those services?

Most important, get references! All reputable production companies offer a list of people they've done work for. Call at least three of those references and evaluate their satisfaction with the production company on all aspects of their project.

2200 Sixth Avenue, Suite 750
Seattle, Washington 98121
(206) 256-0420; Fax (206) 256-0419
E-Mail: eln@eln.com
Web site: www.eln.com

EVENT PRESENTATION SPECIALISTS

from small social gatherings to large national events

- Concept, Creative, & Production Consulting
- Full Video (multi-media) Capabilities
- Live Event Broadcasts & Webcasts
- Design, Construction, Lighting, & Sound
- Projection Systems (including large screen IMAG systems)
- Entertainment Network (booking talent)
- Satellite Services & Videoconferencing

OUR COMMITMENT TO YOU...

"I can't tell you what it means to work with people of your caliber; who you can always count on, professionally and personally."

—Kathy Haggart, Executive Director, Boys & Girls Clubs of Bellevue

"Thank you for all of your efforts in making the PONCHO Wine Auction a success. The addition of the video was tremendous."

—Robert DiPietrae & Marc Sherman, Production Chairs, PONCHO

"In the 25 years I have been with the Institute I have never witnessed such a powerful, and beautiful presentation."

—Peggy Casey, The Pacific Institute

RECENT ELN EVENT PRODUCTIONS

- Poncho Auction & Poncho Wine Auction—Seattle, WA
- Fred Hutchinson Holiday Gala—Seattle, WA
- Cystic Fibrosis Auction—Seattle, WA
- American Foundation for Suicide Prevention (live broadcast of three city event to 55 markets and a simultaneous webcast)—New York, NY
- Miami's 100th Anniversary (350,000 people at Bay Front Park)—Miami, FL
- Camp LeJune (live concert and satellite transmission to 27 cities)—LeJune, NC

Whether you are an individual, corporate planner, marketing agency, or producer, let ELN be your creative partner in providing memorable events!

Call us for a free complimentary consultation.

An Incredible Special Event Video Isn't Expensive...

It's Priceless

PAX VIDEO SERVICES

206-242-2333

Pax Video Services is your high quality, reasonably priced video service for your next special event. Professional, non-intrusive video service needn't be expensive nor complex. Enjoy the luxury of fully digital production: multi-camera service with 3 chip, broadcast quality, digital cameras, stereo wireless microphones, custom music and complete post-production including in-house authoring and DVD mastering. Select one of our popular coverage plans which best suits your special event video needs:

2 Hours Coverage	**$ 499**
4 Hours Coverage	**$ 799**
6 Hours Coverage	**$ 999**
8 Hours Coverage	**$1,299**

Corporate or Political Events, Bar Mitzvahs, Bat Mitzvahs, Parties, Promotions, Roll-Outs, Retirements, Formals, Fund-Raisers, Depositions, Reunions, Anniversaries, Holiday Events, Weddings and General Celebrations

PAX VIDEO SERVICES 206-242-2333

Contact us today for a no-obligation consultation to dicuss your special event plans

Visit our website @ ***www.seattleweddingvideo.com***
E-mail: *paxman@earthlink.net*

See page 537 under Photographers.

Listings: Area Banquet & Event Sites

❖❖❖

ACME

Blue Mountain Farm — PO Box 108, Acme WA 98220
B/X/M/S/R/P/ — Guest Rooms: 9 — Capacity: Outdoors: Up to 100,
Program Room: Up to 30
(360) 595-2114, Fax (360) 595-1144

ANACORTES

The Majestic Hotel Bistro & Pub — 419 Commercial Ave., Anacortes WA 98221
B/X/M/S/R/ — Guest Rooms: 23 — Capacity: Up to 300 (with garden area),
Banquet: Up to 150
Contact: Kathy Baxter, Sales & Catering (360) 293-3355, Fax (360) 293-5214

ANDERSON ISLAND

August Inn — 14117 Lyle Pt. Rd., Anderson Island WA 98303
B/X/M/S/R/ — Guest Rooms: 3 units — Capacity: Indoors: Up to 25,
Outdoors: Up to 60+
(253) 884-4011, Fax (253) 767-3959

ARLINGTON

Gleneagle Golf Club — 7619 Country Club Dr., Arlington WA 98223 *See page 194*
B/X/M/S/R/ — Capacity: Indoors: Up to 180 seated,
Up to 250 with outdoor patio
Contact: Kathy Blumenstein (360) 435-6713, Fax (360) 435-4769

ASHFORD

The Lodge — 38608 SR 706 E., Ashford WA 98304
B/X/M/S/R/ — Guest Rooms: 3 cabins — Capacity: Up to 75
Contact: Nancy Kwon (360) 569-2312, Fax (360) 569-0877

AUBURN

Auburn Senior Center — 910-9th St. S.E., Auburn WA 98002
B/X/M/S/R/ — Capacity: Up to 250
Office (253) 931-3043, Fax (253) 288-3132

Emerald Downs — 2300 Emerald Downs Dr., Auburn WA 98071 *See pages 52 & 184*
B/X/M/S/R/P/C/T/ — Capacity: Banquet, Meeting or
Reception: Up to 500; Picnics: Up to 1,000
(253) 288-7700 or Gen. Info. (253) 288-7000, Fax (253) 288-7710

Federal Way Senior Ctr. — 4016 S. 352nd St., Auburn WA 98001
B/X/M/S/R/ — Capacity: Up to 165
(253) 838-3604, Fax (253) 838-4552

BALLARD

Emerald Center at
The Emerald Chapel — 6556 - 24th Ave. N.W., Ballard WA *See page 183*
B/X/M/S/R/ — Capacity: Speakers Hall: Up to 175;
Conf. Hall: Up to 225 standing or 100 seated;
Garden Courtyard: Up to 75
(206) 789-2964, Fax (206) 297-5939

B=Banquets X=Parties M=Meetings S=Seminars R=Retreats P=Picnics C=Conventions T=Tradeshows

BELLEVUE

Bellevue Club Hotel — 11200 S.E. 6th St., Bellevue WA 98004 *See page 147*
B/X/M/S/R/C/ — Guest Rooms: 67 — Capacity: Banquet: Up to 250, Reception: Up to 300
Catering Dept. (425) 688-3382, Fax (425) 646-0184

Best Western Bellevue Inn — 11211 Main St., Bellevue WA 98004 *See page 149*
B/X/M/S/R/C/ — Guest Rooms: 181 — Capacity: 5 to 450 guests
(425) 455-5240 or (800) 421-8193, Fax (425) 455-0604

Courtyard by Marriott — 14615 N.E. 29th Pl., Bellevue WA 98007
M/S/R/ — Guest Rooms: 152 — Capacity: 40–70
Contact: Carolyn Padre, Sales & Catering (425) 869-5300, Fax (425) 883-9122

Daniel's Broiler –
Bellevue Place — 21st Fl.-10500 N.E. 8th - 21st Fl., Bellevue WA 98004 *See page 168*
B/X/M/ — Capacity: Up to 100
Contact: Manager of Private Dining (425) 462-4662, Fax (425) 451-4312

Doubletree Hotel – Bellevue — 300-112th Ave. S.E., Bellevue WA 98004 *See page 171*
B/X/M/S/R/C/T/ — Capacity: Banquet: Up to 800, Reception: Up to 1000,
Catering Office (425) 455-1300, Fax (425) 450-4119

Doubletree Hotel – Bellevue Center — 818-112th Ave. N.E., Bellevue WA 98004
B/X/M/S/R/ — Guest Rooms: 208 — Capacity: Up to 100
Director of Catering (425) 455-1515, Fax (425) 455-9984

Embassy Suites Hotel – Bellevue — 3225-158th Ave. S.E., Bellevue WA 98008 *See page 181*
B/X/M/S/R/C/ — Guest Rooms: 240 suites
Capacity: Banquet: Up to 360, Meeting/Conf: Up to 500
Contact: Betsy DeLay, Dir of Catering (425) 644-2500 x 612, Fax (425) 865-8065

Grazie Ristorante – Bellevue — 3820-124th S.E., Bellevue WA 98006
B/X/ — Capacity: Indoors: Up to 80, Outdoors: Up to 50
Contact: Manager (425) 644-1200, Fax (425) 644-7538

The Harbor Club – Bellevue — 777-108th Ave. N.E., 25th Fl., Bellevue WA 98004 *See page 199*
B/X/M/S/R/ — Capacity: Banquet: Up to 225, Reception: Up to 450
Catering Office (425) 990-1050, Fax (425) 990-1587

Hilton Bellevue — 100-112th Ave. N.E., Bellevue WA 98004
B/X/M/S/R/C/ — Guest Rooms: 179 — Capacity: Up to 250
Catering Office (425) 455-3330 or (800) 235-4458, Fax (425) 635-0413

Hunan Garden Restaurant — 11814 N.E. 8th, Bellevue WA 98005
B/X/ — Capacity: Up to 80
Contact: Manager (425) 451-3595, Fax (425) 451-3357

Hyatt Regency Bellevue — 900 Bellevue Wy. N.E., Bellevue WA 98004 *See page 209*
B/X/M/S/R/C/ — Guest Rooms: 382 — Capacity: Banquets: Up to 440
Catering Office (425) 462-1234, Fax (425) 698-4281

Kingstad Meeting
Centers — 2445-140th Ave. N.E., #B-100 (at Park 140), Bellevue WA 98005 *See page 221*
B/X/M/S/R/ — Capacity: 7 meeting rooms, for up to 50 each
Contact: Janet Harbold or Tom Edgar (206) 654-6040 or (425) 562-1292

Meydenbauer Center — 11100 NE 6th St., Bellevue WA 98004 *See pages 382 & 383*
B/X/M/S/R/C/T/ — Capacity: Banquet: from 50 to 2000;
Theater: Up to 410; Exhibit Hall: 36,000sq. ft.
Sales Office (425) 637-1020, Fax (425) 637-0166

North Bellevue Senior Center — 4063-148th Ave. N.E., Bellevue WA 98007
B/X/M/S/R/ — Capacity: Up to 300
(425) 452-7681, Fax (425) 882-1968

Overlake Square Conference Center — 14625 N.E. 24th St., Bellevue WA 98007 *See page 246*
B/X/M/X/R/ — Capacity: Up to 325
Managed by Avid Events, Inc. (425) 882-9097, Fax (425) 882-1312

***B**=Banquets **X**=Parties **M**=Meetings **S**=Seminars **R**=Retreats **P**=Picnics **C**=Conventions **T**=Tradeshows*

Residence Inn by Marriott – Bellevue — 14455 NE 29th Pl., Bellevue WA 98007
M/S/R/ — Guest Rooms: 120 — Capacity: Up to 15
Sales & Catering (425) 882-1222

Robinswood House — 2432-148th Ave. S.E., Bellevue WA 98007
B/X/M/S/R/ — Capacity: Indoor: Up to 125, With Outdoor Patio: Up to 200
(425) 865-0795, Fax (425) 452-7825

Rosalie Whyel Museum of Doll Art — 1116-108th Ave. N.E., Bellevue WA 98004
B/X/M/S/R/ — Capacity: Banquet: Up to 50, Reception: Up to 100
Contact: Pat Farwell (425) 455-1116, Fax (425) 455-4793

Spazzo Mediterranean Grill — 10665 NE 4th, 9th Fl., Bellevue WA 98004
B/X/M/S/R/ — Capacity: Up to 120
Contact: Jennifer Covney, Sales & Catering Office (425) 454-8255

Vasa Park Resort & Ballroom — 3560 W. Lake Sammamish Pkwy. S.E., Bellevue WA 98008
B/X/M/S/R/C/ — Capacity: Up to 1,071 (standing), 400 seated
Contact: Manager (425) 746-3260

WestCoast Bellevue Hotel — 625-116th Ave., Bellevue WA 98004 *See page 310*
B/X/M/S/R/C/T/ — Guest Rooms: 176 — Capacity: Up to 250
Banquet Office (425) 455-9444, Fax (425) 646-0229

Wintergarden at Bellevue Place — 900 Bellevue Way N.E., Bellevue WA 98004
B/X/M/S/R/C/ — Capacity: 220 to 300
Catering Office (425) 462-1234

Winters House — 2102 Bellevue Wy. S.E., Bellevue WA 98004
B/X/M/S/R/ — Capacity: Up to 75
Bellevue Parks Dept. (425) 452-6914, Fax (425) 452-6841

BELLINGHAM

Best Western Lakeway Inn & Conference Center — 714 Lakeway Dr., Bellingham WA 98226
B/X/M/S/R/C/ — Guest Rooms: 132 — Capacity: Up to 700
Contact: Catering Manager (360) 671-1011, Fax (360) 676-8519

The Chrysalis Inn & Spa — 804 10th St., Bellingham WA 98225
M/S/R/ — Capacity: Up to 45
(360) 756-1005, Fax (360) 647-0342

Hotel Bellwether — One Bellwether Way, Bellingham WA 98225 *See pages 109 & 207*
B/X/M/S/R/ — Guest Rooms: 68
Capacity: Banquet: Up to 350; Reception: Up to 700
(360) 392-3100 or (877) 411-1200, Fax (360) 392-3101

Lairmont Manor — 405 Fieldston Rd., Bellingham WA 98225
B/X/M/S/R/ — Guest Rooms: 2 Luxury Suites
Capacity: Inside: Up to 150, Outside: Up to 200
Contact: Joyce White (360) 647-1444, Fax (360) 647-9223

North Wood Hall — 3240 Northwest Ave., Bellingham WA 98225
B/X/M/S/R/ — Capacity: Up to 275
(360) 671-8311

Sudden Valley Community Association — 2145 Lake Whatcom Blvd., Bellingham WA 98226
B/X/M/S/R/C/ — Capacity: Banquet: Up to 300
Contact: Events Coord. (360) 734-6430, ext. 242, Fax (360) 734-1915

B=Banquets X=Parties M=Meetings S=Seminars R=Retreats P=Picnics C=Conventions T=Tradeshows

BOTHELL

Courtyard Hall in the Country Village — 720 - 238th St. S.E., Suite H, Bothell WA 98021
B/X/M/S/R/ — Capacity: Up to 210
(425) 402-9818

Grazie Ristorante – Bothell — 23207 Bothell-Everett Hwy. SE, Bothell WA 98021
B/X/M/S/R/ — Capacity: Up to 49
Contact: Barry Munro (425) 402-9600, Fax (425) 402-9644

The Monte Villa Farmhouse — 3300 Monte Villa Pkwy., Bothell WA 98021 *See page 236*
B/X/M/S/R/ — Capacity: Ballroom: Up to 120 guests theatre style;
Living Rm.: Up to 60 theatre style
Contact: Dave Richards or Dana Arnim (425) 485-6115

Northshore Senior Center — 10201 E. Riverside Dr., Bothell WA 98011
B/X/M/S/R/P/ — Capacity: Banquet: Up to 250, Reception: Up to 500
Contact: Maggie Parker (425) 487-2441

Residence Inn by Marriott – Bothell — 11920 NE 195th St., Bothell WA 98011
M/S/ — Guest Rooms: 120 — Capacity: Up to 25
Sales & Catering (425) 485-3030

Teo's Mia Roma — 7614 NE Bothell Wy., Bothell WA 98011
B/XM/S/R/ — Capacity: Private room: 50–100; Entire restaurant: Up to 200
Contact: Ettore Or Teo DiCicco (425) 486-6200

Wyndham Garden Hotel — 19333 North Creek Pkwy., Bothell WA 98011
B/X/M/S/R/C/ — Guest Rooms: 166 — Capacity: Up to 150
Catering Office (425) 485-5557, Fax (425) 486-7314

BREMERTON

Gold Mountain Public Golf Club — 7263 West Belfair Valley Road, Bremerton WA 98312
B/X/P/ — Capacity: Up to 200
(360) 415-5432 or (206) 464-1175, Fax (360) 415-6880

Howard Johnson Plaza Hotel & Conference Center — 5640 Kitsap Wy., Bremerton WA 98312
B/X/M/S/R/C/T/ — Guest Rooms: 145 — Capacity: Up to 400
Sales Dept. (360) 373-9900

BURIEN

Filberto's Italian — 144th & Des Moines Memorial Dr., Burien WA 98168
B/X/M/S/R/ — Capacity: Up to 220
Contact: Mina (206) 248-1944

B=Banquets X=Parties M=Meetings S=Seminars R=Retreats P=Picnics C=Conventions T=Tradeshows

CAMANO ISLAND

Camano Country Club — 1243 S. Beach Drive, Camano Island WA 98282
B/X/M/ — Capacity: Banquet: Up to 200, Reception: Up to 300
Contact: Manager (360) 387-1655, Fax (360) 387-7957

CARNATION

Bors Hede Restaurant — 10320 Kelly Rd. N.E., Carnation WA 98014
B/X/M/ — Capacity: Up to 45
Contact: Roger Shell (425) 788-8624

Carnation Golf Course — 1810 W. Snoqualmie River Rd. N.E., Carnation WA 98014
B/X/M/ — Capacity: Up to 120
Pro Shop (206) 583-0314, Fax (425) 333-6103

Pleasant Hill Estate — 32305 N.E. 8th St., Carnation WA 98014 *See page 252*
B/X/M/S/R/ — Capacity: Indoors: Up to 150; Outdoors: Up to 250
Contact: Birgit Lindvig (425) 333-6770, Fax (425) 333-6799

Remlinger Farms — Carnation WA 98014 *See page 548*
B/X/M/S/R/P/ — Capacity: 100–20,000
Contact: Jaque Remlinger (360) 568-1780, Fax (360) 568-6613

CLINTON

Home by the Sea — 2388 Sunlight Beach Rd., Clinton WA 98236
B/X/M/S/R/ — Guest Rooms: 1 private, 1 suite, 2 cottages
Capacity: Banquet: Up to 20
Office (360) 321-2964, Fax (360) 321-4378

Whidbey Institute — 8898 SR 525, Clinton WA 98236
M/S/R/P/ — Guest Rooms: 3 cabins, 1 house
Capacity: Inside:Up to 150, Outside: Up to 100
(206) 467-0384 or (360) 341-1884

COUPEVILLE

The Captain Whidbey Inn — 2072 W. Captain Whidbey Inn Rd., Coupeville WA 98239
B/X/M/S/R/ — Guest Rooms: 32 — Capacity: Banquet: Up to 25, Reception: Up to 40
Contact: Innkeeper (360) 678-4097 or (800) 366-4097, Fax (360) 678-4110

The Colonel Crockett Farm — 1012 S. Fort Casey Rd., Coupeville WA 98239
B/X/M/S/R/ — Guest Rooms: 5 — Capacity: Up to 15
Contact: Robert (360) 678-3711

DEER HARBOR

Resort at Deer Harbor — PO Box 200, Deer Harbor WA 98243 *See page 112*
B/X/M/S/R/ — Guest Rooms: 26 cottages — Capacity: Up to 100
Contact: NW Waterfront Inns (206) 239-1806 or (360) 376-4420, Fax (206) 239-1801

B=Banquets X=Parties M=Meetings S=Seminars R=Retreats P=Picnics C=Conventions T=Tradeshows

DES MOINES

Anthony's Homeport – Des Moines — 421 S. 227th St., Des Moines WA 98198
B/X/M/S/R/ — Capacity: Up to 50
Contact: Jane Dahl (206) 824-1947, Fax (206) 824-1410

Rose's Highway Inn — 26915 Pacific Hwy. S., Des Moines WA 98198
B/X/ — Capacity: Up to 60
Contact: Jim (253) 839-7277

Salty's At Redondo Beach — 28201 Redondo Beach Dr. S., Des Moines WA 98198 *See page 573*
B/X/ — Capacity: Private seating for 100
(253) 946-0636, Fax (253) 946-5099

Zenith Hall — 1826 - 240th St. S., Des Moines WA 98198
B/X/M/S/R/ — Capacity: Up to 300
Contact: Jane (206) 824-8770 or (253) 520-8685

EASTSOUND

Rosario — 1400 Rosario Road, Eastsound WA 98245
B/X/M/S/R/ — Guest Rooms: 127 — Capacity: Banquets: Up to 200
Group Sales Office (425) 452-8200 or (877) 562-8821

EATONVILLE

Hellyer Natural History Center — 11610 Trek Dr. E., Eatonville WA 98328
B/X/M/S/R/P/ — Capacity: Up to 90
Contact: Gail MacKenzie / Cami Wallin (360) 832-6333, Fax (360) 832-6118

Mill Village Motel — 210 Center St., Eatonville WA 98328
B/X/M/S/R/ — Guest Rooms: 32 — Capacity: Up to 50
Catering (360) 832-3200 or (360) 496-6662

Mountain View Cedar Lodge
Bed & Breakfast — 36203 Pulford Rd. E., Eatonville WA 98328
B/X/M/S/R/ — Guest Rooms: 2 — Capacity: Indoors: Up to 75, Outdoors: Up to 150
Contact: Dana Seitz (360) 832-8080

Northwest Trek Wildlife Park — 11610 Trek Dr. E., Eatonville WA 98328 *See pages 58 & 244*
B/X/M/S/R/P/ — Capacity: Up to 1,000
Group Sales (360) 832-7181

EDMONDS

5th Avenue Grill House — 610 - 5th Avenue, Edmonds WA 98020
B/X/M/ — Capacity: Up to 80
Contact: Manager (425) 672-0660

Arnie's Restaurant & Bar — 300 Admiral Wy., Edmonds WA 98020
B/X/M/ — Capacity: Daytime: Up to 20, Evenings: Up to 20
Contact: Manager (425) 771-5688, Fax (425) 771-7624

B=Banquets X=Parties M=Meetings S=Seminars R=Retreats P=Picnics C=Conventions T=Tradeshows

Edmonds Floral Conference Centre — 201-4th Ave. N., Edmonds WA 98020 *See page 178*
B/X/M/S/R/C/ — Capacity: Chyrsanthemum Room: Up to 350;
Rhododendrom Room: Up to 60; 2 Orchid Rooms: 40 ea.
(425) 640-1808, Fax (425) 640-1024

Edmonds Harbor Inn — 130 W. Dayton St., Edmonds WA 98020
B/X/M/S/R/C/ — Guest Rooms: 92 — Capacity: Up to 50
Contact: Jodi (425) 775-9363, Fax (425) 670-6736

Edmonds Plaza Room — 650 Main St., Edmonds WA 98020
B/X/M/S/R/ — Capacity: Up to 150
Office (425) 771-0230, Fax (425) 771-0253

S.C.S.C. "The Center On The Waterfront" — 220 Railroad Ave., Edmonds WA 98020
B/X/M/S/R/ — Capacity: Up to 300
Contact: Mike Byers (425) 774-5555

ENUMCLAW

King County Fairgrounds — 45224-284th Ave. S.E., Enumclaw WA 98022
B/X/M/S/R/P/C/T/ — Capacity: Up to 1,150, Fieldhouse: 345,
Exhibit Hall: 550, Activity Hall: 400
Contact: Joan Lewis (206) 296-8888 or (360) 825-7777, Fax (206) 296-8891

The White Rose Inn Bed & Breakfast — 1610 Griffin Ave., Enumclaw WA 98022
B/X/M/S/R/ — Guest Rooms: 4 — Capacity: Inside: Up to 65, Outside: Up to 100
Contact: Tami Dunn (360) 825-7194 or (800) 404-7194

EVERETT

Best Western Cascadia Inn — 2800 Pacific Ave., Everett WA 98201
B/X/M/S/R/ — Guest Rooms: 134 — Capacity: Up to 160
Contact: Mary Bartlett (425) 258-4141 or (800) 822-5876, Fax (425) 258-4755

Club Broadway — 1611 Everett Ave., Everett WA 98201
B/X/M/S/R/C/ — Capacity: 4 floors, 50–300
Contact: Diane (425) 259-3551, Fax (425) 339-9488

Everett Inn — 12619-4th Ave. W., Everett WA 98204
B/X/M/S/R/ — Guest Rooms: 72 — Capacity: Up to 100
(425) 347-9099 or (800) 434-9204, Fax (425) 348-3048

Everett Mall Travelodge — 9602 -19th Ave. S.E., Everett WA 98208
B/X/M/ — Guest Rooms: 116 — Capacity: Up to 50
Contact: Manager (425) 337-9090

Holiday Inn Hotel & Conference Center – Everett — 101-128th St. S.E., Everett WA 98208
B/X/M/S/R/C/ — Guest Rooms: 249 — Capacity: Up to 600
Sales (425) 338-4218, Fax (425) 338-4202

Lombardi's Cucina — 1620 W. Marine View Dr., Everett WA 98201
B/X/M/ — Capacity: Up to 65
Contact: Manager (425) 252-1886

The Manor — 13032 Admiralty Wy., Everett WA 98204
B/X/M/S/R/P/ — Capacity: Inside: Up to 300, Outside: Up to 400
Contact: Francesca Cohn (425) 745-4020, Fax (425) 267-0105

B=Banquets X=Parties M=Meetings S=Seminars R=Retreats P=Picnics C=Conventions T=Tradeshows

Marina Village Inn — 1728 W. Marine View Dr., Everett WA 98201
B/X/M/S/R/C/ — Guest Rooms: 26 — Capacity: 1st Room: Up to 80;
2nd Room: Up to 50; Reception: Up to 160
Contact: Richard Luchini (425) 259-4040 , Fax (425) 252-8419

The Marine View Banquet Center — 404-14th St., Everett WA 98201 *See page 233*
B/X/M/S/R/C/ — Capacity: Olympic Room: Up to 350,
Port Gardner Room: Up to 250, Northwest Room: Up to 100
(425) 258-1604

Monte Cristo Ballroom — 1507 Wall St., Everett WA 98201
B/X/M/S/R/ — Capacity: Up to 175
Contact: Scott Gallacher (425) 257-7388

Normanna Lodge – Sons of Norway — 2725 Oakes Ave., Everett WA 98201
B/X/M/S/R/ — Capacity: Two Halls holding up to 220 each
Contact: Head Trustee (425) 252-0291

O'Callahan's – Howard Johnson Plaza Hotel — 3105 Pine St., Everett WA 98201
B/X/M/S/R/C/T/ — Guest Rooms: 250 — Capacity: Ballroom: Up to 600
Catering Office (425) 339-2000, Fax (425) 303-0354

V.F.W. #2100 — 2711 Oakes Ave., Everett WA 98201
B/X/M/S/R/ — Capacity: Up to 150
Contact: Manager (425) 252-2100

FALL CITY

Heritage Garden Farm — 30915 SE Redmond—Fall City Rd., Fall City WA 98024
B/X/M/S/R/ — Capacity: Indoors: Up to 250, Outdoors: Up to 700 (Shown by appt. only)
(425) 881-5115

FEDERAL WAY

Best Western Federal Way Executel — 31611-20th Ave. S., Federal Way WA 98003
B/X/M/S/R/C/ — Guest Rooms: 112 — Capacity: Banquet: Up to 150;
8 Function Rooms: Up to 200
Sales & Catering (253) 941-6000 or (800) 648-3311, Fax (253) 941-9500

Dumas Bay Centre — 3200 S.W. Dash Point Rd., Federal Way WA 98023 *See pages 105 & 174*
B/X/M/S/R/ — Guest Rooms: 80 — Capacity: Banquet: Up to 98
(253) 835-2000, Fax (253) 835-2010

The Keg — 32724 Pacific Hwy. S., Federal Way WA 98003
B/X/ — Capacity: Banquet: Up to 25
Contact: Manager (253) 838-4100

King County Aquatic Center — 650 S.W. Campus Dr., Federal Way WA *See page 219*
B/X/M/S/ — Capacity: Banquets: Up to 300; Theatre Style: Up to 400
(206) 296-4444 or (800) 325-6165, ext. 64444

Knutzen Family Theatre
at Dumas Bay Centre — 3200 SW Dashpoint Rd., Federal Way WA 98023 *See page 94*
M/S/ — Capacity: Up to 250
(253) 835-2025, Fax (253) 835-2010

B=Banquets X=Parties M=Meetings S=Seminars R=Retreats P=Picnics C=Conventions T=Tradeshows

Verrazano's Ristorante — 28835 Pacific Hwy. S., Federal Way WA 98003 *See page 306*
B/X/M/S/R/ — Capacity: Private Rooms for 15 to 300
Contact: Banquet Coordinator (253) 946-4122, Fax (253) 946-1405

Vince's Italian Restaurant — 32411 Pacific Hwy S., Federal Way WA 98003
B/X/M/ — Capacity: Up to 36
Contact: Manager (253) 927-7727

Wild Waves & Enchanted Village — 36201 Enchanted Pkwy., Federal Way WA 98003 *See page 549*
B/X/P/ — Capacity: 100 to 15,000
(253) 661-8001 or (253) 925-8001, Fax (253) 925-1332

FIFE

Best Western Executive Inn Convention Center – Fife — 5700 Pacific Hwy. E., Fife WA 98424
B/X/M/S/R/C/T/ — Guest Rooms: 139 — Capacity: 10 Rooms;
Banquet: Up to 700; Reception: Up to 1,000
Contact: Richard King (253) 922-0080 or (800) 938-8500, Fax (253) 922-6439

Fife Community Center — 2111-54th Ave. E., Fife WA 98424
B/X/M/S/R/ — Capacity: Banquet: Up to 275; Reception: Up to 450
Contact: Kathy Woodard (253) 922-0900, Fax (253) 926-0543

Grand Prix Raceway — 2105 Frank Albert Road, Fife WA 98424 *See page 471*
B/X/M/S/ — Capacity: Up to 150
(253) 922-7722

Royal Coachman Inn — 5805 Pacific Hwy. E., Fife WA 98424
B/X/M/S/R/ — Guest Rooms: 96 — Capacity: Up to 60
Office (253) 922-2500, Fax (253) 922-6443

FRIDAY HARBOR

Mullis Community Center — 489 Nash, Friday Harbor WA 98250
B/X/M/S/ — Capacity: Up to 400, 120 Seated
Contact: (360) 378-9102

Roche Harbor Resort — 248 Reuben Memorial Dr., Friday Harbor WA 98250
B/X/M/S/R/ — Guest Rooms: 53 — Capacity: Up to 150
Contact: Gabe Herda (360) 378- 2155, ext. 403, Fax (360) 378-6809

Friday Harbor House — 130 West St., Friday Harbor WA 98250 *See page 112*
B/X/M/S/R/ — Guest Rooms: 20 — Capacity: Up to 40
Contact: NW Waterfront Inns (206) 239-1806 or (360) 378-8455, Fax (206) 239-1801

GIG HARBOR

Anthony's — 8827 N. Harborview Dr., Gig Harbor WA 98332
B/X/M/S/R/ — Capacity: Up to 100
Office (253) 853-6353, Fax (253) 853-6955

Canterwood Golf & Country Club — 12606-54th Ave. N.W., Gig Harbor WA 98332
B/X/M/S/R/ — Capacity: Up to 300
Office (253) 851-1845, Fax (253) 851-9147

B=Banquets X=Parties M=Meetings S=Seminars R=Retreats P=Picnics C=Conventions T=Tradeshows

Harbor Creek Lodge — , Gig Harbor WA *See page 200*
B/X/M/S/R/P/ — Capacity: Indoors: Up to 300, With Outdoors: Up to 500
Contact: Upper Crust Catering (206) 783-1826, Fax (206) 783-1672

Harbor Inn Restaurant — 3111 Harborview Dr., Gig Harbor WA 98335
B/X/M/ — Capacity: Up to 100
Contact: Tom Drohan (253) 851-5454

The Inn at Gig Harbor — 3211-56th St. N.W., Gig Harbor WA 98335 *See page 212*
B/X/M/R/ — Guest Rooms: 64 — Capacity: Up to 250
Sales & Catering (253) 858-1111, Fax (253) 851-5402

The Olde Glencove Hotel — 9418 Glencove Rd., Gig Harbor WA 98329
B/X/M/S/R/ — Guest Rooms: 2 suites — Capacity: Inside: Up to 50; Combined w/ outside: Up to 100
Contact: Luciann Nadeau (253) 884-2835, Fax (253) 884-4403

GREENWATER

Alta Crystal Resort — 68317 SR 410 E., Greenwater WA 98022
B/X/M/S/R/P/ — Guest Rooms: 24 condos — Capacity: Up to 50
Contact: Vivian & Steven Cadematori (360) 663-2500 or (800) 277-6475

ISSAQUAH

Gibson Hall — 105 Newport Blvd. S.W., Issaquah WA 98027
B/X/ — Capacity: Up to 75
Contact: Issaquah Kiwanis (425) 392-4016

Hedges Cellars — 195 N.E. Gilman Blvd., Issaquah WA 98027 *See page 202*
B/X/M/ — Capacity: Up to 110
Contact: Anne-Marie Hedges (425) 391-6056, Fax (425) 391-3827

Holiday Inn of Issaquah — 1801-12th Ave. N.W., Issaquah WA 98027
B/X/M/S/R/C/ — Guest Rooms: 100 — Capacity: Up to 160
Contact: William Mueller (425) 392-6421

Illusionz Magical Entertainment Center — 1025 N.W. Gilman Blvd., Issaquah WA 98027 *See pages 55 & 413*
B/X/M/S/ — Capacity: Up to 600
(425) 427-2444

Issaquah Community Center — S.E. Bush Street & 1st Avenue S., Issaquah WA 98027 *See page 213*
B/X/M/S/R/ — Capacity: Multipurpose Area: Up to 1,000; Meeting Rms.: 30 to 50
Contact: Jean Sillers (425) 837-3321, Fax (425) 837-3319

Pickering Barn — S.E. 56th & 10th Ave. N.W., Issaquah WA *See page 250*
B/X/M/S/ — Capacity: Up to 400 (Shown by Appointment)
Contact: City of Issaquah (425) 837-3321, Fax (425) 837-3319

Pogacha — 120 N.W. Gilman Blvd., Issaquah WA 98027
B/X/M/ — Capacity: Banquet: Up to 125
Contact: Banquet Manager (425) 392-5550

Tibbetts Creek Manor — 750 Renton-Issaquah Rd., P.O. Box 1307, Issaquah WA 98027 *See page 294*
B/X/M/S/R/P/ — Capacity: Banquet: Up to 120, Reception: Up to 150
Contact: Events Manager (425) 837-3366, Fax (425) 313-0635

B=Banquets X=Parties M=Meetings S=Seminars R=Retreats P=Picnics C=Conventions T=Tradeshows

KENMORE

Bastyr University Conference & Retreat Center — 14500 Juanita Dr. N.E., Kenmore WA 98028
B/X/M/S/R/ — Capacity: Up to 450
Contact: Pamela Vaughn (425) 602-3075, Fax (425) 602-3304

Lake Washington Grillhouse & Tap Room — 6161 N.E. 175th St., Kenmore WA 98028
B/X/M/ — Capacity: Up to 100
Contact: Manager (425) 486-3313

Saint Edwards Grand Dining Hall — 14445 Juanita Dr. N.E., Kenmore WA 98028 *See page 266*
B/X/M/S/R/ — Capacity: Up to 50
(425) 823-2992

KENT

HD Hotspurs — 315 S. Washington, Kent WA 98031
B/X/M/ — Capacity: Up to 100
Contact: Blayne Berry (253) 854-5653

Holiday Inn - Kent — 22318-84th Ave. S., Kent WA 98032
B/X/M/S/R/C/ — Guest Rooms: 125 — Capacity: Up to 125
Sales (253) 395-4300, Fax (253) 395-0116

Kent Commons — 525-4th Ave. N., Kent WA 98032
B/X/M/S/R/C/T/ — Capacity: Up to 900, 2 gyms, 5 meeting rooms
Contact: Doug (253) 856-5000, Fax (253) 856-6000

Kent Parks Resource Center — 315 E. Meeker, Kent WA 98031
B/X/M/S/R/ — Capacity: Up to 175, Saturdays only
Contact: Janet, Rentals Dept. (253) 859-3599, Fax (253) 859-2567

Kent Senior Activity Center — 600 E. Smith, Kent WA 98031
B/X/M/S/ — Capacity: Up to 200
Contact: Monica (253) 859-3342, Fax (253) 856-6150

Victorian Gardens 1888 Bed & Breakfast — 9621 S. 200th St., Kent WA 98031
B/X/ — Guest Rooms: 3 — Capacity: Inside: 35 Reception, Outside: 100 Banquet
Contact: Larry Kiel (253) 850-1776

KIRKLAND

Anthony's Homeport - Kirkland — 135 Lake St., Kirkland WA 98033
B/X/M/ — Capacity: Up to 45 sit-down
(425) 822-0225, Fax (425) 822-8308

Best Western Kirkland Inn — 12223 N.E. 116th St., Kirkland WA 98034
B/X/M/S/R/C/ — Guest Rooms: 110 — Capacity: Up to 100
Contact: Rita (425) 822-2300, Fax (425) 889-9616

Cafe Juanita — 9702 N.E. 120th, Kirkland WA 98034
B/M/S/X/ — Capacity: Up to 24 (by special arrangement only)
(425) 823-1505, Fax (425) 823-8500

Clarion Inn — 12233 N.E. Totem Lake Wy., Kirkland WA 98034
B/X/M/S/R/ — Guest Rooms: 59 — Capacity: Banquet: Up to 100
Contact: Zeri (425) 821-2202

B=Banquets X=Parties M=Meetings S=Seminars R=Retreats P=Picnics C=Conventions T=Tradeshows

Shumway Mansion — 11410-99th Pl. N.E., Kirkland WA 98033
B/X/M/S/R/ — Guest Rooms: 8 — Capacity: Up to 200 with outdoor patio
(425) 823-2303, Fax (425) 822-0421

Third Floor Fish Cafe — 205 Lake St. S., Kirkland WA 98033
B/X/M/ — Capacity: Up to 40
(425) 822-3553, Fax (425) 827-1364

Woodmark Hotel on Lake Washington — 1200 Carillon Point, Kirkland WA 98033 *See page 316*
B/X/M/S/R/C/ — Guest Rooms: 100
Capacity: Indoors: Up to 120, Summer: Up to 225
Catering Dept. (425) 827-1986, Fax (425) 803-5586

Yarrow Bay Grill — 1270 Carillon Point, Kirkland WA 98033 *See page 319*
B/X/M/S/R/ — Capacity: Up to 100
Contact: Vicki McLellan (425) 889-7497

LACEY

Jacob Smith House (in Lacey Corp. Ctr.) — 4500 Intelco Loop S.E., Lacey WA 98503
B/X/M/S/R/P/ — Capacity: Banquet: Up to 85; Reception: Up to 150; Outdoors: Up to 350
Contact: Randy Orth (360) 459-1800

Lacey Community Center — 6729 Pacific Ave. S.E., Lacey WA 98509
B/X/M/S/R/P/ — Capacity: Up to 300
Contact: Mike Rathke (360) 491-0857, Fax (360) 438-2669

LACONNER

Hope Island Inn — P.O. Box 2110, 16846 Chilberg Avenue, LaConner WA 98257-2110
B/X/M/S/R/ — Capacity: Up to 200, (Museum Dining), Waterfront
Contact: Grant Lucas (360) 466-3221, Fax (360) 466-3221

LaConner Quilt Museum in Gatches Mansion — 703 South 2nd St., LaConner WA 98257
B/X/M/S/R/ — Capacity: Up to 125
Contact: Kings Catering (360) 466-4288 or (360) 757-4922

Seafood & Prime Rib House — 614-1st St., LaConner WA 98257
B/X/M/ — Capacity: Up to 130
Contact: Manager (360) 466-4014

The Wild Iris Inn — 121 Maple Ave., LaConner WA 98257
B/X/M/S/R/ — Guest Rooms: 19 — Capacity: Banquet: Up to 75
Sales & Catering (360) 466-1400

LAKE FOREST PARK

Civic Club of Lake Forest Park — 17301 Beach Dr. N.E., Lake Forest Park WA 98155
B/X/M/S/R/ — Capacity: Up to 200
(206) 362-8818, Fax (253) 581-4375

Lake City Elks Lodge — 14540 Bothell Wy. N.E., Lake Forest Park WA 98155
B/X/M/S/ — Capacity: Up to 400
Contact: Linda / Bill (206) 364-1800, Fax (206) 364-2338

B=Banquets X=Parties M=Meetings S=Seminars R=Retreats P=Picnics C=Conventions T=Tradeshows

LAKEWOOD

Lakewold Gardens — 12317 Gravelly Lake Dr. S.W., Lakewood WA 98499 *See page 228*
B/X/M/S/R/P/ — Capacity: Garden: Up to 500, House: Up to 150; Meeting Rms.: Up to 75
Contact: Event Coordinator (253) 584-4106, Fax (253) 584-3021

LANGLEY

Inn at Langley — 400-1st St., Langley WA 98260 *See page 112*
B/X/M/S/R/ — Guest Rooms: 26 — Capacity: Up to 32
Contact: NW Waterfront Inns (206) 239-1806 or (360) 221-3033, Fax (206) 239-1801

LOPEZ ISLAND

The Islander Lopez Marina Resort — P.O. Box 459, Fisherman Bay Road, Lopez Island WA 98261
B/X/M/S/R/ — Guest Rooms: 28 — Capacity: Up to 120
Contact: Kathi Casey (360) 468-2233 or (800) 736-3434, Fax (360) 468-3382

LYNNWOOD

Embassy Suites Hotel Seattle – North/Lynnwood — 20610-44th Ave. W., Lynnwood WA 98036 *See page 182*
B/X/M/S/R/C/ — Guest Rooms: 240
Capacity: Banquet: Up to 400; Meeting/Conf.: Up to 450
Catering Office (425) 775-2500 or Res.: (800) EMBASSY, Fax (425) 774-0485

Hotel International — 5621-196th S.W., Lynnwood WA 98036
B/X/M/S/R/ — Guest Rooms: 54 — Capacity: Reception: Up to 120
Sales/Catering (425) 771-1777

Martha Lake Community Club — 16300 Motor Pl., Lynnwood WA 98037
B/X/M/S/R/ — Capacity: Up to 225, No Sunday Rentals
Office (425) 745-4363

MAPLE VALLEY

Elk Run Golf Course — 22500 S.E. 275th Pl., Maple Valley WA 98038
B/X/M/S/R/ — Capacity: Up to 130
Contact: Roy Humphreys (425) 432-8800 or (800) 244-8631 Golf Course, Fax (425) 432-1907

Lake Wilderness Center – King County Parks — 22500 S.E. 248th, Maple Valley WA 98038 *See page 226*
B/X/M/S/R/P/ — Capacity: Up to 250, 2 meeting rooms, 2 large reception rooms, Kitchen
Contact: King County Park System South District (206) 296-4298 or (800) 325-6165, ext. 4298

Lake Wilderness Golf Course — 25400 Witte Rd. S.E., Maple Valley WA 98038 *See page 227*
B/X/M/S/R/ — Capacity: Indoors: Up to 225; With Outdoor Patio: Up to 400
Contact: Kim Northam Events (425) 432-8038 or Pro Shop (425) 432-9405

B=Banquets X=Parties M=Meetings S=Seminars R=Retreats P=Picnics C=Conventions T=Tradeshows

MARYSVILLE

Battle Creek Public Golf Course — 6006 Meridian Avenue N., Marysville WA 98271
X/M/ — Capacity: Up to 120
Contact: Jim Pulliam (360) 659-7931 or (800) 655-7931, Fax (360) 659-3431

Best Western Tulalip Inn — 6128-33rd Ave. N.E., Marysville WA 98271
B/X/M/S/R/C/ — Guest Rooms: 69 — Capacity: Up to 200
Contact: By The Bay Catering (360) 659-4488, Fax (360) 653-5004

The Marysville Opera House — 1225-3rd St., Marysville WA 98270
B/X/M/S/R/C/ — Capacity: 60 to 300
(360) 657-5532

MERCER ISLAND

Mercerwood Shore Club — 4150 E. Mercer Wy., Mercer Island WA 98040
B/X/M/S/ — Capacity: Up to 200
Contact: Office Manager (206) 232-1622

MILL CREEK

Mill Creek Country Club — 15500 Country Club Dr., Mill Creek WA 98012
B/X/M/S/ — Capacity: Up to 200
Contact: Catering Dept. (425) 743-1444 or (425) 338-4625, Fax (425) 338-7025

MOUNT VERNON

Best Western Cottontree Inn — 2300 Market St., Mount Vernon WA 98273 *See page 150*
B/X/M/S/R/C/ — Guest Rooms: 120 — Capacity: Up to 300
(360) 428-5678 or (800) 662-6886, Fax (360) 428-1844

Hillcrest Lodge — 1717 S. 13th St., Mt. Vernon WA 98274
B/X/M/S/R/P/ — Capacity: Banquet: Up to 150, Reception: Up to 200
Contact: Mt. Vernon Parks & Recreation Reservations (360) 336-6215, Fax (360) 336-6290

MOUNTLAKE TERRACE

The Clubhouse at Ballinger Lake — 23000 Lake View Dr., Mountlake Terrace WA 98043
B/X/M/S/R/P/ — Capacity: Banquet: Up to 175, Reception: Up to 200
Catering (425) 774-4940, Fax (425) 775-6468

Nile Golf & Country Club — 6601-244th S.W., Mountlake Terrace WA 98043 *See pages 243 & 546*
B/X/M/S/R/P/ — Capacity: Banquet: Up to 500;
Reception: Up to 650; 5 Picnic Areas
Events (425) 775-2412 or Pro Shop (425) 776-5154, Fax (425) 744-5622

B=Banquets X=Parties M=Meetings S=Seminars R=Retreats P=Picnics C=Conventions T=Tradeshows

MUKILTEO

A Wedding Place and Conference Center — 13000 Beverly Pk. Rd. #H, Mukilteo WA 98275
B/X/M/S/R/ — Capacity: Banquet: Up to 220, Reception: Up to 400
(425) 267-9383, Fax (425) 267-9850

Arnie's At Mukilteo — 714-2nd St., Mukilteo WA 98275
B/X/M/ — Capacity: Green Room: Up to 35
Contact: Manager (425) 355-2181, Fax (425) 348-4874

Charles At Smugglers Cove — 8340-53rd Ave. W., Mukilteo WA 98275
B/X/M/S/R/ — Capacity: 3 Rooms, Outside: Up to 200, Inside: Up to 90
Contact: Janet Faur (425) 347-2700

Harbour Pointe Golf Club — 11817 Harbor Pointe Blvd., Mukilteo WA 98275
B/X/ — Capacity: Up to 120
Contact: Donna (800) 233-3128 or (425) 355-6060

Rosehill Community Center — 304 Lincoln Ave., Mukilteo WA 98275
B/X/M/S/R/ — Capacity: 3 Rooms, Banquet: Up to 150, Theater: Up to 375
Office (425) 355-2514

NEWCASTLE

The Golf Club at Newcastle — 15500 Six Penny Lane, Newcastle WA 98059 *See page 242*
B/X/M/S/R/ — Capacity: Banquet: Up to 350
Catering Dept. (425) 793-5566

OLGA

Doe Bay Resort — P.O. Box 437, Star Rt. 86, Olga WA 98279
B/X/M/S/R/ — Guest Rooms: 68, Rustic Cabins: 34
Capacity: Café: Up to 50, Beach Mtg Hall: 45
Contact: Tom Stanfield (360) 376-2291, Fax (360) 376-5809

OLYMPIA

Capitol City Golf Club — 5225 Yelm Hwy. S.E., Olympia WA 98513
B/X/ — Capacity: Inside: Up to 50, Outside: Up to 150
Contact: Manager (360) 491-5111, Fax (360) 493-6067

Coach House – State Capitol Museum — 211 W. 21st Ave. , Olympia WA 98501
B/X/M/ — Capacity: Up to 53
Contact: Helene Adams (360) 753-2580, Fax (360) 586-8322

Hands on Children's Museum — 106 11th Avenue S.W., Olympia WA 98501
B/X/M/S/R/ — Capacity: Up to 400
(360) 956-0818, Fax (360) 754-8626

Huber's Gasthaus — 2312 Friendly Grove Rd. N.E., Olympia WA 98506
B/X/M/S/R/ — Capacity: Indoors: Up to 150, With Outdoors: Up to 300
Contact: Caroline Huber (360) 943-6543

***B**=Banquets **X**=Parties **M**=Meetings **S**=Seminars **R**=Retreats **P**=Picnics **C**=Conventions **T**=Tradeshows*

Indian Summer Golf & Country Club — 5900 Troon Ln. S.E., Olympia WA 98501 *See page 211*
B/X/M/S/R/ — Capacity: Up to 500
Contact: Catering Manager (360) 923-1075, Fax (360) 923-9037

Olympia Community Center — 222 Columbia St. N., Olympia WA 98501
B/X/M/S/R/P/ — Capacity: Up to 300
(360) 753-8380, Fax (360) 753-8334

Olympic Flight Museum — 7637A-Old Hwy. 99 S.E., Olympia WA 98501
B/X/M/S/R/ — Capacity: Up to 400
Contact: Event Coordinator (360) 705-3925, Fax (360) 236-9839

The State Room — 1615 State St. N.E., Olympia WA 98506
B/X/M/R/ — Capacity: Up to 299
Contact: Occasions Catering (360) 943-9494, Fax (360) 943-9393

Swantown Inn — 1431-11th Ave. S.E., Olympia WA 98501
B/X/M/S/R/ — Guest Rooms: 4 — Capacity: Inside: Up to 50, Outside: Up to 100
Contact: Lillian & Ed Peeples (360) 753-9123 or (360) 943-4596

Urban Onion at the Olympia Hotel — 116 E. Legion Way, Olympia WA 98501
B/X/M/S/R/ — Capacity: 3 rooms; Accommodates up to 416
Contact: Joy Walker (360) 943-9242, Fax (360) 754-2422

Woman's Club of Olympia — 1002 Washington St. S.E., Olympia WA 98501
B/X/M/S/R/ — Capacity: Up to 150
(360) 753-9921 or (360) 352-2672

PORT ANGELES

**Olympic Park Institute –
Historic Rosemary Inn** — 111 Barnes Pt. Rd., Port Angeles WA 98363
B/X/M/S/R/P/ — Guest Rooms: 26 — Capacity: Up to 100
Contact: Dee Anne Nelson (800) 775-3720 or (360) 928-3720, Fax (360) 928-3046

PORT ORCHARD

**Clubhouse at
McCormick Woods** — 5155 McCormick Woods Drive S.W., Port Orchard WA 98367
B/X/M/S/R/ — Capacity: Up to 350
Catering Dept. (877) 895-0142, Fax (360) 876-2254

PORT TOWNSEND

The Bishop Victorian Guest Suites — 714 Washington St, Port Townsend WA 98368
B/M/R/ — Guest Rooms: 14 — Capacity: Inside: Up to 75, Outside: Up to 200
(360) 385-6122

The Swan Hotel — Water & Monroe St, Port Townsend WA 98368
B/M/R/ — Guest Rooms: 9 — Capacity: Up to 28
(360) 385-1718

***B**=Banquets **X**=Parties **M**=Meetings **S**=Seminars **R**=Retreats **P**=Picnics **C**=Conventions **T**=Tradeshows*

POULSBO

Kiana Lodge — 14976 Sandy Hook Rd. N.E., Poulsbo WA 98370
B/X/M/S/R/P/ — Capacity: Up to 1,000
(206) 282-4633 or (360) 598-4311, Fax (206) 282-2129

Kitsap Memorial Log Hall — 202 N.E. Park St., Poulsbo WA 98370
B/X/M/S/R/P/ — Capacity: Up to 200
(360) 779-3205

Lange's Ranch — 13913 S. Keyport Rd., Poulsbo WA 98370
B/X/M/S/R/P/ — Guest Rooms: 2 — Capacity: Inside: Up to 200, Outside: Up to 500
Contact: Jewell Lange (360) 779-4927, Fax (360) 779-5466

Manor Farm Inn — 26069 Big Valley Rd., Poulsbo WA 98370
B/X/M/S/R/P/ — Capacity: Reception: Up to 50, With Outside: Up to 150
Contact: Suzanne Plemmons (360) 779-4628, Fax (360) 779-4876

Poulsbo Inn — 18680 Hwy. 305, Poulsbo WA 98370 *See page 113*
M/S/R/ — Guest Rooms: 72 — Capacity: Up to 25
Contact: Terri Douglas (360) 779-3921, Fax (360) 779-9737

PUYALLUP

Anton's Restaurant — 3207 E. Main Ave., Puyallup WA 98372
B/X/M/ — Capacity: Up to 110
Contact: Marilyn (253) 845-7569

Best Western Park Plaza — 620 South Hill Park Dr., Puyallup WA 98373
B/X/M/S/R/C/ — Guest Rooms: 100 — Capacity: Up to 200
(253) 848-1500, Fax (253) 848-1511

Liberty Theater Grand Events Hall — 116 W. Main St., Puyallup WA 98371
B/X/M/S/R/C/T/ — Capacity: Reception: Up to 340
Contact: Tom Neumann (253) 864-8116, Fax (253) 435-1658

Noel's Restaurant — 715 Meridian E., Puyallup WA 98371
B/X/M/S/ — Capacity: Banquet: Up to 35
Contact: Manager (253) 927-1809

The Puyallup Fair—
Western Washington Fairgrounds — 110-9th Ave. S.W., Puyallup WA 98371
B/X/M/S/R/P/C/T/ — Capacity: Up to 1,200 (1 Bldg)
Contact: Debbie Baker (253) 841-5011

REDMOND

Champs Karting — 2207 N.E. Bel-Red Rd., Redmond WA 98052 *See page 160*
B/X/M/S/ — Capacity: Up to 250
(425) 455-9999, Fax (425) 646-2722

The Clise Mansion — 6046 W. Lake Sammamish Pkwy. N.E., Redmond WA 98052
B/X/M/S/R/P/ — Capacity: Indoors: Up to 170, Outside: Up to 325
Contact: Competitive Edge Catering (425) 865-0795, Fax (425) 452-7825

Desert Fire Restaurant - Redmond — 7211-166th Ave. N.E., Redmond WA 98052
B/X/M/S/ — Capacity: Up to 48
Contact: Manager (425) 895-1500

***B**=Banquets **X**=Parties **M**=Meetings **S**=Seminars **R**=Retreats **P**=Picnics **C**=Conventions **T**=Tradeshows*

Redmond Inn — 17601 Redmond Wy., Redmond WA 98052
B/X/M/S/R/ — Guest Rooms: 137 — Capacity: Up to 80
Contact: Debbie, Catering & Sales (425) 883-4900, Fax (425) 869-5838
Redmond Senior Center — 8703 160th Ave. N.E., Redmond WA 98052
B/ — Capacity: Up to 200
Contact: Linda Van Loben Sels (425) 556-2314, Fax (425) 556-2365

RENTON

Aqua Barn Ranch — 15227 S.E. Maple Valley Hwy., Renton WA 98058
B/X/M/S/R/P/ — Capacity: 20 to 200
Office (425) 255-4618, Fax (425) 255-4822
City Of Renton Carco Theatre — 1717 Maple Valley Hwy., Renton WA 98055 *See page 93*
M/S/ — Capacity: Theatre: Up to 310
(425) 430-6706, Fax (425) 430-6701
Holiday Inn Select – Renton — One S. Grady Wy., Renton WA 98057
B/X/M/S/R/C/ — Guest Rooms: 226 — Capacity: Up to 300
Contact: Great American Catering (425) 204-6999, Fax (425) 204-8678
Maplewood Greens — 4050 Maple Valley Hwy., Renton WA 98058 *See pages 231 & 484*
B/X/M/S/R/ — Capacity: Banquet: Up to 270, Reception: up to 325
Events (425) 235-5044 or Pro Shop (425) 6800
Renton Community Center — 1715 Maple Valley Hwy., Renton WA 98055 *See page 263*
B/X/M/S/R/ — Capacity: Banquet: Up to 300; Reception: Up to 800
(425) 430-6700, Fax (425) 430-6701
Spirit of Washington Dinner Train — 625 S. 4th St., Renton WA 98055 *See page 64*
B/X/M/S/R/ — Capacity: Up to 338
Contact: Marni Ness (425) 227-8408, Fax (425) 277-8839
Valley Medical Center
Educational Conference Ctr. — 400 S. 43rd St., Renton WA 98055 *See page 97*
M/S/R/ — Capacity: Up to 200
Contact: Kathy Christensen (425) 656-5375, Fax (425) 656-5095

SAMMAMISH

The Plateau Club — 25625 E. Plateau Dr., Sammamish WA 98074 *See page 251*
B/X/M/S/R/ — Capacity: Banquet: Up to 230; Reception: Up to 300
(425) 868-6063, Fax (425) 836-4421

SEABECK

Emel House — Scenic Beach State Park, Seabeck WA
B/X/M/S/R/ — Capacity: Inside: Up to 40, Inside and Outside: Up to 150
Contact: Washington State Parks (360) 830-5079

***B**=Banquets **X**=Parties **M**=Meetings **S**=Seminars **R**=Retreats **P**=Picnics **C**=Conventions **T**=Tradeshows*

SEATAC

13 Coins – SeaTac — 18000 International Blvd., SeaTac WA 98188
B/X/M/ — Capacity: Banquet: Up to 30
Contact: Manager (206) 243-9500, Fax (206) 243-4668

Airport Plaza Hotel — 18601 Pacific Hwy. S., Seatac WA 98188
B/X/M/S/R/ — Guest Rooms: 140 — Capacity: Up to 100
Contact: Banquet Manager (206) 433-0400, Fax (206) 431-2222

Clarion Hotel Sea-Tac — 3000 S. 176th St., Seatac WA 98188
B/X/M/S/R/C/ — Guest Rooms: 214
Capacity: Banquet: Up to 100, Reception: Up to 180
Sales & Catering Dept (206) 242-0200, Fax (206) 242-1998

Funsters Grand Casinos — 15221 International Blvd., SeaTac WA 98188 *See page 193*
B/X/M/ — Capacity: 30 to 750 guests
(206) 988-4888, Fax (206) 988-6166

Holiday Inn – SeaTac — 17338 International Blvd. S., SeaTac WA 98188
B/X/M/S/ — Guest Rooms: 260 — Capacity: Banquet: Up to 200, Reception: Up to 350
Contact: Kathy Hoffman (206) 248-1000

Marriott, Seattle – SeaTac Airport — 3201 S. 176th St., Seatac WA 98188
B/X/M/S/R/C/ — Guest Rooms: 459 — Capacity: Up to 500
Catering Dept. (206) 241-2000, Fax (206) 241-2261

Seatac Community Center — 13735-24th Ave. S., SeaTac WA 98168
B/X/M/S/R/ — Capacity: Banquet: Up to 100, Reception: Up to 120
(206) 439-9273

WestCoast Gateway Hotel — 18220 International Blvd. S., Seatac WA 98188
M/S/R/ — Guest Rooms: 146 — Capacity: Up to 100
Sales & Catering (206) 246-5535

SEATTLE

13 Coins – Seattle — 125 Boren Ave. N., Seattle WA 98109
Capacity: Up to 28
Contact: Manager (206) 682-2513, Fax (206) 682-2847

Alexis Hotel—The Painted Table — 1007-1st Ave. At Madison, Seattle WA 98104 *See page 141*
B/X/M/S/R/ — Guest Rooms: 54 — Capacity: 10 to 120 guests
Contact: Elizabeth Bernstein (206) 340-6710 or (206) 624-8444

Aljoya Conference Center
at Laurelhurst — 3920 N.E. 41st St., Seattle WA 98105-5428 *See page 142*
M/S/R/ — Guest Rooms: 30 — Capacity: 8 meeting rooms for 5 to 100
Contact: Eva Bledsoe (206) 268-7000, Fax (206) 268-7001

Anthony's Homeport – Shilshole — 6135 Seaview Ave. N., Seattle WA 98107
B/X/M/S/R/ — Capacity: Up to 200
Contact: Tracy (206) 783-0780 or (206) 783-7812, Fax (206) 789-8396

The Atrium Cafe — 5701-6th Ave. S., Seattle WA 98108
B/X/M/ — Capacity: Up to 800
Catering Dept. (206) 763-2215, Fax (206) 763-3209

Avalon Ballroom – Washington Dance Club — 1017 Stewart St. , Seattle WA 98101
B/X/M/S/R/ — Capacity: Up to 300
Contact: Marge Hinshaw (206) 628-8939

B=Banquets X=Parties M=Meetings S=Seminars R=Retreats P=Picnics C=Conventions T=Tradeshows

Axis Restaurant — 2214-1st Ave., Seattle WA 98121
B/X/M/ — Capacity: Private Room: Up to 60 seated, 100 receptions, Restaurant: Up to 300
Contact: Liz Nunez (206) 441-9600, Fax (206) 441-4275

Bacon Mansion — 959 Broadway E., Seattle WA 98102
B/X/M/S/R/ — Guest Rooms: 11 — Capacity: Up to 75
Contact: Daryl King (206) 329-1864, Fax (206) 860-9025

The Bay Pavilion — 1301 Alaskan Wy., Seattle WA 98101 *See pages 144 & 340*
B/X/M/S/R/ — Capacity: Banquet: Up to 250, Reception: Up to 350, Whole Pier: Up to 1,500 for receptions
Contact: Lance Fushikoshi or Michelle Blanchard (206) 623-8600

Bell Harbor International Conference Center — Pier 66, 2211 Alaskan Wy., Seattle WA 98121 *See pages 146, 380 & 381*
B/X/M/S/R/C/ — Capacity: 20 to 2,000; Auditorium: Up to 300; Conference Center: 16,450sq. ft.
Sales Department (206) 441-6666, Fax (206) 441-6665

Belltown Billiards & Ristorante — 90 Blanchard St., Seattle WA 98121
B/X/M/ — Capacity: Up to 350
Contact: Lisa Rios (206) 448-6779, Fax (206) 443-9513

Benaroya Hall — 200 University Street, Seattle WA 98101 *See page 148*
B/X/M/S/ — Capacity: Auditorium: Up to 2,500; Banquet or Meeting: 120 to 500 seated; Receptions: Up to 1,100
Contact: Troy Skubitz (206) 215-4804, Fax (206) 215-4801

Best Western Executive Inn Convention Center – Seattle — 200 Taylor Ave. N., Seattle WA 98109
B/X/M/S/R/C/ — Guest Rooms: 123 — Capacity: Up to 250
Contact: Jan Peterson (206) 448-9444 or (800) 351-9444, Fax (206) 441-7929

Best Western Sea-Tac — 20717 Pacific Hwy S., Seattle WA 98198
B/X/M/S/R/ — Guest Rooms: 138
Capacity: Up to 80 classroom style, Up to 150 theatre style
Contact: Catering Manager (206) 878-3300 x344, Fax (206) 824-9000

Big Picture — 2505 1st Avenue, Seattle WA 98121 *See page 152*
B/X/M/S/R/ — Capacity: Up to 125
Contact: Mark or Katie Stern (206) 256-0566

Blue Ribbon Cooking School — At Madison Park, Seattle WA *See pages 153 & 464*
B/X/S/ — Capacity: Ideal for groups of 15 to 65
(206) 328-2442, Fax (206) 328-2863

BluWater Bistro — 1001 Fairview Ave. N. #1700, Seattle WA 98109 *See page 154*
B/X/M/ — Capacity: Banquet: Up to 90, Reception: Up to 175
Contact: Elizabeth Williams (206) 447-0769, Fax (206) 447-6977

Broadway Performance Hall — 1625 Broadway, Seattle WA 98122 *See page 92*
B/X/M/S/ — Capacity: Reception: Up to 100, Conference: Up to 295, Theatre: Up to 295
Contact: Darrell Jamieson (206) 325-3113, Fax (206) 325-3420

The Jerry M. Brockey Center at South Seattle Community College — 6000 16th Ave. S.W., Seattle WA 98106 *See page 216*
B/M/S/C/T/ — Capacity: Banquet: Up to 350; Theatre Style: Up to 700
Contact: Bob Sullivan (206) 768-6613

The Burke Museum of Natural History & Culture — (UofW Campus) N.E. 45th St. & 17th Ave. N.E., Seattle WA 98195 *See page 155*
B/X/M/S/R/ — Capacity: Banquet: Up to 130, Reception: Up to 300
(206) 221-2853 Banquets or (206) 543-5590 Museum

***B**=Banquets **X**=Parties **M**=Meetings **S**=Seminars **R**=Retreats **P**=Picnics **C**=Conventions **T**=Tradeshows*

Canlis Restaurant — 2576 Aurora Ave. N., Seattle WA 98109 *See page 156*
B/X/M/ — Capacity: Exec. Room: 15 to 30; Penthouse: 35 to 90; Caché: 2 to 4
Private Dining (206) 298-9550

CaterArts at the Lakeside — 2501 N. Northlake Wy., Seattle WA 98103 *See pages 157 & 344*
B/X/M/S/R/ — Capacity: Up to 250
Contact: Elisabet Hebrant, or Laura Daley (206) 632-2200, Fax (206) 545-2137

Center for Urban Horticulture
Conference Facilities – U of W — 3501 N.E. 41st St., Seattle WA 98105
B/X/M/S/R/ — Capacity: 10–200
Contact: Becky (206) 221-2500

Center for Wooden Boats — 1010 Valley St., Seattle WA 98109
B/X/M/S/R/ — Capacity: Reception: Up to 75
(206) 382-2628, Fax (206) 382-2699

Century Ballroom — 915 E. Pine St., Seattle WA 98122 *See page 159*
B/X/M/ — Capacity: Banquet: Up to 225, Reception: Up to 300
(206) 324-7263, Fax (206) 324-7263

The Children's Museum — 305 Harrison St., Seattle WA 98109
B/X/M/S/R/ — Capacity: Up to 1,000
(206) 441-1768, Fax (206) 448-0910

China Harbor Restaurant — 2040 Westlake Ave. N., Seattle WA 98109
B/X/M/ — Capacity: Up to 350
(206) 286-1688

Chinatown Discovery, Inc. — P.O. Box 3406, Seattle WA 98114
B/X/M/ — Capacity: Up to 300
Contact: Vi Mar (425) 885-3085, Fax (425) 869-9170

Chinook's at Salmon Bay—
Fishermen's Terminal — 1900 W. Nickerson, Seattle WA 98119
B/X/M/ — Capacity: Up to 50
Office (206) 283-4665, Fax (206) 283-370

The Claremont Hotel — 2000 Fourth Ave., Seattle WA 98121 *See pages 32 & 161*
B/X/M/S/R/ — Guest Rooms: 120
Capacity: Banquet: Up to 150, Receptions: Up to 225
Sales Office (206) 694-7255 or (800) 448-8601, Fax (206) 443-1420

College Club — 505 Madison, Seattle WA 98104
B/X/M/S/ — Capacity: Banquets: Up to 260, Receptions: Up to 350
Contact: Mary Pat Bonus (206) 622-0624, Fax (206) 622-0627

Columbia Tower Club — 701-5th Ave., 75th & 76th Fls., Seattle WA 98104 *See page 162*
B/X/M/S/R/ — Capacity: Banquet: Up to 250, Reception: Up to 500
Private Event Dept. (206) 622-2010

Corinthian Yacht Club – Leschi Clubhouse — 106 Lakeside Ave., Seattle WA 98122
B/X/M/S/R/ — Capacity: Up to 40
Contact: Joe James (206) 789-1919

Corinthian Yacht Club – Seattle — 7755 Seaview Ave. N.W., Seattle WA 98117
B/X/M/S/R/ — Capacity: Up to 100
(206) 789-1919

Costas Opa Greek Restaurant — 3400 Fremont Ave. N., Seattle WA 98103
B/X/M/ — Capacity: Up to 60
Contact: Nina (206) 633-4141

Court in the Square — 401-2nd Ave. S. #100, Seattle WA 98104 *See page 164*
B/X/M/S/ — Capacity: Up to 300
Contact: Robert Payne (206) 467-5533, Fax (206) 467-9798

B*=Banquets* ***X****=Parties* ***M****=Meetings* ***S****=Seminars* ***R****=Retreats* ***P****=Picnics* ***C****=Conventions* ***T****=Tradeshows*

Crêpe De Paris French Restaurant — 1333-5th Ave., Seattle WA 98101
B/X/M/ — Capacity: Banquet: Up to 100, Reception: Up to 200 (including terrace)
Contact: Paulette (206) 623-4111

Crowne Plaza — 1113-6th Ave., Seattle WA 98101 *See page 165*
B/X/M/S/R/C/T/ — Guest Rooms: 415
Capacity: Indoor: Up to 400, Outdoor Patio: Up to 120
Catering Office (206) 464-1980 or (800) 521-2762

Cutter's Bayhouse — 2001 Western Ave., Seattle WA 98121 *See page 166*
B/X/M/ — Capacity: Banquet: Up to 80, Receptions: Up to 100
Contact: John O'Brien (206) 448-4884, Fax (206) 727-2194

D.A.R. - Rainier Chapter House — 800 E. Roy St., Seattle WA 98102
B/X/M/S/R/ — Capacity: Up to 250
Contact: Kaye Theobald (206) 323-0600, Fax (206) 328-4846

Dahlia Lounge — 2001 4th Ave., Seattle WA 98121 *See page 167*
B/X/ — Capacity: Up to 50
(206) 682-4142, Fax (206) 467-0568

Daniel's Broiler – Leschi Marina — 200 Lake Washington Blvd., Seattle WA 98122 *See page 168*
B/X/M/ — Capacity: Private Parties: Up to 18, Restaurant: Up to 110 daytime only
Contact: Manager of Private Dining (425) 462-4662 or
(206) 329-4191, Fax (206) 328-8190

Daniel's Broiler – South Lake Union — 809 Fairview Pl. N., Seattle WA 98109 *See page 168*
B/X/M/ — Capacity: Private Parties: Up to 36, Restaurant: Up to 200 daytime only
Contact: Manager of Private Dining (425) 462-4662 or
(206) 621-8262, Fax (206) 748-7762

Daybreak Star Art Center – Discovery Park — PO Box 99100, Seattle WA 98199
B/X/M/ — Capacity: Up to 300
Contact: Audrey Gray (206) 285-4425 x33, Fax (206) 282-3640

Desert Fire Restaurant – Pacific Place — 600 Pine St., #402, Seattle WA 98101
B/X/M/ — Capacity: Up to 30
Contact: Manager (206) 405-3400

The Dome Room — 700-3rd. Ave., Seattle WA 98104 *See pages 169 & 369*
B/X/M/S/ — Capacity: Banquet: Up to 250, Reception: Up to 350
Contact: Tony's Events & Catering (206) 328-2195

Doubletree Guest Suites
Seattle - Southcenter — 16500 Southcenter Pkwy., Seattle WA 98188 *See page 170*
B/X/M/S/R/C/ — Guest Rooms: 221
Capacity: Banquet: Up to 550, Reception: Up to 700; 11 Conference Rms.
Sales & Catering Office (206) 575-8220, Fax (206) 575-4743

Doubletree Hotel – Seattle Airport — 18740 Pacific Hwy. S., Seattle WA 98188 *See page 172*
B/X/M/S/R/ — Guest Rooms: 850
Capacity: 30 Meeting Rms; 10 to 2,000 guests
Catering Office (206) 433-1881, Fax (206) 901-5902

Drachen Foundation — 1905 Queen Anne Ave N, Seattle WA 98109 *See page 173*
B/M/B/S/ — Capacity: Up to 100
(206) 282-4349, Fax (206) 284-5471

Dragonfish Asian Cafe - Seattle — 722 Pine St., Seattle WA 98101 *See page 572*
B/X/ — Capacity: Private Rms.: 30 to 50
(206) 467-7777 or (206) 467-8891

Eagles Aerie #1 — 6205 Corson Ave. S. (Exit 162 Off Of I-5), Seattle WA 98108 *See page 175*
B/X/M/S/R/C/T/ — Capacity: Banquet or Reception: up to 999
Contact: Todd Solemsaas (206) 762-5203

B=Banquets X=Parties M=Meetings S=Seminars R=Retreats P=Picnics C=Conventions T=Tradeshows

The Edgewater — 2411 Alaskan Wy, Pier 67, Seattle WA 98121-1398 *See pages 33 & 177*
B/X/M/S/R/ — Guest Rooms: 236 — Capacity: Up to 200
Catering & Sales (206) 728-7000 or (888) 316-4449, Fax (206) 448-0255

El Gaucho — 2505-1st Ave., Seattle WA 98121 *See page 179*
B/X/M/S/R/C/ — Capacity: 4 Private Rms.; Banquet: Up to 125, Reception: Up to 200
Contact: Eileen Reimann (206) 728-1337, Fax (206) 728-4477

Elliott Grand Hyatt — 721 Pine Street, Seattle WA 98101 *See page 180*
B/X/M/S/R/ — Guest Rooms: 425 — Capacity: Up to 600
Contact: Tev Marchettoni (206) 774-1234, Fax (206) 625-1221

Elliott's — 1201 Alaskan Wy., Pier 56, Seattle WA 98101
B/X/M/S/ — Capacity: Banquet: Up to 40, Reception: Up to 75
Contact: Ben Steingard (206) 623-4340, Fax (206) 224-0154

Etta's Seafood — 2020 Western Avenue , Seattle WA 98121
B/X/M/ — Capacity: Up to 45
(206) 443-6000, Fax (206) 443-0648

Experience Music Project
(at the Seattle Center) — 325-5th Ave. N., Seattle WA 98109 *See page 187*
B/X/M/S/R/C/ — Capacity: Banquets: Up to 300,
Receptions: Up to 700; Entire Museum: Up to 1,500
Facility Sales (206) 770-2700, Fax (206) 770-2727

F.X. McRory's Steak, Chop &
Oyster House — 419 Occidental S. #602, Seattle WA 98104 *See page 188*
B/X/ — Capacity: 3 rooms accommodate: 40, 60, & 110; Reception: Up to 300
(206) 623-4800, Fax (206) 613-3105

The Fairview Club –
A Grand Affaire at — 2022 Boren Ave. , Seattle WA 98121 *See pages 189 & 337*
B/X/M/S/R/ — Capacity: Banquet: Up to 350, Reception: Up to 450
(206) 623-9003, Fax (206) 623-3315

The Hall at Fauntleroy — 9131 California Ave. S.W., Seattle WA 98136 *See pages 197 & 370*
B/X/M/S/R/ — Capacity: Indoors: Up to 500, Outdoors: Up to 300 (seasonal)
Contact: David Haggerty or David Meckstroth,
Tuxedos N' Tennis Shoes Catering (206) 932-1059, Fax (206) 937-6508

Flying Fish — 2234 1st Ave., Seattle WA 98121 *See page 191*
B/X/M/ — Capacity: Banquet: Up to 40, Reception: Up to 70
(206) 728-8595, Fax (206) 728-1551

Four Seas Restaurant — 714 S. King St., Seattle WA 98104
B/X/M/ — Capacity: Up to 450
Contact: Manager: Al Quan (206) 682-4900

Four Seasons Olympic Hotel — 411 University St., Seattle WA 98101
B/X/M/S/R/C/ — Guest Rooms: 450 — Capacity: Up to 550
Catering Dept. (206) 621-1700, Fax (206) 623-2271

Full House Catering at Key Arena — 305 Harrison St., Seattle WA 98109
B/X/M/C/T/ — Capacity: Seated: Up to 900, Reception: Up to 1,500
Contact: Manager (206) 448-6790, Fax (206) 281-5839

GameWorks — 1511-7th Ave., Seattle WA 98101
B/X/M/C/ — Capacity: Up to 1,500
Marketing Dept (206) 521-0952, Fax (206) 521-9293

The Garage Pool Hall — 1130 Broadway, Seattle WA 98122
B/X/M/S/ — Capacity: Up to 400
Contact: Alex Or Mike (206) 322-2296, Fax (206) 320-8507

B=Banquets X=Parties M=Meetings S=Seminars R=Retreats P=Picnics C=Conventions T=Tradeshows

General Cinema at Pacific Place — 600 Pine St., #400, Seattle WA 98101
M/S/ — Capacity: 11 auditoriums that accommodate 75–600
Contact: Marketing Dir. (206) 652-8908, Fax (206) 652-8909

General Petroleum Museum — 1526 Bellevue Avenue, Seattle WA 98122
B/X/M/S/R/ — Capacity: Banquet: Up to 275, Reception: Up to 450
Contact: Susan Pederson (206) 323-4789

Gordon Biersch Brewing Company — Pacific Place, 600 Pine St., 4th Floor, Seattle WA 98101
B/X/M/ — Capacity: Pilsner Room: Up to 48 seated,
South Dining Room: Up to 60 seated, Entire Facility: Up to 500
Contact: Kaaren Kragerud (206) 405-4207, Fax (206) 405-4204

Graham Visitor Center in
Washington Park Arboretum — 2300 Arboretum Dr. E., Seattle WA 98112
B/X/M/S/R/ — Capacity: Inside: Up to 100, Inside and Outside: Up to 130
Contact: Josey Fast (206) 543-8800

Greenwood Square — 8420 Greenwood Ave. N., Seattle WA 98103 *See pages 196 & 373*
B/X/M/S/R/ — Capacity: Banquet: Up to 125, Reception: Up to 175
Contact: Upper Crust Catering (206) 783-1826, Fax (206) 783-1672

Hale's Brewery & Pub — 4301 Leary Way N.W, Seattle WA 98107
B/X/M/ — Capacity: Up to 90
Contact: Cathy Foote (206) 706-1544

The Hall at Fauntleroy — 9131 California Ave. S.W., Seattle WA 98136 *See pages 197 & 370*
B/X/M/S/R/ — Capacity: Indoors: Up to 500, Outdoors: Up to 300 (seasonal)
Contact: David Haggerty or David Meckstroth,
Tuxedos N' Tennis Shoes Catering (206) 932-1059, Fax (206) 937-6508

The Harbor Club – Seattle — 801 2nd Ave., 17th Fl., Seattle WA 98104 *See page 198*
B/X/M/S/R/ — Capacity: Banquet: Up to 275;
Luncheons: Up to 150; Reception: Up to 450
Catering Dept. (206) 623-3532, Fax (206) 623-0686

Harborside Seafood Restaurant,
McCormick & Schmick's — 1200 Westlake Ave. N., Seattle WA 98109 *See pages 201 & 359*
B/X/M/S/R/ — Capacity: Banquet: Up to 150; Reception: Up to 200
(206) 270-8815

Henry Art Gallery — Univ. of Washington, 15th Ave. N.E. & N.E. 41st St., Seattle WA 98195
B/X/M/S/R/ — Capacity: Auditorium: Up to 150,
Banquets: Up to 60, Receptions: Up to 250
Events Dept. (206) 543-2280 or (206) 616-8627, Fax (206) 685-3123

Hilton Seattle — 6th & University, Seattle WA 98101 *See page 203*
B/X/M/S/R/C/ — Guest Rooms: 237 — Capacity: Up to 350
Contact: Kitty Kuhnly (206) 624-0500

Hilton Seattle Airport &
Conference Center — 17620 Pacific Hwy. S., Seattle WA 98188 *See page 204*
B/X/M/S/R/C/T/ — Guest Rooms: 400
Capacity: 26 Conf. Rms. & Event Space; Banquet: Up to 900; Reception: Up to 1,200
Catering Office (206) 244-4800, Fax (206) 248-4495

Hiram's — 5300-34th Ave. NW., Seattle WA 98107
B/X/M/ — Capacity: Up to 100
Contact: Banquet Coordinator (206) 784-1733

Holiday Inn Express SeaTac — 19621 International Blvd., Seattle WA 98188 *See page 205*
B/X/M/S/R/ — Guest Rooms: 147 — Capacity: Up to 90
(206) 824-3200, Fax (206) 824-0233

B=Banquets X=Parties M=Meetings S=Seminars R=Retreats P=Picnics C=Conventions T=Tradeshows

Holiday Inn Seattle Center — 211 Dexter Ave. N., Seattle WA 98109
B/X/M/S/R/ — Guest Rooms: 198 — Capacity: Banquet: Up to 120, Reception: Up to 158
Sales Dept. (206) 728-8123, Fax (206) 441-9794

Hotel Monaco — 1101 4th Ave. , Seattle WA 98101 *See page 34*
B/X/M/ — Capacity: Up to 200
(206) 516-5007, Fax (206) 624-0060

Icon Grill — 1933 5th Ave., Seattle WA 98101 *See page 210*
B/X/ — Capacity: Up to 22 guests
(206) 441-6330, Fax (206) 441-7037

Ivar's Acres of Clams — Pier 54, Alaskan Wy., Seattle WA 98104 *See page 214*
B/X/M/ — Capacity: Spirit of the Bay Room: Up to 50,
Proclamation Room: Up to 45, Upper Terrace: Up to 110
Contact: Nancy Bogue (206) 587-6500, Fax (206) 624-4895

Ivar's Salmon House — 401 N.E. Northlake Wy., Seattle WA 98104 *See page 215*
B/X/M/ — Capacity: Potlach Room: Up to 100, Makah Room: Up to 25,
Muckleshoot Room: Up to 65, Lake Union Barge: Up to 140, Waterfront Deck: Up to 65
Contact: Nancy Bogue (206) 587-6500, Fax (206) 624-4895

Jackson Park Golf Club — 1000 N.E. 135th, Seattle WA 98125
B/X/ — Capacity: Up to 25
(206) 363-4747, Fax (206) 361-6636

Jefferson Community Center — 3801 Beacon Ave. S., Seattle WA 98108
B/X/M/S/R/ — Capacity: Up to 175
(206) 684-7481, Fax (206) 684-7483

Jefferson Park Golf Club — 4101 Beacon S, Seattle WA 98108
B/X/ — Capacity: Up to 40
(206) 762-4513

The Jerry M. Brockey Center at
South Seattle Community College — 6000 16th Ave. S.W., Seattle WA 98106 *See page 216*
B/M/S/C/T/ — Capacity: Banquet: Up to 350; Theatre Style: Up to 700
Contact: Bob Sullivan (206) 768-6613

Jillian's – Seattle — 731 Westlake Avenue N., Seattle WA 98109 *See pages 56 & 217*
B/X/M/ — Capacity: Up to 1,000
Contact: Chris Weaver (206) 223-0300

Kaspar's Restaurant — 19 W. Harrison, Seattle WA 98119 *See page 218*
B/X/M/ — Capacity: Banquet: Up to 250, Reception: Up to 300
Contact: Catering Coordinator (206) 298-0123, Fax (206) 298-0146

Kells Irish Restaurant — 1916 Post Alley , Seattle WA 98101
B/X/M/ — Capacity: Up to 170
Contact: Patrick McAleese (206) 728-1916, Fax (206) 441-9431

Kingstad Meeting Centers — 1301 1st Ave. at Harbor Steps, Seattle WA 98101 *See page 221*
B/X/M/S/R/ — Capacity: 6 meeting rooms, for up to 50 each
Contact: Janet Harbold or Tom Edgar (206) 654-6040 or (425) 562-1292

Knights of Columbus — 722 E. Union Street, Seattle WA 98122 *See page 222*
B/X/M/S/ — Capacity: Banquets: Up to 250
(206) 325-3410

LaFontana Ristorante — 120 Blanchard St., Seattle WA 98121
B/X/ — Capacity: Up to 50
Contact: Mario (206) 441-1045

Lake Union Cafe — 3119 Eastlake Avenue East, Seattle WA 98102 *See page 223*
B/X/M/S/ — Capacity: Up to 350
Contact: Victoria Haberman (206) 568-1258

B*=Banquets* ***X****=Parties* ***M****=Meetings* ***S****=Seminars* ***R****=Retreats* ***P****=Picnics* ***C****=Conventions* ***T****=Tradeshows*

Lake Union Crew — 11 E. Allison St., Seattle WA 98102 *See page 224*
B/X/M/S/R/ — Capacity: Banquet: Up to 140;
Conf. Rm.: Up to 12; Seminars: Up to 48
Contact: Rome Ventura (206) 860-4199, Fax (206) 860-7826

Lake Washington Rowing Club — 910 N. Northlake Wy., Seattle WA 98103 *See page 225*
B/X/M/S/R/ — Capacity: Banquet Rm.: Up to 150; Board Rm.: Up to 14 seated
Contact: NW Events & Parties (206) 524-4918

Lakeside School — 14050-1st Ave. N.E., Seattle WA 98125
B/X/M/ — Capacity: Up to 250
Contact: Judy Bauer (206) 440-2752

Langston Hughes Cultural Arts Center — 104-17th Ave. S., Seattle WA 98144
B/X/M/S/R/ — Capacity: Up to 290
Contact: Rental Coordinator (206) 684-4757, Fax (206) 233-7149

Laurelhurst Community Center — 4554 N.E. 41st St., Seattle WA 98105
B/X/P/ — Capacity: Inside: Up to 125
Office (206) 684-7529, Fax (206) 522-6029

Lowell-Hunt Premier Catering — 1111 Fairview Ave. N., Seattle WA 98109 *See page 230*
B/X/M/S/R/ — Capacity: Dining Room: Up to 130, Waterview Deck: Up to 240
Contact: Event Coordinator (206) 264-0400 - Seattle or
(425) 486-4072 - Eastside, Fax (206) 264-9445

Madison Park Cafe — 1807-42nd Ave. E., Seattle WA 98112
B/X/ — Capacity: Up to 40
Contact: Karen (206) 324-2626

Marina Club at Shilshole Bay — 7001 Seaview Ave. N.W., Seattle WA 98107 *See page 232*
B/X/M/R/ — Capacity: Banquet: Up to 400, Reception: Up to 450
(206) 706-0257

Mayflower Park Hotel — 405 Olive Wy., Seattle WA 98101 *See page 234*
B/X/M/S/R/C/ — Guest Rooms: 171
Capacity: Six Meeting & Banquet Rms. for groups of 10 to 200
Catering Office (206) 382-6991

**The Mediterranean Inn –
The Inn Apartments** — 425 Queen Anne Ave. N., Seattle WA 98109 *See pages 35 & 235*
B/X/M/S/R/ — Guest Rooms: 180
Capacity: Boardroom: Up to 12; Meeting Rm.: Up to 16 classroom or 20 for receptions
(206) 428-7000 or (866) 425-4700, Fax (206) 428-4700

Merchants Cafe — 109 Yesler Wy., Seattle WA 98104
B/X/M/ — Capacity: Up to 75
Contact: Chuck Curilla (206) 624-1515

Meridian Restaurant at Gasworks — 1900 N. Lakeway, Seattle WA 98103
B/X/M/ — Capacity: Up to 32
Contact: Mike Jallits (206) 547-3242, Fax (206) 547-3239

Metropolitan Grill — 820 2nd Ave. At Marion, Seattle WA 98104
B/X/M/ — Capacity: Banquet: Up to 25, Reception: Up to 50
Catering (206) 624-3287

Michelangelo's Bistro & Bar — Seattle Center, Centerhouse, 305 Harrison, Seattle WA 98109
B/X/M/ — Capacity: Up to 300
Contact: Jim (206) 441-6600, Fax (206) 343-9173

Mount Baker Club — 2811 Mount Rainier Dr. S., Seattle WA 98144
B/X/M/S/R/ — Capacity: Ballroom: Up to 380, Conference: Up to 50
Contact: Manager (206) 722-7209

B=Banquets X=Parties M=Meetings S=Seminars R=Retreats P=Picnics C=Conventions T=Tradeshows

The Mountaineers Building — 300-3rd Ave. W., Seattle WA 98119
B/X/M/S/R/ — Capacity: Up to 600
Sales Office (206) 281-7775

Museum of Flight — 9404 East Marginal Wy. S., Seattle WA 98108 *See page 238*
B/X/M/S/R/C/T/ — Capacity: 10 to 2,500 guests
Special Events Dept. (206) 764-5706 or
Museum (206) 764-5720, Fax (206) 764-5707

Museum of History & Industry (MOHAI) — 2700-24th Ave. E., Seattle WA 98112 *See pages 95 & 240*
B/X/M/S/ — Capacity: Banquet: Up to 200; Reception: Up to 300;
Theatre/Auditorium: Up to 373
(206) 324-1126, Fax (206) 324-1346

New Holly Neighborhood Campus — 7054 - 32nd Avenue South, Seattle WA 98118 *See page 241*
B/X/M/S/ — Capacity: Up to: 250
(206) 760-3280, Fax (206) 760-3290

Nikko Restaurant — 1900 - 5th Ave., Seattle WA 98101
B/X/M/ — Capacity: Up to 50
Catering (206) 322-4641

Nippon Kan Theatre — 628 S. Washington, Seattle WA 98104
B/X/M/S/ — Capacity: Theatre: Up to 400, Banquet Hall: Up to 250
(206) 224-0181

Odyssey - The Maritime Discovery Center — Bell Street Pier, Pier 66, 2211 Alaskan Wy., Seattle WA 98121 *See page 245*
B/X/M/S/R/ — Capacity: Receptions: Up to 500
Catering (206) 441-6666, Fax (206) 441-6665

The Old Spaghetti Factory – Seattle — 2801 Elliott Ave., Seattle WA 98121
B/X/M/ — Capacity: Up to 100
Contact: Manager (206) 441-7724

Pacific Science Center — 200-2nd Ave. N., Seattle WA 98109 *See pages 59 & 247*
B/X/M/S/R/ — Capacity: 200–4,500
Contact: Cindy Messey Events (206) 443-2899 or
General (206) 443-2001, Fax (206) 443-3631

Palisade – Elliott Bay Marina — 2601 W. Marina Place, Seattle WA 98199 *See pages 248 & 573*
B/X/M/S/ — Capacity: Banquets: Up to 125, Receptions: Up to 175
Contact: Laura Adams (206) 285-5865

The Paramount Hotel – A WestCoast Hotel — 724 Pine St., Seattle WA 98101
B/X/M/S/R/ — Guest Rooms: 146
Capacity: Banquet: Up to 60, Theater Style: Up to 80
Sales & Catering (206) 292-9500, Fax (206) 447-4736

The Paramount Theatre & Ballroom — 911 Pine St., Seattle WA 98101 *See pages 96 & 249*
B/X/M/S/R/C/T/ — Capacity: Theatre Style: Up to 2,946; Banquets: Up to 2,500
Contact: Jason Ferguson (206) 467-5510 x 150 or
Gen. Info.: (206) 682-1414, Fax (206) 682-4837

Parker's Sports Bar & Casino — 17001 Aurora Ave. N., Seattle WA 98133
B/X/M/ — Capacity: Up to 850
Contact: Sharon (206) 542-9491, Fax (206) 546-2600

Phinney Neighborhood Center — 6532 Phinney Ave. N., Seattle WA 98103
B/X/M/S/R/ — Capacity: Banquet: Up to 100,
Reception: Up to 150 (No alcohol/amplified music)
(206) 783-2244

B=Banquets X=Parties M=Meetings S=Seminars R=Retreats P=Picnics C=Conventions T=Tradeshows

Piatti, Ristorante — 2800 University Village, Seattle WA 98105
B/X/M/ — Capacity: Banquet: Up to 40
Contact: Manager (206) 524-9088, Fax (206) 524-3116

The Pike Pub & Brewery — 1415-1st Ave., Seattle WA 98101
B/X/M/ — Capacity: Up to 100
Contact: Bruce Raymond (206) 622-6044, Fax (206) 622-8730

Pocock Memorial Rowing Center — 3320 Fuhrman Ave. E., Seattle WA 98102
B/X/M/S/R/ — Capacity: Up to 167
Contact: Wilma Comenat (206) 328-0778, Fax (206) 328-4239

Ponti Seafood Grill — 3014-3rd Ave. N., Seattle WA 98109 *See page 256*
B/X/M/S/R/ — Capacity: Two private rooms,
Sit-down: Up to 25 or Reception: Up to 50
Contact: Richard Malia (206) 284-3000, Fax (206) 284-4768

Pyramid Alehouse — 1201 First Ave. S., Seattle WA 98134 *See page 257*
B/X/M/ — Capacity: Mezzanine: Up to 70 seated, VIP Room: Up to 40 seated,
Executive Room: Up to 60 seated, combined: Up to 115; Alehouse: Up to 400 seated
(206) 682-8322 x323, Fax (206) 682-8420

Queen Anne Masonic Temple — 1608-4th Ave. W., Seattle WA 98109
B/X/M/S/R/ — Capacity: Up to 200
Contact: Dan Newton Or Ted (206) 285-1930

Radisson Hotel Seattle — 17001 Pacific Hwy. S., Seattle WA 98188
B/X/M/S/R/ — Guest Rooms: 308 — Capacity: Reception: 400, Seated: 250
Catering Dept. (206) 244-6000

Rainforest Cafe — 290 Southcenter Mall Blvd., Seattle WA 98188 *See page 258*
B/X/ — Capacity: Banquet: Up to 325 seated; Reception: Up to 600
(206) 248-8882, Fax (206) 248-2026

Rainier Golf & Country Club — 11133 Des Moines Memorial Dr. S., Seattle WA 98168
B/X/M/S/R/ — Capacity: Up to 300
Contact: Jim Ashburn (206) 242-2222, Fax (206) 242-4600

Rainier Valley Cultural Center — 3515 S. Alaska Street, Seattle WA 98118
B/X/M/ — Capacity: Wedding: Up to 250, Reception: Up to 150; Kitchen available
Contact: Jerri Plumridge (206) 725-7517 or (M-F 8am-4:30pm)

Ramada Inn – Northgate Seattle — 2140 N. Northgate Wy., Seattle WA 98113
B/X/M/S/R/ — Guest Rooms: 169
Capacity: Banquet: Up to 125, Reception: Up to 200
Sales & Catering (206) 365-0700, Fax (206) 365-0750

Ray's Boathouse — 6049 Seaview Ave. N.W., Seattle WA 98107 *See pages 259 & 365*
B/X/M/S/ — Capacity: Banquet: Up to 64,
Reception: Up to 120 with canopied deck
Catering Office (206) 789-6309, Fax (206) 781-1960

Red Lion Hotel - Seattle Airport / Southcenter — 205 Strander Blvd., Seattle WA 98188
B/X/MS/R/C/ — Guest Rooms: 198
Capacity: Banquet: Up to 220, Reception: Up to 300
Catering Office (206) 246-8220, Fax (206) 575-4747

REI — 222 Yale Ave. N., Seattle WA 98109 *See pages 261 & 475*
M/S/R/ — Capacity: Conf. Hall: Up to 250
(206) 223-1944 or (888) 873-1938, Fax (206) 223-1407

Renaissance Madison Hotel — 515 Madison St., Seattle WA 98104 *See page 262*
B/X/M/S/R/C/T/ — Guest Rooms: 553
Capacity: Banquet: Up to 450, Reception: Up to 600
Catering Office (206) 583-0300

The Rhododendron Restaurant in the Inn at Virginia Mason — 1006 Spring St., Seattle WA 98101
B/X/M/S/R/ — Guest Rooms: 79
Capacity: Rooftop Garden: Up to 25, Courtyard: Up to 25, Inside: Up to 70
Catering Sales (206) 223-7556

Ristorante Di Ragazzi — 2329 California Ave. SW., Seattle WA 98116
B/X/ — Capacity: Private Room: Up to 15, Restaurant: Up to 70
Contact: Laura (206) 935-1969, Fax (206) 938-0580

Rock Bottom Restaurant & Brewery — 1333-5th Ave. , Seattle WA 98101
B/X/M/S/ — Capacity: Receptions: up to 475
Contact: Lisa Creighton, Banquet Mngr. (206) 623-3070

Rock Salt Steakhouse on Latitude 47° — 1232 Westlake Ave. N., Seattle WA 98109
B/X/M/ — Capacity: 25–400
Contact: Donna Tarrant, Mngr. (206) 284-1047, Fax (206) 784-7856

The Roosevelt—A WestCoast Hotel — 1531-7th Ave., Seattle WA 98101
B/X/M/S/R/ — Guest Rooms: 151 — Capacity: Up to 64
Sales Dept. (206) 621-1200 or (800) 325-4000 room reservations only, Fax (206) 233-0335

Russian Community Hall — 704-19th E., Seattle WA 98112
B/X/M/S/R/ — Capacity: Up to 200
(206) 323-3877

Ruth's Chris Steakhouse — 800-5th Ave., Seattle WA 98104
B/X/M/ — Capacity: Up to 80
Contact: Manager (206) 624-8524

SAFECO Field - Home of Winning Events — 1250-1st Ave. S., Seattle WA 98134 *See page 265*
B/X/M/S/R/T/ — Capacity: 10 to 47,000
Contact: Jennifer Mojo (206) 346-4228, Fax (206) 346-4250

Salty's on Alki — 1936 Harbor Ave. SW., Seattle WA 98126 *See pages 268, 366 & 574*
B/X/M/S/R/ — Capacity: Banquet: Up to 225, Reception: Up to 300
Contact: Catering Sales Manager (206) 937-1085, Fax (206) 937-1430

Sand Point Magnuson Park — 7400 Sand Point Wy. N.E., Seattle WA 98115
B/X/M/S/R/P/ — Capacity: Picnic Shelters: Up to 75; Bldg. 30: 20,000sq. ft.; Bldg. 27: 85,000sq. ft.; Conf. Rms. 30 to 125
Contact: Terri Arnold (206) 386-9873 or , (206) 386-4523

Scottish Rite Masonic Center — 1155 Broadway E., Seattle WA 98102 *See page 269*
B/X/M/S/R/ — Capacity: Up to 500
Contact: Chris Williams or Brian Lorton (206) 324-3330, Fax (206) 324-3332

Seattle Aquarium — 1483 Alaskan Wy., Pier 59, Seattle WA 98101 *See page 270*
B/X/M/S/R/ — Capacity: Up to 600+
Contact: Aquarium Scheduler Events (206) 386-4314 or General (206) 386-4320

Seattle Art Museum — 100 University St., Seattle WA 98101 *See page 271*
B/X/M/S/R/ — Capacity: Reception: Up to 500
Contact: John Ferguson Events (206) 654-3140 or General (206) 625-8900

Seattle Asian Art Museum — 1400 E. Prospect, Seattle WA 98112 *See page 272*
B/X/M/S/R/ — Capacity: Reception: Up to 200
Contact: John Ferguson Events (206) 654-3140 or General (206) 654-3206

B=Banquets X=Parties M=Meetings S=Seminars R=Retreats P=Picnics C=Conventions T=Tradeshows

Seattle Center — 305 Harrison St., Seattle WA 98109
B/X/M/S/R/C/T/ — Capacity: Reception: Up to 800
Contact: Judy Camou Events (206) 684-7202 or General (206) 684-7200

Seattle Design Center — 5701-6th Ave. S., Seattle WA 98108 *See page 273*
B/X/M/S/ — Capacity: 50 to 700
Contact: Schwarz Brothers Catering (206) 689-7300

Seattle Repertory Theatre — 155 Mercer St., Seattle WA 98109 *See page 274*
B/X/M/S/ — Capacity: Banquet: Up to 350, Reception: Up to 1,100
Contact: Michael Betts (206) 443-2210, Fax (206) 443-2379

Seattle University — 900 Broadway At Broadway & Madison, Seattle WA 98122
B/X/M/S/R/ — Capacity: Banquet: Up to 500, Theatre: Up to 470
(206) 296-5620

Sheraton Seattle Hotel & Towers — 1400-6th Ave., Seattle WA 98101 *See page 275*
B/X/M/S/R/C/T/ — Guest Rooms: 840
Capacity: Banquet: Up to 1,400, Reception: Up to 2,400
Catering Dept. (206) 389-5735

Shilshole Bay Beach Club — 6413 Seaview Ave. N.W., Seattle WA 98107 *See page 276*
B/X/M/S/R/C/ — Capacity: South Room: Up to 200,
North Room: Up to 300, Combined: Up to 500
Contact: Special Events Co. (206) 706-0257

Skansonia Ferryboat — 2505 N. Northlake Wy., Seattle WA 98103 *See page 278*
B/X/M/S/R/ — Capacity: Seated: Up to 300; Standing: Up to 400
Contact: Tamara (206) 545-9109

Skyway Park & Bowl — 11819 Renton Ave. S., Seattle WA 98178 *See page 62*
X/
(206) 772-1220, Fax (206) 772-9860

The Smith Tower, Chinese Room at — 506-2nd Ave, 35th Fl., Seattle WA 98104 *See page 280*
B/X/M/S/R/ — Capacity: Banquet: Up to 70, Reception: Up to 99
Contact: Hospitality Director (206) 622-313, Fax (206) 622-9357

Sorrento Hotel — 900 Madison St., Seattle WA 98104 *See page 282*
B/X/M/S/R/C/ — Guest Rooms: 76 — Capacity: Three rooms combined: Up to 200
Contact: Director Of Catering (206) 622-6400 or (800) 426-1265, Fax (206) 343-6159

Southwest Community Center — 2801 S.W. Thistle, Seattle WA 98126
B/X/M/S/R/ — Capacity: Inside: Up to 175
Contact: Seattle Parks (206) 684-7438

Space Needle – Skyline Level — Broad & John St., Seattle WA *See pages 63 & 284*
B/X/M/S/R/ — Capacity: Up to 350
Catering (206) 905-2180 or (800) 964-7695, Fax (206) 905-2107

St. D's Conference & Banquet Center — 2100 Boyer Ave. E, Seattle WA 98112
B/X/M/S/ — Capacity: Banquet: Up to 540
Office (206) 528-8361, Appt. required for viewing

The Stimson-Green Mansion — 1204 Minor Ave., Seattle WA 98101 *See page 286*
B/X/M/S/R/ — Capacity: Reception: Up to 200; Sit-down Dinners: Up to 48
(206) 624-0474, Fax (206) 624-9596

Stone Gardens, Inc. — 2839 N.W. Market St., Seattle WA 98107
B/X/M/S/ — Capacity: Up to 200
Contact: Bruce Andersen (206) 781-9828, Fax (206) 781-9837

Studio 7000 — 1406-10th Ave. Suite 200, Seattle WA 98122 *See page 287*
B/X/M/S/R/ — Capacity: Up to 375
Contact: Kit Vannocker (206) 325-3926, Fax (206) 325-3707

***B**=Banquets **X**=Parties **M**=Meetings **S**=Seminars **R**=Retreats **P**=Picnics **C**=Conventions **T**=Tradeshows*

Studio One Sixteen — 116 Elliott Ave. W., Seattle WA 98109 *See page 288*
B/X/M/S/R/ — Capacity: Seated: Up to 100; Receptions: Up to 203
Contact: Rocky Salskov or Mike Seidl (206) 860-7449, Fax (206) 860-7488

Sunset Hill Community Association — 3003 N.W. 66th St., Seattle WA 98117
B/X/M/S/R/ — Capacity: Rooms for up to 100 or 150 each
Contact: Kathy, Event Coord. (206) 784-2927

The Swedish Cultural Center — 1920 Dexter Ave. N., Seattle WA 98109
B/X/M/ — Capacity: Banquet: Up to 200, Reception: Up to 250
(206) 283-1078, Fax (206) 283-2970

T.S. McHugh's — 21 Mercer St., Seattle WA 98109
B/X/M/ — Capacity: Three banquet areas seating 30, 40, and 45
(206) 282-1910

Tillicum Village — 2200-6th Ave., #804, Seattle WA 98121 *See pages 65 & 295*
B/X/M/S/R/P/C/ — Capacity: Up to 850
(206) 933-8600 or (800) 426-1205

Top of the Market — 93 Pike St., #307, Seattle WA 98101 *See page 297*
B/X/M/S/R/ — Capacity: Up to 150
Contact: NW Events & Parties (206) 447-9994

Town Hall Seattle — 1119-8th Ave., Seattle WA 98101 *See page 298*
B/X/M/S/R/ — Capacity: Banquet: Up to 375,
Reception: Up to 800; Great Hall: Up to 900 seated
(206) 652-4255, Fax (206) 652-5858

Tulio Ristorante — 1100-5th Ave., Seattle WA 98101 *See page 301*
B/X/M/S/ — Capacity: Banquet: Up to 60, Reception: Up to 100
Contact: Gillian Baumann (206) 623-1066

Tyee Yacht Club — 3229 Fairview Ave. E., Seattle WA 98102 *See pages 302 & 369*
B/X/M/S/R/ — Capacity: Banquet: Up to 160, Reception: Up to 200
Contact: Tony's Events & Catering (206) 328-2195, Fax (206) 328-2754

Union Square Grill — 621 Union St., Seattle WA 98101
B/X/M/ — Capacity: Up to 48
Contact: Rae Pearson (206) 224-4321

Union Station – Seattle — 4th Ave. S. & S. Jackson, Seattle WA 98104 *See page 303*
B/X/M/S/C/T/ — Capacity: Banquets: Up to 550, Receptions: Up to 700
(206) 706-0257

University Heights Center — 5031 University Wy. N.E., Seattle WA 98105
M/S/R/ — Capacity: Up to 150
(206) 527-4278

University Inn — 4140 Roosevelt Wy. N.E., Seattle WA 98105
B/X/M/S/R/ — Guest Rooms: 102 — Capacity: Up to 100
Sales Office (206) 545-1504, Fax (206) 547-4937

University Meeting & Friends Center — 4001-9th Ave. N.E., Seattle WA 98105
B/X/M/S/R/ — Capacity: 150 to 200
Office (206) 547-6449

University Plaza Hotel — 400 N.E. 45th St., Seattle WA 98105
B/X/M/S/R/C/ — Guest Rooms: 135 — Capacity: Up to 225
Catering Office (206) 634-0100, Fax (206) 633-2743

Von's Grand City Cafe & Martini Manhattan Memorial — 619 Pine St., Seattle WA 98101
B/X/M/ — Capacity: Up to 50
Contact: Manager (206) 621-8667

B=Banquets X=Parties M=Meetings S=Seminars R=Retreats P=Picnics C=Conventions T=Tradeshows

W Seattle Hotel — 1112-4th Ave., Seattle WA 98101 *See page 307*
B/X/M/S/R/C/ — Guest Rooms: 419
Capacity: Banquets: Up to 350, Receptions: up to 500
Catering Dept. (206) 264-6150, Fax (206) 264-6001

Warwick Hotel — 4th & Lenora Ave., Seattle WA 98121
B/X/M/S/R/C/ — Guest Rooms: 229 — Capacity: Up to 80
Catering Dept. (206) 443-4300, Fax (206) 777-1989

Washington Athletic Club — 1325 - 6th Ave., Seattle WA 98101 *See page 308*
B/X/M/S/R/ — Guest Rooms: 113 — Capacity: 16 Banquet Rooms for 6 to 350
Catering Dept. (206) 464-3050, Fax (206) 464-3052

Washington State Convention
& Trade Center — 800 Convention Pl., Seattle WA 98101 *See pages 384 & 385*
B/X/M/S/R/C/T/ — Capacity: Up to 4,000; 546function rooms,
2 ballrooms: 2,200 banquet, 900 banquet; Six Exhibit Halls totaling 205,700 sq. ft.
Sales & Marketing (206) 694-5111, Fax (206) 694-5398

Washington State Stadium
Exhibition Center — 1000 Occidental Ave. S., Seattle WA 98104 *See pages 386 & 387*
C/T/ — Capacity: Up to 6,000; Main Hall: 165,370 sq. ft.; East Hall: 90,185 sq. ft.;
Stadium North Hall: 60,730 sq. ft.; Stadium Club Level: 62,605 sq. ft.
Contact: Steve Eckerson (206) 381-7575, Fax (206) 381-7557

Waterfront Seafood Grill - Pier 70 — 2801 Alaskan Way, Pier 70, Seattle WA 98121
B/X/M/ — Capacity: Up to 400
(206) 956-9171, Fax (206) 956-8090

WestCoast Camlin Hotel — 1619-9th Ave., Seattle WA 98101
B/X/M/S/R/ — Guest Rooms: 132 — Capacity: Banquet: Up to 75
Sales & Catering (206) 682-0100, Fax (206) 682-7415

WestCoast Grand Hotel On Fifth Avenue — 1415 Fifth Ave., Seattle WA 98101 *See page 311*
B/X/M/S/R/C/ — Guest Rooms: 297 — Capacity: Ballroom: 120 to 630;
Five Meeting Rms.: 15 to 120; Terrace Garden: Up to 190
Contact: Tamara Hall (206) 971-8030 or (206) 971-8030, Fax (206) 971-8101

The Westin Hotel — 1900-5th Ave., Seattle WA 98101 *See page 312*
B/X/M/S/R/C/T/ — Guest Rooms: 891
Capacity: Banquet: Up to 1,600, Reception: Up to 2,000; Theatre Style: Up to 2,120
Contact: Jason Tyler (206) 727-5833

The Wilsonian Ballroom — 4710 University Wy. N.E., Seattle WA 98105 *See page 315*
B/X/M/S/R/ — Capacity: Banquet: Up to 150, Reception: Up to 247
Contact: Lora Kingsley (206) 524-0450, Fax (206) 324-0040

Wolfgang Puck — 1225-1st. Ave., Seattle WA 98101
B/X/M/ — Capacity: Banquet: Up to 190, Reception: Up to 300
Contact: Manager (206) 621-9653

Woodland Park Zoo — 5500 Phinney Ave. N., Seattle WA 98103 *See page 66*
B/X/M/S/R/P/ — Capacity: Rain Forest Pavillion: Up to 300 seated,
Up to 450 receptions; Other settings: 50-5,000
Events (206) 233-7272 or General (206) 684-4800

World Trade Center — 2200 Alaskan Wy., Suite 410, Seattle WA 98121 *See page 317*
B/X/M/S/R/ — Capacity: Banquet: Up to 80, Reception: Up to 120
(206) 956-4590, Fax (206) 374-0410

Yale Street Landing — 1001 Fairview Ave. N., Seattle WA 98109 *See page 318*
B/X/M/S/R/ — Capacity: Up to 300
(206) 344-4757, Fax (206) 447-6977

***B**=Banquets **X**=Parties **M**=Meetings **S**=Seminars **R**=Retreats **P**=Picnics **C**=Conventions **T**=Tradeshows*

Yankee Grill & Roaster — 5300 - 24th Ave. N.W., Seattle WA 98107
B/X/M/S/R/ — Capacity: 30 to 300
Contact: Catering Sales Mngr. (206) 783-1999, Fax (206) 784-0580

SEQUIM

Dungeness Golf & Country Club — 1965 Woodcock Road, Sequim WA 98382
B/M/S/R/ — Capacity: Up to 175
Contact: Julie (800) 447-6826, ext. 4 or (360) 683-6344, Fax (360) 683-1709

SHELTON

Little Creek Casino — West 91 Hwy. 108, Shelton WA 98584
B/X/M/S/C/T/ — Capacity: Up to 400
Marketing Dept. (360) 427-7711

SHORELINE

Richmond Masonic Temple — 753 N. 185th St., Shoreline WA 98133
B/X/M/S/R/ — Capacity: Up to 255
Contact: Norman Miller (206) 784-7154
Shoreline Historical Museum — 749 N. 175th, Shoreline WA 98133
B/X/M/S/R/ — Capacity: Up to 80
Contact: Vicki Stiles (206) 542-7111
Shoreline Lake Forest Park Senior Center — 18560-1st Ave. N.E., #1, Shoreline WA 98155
B/X/M/S/R/ — Capacity: Up to 200
Contact: Marilyn Yeider (206) 365-1536, Fax (206) 364-8930

SMOKEY POINT

A Country Location — 333-156th St. N.E., Smokey Point WA 98223
B/X/M/S/R/P/ — Capacity: Indoors: Up to 100, Outdoors: Up to 200
Contact: Judy Milton (206) 949-0229, Fax (360) 652-4768

B=Banquets X=Parties M=Meetings S=Seminars R=Retreats P=Picnics C=Conventions T=Tradeshows

SNOHOMISH

Craven Farm — 13817 Short School Rd., Snohomish WA 98290 *See pages 466 & 541*
B/X/M/S/R/P/ — Capacity: Indoors: Up to 150, Outdoors: Up to 300
Contact: Judy Craven (360) 568-2601, Fax (360) 568-9001

Echo Falls Country Club — 20414-121st Ave. S.E., Snohomish WA 98296 *See page 176*
B/X/M/S/R/ — Capacity: Up to 200
Contact: Lisa Burke (206) 362-3000, ext. 238

The Farm — 4301 Rivershore Rd., Snohomish WA 98290 *See page 543*
X/M/R/P/ — Capacity: Up to 500 guests; 3,000sq. ft. covered picnic area
Contact: Bob & Carol Krause (425) 334-4124

Lord Hill Farms — 12525 Old Snohomish-Monroe Rd., Snohomish WA 98290 *See page 229*
B/X/M/S/R/P/ — Capacity: Outdoors: Up to 5,000,
Indoors: Up to 800 (Shown by appointment only)
(360) 568-1780

Swan's Trail Chapel — 5427-64th St. S.E., Snohomish WA 98290
B/X/M/S/R/P/ — Capacity: Indoors: Up to 200, Outdoors: Up to 300
Contact: Terry McCullough (425) 334-9989

Victorian Manor at Snohomish — 610-1st St., Snohomish WA 98290
B/X/M/S/R/ — Capacity: Indoors: Up to 90, With Gardens: Up to 150
(360) 568-8597

SNOQUALMIE

Salish Lodge & Spa — 6501 Railroad Ave. S.E., Snoqualmie WA 98065 *See page 267*
B/X/M/S/R/C/ — Guest Rooms: 91
Capacity: Banquet: Up to 150, Outdoors: Up to 200
Contact: Bonny Hawley (425) 831-6598, Fax (425) 888-9634

Snoqualmie Ridge Golf Club — 36005 S.E. Ridge St., Snoqualmie WA 98065 *See page 281*
B/X/M/S/R/ — Capacity: Banquet: Up to 300, Reception: Up to 450
Catering Dept. (425) 396-6000

SNOQUALMIE PASS

Hyak Lodge — 370 Keechelus Boat Launch Road, Snoqualmie Pass WA 98068 *See page 208*
B/X/M/S/R/ — Guest Rooms: 34
Capacity: Banquet: Up to 60, Reception: Up to 100
(360) 902-8600 or Tours: (425) 434-5955

B=Banquets X=Parties M=Meetings S=Seminars R=Retreats P=Picnics C=Conventions T=Tradeshows

STANWOOD

Kayak Point Golf Course — 15711 Marine Dr., Stanwood WA 98292
B/X/M/S/R/ — Capacity: Up to 200
(360) 652-9676, Fax (360) 652-3812

Lake Goodwin Community Club — 17323-42nd Ave. N.W., Stanwood WA 98292
B/X/M/S/R/ — Capacity: Up to 225
Contact: Lorraine (360) 652-9786 or (360) 652-7925

Warm Beach Camp & Conference Center — 20800 Marine Dr., Stanwood WA 98292
B/X/M/S/R/ — Capacity: 18 meeting areas, Auditorium: Up to 1,000, Banquet: Up to 350
Contact: Events Coord. (360) 652-7575

STEILACOOM

E.R. Rogers — 1702 Commercial St., Steilacoom WA 98388
B/X/M/ — Capacity: Sit-down: Up to 40, Buffet: Up to 250
Contact: Gordon or Kristi (253) 582-0280

Steilacoom Community Center — 2301 Worthington, Steilacoom WA 98388
B/X/M/S/R/ — Capacity: Up to 300
Office (253) 581-1076

Steilacoom Town Hall — 1715 Lafayette St., Steilacoom WA 98388
B/X/M/S/ — Capacity: Up to 150
Office (253) 581-1076

SUMNER

Tapp Island Golf Course — 20818 Island Park Wy. E., Sumner WA 98390
B/X/M/ — Capacity: Up to 65
Contact: Eileen Events (253) 862-6616 or Golf (253) 862-7011, Fax (253) 862-3310

TACOMA

Allenmore Restaurant & Lounge — 2125 S. Cedar, Tacoma WA 98405
B/X/M/ — Capacity: Up to 144
Contact: Jackie (253) 627-1161

The Annie Wright School — 827 Tacoma Ave. N., Tacoma WA 98403
B/X/M/S/R/ — Capacity: Reception: Up to 200
Contact: Karen Credgington (253) 272-2216, Fax (253) 572-3616

BBQ Pete's—at 72nd & Portland Ave. — 1314 E. 72nd, Tacoma WA 98404
B/X/M/ — Capacity: Banquet: Up to 70
Contact: Vanessa or Wendy (253) 535-1000, Fax (253) 531-6121

Broadway Center for the Performing Arts –
Rialto, Pantages, Theatre in the Square — 901 Broadway, Tacoma WA 98402
B/X/M/S/R/C/ — Capacity: 3 Theaters, Up to 1,186 Theater style
Contact: Events & Program Assistant (253) 591-5890

B=Banquets X=Parties M=Meetings S=Seminars R=Retreats P=Picnics C=Conventions T=Tradeshows

 Please let these businesses know that you heard about them from the Bravo! Event Resource Guide.

Brown's Point Improvement Club — 5125 Tok-A-Lou N.E., Tacoma WA 98422
B/X/M/S/ — Capacity: Up to 170
Contact: Alice Owen (253) 927-1042

C.I. Shenanigans — 3017 Ruston Wy., Tacoma WA 98402
B/X/M/S/R/ — Capacity: Up to 200
Contact: Banquet Manager (253) 752-8899, Fax (253) 752-8623

Captain Nemo's — 4020 Bridgeport Wy. W., Tacoma WA 98466
B/X/M/ — Capacity: Up to 60
Contact: Kathy (253) 564-6460

The Centre at Norpoint — 4818 Nassau Ave. N.E. , Tacoma WA 98422 *See page 158*
B/X/M/S/R/ — Capacity: Banquet: Up to 250, Reception: Up to 300
Contact: Rental Coordinator (253) 591-5504 or (253) 661-3289

The Cliff House — 6300 Marine View Dr. N.E., Tacoma WA 98422
B/X/M/ — Capacity: 20 to 100
Contact: Guido or Tammy (253) 927-0400

Copperfield's Restaurant & Lounge at the Best Western — 8726 S. Hosmer, Tacoma WA 98444
B/X/M/ — Guest Rooms: 150 — Capacity: Up to 250
Contact: Alice Shifflett (253) 535-2880, Fax (253) 537-8379

Crystal Ballroom — 776 Commerce, Tacoma WA 98402
B/X/M/ — Capacity: Up to 300
(253) 272-9329, Fax (253) 272-1677

David's on Broadway – University Union Club Mansion — 539 Broadway, Tacoma WA 98402
B/X/M/S/R/ — Capacity: Up to 300
Contact: David (253) 572-0099 or (253) 732-9854, Fax (253) 627-5001

Days Inn – Tacoma — 6802 Tacoma Mall Blvd., Tacoma WA 98409
B/X/M/S/R/C/ — Guest Rooms: 123 — Capacity: Reception: Up to 250
Contact: Great American Catering (253) 475-0757, Fax (253) 475-3540

Devoe Mansion — 208 E. 133rd St., Tacoma WA 98445
B/X/M/R/ — Guest Rooms: 4 — Capacity: Outdoors: Up to 100
(253) 539-3991 or (888) 539-3991

Emerald Queen Casino & Night Club — 2102 Alexander Ave., Tacoma WA 98421 *See pages 53 & 185*
B/X/M/C/T/ — Capacity: Bridge: Up to 300;
3rd Deck: Up to 500; Showroom: Up to 1,800
(888) 831-7655, Fax (253 272-6725)

Harmon Pub & Brewing — 1938 Pacific Ave., Tacoma WA 98402
B/X/M/ — Capacity: Up to 70
Catering (253) 383-2739

The Homestead — 7837 S. Tacoma Wy., Tacoma WA 98409
B/X/M/ — Capacity: Up to 63
Contact: Manager (253) 475-3252

Jillian's – Tacoma — 1114 Broadway Plaza, Tacoma WA 98402 *See pages 56 & 217*
B/X/M/S/ — Capacity: Up to 1,000
Contact: Jeff Weinkauf (253) 572-0300, Fax (253) 572-2103

King Oscar Motel & Convention Center — 8820 South Hosmer, Tacoma WA 98444 *See page 220*
B/X/M/S/R/C/T/ — Guest Rooms: 221rms., 12suites — Capacity: 10 to 700
(253) 539-1153, Fax (253)536-3116

The Lobster Shop at Dash Point — 6912 Soundview Dr. N.E., Tacoma WA 98422
B/X/M/ — Capacity: Private Room: Up to 35
Contact: Manager (253) 927-1513

B*=Banquets* ***X****=Parties* ***M****=Meetings* ***S****=Seminars* ***R****=Retreats* ***P****=Picnics* ***C****=Conventions* ***T****=Tradeshows*

The Lobster Lobster Shop South on Ruston Way — 4015 Ruston Wy., Tacoma WA 98402
B/X/M/ — Capacity: Private Room: Up to 40
Contact: Manager (253) 759-2165, Fax (253) 752-9640

Manitou Community Center — 4806 S. 66th, Tacoma WA 98409
B/X/M/S/R/ — Capacity: 30–300
Contact: Center Assistant (253) 591-5484

Mulligans At Meadow Park
Golf Course — 7108 Lakewood Dr. S.W., Tacoma WA 98467 *See page 237*
B/X/M/S/R/ — Capacity: April - Sept.: Up to 100, Oct. - Mar.: Up to 200
(253) 473-7516

Museum of Glass — 934 Broadway, Tacoma WA 98402 *See page 239*
B/X/M/S/R/ — Capacity: Banquet: Up to 340,
Reception: Up to 1,000; Theatre: Up to 180
(253) 396-1768, ext. 2148, Fax (253) 396-1769

North Shore Golf Course — 4101 North Shore Blvd. N.E., Tacoma WA 98422
B/X/M/ — Capacity: Up to 150
Contact: Link Elliott (253) 927-1375 or (800) 447-1375, Fax (253) 838-5898

The Old Spaghetti Factory – Tacoma — 1735 Jefferson St., Tacoma WA 98402
B/X/M/ — Capacity: Up to 150
Contact: Manager (253) 383-2214

On the Greens Restaurant
at North Shore Golf Course — 4101 North Shore Blvd. N.E., Tacoma WA 98422
B/X/M/ — Capacity: Up to 150
Contact: Link Elliott (253) 927-1375, Fax (253) 838-5898

Pacific Lutheran University — Garfield & Park St., Tacoma WA 98447-0003
B/X/M/S/R/C/ — Capacity: Banquet: Up to 700, Reception: Up to 3,000
Contact: Mark Mulder (253) 535-7450, Fax (253) 536-5076

Point Defiance Lodge — 5400 N. Pearl St., Tacoma WA 98407 *See page 253*
B/X/M/S/R/ — Capacity: Banquet: Up to 55, Reception: Up to 75
Contact: Facility Coordinator (253) 305-1010

Point Defiance Park Pagoda — 5400 N. Pearl St., Tacoma WA 98407 *See page 254*
B/X/M/S/R/ — Capacity: Banquet: Up to 100, Reception: Up to 200
Contact: Facility Coordinator (253) 305-1010

Point Defiance Zoo & Aquarium — 5400 N. Pearl St., Tacoma WA 98407 *See pages 61, 255 & 547*
B/X/M/S/R/P/ — Capacity: Banquets: Up to 250, Picnics: Up to 1,000
(253) 404-3643 or Gen. Info.: (253) 591-5337, Fax (253) 591-5448

Portland Avenue Community Center — 3513 Portland Ave., Tacoma WA 98404
B/X/M/S/R/ — Capacity: Up to 250
Contact: Center Supervisor (253) 591-5391

Ramada Hotel – Tacoma Dome — 2611 E. 'E' St., Tacoma WA 98421
B/X/M/S/R/C/ — Guest Rooms: 160 — Capacity: Reception: Up to 130
Sales & Catering (253) 572-7272, Fax (253) 572-9664

Sheraton Tacoma Hotel — 1320 Broadway Plaza, Tacoma WA 98402
B/X/M/S/R/C/T/ — Guest Rooms: 319
Capacity: Ballroom: Up to 400, Convention Center: Up to 1,000
Sales & Catering (253) 572-3200, Fax (253) 591-4105

Slavonian Hall — 2306 N. 30th St., Tacoma WA 98403
B/X/M/S/R/ — Capacity: Reception: up to 300
Office (253) 627-6878 or (253) 752-1741

***B**=Banquets **X**=Parties **M**=Meetings **S**=Seminars **R**=Retreats **P**=Picnics **C**=Conventions **T**=Tradeshows*

South End Neighborhood Center — 7802 S. L St., Tacoma WA 98408
B/X/M/S/R/ — Capacity: Up to 300
Contact: Tom Weathers / Metro Parks Tacoma (253) 591-5098, Fax (253) 591-5216

South Park Community Center — 4851 S. Tacoma Wy., Tacoma WA 98409 *See page 283*
B/X/M/S/R/ — Capacity: Two rooms: 325 and 225 guests
Contact: Centre Supervisor / Metro Parks Tacoma (253) 591-5299

The Tacoma Dome — 2727 E. D St., Tacoma WA 98421
B/X/M/S/C/T/ — Capacity: Banquet: Up to 1,700
(253) 272-3663, Fax (253) 593-7620

Tacoma Executive Inn — 5700 Pacific Hwy. E., Tacoma WA 98424
B/X/M/S/R/ — Guest Rooms: 139 — Capacity: Banquet: Up to 650, Reception: Up to 1,000
Sales & Catering (253) 922-0080 or (800) 938-8500, Fax (253) 922-6439

Tacoma Inns.com — PO Box 7957, Tacoma WA 98407
B/X/M/S/R/P/ — Capacity: 8 member B&B's; Call for event capabilities
(253) 593-6098

Tacoma Lawn & Tennis Club — 502 Borough Rd., Tacoma WA 98403
B/X/M/S/R/ — Capacity: Up to 250
(253) 383-5935, Fax (253) 383-5934

The Tacoma Nature Center — 1919 S. Tyler St., Tacoma WA 98405 *See page 290*
B/X/M/S/R/ — Capacity: Banquet: Up to 65, Reception: Up to 80
Contact: Center Staff (253) 591-6439, Fax (253) 593-4152

The Tacoma Rhodes Center — 949 Market St., Suite #542, Tacoma WA 98402 *See page 291*
B/X/M/S/R/ — Capacity: Up to 700
(253) 597-4141, Fax (253) 597-3606

Tacoma Sheraton — 1320 Broadway Plaza, Tacoma WA 98402
B/X/M/S/R/C/T/ — Guest Rooms: 319
Capacity: Ballroom: Up to 400, Reception: up to 1,000
Sales & Catering (253) 572-3200 , Fax (253) 627-3167

Tacoma Union Station — 1717 Pacific Ave., Tacoma WA 98402 *See page 292*
B/X/M/S/R/C/T/ — Capacity: Banquet: Up to 800, Reception: Up to 1,200
Contact: Rotunda Coordinator (253) 863-5173 x223, Fax (253) 863-2040

Tacoma's Landmark Convention Center — 47 St. Helens Ave., Tacoma WA 98402 *See page 293*
B/X/M/S/R/C/T/ — Capacity: Up to 1,000
(253) 272-2042, Fax (253) 272-3793

Titlow Lodge Community Center — 8425-6th Ave. E., Tacoma WA 98465 *See page 296*
B/X/M/S/R/ — Capacity: Banquet: Up to 140, Reception: Up to 200
Contact: Center Supervisor (253) 591-5297

Trattoria Grazie — 2301 N. 30th , Tacoma WA 98403 *See page 299*
B/X/M/ — Capacity: Up to 250
Contact: Thomas Day (253) 627-0231, Fax (253) 627-4729

University Union Club Mansion — 539 Broadway, Tacoma WA 98402
B/X/M/S/R/ — Capacity: Up to 800
Office (253) 572-0099, Fax (253) 627-5001

The Vaeth Mansion — 422 N. E St., Tacoma WA 98403
B/X/M/S/R/ — Capacity: Up to 150
(253) 272-0150

The Vault — 1025 Pacific Ave., Tacoma WA 98402 *See page 304*
B/X/M/S/R/ — Capacity: Up to 300
Contact: Marnie Jackson (253) 572-2933, Fax (253) 572-0515

The Top Floor at The Vault — 1025 Pacific Ave., Tacoma WA 98402 *See page 305*
B/X/M/S/R/ — Capacity: Up to 200
Contact: Marnie Jackson (253) 572-2933, Fax (253) 572-0515

B*=Banquets* ***X****=Parties* ***M****=Meetings* ***S****=Seminars* ***R****=Retreats* ***P****=Picnics* ***C****=Conventions* ***T****=Tradeshows*

The Villa B&B (A 1925 Historic Mansion) — 705 N. 5th St., Tacoma WA 98403
B/X/M/S/R/ — Guest Rooms: 6 — Capacity: Inside: Up to 75, Outside: Up to 100
Contact: Manager (253) 572-1157 or (888) 572-1157, Fax (253) 572-1805

Washington State History Museum — 1911 Pacific Ave., Tacoma WA 98402 *See pages 98 & 309*
B/X/M/S/R/C/ — Capacity: Indoors: Up to 350, Outdoors: Up to 350
Contact: Amice Barreras or JoAnn Puccia (253) 798-5895 or
(253) 798-5893 or Gen. Info. (888) 238-4373, Fax (253) 272-9518

Yankee Grill & Roaster – Tacoma — 6812 Tacoma Mall Blvd., Tacoma WA 98409
B/X/M/S/R/ — Capacity: Up to 400, Boardroom: Up to 70
Contact: Banquet Manager (253) 475-3006 or (253) 475-0757, Fax (253) 475-3540

THORP

Springwood Ranch Party Barn — PO Box 175, Thorp WA 98946
B/X/M/S/R/P/ — Capacity: 80–600
Office (509) 964-2156

TUKWILA

Best Western at Southcenter — 15901 W. Valley Rd., Tukwila WA 98188
B/X/M/S/R/C/ — Guest Rooms: 140
Capacity: Banquet: Up to 220, Reception: Up to 350
Contact: Michon Wheeler - Catering Mngr. (425) 226-1812 or
(800) 544-9863, Fax (425) 255-7856

Embassy Suites Hotel – Southcenter — 15920 W. Valley Hwy., Tukwila WA 98188
B/X/M/S/R/C/ — Guest Rooms: 238 — Capacity: Up to 220
Contact: Michelle Dress, Sales & Catering (425) 227-8844

Family Fun Center –
Bullwinkle's Restaurant — 7300 Fun Center Wy., Tukwila WA 98188 *See pages 54 & 190*
B/X/M/R/ — Capacity: Amusement Park: Up to 2,500, Dining Room: Up to 300
(425) 228-7300, Fax (425) 228-7400

Grand Central Casino — 14040 Interurban Ave. S., Tukwila WA 98168 *See page 195*
B/X/M/S/ — Capacity: Up to 225
Contact: Greg Bakamis (206) 244-5400, Fax (206) 244-4542

Grazie Ristorante – Tukwila — 16943 South Center Pkwy., Tukwila WA 98188
B/X/M/ — Capacity: Inside: Up to 85
Contact: Manager (206) 575-1606, Fax (206) 575-6773

The Riverside Inn Casino — 14060 Interurban S., Tukwila WA 98168
B/X/M/S/R/ — Capacity: Up to 70
Contact: Panda Moore, Events Dept. (206) 244-5400, Fax (206) 244-4542

Tukwila Community Center — 12424 42ns Ave. S., Tukwila WA 98168 *See page 300*
B/X/M/S/C/T/ — Capacity: Banquets: Up to 650; Exhibits: Up to 1,200
(206) 768-2822, Fax (206) 768-0524

B=Banquets X=Parties M=Meetings S=Seminars R=Retreats P=Picnics C=Conventions T=Tradeshows

TUMWATER

The Schmidt House — 330 Schmidt Place, Tumwater WA 98501
B/X/M/S/R/P/ — Capacity: Indoors: Up to 100, With Outdoors: Up to 350
Contact: Joe Reder (360) 943-2550

VASHON ISLAND

Back Bay Inn — 24007 Vashon Hwy. S.W., Vashon Island WA 98070
B/X/M/S/R/ — Guest Rooms: 4
Capacity: Banquet: Up to 40, Reception: Up to 65, Restaurant: 38–50
Contact: Robert Stowe (253) 759-8084 or (206) 463-5355, Fax (206) 463-6663

WOODINVILLE

Bear Creek Country Club — 13737-202nd Ave. N.E., Woodinville WA 98072 *See pages 145 & 483*
B/X/M/S/R/ — Capacity: Up to 400
Catering Dept. (425) 883-4770

Columbia Winery — 14030 - 145th Street, Woodinville WA 98072 *See page 163*
B/X/M/S/R/ — Capacity: Banquets: Up to 200
(425) 488-2776 or (800) 488-2347, Fax (425) 488-3460

Gold Creek Lodge — 16020-148th Ave. N.E., Woodinville WA 98072
B/X/M/S/R/P/ — Guest Rooms: Dorm Lodging for 40
Capacity: Up to 100 (N/A June-Aug)
Contact: King County Park System (800) 325-6165 x2966 or
(206) 296-2963, Fax (206) 296-1437

The Herbfarm — 14590 N.E. 145th St., Woodinville WA 98072
B/X/M/S/R/P/ — Capacity: Up to 65
Contact: Carrie Van Dyck (206) 789-2279

The Hollywood Schoolhouse — 14810 N.E. 145th, Woodinville WA 98072 *See page 206*
B/X/M/S/R/ — Capacity: Up to 300
Contact: Lori Reeder or Jennifer Diamond (425) 481-7925

Red Barn Country Inn — 16560-140th Pl N.E., Woodinville WA 98072
B/X/M/S/R/P/ — Capacity: Indoors: Up to 50, Outdoors: Up to 300
Contact: Lila & David Chapman (425) 806-4646, Fax (425) 488-7446

Redhook Ale Brewery – Woodinville — 14300 N.E. 145th, Woodinville WA 98072 *See page 260*
B/X/M/S/R/ — Capacity: Banquet: up to 200, Reception: Up to 250
Contact: Teresa Do (425) 483-3232, ext. 222, Fax (425) 481-4010

Willows Lodge — 14580 N.E. 145th Street, Woodinville WA 98072 *See page 314*
B/X/M/ — Guest Rooms: 88 — Capacity: Up to 150
Catering Department (425) 424-3900 or (877) 424-3930, Fax (425) 424-2585

YELM

Lake Lawrence Lodge — 15735 Topaz Dr. S.E., Yelm WA 98597
B/X/M/S/R/ — Capacity: Up to 600
Contact: Arlene (360) 894-3398

B=Banquets X=Parties M=Meetings S=Seminars R=Retreats P=Picnics C=Conventions T=Tradeshows

Notes

Listings: Boats & Trains Banquet Sites

BELLEVUE

Champagne Cruises -
Lake Union Charters — PO Box 3673, Bellevue WA 98009
B/X/M/S/R/ — Capacity: Up to 240
Office (425) 455-5769, Fax (425) 637-1029

Schooner Mallory Todd,
Office — 10042 N.E. 13th, Bellevue WA 98004
B/X/M/R/ — Capacity: Up to 38
Contact: Capt. George Todd, Office (425) 451-8160 or Schooner (206) 467-9940

KIRKLAND

Absolutely
Amazing Cruises — 218 Main Street #143, Kirkland WA 98033 *See page 129*
B/X/M/ — Capacity: 30 to 200 guests
(425) 481-1077, Fax (425) 481-0832

RENTON

Spirit of Washington
Dinner Train — 625 S. 4th St., Renton WA 98055 *See page 64*
B/X/M/S/R/ — Capacity: Up to 338
Contact: Marni Ness (425) 227-8408, Fax (425) 277-8839

SEATTLE

Anchor Bay — 7316-11th Ave. N.W., Seattle WA 98117
B/X/M/S/R/ — Capacity: Up to 33
Contact: Kevin Dahlgren (206) 781-0709

Argosy Cruises —
1101 Alaskan Wy., Pier 55, #201, Seattle WA 98101 *See pages 51, 130 & 131*
B/X/M/S/R/ — Capacities:
Goodtime I & II: Up to 350
Goodtime III:Up to 175
Sightseer: Up to 150
Spirit of Seattle: Up to 400
Queen's Launch: Up to 40
Celebrations: Up to 100
Champagne Lady: Up to 90
Lady Mary: Up to 200
M.V. Kirkland: Up to 150
Royal Argosy: Up to 800
Contact: Charter Representative (206) 623-1445, Fax (206) 623-5474

Catalyst Cruises — 1001 Fairview Ave. N., Seattle WA 98109
B/X/M/S/R/ — Capacity: M/V Sacajawea: Up to 30
Contact: J.E. Nesset (800) 670-7678 or (253) 537-7678

Cristal Charters — Office: 6037-35th Pl. N.W., Seattle WA 98107 *See page 132*
B/X/M/S/R/ — Capacity: M/V Matchmaker: Up to 49
Contact: Ralph (206) 286-9711, Fax (801) 881-8372

B=Banquets X=Parties M=Meetings S=Seminars R=Retreats P=Picnics C=Conventions T=Tradeshows

Ledger Marine Cruises — 1500 Westlake N., #110, Seattle WA 98109
B/X/M/S/R/ — Capacity: 50 Boats, Banquet: 10 to 500
Contact: Robey Banks (206) 283-6160, Fax (206) 283-3041

Royal Argosy
Fine Dining Cruises — 1101 Alaskan Wy., Pier 55, #201, Seattle WA 98101 *See pages 51 & 133*
B/X/M/S/R/ — Capacity: Seated: Up to 600; Reception: Up to 800
Contact: Charter Representative (206) 623-1445, Fax (206) 623-5474

Safari Rose — 1730 Lakeside Ave. S., Seattle WA 98144
B/X/M/R/ — Capacity: Up to 30
Contact: Mary Norris (206) 325-8390, Fax (206) 325-8381

Skansonia Ferryboat — 2505 N. Northlake Wy., Seattle WA 98103 *See page 278*
B/X/M/S/R/ — Capacity: Seated: Up to 300; Standing: Up to 400
Contact: Tamara (206) 545-9109

Victoria Clipper — 2701 Alaskan Wy., Pier 69, Seattle WA 98121
B/X/M/S/R/ — Capacity: Up to 330
Contact: Lian, Events Coord. Resv. (206) 448-5000 or
General (206) 443-2560, Fax (206) 443-2583

Waterways Cruises & Events — 809 Fairview Pl. N., #110, Seattle WA 98109 *See page 134*
B/X/M/S/R/C/T/ — Capacity: 4 Luxury Yachts; Up to 225
Sales Office (206) 223-2060, Fax (206) 223-2066

***B**=Banquets **X**=Parties **M**=Meetings **S**=Seminars **R**=Retreats **P**=Picnics **C**=Conventions **T**=Tradeshows*

Notes

Listings: Brewery & Winery Banquet Sites

❖❖❖

EVERETT

Scuttlebutt Brewing Company — 1524 W. Marine View Drive, Everett WA 98201
B/X/M/ — Capacity: Up to 35
(425) 257-9316

EVERSON

Mt. Baker Vineyards — 4298 Mt. Baker Hwy., Everson WA 98247
B/X/ — Capacity: Up to 100, ceremonies (outsideonly)
(360) 592-2300, Fax (360) 592-2526

ISSAQUAH

Hedges Cellars — 195 N.E. Gilman Blvd., Issaquah WA 98027 *See page 202*
B/X/M/ — Capacity: Up to 110
Contact: Anne-Marie Hedges (425) 391-6056, Fax (425) 391-3827

SEATTLE

Gordon Biersch
Brewing Company — Pacific Place, 600 Pine St., 4th Floor, Seattle WA 98101
B/X/M/ — Capacity: Pilsner Room: Up to 48 seated,
South Dining Room: Up to 60 seated, Entire Facility: Up to 500
Contact: Kaaren Kragerud (206) 405-4207, Fax (206) 405-4204

Hale's Brewery & Pub — 4301 Leary Way N.W, Seattle WA 98107
B/X/M/ — Capacity: Up to 90
Contact: Cathy Foote (206) 706-1544

The Pike Pub & Brewery — 1415-1st Ave., Seattle WA 98101
B/X/M/ — Capacity: Up to 100
Contact: Bruce Raymond (206) 622-6044, Fax (206) 622-8730

Pyramid Alehouse — 1201 First Ave. S., Seattle WA 98134 *See page 257*
B/X/M/ — Capacity: Mezzanine: Up to 70 seated,
VIP Room: Up to 40 seated, Executive Room: Up to 60 seated,
Combined: Up to 115; Alehouse: Up to 400 seated
(206) 682-8322, ext. 323, Fax (206) 682-8420

Rock Bottom Restaurant & Brewery — 1333-5th Ave. , Seattle WA 98101
B/X/M/S/ — Capacity: Receptions: up to 475
Contact: Lisa Creighton, Banquet Mngr. (206) 623-3070

SUMNER

Manfred Vierthaler
Winery & Restaurant — 17136 Hwy. 410 E., Sumner WA 98390
B/X/M/ — Capacity: Up to 45
Contact: Baron Manfred Von Vierthaler (253) 863-1633, Fax (253) 891-7249

B*=Banquets* ***X****=Parties* ***M****=Meetings* ***S****=Seminars* ***R****=Retreats* ***P****=Picnics* ***C****=Conventions* ***T****=Tradeshows*

TACOMA

Harmon Pub & Brewing — 1938 Pacific Ave., Tacoma WA 98402
B/X/M/ — Capacity: Up to 70
Catering (253) 383-2739

WOODINVILLE

Columbia Winery — 14030 - 145th Street, Woodinville WA 98072 *See page 163*
B/X/M/S/R/ — Capacity: Banquets: Up to 200
Contact: (425) 488-2776 or (800) 488-2347, Fax (425) 488-3460

Redhook Ale Brewery – Woodinville — 14300 N.E. 145th, Woodinville WA 98072 *See page 260*
B/X/M/S/R/ — Capacity: Banquet: up to 200, Reception: Up to 250
Contact: Teresa Do (425) 483-3232, ext. 222, Fax (425) 481-4010

***B**=Banquets **X**=Parties **M**=Meetings **S**=Seminars **R**=Retreats **P**=Picnics **C**=Conventions **T**=Tradeshows*

NOTES

Listings: Park Banquet Sites

❖❖❖

LISTINGS: PARK BANQUET SITES

BELLEVUE

Chism Beach Park — 1175 - 96th Ave. S.E., Bellevue WA 98004
B/X/P/ — Capacity: Indoors: Up to 250
Contact: Paula (425) 452-7158, Fax (425) 452-6841

Clyde Beach Park — 2-92nd Avenue S.E., Bellevue WA
P/ — Capacity: Up to 50
(425) 452-6881, Fax (425) 452-6841

Crossroads Park — 16000 N.E. 10th Street, Bellevue WA
P/ — Capacity: Up to 300
(425) 452-6914, Fax (425) 452-6841

Downtown Park Formal Garden — 10201 N.E. 4th Street, Bellevue WA
P/ — Capacity: Up to 2,000 (w/approval)
(425) 452-6914, Fax (425) 452-6841

Enatai Beach Park — 3519-108th Avenue S.E., Bellevue WA 98004
P/ — Capacity: Up to 75
(425) 452-6914, Fax (425) 452-6841

Hidden Valley Sports Park — 1905-112th Avenue N.E., Bellevue WA
P/ — Capacity: Up to 100
Contact: Bellevue Parks (425) 452-6914 or (425) 452-6881, Fax (425) 452-6841

Kelsey Creek Park — 13204 S.E. 8th Place, Bellevue WA 98005
P/ — Capacity: Up to 50
(425) 452-7688, Fax (425) 452-2804

Killarney Glen Park — 1933-104th Avenue S.E., Bellevue WA
P/ — Capacity: Up to 50
Contact: Brad B. (425) 452-6914, Fax (425) 452-6841

Lake Hills Park — 1200-164th Avenue S.E., Bellevue WA
P/ — Capacity: Up to 100
(425) 452-6914, Fax (425) 452-6841

Lakemont Park — 5170 Village Park Drive, Bellevue WA
P/ — Capacity: Up to 200
(425) 452-6914, Fax (425) 452-6841

Meydenbauer Beach Park — 419-98th Avenue N.E., Bellevue WA
P/ — Capacity: Up to 50
(425) 452-6881

Newcastle Beach Park — 4400 Lake Washington Blvd. S.E., Bellevue WA
P/ — Capacity: Up to 300
(425) 452-6914, Fax (425) 452-6841

Spiritridge Park — 16100 S.E. 33rd Place, Bellevue WA
P/ — Capacity: Up to 30
(425) 452-6914

Wilburton Hill Park — 12001 Main Street, Bellevue WA
P/ — Capacity: Up to 150
(425) 452-6914

BOTHELL

Blyth Park — 16950 W. Riverside Dr., Bothell WA 98011
B/X/P/ — Capacity: Up to 115, 2 shelters
Parks & Recreation Office (425) 486-7430, Fax (425) 486-1992

B*=Banquets* ***X****=Parties* ***M****=Meetings* ***S****=Seminars* ***R****=Retreats* ***P****=Picnics* ***C****=Conventions* ***T****=Tradeshows*

BURIEN

Moshier Park & Art Center — 430 S. 156th, Burien WA 98148
P/ — Capacity: Up to 100; Baseball Field
Contact: King County Parks (206) 296-4298, Fax (206) 296-0183
Seahurst Park — 140th Ave. SW & 16th Ave. SW, Burien WA 98166
B/P/ — Capacity: Up to 75 (No alcohol)
Contact: King County Parks (206) 244-5662, Fax (206) 296-0183

CARNATION

MacDonald Park — 31020 NE 40th Street, Carnation WA 98014
B/P/ — Capacity: Barn: Up to 100, 2 covered picnic shelters,
(No alcohol), Campsites available
Contact: King County Parks (206) 296-2966, Fax (206) 296-0183

EATONVILLE

Northwest Trek Wildlife Park — 11610 Trek Dr. E., Eatonville WA 98328 *See pages 58 & 244*
B/X/M/S/R/P/ — Capacity: Up to 1,000
Group Sales (360) 832-7181

ENUMCLAW

Enumclaw Park Community Center — 28511 Hwy. 410, Enumclaw WA 98022
B/X/M/S/R/P/ — Capacity: Log Cabin Style Facility,
Banquet: Up to 345, Assembly: 900+
Contact: King County Parks (206) 296-8892 or (360) 825-7777, Fax (206) 296-8891
King County Fairgrounds — 45224-284th Ave. S.E., Enumclaw WA 98022
B/X/M/S/R/P/C/T/ — Capacity: Up to 1,150, Fieldhouse: 345,
Exhibit Hall: 550, Activity Hall: 400
Contact: Joan Lewis (206) 296-8888 or (360) 825-7777, Fax (206) 296-8891

EVERETT

Floral Hall — 802 Mukilteo Blvd., Everett WA 98203
B/X/M/S/R/ — Capacity: Up to 200
Contact: Everett Parks & Rec. (425) 257-8300
Legion Park — 146 Alverson, Everett WA 98201
B/X/M/S/R/P/ — Capacity: Up to 100
Contact: Sheryl Kallock, Everett Parks & Rec. (425) 257-8300
Lions Hall — 802 Mukilteo Blvd., Everett WA 98203
B/X/M/S/R/ — Capacity: Up to 100
Contact: Everett Parks & Rec. (425) 257-8300
Walter E. Hall — 1226 West Casino, Everett WA 98204
B/X/M/S/R/ — Capacity: Up to 100
Contact: Sheryl Kallock, Everett Parks & Rec. (425) 257-8300

B=Banquets X=Parties M=Meetings S=Seminars R=Retreats P=Picnics C=Conventions T=Tradeshows

FEDERAL WAY

Dumas Bay Centre — 3200 S.W. Dash Point Rd., Federal Way WA 98023 *See pages 105 & 174*
B/X/M/S/R/ — Capacity: Banquet: Up to 98
(253) 835-2000, Fax (253) 835-2010

Five Mile Lake Park — 36429-44th Avenue S., Federal Way WA 98001
P/ — Capacity: Up to 150, 2 picnic sites
Contact: King County Park System
Scheduling Office (206) 296-4287, Fax (206) 296-0183

Lake Geneva Park — S. 344 Street & 46th Avenue S., Federal Way WA 98001
P/ — Capacity: Outside: Up to 20
Contact: King County Park System
Scheduling Office (206) 296-4287, Fax (206) 296-0183

ISSAQUAH

Cougar Mountain Park Regional Wildland — Cougar Mountain Road, Issaquah WA
P/ — Capacity: Up to 50 (no shelter)
Contact: King County Park System (206) 296-4287, Fax (206) 296-0183

Pine Lake Park — 228th Avenue S.E. & S.E. 24th, Issaquah WA 98027
P/ — Capacity: Outdoors: Up to 100 (No alcohol)
Contact: King County Park System (425) 836-7907

KENMORE

Kenmore Park — 6910 N.E. 170th, Kenmore WA 98011
P/ — Capacity: Up to 100 (No alcohol)
Contact: King County Parks (425) 398-8900

KENT

Kent Commons — 525-4th Ave. N., Kent WA 98032
B/X/M/S/R/C/T/ — Capacity: Up to 900, 2 gyms, 5 meeting rooms
Contact: Doug (253) 856-5000, Fax (253) 856-6000

Lake Meridian Park — 14800 S.E. 272nd, Kent WA 98042
B/P/ — Capacity: Shelter: Up to 120
Contact: King County Park System (206) 296-4287, Fax (206) 296-0183

KIRKLAND

Juanita Beach Park — 9703 Juanita Drive N.E., Kirkland WA 98034
B/P/ — Capacity: Two shelters: up to 75 in each, (No alcohol)
Contact: King County Park System (206) 296-2966

O.O. Denny Park — Holmes Point Drive At N.E. 124th St., Kirkland WA 98034
B/P/ — Capacity: Up to 80; sheltered area (no alcohol)
Contact: King County Park System (206) 296-2966, Fax (206) 296-0183

B=Banquets X=Parties M=Meetings S=Seminars R=Retreats P=Picnics C=Conventions T=Tradeshows

MAPLE VALLEY

Lake Wilderness Center –
King County Parks — 22500 S.E. 248th, Maple Valley WA 98038 *See page 226*
B/X/M/S/R/P/ — Capacity: Up to 250, 2 meeting rooms,
2 large reception rooms, Kitchen
Contact: King County Park System
South District (206) 296-4298 or (800) 325-6165, ext. 4298

Lake Wilderness Park — 23601 S.E. 248th, Maple Valley WA 98038
B/P/ — Capacity: Up to 150, Sheltered area outside
Contact: King County Park System South District (425) 836-7907, Fax (206) 296-0183

MERCER ISLAND

Luther Burbank Park — 2040-84th Avenue S.E., Mercer Island WA 98040
B/X/P/ — Capacity: Amphitheater: Up to 300, Picnic Areas
Contact: King County Park System (206) 296-2966, Fax (206) 296-0183

PRESTON

Preston Community Center — 8625-310th Ave. S.E., Preston WA 98050
B/X/M/S/R/ — Capacity: Up to 125, Hall & Stage, (no alcohol)
Contact: King County Park System (206) 296-2966

RAVENSDALE

Gracie Hansen Community Center — 27132 S.E. Ravensdale Wy., Ravensdale WA 98051
B/X/M/S/R/ — Capacity: Up to 500, Meeting room, kitchen, gymnasium
Contact: King County Park System (206) 296-4298

REDMOND

The Clise Mansion — 6046 W. Lake Sammamish Pkwy. N.E., Redmond WA 98052
B/X/M/S/R/P/ — Capacity: Indoors: Up to 170, Outside: Up to 325
Contact: Competitive Edge Catering (425) 865-0795, Fax (425) 452-7825

Marymoor Park — 6046 W. Lake Sammamish, Redmond WA 98052
B/P/ — Capacity: Outside: Up to 2,000, 2 shelters, (No alcohol)
Contact: King County Park System (206) 296-2966

SAMMAMISH

Issaquah Lodge – Beaver Lake — 25201 S.E. 24th, Sammamish WA 98027
B/X/R/P/ — Capacity: Indoors: Up to 125, Outdoors: Up to 250
Managed by: Competitive Edge (425) 865-0795

B=Banquets X=Parties M=Meetings S=Seminars R=Retreats P=Picnics C=Conventions T=Tradeshows

SEATTLE

Bhy Kracke Park — 1212-5th Avenue N., Seattle WA 98109
B/P/ — Capacity: Outside: Up to 150, (No alcohol)
Contact: Seattle Parks (206) 684-4081

Camp Long — 5200-35th Ave. S.W., Seattle WA 98126
B/M/X/R/ — Capacity: Indoor: Up to 72, Outdoors: Up to 100
Office (206) 684-7434, Fax (206) 684-7435

Coleman Viewpoint — 1800 - 19th & Lake Washington, Seattle WA
B/P/ — Capacity: Up to 200
Contact: Seattle Parks (206) 684-4081, Fax (206) 684-4853

Don Armeni — 1222 Harbor Avenue S.W. Off S.W. Maryland, Seattle WA 98136
B/P/ — Capacity: Outdoors: Up to 200
Contact: Seattle Parks (206) 684-4081, Fax (206) 684-4853

Dr. Jose Rizal — 1008 - 12th S. & S. Judkin, Seattle WA 98108
B/P/ — Capacity: Outdoors: Up to 200, Large shelter
Contact: Seattle Parks (206) 684-4081, Fax (206) 684-4853

Gas Works — N. Northlake Way & Meridian Avenue N., Seattle WA 98103
B/P/ — Capacity: Outdoors: Up to 400, Large shelter
Contact: Seattle Parks (206) 684-4081, Fax (206) 684-4853

Graham Visitor Center in
Washington Park Arboretum — 2300 Arboretum Dr. E., Seattle WA 98112
B/X/M/S/R/ — Capacity: Inside: Up to 100, Inside and Outside: Up to 130
Contact: Josey Fast (206) 543-8800

Hamilton Viewpoint — 1531 California Ave. S.W. & S.W. Donald, Seattle WA 98136
B/P/ — Capacity: Outdoors: Up to 200
Contact: Seattle Parks (206) 684-4081, Fax (206) 684-4853

Jefferson Community Center — 3801 Beacon Ave. S., Seattle WA 98108
B/X/M/S/R/ — Capacity: Up to 175
(206) 684-7481, Fax (206) 684-7483

Kubota Garden — 55th & Renton Avenue S., Seattle WA 98118
B/P/ — Capacity: Up to 200
Contact: Seattle Parks (206) 684-4081, Fax (206) 684-4853

Lakewood Park — 11050-10th S.W., Seattle WA 98146
B/P/ — Capacity: Up to 125
Scheduling Office (206) 722-9696

Laurelhurst Community Center — 4554 N.E. 41st St., Seattle WA 98105
B/X/P/ — Capacity: Inside: Up to 125
Office (206) 684-7529, Fax (206) 522-6029

Licton Springs — 9537 N. 97th & Ashworth N., Seattle WA 98103
B/P/ — Capacity: Outside: Up to 200
Contact: Seattle Parks (206) 684-4081, Fax (206) 684-4853

Louisa Boren Lookout — 15th E. & E. Olin, Seattle WA 98112
B/P/ — Capacity: Outside: Up to 100
Contact: Seattle Parks (206) 684-4081, Fax (206) 684-4853

Madrona Park — Lake Washington Blvd. E. & Madrona Drive, Seattle WA 98118
B/P/ — Capacity: Up to 100
Contact: Seattle Parks (206) 684-4081, Fax (206) 684-4853

Magnolia Park — 31st W. & W. Garfield, Seattle WA 98199
B/P/ — Capacity: Outside: Up to 200, Large shelter
Contact: Seattle Parks (206) 684-4081

B=Banquets X=Parties M=Meetings S=Seminars R=Retreats P=Picnics C=Conventions T=Tradeshows

Meridian Park — Meridian Avenue N. & N. 50th St., Seattle WA 98103
B/P/ — Capacity: Outside: Up to 100, Large shelter, and gazebo
Contact: Seattle Parks (206) 684-4081, Fax (206) 684-4853

Parsons Garden — 7th W. & W. Highland Dr., Seattle WA 98119
B/P/ — Capacity: Outside: Up to 150
Contact: Seattle Parks (206) 684-4081, Fax (206) 684-4853

Ravenna/Eckstein Community Center — 6535 Ravenna Avenue N.E., Seattle WA 98115
B/X/M/S/R/ — Capacity: Inside: Up to 50
(206) 684-7534

Rose Garden — Fremont N. & N. 50th St., Seattle WA 98103
B/P/ — Capacity: Outdoors: Up to 200, Gazebo,
4-other facilities available for weddings & recreation
Contact: Seattle Parks (206) 233-7272 or (206) 615-0904

Sand Point Magnuson Park — 7400 Sand Point Wy. N.E., Seattle WA 98115
B/X/M/S/R/P/ — Capacity: Picnic Shelters: Up to 75; Bldg. 30: 20,000sq. ft.;
Bldg. 27: 85,000sq. ft.; Conf. Rms. 30 to 125
Contact: Terri Arnold (206) 386-9873 or , Fax (206) 386-4523

Seward Park Picnic Shelters — Lake Washington Blvd. S. & S. Orca St., Seattle WA 98118
B/P/ — Capacity: 3 sites for up to 40; 1 site for up to 400
Contact: Seattle Parks (206) 684-4081 or (206) 684-4081, Fax (206) 684-4853

Southwest Community Center — 2801 S.W. Thistle, Seattle WA 98126
B/X/M/S/R/ — Capacity: Inside: Up to 175
Contact: Seattle Parks (206) 684-7438

Sunset Hill Viewpoint Park — N.W. 75th & 34th N.W., Seattle WA 98117
B/P/ — Capacity: Outdoors: Up to 100
Contact: Seattle Parks (206) 684-4081

West Seattle Golf Course — 4470-35th Ave. S.W., Seattle WA 98126
B/X/M/S/R/ — Capacity: Banquet: Up to 200
Contact: Don Patin Events (206) 935-0991 or General (206) 935-5187

TACOMA

The Centre at Norpoint — 4818 Nassau Ave. N.E. , Tacoma WA 98422 *See page 158*
B/X/M/S/R/ — Capacity: Banquet: Up to 250, Reception: Up to 300
Contact: Rental Coordinator (253) 591-5504 or (253) 661-3289

Mountaineers Club — 2302 N. 30th, Tacoma WA 98403
B/X/M/S/R/ — Capacity: Up to 175
Contact: Clubhouse Secretary (253) 566-6965

Point Defiance Lodge — 5400 N. Pearl St., Tacoma WA 98407 *See page 253*
B/X/M/S/R/ — Capacity: Banquet: Up to 55, Reception: Up to 75
Contact: Facility Coordinator (253) 305-1010

Point Defiance Park Pagoda — 5400 N. Pearl St., Tacoma WA 98407 *See page 254*
B/X/M/S/R/ — Capacity: Banquet: Up to 100, Reception: Up to 200
Contact: Facility Coordinator (253) 305-1010

Point Defiance Zoo & Aquarium — 5400 N. Pearl St., Tacoma WA 98407 *See pages 61, 255 & 547*
B/X/M/S/R/P/ — Capacity: Banquets: Up to 250, Picnics: Up to 1,000
(253) 404-3643 or Gen. Info. (253) 591-5337, Fax (253) 591-5448

Portland Avenue Community Center — 3513 Portland Ave., Tacoma WA 98404
B/X/M/S/R/ — Capacity: Up to 250
Contact: Center Supervisor (253) 591-5391

***B**=Banquets **X**=Parties **M**=Meetings **S**=Seminars **R**=Retreats **P**=Picnics **C**=Conventions **T**=Tradeshows*

South End Neighborhood Center — 7802 S. L St., Tacoma WA 98408
B/X/M/S/R/ — Capacity: Up to 300
Contact: Tom Weathers / Metro Parks Tacoma (253) 591-5098, Fax (253) 591-5216

South Park Community Center — 4851 S. Tacoma Wy., Tacoma WA 98409 *See page 283*
B/X/M/S/R/ — Capacity: Two rooms: 325 and 225 guests
Contact: Centre Supervisor / Metro Parks Tacoma (253) 591-5299

Tacoma Lawn & Tennis Club — 502 Borough Rd., Tacoma WA 98403
B/X/M/S/R/ — Capacity: Up to 250
(253) 383-5935, Fax (253) 383-5934

The Tacoma Nature Center — 1919 S. Tyler St., Tacoma WA 98405 *See page 290*
B/X/M/S/R/ — Capacity: Banquet: Up to 65, Reception: Up to 80
Contact: Center Staff (253) 591-6439, Fax (253) 593-4152

Titlow Lodge Community Center — 8425-6th Ave. E., Tacoma WA 98465 *See page 296*
B/X/M/S/R/ — Capacity: Banquet: Up to 140, Reception: Up to 200
Contact: Center Supervisor (253) 591-5297

WOODINVILLE

Gold Creek Lodge — 16020-148th Ave. N.E., Woodinville WA 98072
B/X/M/S/R/P/ — Capacity: Up to 100 (N/A June-Aug)
Contact: King County Park System (800) 325-6165, ext. 2966 or
(206) 296-2963, Fax (206) 296-1437

B=*Banquets* ***X***=*Parties* ***M***=*Meetings* ***S***=*Seminars* ***R***=*Retreats* ***P***=*Picnics* ***C***=*Conventions* ***T***=*Tradeshows*

Listings: Getaway Event Sites

❖❖❖

ACME

Blue Mountain Farm — PO Box 108, Acme WA 98220
B/X/M/S/R/P/ — Guest Rooms: 9
Capacity: Outdoors: Up to 100, Program Room: Up to 30
(360) 595-2114, Fax (360) 595-1144

ANACORTES

The Majestic Hotel Bistro & Pub — 419 Commercial Ave., Anacortes WA 98221
B/X/M/S/R/ — Guest Rooms: 23
Capacity: Up to 300 (with garden area), Banquet: Up to 150
Contact: Kathy Baxter, Sales & Catering (360) 293-3355, Fax (360) 293-5214

ANDERSON ISLAND

August Inn — 14117 Lyle Pt. Rd., Anderson Island WA 98303
B/X/M/S/R/ — Guest Rooms: 3 units
Capacity: Indoors: Up to 25, Outdoors: Up to 60+
(253) 884-4011, Fax (253) 767-3959

BELLINGHAM

Best Western Lakeway Inn
& Conference Center — 714 Lakeway Dr., Bellingham WA 98226
B/X/M/S/R/C/ — Guest Rooms: 132 — Capacity: Up to 700
Contact: Catering Manager (360) 671-1011, Fax (360) 676-8519

Hotel Bellwether — One Bellwether Way, Bellingham WA 98225 *See pages 109 & 207*
B/X/M/S/R/ — Guest Rooms: 68
Capacity: Banquet: Up to 350; Reception: Up to 700
(360) 392-3100 or (877) 411-1200, Fax (360) 392-3101

Lairmont Manor — 405 Fieldston Rd., Bellingham WA 98225
B/X/M/S/R/ — Guest Rooms: 2 Luxury Suites
Capacity: Inside: Up to 150, Outside: Up to 200
Contact: Joyce White (360) 647-1444, Fax (360) 647-9223

BLAINE

American Kitchen — Peace Arch State Park, Blaine WA 98230 *See pages 100 & 143*
B/X/M/S/R/P/ — Capacity: Inside: Up to 100,
Inside and Outside: Up to 400
(360) 332-8221

Resort Semiahmoo — 9565 Semiahmoo Pkwy., Blaine WA 98230 *See pages 117 & 264*
B/X/M/S/R/C/ — Guest Rooms: 186rooms, 12suites
Capacity: Banquet: Up to 500, Reception: Up to 1,000
Sales & Catering (360) 318-2000 or (800) 770-7992, Fax (360) 318-5490

BOW

Skagit Valley Casino Resort — 5984 N. Darrk Lane, Bow WA 98232 *See pages 119 & 277*
B/X/M/S/ — Guest Rooms: 103 — Capacity: Banquet: Up to 330
(877) 275-2448, Fax (360) 724-0222

CHELAN

Campbell's, A Resort
On Lake Chelan — 104 W. Woodin Ave., Chelan WA 98816 *See page 102*
B/X/M/S/R/ — Guest Rooms: 170 — Capacity: Up to 300
(509) 682-2561

B*=Banquets* ***X****=Parties* ***M****=Meetings* ***S****=Seminars* ***R****=Retreats* ***P****=Picnics* ***C****=Conventions* ***T****=Tradeshows*

CLE ELUM

Hidden Valley Guest Ranch — 3942 Hidden Valley Road, Cle Elum WA 98922
B/X/M/S/R/ — Guest Rooms: 13 — Capacity: Up to 40
(509) 857-2344 or (800) 526-9269

CLINTON

Home by the Sea — 2388 Sunlight Beach Rd., Clinton WA 98236
B/X/M/S/R/ — Guest Rooms: 1 private, 1 suite, 2 cottages — Capacity: Banquet: Up to 20
Office (360) 321-2964, Fax (360) 321-4378

COUPEVILLE

The Captain Whidbey Inn — 2072 W. Captain Whidbey Inn Rd., Coupeville WA 98239
B/X/M/S/R/ — Guest Rooms: 32 — Capacity: Banquet: Up to 25, Reception: Up to 40
Contact: Innkeeper (360) 678-4097 or (800) 366-4097, Fax (360) 678-4110
The Colonel Crockett Farm — 1012 S. Fort Casey Rd., Coupeville WA 98239
B/X/M/S/R/ — Guest Rooms: 5 — Capacity: Up to 15
Contact: Robert (360) 678-3711

CRYSTAL MOUNTAIN

Crystal Mountain Resort — Crystal Mountain Blvd., Crystal Mountain WA 98022
B/X/M/S/R/ — Guest Rooms: 170 — Capacity: Up to 400
Group Sales (360) 663-2265, Fax (360) 663-3001

DEER HARBOR

Resort at Deer Harbor — PO Box 200, Deer Harbor WA 98243 *See page 112*
B/X/M/S/R/ — Guest Rooms: 26 cottages — Capacity: Up to 100
Contact: NW Waterfront Inns (206) 239-1806 or (360) 376-4420, Fax (206) 239-1801

EASTSOUND

Rosario — 1400 Rosario Road, Eastsound WA 98245
B/X/M/S/R/ — Guest Rooms: 127 — Capacity: Banquets: Up to 200
Group Sales Office (425) 452-8200 or (877) 562-8821

ELBE

Hobo Inn — 54106 Mountin Hwy. E., Elbe WA 98330
B/X/M/S/R/ — Guest Rooms: 7 — Capacity: Reception: Up to 50, Small church: Up to 25
Office (360) 569-2500

FORKS

Kalaloch Lodge — 157151 Hwy. 101, Forks WA 98331
B/X/M/S/R/P/ — Guest Rooms: 62 — Capacity: Up to 50
(360) 962-2271, Fax (360) 962-2271

FRIDAY HARBOR

Friday Harbor House — 130 West Street, Friday Harbor WA 98250 *See page 112*
B/X/M/S/R/ — Guest Rooms: 20 — Capacity: Up to 40
Contact: NW Waterfront Inns (206) 239-1806 or (360) 378-8455, Fax (206) 239-1801
Roche Harbor Resort — 248 Reuben Memorial Dr., Friday Harbor WA 98250
B/X/M/S/R/ — Guest Rooms: 53 — Capacity: Up to 150
Contact: Gabe Herda (360) 378- 2155, ext. 403, Fax (360) 378-6809

***B**=Banquets **X**=Parties **M**=Meetings **S**=Seminars **R**=Retreats **P**=Picnics **C**=Conventions **T**=Tradeshows*

GOLD BAR

Wallace Falls — Gold Bar WA *See page 124*
B/M/R/ — Guest Rooms: 10 — Capacity: Indoors: Up to 60; Outdoors: Up to 100
(360) 793-8784 or (888) 337-7492

GREENWATER

Alta Crystal Resort — 68317 SR 410 E., Greenwater WA 98022
B/X/M/S/R/P/ — Guest Rooms: 24 condos — Capacity: Up to 50
Contact: Vivian & Steven Cadematori (360) 663-2500 or (800) 277-6475

LACONNER

Channel Lodge — 205 N. 1st St., LaConner WA 98257 *See page 110*
B/X/M/S/R/ — Guest Rooms: 40 — Capacity: Up to 75
Contact: Melinda Burghduff (360) 466-3101

Country Inn — 107 S. Second Street, LaConner WA 98257 *See page 110*
B/X/M/S/R/ — Guest Rooms: 28 — Capacity: Up to 75
Contact: Melinda Burghduff (360) 466-3101 or (888) 466-4113

Hope Island Inn — P.O. Box 2110, 16846 Chilberg Avenue, LaConner WA 98257-2110
B/X/M/S/R/ — Capacity: Up to 200, (Museum Dining), Waterfront
Contact: Grant Lucas (360) 466-3221, Fax (360) 466-3221

Seafood & Prime Rib House — 614-1st St., LaConner WA 98257
B/X/M/ — Capacity: Up to 130
Contact: Manager (360) 466-4014

The Wild Iris Inn — 121 Maple Ave., LaConner WA 98257
B/X/M/S/R/ — Guest Rooms: 19 — Capacity: Banquet: Up to 75
Sales & Catering (360) 466-1400

LANGLEY

Inn at Langley — 400-1st St., Langley WA 98260 *See page 112*
B/X/M/S/R/ — Guest Rooms: 26 — Capacity: Up to 32
Contact: NW Waterfront Inns (206) 239-1806 or (360) 221-3033, Fax (206) 239-1801

LEAVENWORTH

Best Western Icicle Inn — 505 Highway 2, Leavenworth WA 98826 *See pages 101 & 151*
B/X/M/S/R/ — Guest Rooms: 93 — Capacity: Up to 250
(509) 548-7000 or (800) 558-2438

The Enzian — 590 Highway 2, Leavenworth WA 98826 *See pages 106 & 186*
B/X/M/S/R/ — Guest Rooms: 104 — Capacity: Up to 250
(509) 548-5269 or (800) 223-8511, Fax (509) 548-9319

Mountain Springs Lodge — 19115 Chiwawa Loop, Leavenworth WA 98826 *See page 111*
B/X/M/S/R/ — Guest Rooms: 18
Capacity: Inside: Up to 100, Outside: Up to 300
Contact: Lyn Kay (800) 858-2276 or (509) 763-2713

Sleeping Lady — 7375 Icicle Road, Leavenworth WA 98826 *See pages 120 & 279*
B/X/M/S/R/ — Guest Rooms: 50 — Capacity: Up to 200
Contact: Michael Molohon (800) 574-2123, Fax (509) 548-6312

LOPEZ ISLAND

The Islander Lopez Marina Resort — P.O. Box 459, Fisherman Bay Road, Lopez Island WA 98261
B/X/M/S/R/ — Guest Rooms: 28 — Capacity: Up to 120
Contact: Kathi Casey (360) 468-2233 or (800) 736-3434, Fax (360) 468-3382

B=Banquets X=Parties M=Meetings S=Seminars R=Retreats P=Picnics C=Conventions T=Tradeshows

MAZAMA

Freestone Inn — 31 Early Winters Dr., Mazama WA 98833 *See page 108*
B/X/M/S/R/ — Guest Rooms: 21 rooms, 15 cabins — Capacity: Up to 125
(800) 639-3809, Fax (509) 996-3907

MOSES LAKE

Best Western Hallmark Inn — 3000 Marina Drive, Moses Lake WA 98837
B/X/M/S/R/C/ — Guest Rooms: 161 — Capacity: Banquet: Up to 250, Reception: Up to 350
Sales & Catering (509) 765-9211, Fax (509) 766-0493

MOUNT VERNON

Best Western Cottontree Inn — 2300 Market St., Mount Vernon WA 98273 *See page 150*
B/X/M/S/R/C/ — Guest Rooms: 120 — Capacity: Up to 300
(360) 428-5678 or (800) 662-6886, Fax (360) 428-1844

OAK HARBOR

Best Western Harbor Plaza — 33175 State Route 20, Oak Harbor WA 98277
B/X/M/S/R/ — Guest Rooms: 80 — Capacity: Up to 250
Sales & Catering (360) 679-4567 or (800) 927-5478, Fax (360) 675-2543

Coachman Inn — 32959 Hwy. 20, Oak Harbor WA 98277
B/X/M/S/R/ — Guest Rooms: 102 — Capacity: Banquet: Up to 50, Reception: Up to 70
Contact: Randy Bradford (360) 675-0727 or (800) 635-0043, Fax (360) 675-1419

OCEAN SHORES

The Canterbury Inn — PO Box 310, 643 Ocean Shores Blvd., Ocean Shores WA 98569
B/X/M/S/R/ — Guest Rooms: 44 — Capacity: Up to 40
Contact: Manager (360) 289-3317 or (800) 562-6678, Fax (360) 289-3420

Ocean Shores
Convention Center — PO Box 1447, 120 W. Chance Ala Mer, Ocean Shores WA 98569
B/X/M/S/R/C/T/ — Capacity: Up to 1,000
Contact: Lori Mason (360) 289-4411 or (800) 874-6737, Fax (360) 289-4412

The Polynesian — PO Box 998, 615 Ocean Shores Blvd., Ocean Shores WA 98569
B/X/M/S/R/ — Guest Rooms: 71 — Capacity: Up to 60
Sales Dept. (360) 289-3361 or (800) 562-4836, Fax (360) 289-0294

Quinault Beach
Resort & Casino — 78 State Route 115, P.O. Box 2107, Ocean Shores WA 98569 *See page 114*
B/X/M/S/R/ — Guest Rooms: 150
Capacity: Banquet: Up to 400; Theatre Style: Up to 1,100
(360) 289-9466 or (888) 461-2214, Fax (360) 289-5833

Shilo Inn Ocean Shores — 707 Ocean Shore Blvd. N.W., Ocean Shores WA 98569 *See page 118*
B/X/M/S/R/ — Guest Rooms: 113 — Capacity: Ballroom: Up to 500
Sales & Catering (360) 289-4600 or (800) 222-2244, Fax (360) 289-0677

OLGA

Doe Bay Resort — P.O. Box 437, Star Rt. 86, Olga WA 98279
B/X/M/S/R/ — Guest Rooms: 68, Rustic Cabins: 34
Capacity: Café: Up to 50, Beach Mtg Hall: 45
Contact: Tom Stanfield (360) 376-2291, Fax (360) 376-5809

ORTING

High Cedars Golf Club — 14604 149th Street Court E, Orting WA 98360
B/X/M/S/ — Capacity: Up to 300
(360) 893-3171

B=Banquets X=Parties M=Meetings S=Seminars R=Retreats P=Picnics C=Conventions T=Tradeshows

PORT LUDLOW

Port Ludlow Golf Course — 751 Highland Drive, Port Ludlow WA 98365
B/X/ — Capacity: Up to 40
(360) 437-0272

Port Ludlow Resort
& Conference Center — 200 Olympic Place, Port Ludlow WA 98365
B/X/M/S/R/ — Guest Rooms: 135 — Capacity: Up to 250
Contact: Event Coordinator (360) 437-2222 or
(800) 732-1239, Fax (360) 437-2482

The Resort at Ludlow Bay — 200 Olympic Pl., Port Ludlow WA 98365 *See page 115*
B/X/M/S/R/ — Guest Rooms: 200
Capacity: Variety of rooms accommodating 12 to 200
Contact: Debi Bainbridge (360) 437-2222, Fax (360) 437-2482

PORT ORCHARD

Horseshoe Lake Golf Course
& Restaurant — 1250 S.W. Clubhouse Court, Port Orchard WA 98367
B/X/M/S/ — Capacity: Up to 100
(253) 857-3326, Fax (253) 857-4352

McCormick Woods
Golf Course — 5155 McCormick Woods Drive S.W., Port Orchard WA 98367
B/X/M/P/ — Capacity: Up to 300
(800) 323-0130 or (360) 895-0130

PORT TOWNSEND

Ann Starrett Mansion Bed & Breakfast — 744 Clay, Port Townsend WA 98368
B/X/M/S/R/ — Guest Rooms: 11 — Capacity: 22-40
Contact: Office (360) 385-3205 or (800) 321-0644, Fax (360) 385-2976

Fort Worden State Park
& Conference Center — 200 Battery Wy., Port Townsend WA 98368 *See pages 107 & 192*
B/X/M/S/R/P/C/ — Guest Rooms: dorms: 32-365, houses: 23
Capacity: 12 to 1,200
Contact: Washington State Parks (360) 344-4400, Fax (360) 385-7248

Manresa Castle — 7th & Sheridan, P.O. Box 564, Port Townsend WA 98368
B/X/ — Capacity: Up to 75
Contact: Roger O'Connor (360) 385-5750 or (800) 732-1281

POULSBO

Lange's Ranch — 13913 S. Keyport Rd., Poulsbo WA 98370
B/X/M/S/R/P/ — Guest Rooms: 2 — Capacity: Inside: Up to 200, Outside: Up to 500
Contact: Jewell Lange (360) 779-4927, Fax (360) 779-5466

Poulsbo Inn — 18680 Hwy. 305, Poulsbo WA 98370 *See page 113*
M/S/R/ — Guest Rooms: 72 — Capacity: Up to 25
Contact: Terri Douglas (360) 779-3921, Fax (360) 779-9737

QUINAULT

Lake Quinault Lodge — 345 South Shore Road, Quinault WA 98575
B/X/M/S/R/P/ — Guest Rooms: 92 — Capacity: Up to 100
(360) 288-2900 or (800) 562-6672, Fax (360) 288-2901

SEABECK

La Cachette B&B — PO Box 920, 10312 Seabeck Hwy., Seabeck WA 98380
B/X/ — Guest Rooms: 4 suites — Capacity: Up to 30, (no weddings)
Contact: Drs. Chris & Michael Robbins (360) 613-2845, Fax (360) 613-2912

B=Banquets X=Parties M=Meetings S=Seminars R=Retreats P=Picnics C=Conventions T=Tradeshows

SEQUIM

Best Western Sequim Bay Lodge — 268522 Hwy. 101, Sequim WA 98382
B/X/M/S/R/ — Guest Rooms: 54 — Capacity: Conference Room: 30, (restaurant adjacent)
Sales & Catering (360) 683-0691 or (800) 622-0691, Fax (360) 683-3748

SILVERDALE

WestCoast Silverdale Hotel — 3073 N.W. Bucklin Hill Road, Silverdale WA 98383
B/X/M/S/R/C/ — Guest Rooms: 150 — Capacity: Banquet: Up to 250
Sales & Catering (360) 698-1000, Fax (360) 692-0932

STEVENSON

Dolce Skamania Lodge — 1131 Skamania Lodge Way, Stevenson WA 98648 *See page 104*
B/X/M/S/R/C/ — Guest Rooms: 195 — Capacity: Up to 500
Sales & Catering (509) 427-2503 or (800) 376-9116

UNION

Alderbrook Resort Golf & Conference Center — 7101 E State Rd 106, Union WA 98592
B/X/M/S/R/ — Guest Rooms: 76rooms,15cottages
Capacity: Indoors: Up to 225, Outdoors: Up to 200 (2 outside areas),
Non-Alcoholic, Non-Smoking
Sales & Catering (360) 898-2200 or (800) 622-9370, Fax (360) 898-4610

VANCOUVER

The Heathman Lodge — 7801 N.E. Greenwood Drive, Vancouver WA 98662
B/X/M/S/R/C/T/ — Guest Rooms: 22 suites, 121 rooms — Capacity: Up to 300
Sales Office (888) 475-3100 or (360) 254-3100

WENATCHEE

Wenatchee Center —
c/o The Wenatchee Valley CVB, 116 N Wenatchee Ave., Wenatchee WA 98801 *See page 125*
B/X/M/S/R/C/T/ — Capacity: 7 meeting rms; Up to 600
(800) 572-7753, Fax (509) 663-3983

Wenatchee Red Lion — 1225 N. Wenatchee Ave., Wenatchee WA 98801
B/X/M/S/R/ — Guest Rooms: 149 — Capacity: Up to 400
Sales & Catering (509) 663-0711 or (800) Red-Lion

WINTHROP

River Run Inn — 27 Rader Road, Winthrop WA 98862
B/X/M/S/R/ — Guest Rooms: 1cabin, 20rooms — Capacity: Up to 65
Contact: Carol Lints (509) 996-2173, Fax (509) 996-2173

Sun Mountain Lodge — P.O. Box 1000, Winthrop WA 98862 *See pages 122 & 289*
B/X/M/S/R/C/ — Guest Rooms: 114 — Capacity: Up to 200
Contact: Lisa Adair - Seattle Office (425) 487-6638 or (800) 572-0493, Fax (425) 487-1278

COEUR D'ALENE, IDAHO

The Coeur D'Alene Resort — 115 S. 2nd St., Coeur D'Alene ID 83814 *See page 103*
B/X/M/S/R/C/T/ — Guest Rooms: 337 — Capacity: 50 to 2,000 in 29 meeting locations
Catering & Sales (208) 765-4000 or (800) 365-8338, Fax (208) 664-7278

B=Banquets X=Parties M=Meetings S=Seminars R=Retreats P=Picnics C=Conventions T=Tradeshows

GLENEDEN BEACH, OREGON

The Westin Salishan Lodge & Golf Resort — 7760 Highway 101 N., Gleneden Beach OR 97388 *See pages 126 & 313*
B/X/M/S/R/C/ — Guest Rooms: 205 — Capacity: 5 to 500
Sales & Catering (800) 890-9316, Fax (541) 764-3510

GRAND RONDE, OREGON

Spirit Mountain Casino — PO Box 39, Grand Ronde OR 97347 *See pages 121 & 285*
B/X/M/S/R/C/ — Guest Rooms: 100
Capacity: Banquets: Up to 200; Receptions: Up to 250
Group Sales (800) 760-7977

LINCOLN CITY, OREGON

The Inn at Spanish Head — 4009 S.W. Hwy. 101, Lincoln City OR 97367
B/X/M/S/R/C/ — Guest Rooms: 120 — Capacity: Up to 150
Sales & Catering (800) 452-8127

NEWPORT, OREGON

Shilo Inn Newport — 536 S.W. Elizabeth Street, Newport OR 97365
B/X/M/S/R/C/ — Guest Rooms: 179 — Capacity: Up to 600
Catering Office (541) 265-7701 or (800) 222-2244

SEASIDE, OREGON

Shilo Inn Seaside Oceanfront Resort — 30 N. Prom, Seaside OR 97138
B/X/M/S/R/C/ — Guest Rooms: 112 — Capacity: Up to 400
Catering Office (503) 738-9571 or (800) 222-2244

WARM SPRINGS, OREGON

Kah-Nee-Ta Resort — PO Box 1240, Warm Springs OR 97761
B/X/M/S/R/C/ — Guest Rooms: 139 — Capacity: Up to 550
(541) 553-1112 or (800) 831-0100, Fax (541) 553-1071

WELCHES, OREGON

The Resort at the Mountain — 68010 E. Fairway Avenue, Welches OR 97067 *See page 116*
B/X/M/S/R/C/ — Guest Rooms: 160 — Capacity: Up to 700
Office (800) 733-0800

HARRISON HOT SPRINGS, BC, CANADA

Harrison Hot Springs Hotel — 100 Esplanade, Harrison Hot Springs BC Canada V0M1K0
B/X/M/S/R/ — Guest Rooms: 323 — Capacity: Banquet: Up to 650
Contact: Catering & Sales (800) 663-2266, Fax (604) 796-9374

VICTORIA, BC, CANADA

The Empress — 721 Government Street, Victoria BC Canada V8W1W5
B/X/M/S/R/ — Guest Rooms: 472
Capacity: Banquet: Up to 500, Reception: Up to 350
Contact: (250) 384-8111, Fax (250) 381-5959

B=Banquets X=Parties M=Meetings S=Seminars R=Retreats P=Picnics C=Conventions T=Tradeshows

INDEX BY NAME & SUBJECT

B

D

E

F

I

J

K

L

M

N

O

P

S

T

U

V

W

X–Y–Z